汉 英 对 照
Chinese-English

外教社中国文化汉外对照丛书
SFLEP Bilingual Chinese Culture Series

英译中国当代短篇小说精选

SELECTED CONTEMPORARY CHINESE SHORT STORIES

赵丽宏　主编　Edited by Zhao Lihong
李　洁　译　Translated by Li Jie
汪榕培　审订　Revised by Wang Rongpei

上海外语教育出版社
外教社 SHANGHAI FOREIGN LANGUAGE EDUCATION PRESS

图书在版编目（CIP）数据

英译中国当代短篇小说精选：汉英对照 / 赵丽宏主编；李洁译.
—上海：上海外语教育出版社，2012（2014重印）
（外教社中国文化汉外对照丛书）
ISBN 978-7-5446-2806-8

Ⅰ.①英… Ⅱ.①赵… ②李… Ⅲ.①英语－汉语－对照读物
②短篇小说－小说集－中国－当代 Ⅳ.①**H319.4:I**

中国版本图书馆CIP数据核字（2012）第**118373**号

出版发行：**上 海 外 语 教 育 出 版 社**
（上海外国语大学内） 邮编：200083
电　　话：021-65425300（总机）
电子邮箱：bookinfo@sflep.com.cn
网　　址：http://www.sflep.com.cn　http://www.sflep.com
责任编辑：梁瀚杰

印　　刷：上海华业装璜印刷厂有限公司
开　　本：787×965　1/16　印张32.75　字数585千字
版　　次：2013年2月第1版　2014年1月第2次印刷
印　　数：2 100 册

书　　号：**ISBN 978-7-5446-2806-8 / I · 0212**
定　　价：65.00 元

本版图书如有印装质量问题，可向本社调换

序

赵丽宏

最近三十多年，中国发生的变化举世瞩目。经历了"文化大革命"的风雨之后，中国走出了闭锁和迷茫，走向开放，走向强盛，走向民主。经济的飞速发展，牵动了社会的变革，也改变了中国人的生活。在这一时期中，中国的作家打破思想的桎梏，展示出丰富多姿的创造才华，佳作浩如烟海。这三十多年文学创作的本身，见证了中国的变化。要为这三十年的中国文学编一本选集，好比银河摘星，花海寻蕾，让人眼花缭乱，不是一件容易的事情。

这本选集中的作品，选自这三十多年来在《上海文学》发表的短篇小说佳作。这些短篇小说的作者来自全国各地，有名满天下的重量级作家，也有初出茅庐的文坛新秀。其中的很多作品，发表后曾广为流传，引起强烈的反响，成为那一时期的代表之作，有些也成为年轻作家的成名之作。这些作品，题材多样，反映的生活和主题丰富多彩，写作的风格也都是独具个性。这些年中，中国文坛各种文学流派风云一时，如"伤痕文学"、"寻根文学"、"先锋文学"和"新写实主义"等等，中国的作家如饥似渴地汲取着外国文学的养料，也呼唤着优秀民族传统的回归。作家真诚的态度，不拘一格求创新的艺术追求，使得这一时期的中国短篇小说创作呈现出极为丰繁灿烂的景象。这个选本，尽管只收入34篇小说，但是读者可以管中窥豹，从中看到这样的景象。

中国对外国文学的翻译和介绍，一直采取一种积极开放、不遗余力的态度，这使得中国读者对当代的外国文学有比较全面的了解。而西方世界对中国当代文学的介绍，却少得可怜；西方读者对中国当代文学的了解，仍处于一种茫然无知的状况。这种不对等的状况，一时难以改变，但不应该一直这样延续下去。上海外语教育出版社能翻译出版这类中国当代文学选集的中英文对照读本，是一件非常有意义的事情，这是改变这种不对等状况的一种卓有成效的努力。

我相信，读这样的文学选本，英文读者会产生一点惊讶：中国作家的小说，原来这样有意思！中文读者会产生一点自信：中国当代文学，可以毫无愧色地面对世界。

2011年2月27日于四步斋

Preface

© *Zhao Lihong*

The past 30 years have witnessed great transformations in China. After the tumultuous "Cultural Revolution", out of the isolation and confusion, China has stepped on a road toward openness, prosperity and democracy. The rapid economic development has exerted a great influence on the social changes and the people's life. In this period, Chinese writers freed their minds from the shackles of the outdated notions and demonstrated their creative writing talents in various ways. As a result, a great number of masterpieces emerged, which bore witness to the great changes taking place in China during these 30 years. Like plucking stars from the boundless sky and looking for buds among waves of flowers, to compile an anthology of Chinese literary works, therefore, is no easy job.

The short stories in this book are selected from the pieces published in *Shanghai Literature*, a well-known literary magazine in China, during these 30 years. The writers of these excellent works come from all parts of the country; some are famous and influential writers and some are promising young writers. Quite a lot of pieces in this book have been circulated widely and evoked nation-wide responses since their publications. They have either become the representative works in a particular period or helped some young writers establish their initial reputations. These short stories vary in themes and styles. They depict the colorful life of a contemporary China in their unique literary styles. During the past 30 years, such various schools as "scar literature", "root-seeking literature", "pioneer literature" and "neo-realism literature" flourished one after another in the Chinese literary field. The Chinese writers have been devoted not only to absorbing the quintessence from foreign literatures but also to calling for the return of the brilliant Chinese national tradition in literary creation. Their sincere attitude and their outstanding creativity in artistic pursuit make Chinese short-story writing thrive and prosper. Though only 34 pieces are selected in this book, readers can easily have a view of our literary development and prosperity.

We have been sparing no effort in translating and introducing foreign literature into China. As a result, Chinese readers have an easy access to foreign literary works and have a relatively all-round understanding of contemporary foreign literature. In contrast, western readers know little about Chinese literature. This unequal state should not continue, though it is hard to be changed in a short period of time. Now, it is significant and quite meaningful for Shanghai Foreign Language Education Press to publish such books with English translation which not only introduce the contemporary Chinese literature to the world but also play a positive role in changing the present unequal state.

I believe that this book will amaze the English-speaking readers with the fact that the Chinese fiction can be so interesting, and that it will also make our Chinese readers confident: the contemporary Chinese literature can stand proudly in the world's literature landscape.

February 27, 2011
In the Four-step Study

目 录

海的梦

○ 王 蒙

　　下车的时候赶上了雷阵雨的尾巴。车厢里热烘烘、乱糟糟、迷腾腾的。一到站台，只觉得又凉爽，又安静，又空荡。潮润的空气里充满了深绿色的针叶树的芳香。闻到这种芳香的人，觉得自己也变得洁净和高雅了。从软席卧铺车厢下来了几个外国人，他们叽叽喳喳地说笑着，噢、噢地拉长着声音。"哈啰，"他们向缪可言挥了挥手，缪可言也向他们点头致意。有一个外国女人笑得非常温和，她长得并不好看，但是有很好的身材，走起路来也很见精神。此外没有什么人上车和下车。但是站台非常之大，一尘不染，清洁得令人吃惊。一幢幢方方正正的小房子，好像在《格林童话集》的插图里见到过似的，红色的瓦顶子晶晶地闪光。这个著名的海滨疗养胜地的车站，有自己的特别高贵的风貌。

　　说来惭愧。作为一个翻译家，作为一个搞了多半辈子外国文学的研究与介绍的专门家，五十二岁的缪可言却从来没有到过外国，甚至没有见过海。他向往海。年轻的时候他爱唱一首歌：

　　　从前在我少年时……
　　　朝思暮想去航海，
　　　但海风使我忧，波浪使我愁……

　　这是奥地利的歌儿吗？还有一首，是苏联的：

　　　我的歌声飞过海洋……
　　　不怕狂风，不怕巨浪，
　　　因为我们船上有着
　　　年轻勇敢的船长……

览公路，以及海和天和码头，都模糊了，都温柔了，都接近了，都和解了，都依依地联结在一起。所有的差别——例如高楼和平地，陆上和海上——都在消失，所有的距离都在缩短，所有的纷争都在止歇，所有的激动都在平静下来，连潮水涌到沙岸上也是轻轻地，试探地，文明地，生怕打搅谁或者触犯谁。

而超过这一切，主宰这一切，统治着这一切的是一片浑然的银光。亮得耀眼的、活泼跳跃的却又是朦胧悠远的海波支持着布满青辉的天空，高举着一轮小小的、乳白色的月亮。在银波两边，月光连接不到的地方，则是玫瑰色的，一眼望不到头的黑暗。随着缪可言的漫步，"银光区"也在向前移动。这天海相连，缓缓前移的银光区是这样地撩人心绪，缪可言快要流出泪来了。这一切都是安排好了的，海在他即将离去的前一个夜晚，装扮好了自己，向他温存，向他流盼，向他微笑，向他喁喁地私语。

海——呀——我——爱——你——！他终于喊出了声，声音并不大，他已经没有当年的好嗓子。然而他惊起了一对青年男女。他完全没有注意到，就在他脚下的岩石上，有一对情侣正依偎在一起。他完全没有思想准备，完全想不到他会打扰年轻人。因为这里和城市的公园或者游泳池不同，这里简直就没有什么年轻人。但是，他确实已经打扰了人家，女青年已经从岩石上站了起来，离开了男青年的怀抱。他恍惚看到了女青年的淡色的发结。他怀着一种深深的歉疚，三步并两步地离开了这个地方。他非常懊悔，却又觉得很高兴，很满意。年轻人在月夜海滨，依偎着坐在一起，这很好。海和月需要青春。青春也需要海和月。但他们是谁呢？休养员里没有这样年轻的，服务人员里也没有这样年轻的。事后他才依稀感到了在自己的耳膜上残留着轻微的本地口音。那么说是农民！一定是农民！是社员？是回乡知识青年？是公社干部？还只是最一般的农民？反正是青年。反正农民也爱海，爱月，爱这"银光区"。那就更好。这天和地，海和人，都显得甜甜的了。

这是什么声音？哗——哗——，不是浪，不是潮，这只能是人的手臂划动海水的声音。他顺着这声音找去，他看到了在他刚离去的岩石下面，似乎有两个人在游海。难道是那两个青年下去游水了么？他们不觉得凉么？他们不怕黑么？他们把衣服放到了哪里？喔哟，看，那两个人已经游了那么远，他们在向着他向往过许多次，却从来没有敢于问津的水天相接的亮晶晶的地方游去了呢。

缪可言觉得有点眼花，这流动的、摇摆的、破碎的和粘连的银光真叫人眼花缭乱。是不是他看错了呢？那里是两个人吗？人有这样的游水速度吗？难道是鱼？人鱼？美人鱼？

不，那不会错，那就是人，就是刚刚被惊动了的那两位热恋中的青年人。缪可言又有什么怀疑的呢？如果是他自己，如果倒退三十年，如果他和他的心爱的姑娘在一起，他难道会怕黑吗？会嫌冷吗？会躲避这泛着银光的波浪吗？不，他和她会一口气游出去八千米。就是八公里，就是那个极目所至的地方。爱情，青春，自由的波涛，一代又一代地流动着，翻腾着，永远不会老，永远不会淡漠，更永远不会中断。它们永远和海，和月，和风，和天空在一起。

他唱起了一支歌。他怀着隐秘的激情回到了休养所。入睡之前，他一下子想起了好几首诗，普希金的，莱蒙托夫的，拜伦的，雪莱的，惠特曼的，还有他自己的。他睡了，嘴角上带着微笑。

"怎么样？这海边也没有太大的意思吧？"送他走的汽车驾驶员说。这位驾驶员是一个善知人意的心理学家，而且他已经得悉缪可言是个古板的、其貌不扬的老单身汉。然而这回他错了。缪可言回答道：

"不，这个地方好极了，实在是好极了。"

（载1980年6月号）

9

The Sea Dream

○ *Wang Meng*

When he got off the train, the thunder shower was going to stop. Hardly had he set foot on the platform when he was refreshed by the cool air. The station was empty and quiet, so the travel experience of swelter, hubbub and dizziness on the train was finally thrown behind. The fragrance of the dark-green pine trees pervaded the humid air and he felt himself clean and elegant in such aroma. Several foreigners off the soft-class sleeper were talking in an excited manner. They said "Hi" to him with a prolonged voice and waved to him. He, to show his politeness, also nodded a greeting to them. A woman among them smiled at him gently. Her face was not so good-looking but she had a good figure and a brisk gait. Except them, few people were getting on and off the train.[1] The platform looked spacious and spotlessly clean. The houses, square-shaped and not tall, with glistening red roofs, were much like those in the pictures in *Grimm's Fairy Tales*. Obviously, the station of this seaside recuperation resort had its unique noble look and style.

A sense of shame gradually welled up in his heart. As a translator, a researcher and a specialist who studied foreign literature for more than half of his lifetime, he, Miao Keyan, had never been abroad! He even had no opportunity to have a look at the sea! He had been longing for the sea all his life, though. Until now, he still remembered a song he was fond of when he was young.

> When I was a teenager…
> I longed for a journey on the sea,
> But the sea wind made me worry,
> And the huge waves made me tarry…

Was it an Austrian song? The other song he favored much was from the Soviet Union.

> My songs are flying across the sea…
> Dauntless of wild wind and angry billows,
> For the young and courageous captain
> Is by my side and supporting me…

These two songs ran through his youthful days and his bitter-sweet first love. The love, the sea and the anxiety of flying high beckoned his thirsty soul. A, B, C, D… He started his career and later was brought down as a "Secret Agent Suspect". Since then, big waves have come one after another, and now he was fifty-two years old, out of love and never getting a chance to see the sea, let alone flying high… He was almost gobbled up by the big wind and wave.[2] Where are you, my young and courageous captain?!

The bus rode on the pavement which was slightly wet after the rain. On both sides were the tall and dense pagoda trees which appeared noble and arrogant. Seeing the black clouds scattering away, the driver said to the passengers, "We are going to see the sea soon!" He could read his guests' mind.

Sea, sea! Was it the sea before the thunderstorm under Gorky's pen? Or that colorful, splendid and fantastic sea in Andersen's story? Or the sea in Jack London's and Hemingway's novels that he once took great pains in translating? Ah, yes! Maybe it was that ancient Arabian sea in Nikolai Rimsky-Korsakov's *Scheherazade*?

No. It was nothing like what he had imagined. There it was, placid, serene and listless, like a piece of silk satin sewn into the misty sky, but a lot darker, brighter and purer than the sky, or a dense layer of emulsion hanging high above the horizon. He saw the satin waving softly; he saw the emulsion slightly shivering; he saw the curving line, now visible and now invisible along the horizon; and he saw the white foams and waves appearing and disappearing from time to time. What sound? Was it real? Between the droning of the engine and the rustling of the wheels, he heard, if any, the sound of the blowing sprays.[3] As they rode forward, the dark clouds were quickly left behind. It was afternoon. The sunshine was warm and dazzling and the gray clouds were turning into white. Oh, God! The sea also changed! It turned into a glistening blue jade on which golden waves and dark shadows of clouds added irresistible charm to each other. Seagulls flew close to the surface of the water and their white belly could be clearly seen. In the distance where the sky and the sea met, a black speck and a white speck gradually came into view — a ship with white sails or white sails on a ship. "Ah, sea, finally I see you! After a half century's yearning, finally I come to your side! But after so many trials and tribulations my hair has turned white, and yours, too — white waves!"

Late! It was too late! His prime time had gone! He recalled the days when he was accused of being a "Secret Agent Suspect" and a "Vicious Attacker". He was put into a small cell, and after the door was heavily shut with a bang, he no longer had the opportunity to see the blue sky and the golden sunshine, except the time when it was his turn every six days to pour the toilet bowl. In those hard days, in either freezing cold or scorching heat, was it likely for a man to yearn for the sea? Now, finally, he came to the sea's warm embrace! Backstroking in the water, with his eyes closed, enjoying the caress of the waves as smooth as silk satin, he felt relaxed and intoxicated. After years of physical and mental exhaustion he felt relieved. He was contented, indifferent to all the things around. Perhaps, he felt like lying on the waves for the rest of his life! But where was his passion? Where was his youth? Where were his vigor and vitality burning with eagerness? Where was the heat of his tears filled with joys and sorrows?

He felt sorry for his friends and former colleagues. In the past years they gave him much care and solicitude but now he could not find a way to repay them. "Rehabilitation" — the Chinese people might, one day, turn to the *Ancient Chinese Dictionary* to find such a complicated word? Besides, such awkwardly coined acronyms as SAS ("Secret Agent Suspect"), VA ("Vicious Attacks") and RS ("Reactionary Slogans")[4] added confusion to the absurdity of those years. Nevertheless, thanks to them, the disorder and reversal were blurred with a layer of mist. Now, what his leaders and his colleagues most cared about were two things. First, he was advised to take a good rest, relax himself and recover his health; second, he was urged to build a family.

He agreed upon the former but as for the latter he felt confused, confounded and depressed. "You were too romantic and impractical when you were young, and later you were involved in the political movement. Now, isn't it the fullness of time to settle down and have a family?" His colleagues urged him over and over again.

But he had his own logic. Peach flowers, jujube flowers and any other flowers had their own blossoming seasons; carrots, cabbages and any other vegetables had their own seeding periods. The wrong time must lead to the wrong result. In *The Arabian Nights*, that devil in the bottle at first promised to give the one who came to let him out the whole world's wealth; however, after the long and desperate wait, he had got exhausted and changed his mind, determining to devour his tardy savior. Of course, the result was, inevitably, that he was put back into the bottle again.

He had no idea why he thought of this story when he was introduced to a sequence of "girlfriends". Of course, he had no intention of devouring somebody or repaying kindness with hatred. He just thought that he missed the right time and that he was no longer young. Any good wine over-fermented might turn sour. To him, all were gone, never to return … his youth, his love and his sea dream!

Therefore, the moment he heard the word "girlfriend", he slipped away. Of course, he himself felt his escape revolting. He thought of Andersen's fairy tale *The Old Bachelor's Sleeping Hat* and Oscar Wilde's *Selfish Giant*. Spring would not come to a garden with no kids. Ah, yes! His heart, like a bare garden, was still covered with ice and snow.

Nonetheless, the sea never left him. She was his old friend — they had enjoyed the mutual understanding and trust to each other for such a long time; she was his new friend — now they finally got the chance to make acquaintance. She had been faithful to him all the time and she had been welcoming him all the time! She was embracing him, kissing him, caressing him, tapping him, bumping into him, washing him, cleaning him and pressing him, never thinking of fatigue or withdrawal in the least. Sometimes, it was blue, sometimes, it was yellowish green, and sometimes, it turned silvery gray. When the wind was roaring, the waves suddenly turned reddish brown like the dense boiling malted milk with sticky foams on the top. A billow was like a mountain, falling down overwhelmingly and scattering away immediately with no trace at all. The sea was merciless in others' eyes, but tender and affectionate in his.[5]

The great waves cheered him up. He quickly adapted himself to them. When a big wave came, he had a deep breath and put his head into the water to exhale, where he opened his eyes, saw the wave surging over his head and heard it roaring like thunders. After it passed, he raised his head out of the water to inhale again and stroked with his two arms, facing and welcoming another awesome wave. He turned elated, for such big waves could do nothing with him. In high spirits, he swam a thousand meters away, already out of the shark-proof net. "I am so skinny, the third-grade meat at best, and sharks don't like me." He said to himself. As he was boasting to be a good swimmer braving the winds and waves and a proud conqueror of the sea, he suddenly got a cramp in his left shank. As he was accused of a "Vicious Attacker", in an "interrogation", his left shank was seriously injured when someone kicked it heavily in order to make him kneel down. Now, looking about, except mountain-like billows, he could see nothing else. "Am I going to finish here?" At the thought of this, he trembled. Swallowing a mouthful of bitter and salty water, he suddenly turned furious. No! He could not die here! He was unwilling to die! He felt wronged by the fate! He began to struggle. He went all out to fight. He was an excellent swimmer when he was young. Although he learned to swim in a small pool, he thought his skill was good enough to fight with the turbulent waves here. He moved his left foot with his hands and stretched his left leg with great efforts. At last, he pulled himself onto the bank. He, Miao Keyan, had not been devoured by Jiang Qing (who played a major role in the Cultural Revolution 1966-1976 and formed the radical political alliance known as the Gang of Four) and now surely it was impossible for him to be devoured by sea sirens.

"Nevertheless, I have to admit I am old." After this accident, he felt strongly about it. Such lovely remarks as "many a good tune played on an old fiddle", "bursting with youthful energy", "becoming more vigorous with age" and "leading your 52-year-old life as if you were just 25"[6] could not change the law of nature. He was already fifty-two. And his cells were aging; his calcareous infarct was increasing; his elasticity of muscles was lessening; his heart was declining; his teeth were decaying; his wrinkles were multiplying; and his memory was waning…

He found that people coming to this resort were close to his age, if not older. Some were about fifty years old with graying hair; some were aged with bent backs; and some wore hearing aids or walked with the support of walking sticks. Quite a few of them had nitroglycerin tablets in their pockets, and wherever they went, they were followed by doctors, and wherever they slept, they asked whether there were oxygen facilities ready and at call. There were just a few women here, who looked no longer young and most of whom gathered flesh in their waist and belly. Even the sellers in the department stores and food stores or the waiters in the western and Chinese restaurants were about forty years old. They were skilled and calm, and served their guests with great patience. Under no circumstances were they likely to fail to serve leaders or foreign guests well.

So he could not find one in company with him to swim. When the wind was slightly strong or the sky was a little overcast, people no longer went to the shore. However, when the weather was good with golden sunshine and white clouds, when the sea was calm, clear and tranquil in which every fish and every cluster of seaweed was visible, when the tapping of the waves was as gentle as a mother's soft breath puffed onto her injured kid, most people still kept a distance to it. They just played in the places twenty meters away from the bank where the water just reached their ankles or knees at most. Only at dawn or at dusk when the tide was ebbing and flowing did more people come to the shore, picking up some seashells or taking a walk along the beach. They moved slowly in a leisurely and majestic manner like the clouds adrift in the sky.

Without a companion he no longer dared to swim far beyond the shark-proof net. Each time, after thirty or forty minutes at most, he would climb onto the bank and lay on the silver sand in the sun. Closing his eyes, he saw some dark red dots flying, changing and assembling into different shapes, like the signals on a computer monitor. He felt sorry to the sea. She was so big, so ardent and whole-hearted to embrace him. "Come — come here —," every roll of waves gushed onto the bank and beckoned him; "Play here — play here —," every roll of waves surged back and called at him.

"Oh — sea — I — love — you — !" Sometimes, he also wanted to shout at the salty, fishy, vast and free wind on the sea, but he did not. Around him were those polite, moral and respectable people, and his "petty bourgeois" yells might be considered one of his lunatic symptoms.

Most of the time, he just walked to and fro on the sightseeing road along the shore. It often took him one and a half hours to walk from the West Hill to the East Hill. (These were two tiny peninsulas flanking a small bay.) He was always moved and encouraged by the rose willows, which, under the force of the yearly wind, grew inclined to one side. Normally, rose willows grew on the Gobi Desert in the northwest. He had never expected that they could also grow near the sea. It was true that different lifestyles and living areas shared some common features. The shore stretched upward and several small houses stood on the higher place. It must be agreeable to enjoy a distant view of the sea there! He guessed. Now, standing on the shore, he looked as far as he could, but the boundless sea in his imagination did not come into view.

His field of vision was confined by a level line in the distance (called the "horizon", it would seem?), which was much like the rim of a frame. Oh, the sea was also confined in a frame, which, of course, was his optical illusion. When he looked sideways to the eastern or western directions, instead of facing the sea directly, he saw the sea stretching and extending endlessly, but when he looked at the sea straight on, the horizon and the shoreline severed his vision; besides, the waves far and near were of the same color, which made it hard to judge how far the sea stretched. In contrast, when he looked at the sea sideways, the two lines extended forward and the scenery alongside the banks gave him a real sense of distance. Hence, different perspectives gave people different senses. One might constantly remind himself of the fact that the earth was round and that a person's eyesight could only reach as far as eight kilometers even when not blocked at all, and no matter what aspect a person adopted, straight on or sideways, his range of vision was about the same. However, this scientific reminder could not change the real feeling that the unscientific eyes brought about.

As a matter of fact, the genuinely boundless was not the sea but the sky. Go to the beach and look up at the sky! How he wished he could soar to the sky! A person in the plane might never sense the happiness of a swallow, even if the plane flew ten or twenty thousand meters high. A swallow depended on its own wings, its own body, its own feathers and its own efforts to become an inseparable part of the sky, while a person in an airtight Boeing 707 could not sense such freedom and excitement. Only those on the ground knew the plane flew very high.

So it is better to admire the layers and layers of rosy clouds by the sea, he thought. He was so much enchanted by the widespread fan-shaped clouds at dusk. At first, they looked like snow-white cotton balls, and after a while, they turned into golden pineapples; later, they were dyed with such various colors as rose-red, dark purple, snow-gray, grayish black, brown and light yellow. Different colors mixed together and made the clouds look like a beautiful flowerbed, now appearing, now disappearing, in the distance. The whole sky and the sea darkened with the changing colors of the clouds. All of a sudden, the sun escaped the embrace of the clouds and fell onto the sea. Like a big egg-yolk, it changed its color from orange, orange-red, to bright red, and changed its shape from round to oblate, and in the end, disappeared in the surging waves.

He enjoyed looking up at the sky by the sea. Here, the sky was not dazzlingly bright and the sun was not scalding, for the dense foggy mist had absorbed much heat and light. Looking at the sky, a subtle inexpressible sense of sadness welled up in his heart. Under the vast eternal sky, the human life was so insignificant and so limited! And the bygone days would never return.

Thinking of this, he had a strong impulse to take off his clothes at once and plunge himself into the sea, regardless of the heavy waves, the changing temperatures of the water, the dangerous sharks and jellyfish, and even regardless of the darkening sky and the long black night after sunset. He just wanted to swim toward the place where the sky and the sea met, directed by the point of the cone-shaped cloud which had been fan-shaped a moment ago. The true sea, the true sky, and the true infinity were right there. He had lived much of his lifetime and got nothing in his hands, and only there could he see his dream sea and realize his day-and-night sea dream. The stars, the sun, the iridescent clouds, the free wind, the dragon king, the mermaids, the white whales, the fairy on the green ripples were all there! Yes! They were all waiting for him!

"Ah, you have been dwelling in my thirsty soul, my dancing zest, my whimsical illusion and my childish longings for such a long time! Where are you, my dream sea?"

Indeed, he was not able to reach there. His damned left shank! Fifty-two years had passed! He had no way to return to his youthful days!

Perhaps, for him, it was better not to go there? A Scandinavian writer once wrote about a mystical small island which was incomparably beautiful. Greatly attracted by it, several young fellows made up their minds to go there and have a look. They underwent the freezing coldness and all kinds of hardships, and after a whole day's skiing, they finally got there, only to find nothing but dry and drab stones. The story vividly depicted the pains a person experienced when he lost his dream in the wake of realizing it. After all, Miao Keyan had passed the age of dreaming.

As a result, he planned to leave. After fifty years of yearnings, he stayed by the sea for only five days. Compared with the damp, rancid and desperate prison or his busy, simple and hard daily life, this seaside resort was really a paradise. Rows and rows of luxuriant trees stood in order and one could never confuse French phoenix trees with Chinese phoenix trees. The resort was so clean that the traffic police-men's white uniform looked glaring and even the strongest wind brought no dirt. Here, the ground was covered with brownish red sands, a kind of fine sands with no adhesion or pollution, as if repeatedly washed by the medical normal saline. The streets here were cleaned and sprinkled with water every day, and people here need not frequently change their shirts, for collars and cuffs remained clean for several days.

The sanatorium had various flowers. He could enjoy the sea in the distance and admire the flowers before his window. In the daytime, he could stand in the porch and count the numbers of the passing ships and at night, after people went to sleep, he could hear the waves murmuring like his mother's soft sleeping breaths he had heard in his childhood. At this time, the sea was age-old and so was its breath; the sea was composed and so were its ups and downs. When the wind blew and stirred up the waves, he could hear the sea roaring, shouting and exclaiming, as if tens and thousands of soldiers were fighting and grappling.

In addition, the meals here were quite good. A person didn't always have the luck to enjoy good meals. He recalled the days when he was persecuted and shut in the "cell", where tedium and monotony almost drove him and his fellow prisoners crazy. Then, one of them, in one way or another, got an old worn-out idiom dictionary, which at once became the apple of their eyes. To dispel the tedium, they made use of the dictionary to tell fortunes. One was asked to say a page number and an entry number on that page, and accordingly, they looked up the dictionary and found that entry on that page. The corresponding idiom indicated one's fate. If they came across such idioms as "being guilty of a crime for which even death can't atone", "being condemned for generations", or "one punished as a deterrent to others", they would sigh and turn dejected; however, if the idioms were "having a promising future", "sweet after sweat" or "having a sudden glimpse of hope in the dark mist of bewilderment", they would shout and jump with joy. The only idiom Miao Keyan met was "delicacies from land and sea", which brought him so much hope and happiness and gave everyone a grand spiritual feast (as everyone was asked to describe what delicacies he had ever eaten). Now, in this seaside resort, there were little delicacies from land, but a lot from sea, which were enough to

gratify everyone's palate. Fish, crabs, shrimps, jellyfish, seaweed, and sea kale…
And everyone here was provided with a kilogram of cooking oil per month, four
times the ration of urban residents. He just spent sixty cents for his meals every day,
but actually what he ate would cost one yuan and eighty cents. In addition, various
entertainments were provided. 20-inch color TV set, table tennis, cards, miniature
billiards, *weiqi*, Chinese chess, etc. New foreign films were often shown in the
neighboring sanatorium.

Then, what on earth did he want? What on earth was the sanatorium in lack of?
He could not call back the souls of his comrades-in-arms who died unnatural deaths
and he could not call back his ambitions! At his request of leaving, the head of the
sanatorium turned uneasy. "Have we done something wrong? Aren't you satisfied
with our service? Don't our meals agree with your taste? Doesn't our mosquito net
work? Or can't you get on well with other guests here?" The head of the sanatorium
showed deep concern for him and repeatedly urged him to stay longer. After all, his
recommendation letter said that he planned to stay for a month.

He, indeed, felt something missing. The sky was too boundless; the sea was too
spacious; there were too many people, who were too old; his swimming postures
and movements were too simple; he lacked courage and strength; the coating on his
tongue was too thick; his conversations with others were too monotonous; he had
too much cholesterol; his dream was too long; his bed was too soft; the air was too
damp; he had too much complaint; the books were too thick — hence, he insisted
on leaving.

After he made his decision, his mood got better. In the evening, he had one
more bowl of porridge made by rice and green peas and ate more pickled vegetables
mixed with sesame oil. After dinner, as usual, he took a walk with other guests in
the sanatorium along the beach. Looking at the sky, the clouds, the sea, the waves
and the fishing boats, he murmured in his heart, "Farewell! Please forgive me!" Like
a grown-up child who was unwilling to lead his life by his mother's side, he was
asking for forgiveness. "Good-bye! I am leaving."

Before going to sleep, he got up and went to the lavatory in the garden. On his
way back, when he passed the porch, he stretched his neck and took a look at the
sea. Ah! He had never seen such a beautiful scene. The surface of the sea was gilded
with a layer of silvery light. Oh, he could not help but wonder what bright moon
there was on such a serene night.

Over the sea the moon shines bright,
And we gaze at it far far apart.[7]

"Under the full moon, what does the sea look like? Let me, the unfilial son, say goodbye to you again!" Thinking of this, he returned to his room, put on his coat and shoes and went out alone.

He was stunned! He had never realized that the night and the moon had such great enchantment! They embraced, altered, repainted, and reshaped everything, which was no longer what it was in the daytime. Now, on such a tranquil night, bathed in the moonlight, all the things became vague and gentle. Rose willows, pines and cypresses, phoenix trees, pagoda trees, attics, houses, dressing rooms, bathing pools, coast, beach, caves, winding sightseeing road as well as the sea, the sky and the pier... They closed in to one another, reconciled to one another and attached to one another. All the differences and contrasts — such as tall buildings and level ground, land and sea — were fading away; all the distances were being shortened; all the disturbances were coming to an end; and all the excitements were calming down. Even the tidewater became tender and soft. It lightly, tentatively and politely tapped the bank for fear of disturbing or offending someone.

Transcending, presiding and dominating over all these was an integral whole of the silvery light.[8] With the glaring, vivacious, misty and expansive sea beneath, the sky appeared more boundless and profound, in which the small milky moon was especially conspicuous. The moon shed its light and formed a "silvery light area" on the surface of the water, while outside that area the sea was rosy and endlessly dark. As he sauntered, the "silvery light area" moved together with him. Under such a moon and sky, with such an inviting silvery light area by his side, he was almost moved to tears. It seemed that all these had been planned and arranged for him in advance. On the night before his departure, the sea dressed herself up, showed him all her tenderness, lingered lovingly with him, smiled gently to him and whispered affectionate words to him.

"Oh — sea — I — love — you — !" Finally, the call burst out of his heart. His voice was not loud. After all, he was no longer young, but a young couple flushed. He did not notice at all that under the rock where he stood there were two young lovers snuggling each other. He had never thought he might disturb someone, especially young people, for different from the parks or the swimming pools in the city, there were few young people here! Indeed, they were startled. The girl got out of her lover's arms and stood up. He could vaguely see her light-colored hair-knot. Feeling sorry to them, he quickly left. He felt sorry to have disturbed them but meanwhile he was happy and satisfied. It was so wonderful for the young people to date and nestle up to each other under such a romantic moon on the beach. The sea and the moon needed the youth and the youth also needed the sea and the moon! Who were they? He wondered. The guests and waiters here were not very young.

The local accent left over in his ears told him the answer. They were farmers! They must be farmers here! The local farmers! The "educated youth" (secondary school graduates who were sent to the countryside for reeducation during the Cultural Revolution 1966-1976)? The cadres in the village? The ordinary farmers? Anyway, they were young and loved the sea and the moon. They loved this "silvery light area". That's enough! Now, to him, the sky and the sea and the young lovers were all pleasantly sweet.

What sound? Swoosh — swoosh —. It was not the sound of waves or tides but what human arms produced. Under the rock he left just now, two people were swimming. Were they those two young lovers? Did not they feel cold? Were they not afraid of darkness? Where did they put their clothes? Ah, look! They swam so far! They were swimming toward the place which he had been looking forward to, the place he had no courage to reach, the place where the sky and the sea met, the place full of hope and light.

His eyes blurred. The flowing, flickering, fragmented and jointed silvery light dazzled his eyes![9] Did his eyes deceive him? Were there two people? Could people swim so fast? Were they fish? Mermen? Or mermaids?

No, he could not be wrong. They were human beings. They were those two young lovers. What did he doubt? If he were young, thirty years younger, if he were together with his beloved girl, would he be afraid of the darkness and the coldness? Would he miss this silvery night? Of course not! He would swim eight thousand meters away in one breath with his girlfriend to as far as he could see. Love, youth, and waves of freedom kept moving forward generation after generation and they would never become old and cold. They would last eternally, together with the sea, the moon, the wind and the sky.

He began to sing a song. With secret passions in his heart, he returned to his room. On the bed he thought of several poems — Pushkin's, Lermontov's, Byron's, Shelley's, Whitman's and his own. He fell asleep with a smile.

"What about your seaside tour? Just so so, right?" The driver who came to send him off asked. The driver might consider himself a psychologist with a profound insight, and he was told that Miao Keyan was just an old starchy bachelor. However, this time, the driver was wrong. Miao Keyan replied,

"No, this place is great — really fantastic!"

(Published in No.6, 1980)

1. 英语中的成对词，是语言的一大亮点，可以增强作品的文学性。下面列举一下英语中常用的成对词：alive and kicking 活泼的/ stuff and nonsense 胡说八道/ odds and ends 零碎/ lean and lanky 瘦而长/ high and mighty 趾高气扬/ by leaps and bounds突飞猛进地/ one and only 唯一的，最喜欢的/ open and aboveboard 坦率，正大光明/ through thick and thin 不顾艰难险阻的/ off and on 断断续续/ in and out; high and low 到处/ come and go 来来往往/ to and fro 来来往往/ rank and file 普通士兵，老百姓/ every hole and corner 每个角落/ whip and spur 快马加鞭。

2. 这里wind and wave押头韵，可以增强语言的音乐美。例如：twist and turn 曲折/ might and main 尽全力/ part and parcel 重要部分/ safe and sound平安无恙/ spick and span 崭新的/ time and tide 时光/ rack and ruin 毁灭/ slow and sure 稳而慢，稳妥/ hale and hearty 老当益壮/ chop and change 变幻莫测/ fair and foul 在任何情况下/ weal and woe 福祸/ forgive and forget 不念旧恶/ wax and wane 盛衰。

3. 全文多处提到海、树叶、风的声音。英语中的大多数拟声词(onomatopoeia)既可以作名词也可以作动词用，声音与意义联动，增强语言的注意价值和记忆价值，使语言更具形象性、文学性。例如：babble 潺潺声，叽叽喳喳/ click 轻微的尖声，咔嗒声/ clank 低沉的金属声，叮当声/ creak 嘎吱声/ crack 爆裂声，噼啪声/ crash 撞击声，破裂声，坠落声/ flop 扑通一声/ gurgle 水流汩汩声/ jingle 硬币、钥匙等金属的叮当声/ rattle 短促而尖利的声音/ sizzle 咝咝声/ pit-a-pat 噼啪声/ splash 溅泼声/ toot 号角、喇叭等的嘟嘟声。

4. "'特嫌'、'恶攻'、'反标'这些古老的汉语的生硬的缩写……"这是特定时代出现的一些特殊词汇，而且用了简称。由于汉英两种语言的差异，译文用首字母略缩词(acronym) 并加括号注释的方式来处理：... such awkwardly coined acronyms as SAS ("Secret Agent Suspect"), VA ("Vicious Attacks") and RS ("Reactionary Slogan")…

5. 这一段的描写形象感人。拟人、比喻等修辞手法的运用、对色彩的描摹、动词的生动使用，使作者眼中的大海栩栩如生。此外，汉语的意合特点也非常明显，主语不断变化，分句多，流散铺排。在翻译时，一是注意词汇的选择，务求准确、形象，以再现原文所描述的生动景象；二是由于英语是形合语言，译文的句式结构可以灵活处理，重新组织，不要拘泥于原文句式结构。

6. 汉语中有大量成语或者四字习语，比如此处的"老当益壮"、"青春焕发"、"越活越年轻"，以及下文的"杀一儆百"、"遗臭万年"、"罪该万死"、"前程似锦"、"苦尽甘来"等，翻译时，尽量在英语的idiom中找到对应的表达。要特别注意英汉idiom内涵的细微不同，比如喻体的不同、感情色彩的不同等等，准确使用。例如：*血流如注* to bleed like a pig /*艳若桃李* as red as rose; like lilies and roses /*一贫如洗* as poor as a church mouse /*白费口舌* to speak to the wind /*妖魔鬼怪* the power of darkness /*巧舌如簧* to have a silver mouth /*大海捞针* to look for a needle in a haystack /*打草惊蛇* to wake a sleeping dog.

7. 文学性较强的作品中，常常会出现诗歌，比如此处的"海上生明月，天涯共此时"和上文的奥地利歌曲。在翻译时，应该考虑到诗歌语言的特点，注意韵律，比如头韵、腹韵、尾韵等，注意意象的生动，注意句式的对仗，尽量做到音美、意美、形美。此处译文引自许渊冲译文"Over the sea the moon shines bright, / And we gaze at it far far apart."

8. "而超过这一切，主宰这一切，统治着这一切的是一片浑然的银光。"此句译为Transcending, presiding and dominating over all these was an integral whole of silvery light. 英语句式有尾重的特点。此处翻译采用了倒装，把句子要表达的重点放到最后，突出效果。

9. 毛荣贵说："英语音韵之美，其半壁江山归功于头韵。"(《翻译美学》，114页)此处，flowing, flickering, fragmented可以使得译文语言具有音韵美，对原文情感的表达具有辅助作用。

高女人和她的矮丈夫

◎ 冯骥才

一

你家院里有棵小树，树干光溜溜，早瞧惯了，可是有一天它忽然变得七扭八弯，愈看愈别扭。但日子一久，你就看顺眼了，仿佛它本来就应该是这样子。如果某一天，它忽然重新变直，你又会觉得说不出多么不舒服。它单调、乏味、简易，像根棍子！其实，它不过恢复最初的模样，你何以又别扭起来？

这是习惯吗？嘿，你可别小看了"习惯"！世界万事万物中，它无所不在。别看它不是必须恪守的法定规条，惹上它照旧叫你麻烦和倒霉。不过，你也别埋怨给它死死捆着，有时你也会不知不觉地遵从它的规范。比如说：你敢在上级面前喧宾夺主地大声大气说话吗？你能在老者面前放肆地发表自己的主见吗？在合影时，你能叫名人站在一旁，你却大模大样站在中间放开笑颜？不能，当然不能。甭说这些，你娶老婆，敢娶一个比你年长十岁，比你块头大，或者比你高一头的吗？你先别拿空话呛火，眼前就有这么一对——

二

她比他高十七厘米。

她身高一米七五，在女人们中间算做鹤立鸡群了；她丈夫只有一米五八，上大学时绰号"武大郎"。他和她的耳垂儿一般齐，看上去却好像差两头！

再说他俩的模样：这女人长得又干、又瘦、又扁，脸盘像没上漆的乒乓球拍儿。五官还算勉强看得过去，却又小又平，好似浅浮雕；胸脯毫不隆起；腰板细长僵直，臀部瘪下去，活像一块硬挺挺的搓板。她的丈夫却像一根短粗的橡皮滚儿：饱满，结实，发亮；身上的一切——小腿啦，脚背啦，嘴巴啦，鼻头啦，手指肚儿啦，好像都是些溜圆而有弹性的小肉球。他的皮肤柔细光滑，有如质地优良的薄皮子。过剩的油脂就在这皮肤下闪出光亮，充分的血液就从这皮肤里透出鲜美微红的血色。他的眼睛简直像一对电压充足的小灯泡。他妻子的眼睛可就像一对糊里糊涂的玻璃球儿了。两人在一起，没有谐调，只有对比。可是他俩还总在一起，形影不离。

有一次，他们邻居一家吃团圆饭时，这家的老爷子酒喝多了，乘兴把桌上的一个细长的空酒瓶和一罐矮墩墩的猪肉罐头摆在一起，问全家人："你们猜这像嘛？"他不等别人猜破就公布谜底，"就是楼下那高女人和她的矮爷儿们！"

全家人轰然大笑，一直笑到饭后闲谈时。

他俩究竟是怎么凑成一对的？

这早就是团结大楼几十户住家所关注的问题了。自从他俩结婚时搬进这大楼，楼里的老住户无不抛以好奇莫解的目光。不过，有人爱把问号留在肚子里，有人忍不住要说出来罢了。多嘴多舌的人便议论纷纷。尤其是下雨天气，他俩出门，总是那高女人打伞。如果有什么东西掉在地上，矮男人去拾便是最方便了。大楼里一些闲得没事儿的婆娘们，就对着他俩这不相称的背影指指划划。难禁的笑声，憋在喉咙里咕咕作响。大人的无聊最能纵使孩子们的恶作剧。有些孩子一见到他俩就哄笑，叫喊着："扁担长，板凳宽……"他俩闻如未闻，对孩子们的哄闹从不发火，也不搭理。可能为此，也就与大楼里的人们一直保持着相当冷淡的关系。少数不爱管闲事的人，上下班碰到他们时，最多也只是点点头，打一下招呼而已。这便使真正对他俩感兴趣的人，很难再多知道一些什么。比如，他俩的关系如何？为什么结合一起？谁将就谁？没有正式答案，只有靠瞎猜了。

这是座旧式的公寓大楼，房间的间量很大，向阳而明亮，走道又宽又黑。楼外是个很大的院子，院门口有间小门房。门房里也住了一户，户主是个裁缝。裁缝为人老实；裁缝的老婆却是个精力充裕、走家串户、专好说长道短的女人，最喜欢刺探别人家里的私事和隐秘。这大楼里家家的夫妻关系、姑嫂纠纷、做事勤懒、工资多少，她都一清二楚。凡她没弄清楚的事情，就要千方百计地打听到；这种求知欲能使愚顽成才。她这方面的本领更是超乎常人，甭说察言观色，能窥见人们藏在心里的念头；单靠嗅觉，就能知道谁家常吃肉，由此推算出这家的收入状况。不知为什么，六十年代以来，处处居民住地，都有这样一类人被吸收为"街道积极分子"，使得他们的能力、兴趣和对别人的干涉欲望合法化并得到发挥。看来，造物者真的不会荒废每一个人才的。

尽管裁缝老婆能耐，她却无法获知这对天天从眼前走来走去的怪夫妻结合的缘由。这使她很苦恼。好像她的才干遇到了有力的挑战。但她凭着经验，苦苦琢磨，终于想出一条最能说服人的道理：夫妻俩中，必定一方有某种生理缺陷。否则谁也不会找一个比自己身高逆差一头的对象。她的根据很可靠：这对夫妻结婚三年还没有孩子呢！于是团结大楼的人都相信裁缝老婆这一聪明的判断。

事实向来不给任何人留情面，它打败了裁缝老婆！高女人怀孕了。人们的眼睛不断地瞥向高女人渐渐凸出来的肚子。这肚子由于离地较高而十分明显。不管人们惊奇也好，置疑也好，困惑也好，高女人的孩子呱呱坠地了。每逢大太阳或下雨天气，两口子出门，高女人抱着孩子，打伞的事就落到矮男人身上。人们看他迈着滚圆的小腿、半举着伞儿、紧紧跟在后面滑稽的样子，对他俩居然成为夫妻，居然这样形影不离，好奇心仍然不减当初。各种听起来有理的说法依旧都有，但从这对夫妻身上却得不到印证。这些说法就像没处着落的鸟儿，啪啪地满天飞。裁缝老婆说："这两人准有见不得人的事。要不他们怎么不肯接近别人？身上有脓早晚得冒出来，走着瞧吧！"果然一天晚上，裁缝老婆听见了高女人家里发出打碎东西的声音。她赶忙以收大院扫地费为借口，去敲高女人家的门。她料定长久潜藏在这对夫妻间的隐患终于爆发了，她要亲眼看见这对夫妻怎样反目，捕捉到最生动的细节。门开了，高女人笑吟吟迎上来，矮丈夫在屋里也是笑容满面，地上一只打得粉碎的碟子——裁缝老婆只看到这些。她匆匆收了扫地费出来后，半天也想不明白这夫妻之间到底发生了什么事。打碎碟子，没有吵架，反而像什么开心事一般快活。怪事！

后来，裁缝老婆做了团结大院的街道居民代表。她在协助户籍警察挨家查对户口时，终于找到了多年来经常叫她费心的问题答案。一个确凿可信、无法推翻的答案。原来这高女人和她的矮丈夫，都在化学工业研究所工作。矮男人是研究所总工程师，工资达一百八十元之多！高女人只是一名普普通通的化验员，收入不足六十元，而且出生在一个辛苦而赚钱又少的邮递员家庭。不然她怎么会嫁给一个比自己矮一头的男人？为了地位，为了钱，为了过好日子，对！她立即把这珍贵情况，告诉给团结大楼里闲得难受的婆娘们。人们总是按照自己的思维方式去解释世界，尽力把一切事物都和自己的理解力拉平。于是，裁缝老婆的话被大家确信无疑。多年来留在人们心里的谜，一下子被打开了。大家恍然大悟：原来这矮男人是个先天不足的富翁，高女人是个见钱眼开、命好有福的穷娘儿们。当人们谈到这个模样像匹大洋马、却偏偏命好的高女人时，语调中往往带一股气。尤其是裁缝老婆。

三

人，命运的好坏不能看一时，可得走着瞧。

一九六六年，团结大楼就像缩小了的世界，灾难降世，各有祸福，楼里的所有居民都到了"转运"时机。生活处处都是巨变和急变。矮男人是总工程师，迎头遭到横祸，家被抄，家具被搬得一空，人挨过斗，关进牛棚。祸事并不因此了结，有人说他多年来，白天在研究所工作，晚上回家把研究成果偷偷写成书，打算逃出国，投奔一个有钱的远亲，把国家科技情报献给外国资本家——这个荒诞不经的说法居然有很多人信以为真。那时，世道狂乱，人人失去常态，宁肯无知，宁愿心狠，还有许多出奇的妄想，恨不得从身旁发现到希特勒。研究所的人们便死死缠住总工程师不放，吓他、揍他、施加各种压力，同时还逼迫高女人交出那部谁也没见过的书稿，但没效果。有人出主意，把他俩弄到团结大楼的院里开一次批斗大会；谁都怕在亲友熟人面前丢丑，这也是一种压力。当各种压力都使过而无效时，这种做法，不妨试试，说不定能发生作用。

那天，团结大楼有史以来从未这样热闹。

下午研究所就来了一群人，在当院两棵树中间用粗麻绳扯了一道横标，写着那矮子的姓名，上边打个叉；院内外贴满口气咄咄逼人的大小标语，并在院墙上用十八张纸公布了这矮子的"罪状"。会议计划在晚饭后召开，研究所还派来一位电工，在当院拉了电线，装上四个五百烛光的大灯泡。此时的裁缝老婆已经由街道代表升任为治保主任，很有些权势，志得意满，人也胖多了。这天可把她忙得够呛，她带领楼里几个婆娘，忙里忙外，帮着刷标语，又给研究所的革命者们斟茶倒水，装灯用电还是从她家拉出来的呢！真像她家办喜事一样！

晚饭后，大院里的居民都给裁缝老婆召集到院里来了。四盏大灯亮起来，把大院照得像夜间球场一般雪亮。许许多多人影，好似放大了数十倍，投射在楼墙上。这人影都是肃条不动的，连孩子们也不敢随便活动。裁缝老婆带着一些人，左臂上也套上红袖章，这袖章在当时是最威风的了。她们守在门口，不准外人进来。不一会儿，化工研究所一大群人，也戴袖章，押着高女人和她的矮丈夫，一路呼着口号，浩浩荡荡来了。矮男人胸前挂一块牌子，高女人没挂。他俩一直给押到台前，并排低头站好。裁缝老婆跑上来说："这家伙太矮，后边的革命群众瞧不见。我给他想点办法！"说着，带着一股冲动劲儿扭着肩上的两块肉，从家里抱来一个肥皂箱子，倒扣过来，叫矮男人站上去。这样一来，他才与自己的老婆一般高，但此时此刻，很少有人对这对大难临头的夫妻不成比例的身高发生兴趣了。

大会依照流行的格式召开。宣布开会，呼口号，随后是进入了角色的批判者们慷慨激昂的发言，又是呼口号。压力施足，开始要从高女人嘴里逼供了。于是，人们围绕着那本"书稿"，唇枪舌剑地向高女人发动进攻。你问，我问，他问；尖声叫，粗声吼，哑声喊；大声喝，厉声逼，紧声追……高女人却只是摇头。真诚恳切地摇头。但真诚最廉价；相信真诚就意味着否定这世界上的一切。

无论是脾气暴躁的汉子们跳上去，挥动拳头威胁她，还是一些颇工心计的人，想出几句巧妙而带圈套的话问她，都给她这恳切又断然的摇头拒绝了。这样下去，批判会就会没结果，没成绩，甚至无法收场。研究所的人有些为难，他们担心这个会开得虎头蛇尾；乘兴而来，败兴而归。

裁缝老婆站在一旁听了半天，愈听愈没劲。她大字不识，既对什么"书稿"毫无兴趣，又觉得研究所这帮人说话不解气。她忽地跑到台前，抬起戴红袖章的左胳膊，指着高女人问："你说，你为什么要嫁给他？"

这句突如其来的问话使研究所的人一怔，不知道这位治保主任的问话与他们所关心的事有什么奇妙的联系。

高女人也怔住了。她也不知道裁缝老婆为什么提出这个问题。这问题不是这个世界所关心的。她抬起几个月来被折磨得如同一张皱巴巴枯叶的瘦脸，脸上满是诧异神情。

"好呵！你不敢回答。我替你说吧！你是不是图这家伙有钱，才嫁给他的？没钱，谁要这么个矮子！"裁缝老婆大声说，声调中有几分得意，似乎她才是最知道这高女人根底的。

高女人没有点头，也没摇头。她好像忽然明白了裁缝老婆的一切，眼里闪出一股傲岸、嘲讽、倔犟的光芒。

"好，好，你不服气！这家伙现在完蛋了，看你还靠得上不！你心里是怎么回事，我知道！"裁缝老婆一拍胸脯，手一挥，还有几个婆娘在旁边助威，她真是得意到达极点。

研究所的人听得稀里糊涂。这种弄不明白的事，就索性糊涂下去更好。别看这些婆娘们离题千里地胡来，反而使会场一下子热闹起来。没有这种气氛，批判会怎好收场？于是研究所的人也不阻拦，任使婆娘们上阵发威。只听这些婆娘们叫着：

"他总共给你多少钱？他给你买过什么？说！"

"你一月二百块钱不嫌够，还想出国，美的你！"

"邓拓是不是你们的后台？"

"有一天你往北京打电话，给谁打的，是不是给'三家村'打的？"

会开得成功与否，全看气氛如何。研究所主持批判会的人，看准时机，趁会场热闹，带领人们高声呼喊了一连串口号，然后赶紧收场散会。跟着，研究所的人又在高女人家搜查一遍，撬开地板，掀掉墙皮，一无所获，最后押着矮男人走了，只留下高女人。

高女人一直呆在屋里，入夜时竟然独自出去了。她没想到，住在大院门房的裁缝家虽然闭了灯，裁缝老婆却一直守在窗口盯着她的动静。见她出去，就紧紧尾随在后边，出了院门，向西走过了两个路口，只见高女人穿过街在一家门前停住，轻轻敲几下门板。裁缝老婆躲在街这面的电线杆后面，屏住气，瞪大眼，好像等着捕捉出洞的兔儿。她要捉人，自己反而比要捉的人更紧张。

咔嚓一声，那门开了。一位老婆婆送出个小孩。只听那老婆婆说：

"完事了？"

没听见高女人说什么。

又是老婆婆的声音：

"孩子吃饱了，已经睡了一觉。快回去吧！"

裁缝老婆忽然想起，这老婆婆家原是高女人的托儿户，满心的兴致陡然消失。这时高女人转过身，领着孩子往回走，一路无话，只有娘俩的脚步声。裁缝老婆躲在电线杆后面没敢动，待她们走出一段距离，才独自怏怏地回家了。

第二天一早，高女人领着孩子走出大楼时眼圈明显地发红，大院里没人敢和她说话，却都看见了她红肿的眼皮。特别是昨晚参加过批斗会的人们，心里微微有种异样的、亏心似的感觉，扭过脸，躲开她的目光。

四

矮男人自批判会那天被押走后，一直没放回来。此后据消息灵通的裁缝老婆说，矮男人又出了什么问题，进了监狱。高女人成了在押囚犯的老婆，落到了生活的最底层，自然不配住在团结大楼内那种宽敞的房间，被强迫和裁缝老婆家调换了住房。她搬到离楼十几米远孤零零的小屋去住，倒也不错。省得经常和楼里的住户打头碰面，互相不敢搭理，都挺尴尬。但整座楼的人们都能透过窗子，看见那孤单的小屋和她孤单单的身影。不知她把孩子送到哪里去了，只是偶尔才接回家住几天。她默默过着寂寞又沉重的日子，不过三十多岁，从容貌看上去很难说她还年轻。裁缝老婆下了断语：

"我看这娘儿们最多再等上一年。那矮子再不出来，她就得改嫁。要是我呵——现在就离婚改嫁，等那矮子干嘛，就是放出来，人不是人，钱也都没了！"

过了一年，矮男人还是没放出来，高女人依旧不声不响地生活。上班下班，走进走出，生着炉子，就提一个挺大的黄色的破草篮去买菜。一年三百六十五天，天天如此……但有一天，矮男人重新出现了。这是秋后时节，他穿得单薄，剃了短平头，人大变了样子，浑身好似小了一圈儿，皮肤也褪去了光泽和血色。他回来径直奔楼里自家的门，却被新户主、老实巴交的裁缝送到门房前。高女人蹲在门口劈木柴，一听到他的招呼，刷地站起身，直愣愣看着他。两年未见的夫妻，都给对方的明显变化惊呆了。一个枯槁，一个憔悴；一个显得更高，一个显得更矮。两人互相看了一忽儿，赶紧掉过头去，高女人扭身跑进屋去，半天没出来；他蹲在地上拾起斧头劈木柴，直把两大筐木块都劈成细木条。仿佛他俩再面对片刻就要爆发出什么强烈而受不了的事情来。此后，他俩又是形影不离地一起上班，一起下班回家，一切如旧。大楼里的人们从他俩身上找不出任何异样，兴趣也就渐渐减少。无论有没有他俩，都与别人无关。

一天早上，高女人出了什么事。只见矮男人惊慌失措从家里跑出去。不会儿，来了一辆救护车把高女人拉走。一连好些天，那门房总是没人，夜间灯也闭着。二十多天后，矮男人和一个陌生人抬一副担架回来，高女人躺在担架上，走进小门房。从此高女人便没有出屋。矮男人照例上班，傍晚回来总是急急忙忙生上炉子，就提着草篮去买菜。这草篮就是一两年前高女人天天使用的那个，如今提在他手里便显得太大，底儿快蹭地了。

转年天气回暖时，高女人出屋了。她久久没见阳光的脸，白得像刷一层粉那样难看。刚刚立起的身子左倒西歪。她右手拄一根竹棍，左胳膊弯在胸前，左腿僵直，迈步困难，一看即知，她的病是脑血栓。从这天起，矮男人每天清早和傍晚都搀扶着高女人在当院遛两圈。他俩走得艰难缓慢。矮男人两只手用力端着老婆打弯的胳膊。他太矮了，抬她的手臂时，必须向上耸起自己的双肩。他很吃力，但他却掬出笑容，为了给妻子以鼓励。高女人抬不起左脚，他就用一根麻绳，套在高女人的左脚上，绳子的另一端拿在手里。高女人每要抬起左脚，他就使劲向上一提绳子。这情景奇异，可怜，又颇为壮观，使团结大楼的人们看了，不由得受到感动。这些人再与他俩打头碰面时，情不自禁地向他俩主动而友善地点头了……

五

高女人没有更多的福气，在矮小而挚爱她的丈夫身边久留。死神和生活一样无情。生活打垮了她，死神拖走了她。现在只留下矮男人了。

偏偏在高女人离去后，幸运才重新来吻矮男人的脑门。他被落实了政策，抄走的东西发还给他了，扣掉的工资补发给他了。只剩下被裁缝老婆占去的房子还没调换回来。团结大楼里又有人眼盯着他，等着瞧他生活中的新闻。据说研究所不少人都来帮助他续弦，他都谢绝了。裁缝老婆说：

"他想要什么样的，我知道。你们瞧我的！"

裁缝老婆度过了她的极盛时代，如今变得谦和多了。权力从身上摘去，笑容就得挂在脸上。她怀里揣一张漂亮又年轻的女人照片，去到门房找矮男人。照片上这女人是她的亲侄女。她坐在矮男人家里，一边四下打量屋里的家具物件，一边向这矮小的阔佬提亲。她笑容满面，正说得来劲，忽然发现矮男人一声不吭，脸色铁青，在他背后挂着当年与高女人的结婚照片；裁缝老婆没敢掬出侄女的照片，就自动告退了。

几年过去，至今矮男人还是单身寡居，只在周日，从外边把孩子接回来，与他为伴。大楼里的人们看着他矮墩墩而孤寂的身影，想到他十多年来一桩桩事，渐渐好像悟到他坚持这种独身生活的缘故……逢到下雨天气，矮男人打伞去上班时，可能由于习惯，仍旧半举着伞。这时，人们有种奇妙的感觉，觉得那伞下好像有长长一大块空间，空空的，世界上任什么东西也填补不上。

1982年2月16日天津

（载1982年5月号）

The Tall Woman and Her Short Husband

○ Feng Jicai

I

You have been accustomed to the shape of the small tree in your yard. With few branches, bare of leaves, it stands straight like a stick. One day, it changes and becomes crooked, uneven and irregular. You may feel awkward and uneasy at first, but after a few days you will get used to the new sight of it, as if it has always looked like this. However, one day, it suddenly turns straight again, which consequently becomes an eyesore for you in an instant. You will frown upon it. This tree is so boring, simple and dull like a stick! As a matter of fact, it is what it used to be. What's the matter with you?

Is the "power of habit" working on you? Yes! Don't make light of it! It breaks through every pore of God's own earth and it is everywhere around you. Habit is not a decree or a regulation that you must abide by but it is powerful enough to bring about trouble and bad luck if you belittle it. You cannot say you are tightly bound by it, for, more often than not, you succumb to its force and follow it consciously or unconsciously. For instance, dare you speak aloud in front of your superiors? Have you ever given any of your lip wantonly in front of the venerable seniors? When having a group picture taken, have you stood in the middle, giving unbridled smirks with celebrities standing aside? Of course not! Putting all these aside, even in your marriage, are you willing to marry a woman who is ten years older, much bigger and a lot taller than you? Don't butt in or retort so rapidly! Now let me show you such a couple —

II

She was 17 centimeters taller than her husband.

She was 175 centimeters tall, like a crane among chickens, while he had a body

31

of only 158 centimeters and thus got a nickname "Wu Dalang" (a character in one of China's greatest classical novels *Outlaws of the Marsh*, nicknamed "Three-inch Nail" for his short stature and ugly appearance).[1] He reached her earlobe but looked almost two heads shorter than her!

Their appearances contrasted a lot. She looked withered, skinny and flat. Her face, like an unpainted ping-pong bat, was narrowly acceptable, and her facial features looked small and flat as if carved in low relief. Her breasts were not plump at all. Under her thin and stiff waist, that pair of buttocks were dented much like a hard washboard. In contrast, her husband looked stout, strong and shiny, like a short thick rubber rolling stick. His shanks, insteps, mouth, nose, faces of the fingertips, and all the other things on his body were round, fleshy and elastic. His skin, a piece of best-quality thin leather for sure, was smooth and soft. And thanks to the superfluous grease and the abundant blood circulation underneath his skin, his face glowed with a rosy luster. As opposed to her blurry eyes, his eyes, like a pair of bulbs with sufficient electric voltage, always shed bright light. In appearance, they did not match in the least but strangely enough, they kept each other's company every day, inseparable as body and shadow.[2]

One day, a family of their neighbors had a reunion dinner. To add more fun, the old man in that family put a winebottle and a pork can side by side on the table. Pointing to the slender bottle and the stumpy can, he asked, "What do they look like? Guess!" "The tall woman and her short man downstairs!" The old man could not wait for the reply and announced excitedly.

All the family burst into a riotous laughter. They kept laughing till the dinner was over.

How did the tall woman and the short man get to know each other and become a couple?

This was the question that all the residents in Solidarity Building were interested in. When the couple moved into this building, all the residents looked at them curiously and skeptically. Some kept their doubts in their own hearts, while some loose-tongued people could not help but begin to be garrulous. As a result, gossips came pell-mell.[3] When it rained, it was always the tall woman who held the umbrella, and if something fell onto the ground it was invariably the short man who bent down and picked it up. At this occasion, some nosy and idle women would always point at their backs and start teasing and gossiping. After all, when the giggle began to gurgle in one's throat, it was hard to hold it back.[4] Adults' tomfoolery easily triggered kids' pranks, and the moment they saw this couple, the kids guffawed and shouted in an excited way, "The carrying pole is long while the stool is short …"

Turning a deaf ear to the kids' mischief, the couple never got angry. The tall woman and her short husband went on their lives as usual but they deliberately kept a distance from their neighbors. Only a few people occasionally nodded a greeting to them when they met the couple on their way to work or back home. Thus, people found it hard to know more about the couple. By and by, the couple became a mystery in their neighbors' eyes. Did the couple get on well with each other? How did they get married? Who always gave way in their family? — Nobody could give a reliable answer. They could only think about the answers by guess and by god.[5]

This was an old-style apartment building. The rooms facing the south were big and bright and the corridor was wide but dark. Outside the building, there was a spacious yard, at the entrance of which lived a tailor and his wife. The tailor was honest and simple while his wife energetic and nosy, who loved gossiping, dropping around, and poking her nose into others' privacy. She knew everything in this building like the palm of her hand.[6] The spousal relationships in each family, the conflicts among relatives, who's diligent and who's lazy, and so on and so forth, and even the income of each family was as clear as day to her. If she found something unknown, she would use all sorts of wiles and methods to get it.[7] Such a spirit could turn a fool into a king! Indeed, she had the supernatural ability in this respect. She could read people's faces and minds; she knew whose family was having meat for dinner just with the help of her nose and accordingly she could guesstimate the income of that family. For this reason or that, since the 1960s, there were many such people, who were regarded as "positive models" in each residential area. Thus, their behavior was justified and they had more opportunities to bring into full play their unparalleled abilities and their interest in meddling with others' private affairs. It was true that the Creator gave everyone the chance to display himself.

However, the tailor's wife felt greatly frustrated at this particular case. She was capable but she knew little about this strange couple who went to and fro in front of her eyes every day. She felt her talent was challenged! Racking her brains day and night, she finally hit upon a convincing explanation. One of them must have some physical defects; otherwise, why would a woman marry a man who was a head shorter than her! She was convinced by her own deduction. The couple had been married for three years and still they had no kid! Soon, people in Solidarity Building all took her explanation for granted and accepted it as true.

However, the subsequent fact dealt a heavy blow to her and shattered her confidence completely. The tall woman was pregnant. People kept casting curious and doubtful looks at the tall woman's gradually protruding belly, which, high above the ground, appeared quite noticeable. In their surprise, query and puzzlement,

33

the tall woman's child came to the world. After that, when the couple went out on a sunny or a rainy day, the tall woman would hold the child in her arms and it was her short husband who held the umbrella for them, moving his clumsy and fleshy short legs and following her closely. His ridiculous and arduous manner made people more curious. How could such two people be glued to each other! All sorts of seemingly reasonable guesses and explanations turned up but none of them was verified and confirmed. Thus, gossips went on and on, fluttering here and there like birds unable to find a place to perch on. The tailor's wife asserted, "They must be having something under the table; otherwise, why don't they approach others? The pus will ooze out sooner or later. Let's wait and see!" One night, sure enough, she heard a smash from the couple's room. With the excuse of collecting fees for sweeping the yard, she hurried to the couple's home. Knocking at their door, she felt complacent that the snake in the grass finally showed up — the couple's secret would come to light! She could not lose the opportunity to see their quarrel with her own eyes and thus get the most detailed detail then and there.[8] But the tall woman opened the door with a smile and her husband was sweeping a smashed plate behind her, with a smile, too! How disappointing! The tailor's wife collected the fee and left in a hurry. What happened? A plate was smashed but neither of them got angry; instead, they smiled. What a strange couple!

Later, the tailor's wife was elected deputy of the residents in Solidarity Building. Once, when she accompanied the neighborhood policemen to check on the residential occupants, she finally discovered the answer to the mystery which had been pestering her heart for so many years, a conclusive and irrefutable answer. The tall woman and the short man both worked in a chemical industry research institute. The short man was the chief engineer and earned the high salary of 180 yuan per month! The tall woman, born in a poor family of a postman, was just an ordinary technician with a salary of less than 60 yuan every month. So that's how matters stood! No wonder the tall woman would like to marry a man who was a head shorter! Obviously, for his position, his money, for the sake of having a good life! The tailor's wife immediately told her invaluable discovery to every woman plagued with idleness in Solidarity Building and they all had a firm belief in her words. It was true that people were willing to explain the world in their own logic and they tended to conform everything to their own understanding. Finally, the mystery haunting their hearts for years was unveiled! The truth suddenly dawned upon them. The husband was a rich man with some inborn defect and the wife was a money-hungry woman with some good luck. Since then, when they talked about the tall woman, about her lank figure, about her good luck, they would turn unpleasantly sour,[9] especially the tailor's wife.

III

Happiness and misfortunes can never be foretold.

When calamity came, people's fates turned different. In 1966, great changes and abrupt crises occurred everywhere, and all the residents in Solidarity Building got their opportunity to "change their fates". Disasters fell onto the short man. His home was searched and his properties were totally confiscated; he was publicly criticized and denounced and put into a "cowshed", a detention house (set up by the "Red Guards" during the Cultural Revolution for those considered as "monsters and demons"). To add more crimes to him, someone came up with the charge that the short man, during those years, collected research findings in the daytime when he worked in the institute and wrote them into a book at night, and that he planned to escape with his book to one of his rich relatives abroad. He was accused of divulging the national technological information to foreign capitalists! It was really absurd that many people accepted the accusation as true. In those days, everything was in a disorderly and frenzy state and everyone turned abnormal and even hysterical. Quite a lot of people would rather be ignorant and cruel-hearted. They were obsessed with uncovering "hidden evildoers" at their side and they would ferret out Hitler if they could! Some people who once worked in the institute made frantic attacks on the short man, their former chief engineer. They threatened him, beat him, put all sorts of pressures on him and forced his wife to surrender that book which actually nobody had ever seen. However, their intimidations yielded no result. Then, someone suggested that a criticism and denunciation meeting be held in front of Solidarity Building and said that the short man might feel disgraced in front of his relatives and acquaintances. Since all their former attempts had failed, it was worth a try.

That day, there was an unprecedented hubbub around Solidarity Building.

In the afternoon, a group of people came from the institute. They hustled and bustled,[10] tying a thick rope between two trees and hanging on it a banner on which the short man's name bearing a big cross was painted. The aggressive slogans were put on everywhere inside and outside the yard and the short man's crimes were shown in public on 18 pieces of paper. The meeting was scheduled to be held after supper. An electrician was sent in time, who installed four big bulbs of 500-watt power. The tailor's wife was a lot fatter. She had been promoted to be the director of public security. Complacent with her power and influence, she was elated and contented. On that day, she busied herself with the neighborhood women, painting slogans and pouring tea for the "revolutionaries" from the institute. And even the electricity wire for the bulbs was threaded from her house to the meeting. She was so excited as if she were hosting a wedding ceremony!

After supper, summoned by the tailor's wife, all the residents in the building gathered in the yard. Those four big bulbs lit up the whole yard and made it as bright as a football field under spotlights at night. People stood there motionless and even children dared not move about. Their shadows on the walls, dark and still, were tens of times bigger than their real figures. The tailor's wife, together with several other guys, wore red armbands on their left arms, the most majestic thing in those years. They guarded the gate to prevent irrelevant people from coming in. After a while, a mob of people came,[11] wearing red armbands and shouting slogans on the way. The short man and the tall woman were escorted into the yard. A board hung in front of the short man's chest and another board was reserved for his woman. The couple was forced to lower their heads and stand side by side on the stage. The tailor's wife rushed forward and yelled, "This man was too short and people standing behind can't see him. Let me see …" While screaming, she turned and ran to her home, the two hunks of flesh on her shoulders bumping up and down all the way. Soon, she brought back a soap box. Turning it upside down, she put it on the ground and let the short man stand on it. Now, finally, he was as tall as his wife. However, at this time, few people showed interest to their disproportionate statures. The couple was facing an imminent disaster!

The meeting was conducted in accordance with the then popular form. The announcement of the opening of the meeting was followed by shouting slogans, delivering vehement speeches and shouting slogans again. After all these procedures, after all these pressures were exerted, people began their frenzied attacks on the tall woman. They threw verbal swords at her one after another. Some shrieked, shouted and roared at her, and others snapped or rapped out abuses,[12] all with the intent of making her hand over the manuscript of the "book". In the cut and thrust of the noise, she remained silent, shaking her head sincerely and earnestly. But sincerity was the most valueless thing in those days and the belief in sincerity meant disbelief in all the other things.

Some bad-tempered men jumped up and threatened the tall woman with their fists, and some threwd people with a calculating mind asked her a few wily and tricky questions, trying to extract some useful information out of her mouth. In face of the noisy crowd, the tall woman kept shaking her head in a resolute and earnest manner. Obviously, the meeting would yield no result and even end in commotion and failure. People began to scratch their heads. The meeting might have "a tiger's head and a snake's tail" — they came in high spirits and might depart in dejection.[13]

The tailor's wife got more and more impatient. She was illiterate and had no interest at all in that "book". To vent more anger, she, all of a sudden, jumped onto the stage. Raising her left arm with the red armband and pointing at the tall woman, she blurted out, "You! Why did you marry him? Why?"

All the people were taken aback by her question and her sudden surge of anger, having no idea about the delicate and wonderful relation between her strange question and their predominant concern.

The tall woman was also dumbfounded. She did not expect that the tailor's wife would ask her such a strange question, which actually had nothing to do with her "crimes". Raising her emaciated face, which, after months of torture, was much like a wrinkled and withered leaf, she looked at the tailor's wife in great surprise.

"OK, you dare not speak out. Let me help you! You married him for his money, right? Otherwise, who is willing to marry such a pigmy!" The tailor's wife shrieked in a triumphant tone, believing that it was she alone who knew the ins and outs of the matter.

Now, the tall woman neither nodded nor shook her head. A flash of proud, mocking and rebellious light glowed in her eyes. She was suddenly wide awake.

"OK, OK, you are still unwilling to submit! It's all over with him. Don't you know? You can no longer rely on him! I know what you are thinking about!" Patting her chest and waving her hand, the tailor's wife shouted, beside herself with excitement. Several garrulous old women cheered for her by her side.

People from the institute could not understand what the tailor's wife was talking about. Feeling puzzled, they had no other choice but to go on listening. They knew that a woman's whimsical and digressing nonsense sometimes could help build a boisterous atmosphere, and now, undoubtedly, they needed such a noisy situation. Hence, nobody came up to stop her. The tailor's wife and some other women got more excited. They yelled,

"How much did he give you? What did he buy for you? You must confess!"

"Isn't 200 yuan a month enough for you? You even want to go abroad. Stop daydreaming!"

"Is Deng Tuo your backstage supporter?" (Deng Tuo once served as the editor-in-chief of *People's Daily* and he committed suicide in 1966 when the Cultural Revolution began.)

"You phoned to Beijing one day. To whom? The Village of Three Homes?" ("The Village of Three Homes" is a column of a magazine, written by three writers who were severely criticized and denounced in the Cultural Revolution.)

As was known, the success of a meeting totally depended on the atmosphere. Seeing the people so excited and the air so lively, the leader of the meeting announced the adjournment in a hurry. After shouting a series of slogans, people scattered away. The tall woman's home was searched once again. They pried up the floor and peeled off the wall, only to find nothing. In the end, they escorted the short man away, leaving the tall woman alone at home.

The tall woman did not go out until night fell. The light in the tailor's had been turned off already but the tailor's wife had been sitting by the window in the darkness, watching the tall woman's movement. Seeing the tall woman going out, the tailor's wife followed her stealthily. Out of the yard, after two crossings westwards, the tall woman stopped at a door. She knocked at it lightly. The tailor's wife hid herself behind a telegraph pole on the opposite side of the street, holding her breath, opening her eyes wider, as if waiting to catch a rabbit which was about to get out of its hole. She was much more nervous than her prey.

With a click, the door opened. An old granny brought out a small kid.

"It was over?"

No answer could be heard.

The old granny said,

"The kid has taken his supper and had a sleep. Go back soon."

The tailor's wife suddenly remembered that it was this old woman who had been helping the couple take care of the kid. She felt disappointed! The tall woman came here just for her kid, which really threw a wet blanket on her. Her high spirits and zest instantly vanished. At this moment, the tall woman turned around and left with her kid. The tailor's wife heard nothing but the sound of their footsteps. Seeing them walking away, she went home sullenly.

The next morning, when the tall woman led her kid out of the building, nobody dared accost her. Seeing her red and swollen eyes, they, especially those who attended the meeting last night, experienced a peculiar feeling toward her. Secretly, they felt guilty. They looked away to avoid her eyes.

IV

Since that meeting, her husband had not returned home. The well-informed tailor's wife blatted that he was charged with more crimes and was put into prison. Thus, the tall woman became the prisoner's wife, totally falling into the unfathomable abyss of life. She was not allowed to continue living in Solidarity Building and was forced to exchange her room with the tailor's family. She moved into that isolated small room several meters away. In fact, it was not so bad. At least, it saved her the trouble of seeing those people in the building. It seemed that even nodding a greeting was embarrassing to them all. Every day, the residents in the building saw her lonely house and her lonely figure through their windows. Nobody knew where she had sent her kid, who came back occasionally. In most of the time, she was alone. The lonely and hard life made her older. It was hard to tell her age. As a matter of fact, she was no more than thirty. The tailor's wife made an assertion.

"I bet that she will remarry if her husband continues to stay in prison. If I were her, I would remarry now. What's the point of waiting for him? Even if he comes back, he is not what he used to be. Just a poor fish!"

One year passed. Her husband still did not return. The tall woman led her life as before. Every day, she went to work and came home lonely and silently. To warm herself, she lit the stove in her room, and while the stove was burning, she went to the vegetable market with a big yellow beat-up basket. Day in and day out, her life went on and on like this … One day, her short man came back! It was in late autumn. He had changed a lot. His hair was crew-cut; his skin was pale, no longer lustrous as it had been; and his body was greatly trimmed down. He went directly to his former home, only to find the tailor there. The kind-hearted tailor sent him to the small room where the tall woman lived. She was chopping wood to light up a fire. On hearing his voice, she stood up at once, gazing at him with astonishment, stupefied. Both of them were surprised at each other's changes. One was withered and the other exhausted; one looked taller and the other much shorter. They stared at each other for a while and the woman turned her head and went into the room. He picked up the axe and began to chop firewood. He dared not stop as if something vehement and violent would happen between them if they were face to face again. He did not stop until two big baskets of wood were chopped into thin slices. After that, as before, they went to work together and came home together. People in the building found nothing strange about them and by and by they lost interest in them. The couple was no longer their concern.

One morning, something happened to the tall woman. Her husband ran out of the home in a hurry, and after a while, an ambulance came and brought the woman away. Their room was locked with lights off for several days and after more than twenty days the short man carried a stretcher back with a stranger, on which the tall woman lay quietly. After that day, the woman no longer came out of the room. Every day, her husband went to work in the morning and hurried back in the evening. After lighting the stove, he hurried to the market with that yellow beat-up basket, which had been used by his wife one or two years before. Now, the basket in his hand appeared bigger, its bottom almost touching the ground.

When the spring came the next year, the tall woman finally walked out of the room. For the lack of suntan, her face was very pale, as if coated with a layer of white paint. She staggered and lurched forward with a bamboo stick in her right hand. Her left arm curled in front of her chest and her left leg was so stiff that it was hard to move a step. Obviously, she got cerebral thrombosis. At each dawn and dusk, the short man helped her walk around the yard, taking great efforts to hold her curled left arm. She walked very slowly with great difficulty. As he was too short, he had to try his best to raise both of his shoulders so as to hold her arm tightly. Nevertheless, he was smiling. He kept encouraging her. He tied a rope around her left foot and exerted himself to pull it up with the rope. In this way, she could move forward. Somewhat moved by this spectacular scene, the people of Solidarity Building began to give the couple a voluntary and friendly greeting when they met the couple …

V

However, the tall woman was not so much blessed. She was, in the end, beaten down by the merciless fate of life and death. She died, leaving her beloved short man alone in this world.

After she died, good luck once more came to kiss the forehead of the short man. The government policy to right the wrongs was implemented and the confiscated property was returned to him. Besides, his salaries which had been taken away or held up in the past years were given back to him. Only his former home was still occupied by the tailor's family. At this time, some people, again, started to pay attention to him. It was said that his colleagues persuaded him to remarry and he declined for several times. The tailor's wife went chatterbox again,

"I know what kind of a woman he wants. Let me try!"

Now the tailor's wife had passed her prime and became modest and soft. Without power, she had to wear a smile on her face all the time. She went to the short man's home with a picture of her niece who was young and good-looking.

She sat in his room, looking about closely. With smiles all over her face, she brought up a proposal of marriage to him. As she was speaking excitedly, his face turned pale. He sat there, remaining silent, and behind him his wedding photo hung on the wall. Seeing his response, the tailor's wife did not dare to take out her niece's picture and had to leave quickly.

Several years passed. The short man was still single. Only on Sundays did he bring his kid back. Seeing his short and lonely figure every day and thinking of his years of hardships, little by little, people began to understand his persistence … When it rained, on his way to work, he held his umbrella the way he did before. At such times, people always got a strange feeling — under his umbrella there was a big empty space which could be filled with nothing and nobody in this world.

February 16, 1982 Tianjin
(Published in No.5, 1982)

1. 在翻译中，会涉及一些与原语历史、地理、政治等有关的文化信息。原语读者对于这些信息是理解的，但是对于译语读者来说，由于相关文化知识的缺乏，头脑中相关文化图式缺省，他们是很难理解的。文内夹注是一个有效的补偿手段，可以为译文读者补充相关知识，有助于读者的理解。本文中"武大郎"、"三家村"等，译者都在括号中加了简单的注解。

2. 人物的形象描写，是翻译的难点。好的翻译可以使人物形象跃然纸上，给全文起到画龙点睛的作用。在这一段中，丈夫和妻子的形象反差很大。原文多次运用比喻的修辞方法，形容词的使用也非常精彩，人物形象栩栩如生。在翻译时，尽量保留原文的修辞，注意选择生动形象的形容词进行翻译，比如这里的small、flat、plump、fleshy、elastic、smooth、soft、rosy、blurry、superfluous 等。

3. pell-mell 可以作名词、形容词和副词使用，是"鲁莽、匆忙、混乱"的意思。这里Gossips came pell-mell，形容谣言或者背后的各种议论纷至沓来。pell-mell为押韵词，读起来也可以有一些韵律效果，增添文采。这样的押韵的词汇在英语中很多，应注意积累。例如：airfare 飞机票价 / backtrack 走回头路 / cookbook 食谱 / deadhead 使用免费优待证的人 / fair hair 金发 / grandstand 体育场的正面看台 / hi-fi 高保真的音响设备 / willy-nilly 不管愿意不愿意 / teeny-weeny 很小的 / razzle-dazzle 骚动、欢闹。再比如成对的词：fair and square 公平地 / high and dry 孤立无援地 / toil and moil 辛苦工作 / wear and tear 磨损劳累 / wheel and deal 胆大妄为 / wine and dine 吃喝款待 / dear and near 亲近的 / town and gown 城镇居民和大学师生，等等。(汪榕培，《说东道西话英语》，347页)

4. "难禁的笑声，憋在喉咙里咕咕作响。"译为: When the giggle began to gurgle in one's throat, it was hard to hold it back. 原文"咕咕作响"译为 gurgle。译文中giggle与gurgle 押头韵，有利于再现原句的幽默效果。

41

5. They could only think about the answers by guess and by god. 句中by guess and by god意思是胡乱猜想。

6. like the palm of one's hand 了如指掌，下文中的as clear as day 一清二楚，这些都属于英语中的常用短语或习语。掌握这些常用习语，对翻译有很大帮助。例如：as poor as a church mouse 一贫如洗 / as obstinate as a mule 非常固执/ as like as two peas 二者看起来很像 / as easy as ABC 很容易，等等。

7. wiles and methods 各种办法。注意下文的几个短语：read one's mind 了解某人的想法，for this reason or that 为了这样那样的原因。

8. then and there 当时当地、当场，还可以用on the spot。英语中的有些短语用起来简单又生动。

9. 汉语中的"酸"的意思是醋的味道、不好的、伤心的、迂腐的、嫉妒的。英语中的"sour"意思是不好的、坏脾气的、生气的、刺耳的等等。汉语"酸"的隐喻意义与英语"sour"的隐喻意义不尽相同。在翻译时，要注意这一点。例如：你这人就爱吃醋，吃不相干的醋。You like being jealous, and it's over nothing.

10. hustle and bustle 熙熙攘攘，形容忙乱。

11. 这里用a mob of people 指出这群人是乌合之众，有混乱、嘈杂之感。英语中的单位词是非常丰富的，当谈到"一群人"时，可以根据这些人的特点或职业，选择最合适、最生动的单位词来翻译。例如：a band of musicians / a batch of students / a bench of judges / a board of directors / a choir of singers / a crew of sailors / a gang of hooligans / a mob of demonstrators / a pack of thieves / a party of guests。

12. "你问，我问，他问；尖声叫，粗声吼，哑声喊；大声喝，厉声逼，紧声追……"原文用了一系列有关喊叫的词，描述当时的场面的混乱和人们的疯狂。在翻译中，注意动词的选择，例如这里的shriek、shout、roar、snap、rap out 等等。有关人的说话或叫喊的动词，要注意多积累，例如：state / chat / chatter / gossip / announce / declare / scream / shout / exclaim / utter / prattle / babble / assert / affirm 等等。

13. "虎头蛇尾"是汉语中常用的成语，破折号后加上适当解释，有助于译文读者理解。

大坂

○ 张承志

从邮电局的绿漆窗口里伸出一只手臂，朝他拼命地挥舞着。

"嗬依！jihder！嘿！jihder！"那邮递员用生硬的乌梁海方言朝他吼着。——就这样知道了那个消息。他茫然信马走去时，已经听不见雇来带路的瘸老头怎样和那乌梁海人胡扯。远山像一条刺目的闪烁银霞。

他皱紧眉头，心里感到一片苍凉。马缰一下下地扯着他的手。

一个精光赤裸的小孩正在路边厚厚的尘土里爬着蠕动。细细的淡黄色粉末均匀地涂遍所有的小胳膊小腿，还有肚皮、屁股、脸蛋。他盯着那干土堆里玩得专心致志的土黄色肉体，"是男孩，"他想。这光洁的肤色和白亮炫目的远山都频频向他闪着捉摸不定的光。

这是什么信号呢？马儿却自顾自地走着。她的眼睛里一定也闪着光或信号，也可能是泪光，她是挺软弱的。

走过县文化馆。吴二饼站在台阶上，正慢腾腾地擦着那副变色眼镜。"真的上么？小伙子？"他问。显然声音里带着点酸味儿。

"还有假的？咱爷们又不是你这号废物！"向导李瘸子不屑地插嘴骂道。

"别吹啦，瘸子！"吴二饼戴上眼镜，反唇相讥道，"你能。从青海，到新疆，咋连个老婆也没混上？……"

他费劲地听着。两个老家伙的声音极淡极远，飘忽不定。jihder应当是信件，而不是电报。但又是走了他妈的四天的电报。电波总不会在哪里排队、等车、喂马料吧？居然四天才到达目的地。

干燥黄尘里那裸着的小孩朝前爬着，强烈的阳光晒着那涂匀了一层粉末的小光屁股。马喘着，牢牢跟定那小孩前行。再向前就是汽车站了：赶下午班车，明天能回到城里。接着，坐火车需要七十多个小时。——也就是说，一共需要六天才能赶回她身旁。

这内陆亚洲的山前平原酷热无比。大地不仅爆烤在白日之下，而且蒸腾着昨天和几天前饱存的热气。马无言地走着，向导老李跟在后面。汗水淌在胸脯上。电报，jihder。横亘前方的天山遮断了视线，像一线狰狞的银色屏障。她此刻一定在流泪。一定那样：默不出声，任泪水在颊上流淌。单调的马蹄音也随着这一切，踏着枯燥的节奏，啮咬着人心。

不管那乌梁海蒙古人怎样称呼电报，这该死的消息已经走了四天。而且他至少要六天才能赶回去。十天，十天后她会怎样呢？平安地度过这场劫难，还是死于大出血？

"流产。大出血。住院。能回来吗？"这电报语言也和马蹄声、和倾泻在大地上的白晃晃阳光、和这肮脏街镇的呼吸，和一切保持着同样的可憎节奏。踢踏，踢踏。马耳朵一耸，一耸。树叶子哗啦，哗啦。十天，十天。

"走哟，尕兄弟！"瘸老李催促着。光屁股的小孩儿在阳光里蠕行。前方的天山像露着牙齿。他感到头疼起来，似乎牙龈也肿起来了。毒阳狠狠地灼着他的脸，烤着他的心。他觉得心里也燃起了一片毒火，那火苗烧得他要发疯了。

这县城的土街很长，他收着马，慢慢走着，一言不发。他紧张地想着什么，汗流浃背。耀眼的阳光下，那小孩还在土堆里滚着，爬着，若有所思地。奇怪的孩子！他不觉被那赤裸的小小肉体吸引住了。

"大出血。能回来吗？"这样的电文一定会使邮电局的人投去惊奇的一瞥。十天以后，她会怎样呢？难道她真的会从这世上消失么？那可能消失的，难道真的能是她——那还在少年就结识了的、温柔而真诚的她么？

当他坐在西去列车的窗口时，曾默默地下决心要干成件什么事。他想到过那些当装卸工和卖大碗茶的同学，想到那些在麻省理工学院已经读到博士课程第二年的朋友，也想到过那些拆开了能熏死人的、文质彬彬的文痞。他们都似乎催着他到这儿来。

这条尘土飞扬的街一会儿就将走完。十天，这个冷冰冰的数字。他还什么都没干成。而十天之后一切只会剩下结局。还有五千公里以上的路程。——不管结局怎样，反正他已经绝不可能跨越这十天和五千公里的时间和空间了！

那孩子在黄土粉末里沐浴够了，站起来朝前跑去，横着穿过他面前的土街。

哦，这挺着鼓鼓的圆肚皮，逆着阳光奔跑的小崽子简直就是一个玩弄大自然的、胜利的生灵。而自己的那一个却——失败了，夭亡了，悄无声息地无影无踪了。

她也是一样。如果十天以后他捧着一个骨灰盒从地铁车站里走出来，那些大都市里流水般涌来的姑娘们女人们照旧会快乐喧嚣，向着他迸射出生的活力。就是这样：弱者的悲哀分文不值。

"能回来吗？"她真能选择语汇。电报纸上这行打印的灰色字迹里，既有她的心境，又有她的冷静。马儿走着，前面是银行的高台阶。

他慢慢地收着马缰，手上青筋突起。马儿站住了。让艰辛奋斗的弱者也得到一份成功，一份补偿吧……他目不转睛地盯着那白漆的银行牌子。

"牵着马。"他低声吩咐向导。

当他从银行大门里走出来时，全部公款都已汇至大坂彼侧的县城。这是一种自带凭证的汇寄方法。

现在即使后悔也晚了。只有翻过那道银色的、像大地狰狞尖牙般的大坂。

路过长途汽车站时，他闭上了眼。两匹马用力跺着坚硬的土路，甩着鬃走着。心头那火苗变小了，开始持久地一舐一舐地燎着他。牙龈完全肿了起来，生理的反应居然这么迅速。

他踢踢马腹，两骑马奔跑起来。

前面那大坂冷漠地矗立着。

李瘸子爱吹牛。据他说，他精通各大山脉里的每条道路，几十年专给各路军头、诸色衙门当向导。

"你这匹马，"他怀疑地盯着这瘸老汉胯下的那匹三岁杂毛红马，"这马能上大坂？"

"行，行呢。"老头不介意地应着，"那一年，我们的马子全垮啦。走到贼疙瘩梁，有个庄户。日他妈，门口绊着个马子。我枪栓一拉——"

他厌恶地打断了这老江湖："你专门给盛世才的兵带路？"

"还有老毛子俄娄斯。那年回回马仲英进来，也掂摆子银洋求咱。再后，帮咱解放军干过。再后——"

他不愿再听这青海老汉吹牛。马放开大步，茇茇草丛唰唰擦过马腿。松树林子近了，白桦林子近了，大山四下围合过来。那个光屁股的娃娃在阳光烤透的尘埃里安静地爬着，肤色像熟透的小麦。世界多丰富：钻山钻熟了也成了一种职业。这老头为着每天两块五的工钱，骑上匹小马就往冰山上爬，而且像去娶媳妇那么瘾头十足。雪线稍稍上移了，大约在两千米海拔以上。广播说山口风力七级。山口就是大坂，在那道传说是冰封的大坂面前，科学院的考察队撤退了。

他只担心瘸老李那匹粉杂毛的三岁马。

"这马是春天驯的？"他问。

"不价！去年它才两岁口，咱就把狗日的压出来啦。"

他不快地说："去年你骑的就是它？"

"哪！人家科学院一下就雇了好几匹！又驮人又驮料。就是走个半截子。日他妈，工钱少挣十几块。"

他敏感地想，这回你骑个癞皮狗找我开心来啦……"快走。"他吩咐。

牙疼。用舌头轻轻一舐，妈的，所有牙齿都松动了。他皱紧眉头，阴沉地望着前面的深谷。潮闷的风从云杉林子和密丛丛的草棵里吹来，马蹄踢动石块，单调地响着。

你骑着个马，我扛了个枪
诺们子两个嘛——浪新疆

老李乐滋滋地甩开右镫，弯过瘸腿在马脖子上盘了个二郎腿。这小调八成是个青海的土匪调。"诺们子两个"，他知道就是"我们俩"。可这歌调门很野，他感到山谷里明显地被这老头嚎得变成了绿林世界。

"老李，"他喊道，"走快点！"

马蹄重重地踏着石块。山脉正缓缓向背后迂回。蹄声嗒嗒——离妻子，离夭亡的孩子，离电报或者jihder都愈来愈远了。

"能回来吗？能回来吗？"他紧闭上干裂的眼角。这已经是第二次了。

上一次是在婚后不久。

"怎么办？我们刚刚开始补习呵，生孩子时，正赶上结业考试……"她注视着他。

他心烦意乱地大口吸着烟，坐立不安。

"……而且，那会儿也正好是研究生考试的日期，你怎么温书呢……"她自言自语地和他商量着。

他一口烟呛在肺里，剧烈地咳起来。

"咱们不要了吧——不要了吧？"她扶住他，轻轻地问。奇怪的是，她像是在哄他。

他心乱如麻，一拳猛砸在墙上。几个指关节都沁出血滴。

生活，你对这一代人太苛刻了……"不，我们回家！回家！"他疯狂地吼着，在妇科门诊"男同志止步"的玻璃牌子下，他一把抓住她的手，转身就走。

这是真实的么？……其实这是一种懦弱的推托。把残酷的选择推给一个弱女子来作。只是那烦恼是真的，现实从四面八方压来的烦恼。也许，这烦恼的气氛混淆了夫妻双方本质完全不同的心境。

他们太年轻了。当年轻的夫妇在社会的选择面前挣扎的时候，他们还没能体会诸如"父亲""母亲"这些深沉的字眼儿。

"你知道么，"从手术室出来时，她虚弱地倚着他的肩，缓慢地沿着医院昏暗的楼道走着，"我们组里的徐玲，想要孩子有好些年啦。我说我不要这个了，她说我不敢。哦——"她惨白的额上沁出细汗，露出一个疲倦的笑容。好像她终于攀过了一道冰大坂，很欣慰似的。"好啦，不怕那些考试啦——"她沉重地吐了一口气，闭上了眼睛。她用手指抚弄着他结实的臂肌，"别烦，只要你心里别烦，我就不怕。"她径管低柔地喃喃着，缓缓地走着。

也许她觉得很高兴：熬过了这一场苦难，又能倚着这么高大健壮的男子汉。

向导李老汉得意洋洋地甩着缰绳头，指着山崖上的小路："那一年，阿勒泰的哈萨反啦，盛世才派兵杀。走的就是这个道。"

牙疼得难忍，一跳一跳的，像是在跳脓。天山腹地的景观应当是迷人的：黛色的流雾，翠郁的松林。而现在充斥他视野的却是一片铁色。他盯着那些石砬子和断崖，马蹄无止无休地踏在那冰冷的铁色之上。

"……一个哈萨丫头子躲在水渠里头哩。妈的，老子正饮马，马子吓得蹦高。"瘸老李还在吹着牛。这老汉每时每刻都在絮叨，瘾头十足地吹牛皮。为着几壶酒钱，他美滋滋地朝大山里钻，骑着个小杂毛三岁马。

这老头一定没有孩子。

"……后来，我给那丫头子披了个军服，扣上个军帽子。趁黑，把她窝在艾比滩一个把兄弟家里啦。"

"老李，生火煮茶吧，歇会儿。"

老汉从脏污的马褡子里摸出两个又黑又硬的包谷馍。

他用力掰下一小块。咬了一下，松动的牙根立即刺入牙龈。他痛得眯起了眼。从嘴里掏出那块烤馍，上面染着红红的血。

"后来呢老李？那哈萨克丫头——"

老头大嚼着，不经意地回答说："她非不走嘛——咱还不拿上。咦，你吃呀！"

"不吃，不饿。"

"再说，那阵子，她只要一露头，骑巡队见了就是一刀。嘿，山上那死人

47

哪——"

他截断了话头："有娃娃么？"

"……呃，养了一个，唔，尕小子。"老汉咽下了一大口。

这瘸老汉也有罗曼史。被搭救的哈萨克姑娘哭着抱住了他的瘸腿。牙齿会全烂掉的，现在已经不能吃东西了。十天——已经不是十天，而是更多。一个肮脏而结实的光屁股小孩在爬着，他一定是在追着一只蚂蚁，他也一定是在一个蓬头垢面的哈族女人身旁。也许年青时代的李瘸子也站在旁边。

他啜着茶水，一杯接一杯。现在只有喝水，要多喝水。他凝神望着前方的冰山，牙龈还在一跳一跳地疼。那冰山轻蔑地朝他闪着冷光。

"走吧，老李。"他站起来。

自从二十世纪初法国探险队在敦煌发现了一份珍贵的唐代写本卷子以来，这条空寂的山峡连同它中间的那道冰大坂，就成了历史、考古、地理世界里的响亮名字。

"你们为什么撤回来了呢？"他曾经奇怪地问过科学院那几位中年人。

"我们不会骑马。"

"什么？"

"我们不会骑马，屁股疼得厉害。"

他愕然了。真不是一代人哪。不会骑马，屁股疼。他们就这样轻易地放弃了光荣。那份敦煌地理文书现在锁在巴黎的博物馆里，而关于它描述的那古道上的种种，至今没有一个中国人考察。

"我打算过冰大坂。"他对县文化馆的权威吴二饼说，"麻烦您帮我找找马匹和向导。"

"你过不去，过不去。雪线还低呢。去年我都没敢过。你不懂，山口风力七级。算啦，过不去。"这是县境之内唯一的一个眼镜。他看见镜片里反射着嫉妒的光和一种地头蛇式的恼怒。"马么？马匹困难哪！向导也难找——都搞包产啦，谁愿意跟上你钻大山？"那镜片里甚至闪射着快乐的、得意的光。

他默默地把桌子上那杯白开水喝下去。

"那么再见。我明天就上山。现在，和您辞行啦。"他站起来，冷冷地和那人握了握手。

多么狂妄的口气。简直是锐气逼人。而此刻，哪怕妻子丧亡的电报飞到身后的县城，不管那乌梁海人怎样再次把它称为jihder，他也无从知道了。一步的勇敢，一次男性的证明，背后深埋着多少难言的牺牲呐。牙齿又疼起来了，头晕。他摸出一包土霉素片，数也不数地吞了下去。

两骑马攀到了雪线以上。

"人哪，谁也有个山穷水尽，"老李又把二郎腿盘上了马脖子，"那回在贼疙瘩梁，咱不是拿了那老回回一个马子么——后来，日他哥；有一回我领着兵上北道桥子浪。沙窝上边边上，嘿！两个土匪绑了一伙淘金的客。顺着跪了一溜，吭吭大刀抡着砍头。"

"里头有那个人？"他问。

"啊呀！"老汉嚷出一句青海话，"——见了面就哭着磕头。咱一说情，就留下他一个。你看：这家伙赚不赚？给了咱个马，落下了一条命。"老头吹得唾沫星子乱溅。

走着，走着。马喘着粗气。

薄暮时，见到了一座哈萨克人的毡房。一个肤色黧黑的女人正在门口忙碌。夕阳染黄的山坡上散着羊群。

那个女人惊讶地望着这两个装束奇怪的骑者。她的眼睛是标准突厥式的，深陷的双眼皮俊目。"她也像这个哈萨克女人一样，"他心里想道，"在都市的险谷里迎送生涯。"女人，为什么也把她们驱赶到这种险恶的生涯里来呢？难道这儿不是男人们拼斗的世界么。

"住下吧？这地场美得很！"瘸老汉问。

"离大坂还有多远？"他犹豫了一下。

"嗨，远得很，那狗日的冰大坂。那一年，盛世才的兵——"

突然，他看见一个小孩，一个光屁股的哈萨克小男孩，追着一条小花狗崽儿朝山坡跑去。金灿的斜阳照得那小小的肉体分外明亮。

"够啦，接着走！"他猛地抽了马一鞭。

"哎，急啥嘛！公家人，住几天也不花自家的钱……哎，下马，下马呀。"

"快，走着说。"马匹已经跑起来。

"走着说，"老汉急了，"走着还说啥！"

"天黑再住。再赶一程。"他头也不回。

"哎呀你个尕娃娃！那年盛世才的兵——"

"老李，看看黄历。别一嘴一个盛世才。"

"……"

他们不再顶嘴，默默地走着。黄昏的山谷清脆地回响着倦乏的蹄音。山道陡峭起来。他们下了马，牵着马登上了一道山脊。

他吃惊地、用劲一把拽住了马嚼子。

——山体在此分成几脉，磅礴地朝四方滚滚而去。来路像一根线，缝在深谷崇山之中。层峦叠嶂移开了，正前方是一道明亮耀眼的冰岭。

那冰岭拦住了没有阻挡的夕阳余晖，闪烁着，静卧着，冷酷地斜睨着这渺小的两骑马。"狗日的，就是它。妈的大坂。"瘸子老李恶狠狠地嘟哝着。

天将黑的时候，在紧挨大坂脚下的石崖旁发现了一个松枝石块搭的窝棚。

"啧啧，美得很！"老汉打量着窝棚，赞不绝口。"猫下！就这儿猫下。"他嚷着，也许这里比帐房人家更对他胃口。

水烧开了，老汉撒上一把砖茶末子。

他试着咬了一口馍，疼得嘴角又抽搐起来。"饿了么？啧啧。"老头子吃得喷香，用狡猾的眼神瞅着他。夜幕正在降临。她如果——她一定正躺在医院里，在昏暗中睁大着眼睛，凝望着漆白的板壁。他用手指轻轻捻着烤馍块，用茶水泡了一缸糊糊。篝火烧旺了，毕剥响着。烤焦的苞米馍块没有泡软，他使劲嚼着，咽下一些咸咸的东西。篝火跳跃着，火苗黄得透明，像一个赤裸在炫目阳光下的小孩在舞蹈。

绊马时，发生了冲突。

瘸子老李摸出一根细细的硬麻绳，把马的两条前腿捆在一起，像捆一个贼。

"不行吧，老李，"他担心地望着老头，想起以前在军马场当牧工时的一些往事，"老李，马腿会淤血呀，不行吧！"

"哪里的话！嗨，就这个章法！"

"马走了十来个钟头，这么一捆，明天就瘸啦。"他劝道。

"管它！畜生么！明天睡醒，狗日的在眼皮底下要紧！"

"你这是在盛世才队伍上学下的章法？"他生气了，恶意地问。

"哈，就是嘛！尕娃子！"老汉却乐了，龇出一口黄板牙。

"明天马瘸了，咱们也去抢两匹换上？"他愤怒了。

"瘸不瘸，在它的命。人安生要紧。不行，真不行——回去哈萨帐房浪上两天嘛。"

"解开马腿。"他命令道。

"你——"老头子也火了。

"解开！"他低低地喝道。

老头双手叉起腰，蔑视地打量着他："你懂还是我懂？尕娃，老李咱五十六岁喽！"

正在这时，那匹粉红杂毛马一下子摔倒在地，而那土匪式的麻绳绊仍死勒在它腿上。小杂毛马绝望地放松了肢体，呼呼地喘着。

他决心乘机压住这江湖老汉："看见了么？论骑马，你得喊我先生！"

老汉一抢鞭子，喊起来："这么个难伺候！妈的，咱回呀，不干啦！"

"随你的便！"他吼道，双手攥成拳头："老子自己走！你卡不住老子的脖子！不信我就能死在这鬼大坂上！"

他狂怒地推开瘸老汉，劈手夺下马缰，把自己骑的红马解下来。土匪！兵痞！老江湖油子！他拔下一束马尾。大坂！大坂！万恶的大坂！他用马尾编着一根辫子。刹那间他看见了许多人的脸。吴二饼，"科学院"，还有别的一些。他用马尾辫联住两条前腿绊。红骠马低头吃草了，——它走不动，但又没有勒疼。他飞快地干着，一声不吭。心里那毒火吞噬了他。

老头子呆呆地站着。浓暮中看不清他的脸色。瘦骨嶙峋的、翘着一条瘸腿的身影，显得可怜巴巴。他迟疑着，迈开瘸腿，一拐一拐地解开了那根硬麻绳，小杂毛粉马站起来了。他扣好皮绊，与红骠马联上。他又一拐一拐地走开，抱来一捧松枝，添在快要熄灭的篝火上。——他顺服了。

怒涛平息了，一丝羞耻浮了上来。为了马，伤了人。而且是为了马腿，伤了人心。但他又必须使这自行其是的老江湖就范。他抬起眼睛，夜空星汉灿烂。那些星星在凝望着他。妻子和夭折了的小生命也在凝望着他。

又是这种莫名的烦躁的发泄。上一次的烦躁是为了让一个女人承担一切。这一次是要对付一个瘸老头。老李当然会顺服的。他要挣你的钱。当向导一天两块五毛钱，你是公家的人么……他慢慢地咬紧了牙关。三十二个牙齿的尖尖齿根一齐向肿胀溃烂的牙床刺进去。你用金钱的优势压服了一个穷人，一个老人，一个男人。星光下，青蓝色的大坂一片朦胧。哦，为了越过这大坂，他已经不择手段，不惜丑恶。莱辛说过，古代艺术家即使在表现痛苦时也避免丑，他们的法律是美。他觉得，这位德国古典美学家的眼睛，似乎也在那永恒夜空的星群中注视着他，像注视着一个渺小的例子。他垂下了头。咸咸的液体流向喉咙。

篝火熄了，只剩下暗红的灰烬。

两人枕着马鞍，裹着毡毯和皮袄睡下了。

天地一片漆黑。一股刺骨的寒气无声无息地浸入了膝盖以下没有盖上的肢体。双腿渐渐麻木了。

他一动不动地躺着，睁着眼睛。

李老汉似乎轻轻一动：大概也冻得睡不着。

"老李，抽根烟么？"他侧过脸去。

51

"嗯，不，咱……"

"喏，抽这个。我白天在马背上卷的。"

嗤的一声，火柴的亮光照亮了那张干枯的脸。"这莫合烟，……是伊犁的么？"

"不，县城买的。"

"怪。咱这烂县城能出这号好烟？"

"不坏吧？真有点伊犁烟的味儿。"

"就是。好烟。"

两个烟头一闪一闪。红光映亮两人的嘴唇和鼻尖。他们小声地谈着。

"狗日的，真冻人。"

"老李，你常在大山里睡么？"

"嗯……不。日他哥，这鬼地方。"

"抽烟，接上一根。"他又摸出莫合烟。

"不，抽我的，尕娃。给——"

"冷哪，忘了带上瓶酒。"

"狗日的，是忘啦。有瓶子古城大曲才美。"

"三台白酒也行啊。"他赞同地附和道。

"河南大裤裆的红薯干烧酒也行啊。"老头向往地说。

两个人都嘿嘿地笑了。

"尕娃子，我有个章法。"老头来精神了。

"什么章法？"他问。

"插筒子睡。你脚伸我怀里，我脚伸你怀里。就是——咱臭脚。"

"好！"他蹦起来，"插你老的筒子！"接着他又笑道："不然，明天马腿不瘸，人腿倒瘸了！"

"咱反正是瘸子。怕可惜了你城里人。"老头子狡猾地回答。

两人调整了睡法。脚和膝盖立即暖和过来。老汉放肆地把脚丫子蹅到他胸前，恶臭阵阵袭来。他也痛快地伸直两腿，满心希望把脚伸到老汉鼻头上去。

两个旅人沉沉地睡熟了。

他梦见了一座冰雪砌成的大坂。梦见了两匹联着绊子吃草的马。他看见了妻子。他走过去，想用双臂使劲地搂住她。但她却飘忽难即。他眼前闪过一道金黄色的电光，一个赤裸着胖乎乎屁股的小孩在正午的太阳地里爬着。满天的星斗都深不可测地望着他。妻子也用那星斗般的眼睛在望着他。不是每个女人，不是漂亮的女人和热恋中的女人就能有这样的眼神的。他好像搂了那当向导的瘸老汉。老汉哭了，又笑了。邮局的那个乌梁海人喊道："jihder！"文化馆门口，吴二饼慌张地跑来想拦住他。"能回来吗？"他终于从妻子的眼神中看到了这句话。"大坂，大坂。"他在梦中沙哑地嘟哝着。

大坂，在探险家A·斯坦因爵士的地图上写为Daban或Dawan。几乎中亚和蒙古的一切语言中都有这个语汇。已经很难判定它究竟是一个古老的汉语借词，还是一个汉语对某种民族语的谐声切意的译写。谁都知道，大坂是指翻越一道山脉的高高山口，是道路的顶点。

清晨，两骑马越过了松林，登上了植被稀疏的高海拔山顶地带。

"老李，你常年在山里跑，不想家么？"

"啥家！吴二饼不是说么，咱是光棍子。"

他想起老汉的浪漫故事："咦，你不是娶了个哈族丫头，还养了个儿子吗？"

"嗨！早跑了个毬的啦！"老头不耐烦地一甩鞭子，像轰了个苍蝇。

石头上有一处游牧人的岩画。一只印象派的岩羊。他取出笔记本、地图和罗盘。临摹着，他又问道：

"老婆儿子还能跑么？"

"日他哥，一块过了六、七年，她家里亲戚闹事，马队来了把她拿上跑啦。咱也没敢声张。"

"你也没去看看她？"

"前些年，我给地质队带路，山里见着她一次。妈的，一进帐房——"

他举起手止住老汉。石头裂隙中有尊残破的石窟造像。他举起照相机，按下快门。

"接着说呀，老李。"

"我一进门，她哇地他妈的就嚎开啦。"

马匹汗水淋漓，停住了脚步。他们下了马，朝上步行攀登。老汉一歪一拐地走着，说着。

"我吆喝她说，你嚎个啥，嚎得你男人回来一准揍你。快烧些茶，咱喝了上路。她不听，捂着脸，哇哇地嚎。狗日的，嚎得昏天黑地。"

"后来呢？"年轻人听得很紧张。

"后来没喝上茶。地质队那些人说，别惹个民族矛盾。嘿，帐房外头挤了不少人，偷听哪……她男人回来准揍了她。"

年轻人问："后来呢——再也没见她？"

"没。也不知他们上了哪处，是死是活。"瘸老汉擦了擦汗，想了一下，叹了口气："唉，那丫头，是个好丫头。"

远处那鞍形的冰大坂白雪皑皑。他想起了那双凝视着的眼睛。哦，她也是个好丫头。她现在也不知是死是活……现在他和老人心里体会到的，可能是一样的、过来人的滋味。

他们默默地上了马，穿上了皮袄。马弓着背，在青灰色的缓坡上一步步走着。山风带着尖锐的哨音掠过耳边。他觉得头晕得更厉害了。巉岩陡崖已低低沉向脚底，两侧山沟里满盛着白沙般的粉雪，明晃晃的。

在这片青色砾石的漫坡尽头，就是那鞍形的大坂之顶。

他转过身来，向老头问道：

"儿子呢？也和他妈在一块？"

"嗯。"老汉点点头，"那回没见上他。"

他失望地转回身去。这时，一股寒气逼人的风突然迎面冲来。他抬眼一望，前面是一道白色的山口。

他的心突然激烈地跳了起来。摸摸前额，有些发烫。

那快要伸手可触的山顶突然传来了一声呼唤，像是他逆境中的妻子发出的绝望叫声。他突然无比强烈地仇恨起这凶险的巨大山脉，仇恨起这高踞在上的大坂和这强大地欺凌人类的大自然。刹那间他也记起了吴二饼和他熟知的那些文痞，记起了所有侮辱过他和侮辱过他热爱的人们的人。他还记起了那制造又消灭了老李的家庭和使他沉默寡言的因素。肿起的牙龈一跳一涌地折磨着他，但他没有向挎包里去摸那些消炎药。他使劲地咬着那些背叛的牙齿，任咸咸的血向嗓子里流。他已难以压抑一股冲动，一股野兽般的、想蹂躏这座冰雪大山的冲动。他想驰骋，想纵火焚烧，想唤来千军万马踏平这海洋般的峰峦。他疯狂地感到一种快乐，感到自己终于找到了什么。他想呼喊，想喊来世上一切英雄好汉和一切专会向生活耍光棍的坏种，在这里和他一比高低。他想告诉无病呻吟的诗人和冒充高深的学者：这里才是个够味儿的战场，才是个能揭露虚伪的、严酷的竞争之地。他的胸中正升起着勇敢，升起着男子汉的气概。他想一步跨过这可怕的大坂，纵身飞下彼岸的绿洲，然后向那无援的女人飞奔。"能回来吗？"她用了问号。她已经安心承受一切苦难，为他留下了向这座大坂冲击的可能。"坚持住！"他默默地向她喊着，"等着我，坚持住！"他坚信只要迈过这最后一步她就能得救。但是——这里海拔已近四千米，他不仅无法驰骤，甚至不能加快一步。他僵硬地屹立在马背上，颜色铁青的脸上，两只血丝密布的眼睛死死盯着前方那白色的、迷蒙的大坂。

马匹喘着，拐着之字形，缓慢地向大坂顶端的分水线蠕动。其实，从远处或从空中看去，那黑甲虫似的两个影子已经和那鞍形的山口融为一体了。

他在霎时间平静了。

世界化成了斑斓的地图。在分水线上，他同时看见了山脉两侧的准噶尔和吐鲁番两大盆地。唐代敦煌文书描述的古道正静静地深嵌在弯曲的峡谷之底。山顶的一块巨石上铭文剥落，旁边堆着一匹驿马的骸骨。大地峥嵘万状地倾斜着，向着南方的彼岸俯冲而去。这是从海拔四千米向海平面以下伸延的、大地的俯冲。剧烈抖动的气浪正从吐鲁番低地淡白色的中央地带扶摇而起，化成长长一片海市蜃楼。在赤褐色的南侧深涧里，嵌着一条蓝莹莹的冰川。

他从未见过如此雄壮的景观。

大坂上的那条冰川蓝得醉人。那千万年积成的冰层水平地叠砌着，一层微白，一层浅绿，一层蔚蓝。在强烈的紫外线照射下，冰川幻变出神奇的色彩，使这荒凉恐怖的莽苍大山陡添了一分难测的情感。"大坂——"他失声叫道。他想不到这大坂、这山脉、这自然和世界会用这样的方式来安慰他。他久久勒着马伫立着，任那强劲的山风粗野地推撞着他。

"他妈的，这大坂。老子的马子累垮了！"拐子老李满头大汗，咒骂着走上山顶。那匹粉色的三岁马浑身透湿，簌簌地打着战。

"畜生！这么个熊样！"老汉恶煞般朝小马怒吼着，"趴蛋啦？挨刀子啦？这号熊样，能回来吗？"他颤抖了一下。"能回来吗？"他听见一个低柔的声音。一个最后的声音。他下了马。豪迈和勇敢突然消逝了。他慢慢把照相机放进了挎包。"不能在山顶上冒充英雄。"他想。他把马料倒在雨衣上，看着那匹精疲力竭的小马嚼着。风卷着积雪，在冰川顶上堆起乳色的一层。这层层砌起的冰川里不知葬着多少人的不幸。今天的这层雪会在夜里结成新的一层冰。每天冰川上都结着新的冰。不要照相，哪怕为着已经粗现轮廓的论文。——留下些缺憾吧。

"喂，抽些烟吧，尕娃。"

"抽莫合烟——帮我卷一根粗的。"

"这王八大坂，真难走。"

"喏，老李，点上火。"

他吸着浓烈的莫合烟，望着冰川顶的乳色积雪。今天的这一层里埋着他夭亡的孩子。这一定也是一个在阳光中光彩照人的，赤裸着的小男孩。他在今天被父亲葬到了这冰川之中。

他们休息了很久。粉色杂毛小马吃饱了苞米粒子。马褡子捆扎稳当。他们上了马，走向古道的另一半路程。

你骑着个马，我扛了个枪

诺们子两个嘛——浪新疆

　　瘸老李又乐陶陶地唱起了那支野蛮的青海小调。马蹄又在岩石上敲出单调的响声。南来的骄阳烫着脸颊，他们走离了分水线。

　　古希腊的艺术家是对的，经过痛苦的美可以找到高尚的心灵。这一点，她已经做到了。她不会死，她只会得到更坚实的爱情。因为，她以一个女人的勇敢，早已越过了她的大坂。死去的儿子也做到了，他将在这永恒的冰川上化成一个洒满阳光的胜利的小精灵。

　　下山道上，马儿走得很快。他朝那冰川，朝大坂投去了告别的、父亲的一瞥，然后不动声色地追上了他的向导。

1982年7月15日改定于博尔塔拉

（载1982年11月号）

Daban[1]

○ *Zhang Chengzhi*

An arm, out of the window which was painted green, was waving to him wildly.

"Hi! *Jihder*! Hi! *Jihder*!" The postman shouted at him in a clumsy Wulianghai dialect — he got the news in this way. Riding his horse forward in a daze, he could not hear the blabs between that postman and the old lame man, whom he hired to lead the way. Now, the mountains, much like glittering silvery clouds, appeared dazzlingly bright in the distance.

Knitting his brows tightly, he suddenly found his heart turning into a desolate wilderness. Dragged now and then by the rein in his hand, he moved on, at a loss.

Beside the path, a naked boy was crawling in the thick earth, with light yellow dirt all over his arms, legs, abdomen, hips and cheeks. Staring at this brownish fleshy ball playing wholeheartedly in the dirt, he could not help but utter a sigh, "It's a boy." Now, to him, the boy's lustrous skin and the dazzling mountain in the distance were both sparkling with some uncertain and unpredictable light.

Was it a sign? His horse trotted forward by itself. Now, her eyes must also be sparkling with light and signs, perhaps tears. She was fragile, indeed.

On the stairs of the County Cultural Center, Wu Erbing was cleaning his sunglasses in a leisurely manner. "Are you serious, young man?" He asked. Obviously, his tone was scornfully sour.

"Of course! We are not good-for-nothings like you!" Lame Li, the old guide he hired butted in contemptuously.

"Stop bragging! You old lame man!" Wu Erbing retorted, putting on his glasses, "From Qinghai to Xinjiang, you've covered such a long journey! If you are so capable as you said, how come you still cannot get a wife! ..."

He took great efforts to make sense of what these old fellows were talking about. Their voices gradually scattered, drifted, and faded away. *Jihder* must be a letter, not a telegraph.

But it was a telegraph! It took four days to arrive here! Damn it! Did telegraph

57

waves also need to line up and wait for the bus or the train? Did it need time to feed its horse? How could it be so slow!

The naked boy was still playing in the dry earth. Strong sunlight shone onto his naked buttocks which were covered with an even layer of dirt. The horse gasped and panted, following the boy closely. The bus station was ahead and if he caught the bus in the afternoon he could arrive at the town tomorrow, and after more than seventy hours in the train he could reach her. Altogether he needed six days.

It was sweltering. The plains before the mountains in inland Asia had been scorched by the blazing sun and the intense heat for several days. The horse trotted on silently and Lame Li, his guide, followed it closely. Sweat continuously dripped down to his chest. Telegraph, *Jihder*. The Tianshan Mountains ahead, which looked like a terrifying silver barrier, tortured his heart. She must be crying silently now. Her tears must be streaming down her cheeks now. The monotonous clattering of horse hoofs began to gnaw into his heart.

No matter how the Wulianghai Mongolian called it, the damned telegraph reached him too late! It took the bad news four days to reach him! And he needed at least six days to go back home. Altogether ten days … What would happen to her in these ten days? Could she survive the disaster? Would she die of profuse bleeding?

"Abortion. Massive hemorrhage. In hospital. Come back?" Her telegraph was in tune with the abominable rhythm around him — the clattering of the horse hoofs, the white glaring sunlight, the breath of the filthy streets — trit-trot, trit-trot, tick-tock, tick-tock … The horses' ears moved up and down … The tree leaves were rustling pit-a-pat, pit-a-pat … Ten days! Ten days![2]

"Let's go, buddy!" Lame Li urged. The naked boy kept crawling his way in the sun. The mountain ahead looked as if it were showing its teeth. He felt a strong headache and his gums began to swell. The sun was scorching his face and searing his heart. He felt that a fire was burning within his heart, which was going to drive him out of his mind.

The road in this small county seemed very long. Riding on his horse, he moved on slowly and silently. He was pondering over something. He was nervous, soaked through with sweat.

Under the glaring sun, the naked boy was still there as if he were thinking about something. What a strange boy! He was attracted by that small fleshy ball, rolling and crawling on that heap of earth.

"Massive hemorrhage. Come back?" Such words must have surprised the man in the post office. In ten days, what would happen to her? She would faint away? She would disappear from this world? His beloved, that tender and earnest girl whom he knew from his childhood, was going to die? Was it possible?

On the day when he sat in the westward train, he made up his mind to make some achievement. He thought of his classmates who were either working as a stevedore or selling bowls of tea at a stall; he thought of his friends who were the second-year students in MIT, going after their doctoral degrees; He thought of those stinky refined gentlemen who were accustomed to confusing facts by means of writing.[3] All of them were urging and prompting him to come here. He thought so.

He would soon walk to the end of the street where the dust was blown about by the wind. Ten days, what a cold number! He had achieved nothing. However, in ten days, all would be over. He was more than five thousand kilometers away from her — anyhow, it was impossible for him to transcend the time and space!

Bathed in the dirt long enough, the naked boy finally stood up. He saw the little boy crossing the road in front of him.

The little boy with a lovely protruding belly ran to the sun. Oh! The boy was like a mischievous sprite, playing with the nature and in the end conquering the formidable nature! However, his own child … was aborted and died silently.

So was she. After ten days, if he, holding her funerary urns, went out of a subway station, girls and women around him would continue their colorful ways of living and they would go on elbowing their way among the flood of crowds with vigor and vitality. He could imagine it. This was life. Nobody would care about the weak whose sadness was worthless.

"Come back?" She chose such words! The gray words printed on the telegraph paper conveyed not only her anxious expectation but also her composure. The horse moved on. He saw the bank's stairs ahead.

Slowly he pulled the reins, the blue veins standing out on the back of his hands. The horse stopped. The laborious and strenuous weak might as well have a share of success and compensation … He fixed his eyes on the white signboard of the bank.

"Lead the horse!" He said to Lame Li.

When he walked out of the bank, he knew all the available money had been remitted to the county on the other side of Daban. The remittance slip had a voucher.

Now it was too late to regret. The only thing he could do was to surmount Daban, the silvery, terrifying and sharp-teethed Daban.

While passing the long-distance bus station, he spurred his horse on, with his eyes tightly closed. His horse and Lame Li's trotted along the hard road, their manes flying in the wind. The fire in his heart abated, but it started to singe and gnaw at him little by little. His gums were swollen through and through. The physiological response was so fast!

He kicked his horse on the abdomen and it began to rush forward. Lame Li's horse followed at once.

Daban was standing ahead, indifferent and merciless.

Lame Li was fond of bragging, boasting that he was familiar with every path in every mountain. He had been a guide for various armies and governments.

"Your horse," looking at that three-year-old horse with shaggy pink hair, he asked Lame Li in a doubtful tone, "Your horse can climb onto Daban?"

"Of course!" Lame Li said, "That year, all the horses were exhausted and broke down. When we got to the Bandits' Gnarled Ridge, we found a horse at the gate of a farmhouse. Damn it! I cocked my rifle and …"

He interrupted Lame Li and asked, "Was it your job to lead the way for Sheng Shicai's soldiers?" (Sheng Shicai was a Chinese warlord who ruled Xinjiang from 1933 to 1944.)

"And for Russian soldiers, too. One year, Ma Zhongying gave me much money and asked me to lead the way for his army. And I also led the way for PLA soldiers. And …" (Ma Zhongying was a Hui Chinese warlord of Gansu Province during the 1930s. He wanted to expand his territory into southern Xinjiang by launching campaigns but was eventually repelled by Xinjiang's warlord Sheng Shicai.)

Tired of the old man's ramblings, he urged his horse forward. The horse quickened its steps and the grass underneath kept rustling. They were close to the pine woods … They were close to the birch woods … The mountains loomed and overwhelmed them from all sides. The naked boy was still lingering in his mind, who was crawling quietly on the heap of dirt which had been seared through by the sun. The boy's skin looked like that of the ripest wheat. What a wonderful world! Familiarity gave rise to a job! This old lame man, for the sake of a meager sum of money, would be willing to climb the icy mountain on his little horse! The old man was so addicted to his "job" that he looked as if he were going to his wedding. The snowline rose to about two thousand meters above the sea level. The radio said that wind force reached seven degrees at the mountain pass. Daban was the mountain pass, the legendary icy barrier which even scared away the expedition of the Science Academy.

What worried him most was Lame Li's three-year-old shaggy horse.

"Your horse was tamed this spring?" He asked Lame Li.

"No. Last year it was only two years old, but I already brought the damned animal into use!"

He turned a little fretful, "You mean you rode it last year?"

"Yup! The Science Academy hired several horses to carry people and stuff. It was a pity that we stopped halfway. Damn! I earned less money."

Hearing Lame Li's words, he turned sensitive and vexed. "Oh, this time, you are having fun with your 'mangy dog' at my expense ..." He said to himself. "Let's go! Be quick!" He ordered.

Toothache! He licked his teeth. Damn it! All his teeth loosened. He frowned and cast a gloomy glance at the deep valley ahead.

The damp and suffocating wind came from the fir woods and the dense grass. Their horses kicked stones under their hoofs, producing some monotonous sounds.

You ride your horse and I carry my gun;

We two brothers wander about the vast Xinjiang.

In a good mood, Lame Li began to hum a folk tune in a leisurely manner, as he took his lame feet out of the stirrup and crossed his legs around the horse's neck. The tune must be a Qinghai folk song, and bandits in Qinghai must always be singing it.[4] It sounded high-pitched and wild, and in his gruff voice the whole valley suddenly turned into a world of outlaws.

"Li," He cried out to the old man, "Be quick!"

The horse hoofs tramped and stamped upon rocks and stones and the mountain ranges were left behind by and by. In the clattering of the horses, his wife, his deceased child, the telegraph and that "*Jihder*" were farther and farther left behind.

"Come back? Come back?" Tightly he closed his eyes, which were cracking in the corners. This was his wife's second abortion.

The first abortion happened shortly after they got married.

"What can we do? Our remedial course just started, and the time I give birth to our child will be the final examination ..." She said to him, worried and anxious, gazing at his eyes.

He, too, was frustrated and fidgety, taking big puffs at his cigarette.[5]

"And ... the entrance examination for the post-graduate program will also be held on that day. How will you manage to go over your books ..." She said to herself and also to him.

He was heavily choked by a puff of smoke and began to cough roughly.

"We may as well ... abort it?" She held his arm and asked softly and tentatively. She seemed to be consoling him.

His mind was whirling. He could hardly compose his heart. Stretching his arm, he punched the wall with his fist. His finger joints began to bleed.

Life! You were so cruel to this generation of people ... "No! Let's go home! Go home!" He roared madly.

Under that "Women Only" glass signboard in the Department of Gynaecology, he grabbed her hand and left.

Was he right? … As a matter of fact, he evaded his duty like a coward. He left the cruel choice to his fragile wife. He was indeed annoyed. He was annoyed by the pressures and frustrations from all sides. Perhaps, it was these frustrations that confused the young couple's essentially different states of mind.

Yes, they were too young. When young couples struggled in the world, it was hard for them to understand the profound meaning of "father" and "mother".

Coming out of the operation room, she leaned languidly against his shoulder and shambled with him along the hospital's dark corridor.

"Do you know my associate Xu Ling? She has been longing for a child for many years, and this time when I told her I wanted to do an abortion, she said that she did not dare to do it. Ouch!" She felt painful, sweating all over her pale forehead. But she smiled at him as if she had surmounted the icy Daban and felt greatly pleased and relieved. Uttering a long sigh, she continued, "Now, I am not afraid of those exams …" Closing her eyes, caressing his strong arm with her fingers, she murmured gently to him, "Don't worry! As long as you are not upset, I am not afraid." They walked slowly forward.

Perhaps she was happy that she survived such a torture and that she could lean on the strong body of her man again.[6]

Swinging the rein, pointing at the small path in the mountain, Lame Li said in a complacent tone, "That year when people in Aletai rebelled, it was along this path that Sheng Shicai's troop came."

The teeth were throbbing with great pain. Perhaps they were suppurating. The scenery in the central region in the Tianshan Mountains should have been charming: the dark flowing fog, the green luxuriant pine trees … However, now, in front of his eyes it was a stretch of cold grayness. Staring at the iron-colored stones and broken cliffs, he spurred his horse on, leaving behind the incessant clattering of his horse hoofs on the cold and gray land.

"… At that time a Kazakh girl was hiding in the ditch. Damn! I was about to water my horse and she gave it a start!" Lame Li continued bragging about his past story. This old man kept nagging all the time, never to stop for a minute! He was so fond of talking big before others! Now to make a little money for alcohol, he would risk his life in the mountains, full of zest, on his three-year-old shaggy horse.

Lame Li must have no kids.

"… Later, I covered her with an army uniform and put an army cap on her head, and hid her in one of my brothers'."

"Li, let's set a fire and make some tea. Have a rest!"

Lame Li fumbled into his dirty bag and took out two corn pies, which were black and hard already.

He took one from Lame Li's hand, made efforts to break off a small piece and put it into his mouth. He gnawed slowly and lightly. The loosened teeth at once thrust into his gums. He felt so painful that he could not but close his eyes and take out that blood-stained corn pie from his mouth.

"Li, what happened later? That Kazakh girl …"

Lame Li, eating his pie ravenously, replied, "She did not want to leave me — then, why not take her? Em, hey, why don't you eat it?"

"I am not hungry."

"Besides, at that time, when she was found by the mounted patrols, she would be killed. Ah, so many people were killed … "

He stopped the old man's chattering, "Do you have kids?"

"… Oh, we had one boy." The old man swallowed a big mouthful.

He did not expect that even this old lame man had a romance — that Kazakh girl cried and hugged his lame leg, begging him to let her stay. His teeth would totally go rotten and now he could not eat with them. Ten days — not ten days, more than ten days! A dirty naked boy was crawling, who must be chasing an ant, and beside the boy stood a Kazakh girl with disheveled hair and a dirty face. And Lame Li in his prime was standing beside her.

He drank one cup of tea after another. What he could do now was to drink water. The more, the better. Fixing his eyes on the icy mountain in the distance, he felt his gums were throbbing more violently and the mountain far away was casting a cold and contemptuous look at him.

"Let's go, Li!" He stood up.

Since the French expedition discovered the precious manuscripts of the Tang Dynasty in Dunhuang at the beginning of the 20th century, the secluded valley with that icy Daban in the middle became a resounding name in the academic world of history, archeology and geography.

"Why did you retreat?" Once, out of curiosity, he asked those middle-aged men working in the Science Academy.

"We can't ride horses."

"What?"

"We are not able to ride horses. You know, our buttocks ache a lot on horseback."

He was surprised. Indeed, he and these men belonged to different generations. Could not ride horses? Buttocks ached? How could they give up the honor of doing the research with such an excuse! Now, the manuscripts discovered in Dunhuang were locked up in a museum in Paris, and until now, no Chinese had ever made an exploration or investigation on what the manuscripts depicted about the ancient road.

"I am going to climb over Daban." He said to Wu Erbing, the chief of the County Cultural Center, "I have to ask you to find a horse and a guide for me."

"It's impossible for you to pass it! The snowline is still low now. I did not dare to pass it last year, when the snowline was higher. Do you know? The wind force at the mountain pass reaches seven degrees. Forget it, young man! You can't pass it. I am sure." Wu Erbing was the only one wearing glasses in the county. A ray of jealousy and a fit of a local tin god's fury hid behind the glasses. "Horse? It's hard to find a horse! It's much harder to find a guide! Farmers have made a production contract and they are busy working in their fields. Who has the spare time to go with you into the mountains?" A flash of happy and even complacent light shot out of the glasses.

Saying no more words, he took up the cup of water on the table and drank it up.

"All right. Tomorrow I'll go to the mountains. Now let me say goodbye to you!" He stood up, shaking hands with Wu Erbing in a cold manner.

How arrogant and overbearing he had been! Now, he had no other choice but to go forward, regardless of possibly another telegraph (or *Jihder*, as the Wulianghai postman might call it) sent to the town behind him bearing the news of his wife's death. To him, this was a display of courage, a proof of his masculinity. Nobody knew how many sacrifices he had made and would make. His teeth began to ache again. He felt dizzy, so he took out a pack of oxytetracycline tablets and without counting the number he swallowed all of them.

Two horses climbed above the snowline.

"Whoever he is, he may come to the end of the road someday,"[7] Li continued, crossing his legs around the horse's neck. "Remember? I once grabbed a horse from a Hui man on the Bandits' Gnarled Ridge — later, I led some soldiers to the Land Bridge in the north, where we encountered two bandits by the sandpit. They caught a group of gold diggers, let them kneel down in a line, and were about to chop their heads off one by one."

"That Hui man was among them?" He asked.

"Yup!" Lame Li raised his voice, "As soon as he saw us, he kept kowtowing to us. Then we interceded for him and saved his life. So look! Was he lucky? He earned his life at the cost of a horse." Lame Li said in the Qinghai dialect, his spit spraying and flying with excitement.

As they went forward, their horses began to breathe heavily.

At sunset, they came to a Kazakh yurt. A woman with dark skin was busying herself at the gate. Looking afar, they could see herds of sheep scattering on the hillside gilded with a layer of golden sunlight.

The woman was surprised at the sight of the two riders in their strange outfits. Her nice, deep-set eyes with double-fold eyelids were typically Turkic. "Like that Kazakh girl, this woman is leading her life in such a dangerous place." He said to himself. Women, why did they come to such a place? Wasn't it the battlefield only for men?

"Let's stay here for some time. It is beautiful here." Lame Li suggested.

"How far is it to Daban?" He hesitated.

"Much farther. That damned Daban! That year when Sheng Shicai's army …"

All at once, he saw a boy, a Kazakh boy, naked, who was chasing a small puppy down the hillside. The glittering golden sun shone onto the boy's small body and made it very bright.

"Stop your idle talk! Let's go on!" He flung his whip onto his horse heavily.

"Why are you in such a hurry! Since you are working for the government, you don't need to pay for the boarding from your own pocket … Hey, guy, get off, get off the horse."

"Hurry up. You can go on your talk while riding forward."

"How can I chat with you on a galloping horse?" The old man turned restless.

"Don't stay until it gets dark. Now let's press on with our journey." He answered Lame Li even without turning his head.

"Ah, you young man! That year Sheng Shicai's army …"

"Oh, please! Li, look at the calendar! Stop talking about Sheng Shicai!"

"…"

They no longer talked to each other. Silently, they hastened their way in the valley, where the clattering of their weary horses resounded and lingered. As the mountain path turned steep, they dismounted. Dragging the horses, they ascended a ridge.

He was amazed. He pulled the curb and stopped his horse.

The mountain spread and rolled in all directions. Seen from afar, the small path they took was much like a thread in the deep valley. Now, layers upon layers of peaks and knolls no longer blocked their eyes and right ahead they saw a dazzling ice ridge.

The ice ridge stood there, quietly, sparkling with the afterglow of the sun, looking at them indifferently.

"Damn it! Here we are! It is the damned Daban." Lame Li grunted ferociously.

It was getting dark. By the cliff at the foot of Daban, they found a hut set up with pine branches and stones.

"Hey, great!" Lame Li looked at the hut up and down and kept praising it. "Stay here. Let's stay for the night!" He shouted. Perhaps, to him, this small hut agreed with him more than a Kazakh yurt.

The water was boiling in the kettle. Lame Li put a handful of crumbly brick tea into the water.

He tried eating the pie but just a small nibble of it gave him so great a pain that his mouth twitched. "Hungry, right?" Lame Li ate with relish, casting a cunning look at him. Night was falling. Now she must be lying in the hospital, opening her eyes wider and peering at the white walls and the ceiling. He pinched a little piece of the pie and put it into his tea. They got mixed and became a sticky congee. The fire they set up just now was burning with a pit-a-pat. The corn pie in the tea still kept hard and he had to force himself to chew and digest that salty thing. The yellow flames flickered, like a naked boy dancing in the dazzling sun.

They had a quarrel when tying the horses.

Lame Li tied his pink horse's two forelegs with a hard thin string as if binding a thief.

"No, Li." He turned uneasy. Lame Li's action reminded him of his past experience when he worked on an army horse-breeding farm. He stopped Lame Li and said, "Li, its legs may get bruised. You should not tie its legs like this."

"What are you talking about? We do it this way!"

"It has walked more than ten hours, and now, if you tie its legs this way, tomorrow it will become lame!" He explained.

"Who cares! They are just animals! Tomorrow when we wake up, it'll be more important that these damned animals are still here."

"Sheng Shicai did this to his horses?" He got angry and asked relentlessly.

"Oh, yes! Young man!" Lame Li laughed, showing his yellow teeth.

"If they become lame we'll plunder two horses as Sheng Shicai's army did?" He was exasperated.

"Whether it will be lame depends on its fate. It's more important to set our hearts at rest. If it becomes lame — we can go back to the Kazakh's home and stay there for a couple of days. "

"Untie its legs!" He ordered Lame Li.

"You …" The old man looked irritated.

"Untie them!" He ordered again in a low harsh voice.

Lame Li, with his hands on his hips, looked at him and shouted in a contemptuous tone, "Hey, young man, I am fifty-six! Is it possible that I know less than you?"

At this time, Lame Li's little horse fell down suddenly, and its two legs were tied so tightly that it desperately gave up struggling and fell onto the ground, out of breath.

"See? When it comes to riding horses, you'd better call me teacher!" He was determined to take this opportunity to repress this old man's swelling arrogance.

Lame Li flung his whip away and yelled, "So hard to wait on! Damn it! I want to go home. I quit!"

"Do as you please!" He roared, clenching his fist. "I'll go alone! Don't threaten me! I bet I won't die on this damned Daban!"

In great rage, he grabbed Lame Li's rein, pushed the old man away and untied his red horse's legs. Bandit! Army ruffian! Foxy old hand! He plucked off a wisp of hair from the horse's tail. Daban! Daban! The evil Daban! While braiding the horsehair, he saw many faces flashing in front of his eyes. Wu Erbing, "the Science Academy" and some others. He connected the horse's two forelegs with the horsehair braid. The red horse lowered its head and began to eat grass — it was effectively immobilized and didn't feel any pain from the braid. Without saying a word, he went on braiding another wisp of horsehair. His heart exploded with vexation and exasperation. The flame in his heart almost gobbled him up.

Lame Li said nothing but stood there, staring blankly. The old man's face was almost invisible in the dusk. His lean figure and that lame leg made him appear more deplorable. After a short hesitation, he staggered to his horse and untied its two legs. His pink little horse stood up at once. After tethering it with that red horse, the old man staggered to fetch a bundle of pine sticks to make a fire. Lame Li surrendered.

Thus, the surge of exasperation in his heart soothed. But in the wake of it, a flicker of guilt popped up.[8] He felt guilty to hurt his companion just for the sake of horses. For horses' legs, he hurt Lame Li's heart. He had to do so. He must subdue this old man. Looking up at the sky, he saw all the stars peering at him. His wife and his aborted little child must be looking him in the eye.

He knew that he was giving vent to his vexation and frustration. He felt frustrated last time because he had to let his wife bear all the burdens, while this time, he felt frustrated because he had to subdue an old lame man. He knew that Lame Li would give in for the sake of money — 2.5 yuan per day as a guide for someone working for the government. He clenched his teeth. The tips of his thirty-two teeth all thrust into his festered gums. Lame Li was a poor man, an old man, a man in need of money! He even forced such an old man to submit! Under the starry sky, the grayish blue Daban looked indistinct. Alas! In order to pass Daban, he became so unscrupulous! He stopped at nothing to get what he wanted. Gotthold Ephraim Lessing once said that the ancient artists avoided showing the foul or ugly side of life even when they were expressing their pains and sorrows, and that to them beauty was the eternal law. At this moment, he felt that this German aesthetician was also looking at him, a tiny insignificant negative example. He lowered his head, some salty fluid flowing into his throat.

The fire gradually went out and only a few dark red cinders were left, glowing with sparkles.

Wrapped by a blanket and a fur coat, they lay down on the ground, with saddles under their heads.

Endless darkness loomed over them and enclosed them. After a while, the chilly coldness silently crept over their body and numbed their shanks.

However, he lay there still, gazing at the sky.

Lame Li's body jerked lightly. Perhaps he was too cold to go to sleep.

"Li, have a smoke?" He turned to Lame Li and asked.

"Eh, no, we ..."

"Have this one!" He passed a cigarette to Lame Li. "I rolled it on the horseback today."

Scratch — the light of the match lit up Lame Li's withered face. "Did you buy it from Yili?" Lame Li asked.

"No. I bought it from the county."

"Oh? Our county produces such good cigarette?"

"Not bad, eh? Like the Yili cigarette, sort of."

"Em. Good."

The light on their cigarettes sparkled, lighting up their lips and nose-tips. They chatted in a low voice.

"It is damned cold."

"Li, do you often sleep in the mountains?"

"Em ... no. Who likes sleeping in this damned place?"

"Have one more cigarette!" He took out another one.

"No. Have mine, young man! Here ..."

"How cold! I forgot to bring some liquor."

"Damn! I also forgot it! If only we had some Gucheng liquor here!"

"The Santai liquor will also be OK." He agreed.

"The Henan liquor made from sweet potatoes is also good." Lame Li said, full of expectations.

They chuckled[9].

"Young man, I have an idea." The old man perked up.

"What idea?"

"You put your feet into my arms and I put mine into yours. The only problem is ... my feet stink."

"Good!" He almost jumped up. "I'll put my feet into your arms!" He laughed, "Otherwise, I am afraid that our legs may become lame tomorrow morning."

"I am already lame. I just think more of you, the man from the city." The old man answered with a cunning smile.

They adjusted their positions and lay down again. Their feet and knees turned warm quickly. The stinky smell of Lame Li's feet on his chest pelted at him, and he, too, stretched his legs into the old man's arms, hoping to raise his feet above the old man's nose.

Both of them fell asleep soon.

In his dream, he saw that icy and snowy Daban. He saw those two horses linked together with a braid, grazing on the meadow. He saw his wife! He walked to her, hoping to embrace her. But she was too vague and distant to reach. A golden flash of light dazzled him and he saw a naked fleshy boy crawling in the sun. All the stars cast an unfathomable look at him. His wife peered at him, too. Not every beautiful woman or every woman in love had such a pair of eyes. He seemed to beat old Lame Li, who sobbed and after a while burst into laughter. The postman cried out in the Wulianghai dialect, "*Jihder!*" At the gate of the County Cultural Center, Wu Erbing hurried to him, trying to stop him. "Come back?" He read these words in his wife's eyes. "Daban, Daban ..." He murmured in his dream.

"Daban" or "Dawan" appeared in the maps of the Hungarian-British explorer Sir Marc Aurel Stein. The word could be found in almost all the Central Asian and Mongolian languages. Nobody knew whether it was an ancient word borrowed from Chinese or a word transliterated from some other national language. Anyway, everyone knew that Daban was the highest mountain pass, the end of the mountain path.

In the morning, they passed the pine forest and climbed onto the top of the mountain where few trees or grass grew.

"Li, you keep going into the mountains all the year round. Don't you miss your home?"

"Home! Didn't Wu Erbing tell you? I am single!"

Thinking of that romantic story, he asked curiously, "Why? You said you married the Kazakh girl and have a son."

"Ah! She left me long ago!" Lame Li swung his whip impatiently as if driving a fly away.

A petroglyph by the ancients nomads caught his eye — a blue sheep in the style of impressionism. He took out his notebook, map and compass, and began to make a copy of it.

"Your wife and son left you? How come?" While drawing the picture, he asked.

"Damn! We had been together for six or seven years. Then her relatives came and took her away. I dared not say a word and had to hush it up."

"Didn't you see her later?"

"Several years ago, when I led the way for the geological expedition, I had a chance to see her in the mountains. Damn it! Hardly had I stepped into the yurt …"

Raising his hand, he stopped Lame Li. He was attracted by a dilapidated grotto statue standing in the crack of a rock. He held the camera up and clicked its shutter.

"Go on, please, Li!"

"Hardly had I stepped into the yurt when she began to cry."

Their horses were soaked with sweat all over. They got off the horses and tried to climb on foot. Lame Li staggered forward while chatting about his past story.

"I shouted to her. 'Why are you crying? Your husband will beat you up if he comes back and hears you crying. Be quick! Get some tea for us! We are thirsty. We'll go on our ride.' But she went on crying, putting her face in her hands. She cried and cried and cried her heart out."

"Then?" He asked nervously.

"Later, we had to leave without drinking her tea. The men from the geological expedition were afraid of causing a conflict between different nationalities, which was big trouble, for many local people huddled outside the yurt listening to our conversation. Her husband would surely beat her up when he came back."

He asked, "And then — you never saw her?"

"Never. I don't know where they are or whether they are still alive." Lame Li wiped off his sweat and uttered a sigh, "She is a good girl, a really good girl."

The saddle-like icy Daban lay in the distance. He thought of his wife's eyes. Oh! She was a good girl, too. Was she alive now? Now, he could understand Lame Li's experience and feeling. Both of them had trodden on the same path.

Silently they mounted their horses and put on their fur coat. Bending their backs, the horses plodded forward on the gray slope of the mountain. The wind whistled across their ears. He felt the dizziness even more overbearing. The sheer cliffs with craggy rocks were left behind them by and by. The valleys on two sides were filled with white glaring snow.

At the end of the slope was the top of that saddle-like Daban.

He turned to the old man and asked,

"Where is your son? By his mother's side?"

"Yes." Lame Li nodded, "But I did not see him last time."

He turned around in disappointment. A gust of chilly air blasted at them. Looking ahead, he saw a white mountain pass.

His heart began to beat violently and his forehead is burning.

He heard a call, much like the call of his desperate wife in hardships, from the mountaintop which was now almost within his reach. All of a sudden, a crushing resentment welled up in his heart. He hated this dangerous mountain, the arrogant Daban on top of it and the powerful unconquerable nature. He thought of Wu Erbing and those so-called writers, of those who insulted him and who put to shame the people he loved, and of those "convincing reasons" which helped build and finally destroyed Lame Li's family. His teeth were aching, but he did not reach for the anti-inflammatory pills in his bag; instead, he clenched his rebellious teeth in a forceful and resolved manner, regardless of the salty blood gushing into his throat. He could not repress his impulse, a beast-like impulse to make attacks at this mountain. He was eager to rush onto it, to set on fire all the things on the mountain and to call forth thousands and thousands of army men to stamp down all the forests and mountain ridges here. He enjoyed immersing himself in such a wild and zealous rhapsody, feeling that he finally achieved something. He yearned for calling out loud. He wanted to summon all the heroes and scoundrels here to fight each other. He wanted to tell those moaning and groaning poets and those sham scholars: this is the true battlefield, a place full of fierce competitions, a place without hypocrisy and fraud. Courage, of a masculine kind, gradually swelled in his heart. He longed for crossing Daban in one stride and plunging himself into the green oasis beyond it, into the bosom of his beloved wife over there. "Come back?" A question mark revealed her determination. She would rather endure all the pain by herself so as to give him more chances to fight with Daban. "Hold on!" He shouted to her in his heart. "Hold on! Wait for me!" He firmly believed that she could be saved if both of them persisted. However, it was four thousand meters above sea level and he could not speed up at all, let alone scud forward. He sat erect on the horse, stiff and serious, his face turning bluish pale and his bloodshot eyes glaring at that white misty Daban ahead. The horses gasped and plodded in a zigzagging line to the watershed on the top of Daban. At this time, seen from afar or from the sky, they, like two beetle-like black dots, had merged with the saddle-shaped mountain pass.

In a split second, he composed himself.

The whole world changed into a colorful map, spreading in front of his eyes. On the water-parting line, he saw the Junggar Basin and the Turpan Basin on the two sides of the mountain. The ancient road recorded in the Dunhuang manuscripts of the Tang Dynasty was quietly lying at the bottom of the valley. The inscriptions on a vast rock on the top of the mountain were already indistinct and beside the rock skeletons of a horse scattered. The ground dived southward with all its majesty, austerity, ruggedness and sheer strength. This was a dive from four thousand meters high! Streams of air waves shuddered and rose up from the white center of the Turpan Basin, and finally turned into a mirage, a large fantastic picture in the sky. The reddish brown valley in the south was inlaid with a blue and clear glacier.

Indeed, he had never seen such majestic and splendid scenery.[10]

The blue glacier on Daban was an intoxicating sight. The ice layers formed in tens of thousands of years piled in order and stretched horizontally forward. One layer was milky white; another was light green; and yet another layer was sea blue. Under the strong sunlight, the glacier miraculously changed its colors and gave off a magical light, which added an irresistible charm and a romantic hue to the isolated and dreadful mountain. "Daban —" He could not help but utter a cry from the bottom of his heart. The abominable Daban, the mountain, the nature and the world in the end soothed him in this way! He had never thought of this. For a long time he remained there, whipped by the strong wind.

"Damn it! Daban! My horse broke down!" Lame Li cursed, sweat all over his forehead. His three-year-old pink horse kept shivering, wet through with sweat.

"Clumsy! How can you be like this!" Lame Li yelled at his small horse. "Broke down? Can't stand up? Look at you! You wanna come back?"

He suddenly thrilled. "Come back?" He heard her gentle voice, her last voice. He got off the horse. His courage and heroic ambition disappeared abruptly. Putting the camera into his bag, he said to himself, "Don't pretend to be a hero here!" He spread his raincoat on the ground and put the horse feed onto it. His exhausted horse lowered its head and began to eat greedily. Rolls of snow on the rising wind piled on the glacier, which might have buried many unfortunate people and their dreams. Snow would freeze into ice at night. New layers of ice are formed every day on this glacier. They should not linger here too long. He should not indulge himself in taking pictures here even for his roughly outlined thesis. — It was OK to leave some regrets here.

"Hey. Have a cigarette, young man!"

"OK. Help me roll one! A thick one!"

"This damned Daban. Too rough and hard!"

"Here, Li, light it!"

Smoking the strong cigarette and looking at the snow on top of the glacier, he had the feeling that his child was buried there. His child must be a naked beautiful boy who also liked running in the sun! Today, the boy was buried by his father into the snow and ice.

He and Lame Li had a long rest. Li's small horse finally had its fill of corns.

They settled their bags on the horseback and tied them tightly. They mounted the horses and rode toward the other half of the ancient road.

You ride your horse and I carry my gun;
We two brothers wander about the vast Xinjiang.

Lame Li sang his Qinghai folk tune again. Horse hoofs began to produce the monotonous sounds again. With the southward sun scorching on their faces, they left the watershed.

The ancient Greek artists were right. Beauty which went through pain could stay in a noble man's heart for ever. She had a noble heart. She would not die. She would gain his true love. She had already transcended her Daban with a brave heart. Their dead son was noble, too, and would become a sprite, dancing triumphantly on this eternal glacier in the sun.

Their horses trod fast down the mountain. He turned his head, casting a farewell and a fatherly look at Daban. Then, he spurred his horse and quickly caught up with his guide.

Finished in Boertala on July 15, 1982
(Published in No.11, 1982)

1. 整篇小说是以第三人称叙述的，故事中穿插着大量主人公的心理活动以及对往事的回忆，即故事的叙述、人物的心理活动、回忆全都交织在一起，翻译时要注意脉络，让读者理解时间的跳跃。另外，小说提到的几个人物都为男性，人称代词的使用要谨慎，防止指代不清。

2. "踢踏，踢踏。马耳朵一耸，一耸。树叶子哗啦，哗啦。十天，十天。"原文作者用了象声词，语言富于节奏感。译者也用了拟声词，力图再现原句的声音和节奏：Trit-trot, trit-trot, tick-tock, tick-tock … The horses' ears moved up and down … The tree leaves were rustling pit-a-pat, pit-a-pat … Ten days! Ten days!

3. He thought of those stinky refined gentlemen … 矛盾修辞(oxymoron)就是指把一对语意相反、相对立的词巧妙地放在一起使用，来表达复杂的心理矛盾或人生哲理。这里，stinky refined 放在一起使用，有幽默效果。矛盾修辞在英语中很常见，例如：crowded solitude / thunderous silence / a wise fool / successful failure / painful pleasure / a cold and warm embrace / bad good news，等等。

4. "'诺们子两个'，他知道就是'我们俩'……"省去不译。

5. 英语中表示消极情绪的形容词很多，例如，这里worried、frustrated、anxious、fidgety的使用，有助于再现人物的情感。vexed、perturbed、wrought-up、disturbed、uneasy、restless等都有不安、心烦、着急的意思，可以根据上下文选择最恰当的来进行翻译。

6. survive、last、patent、inhabit、serve 等英语动词翻译时要谨慎，这些词的后面一般不加介词。

7. "山穷水尽"译为英语习语come to the end of road。英语中的这些习语对翻译非常有帮助，例如：a bolt from the blue 晴天霹雳 / a man of his word 说话算数的人 / a case in point 佐证 / a square peg in a round hole 格格不入 / be all eyes and ears 专心致志 / be all thumbs 笨拙 / as luck would have it 碰巧 / call a spade a spade 有话直说 / cast pearls before swine 对牛弹琴 / Jack of all trades 万事通 / know the ropes 知道内情 / lead a dog's life 过着悲惨的生活 / through thick and thin 经历苦难挫折，等等。学习中应该注意积累和运用。

8. "一丝羞耻浮了上来"翻译成：A flicker of guilt popped up。用 a flicker 来修饰guilt，形容羞耻感的不确定性。

9. 英语中有关"笑"的动词有很多，比如：smile 微笑 / laugh 大笑 / chuckle 咯咯地笑，表示满意、欣赏、得意 / giggle 咯咯笑，用于妇女和儿童 / snicker 窃笑 / snigger 窃笑，暗笑 / guffaw 哄堂大笑 / titter 傻笑，窃笑，偷偷地笑 / beam 面露喜色，带有笑容 / howl 狂笑 / cackle 妇女大笑 / smirk 傻笑，假笑 / snort 嘿嘿地笑 / sneer 冷笑，等等。注意根据上下文选择恰当的词来进行翻译。

10. 这部分是全文的高潮，有大段的景物描写，有丰富的情感和心理活动。在翻译时，尤其注意形容词的使用，注意形容词的感情色彩。

北京人

（节选）

◎ 张辛欣
桑晔

绒线帽

肖凤贞，三十六岁，北京电镀总厂女工。

我这辈子别的什么也没图着，就是找了个好丈夫。我六六年就进厂当工人，年轻的时候，周围也有不少人追呢；他来我们厂帮着修机器，是济南人，你说怪不怪，隔着那么老远，就那么一个碴儿，跟谁也没好，就跟他好了。他没有父母，父母跑台湾去了。他出身不好。我们俩好，真是命。他在四机部的厂子，跟我一样，也是四级工。

我们那位不怎么会说话，可非常能干。在家，我就管织绒线，不会裁衣服，就会织，这件还没织完呢，又开始琢磨下一件怎么织。其余的活儿全叫他包了，打酱油、买煤、做饭、洗衣服，他爱干，最近他还给自己买了个洗衣机，说是这下在家干活也开始使机器了，跟厂子干活一样。

前不久，《现代时装》杂志和中央电视台联合举办了一个绒线帽编织比赛，我的帽子得了二等奖。那帽子是在家歇病假时织的。

我病，全怪我这人心强，又爱生气。我干活手快，人家两小时的活儿，我一个小时能干完。在车床上好，谁干多少是多少，在我们氧化车间不行，一个氧化槽七个人，你愿意干，干得快，就老得干。我这人不会溜呀、拍呀什么

75

的，咱们不靠那个，就靠干活，你不是不成吗？我成。可老这么着，活该你累死！心里实在怪生气。跟车间说了多少回，这槽子上的事儿我不管了，车间说不行，老师傅得带头。五月份，我上医院了，开了病假条，回家歇了，奖金也没了。歇了也一点儿不轻闲，天天在家织绒线，赶着把一家大小今年的衣服都织完，还有邻居的、朋友的、同事的。人家来求你，"小园的妈妈，给织个帽子吧"。小园是我女儿，上二年级，你能回绝吗？一起住着，一块儿干着，谁还没有求着谁的时候？这帽子就是关系呢。我去人家家里作客，有时候也带个帽子去，送什么礼都挺贵，也不见得出数，送顶帽子，又实惠，又自然，我的帽子也拿得出手。昨晚我躺在床上算了算，好，把送去参加比赛的三个帽子也加上，歇这病假，光帽子就织了五十多个！

起先我也不知道比赛的事儿，还是我们那位买了份《电视周报》回来，说，你不是挺爱好吗？瞧瞧这个，你成吗？我看了报，就想，全国比赛，谁知道都有些什么样的能人呢？赛花样，人家上海人最"海"啦。我呀，干脆织一顶适合中年人戴的帽子，你知道现在我们中年人想要打扮最费神儿了，太花太怪的穿不出去，得合我们这个年纪。我可不是中年人吗！

你看我这个帽子，这么一戴，把眉毛露出来。冬天穿薄呢子大衣，把领子竖起来，真丝头巾系在领子外边，挺暖和，挺端庄，就这样，好吗？这个样式，换奶白色的线，我们戴有点惹眼，年轻人戴，帅啦！

中奖呀？是这样，我们家住平房很不好找，电视台的同志按我给的那地址找到我妈家去了，我妹过来说，姐，你中奖了。一会儿又说，你怎么也不显得特别兴奋呀？我说，这有什么？过了几天，电视台来一信，写明了，拿着这信，可以上厂子请假，算公差，去中央台"为您服务"节目拍电视。厂子里就这么都知道了。嚯，就我们三个得奖人介绍织帽子那几分钟的电视，拍了一礼拜呢。在宣武公园拍的，开头我还做了做头发，后来都懒得弄了，拍一会儿，风来了，树叶子哗哗响，叫停，等半天，又拍一会儿，又出点儿什么事儿。后来挪屋里拍成的。紧张？怎么不紧张呢，头一个说话的，得一等奖那姑娘，二十三岁，直跟我说，大姐，您摸摸我这膝盖，怎么老抖呀？化妆师还往我脸上拍点红。等播放那天晚上，我坐家里一看，哎哟，又老又丑的，我怎么那样儿呀？

还真有人把我认出来了。前两天坐公共汽车，车上有一群姑娘就问，电视上那是您吧？我说是，人家问，您帽子上那蜜枣花到底怎么织没看清楚，我说，上电视就是那么一比划，是看不明白。在车上我又跟她们比划半天，可能也没说清，这东西就得手把手，其实一点儿也不难，只要是会做活的妇女，你给她勾几道，她就明白啦。这蜜枣花编织书上有，可我又把它改造了。我这帽子边呀，是用浑身刺的草果把毛刮起来的。那是南方一种植物，咱们没地方找。我们一位同事的爱人在羊毛衫厂工作，人家机器够不着的地方，就拿草果刮刮。我们同事拿来，把赶了毡的拉毛围巾刮顺了，我就琢磨，把我这帽子边刮刮，不是很好看吗？是挺好看吧？我又想，以后人家个人弄不着草果怎么办呢？就去市场上买铜丝刷子，这是我们那位的主意，回来一刮，铜丝软，我们那位就把铜丝剪断一半，效果跟草果一样！那天，我在街上看见一个个体户在卖帽子，猛一看，外形和我的帽子有点像，拿到手里一瞧，唉，稀稀拉拉的。他那还卖五块钱一个，我这个成本两块五，要是站在他旁边卖，保险抢我这个！厂子里，会做活的都织帽子，各织各的，各有所好；不过，有的那帽子看着挺好，用手一撑，尽是大窟窿眼儿，一洗，那帽子就搭拉了，变形了，我的帽子不！

要说爱美，我从年轻的时候就爱美，可是没美过。又是"文化大革命"，我又出身不好。生父是个国民党军官，我生下不久他就进了监狱，我两岁的时候我妈带着我和哥哥改了嫁，我现在这个父亲人非常好。生父还在，他再有钱我也不想他，不认他，他一天都没尽过责任，还叫我们背黑锅。过去，你出身不好就老觉着做错了天大的事，我最最怕填各种表，一看见"家庭出身"这一栏就发怵，还得填"反动军官"出身。我妈出身也不好。那些年，总走背字，偏又要强，人都看着你，挤兑你，倒霉的时候，没有什么人伸出手拉你一把……就是我丈夫好，结婚的时候我就说，我们都是苦人，要好好相依为命，又都没有父亲了，得好好孝敬这个父亲，好好孝敬我妈，我妈这辈子不容易……不能说，从前那些事说起来心里不好受。

当然，美不成的时候心里也没断过琢磨。琢磨什么呢？一件白衬衫，配一个驼色的裤子，那是挺雅致的。我结婚也没赶上穿好的，当天夜里来砸我们家门，问我去没去天安门，对啦，是七六年。我结婚穿的是四个兜的蓝色军便装。真的，就是军便装，一辈子的大事儿嘛！那衣服现在我妈穿着呢，她说，还挺新的，立领，挺暖和的……现在变化太快了，就说绒线帽，去年流行过一阵带帽沿儿的小帽子，小孩戴，大人戴，男的戴，女的也戴，一出来疯抢，国营商店没啦，个体户那儿价涨一倍，还是抢，过一阵子，不行了。今年更让人眼晕！我就爱在大街上看人，看谁穿得好看，样式新，不过，人的打扮得跟自己符合，你说挺大的脸上楞拔细细的眉毛那好看吗？

我的帽子获了奖，我又赶织了一件毛衣，跟那帽子配套，电视上戴我那帽子的演员，就是穿着我织的那件毛衣。人家那衣服好多都是现凑的。得了奖，厂子里开大会的时候也表扬了我，挺重视的，还想叫我负责带一批有孩子、长期病假的女工织帽子，增加个人和厂子的收入。我原本想调工作，去公园看看电动玩具，不再为厂子里的事操心、生气，现在，不走了。

那天我跟我丈夫说，不知怎么回事，这几天我老想起中学在农村劳动的时候，批判一个地主和他写的"变天诗"，那诗大约是：脱毛的凤凰不如鸡，有朝一日，凤凰还是凤凰，鸡还是鸡！

好像就是这么回事。

我是自信，因为我活得有乐趣。什么乐趣？咱们不说大话，说实在的行吗？我的乐趣就是我女儿的成长。我老跟她说：园园，妈妈这辈子不顺，就是给你铺一条顺道儿……

兄弟

有两座武当山。太和武当在湖北，田州武当在宁夏。傍晚。田州武当附近的一座寺庙。

葛尔丹，五十岁上下；一面搅拌胶泥，一面同我们讲不纯熟的汉语。

我不知道很多你们的事情，你们要我说我是什么人？你们说我是什么人好？对，我是一个做佛的人。我们是施工队，专门做佛的，还画庙里的柱子和梁上的彩色画。我们不是县里公家的，人民公社的人也没有很大权力和时间管我们。我们走到一个地方，有一个合同订，就干一个时间，做完要走另一个地方，走很多的地方。我们有政府里开出来的证明信，证明我们是组织起来做佛的手艺人；我们一个队里有蒙古人，和我一样的，也有汉人，和你们一个民族；证明在队长的口袋里。他今天到另一个地名的地方去了，他会知道你们问的话。大概……大概是集体所有制吧？

不，我不信佛，我什么东西也不信，做佛是我的工作。我以后还可能会学习做外国的一种佛，叫圣母和叫基督的一种外国佛。你们可以问我做佛的事情，做佛的事情我懂很多。我是老师傅。

什么是像，什么是不像，没有办法比。你见过佛吗？没有。真的佛谁也没有见过一次，凭什么道理讲像不像？你讲，我若是把观世音的手做六个指头，你有办法吗？一个办法也没有。你讲他是五个指头一只手，只是看到别的人做的佛全是五个指头；到底几个指头，到底有没有一只手，谁也不知道，因为谁也没有见过这个人——不是，是这个佛的活的时候的样子。做佛，只要做成和人的样子不远也不近的样子，人们就会同意说：做得好极了！

有一个人讲做佛"心诚则灵，心至则慧"，我不信。我根本不理佛，照样可以做得很好。我没有诚心，我为赚钱卖我做佛的手艺。

我研究过最早的佛、过去的佛和现在的佛。是在须弥山研究的，那里有最早的佛。最早的佛像口里（即张家口以南的华北地区——作者注）的羊，我们叫狗羊的瘦山羊，书里的说法是"秀骨清相"；过去的佛呢，做得很笨，像我们内蒙古的羊，真正的羊，书里面叫"朴拙持重"；现在的佛呢，成了很有福气的样子，我们行里叫"面丰体广"，就是脸很大，身体也很肥的样子。我研究过，不是佛变了，是人变了。人的眼睛出了问题。

我是做胎的师傅，是顶重要的工作，他们刷彩的人、做木架子的人，都没有我重要。我不干了，他们就完蛋了，只能买车票回去。我已经同宁夏的人讲了，这里的佛我不负责任，他们没有很多的猪血，也没有树上长出来的真正的漆，我做的泥胎很好也没有用。我的好手艺要留给真正的武当山庙用，他们有很多东西和钱。

不，我不和刚刚见面的朋友讲我自己。我可以讲我的爷爷和爸爸。我的爷爷是被清朝的旗兵打死的人，他是反对满族压迫汉人和我们真正的蒙古人的。我的爸爸也死掉了，阿妈也死掉了，他们死掉的时候，我很小。他们是很穷的人。我是和另外一个人长大的，他是我爸爸的弟弟。我原来也没有钱，现在有钱，很富。"文化大革命"的造反学生兵把寺庙和佛砸去了，现在要我们做佛，所以很有钱。我没有读过书，不认识蒙文，也不认识汉文，我要我的徒弟读有用的书，比方做佛的书，讲什么地方有最早的佛的书给我听。听了就会记住。

县里——你们汉族叫县里，我们是叫旗里的——很同意我们在四处做佛，他们要听党中央邓小平的话。邓小平是很好的人，他不止让我们做佛或者修房子的蒙古人富，也让我们整个内蒙古好了。现在是我从很小到现在最富的时候。

我们没有工资，我们是在一个地方做完佛算钱。算好之后分掉。我的钱放在我自己知道的一个地方。

我还会画人像，画得很好。同照相一样的人像，用铅笔画。我可以告诉你们：画像是不用花很多钱到北京上美术学院的，我看过他们的展览会，画得很不好！我的爸爸的弟弟——他也死掉了——不止教给我做佛的办法，还留下一本很有用的画书。那是"百首图谱"，内面有一百种眉毛们，一百种嘴们，一百种眼睛们和别的一百种人头上的东西们。你把它们全记住和画好以后，就是最好的画家了。你要画一个你刚刚见到的朋友，就认真看他的头，记住眉毛是几号的，嘴是几号的，别的东西是几号的，一下子画出来就很好，很像。是最好的画！

我没有老婆，也就是没有爱人的意思。我以后会把书留给我最好的徒弟，他是你们汉族人。但是也可能明年有一个老婆，然后有孩子。

（载1985年1月号）

The Beijing People (Excerpts)

Zhang Xinxin & Sang Ye

A Hand-knitted Bonnet

Xiao Fengzhen, at the age of thirty-six, works in Beijing Electroplating General Factory.[1]

In my life my biggest accomplishment is my husband. I began to work in my factory in 1966. When I was young, quite a few guys went after me, yet my husband was just an ordinary worker from his hometown of Jinan. Once, he came to my factory to help fix machines and from afar I took a look at him. As a matter of fact, he was too far to be seen clearly, but strangely enough, later, I fell in love with nobody else but him! He had a disgraceful parentage: His parents escaped to Taiwan long ago. Perhaps, we were destined to meet each other and fell in love with each other. At that time, he worked in a factory affiliated to the Fourth Machinery Department. He was a fourth-grade worker, and I, too.

My husband is not a good talker but he is very capable of doing all the housework. I don't know how to cut out and make clothes, and the only thing I do at home is knitting. At the close of one knitting work I begin to think about another. My husband, therefore, does all the housework — cooking, washing and buying soy sauce and coal. He enjoys doing these and recently he bought a washing machine, saying that he was happy to lead a mechanized life at home, like in the factory!

Not long ago, I won the second prize in a Hand-knitted Bonnet Contest held by *Modern Fashion Magazine* and China Central Television Station. I knitted the bonnets when I was on my sick leave at home.

My hot temper should take the blame for my sickness. I am swift-handed and I can finish the work in one hour which may take others two hours. It was OK to work on a lathe but in an oxidation workshop my efficiency put me at an unfavorable condition. Seven people worked on one oxidation tank and it was always I who did more work than the others. Of course, I am not an apple-polisher. I am not good at flattery or compliment. And I would rather do more work with my own hands. However, too much work made me exhausted. I certainly didn't deserve it to be so worn and torn! And none of them showed pity on me! I was really angry! I talked to the head of my workshop, telling him that I wanted to quit the tank job, but he disapproved and said that as a veteran worker I was supposed to set a good example for the other young workers. In May, I went to hospital. I had no other choice but to ask for a sick leave. Since then, they stopped my bonus. Nevertheless, I didn't idle away my time at home. I kept knitting all day long, for my family, my neighbors, my friends and my colleagues. From time to time, they came to me, "Xiaoyuan's mother, would you please knit a bonnet for me?" Xiaoyuan is my daughter, a second-grade student in an elementary school. How could I refuse them? We work or live together and one day I may be in need of their help. Who knows? These bonnets may play a role in building our relationships. So I never refused their requests. Besides, during those days when I called on someone's, I always brought a bonnet with me and sent it to them as a gift. You know, gifts cost money and sometimes are not quite presentable, while my hand-knitted bonnets are money-saving and good-looking. Last night, lying on bed, I made a rough calculation. During my sick leave, I had knitted altogether more than fifty bonnets, including those three sent to the contest!

In fact, I didn't know about the contest at the beginning. It was my husband who brought the newspaper *Television Weekly* to me. "Look! Aren't you fond of knitting? Will you take part in it?" My husband asked me. I read the newspaper carefully. Oh, it was a nationwide contest! The contestants must be very skillful; besides, in terms of fashion, who can compete with those stylish Shanghai people![2] Thinking of this, I decided to knit a bonnet suitable for the middle-aged. You know, it's hard for us middle-aged women to dress ourselves up beautifully! Some colors or styles are too loud for our age.[3] Yes, I am already middle-aged!

Look at my bonnet! You can wear it this way. Leave your eyebrows outside. In winter when you wear a thin woolen overcoat, you may as well erect your collar and put on a silk scarf around it. Together with my bonnet, you'll be warm and beautiful. The bonnet of the same design, knitted with milk-white threads, is particularly suitable for young people. Of course, this color is a little glaring to us middle-aged, but to the young it's gorgeous!

The prize? Oh. I live in a bungalow and the people from the television station had trouble finding my home. They found my mother's home with the address I gave them. My little sister came to tell me. "Sister, you win the prize! Why aren't you happy?" She asked me curiously. "Is it a big deal?" I replied. After several days, I got a letter from the television station. It said clearly that I could ask for a leave with the letter and take a trip on business to CCTV to shoot the program called "Serving the People". The whole factory knew about this. It took us a whole week to make that program which lasted only a few minutes. Three prize winners were invited to introduce how to knit bonnets on the screen. The program was shot in the Xuanwu Park. At the beginning, I was in a good mood and I even had my hair done, but later, I grew impatient. As long as the tree leaves were rustling in the wind, we stopped, and after a while, as something else happened, we stopped again. And at last, we had to move indoors. Nervous? Of course, yes. That girl, the first prize winner at the age of 23, kept asking me: "Sister, put your hand on my knees. They keep shivering! Why?" ... The makeup dresser put some blusher on my cheeks. On the day when the program was shown on TV, I sat at home and watched attentively. "Oh! I am so old and ugly! How can I look like that?" I exclaimed.

Several days ago, in a bus, a group of girls recognized me! "Are you that lady on the TV program?" "Yes." I answered. "How do you knit the jujube-flower pattern on the bonnet? We didn't see it clearly that day." I replied, "In the program I showed the basic steps and of course you couldn't grasp them in that short period of time." Then, gesturing with my hands, I tried to show them the knitting procedures again, but the girls still couldn't grasp them. In fact, it was not so hard to knit that jujube-flower, I simply needed a real demonstration to make myself understood. If a woman had ever done some knitting before, by seeing me do a few stitches she would know how to knit it. Actually, I learned it from a book, but I made some changes. To make the rim of my bonnets hairy and downy, I scraped it with a kind of berry which had sharp thorns. The berry is a southern plant and we cannot find it here. My colleague's wife works in a sweater knitting factory where berries are used to scrape the place which machines cannot reach. Once, my colleague had his disheveled napped scarf scraped with the berries and it became very smooth. Seeing this, I thought if I scraped the rim of my bonnets in such a way, they must look more beautiful! But how could I get the berries? I was anxious to find a way to solve my problem. Later, following my husband's advice, I bought a copper wire brush on the market. I tried it but found the wires too soft. Then, my husband cut them by half. To my amazement, it worked! It produced the same effect as the berries did! One day, I saw a man selling bonnets on the street. His bonnets looked much like mine but upon a closer look they were loosely knitted. He sold each of his bonnets for 5 yuan while mine was only 2.5 yuan. If I stood beside him, people, sure enough, would go for mine! I know that many people in my factory are good at knitting and their bonnets have different designs and patterns, but when propped open with your hand their bonnets are full of big holes — they look good, though. Their bonnets easily go out of shape after being washed, which has never happened to mine.

Women are born with a love for beauty. I have been pursuing it but I have never been beautiful. "The Cultural Revolution", my disgraceful parentage and a series of matters inflicted great distress on me, so how could I be beautiful? My father was a Kuomintang official and not long after I was born he was put into prison. When I was two years old my mother remarried. Fortunately, my stepfather is a good person, who treats me and my elder brother well. My biological father is still alive now but I don't miss him in the least! No matter how wealthy he is, I won't take him as my father, for he has never done his duty! Just because of him, we were unjustly blamed and tortured. In that age, a person with disgraceful parentage always felt humiliated as if he had made a great mistake. At that time, what I hated most was to fill out various forms. At the sight of "family parentage", I was weighed down by fear and nervousness, for I had to write "reactionary army official" in the blank.[4] My mother was not born in a good family, either. Not favored by fortune, she led a hard life in those years. People kept fixing their eyes on her, trying to find fault with her, and nobody was willing to give her a hand … but every cloud has a silver lining,[5] and I am lucky that I have a good husband! When we got married, I told him: "Two in distress makes sorrow less. From now on, we are bound to each other. Since both of us lost our biological fathers, we should treat my stepfather and my mother whole-heartedly with filial respect. My mother has had a hard life ..," Now, I really don't want to relate the past. The slightest mention of it makes me sad.

Of course, all these couldn't stop my pursuit for beauty. Even in those days when we were poor, I kept dreaming. Dreaming for what? A white shirt with a pair of brown trousers, which must make a woman good-looking! I had no beautiful dress when I got married. On the night of my wedding, someone kept knocking at our door and questioned if I had been to the Tian'anmen Square. Oh, that was the year of 1976. On the day I got married, I wore a blue army uniform with four big pockets. After all, wedding was a big event in my life and the army uniform suited that occasion. Later, I gave it to my mother. She said it was new and warm, with a stand-up collar … Now, great changes have taken place in China. Take the knitted bonnets for example. Last year, hats with a brim were popular among children and adults. Men and women all rushed for that kind of hats. After they were sold out in the state-owned shops, the self-employed businessmen doubled the price. People went on struggling to buy them even at a much higher price. But soon, they were out of fashion. This year, I am more dazzled by people's crushing desire for fashion! I love watching people on the streets. Whose dress is beautiful? Whose dress has a new style? I am so attracted! In my view, people must find a suitable match of what they wear. Do you find it attractive if a person with a big face wears a pair of thinly trimmed eyebrows?

After my bonnet won the prize, I knitted a sweater to go with it. The actress on television wore the bonnet and the sweater I knitted. The heads of my factory also praised me in a meeting and advised me to teach those female workers who had children and stayed at home on long-term sick leave, so that they could earn some money for themselves and for the factory as well. I had planned to transfer my job and go to take care of the electric toys in the park, but now I have changed my mind.

The other day, I said to my husband: "I don't know why? Recently I always recall my high school days when I labored in the countryside. At that time, we criticized a landowner and his 'erroneous' poem: A phoenix without feathers is no better than a chicken but phoenix is phoenix and chicken is chicken — that can never be changed!"

His poem is reasonable.

I am confident, for I enjoy my life now. What do I enjoy in my life? To be frank, with no brags, I enjoy seeing my daughter growing up. I often tell her: "Xiaoyuan, Mom's bumpy life will pave a smooth way for you …"

Brothers

There are two mountains by the name of Wudang in China: Taihe Wudang in Hubei Province and Tianzhou Wudang in Ningxia Hui Autonomous Region. At dusk, in a temple near Tianzhou Wudang Mountain, Geerdan, at the age of about 50, is chatting with us in his clumsy mandarin Chinese while mixing and stirring the gel-cement.[6]

I don't know much about your things. What do I do? What do you think of me? Yes. I am a person who makes a living by making Buddha statues. I work in a construction team specializing in making Buddha statues. In addition, we do some painting on columns and crossbeams for some temples. We are not affiliated to the county government, and the People's Commune also had no time or power to control us. After a contract is signed in one place we work there for some time, and when the work is finished we'll move to other places. Our construction team has worked in quite a lot of places. We have the certificate issued by the government, which proves that we are a group of organized craftsmen. Among us, there are Mongolians like me and people of Han nationality like you. The certificate is in our team head's pocket. He is not here today. He must be able to answer your questions. Maybe … collective ownership?

No. I don't believe in Buddha. I don't believe in any god. Making Buddha statues is just my job, and in future, I may learn to make some foreign gods such as Virgin Mary or Jesus Christ. You can ask me anything about how to make Buddha statues. I am a veteran master. I know a lot about it.

Do the statues we make resemble Buddha? Like or unlike? It's hard to say. Have you seen a Buddha before? Nobody has ever seen one and nobody can say whether our statues are like Buddha or not. If I make a Guanyin Bodhisattva with six fingers on a hand, can you say it is unlike the real Guanyin Bodhisattva? No! I know all the Buddhas you have seen have five fingers, so you think Guanyin has five fingers. But how many fingers on earth does Guanyin have? Does Guanyin have a hand? Nobody knows! Nobody has ever seen Guanyin — I should say, the living Guanyin. As long as we make statues a bit like human beings, people will say: "Well done!"

Someone tells me that one can make the perfect Buddha if his heart is faithful and sincere enough.[7] I don't believe it. I never worship Buddha but still I do my work well. I am not faithful. I do my work just to make a living.

I did some research about the earliest Buddha, the previous Buddha and the present Buddha. I did it in Xumi Mountain. The earliest Buddha is there. The earliest Buddha, like the thin sheep to the south of Zhangjiakou in north China, is slender and elegant; the previous Buddha, like our Inner Mongolian sheep, the true sheep, looks clumsy, as described in books — plain and modest; the present Buddha is blissful with a strong figure and a plump face, which means it has a big face and a thick-set body. It is not the Buddha that changes, but people. The problem lies in people's eyes.

I mold the shape for statues. My work is more important than theirs — painting or making wooden frames. If I wash my hands of my job, it is all over with them and what they can do is to buy train tickets and go home. I have talked to people from Ningxia that I cannot guarantee to make good-quality statues here, for they haven't enough pig blood or the natural lacquer abstracted from trees. Without the good painting materials, it's useless to make good molds. I'd better reserve my good handicraft to the temples in the real Wudang Mountain. They have enough money and necessary materials.

No. I never talk about myself with strangers, but I can tell you something about my grandpa and my father. My grandpa was killed by the soldiers of the Qing Dynasty. At that time, people of the Manchu nationality (which was the dominating class in the Qing Dynasty) often oppressed the people of other nationalities such as Han and Mongolia. My grandpa was strongly against it. My father and my mother died when I was very young. Both of them were poor. And I grew up with my father's little brother. I used to be very poor, and as luck would have it, now I am rich. Why? Those rebel students battered down the temples and Buddha statues in "the Cultural Revolution", and now we are paid to repair or rebuild Buddha statues. I am illiterate. I don't know the Mongolian characters, and I don't know the Han characters, either. I require that my apprentices should read more useful books, such as books on how to make Buddha statues. I often ask them to read the books on the earliest Buddha to me. I can bear in mind the information in those books.[8]

The heads of the county, which we call "banner", show an affirmative attitude to our work — they permit us to make Buddha statues in different places. They abide by the Central Government's policy. Deng Xiaoping is a very good man, under whose leadership, we, the Buddha makers, have become rich and the people in the whole Inner Mongolia have led a good life now. So far I can say I am the richest in my life.

We have no salaries. After we finish our work in one place and get the payment, we divide it. And I always put my money in a place which only I know.

And I am also good at drawing pictures for people. My pencil drawings are very good, as good as the pictures taken with cameras. In fact, one doesn't need to spend much money learning drawing or painting in the Fine Arts Institute in Beijing. I visited their exhibitions. Their drawings are really not good! My father's little brother, who died years ago, left me not only the statue-making skills but also a very useful book about drawing pictures. The book is *A Hundred Human Heads*, which shows a hundred different eyebrows, a hundred different mouths, a hundred different eyes and other features on a human head. If one keeps all these in mind and practices drawing them accordingly, he must become the best artist. For instance, if you want to draw a portrait for a friend you see for the first time, you just need to observe his head closely and associate his brows, his eyes and his other facial features with their corresponding numbers in that book, thus, you can draw a picture of him quickly. And the portrait is very much vivid and alive. Of course, it is the best portrait!

I have no wife. You city people may call it "lover".[9] I'll leave my book to my best apprentice, who is a person of Han nationality, like you. I may have a wife next year, and a kid.

(Published in No.1, 1985)

1. 小说《绒线帽》采用第一人称讲述故事。故事的主人公，即讲述者肖凤贞，是一个在工厂工作的普通劳动者，语言简单朴实，这符合人物的社会地位和教育背景。在翻译时，应注意原文的这种口语化风格，译文也多运用有口语特点的词汇和句型，不刻意进行过多修饰。另外，在主人公的叙述中，既有发生在过去的事，也有对现在情况的讲述，所以译文中既有过去时态也有现在时态。

2. "赛花样，人家上海人最'海'啦……"这是口语化的用词，上海人最"海"，就是最洋气、最时髦的意思，故译文处理为"those stylish Shanghai people"。stylish的意思是有风度、有格调、新潮、高雅，而且这个词也比较口语化。

3. "太花太怪的穿不出去，得合我们这个年纪……"。译文处理为：Some colors or styles are too loud for our age. loud在这里有刺眼、俗艳、招摇、花哨之意，而且这个词简单易懂，符合口语特点，用在这里比较合适。

4. 主人公的叙述中出现了"文化大革命"、"家庭出身"、"反动军官"以及下文的"变天诗"等属于某个特定时代的用词，译文对这些词的翻译都加了引号，目的是让读者明白这是专有名词。为了便于读者更好理解，有时还可以加一些注释，为读者提供一些背景知识，补充读者头脑中缺省的文化图式。

5. "……就是我丈夫好，结婚的时候我就说……"。英语是形合语言，译文要注意上下文的衔接，注意逻辑关系。这里，主人公讲述了自己的出身和困苦后，一转折，开始说：庆幸的是自己有个好丈夫。译者在"... I am lucky that I have a good husband!"前面加了一句："Every cloud has a silver lining,"意思是黑暗中总有光明，"山重水复疑无路，柳暗花明又一村"的意思。这样可以体现上下文之间的逻辑关系，也增加一些文采。

6. 小说《兄弟》是一个做佛的手艺人的自述。第一人称，语言通俗，口语化特征明显。翻译时注意文体对应，语言尽量符合一个没有受过太多教育的民间手艺人的语言特点。时态采用了一般现在时。

7. "心诚则灵，心至则慧"，汉译英中会遇到很多这样的四字词组，中国人喜欢用四个字的词组或成语，它们对仗工整，言简意赅，音韵和谐，给人美感。在英译时，有时我们可以找到英语中对应的习语或一些固定的表达，比如：穷则思变 Adversity leads to prosperity. / 江山易改，本性难移 A fox may grow gray, but never good. / 海纳百川 All rivers run into sea. 等等。但是有时候，为了上下行文的连贯，不用刻意去追求译文的对应，这里译文处理为：… one can make the perfect Buddha if his heart is faithful and sincere enough.

8. 在以上这段译文中，简单句较多，读起来很琐碎，但符合说话人的语言特点。

9. "我没有老婆，也就是没有爱人的意思。"在英语中老婆为wife，爱人为husband 或wife。这里处理为：I have no wife. You city people may call it "lover". lover可以是爱好者、情人、情侣之意，放在这里用于形容城里人的礼貌或浪漫。

遍地风流（节选）

○ 阿 城

峡 谷

山被直着劈开，于是当中有七八里谷地。大约是那刀有些弯，结果谷地中央高出如许，愈近峡口，便愈低。

森森冷气漫出峡口，收掉一身粘汗。近着峡口，倒一株大树，连根拔起，似谷里出了什么不测之事，把大树唬得跑，一跤仰翻在那里。峡顶一线蓝天，深得令人不敢久看。一只鹰在空中移来移去。

峭壁上草木不甚生长，石头生铁般锈着。一块巨石和百十块斗大石头，昏死在峡壁根，一动不动。巨石上伏两只四脚蛇，眼睛眨也不眨，只偶尔吐一下舌芯子，与石头们赛呆。

因有人在峡中走，壁上时时落下些许小石，声音左右荡着升上去。那鹰却忽地不见去向。顺路上去，有三五人家在高处。临路立一幢石屋，门开着，却像睡觉的人。门口一幅布旗静静垂着。愈近人家，便有稀松的石板垫路。

中午的阳光慢慢挤进峡谷，阴气浮开，地气熏上来，石板有些颤。似乎有了噪音，细听却什么也不响。忍不住干咳一两声，总是自讨没趣。一世界都静着，不要谁来多舌。

走近了，方才辨出布旗上有个藏文字，布色已经晒退，字色也相去不远，随旗沉甸甸地垂着。

忽然峡谷中有一点异响，却不辨来源。往身后寻去，只见来路的峡口有一匹马负一条汉，直腿走来。那马腿移得极密，蹄子踏在土路上，闷闷响成一团。骑手侧着身，并不上下颠。

愈来愈近，一到上坡，马慢下来。骑手轻轻一夹，马上了石板，蹄铁连珠般脆响。马一耸一耸向上走，骑手就一坐一坐随它。蹄声在峡谷中回转，又响又高。那只鹰又出现了，慢慢移来移去。

骑手走过眼前，结结实实一脸黑肉，直鼻紧嘴，细眼高颧，眉睫似漆。皮袍裹在身上，胸微敞，露出油灰布衣。手隐在袖中，并不拽缰。藏靴上一层细土，脚尖直翘着。眼睛遇着了，脸一短，肉横着默默一笑，随即复原，似乎咔嚓一响。马直走上去，屁股锦缎一样闪着。到了布旗下，骑手俯身移下马，将缰绳缚在门前木桩上。马平了脖子立着，甩一甩尾巴，曲一曲前蹄，倒换一下后腿。骑手望望门，那门不算大，骑手似乎比门宽着许多，可拐着腿，左右一晃，竟进去了。

屋里极暗，不辨大小。慢慢就看出有两张粗木桌子，三四把长凳，墙里一条木柜。木柜后面一个肥脸汉子，两眼陷进肉里，渗不出光，双肘支在柜上，似在瞌睡。骑手走近柜台，也不说话，只伸手从胸口掏进去，捉出几张纸币，撒在柜上。肥汉也不瞧那钱，转身进了里屋。少顷拿出一大木碗干肉，一副筷，放在骑手面前的木桌上，又回去舀来一碗酒，顺手把钱划到柜里。

骑手喝一口酒，用袖擦一下嘴。又摸出刀割肉，将肉丢进嘴里，脸上凸起，腮紧紧一缩，又紧紧一缩，就咽了。把帽摘了，放在桌上，一头鬈发沉甸甸慢慢松开。手掌在桌上划一划，就有嚓嚓的声音。手指扇一样散着，一般长短，并不拢。肥汉又端出一碗汤来，放在桌上冒气。

一刻功夫，一碗肉已不见。骑手将嘴唷进酒碗里，一仰头，喉结猛一缩，又缓缓移下来，并不出长气，就喝汤。一时满屋都是喉咙响。

不多时，骑手立起身，把帽捏在手里，脸上蒸出一团热气，向肥汉微微一咧嘴，晃出门外。肥汉梦一样呆着。

阳光已移出峡谷，风又窜来窜去。布旗上下扭着动。马鬃飘起来，马打了一串响鼻。

骑手戴上帽子，正一正，解下缰绳，马就踏起四蹄。骑手翻上去，紧一紧皮袍，用腿一夹，峡谷里响起一片脆响，不多时又闷闷响成一团，越来越小，越来越小。

耳朵一直支着，不信蹄声竟没有了，许久才辨出风声和布旗的响动。

溜　索

不信这声音就是怒江。首领也不多说，用小腿磕一下马。马却更觉迟疑，牛们也慢下来。

一只大鹰旋了半圈，忽然一歪身，扎进山那侧的声音里。马帮像是得到信号，都止住了。汉子们全不说话，纷纷翻下马来，走到牛队的前后，猛发一声喊，连珠脆骂，拳打脚踢。铃铛们又慌慌响起来，马帮如极稠的粥，慢慢流向那个山口。

一个钟头之前就感闻到这隐隐闷雷，初不在意，只当是百里之外天公浇地。雷总不停，才渐渐生疑，懒懒问了一句。首领也只懒懒说是怒江，要过溜索了。

山不高，口极狭，仅容得一个半牛过去。不由捏紧了心，准备一睹气贯滇西的那江，却不料转出山口，依然是闷闷的雷。心下大惑，见前边牛们死也不肯再走，就下马向岸前移去。行到岸边，抽一口气，腿子抖起来，如牛一般，不敢再往前动半步。

万丈绝壁飞快垂下去，马帮原来就在这壁顶上。转了多半日，总觉山低风冷，却不料一直是在万丈之处盘桓。

怒江自西北天际亮亮而来，深远似涓涓细流，隐隐喧声腾上来，着一派森气。俯望那江，蓦地心中一颤，惨叫一声。急转身，却什么也没有，只是再不敢轻易向下探视。叫声漫开，撞了对面的壁，又远远荡回来。

首领稳稳坐在马上，笑一笑。那马平时并不觉雄壮，此时却静立如伟人，晃一晃头，鬃飘起来。首领眼睛细成一道缝，先望望天，满脸冷光一闪，又俯身看峡，腮上绷出筋来。汉子们咦咦喂喂地吼起来，停一刻，又吼着撞那回声。声音旋起来，缓缓落下峡去。

牛铃如击在心上，一步一响，马帮向横在峡上的一根索子颤颤移去。

那索似有千钧之力，扯住两岸石壁，谁也动弹不得，仿佛再有锱铢之力加在上面，不是山倾，就是索绷。

首领缓缓移下马，拐着腿走到索前，举手敲一敲那索，索一动不动。首领瞟一眼汉子们。汉子们早蹲在一边吃烟。只有一个精瘦短小的汉子站起来，向峡下弹出一截纸烟，飘飘悠悠，不见去向。瘦小汉子迈着一双细腿，走到索前，从索头扯出一个竹子折的角框，只一跃，腿已入套。脚一用力，飞身离岸，嗖地一下小过去，却发现他腰上还牵一根绳，一端在索头，另一端如带一缕黑烟，弯弯划过峡顶。

那只大鹰在瘦小汉子身下十余丈处移来移去，翅膀尖上几根羽毛被风吹得抖。

再看时，瘦小汉子已到索子向上弯的地方，悄没声地反着倒手拔索，横在索下的绳也一抖一抖地长出去。

大家正睁眼望，对岸一个黑点早停在壁上。不一刻，一个长音飘过来，绳子抖了几抖。又一个汉子站起来，拍拍屁股，抖一抖裤裆，笑一声："狗日的！"

三条汉子一个一个小过去。首领哑声说道："可还歇？"余下的汉子们漫声应道："不消。"纷纷走到牛队里卸驮子。

牛们早卧在地下，两眼哀哀地慢慢眨。两个汉子拽起一条牛，骂着赶到索头。那牛软下去，淌出两滴泪，大眼失了神，皮肉开始抖起来。汉子们缚了它的四蹄，挂在角框上，又将绳扣住框，发一声喊，猛力一推。牛嘴咧开，叫不出声，皮肉抖得模糊一层，屎尿尽数撒泄，飞起多高，又纷纷扬扬，星散坠下峡去。过了索子一多半，那边的汉子们用力飞快地收绳，牛倒垂着，升到对岸。

这边的牛们都哀哀地叫着，汉子们并不理会，仍一头一头推过去。牛们如商量好的，不例外都是一路屎尿，皮肉疯了一样抖。

之后是运驮子，就玩一般了。这岸的汉子们也一个接一个飞身小过去。

战战兢兢跨上角框，首领吼一声："往下看不得，命在天上！"猛一送，只觉耳边生风，聋了一般，任什么也听不见，僵着脖颈盯住天，倒像俯身看海。那海慢慢一旋，无波无浪，却深得令人眼呆，又透远得欲呕。自觉慢了一下，急忙伸手在索上向身后拨去。这索由十几股竹皮扭绞而成，磨得赛刀。手划出血来，粘粘的反倒抓得紧索。手一松开，撕得钻心一疼，不及多想，赶紧倒上去抓住。渐渐就有血溅到唇上、鼻上，自然顾不到，命在天上。

猛然耳边有人笑："莫抓住鸡巴不撒手，看脚底板！"方才觉出已到索头，几个汉子笑着在吃烟，眼纹一直扯到耳边。

慎慎地下来，腿子抖得站不住，脚倒像生下来第一遭知道世界上还有土地，亲亲热热踩几下。小肚子胀得紧，阳物酥酥的，像有尿，却不敢撒，生怕走了气再也立不住了。

眼珠涩涩的，使劲挤一下，端着两手，不敢放下。猛听得空中一声唿哨，尖得直入脑髓，腰背颤一下。回身却见首领早已飞到索头，抽身跃下，拐着腿弹一弹，走到汉子们跟前。有人递过一支烟，嚓地一声点好。烟浓浓地在首领脸前聚了一下，又忽地被风吹散，扬起数点火星。

牛马们还卧在地下，皮肉乱抖，半个钟头立不起来。

首领与两个汉子走到绝壁前，扯下裤腰，弯弯地撒出一道尿，落下不到几尺，就被风吹得散开，顺峡向东南飘走。万丈下的怒江，倒像是一股尿水，细细流着。

那鹰斜移着，忽然一栽身，射到壁上，顷刻又飞起来；翅膀一鼓一鼓地动。首领把裤腰塞紧，曲着眼望那鹰，抖一抖裆，说："蛇？"几个汉子也望那鹰，都说："是呢，蛇。"

牛们终于又上了驮，铃铛朗朗响着，急急地要离开这里。上得马上，才觉出一身粘汗，风吹得身子抖起来。手掌向上托着，寻思几时才能有水洗一洗血肉。顺风扩一扩腮，出一口长气，又觉出闷雷原来一直响着。俯在马上再看怒江，干干地咽一咽，寻不着那鹰。

（载1985年4月号）

The True Heroes[1] (Excerpts)

A Cheng

The Valley[2]

The mountain was cleaved apart from the top to the bottom. The valley plain in between stretched about three or four kilometers long. Perhaps the broadsword which split the mountain apart was curving inward, so the central part of the valley plain rose up; the closer to the mouth of the valley, the lower the plain declined.

The whole valley was pervaded with dense chilly air, which was cold enough to hold back one's sticky sweat all at once. At the mouth of the valley lay a big uprooted tree, as if something terrible had happened in the valley and the tree had been so frightened that it had fallen over itself and lain on its own back. Overhead, a strip of the blue sky between the two cliffs looked so overwhelmingly remote that one dared not look up at it for too long. A hawk was hovering to and fro, lingering in that strip of sky.

Few grasses or trees grew on the steep precipices, and the rocks looked rusty like pieces of iron put aside for a long time. A gigantic rock and hundreds of big stones lay at the foot of the cliff, motionless and lifeless. Two lizards huddled on the rock, their eyes immobile and their tongues shooting out once in a while, as if they were competing with those stones so as to see who were more sluggish and listless.

Small stones fell down occasionally due to people's movement in the mountain and the sound resounded and slowly drifted upwards. That hawk disappeared suddenly.

Along the path up the mountain stood four or five houses, among which a stone house looking out on the path seemed to be in a sound sleep. Its door was open and in front of the door a cloth banner drooped down, still and silent. A few stone slates, which were sparsely laid, paved the way to the door.

At noon, the sunlight slowly squeezed into the valley. The cold air dispersed and the valley plain turned warm. The slates started to tremble. Someone was coming? But listening attentively, one could hear nothing. Right now, a tentative

94

deliberate cough would be asking for a snub. The whole world was dormant, still and silent, unwilling to be disturbed by anyone.[3]

The banner, with a faded color, drooped down heavily and listlessly, on which the Tibetan characters were vague and hard to tell.

All of a sudden, an unusual sound broke the silence of the valley. It was hard to tell where it came from. After a moment, a horse was seen galloping toward this stone house from the mouth of the valley. The horse ran fast and its hoofs clattered and tramped on the path, producing a dull and monotonous sound. The man on the horse tipped his body but kept steady and calm.

The horse was approaching. When it came to the slope linked to the slates, it slowed down. Spurred by its master, it lightly jumped onto the stone slates immediately and trotted forward, clicking and clanking in succession. In tune with each step of the horse, the horseman moved rhythmically. A volley of sound echoed in the valley, loud and clear. That hawk appeared again, shifting slowly in the strip of sky overhead.

The horseman turned out to have a strong build as he rode by. His face was dark and husky, and his straight nose, tightened lips, narrow eyes, prominent cheekbones, pitch-black brows and eyelashes made him appear stiff and tough. His muscular body was tightly wrapped in a fur coat, except in chest where a gray cloth shirt could be seen. Without holding the horse rein, he put his hands in his sleeves. His boots, with a tilting tip, were covered with a layer of dirt. The moment his eyes met others', the muscles on his face moved slightly, producing a silent smile, as if his face turned even shorter in a split second. Then, in a flash, his transient smile vanished and his face restored to seriousness.[4] His horse carried him toward the stone house, the smooth and lustrous hair on its hips glistening like silk or satin.

Under the banner, the horse stopped and the man jumped off. He tied the horse to a wooden pole in front of the house. The horse set its body straight, swung its tails, bent its forelegs and took turns to rest its hind legs. The man cast a look at the door, which seemed too narrow for him. He was much bigger than the door! Nevertheless, huddling his legs, in one way or another, he entered the house.

The room was awfully dark. Slowly he saw two wooden tables, three or four benches and a wooden counter. Behind the counter stood a fat-faced man whose eyes were deeply set in the flesh, dull and dim, with no glows at all. He sat with his two elbows on the counter and seemed to be dozing off. The horseman silently walked forward, took out some paper money and scattered it on the counter. Casting no glimpse at it, the fat-faced man turned around and entered the inner room. After a while, he came out with a big bowl of meat and a pair of chopsticks.

After putting all of these on a wooden table, he returned to ladle out a bowl of wine for the horseman and swept the money into the closet by the way.

The horseman took a mouthful of wine, wiped his mouth with his sleeve, took out his knife and cut the meat into pieces. He took up a piece and threw it into his mouth. His cheeks bulged at first and then they shrank. By the second shrinking, he had been done with the piece of meat. As he took off his hat and put it on the table, his curly hair slowly loosened and drooped down. When his fingers — almost of the same length, stretching in a fan-like shape for they couldn't close up — touched the table, they were so hard and tough that some scratching sound was produced.[5] While the horseman was eating and drinking, the fat-faced man brought out a bowl of steaming hot soup for him.

In a matter of minutes, the horseman ate up the meat. Then, burying his upper lip into the wine bowl and then raising his head, he let the wine flow down his throat; his adam's apple suddenly jerked upward and then dropped slowly. After drinking the wine, he turned to the soup. Soon, the room was filled with the gurgling sound produced by his throat.

All these done, he stood up, picked up his hat and made a slight grin at the fat-faced man. Then, he staggered out of the room, his face red and hot.

The fat-faced man, as if returning to his dream, didn't make any movement at all.

Now the sunlight had moved out of the valley. Wind began to stir the cloth banner. The horse snorted, its mane flying in the wind.

The horseman put on his hat, straightened it and untied the rein. The horse began to move his legs. He mounted the horse, fastened his fur coat, pressed the horse's underbelly with his legs, and rode away as fast as he could. The trit-trot, the clatter and the tramping sound combined together and gradually faded away.[6]

Incredibly, the sound of the hoofs disappeared in an instant, leaving the cloth banner alone fluttering in the wind.

The Cableway[7]

Was it the sound of Nujiang River? Saying no words, the chief urged his horse with a kick on the underbelly but the horse turned more hesitant. The oxen also slowed down their steps.

A big hawk was soaring overhead. After half a circle, the hawk, all of a sudden, tilted down into the wild furious sound beyond the mountain. The caravan stopped as if getting some signal. All the men dismounted one after another and rushed to the herd of oxen, shouting, cursing, beating and kicking in a helter-skelter manner.[8] After a while, the bells around the oxen's necks began to ring again. The caravan, like thick porridge, slowly flowed toward the mountain pass.

The muffled thunders came into my ears an hour ago but I didn't think too much. Maybe it was God watering his land hundreds of kilometers away. The thunders kept rolling and resounding. "Where are we?" Out of curiosity, I asked listlessly. "Nujiang River, and we are going to cross it by the cableway." The chief replied also in a languid tone.

The mountain was not high but the mountain pass was quite narrow, at the width of only one and a half oxen. I couldn't help holding my breath. My heart was in my mouth now. Through this narrow pass, I would finally see that great river which ran through the west of Yunnan. But out of my expectation, after we squeezed through the pass, the oxen stopped! The dull and insipid thunders were still echoing incessantly by our ears. I jumped off my horse and walked forward to have a look. As I walked to the rim of the cliff, I gasped in wonderment and terror. My legs began to tremble and, like those oxen, I didn't dare to move a step.

Right below us was the sheer precipice, which sank vertically thousands of feet downward! I had thought that the mountain was not high. Who could expect that we spent half a day winding our way on the top of the cliff under which was such an unfathomable abyss!

Underneath, Nujiang River rolled to us from the northwest. It was so far that it looked like a gurgling and glistening stream, but as the sound of its turbulent surges rose up faintly, we were thrilled by its awe-inspiring magnificence.[9] Looking down from the edge of the cliff, I felt my heart beating wildly at once. I couldn't help but utter a fearful cry and turn round abruptly. Although I saw nothing, I had no courage to look down again. My voice echoed in the mountain, hitting the opposite cliff wall and bouncing back from afar.

The chief sat steady on his horse, smiling. His horse was not a big one and right now it stood there silently, composed and majestic like a great man. As it shook its head, the long mane flew in the wind, which added valiance to its majesty. As the chief narrowed his eyes and looked up at the sky, a ray of cold light flashed across his face. The moment he looked down, blue veins stood out on his cheeks. We howled and growled and our cries bumped into one another and echoed in the valley, rising, swirling and at last drifting down slowly.[10]

The bells around the oxen's necks jingled and hit our heart. Amid the jingling sound we moved toward the cableway hanging over the deep gorge.

The two opposite cliff walls were connected by the cableway which looked so tight that it would break apart and the whole mountain would consequently topple and collapse if a little force were applied to it.

The chief slowly got off his horse and staggered to the cableway. He tapped it with his hand. It didn't budge at all. He cast a glance at his companions who were crouching aside and smoking silently. A lean and small man among us stood up. He walked toward the edge of the cliff and flipped into the gorge his cigarette stub, which drifted down and disappeared soon. The small man walked to the cableway, pulled a bamboo-made frame out and put his legs into the frame with a leap. A push from his legs sent him sliding away along the cableway. A rope was tied around his waist, with one end fastened to the cableway and the other end, like a wisp of black smoke, flying across the gorge.

The hawk flew below the small man, keeping a distance of about tens of feet, its wings fluttering and shuddering in the wind.

In the twinkling of an eye, the small man had reached the place where the cableway tipped upward. He quietly put his hands behind his back and pulled at the cableway, while the rope dangling below the cableway jiggled and extended with every pull in his skillful hands.

Quickly, a little black dot stopped on the opposite cliff wall. After a while, a long cry came to us and the rope was waved several times. The second one stood up, patting the dirt off his hips and hitching up his trousers. "Damn it!" He cursed and smiled.

One after another, three men slid across the valley. The chief asked in a hoarse voice, "Go on having a rest?" "No," the rest men quickly responded and walked to the cattle to unload the sacks.

The oxen were all lying on the ground, blinking their eyes at us, appealing for mercy. Two men hauled an ox up and drove it to the cableway — with the help of some foul language. The ox was so frightened that it began to tremble, tears gushing down from its big vacant eyes. They tied its four feet, hung it onto the frame and tied the rope to the frame. Heaving a great shout, they pushed it forward into the air with concentrated efforts. The ox opened its mouth wide but uttered no sound. In great terror, it shivered and shook violently, incontinent of feces and urine, which scattered, flew up and fell down to the valley. After it arrived at the middle part of the cableway, the men on the other side began to pull the rope with great exertion. The ox, upside down, finally slid across the valley and arrived at the destination.

The rest of the oxen begged with tears and sorrowful bellows but failed to get any mercy. They were pushed onto the cableway one after another. As if they had rehearsed it beforehand, they all trembled crazily on the cableway, with feces and urine scattering all the way.

Then we began to put the sacks of goods on the cableway and pushed them across, which, to us, was much easier. After all the things done, it was our turn to cross the gorge by the cableway.

Meticulously I put my legs into the frame. The chief shouted aloud, "Don't look down. Your life is in the sky!" Pushed ahead with great efforts, I began to fly, wind zooming and rubbing my ears. I had no other choice but to look up at the sky, my neck stiff and my head dizzy. The sky in my eyes turned into a vast sea, peaceful and tranquil, with no waves or billows, deep enough to freeze my eyes and far enough to make me sick. When I felt slow, I rushed to pull the cableway so as to speed up again. The cableway was made of several slices of bamboo peel, and it felt sharp like a knife. Scraped by it, my hands were wet with sticky blood, which nevertheless helped me clutch the rope more tightly. However, as I let go the cableway, I felt a stinging pain. In a hurry I clutched it again. After a while, the blood spattered onto my lips and my nose. Of course, I had no time or mood to care about it. My life was in the sky!

All of a sudden, I heard someone shouting, "Let go of your cock! Look at your feet!"[11] Right now, I came to know that I had crossed the gorge and arrived safe and sound. The men on this side were smoking, much relieved, laughing with the corner of their eyes to their ears.

With great caution, I set my foot on the ground, still shivering a lot. After a while, as if touching the ground for the first time in my life I stamped on the ground heavily and happily. I felt my abdomen bloating and my penis tingling. I wanted to pass water but I didn't dare to do it for fear that my energy might flow out of my body and I could no longer stand up.

My eyes were still stiff and dry. Abruptly a sharp whistle thrust into my head and stirred me. Turning around, I saw the chief arrive, as nimble as a squirrel. He jumped down from the cableway and hobbled toward us. Someone handed him a cigarette. He lit it up. Soon, the dense smoke began to gather over his face and instantly it was scattered away by the wind, sparkles adrift here and there.

The oxen and the horses were still lying on the ground, shuddering in terror. Perhaps they needed more than half an hour to recover.

The chief and two men walked to the edge of the cliff. Taking off their pants, they let the urine fly, which fell down several feet and was quickly scattered away toward the southeast. Nujiang River, like a stream of urine, was flowing silently in the deep unfathomable valley.

That hawk tilted and touched the cliff wall, and after a while, it flew up again with its wings fluttering up and down. The chief fastened his pants and looked at the hawk from the corner of his eyes. Jerking the crotch of his pants, he asked, "Going for a snake?" The men looked at the hawk and replied in a chorus, "Yes, a snake."

The oxen finally recovered and were loaded with heavy sacks again. The bells began to ring on the mountain path. We were eager to leave. On mounting the horse, I felt my sweaty body shivering in the wind. How I hoped to have a bath! I uttered a long sigh and let out a long deep breath. The thunders kept rumbling in the distance. Looking down at Nujiang River, I could do nothing but take a gulp. That hawk had disappeared.

(Published in No.4, 1985)

 注 释

1. 这里节选了《遍地风流》的两个小故事《峡谷》和《溜索》。译者对 "遍地风流" 的理解是：在这个熙熙攘攘的世俗社会，平庸苟且的人很多，而阿城笔下的人物，看似渺小平凡，却有着顽强的生命力和坚韧勇敢的豪情，他们是真正的风流人物。所以译者把标题译为The True Heroes。

2. 从这篇小说的翻译上，可以看出汉英语言的巨大差异，以及这些差异给翻译带来的困难。汉语重主体意识，以意役形，不期待形式的规约；汉语重意，句子以意念主轴展开；汉语重直觉感应，是感性语言。这些汉语的特点在《峡谷》一文中表现得很明显：原文句子的主语经常缺省，句子主语不断变化，句子流散铺排，逻辑关系靠意合。而英语重分析，重视逻辑，是拼音文字，有屈折变化，是形合语言，靠形式彰显逻辑关系。在翻译时，对原文句子的主语缺省、主语变化等要非常注意，对人称代词、指示代词的使用要谨慎。

3. 从这几段中，可以看出作者的写作风格：句子短小凝练，简洁内敛，含蓄不露，三四个字即可以是一句；主语经常缺省，或者在一句中，主语频繁变化；语言几近诗性。王蒙这样评价阿城的语言："美不胜收——口语化而不流俗，古典美而不迂腐，民族化而不过'土'。" (http://www.csscipaper.com/literature/xdwxyj/14184_2.html)这些都给翻译带来了困难。小到用词、句式，大到风格的再现，都是翻译的困难。译者从词的选择、意象的再现方面，力图用英语还原阿城笔下的宁静而又蕴含无限张力的意境。

4. 人物的形象描写非常关键。这里骑手的形象很有特点："结结实实一脸黑

肉，直鼻紧嘴，细眼高颧，眉睫似漆。皮袍裹在身上，胸微敞，露出油灰布衣。手隐在袖中，并不拽缰。藏靴上一层细土，脚尖直翘着。眼睛遇着了，脸一短，肉横着默默一笑，随即复原，似乎咔嚓一响。"原文每个小句都四五个字，小句的主语不尽相同，有些还省略了主语，还有夸张而形象的"咔嚓一响"这样的表达。在翻译时，不用拘泥于原文句子的结构特点，可以重新组句，但要把原文中的关键词体现在新组的译句中。要注意句子主语的变化，添加合适的主语，长短句搭配。注意选择形象的形容词，把人物形象勾勒出来。

5. 这是对骑手吃饭喝酒动作的细节描写。在翻译时，注意动词的使用，例如take、wipe、throw、bulge、shrink、loosen、droop、touch、scratch，等等。选择合适的动词，可以使人物形象和动作更加栩栩如生。

6. "峡谷里响起一片脆响，不多时又闷闷响成一团，越来越小，越来越小。"这里"脆响"、"闷闷响成一团"、"越来越小"，都是形容马蹄渐远的声音的。译文处理为：The trit-trot, the clatter and the tramping sound combined together and gradually faded away. 其中trit-trot是踢踏、踢踏的马蹄声，clatter是连续发出的清脆的咔哒声，tramp是沉重的脚步声。

7. 阿城小说的写作经常不出现叙述者的人称。这篇《溜索》中，第一人称的"我"字从未出现。有评论说，这是一种强调手法，使讲述者和所描述的风景和情景融为一体。在翻译时，这个问题应特别重视，如果不添加主语，很多地方则无法正确翻译。

8. "……猛发一声喊，连珠脆骂，拳打脚踢。"这个有声音、有动作的混乱的场面，译文处理为：... rushed to the herd of oxen, shouting, cursing, beating and kicking in a helter-skelter manner. 译者通过动词shout、curse、beat、kick 来再现当时混乱的场景，通过helter-skelter（匆促忙乱的）来渲染氛围，同时这个词押韵，也有一定的音响效果。

9. "怒江自西北天际亮亮而来，深远似涓涓细流，隐隐喧声腾上来，着一派森气。""亮亮而来"、"涓涓细流"、"隐隐喧声"、"一派森气"，这些极富汉语美感的词汇和表达方式，在英语中是无法对应翻译的。译者取其关键词"亮亮"、"深远"、"涓涓"、"隐隐"、"森气"，根据英语特点重新组句，力图在符合英语表达习惯的语句中再现所有关键词。译文处理为：Nujiang River rolled to us from the northwest. It was so far that it looked like a

gurgling and glistening stream, but as the sound of its turbulent surges rose up faintly, we were thrilled by its awe-inspiring magnificence.

10. "汉子们咦咦喂喂地吼起来，停一刻，又吼着撞那回声。声音旋起来，缓缓落下峡去。"这一句是对声音的描写，译文为：We howled and growled and our cries bumped into one another and echoed in the valley, rising, swirling and at last drifting down slowly。这里使用了 howl、growl、cry、echo 这些表声音的词以及 rise、swirl、drift 这些表动作的词，目的是烘托出一种效果，给读者身临其境的感觉。

11. cock 为粗语，符合语境和说话人的语言特点。

苍穹下

（节选）

◎ 赵 长 天

天 嚣

像是条轮船。巨浪狠劲儿冲来，钢板便吱吱叫唤、呻吟……

这里也是海。人们称作瀚海。风，绝对是有形的实体，像浪一样，或许比浪还硬，梗着头向钢架房冲撞。钢架房，便发疟疾般一阵阵战栗、摇晃，随时都像要散架。

也许不用担心墙倒屋倾，因为根本没墙。露出地面的只是房顶。房顶或许也会卷走，也有理由担心。但此刻，屋里没人担这个心，顾不上担这个心，没心思担这个心。

渴！难忍难挨的渴，使人的思想退化得十分简单、十分原始。欲望，分解成最简单的元素，简化成最起码的要求：水！只要有一杯水，哪怕半杯，不，一口也好哇！

"望梅止渴"的故事早讲过了，甚至讲到醋酸、醋晶；但"酸"字也已经麻木，已经刺激不了唾腺。口舌之间，又粘又腻，唾液都制成了胶水。

屋子本来就暗，只有近屋脊的山墙处有扇小窗，现时，窗玻璃混混沌沌，像拉严了厚重的窗帘。空气失去了气体的性质，像液体，甚至像固体，厚重而凝滞。这决不是人的心理错觉，而是客观状态。就像水中掺杂了细密的油珠，而成乳化液一般，空气，也乳化了。只要按一按手电，光线到处，必定像一根白色的石柱。那是粉尘，被风化得极细极小的砂粒无孔不入，无隙不钻，从昏天黑地的旷野钻入小屋，在人的五脏六腑间自由遨游。它无情地和人体争夺着仅有的一点水分。

他躺着，注视着那扇混浊的玻璃窗。喉头有梗阻感，大概食道癌患者就是这种感觉。他怀疑粉尘已经在食道结成硬块。会不会引起别的疾病，比如矽肺？但他懒得想下去。疾病的威胁，似乎已退得十分遥远，遥远得就像不存在什么威胁一样。

他闭上眼，调整头部姿势，让左耳朵不受任何障碍，他左耳听力比右耳强。

风声。丝毫没有减弱的趋势。

他仍然充满希望地倾听。只能寄希望于天气转好，这是唯一的希望。

基地首长一定牵挂着这个小试验队，但无能为力。远隔一百公里，运水车不能出动，直升飞机无法起飞，在狂虐的大自然面前，人暂时还只能居于屈辱的地位。

他又动了动脑袋，不想再费劲去听了。目前最明智的，也许就是进入半昏迷状态，减慢新陈代谢的速度，减少消耗，最大限度地保存体力。

于是，这间屋子，便沉入无生命状态……

不知过了多久。没人看表，没人计算时间。忽然，处于混沌状态的他，像被雷电击中，浑身一震。听到一种声音！他转过头，他相信左耳的听觉，没错，滤去风声、沙声、钢架呻吟声、铁皮震颤声，还有一种虽然微弱，却执着，并带节奏的敲击声。

"有人敲门！"他喊起来。

遭雷击了，都遭雷击了，一个个全从床上跳起，跌跌撞撞，竟全扑到门口。

是的，真真切切，有人敲门。谁？当然不可能是运水车，运水车会揿喇叭，运水车根本开不来。微弱的敲门声已经明白无误地告诉大家：不是来救他们的天神，而是需要他们援救的弱者。

人的生命力，也许是最尖端的科研项目，远比上天的导弹玄秘。如果破门而入的是一队救援大军，屋里这几个人准兴奋得瘫倒在地，任人搬上担架，抬上救护车去。而此刻，个个都像喝足了人参汤。

"桌上有资料没有，当心被风卷出去！"

"门别开得太大！"

"找根棍子撑住！"

每个人都找到了合适的位置，摆好了下死力的姿势。

他朝后看看。"开啦！"撤掉顶门柱，他慢慢移动门闩。

门闩吱吱叫着，痛苦地撤离自己的岗位。当门闩终于脱离了销眼，那门，便砰地弹开来，紧接着，从门外滚进灰扑扑一团什么东西和打得脸生疼的砂砾石块，屋里刹时一片混乱，像回到神话中的史前状态。

"快，推呀，推，关门！"他喊，却喊不出声。但不用喊，谁都调动了每个细胞的力量。

有点像拔河比赛，不过不是拉，是推，当然也没有拔河比赛的欢乐，有的倒是恐惧和悲壮。这本是生命的最后搏斗。

经过一番争夺、拼搏，经过一番拉锯、胶着，门，终于关上了。一伙人，都顺门板滑到地上，瘫成一堆稀泥。

屋里依然混沌，空气越发厚重，就是拧亮灯，怕也伸手不见五指。

谁也不作声。谁也不想动。甚至忘记了开门的目的。直到桌上亮起一盏暗淡的马灯，屋子里的一切朦朦胧胧地显影出来，大家才记起滚进来的那团灰扑扑的东西。

是个人。马灯就是这人点亮的。穿着毡袍，说着叽叽咕咕的蒙语，谁也听不懂。他知道别人听不懂，所以不多说，便动手解皮口袋。

全都惊呆了。西瓜！从皮口袋里滚出来的，竟是大西瓜！绿生生，油津津，像是刚从藤上摘下，有一只还带着一片叶儿呢！

戈壁滩有好西瓜，西瓜能一直吃到冬天，这不稀罕。稀罕的是现在，当一口水都成了奢侈品的时候，谁敢想西瓜！

蒙胞利索地剖开西瓜。红红的汁水，顺刀把滴滴嗒嗒淌，馋人极了！

应该是平生吃过的最甜最美的西瓜，但谁也说不出味儿来，谁都不知道，那几块西瓜是怎么落进肚子里去的，仿佛根本没经过牙齿和舌头。

至于送瓜人是怎么冲破风沙，奇迹般地来到这里，最终也没弄清，因为谁也听不懂蒙语。只好让它成为一个美好的谜，永久地留在记忆中。

浅　水

蹲着，像是怕被别人发现。讲起来总是很难听，为一个洗澡的女人放哨，算什么呀！但似乎恰恰是这一点，又使他暗暗得意——十个男人，她独独选中他！

野外试验，实在不是女人干的活，她却偏偏挤进来，还逞能地表现自己的适应性，处处自在。其实，谁不偷偷地让着她？能为女人献殷勤的机会，任何一个小伙子都很敏感。

但独独没有想到，她需要洗个澡。也许不是没人想到，想到也说不出口。这类话题，稍一偏轨，便会滑入猥亵的境界。都是大学毕业生，谁都觉得自己很高尚。

但洗澡却是生理需要。尤其在大戈壁，温差悬殊，正午的太阳，能从皮肤里烤出油来。背仪器东奔西跑，天天几身臭汗。一个礼拜，就能腌咸肉。

她毕竟是女人，居然还没有腌成咸肉，真了不起。但大概实在维持不下去了，才老老脸皮求他。

换个地方，也许不用求人。咬牙壮胆，挑个月黑天，黑漆墨涂地溜到个河汊堰塘，往水里一泡，就洗了。戈壁滩可不行，天一黑，气温便嗖嗖往下落。洗澡，非得在正午的太阳下。哪个女子有这般胆量，在光天化日之下脱净皮肉？何况总共只有这一弯刚刚及腰的浅水。

她求他，尽量显得大方自然，把性质降低到极普通一件小事，好像随便地问："喂，有八分的邮票没有？"

他却呼地一热。信任，本是任何金钱都买不到的东西。

草叶，在他眼前晃来晃去。样子像芦苇，比江南的芦苇矮。这就是芨芨草吧？想挪个位子，又不想站起来。刚才位置没选对，不该蹲在草丛里，叶子晃来晃去，脸搔得痒痒。

腿也酸了。他想挪到那个树桩去，一动，草叶就哗哗响，他忙稳住，依旧在原地。别惊了身后的人，她准提心吊胆，像惊弓之鸟。想像她的模样，准怪有趣的。忽然，一个念头，像条虫子似的钻进他心里：真想看看她，只看一眼。只须稍稍偏过头去，透过草叶的缝隙。他在草丛里，她在开阔的水面；他能看见她，她却看不见他。选择这个位置，真像事先精心策划的阴谋！

他顿时被自己的念头惊呆了，骇怕地不敢想下去。他一动不敢动，颈脖像僵成一柱石膏，仿佛转动一下，便是企图实现那不轨的预谋。

脚不由自主地抖起来，身体便跟着摇晃。越使劲屏住，越晃。全身的汗，也哗哗地淌出来。热。正午的毒日，尖嘴利牙地啃你的皮肤。平日，总嫌戈壁干燥，蹲在河边，才发现潮湿中的热，更难熬。偏偏还在草丛中，草叶在皮肤上浅浅地划出些细痕，刚才并无感觉，经咸汗一蜇，便热辣辣痛起来，痛得你全身不自在。

他低头咬牙。熬吧，大不了再熬半小时！

没想到好事才开头。嗡嗡的小咬围上来了。全冲着这身汗味儿来的，臭汗是诱虫剂，他知道。只要往后走几步，到那小河边，掬一捧清水，洗洗脸，洗洗颈项，洗洗手臂，清爽凉快不说，小咬也不会过分热心。

但是，这绝对不行。此时此刻，这选择，无异于让他挑选投降还是牺牲。

他也不明白事态怎么变得如此严峻。他们这代青年，并没有太古板的封建意识。刚到野外那天，十一人挤在一个小帐篷，被窝挨被窝，没有谁想过男女之别。仅仅从照顾的角度，安排她睡避风的角落。

可现在，情况明显起了变化。就是因为刚才的那个念头。

仿佛在观察一种生物学实验。手臂被蜇出一个个红点，慢慢肿成一坨坨红疱。难忍的痒，便荡漾开去。

他眼睛忙移开手臂。虱多不痒，随它去！

身后，杳无声息。草丛间，悠悠飘来皂液的香味。不知名的虫儿，从一株草尖跳到另一株草尖，划出漂亮的弧线。

平静的小河。平静的中午。

蓦地，前方，弯弯曲曲的小路那边，隐隐飘来人声。杂沓的脚步，跑调的歌声，敲脸盆伴奏，吹口哨和弦。

他全身悸动，子弹般射出草丛，向同伴奔去，摇晃双手惊呼："站住！回去！向后转！"

脚步停了。歌唱停了。脸盆停了。口哨停了。却没有转身，没有回头。九个男人，都呆呆地站着，屏息静气，向着那弯美丽的浅水。

他慢慢回过头去……

（载1985年8月号）

Under the Sky (Excerpts)

○ Zhao Changtian

The Hubbub of the Sky

The house was like a ship. Lashed by great billows, its steel plates squeaked and groaned …[1]

This place was called Vast Sea (a part of the Gobi Desert), which was really like a sea. The wind here was visible and, much like waves on the sea, it madly bumped onto the steel-framed house with harder and stronger force than that of the waves. Under such a terrible attack, the house shuddered and shook violently. As if suffering from pernicious malaria, the house might break apart at any moment.[2]

Perhaps he didn't need to worry about the walls, for there were no walls at all. What stood aboveground was the roof anyway. Of course, the roof might be blown away soon, but nobody in the house took it to heart. They had no time to worry about it. They had no mood to take thought for it.[3]

Thirst! The unquenchable thirst had numbed their minds. The complexity of the human minds had degraded to a simple and primitive state. All kinds of human desires were broken down to the most basic form of sustenance — water! Only a cup of water. Oh, half a cup was OK! No! A mouthful would suffice!

They had told the story of "quenching thirst by watching sour plums" (a Chinese idiom, which means seeking comfort in one's imagination) and they even talked about acetic acid and vinegar essence. But such words as "sour" or "acid" could no longer stimulate their salivary glands.[4] Now their tongues became sticky and their saliva had turned into glue.

The room was very dark. The only window near the ridge of the roof was obscure and opaque as if blocked by a thick curtain. The air in the room, which actually was no longer gaseous at all, felt as heavy and dense as liquid or solid. Like water mixed with oil, the air in the room was emulsified. Absolutely, this was not the human illusion but the actual situation. They turned on a flashlight and a beam of white column emerged. Dust! The all-pervasive dust, which squeezed into the room from the dark field outside, was running wildly in the room and freely lousing around in the internal organs of the human bodies, mercilessly scrambling for the limited amount of water left there.[5]

He lay there still, gazing at that blurry window pane. Something plugged up his throat, which might be the symptom of esophagus cancer. Perhaps too much dust had stuck together and formed a lump in his gullet. Would it cause other diseases? Silicosis? He didn't want to think more about it. Now, to him, the threat of diseases seemed too distant, too far away to be sensed.

Closing his eyes, he readjusted his head's position so as to keep his left ear unblocked. He had better hearing in the left ear than in the right one.

The wind was roaring outside, with no hint of subsidence.

He kept listening attentively, full of hope. He hoped the weather could get better. It was his only hope now.

The head of the base must be worried about them, the small experimental team, but had no way to help them out. Neither water wagons nor helicopters could reach the team which was 100 kilometers away from the base. In face of the cruel and powerful nature, human beings had to retreat to indignity and humiliation.

He moved his head, unwilling to go on listening. At present, the wisest way for him was to fall into a semi-coma so that his metabolism could slow down. Low consumption of energy might save his life.

Consequently, the room fell into lifeless silence …

None of them knew how long had passed. No one looked at the watch or calculated the time. All of a sudden, he, as if hit by a flash of lightning, trembled and came to himself from his deadened daze. He heard some sound! He trusted his left ear! Yes, it was true. Among the rustles of the wind, the roars of blowing sand, the groans of steel frames and the tremors of iron sheets, a sound, faint but firm, even with rhythm, persisted in the racket.[6]

"Someone was knocking at the door!" He cried.

As if stricken by a thunder, the others all jumped up from bed, hobbled and rushed to the door.

Yes, it was true. Someone was knocking at the door. Who was it? The water wagon? Impossible! It would honk, but it simply couldn't be driven here. The faint rat-tat sound clearly told them that it was not God who came to their rescue but another person who was in urgent need of their help.

The human vitality, a great deal more magical and mysterious than rockets, must be the most advanced subject in scientific research. At this moment, if a rescue team broke into the room, they would be too excited to stand up and too faint to say a word, and they would put themselves at the mercy of the rescue team to be carried out on stretchers into an ambulance. But now, instead of fainting away, everyone was on alert, full of energy, as if they had just had some ginseng soup.

"Are there any materials on the table? Be careful! Don't let the wind blow them away!"

"Do not open the door wide!"

"Prop it up with a stick!"

Each of them found his own position and each of them got himself ready.

He looked back and shouted, "OK, are you ready? I'll open the door!" He took the gatepost away and slowly moved the bolt.

The bolt squeaked and in great pain it left its place. The moment the bolt was taken off, the door flung open with a big bang, and in the wake of it, something gray burst into the room together with sand and stones which heavily slapped their faces. The room was in turmoil like the scene in the prehistoric age described in mythology.

"Be quick! Push, push! Close the door!" He shouted but was too weak to utter the voice. As a matter of fact, he didn't need to shout. Everyone in the room was making their exertions.

As if in a tug-of-war, they called on each cell in their bodies into action. Instead of tugging, they were pushing hard with all their efforts. Without the happiness in a typical tug-of-war, they felt fearful, sad but heroic. This might be their last struggle in their lives.

After a hubbub of struggling and scrambling, the door was closed in the end. In fatigue and fright, they were paralyzed and slipped down to the floor, panting.[7]

Now, the air in the room grew thicker and dustier, and even with a light on they couldn't see each other clearly.

The room was quiet again. Nobody wanted to say a word and nobody wanted to move. And they even forgot why they took such great trouble to open the door. A lamp was lit, and in the dim light everything in the room gradually became distinct. At this time, they thought of that gray thing which rolled into the room just now.

It was a man. And it was he who lit the lamp. In a thick gown, that man spoke to them in the Mongolian language which none of them understood. Realizing that he had no way to make himself understood, the man began to unfasten his bag.

All of them were surprised and dumbfounded. Watermelons! Rolling out of his bag were watermelons! They were green and their skins were smooth and bright. As if just picked off the vine, one of them even had a leaf on!

Watermelons were not rare on the Gobi Desert. They could eat it even in winter. But now, it became a rarity of rarities. When a mouthful of water was a luxury, who could be so bold as to entertain an extravagant hope for a watermelon?

The Mongolian man cut the watermelons quickly and deftly. The red juice dripped down from his knife. How inviting!

To them, these must be the most delicious watermelons they had ever eaten. But none of them could tell the taste and none of them knew how the melons went down their throat — the melons just passed as if there were no such things as teeth and tongue at all.

How did the Mongolian man fight his way in the sandstorm and come to them in time? Nobody knew it, for none of them understood the Mongolian language. They had to treasure this beautiful mystery in heart and bear it in mind for ever.

The Shallow Water

He crouched lest he should be discovered by others. It was embarrassing to talk about it! He was standing sentry for a woman who was having a bath. It was humiliating to let others know it! But he felt elated secretly — among ten men she picked him!

The field experiment was really not suitable for a girl. She insisted in joining them and tried to show her comfort and adaptability to them. As a matter of fact, who wasn't willing to give way to a girl? To any young man, an opportunity to please a girl was really hard to come by.

He never thought that the opportunity came in the form of guarding a bath. Perhaps she needed a bath but felt reluctant to bring the matter up. Even if someone did consider such a possibility, a slightest mention of it would easily put that person into an embarrassing or even obscene situation. They were all university graduates, who always considered themselves noble and sublime.

But taking a bath was the physiological need of human beings, especially in the Gobi Desert where the temperature varied a lot. At noon, the scorching sun burned their skin into butter. Carrying the heavy instruments here and there, they were soaked through with sweat. After a week, their flesh turned into salted meat!

After all, she was a woman. She was so great that she even kept her flesh unsalted. Now, maybe feeling extremely uncomfortable, she had to summon up courage and ask for his help.[8]

It was not so difficult if they were living elsewhere. One just needed to go out on a dark night, find a pond or a stream and steep himself in the water. Everything would be OK, and he didn't need anyone's help. But it was absolutely different here. As soon as it got dark, the temperature of the Gobi Desert dropped dramatically.

Doing it in the sun at noon when the temperature was high seemed to be the only option for one to take a bath. However, no girls were brave enough to go naked in the daylight, bathing in an outdoor pond with waist-deep water.

When she approached him, she tried to appear natural as if discussing with him about a daily trivial matter, as if simply asking, "Do you have an eight-cent stamp?"

His heart felt warm. Trust was priceless in the world.

Now, he was crouching among clusters of grasses. The grass leaves wavered, much like reeds growing in the ponds south of the Yangtze — a little shorter than reeds, though. Perhaps they were splendens? He thought. He wanted to change his place but he didn't move. He hadn't picked a good place. Clusters of grasses were waving to and fro around him, which made his face itch.

As a result of long-time crouching, his legs began to ache. He wanted to walk to the stump over there but he didn't. A slight movement would make the grass leaves rustle. For fear of scaring her, he remained there, still and silent. She must be frightened if she heard something, like a bird startled by the mere twang of a bowstring. In a sorry plight, she must be looking very funny and interesting, he imagined. All of a sudden, an idea popped up and wormed into his heart. He wanted to turn around and take a look at her! He just needed to turn his head slightly and peep through the dense grasses. He hid himself among clusters of grasses while she was bathing in the water. He could see her but she could not see him. Without planning beforehand, he had chosen such a vantage point!

He was horrified by his own thought.[9] He kept motionless in the grasses. His neck turned as stiff as a plaster stone, as if a slight turning would incur his malicious misconduct.

His feet began to shiver and after a while his whole body trembled. The more he tried to stop it, the more violently he shuddered. He was wet with sweat all over at once.

The scorching sun at noon was gnawing his skin. Usually, the Gobi Desert was dry and hot, but now he realized that the damp heat beside the river was much more tormenting! Clusters of grasses enveloped him and the grass leaves left some minor scratches on his skin. He didn't feel the pain at the beginning but now stung by the sweat those scratches began to ache. He felt painful and uneasy.

Clenching his teeth, he resolved to endure this unbearable pain. Hold on! Only half an hour at most!

Out of his expectation, biting flies began to charge and attack him. The stinky sweat all over his body was inviting them. He knew it. As long as he went to the small stream behind and washed his face, neck and arms, the biting flies would lose interest in him and he would feel much better.

Absolutely, he couldn't do it. Now, to surrender or to sacrifice, he was facing a serious choice.

He had no idea that the situation could develop to such a serious state. He and his generation didn't have much exposure to the old conservative ideas of male-female separatism. On the first day they came here, eleven young people huddled in one small tent. They slept close to each other and didn't think too much. For the sake of her health, she was arranged to sleep in the corner sheltered from wind.

But now, the situation changed obviously, just because of that terrible thought.

He squatted there as if he were doing a biological experiment attentively. His arm was stung and red spots appeared, which slowly swelled and became red lumps. The unbearable itch quickly spread in his arm.

He shifted his eyes from his arm right away. Let it be! He had no mood to think about it!

It was quite silent behind him. The fragrance of soap drifted to him and tantalized his nostrils.[10] A nameless insect was jumping from the tip of one grass to another, making a beautiful arch.

The peaceful river. The tranquil noon.[11]

All of a sudden, right ahead of him, at the other end of the path over there, came men's voices, their hurried footsteps, out-of-tune songs, knocks on basins and a choir of whistles.

He was so nervous and worried that he sprang up from the grasses and waved his hands to them, "Stop! Turn around! Turn around!"

The footsteps stopped. The songs stopped. The knocks on the basins stopped. The whistles stopped. None of them turned back. All the nine men held their breath and gazed at the waist-deep water, in a daze.

Slowly, he turned his head …

(Published in No.8, 1985)

 注 释

1.　"钢板便吱吱叫唤、呻吟……"这是拟人的修辞手法，也有描摹声音的词的使用。译者处理为：… its steel plates squeaked and groaned …。squeak表示吱吱响，groan表示呻吟声。英语中有些表示声音的词很生动，例如：潺

潺声babble/ 嘎吱声creak/ 扑通一声flop/ 汩汩声gurgle/ 咝咝声sizzle/ 嘟嘟声toot/ 嗡嗡声zoom/ (鼓的)咚咚声rub-a-dub/ (轻风的)瑟瑟声sough/ 短促而尖利的声音rattle/ (敲门的)砰砰声rat-tat-tat。

2. 英语里表示某一个动作会有多个动词，例如：发抖，可以是shiver、quiver、tremble、shudder、shake，摇晃可以是shake、wave、waver、sway、wobble，等等。在翻译时，选择最恰当的词来进行翻译才能准确生动。"钢架房，便发疟疾般一阵阵战栗、摇晃，随时都像要散架"译为：Under such a terrible attack, the house shuddered and shook violently. As if suffering from pernicious malaria, the house might break apart at any moment.

3. … but nobody in the house took it to heart. They had no time to worry about it. They had no mood to take thought for it. 这里的take it to heart、worry about it、take thought for it 都是担心的意思。同样的意思，分成三小句，重复三次，为了营造一种紧迫的氛围。

4. "'望梅止渴'的故事早讲过了，甚至讲到醋酸、醋晶；但'酸'字也已经麻木，已经刺激不了唾腺。" "望梅止渴"是中国的一个成语，"梅"是酸的，下面还谈到了醋酸、醋晶，酸的东西刺激人的唾腺，产生唾液，可以解渴。所以，"望梅止渴"必须直译，而且里面要有sour这个词，这样才可以与下文连贯，意思承接。为了帮助读者理解，译者对"望梅止渴"加了文内注解。They had told the story of "quenching thirst by watching sour plums" (a Chinese idiom, which means seeking comfort in one's imagination) and they even talked about acetic acid and vinegar essence. But such words as "sour" or "acid" could no longer stimulate their salivary glands.

5. 这一段描写屋子里的混乱、充满粉尘的空气、人的饥渴和绝望。原文多处使用比喻、拟人、夸张等修辞手法，翻译时，对形容词、动词以及原文的修辞手段都要重视，尽量对应，以再现当时的紧张混乱场面。

6. "……滤去风声、沙声、钢架呻吟声、铁皮震颤声，还有一种虽然微弱，却执着，并带节奏的敲击声。"译为：Among the rustles of the wind, the roars of blowing sand, the groans of steel frames and the tremors of iron sheets, a sound, faint but firm, even with rhythm, persisted in the racket. 译文中rustle、roar、groan、tremor 以及押头韵的词faint and firm，都可以很好地对应原文，烘托出声音的效果。

7. "经过一番争夺、拼搏，经过一番拉锯、胶着，门，终于关上了。一伙人，都顺门板滑到地上，瘫成一堆稀泥。" After a hubbub of struggling and scrambling, the door was closed in the end. In fatigue and fright, they were paralyzed and slipped down to the floor, panting. hubbub指嘈杂混乱，"争夺"、"拼搏"、"拉锯"、"胶着"，译者用了struggling and scrambling 两个押头韵的词来处理，in fatigue and fright 和后面的 panting 是译者加上的，用来表达他们劳累、恐惧、瘫成一堆稀泥的状态。

8. "才老老脸皮求他"翻译成：She had to summon up courage and ask for his help. summon up courage是鼓起勇气的意思，用在这里翻译"老老脸皮"。

9. 这篇小说中，"疼痛"、"哆嗦"、"吃惊"等词重复出现过很多次。翻译时，根据语境，换词使用，可以使译文富于文采。例如：此处"惊呆了"或者"吃惊"，可以译为surprised、shocked、astonished、be taken aback、horrified、scared 等等；"哆嗦"可以译为shiver、quiver、shudder、chill等；"疼痛"可以译为painful、hurt、ache、pang、sore、agony等。

10. "草丛间，悠悠飘来皂液的香味。" The fragrance of soap drifted to him and tantalized his nostrils. 后半句是译者所加，有助于烘托人物心理。

11. "宁静"可以译为：calm、tranquil、peaceful、serene、silent、still 等等。应该根据上下文，选择最合适的。例如：serene和 tranquil都有宁静和美好的意思；calm 强调宁静、镇静；peaceful 意为平和、无纷扰; silent 多指沉默不说话；still 常指无动作、一动不动、安静。积累丰富的词汇，并注意词汇之间的细微差别，有助于翻译。

古井

◎ 陈 村

1

村边有一口古井。

老人说，这井通着东海。难怪，地再怎么旱，井水从来不少。井活了许多人的命，张家村的村民便十分地爱惜它。

多少代了，古井老了就像没老一样，总是这么出水，从不用淘它。方圆百里，这井出了名，提起这地方，就叫它"井边儿"。说"离井五里地"，谁都听得明白，张家村反倒没人提。

村里的老头没事，爱上井边坐坐，有事无事朝古井里瞅一眼。其实，水总那么高，平那块稍高起的黑石，瞅也白瞅。老头还是瞅，瞅惯了，瞅一眼心里乐。

姑娘媳妇在井沿洗衣，又笑又闹的，也不顾忌尊长。村风比较开明，倒也没生出什么丑事。小子们很想来凑凑热闹的，无奈老爷子们总在那儿镇着，去也没意思。

一个村的人活得有滋有味。

这天，张家村的三大爷一早又到古井边，背着手朝井里一瞅，吓了一跳：井壁那块黑石不见了。他暗想事情不好。改朝换代也见多了，这黑石从来是见天的，今天淹没在水里，怕有什么讲究。三大爷连忙叫人来看。

一村的人都看。一村的人都怕。

实在想不出这古井想干什么，村里最老的八太爷也说不上。祖宗没有留下话。

偷偷去请阴阳先生。阴阳先生先说"万死不敢从命"，见了钱又说"老夫敢不从命"，来了。饭后由八太爷三大爷等族尊陪去井边，吆五喝六地一阵忙，闭上两只小眼约有半个时辰，说话了。

"此井阴阳不调，腹中有祟。"

"什么祟？"

"祟者，天之秘也。凡天秘者不可预宣也。知者为知之，不知者不知之，以知为不知者……"

阴阳先生说得手也舞了足也蹈了。三大爷心里急，冒昧截断：

"可有什么利害？"

"害者，利之反也。有利则必有害也。一害一利，如一月一日，一阴一阳，一牝一牡，一死一生……"

"究竟什么害？"

阴阳先生小眼稍稍一开，转瞬又合上，并不发话。八太爷知他脾气，忙递过红包。先生翻掌接去，轻轻一笑，用指尖在泥地划出个大字：

杀

划完即用掌抹去。"再勿多言，此已罪过。"拱拱手，竟扬长而去。

一村的人被那"杀"字搅得心里害怕。天未尽黑，家家闭上门，熄了灯，暗地里等那天亮。

狗也乖觉，竟吠了一夜。

第二天，没人下地，如此不是办法。再说那先生话说得阴阴阳阳，不免叫人半信半疑。小子们商量，去请县上的水文队。那几位师傅靠水吃饭，想必能看出名堂。

井里的水，又高出几分。

水文队派来师傅，喝过酒吃过鸡非常好说话。在古井边默不作声地忙了半个时辰，指指那三架仪器，说：

"井，怕是要喷。"

大爷们不懂什么叫井喷，忙请教。师傅从星云说起，讲到板块、应力，讲得比阴阳先生更叫人糊涂。

"您说吧，有什么不福气的事？"老人忌讳说"祸"。

"井要喷，喷水或喷沙。地也要震，震得屋倒楼垮。地要裂缝，缝里能掉进牛去。震得凶呢，至少死一村子。"

果然是"杀"啊，竟不谋而合。祸事了！

"有……有啥子办法？"张三大爷着了急，"咱把井堵上，中不中？"

"堵井？"师傅乐了，"您堵，一堵就炸。别看这好好一个村子，眨巴一下眼睛就成了深坑，底都不见。哼，堵井！"

师傅们吃了鸡喝了酒走了。走前扔下话，还是赶紧避避的好，至少避十里远。这地下的事，谁也说不准。说完，背着仪器慌忙回县。他们也怕。

那就逃命吧。

2

一村的人连夜逃到山上，离村十五里。

进了山可就难了，别说吃饭睡觉，连喝口水都不易。性命要紧，就顾不上这许多了。老婆子天天念佛，保佑村子别炸，保佑平平安安。

等了五天，没有动静。

逃命时匆忙，粮也不够，菜也没有。有胆大的小伙子愿冒死回村，被当娘的一巴掌打了回去。后来，实在捱不过，与其饿死，不如派一个人去抢点东西出来，或许不死呢。

要派只能派小伙子，老人孩子去也背不回什么。那就抽签，抽到谁就是谁。抽签时，手都一抖一抖的。抖出个白签，心里一阵喜欢，抽到黑签，难免一家子哭一夜。第二天天亮，合村送他到路边，又哭又喊，有如出丧。

小伙子总是活着回来，叫父母心里石头落地，也叫乡亲们过意得去。

小伙子轮着去过三回了，并没出险。有天回来报告：那井水又长了一些，但不冒气也不喷沙。老爷子说他孬，一喷就完蛋了，你能回得来？小伙子缩缩头，不再作声。

山里可不比村里，野得很。姑娘小伙成天不干活，厮混一处，没人收治得住。再说大爷太爷们心里烦，顾命都觉得烦难，顾不到这些。好好的一口井，一辈辈传下来都不生事，偏偏坏在自己手里。先是长水，长得黑石头给淹了，后来又说喷水喷沙，还说要炸。面对祖宗儿孙，老头们仿佛心里有愧。

那井还是不喷。

大家等得心里烦，一天天如坐在火上，反倒盼它要喷快喷要炸快炸。可是那井偏偏不炸，只把水慢悠悠长起来，长起来。

地都要荒了，荒了地不炸死却要饿死。长辈们开了会，决定还是种。不过要派个人去守着那井，看到不祥之兆便敲钟，大家也能逃命。

这可是送死的活，虽未明说人人心里明白。那就还是抽签。

人在地里，心却悬着，耳朵竖起老高。一连三天，没有钟声，大家才稍稍松懈。

第四天下午，钟疯了一样乱响。

大家撒腿逃命，只有那个敲钟人的娘，脚软了瘫在地上。众人念他儿子义气，不忍撇下她，便架着她跑。

半天没动静。

守钟的小子脸吓得煞白走来，说水又长了，还冒起泡来。泡一上水面就破，还带响。

众人再不敢下地。

井还是不喷。只好又抽签。

冒了一秋的泡，井还是没喷。水升到齐井口就不再升了，水的中央稍稍高出个肚皮，肚皮上升起水泡，叭叭地响。

每天换一个值班的，换得太烦人，渐渐三天一换，一周一换。起先值班的小伙子还天天上山，久了不耐烦起来，干脆宿在村里。姑娘爱耍个花枪，说要回村取衣，去去就半日不回。一女一男耍够了，在村里炒个鸡蛋，烙张脆饼，嘴上吃得噌亮。

再朝后，人人都抢着去值班。即使不为亲嘴的快活，也图个省力省心。按早先订下的规矩，值班的工分最高。

家有大闺女的那些当娘的，知道事情要坏，赶紧托谁做个顺水媒人，草草打发闺女过门。对早先不答应的儿女私情，现也开通了，免得事情败了遭人耻笑。

初冬时分，全村搬下山去。

3

古井如今成了名胜，慕名来参观的人一批又一批。他们走下汽车，望着一串串"叭叭"的水泡，摸摸井的肚皮，全都赞叹不已，都说从来没见过这么好看的景致。

村里的老婆子，在井边坐成一排，卖着鸡蛋、茶水、枣儿、核桃。价格还公道。

村里的小伙子，学着戴起了"盲公镜"。村里的姑娘，穿起窄窄的裤，把屁股包得凹进凸出。

村里的老头，坐在井边直叹气。早先的乡风，有这么不堪的吗？

1985年6月于昆山

An Old Well

O *Chen Cun*

I

There was an old well in Zhang Village.[1]

The old men in the village said that the well was linked to the East Sea. No wonder it never ran dry even in a drought, nor did its water decline. The well had saved many people's lives and all the villagers took it as their treasure.

The old well had never needed dredging. For generations it kept vigorous, with water gushing out continuously and vivaciously. It became so well-known far and near that the village became to be called "By the Well" or "Five *Li* to the Well", instead of "Zhang Village".

The old men in the village loved sitting on the rim of the well. The water level kept unchanged for many years and in it a big black rock stood out of the surface of the water. From time to time, the old men couldn't help casting an affectionate look at the well. After all, they were used to looking at it and at the sight of it, they were filled with joy and contentment.[2]

Girls always washed clothes by the well, laughing and chatting, regardless of the presence of their seniors. The custom here was enlightened and not very conservative, but nothing disgraceful happened. Those guys really wanted to join the girls by the well but they were stopped by the old men's august eyes.

Villagers led a zestful life here.[3]

One morning, as usual, Third Grandpa[4] sauntered to the rim of the well. As he looked down at the water inside, with his hands behind his back, he was taken aback. That black rock disappeared! He thought it was not a good omen. For so many years the black rock was revealed out of the water, but today it was submerged. Something special and terrible might happen! He hurried to call for other villagers to have a look at it.

All the villagers came. They all felt scared.

What was wrong with the well? They really couldn't make head or tail of it.[5]

Even the oldest Eighth Great-grandpa in the village could not reason out an answer. Their ancestors had never talked of such a phenomenon before.

They could do nothing but send for a fortune-teller called "Mr. Yin and Yang". The fortune-teller refused them at first, "I dare not obey you". When they took out money, he changed his attitude, "I dare not disobey you."[6] After supper, accompanied by Third Grandpa, Eighth Great-grandpa and other seniors in the village, the fortune-teller came to the well. After some calling, crying and clapping[7], he closed his narrow eyes. After a while, he opened his mouth,

"Yin and yang are not in harmony in this well and there is something terrible within."

"What's it?"

"It is Heaven's mystery, which can't be spoken out. The one who knows it knows it and the one who doesn't know it doesn't know it. And the one who knows it doesn't know he knows it…"

Waving his hands, bobbing his head and stamping his feet, the fortune-teller explained to the villagers in an excited manner. Third Grandpa turned impatient and interrupted him,

"Is there anything bad going to happen?"

"The bad is the opposite of the good. The good and the bad come at the same time. The good and the bad, just like the moon and the sun, yin and yang, the female and the male, death and life…"

"What on earth is it?"

The fortune-teller opened his narrow eyes but closed them immediately. He didn't say a word. Eighth Great-grandpa knew the fortune-teller's hint and hurried to cram a red packet filled with money into his hand. The fortune-teller took it and smiled. Bending down, he wrote a word on the mud with his finger tip —

KILL

Before they understood it he quickly wiped it off with his palm. "Do not ask more. I have already sinned by letting out the secret." Cupping one hand in the other before his chest, the fortune-teller said goodbye to them and left quickly.

The villagers were all frightened by that word "Kill". And before it got dark they shut their doors and turned off the lights, waiting for the dawn silently.

Dogs kept barking all the night.

The next day, nobody went to work in the field. Things couldn't go on like this; besides, the fortune-teller's evasive words were rather dubious. Half believing and half doubting, some young people had a discussion and sent for the county's hydrological team, who made a living by studying water. Perhaps they could work out the reason.

The water rose higher.

The hydrological team sent some workers to the village. After they drank the wine and ate the chicken served by the villagers, they turned easy-going and began to busy themselves at the well without saying a word. After some time, they pointed at the three devices they had used and concluded,

"This well is going to blow, perhaps."

The old men hurried to consult them. A blowing well? What would it be like? The workers patiently explained, starting with stars and nebulas, relating the earth plates and elaborating on the internal stress. Their complicated explanation left the villagers totally in the dark![8]

"Just tell us directly. What is the unblessed matter?" The old men butted in. To them, "disaster" was a taboo word.

"The well may blow out water or sand. An earthquake may happen. Your houses may collapse in the earthquake. And the ground may break open and your cows may fall into the cracks. If the earthquake is serious, all the villagers may die."

Ah! They might be "Killed"! The words of the hydrological team coincided with the fortune-teller's prediction! A disaster was coming!

"Do you have any way to help us out?" Third Grandpa got worried very much. "Can we block the well?"

"Block the well?" The workers laughed. "The moment you block it, it will blow. The whole village will become a big hole in a minute. How can you think of such an idea?"

The workers from the hydrological team wined and dined[9] and then planned to leave. Before their departure, they gave their advice: "You'd better escape, at least to a place ten *li* away. What will happen under the ground? Heaven knows!" They carried their devices on their backs and left immediately. Obviously, they were scared, too.

Then, fleeing for life was the only choice for the villagers.

II

The whole villagers escaped into the mountain overnight, fifteen *li* away from their village.

But life was so hard in the mountain. Even a mouthful of water was hard to come by, let alone eating and sleeping. Nonetheless, they had to endure. After all, survival was the most important. The old women prayed to Buddha every day, begging for blessings for the peace of their village.

After five days, nothing happened.

When they fled, they were in such a hurry that they didn't bring enough grains and vegetables with them. Then, some daring guys wanted to go back to the village to fetch something, only to be stopped and even slapped by their mothers. However, after several days, the unbearable hunger tortured them so much that they decided to send one back to the village to fetch something to eat. Maybe, they could survive.

Since old men and little kids didn't have the strength to carry enough food back, a capable young man was their only choice. So they decided to draw lots — with shivering hands. Those getting the white lots were happy as they could stay in safety, while the one getting the black lot burst into tears as he had to go back to the village. His family cried all night. And the next day, they saw the young man off by the roadside, screaming and crying, as if holding a funeral procession.

The young man finally came back, alive and kicking, which made his parents fully relieved. And the villagers no longer felt sad and sorry.

Three young fellows took turns to go back and nothing dangerous happened. The other day, a young man told them: "The well water rises but the well neither gives off fumes nor blows off sand." The old men replied: "How stupid you are! Is it possible for you to come back if it blows?" The young man recoiled and said nothing.

Life in the mountain was different from that in the village. Girls and guys hung together every day, as they went totally unrestrained in the mountain. Nobody could control them. Since grandpas' and great-grandpas' predominant concern was survival, they had no mood to care about young people's intimate relations. The well was handed down from generation to generation and nothing bad had happened, but now it was going to be destroyed in their hands. The water rose at first, and then the black rock disappeared, and later it was said that it might blow out water and sand, and in the end it might explode! — A series of conjectures made the old men upset and fidgety. They felt guilty and ashamed to face their ancestors and their descendants.

However, the well didn't blow.

The villagers got more and more impatient, as if sitting on the flames. They even expected it to blow soon, as quickly as possible. But it didn't. The water kept rising in the well.

The land would be barren if left unattended. They made a living off the land. Without it, they would starve to death, if not die of the blowing well. The old men held an urgent meeting and decided to send some people back to cultivate the land. They decided to ask a person to stay by the well. Thus, in case of any emergency, he could ring the bell and they could escape in time.

Obviously, they all understood this was a life-or-death job. They had to draw lots again.

Working in the field, they felt nervous, their ears on the alert. Three days passed. The bell didn't ring. They turned a little relaxed.

On the afternoon of the fourth day, the bell rang madly.

They made off as fast as they could. An old woman, the mother of the young man who rang the bell, became upset and fell onto the ground. For the sake of her son's braveness, they helped her up, held her arms and ran away.

Nothing happened.

The young man who rang the bell came with a pale face, saying that the water kept rising with bubbles, which burst at the surface and produced a loud sound.

They no longer dared to cultivate the land.

The well didn't blow. They had to draw lots again.

The bubbles kept popping up for the whole autumn. The well didn't blow. When the water was level with the mouth of the well, it stopped rising. The center of the water surface bulged a little, with a stream of bubbles gurgling up.

Every day, they took turns to watch the well. By and by, they took turns every three days, and later, every seven days. At the beginning, the young fellows on watch duty returned every day to give report, but as time went on, they grew impatient and lazy. They slept in the village. Girls, with the excuse of fetching some clothes, always went to the village and stayed there for almost half a day. A guy and a girl could have a wonderful time in the village. They played to their hearts' content, feasted themselves with scrambled eggs or crisp pies, and with greasy lips they came back.

Later, people vied for the watch shifts in the village. If not for those happy hours and secret kisses, they could at least save some efforts. According to the rules set beforehand, the one on duty could get more work points.

Mothers were getting much more concerned. For fear that something disgraceful might happen, they anxiously found some matchmakers and married their daughters in a hurry. The previous secret love affairs were finally permitted and made public.

In the early winter, all the villagers returned to the village.

III

Now the village has become a tourist resort, attracting people far and near. Tourists got off the bus, looked at the bubbles in the well, put their hands on the bulging center of the well and felt happy. They sang high praise for it and said they had never seen such a fantastic view.

The old women in the village sat in a line by the well, selling eggs, tea, jujubes and walnuts at reasonable prices.

Young men in the village loved wearing dark sunglasses and girls were fond of the fashionable pants which tightly wrapped their buttocks into bulges and dents with inviting temptation.[10]

The old men still liked sitting by the well. They always sighed and sighed: "The good old custom has gone!"

Kunshan, June 1985

 注 释

1. 小说以There was an old well in Zhang Village开始，按照时间顺序，娓娓道来，讲述了一个村子里的一口井的故事，文风朴实自然，节奏舒缓，语言平实。译文尽量做到文风对应。

2. "其实，水总那么高，平那块稍高起的黑石，瞅也白瞅。老头还是瞅，瞅惯了，瞅一眼心里乐。"原文三五个字就是一个分句，"瞅也白瞅"、"老头还是瞅"、"瞅惯了"、"瞅一眼心里乐"，这些表达简洁、朴实、有趣，译文从结构上很难对应了，只能根据英语特点重新组句，把意思表达出来：
The water level kept unchanged for many years and in it a big black rock stood out of the surface of the water. From time to time, the old men couldn't help casting an affectionate look at the well. After all, they were used to looking at it and at the sight of it, they were filled with joy and contentment.

3. "一个村的人活得有滋有味。"zest 的意思是"滋味"、"风味"、"香味"、"兴趣"、"热情"、"极大的快乐"。这里，"活得有滋有味"译成：to lead a zestful life。

4. 汉语的亲属称谓体系具有多成分性、多层次性构成的特点，体现在男女有别、长幼有序、系脉分明、宗族有别。在汉语文化中，人们习惯于"排行称谓"，如大哥、二嫂、三姨、四舅，等等。翻译这类称谓，有时可以直译，有时要灵活变通，有时要省略不译。这里，为了让译文读者了解并接受汉语文化的称谓习惯，可以采用异化法处理。这里"三大爷"、"八太爷"

分别译作Third Grandpa和Eighth Great-grandpa。一定要翻译"三"或者"八"，是为了符合原文风貌，体现这两位老人在村里资历深。英语中是没有Third Grandpa这样的称谓的，但这种表达应该能为英语读者理解。例如：杨宪益的《红楼梦》英译本中把"四姑娘"译为The fourth young lady, 在《朝花夕拾》译本中把"沈四太太"译为Fourth Mrs. Shen; 珍妮·凯利的《围城》英译本中把"三奶奶"译为Third Daughter-in-law, 把"三叔"译为Third Uncle。

5. cannot make head or tail of sth. 意思是"摸不着头脑、闹不清楚"，是非正式用语，用在这里指村民们搞不清楚为什么井水上涨了，搞不清楚前因后果。

6. 从"不敢从命"到"敢不从命"，阴阳先生的态度有所变化。原文这两个词只是调整了词序，就产生了一种幽默效果，把阴阳先生的形象和态度变化刻画得惟妙惟肖。译文最好也能通过文字的细微变化，体现这种幽默效果：I dare not obey you和I dare not disobey you。

7. "吆五喝六地一阵忙"译为：After some calling, crying and clapping。可以想象，阴阳先生吵吵嚷嚷、手舞足蹈，所以用了call, cry, clap这三个押头韵的动词，有动作，也有声音效果。

8. leave sb. in the dark. 使某人摸不着头脑，不明白。in the dark 处在蒙昧中，处在不知情状态，摸不着头脑，例如：He kept me in the dark about it. 他隐瞒此事，不让我知道。

9. 上文已经提到水文队的师傅吃鸡喝酒，干完活后，再次得到吃鸡喝酒的款待。这里译为wine and dine，就是好吃好喝款待之意。

10. "村里的姑娘，穿起窄窄的裤，把屁股包得凹进凸出。"... and girls were fond of the fashionable pants which tightly wrapped their buttocks into bulges and dents with inviting temptation。"凹进凸出"说明性感，所以译者加了with inviting temptation。

旷野里

○ 残雪

那天晚上，她睡下去，忽然发现自己没睡着。于是起身，在没点灯的房间里踱来踱去，踩得朽烂的地板阴森森地作响。黑暗里，有一团更黑的东西蹲在墙角，隐隐约约的像一只熊。那团东西移动着，也踩得地板阴森森地作响。

"谁？"她的声音冻结在喉头。

"我。"丈夫骇怕的声音。

他们相互都被对方吓着了。

从此，每天夜里，他们如两个鬼魂，在黑暗中，在这所大寓所的许多空房间里游来游去。白天，她低垂着眉眼，仿佛不记得夜里发生的事。

"玻璃板上的镇纸被打破了。"他抬起血红的眼，偷偷地看了看她。

"自己怎么会掉下去，夜里风真大。"她说，耸起两个肩胛骨，同时就感到肋骨在受苦地裂开。"鬼鬼祟祟真可恶！"她莫名其妙地冲口而出。

"有些房间里有蛇，因为常年空着，而且……"他继续说，手中舞弄着一根橡皮止血带，那上面有一个粗大的注射针头，亮闪闪的。"刚才我说到哪里来了？对，有一天，一条蛇伴着墙根沙沙地游，你要担心蛇咬……"

她是五天前在枕头下发现橡皮管和注射针头的，那东西是崭新的，一股橡胶味儿。当时她一点也没在意。这几天中，丈夫每每将那东西拿在手中玩弄，还在睡觉的时候将橡皮管含在口中咀嚼。

"你应该去听一听气象预报。"他眨巴着一只眼又说。

房间又大又虚空，北风撞击着坏了风钩的窗户。

为了避免在黑暗中相撞，两人都故意把脚步踏得更响些。

他出去了，将橡皮管和针头挂在墙壁的一颗钉子上，她闻见满屋子都是那种味儿。

"我要试验一下。"他打转回来对她说，"我要逮一头野猫。这地方这么大，这么黑，必定有一个地方藏得有各种野物。你知道，在夜里，旷野里落着冻雨，我在那里悠转，背上全湿透了，结出了冰壳。什么地方响着一种陌生的脚步，什么人在那里走呢？"

"那是我在另一头行走。"她淡淡地说，一边将肿胀的脑袋偏进阴影里，想要遮住眼圈周围的黑晕。

他从她面前一步跨过，从墙上取下止血带和针头来摆弄。"有时候，人生中会发生预计不到的转折。"针头在一道闪电中爆起一朵火花。

已经记不得有多久，他们俩再也没睡觉了。她躺下，耳边立刻响起那种奇怪的声音，睁开眼来，发现丈夫闭着眼在嚼咬那根止血带，粗大的针头正插在他的心脏上。她穿好衣站起来，立刻有一个梦追随她。墙壁湿漉漉的，向上面一靠，衣服就被粘住了。

"镇纸打破了，谁干的呢？"他在墙角说起话来，口里嚼得嘎吱作响。

"有一个梦追随我，就从那个小窗口进来的。它像鲨鱼一样游进来，向我的后颈窝呼出大股冷气。这些天没睡，你看我全身的皮肤都是皱皱巴巴的。昨天我在惊慌失措中打坏了镇纸，就是为了躲开那条吃人的鱼。这场追逐的把戏还得延续多久啊？"她不知不觉用了诉苦的口气，"我简直分不清是在做梦还是醒着，我在办公室里讲起胡话来，把同事们吓坏了。"

"这种事谁心中有底呢？有人一辈子就在这种情形中度过。他们不得不在走路的时候，在谈话的时候睡起觉来，或许我们也会是那样。"

"我害怕遇见人，他们会发现我神情恍惚，我尽量不开口。"

他走到另一个房间去了，她依然看见针头在他手上爆出火花。

雷声隆隆响个没完。

从她是小孩子的时候起，寓所里就有这么多空房间，又大，又黑，一个又一个，全是一式一样的。她从来也没数清它们究竟有多少个。后来他来了。一开始，他兴致勃勃地在那些房间的窗台上种上黄杨木，还蓬着头翘着屁股，把那些房间扫得灰雾腾腾。一有人来，他就提高了嗓门说："整个房间变了样！"他一次也没浇过水，黄杨木全枯死了。他扔了它们，剩下许多空钵子摆在窗台上，夜间看去酷似许多骷髅。

"倒不如不种干净。"她蜡黄着脸，丧气地埋怨。

"这地方什么也长不成。"他恶狠狠地踩着脚，"一片荒蛮。"

他不再种什么东西，年纪轻轻却患起老年性气喘来。失眠是无意中到来的。有一天，他一觉醒来，看见窗外墨黑，一瞥壁上的挂钟，他还才睡下呢。他从一个房间走到另一个房间，撞翻了窗台上的瓦钵，瓦钵咚的一声落到外面的水泥地上。

"昨天你打破了镇纸，就是狮子头的那个，你就不能克制一点。"他愚顽不化地又提起那件事。

"窗台上的那些钵子，夜里看起来特别恐怖，能不能扫下去。"她停了一下，语调又变得飘忽不定，"有那么一天，我终于下了决心，将它们一古脑全扫下去了，那时窗台上光秃秃的，真叫人开心。"

他窘得一脸通红，牙齿格格地响。

夜里，他们俩醒着做梦的时候，她发现他的脚伸得那么长，长得给人一种陌生的感觉。那冰冷的、骨节分明的脚掌触着了她的枕头，一个脚趾肿得像胡萝卜。

"你占了那么大的地方，"他在被头里嗡嗡地说，"你把我挤到了墙上，针头就挂在墙上。天上下着雨，你那么快意，我在旷野里东走西走，踩着了蝎子……"

她打开灯，朦胧的双眼睁得大大的。针头挂在靠床的那面墙上，一滴大大的黑血正从针孔里滴下来。橡皮管子在可怕地痉挛，挤压着内部的液体。她走到旷野里，那地方正落着冻雨，冰渣嚓嚓地从树上掉下，她的全身臃肿不堪，发胀的指头渗出水来。她想睡，却又听见什么人在沼泽地里呻吟。她向那发出呻吟的地方笨拙地移动，一边昏昏地打着瞌睡，踩得一个个水洼哀哀叫痛。

他的确踩着了蝎子，一个脚趾迅速地胀大，红肿很快地向膝部蔓延。风一吹，各式各样的水洼叮咚作响，一条陷进沼泽的腿子怎么也拔不出来了。在寂寞中，他听见那可怕的脚步声的临近。

"这不过是一个梦，我自己愿意的梦！"他大声抗拒着，他害怕她的临近。

脚步在他身旁停住了，然而并没有人。这旷野里空无一人。那脚步不过是他的想像，想像中的脚步停在他的身旁。

一只无形的手故意触痛他的脚趾，躲也躲不开。冰冻的汗毛竖起来，如一枚枚大头针。

壁上的挂钟在打完最后一下时破碎了，齿轮像一群小鸟一样朝空中飞去，扭曲的橡皮管紧紧地巴在肮脏的墙上，地上溅着一滩沉痛的黑血。

1984年12月20日

（载1986年8月号）

The Wilderness[1]

⊙ Can Xue

That evening, she went to bed but found it hard to fall asleep. She got out of the bed and paced to and fro in the dark room. Under her feet, the rotten floor squeaked gloomily. Something darker was crouching in the corner of the room like a black bear. As it moved, the floor squeaked gloomily, too.

"Who is it?" She asked nervously, her heart in her mouth.

"Me." It was her husband's voice, filled with fear.

They were taken aback by each other.

Since then, every night, they haunted this big apartment. In the darkness, they loitered from one empty room to another like two ghosts. But in the daytime, she appeared normal and obedient as if nothing had happened at night.

"The paperweight on the glass plate is broken." He peeped at her with his bloodshot eyes.

"How could it fall off by itself? The wind was so strong at night." She said. Shrugging her bladebones, she felt her ribs hurt a lot as if they were splitting. "It's so abominable to sneak about at night!" She blurted out suddenly, with no rhyme or reason.[2]

"There are snakes in some rooms which are empty for years, and ..." He continued, holding a rubber tourniquet, on which a big and thick injecting needle was glistening. "Where am I? Oh, right. One day, I found a snake hissing at the foot of the wall. If you are afraid of being bitten ..."

Five days ago, she found the tourniquet and the needle under the pillow. They were brand-new with a strong smell of rubber. She didn't care about it at first but during these days her husband always held them in hand and even put the rubber tube into his mouth and chewed it.

"You'd better listen to the weather forecast." He suggested, blinking one of his eyes.

The room was spacious and empty. The north wind was heavily slapping the

130

window whose clasp was broken.

To avoid bumping into each other in the darkness, they deliberately stamped heavily on the floor.

He hung his rubber tube and needle onto a nail on the wall and went out. She could smell the rubber all over the room.

"I want a try." He returned and said to her. "I want to catch a wild cat. The wilderness is so big and dark and all kinds of wild animals must be hiding somewhere. You know, the freezing rain was so cold that an ice shell was formed on my back. Someone is walking at the other end. Who is it over there?"

"It is me." She said indifferently, hiding her swollen head into the shadow so that the dark circles around her eyes became invisible to him.

He abruptly walked in front of her and took the rubber tourniquet and the needle off the wall. Holding them in hand, he said, "The unexpected always happens."[3] The needle sparkled in a flash of lightning.

She couldn't remember how long they hadn't had a sleep. Hardly had she lain down on the bed when that strange sound came. Opening her eyes, she found her husband biting that rubber tourniquet beside her, the big needle thrusting into his heart. She put on her clothes and stood up, but a terrible dream followed her right away. The wall was wet and leaning against it she found her clothes glued to it at once.

"The paperweight is broken. Who did it?" He spoke up in the corner, the rubber tube creaking and groaning in his mouth.

"A dream keeps following me these days. It comes in from that small window. Like a shark, it swims to me and puffs cold breath behind my neck. I haven't slept for several days. Look! The skin all over my body turns dry and winkled. Yesterday, in great terror, I broke the paperweight while escaping from that man-eating shark. I don't know how long it is going to chase me. How long?" She grumbled unconsciously in a tone of complaint.[4] "And I really couldn't tell whether I was asleep or awake. I even talked nonsense in my office. My associates were scared by me."

"Who can say it clearly? Some people lead all their lives in this state, therefore, they have to sleep while they are walking or talking. Maybe we'll do the same thing."

"I am afraid to meet people. I am afraid to be found in a trance.[5] I have to keep silent."

He walked to another room. She could see the needle in his hand sparkling.

Thunders were rumbling endlessly.

From her childhood, she had been living in this apartment in which there were many empty rooms. They were big and dark and had the same size and style. She had never counted how many rooms there were. Later, he came. At the beginning, he, with great zest, grew some potted boxwood and put them on the window sills. He even took trouble to sweep the rooms and got his hair disheveled and his face dirty, while the rooms were made hazy with dust. Once someone passed by the door, her husband would raise his voice and shouted, "The whole room has had a change!" He had never watered his potted boxwood and they all died later. He threw them away, leaving the empty pots on the sill, which, seen at night, were much like skeletons.

"Better not grow them." She turned a sallow face to him and complained despondently.[6]

"Nothing can grow here." He tramped heavily on the floor and cursed, "A field of wilderness."

Since then he grew nothing. When he was quite young, he suffered from senile asthma. Later, insomnia came accidentally. One night, he woke up and looked out of the window. It was dark outside. Looking at the clock on the wall, he found it was about the time he went to bed just now. He walked from one room to the other, bumping onto one of the pots on the sill which fell down to the cement floor outside with a big flop.

"Yesterday, you broke the paperweight, the one with the design of a lion's head. Can't you restrain yourself?" He related it again, obstinate as a mule.[7]

"The pots look horrible at night. Can't you get rid of them?" She paused for a while and continued in an indeterminate tone, "One day I'll make up my mind to clear all of them away. The window sill will be clean at that time. That'll be great."

Embarrassed, he clenched his teeth. His face turned red.

At night, when they had a dream — awake, though — she found his legs stretching unnaturally long to make her feel strange, his cold feet, with obvious joints of bones, reaching her pillow. One toe was swollen like a carrot.

"You've taken up too much room." He murmured, his head in the quilt. "You jostled me to the wall and the needle was hung on the wall. It was raining. You were so happy while I was walking on the wilderness. And I stepped on a scorpion…"

She turned on the light. Opening her eyes wider, she saw the needle hanging on the wall by the bed. A big drop of black blood was dripping down from the needle. The rubber tube was moving with convulsions, pressing the liquid inside to flow out. She walked to the wilderness. The freezing rain was heavy and small pieces of ice fell off trees. Her swollen body made her uneasy and she felt her swollen fingers oozing water. She wanted a sleep but found someone groaning in the marsh. While dozing off, she moved her clumsy body to where the groans came, only to find her feet stepping on puddles over and over again. The puddles felt painful and they cried, begging for mercy.[8]

Indeed, he stepped on a scorpion. One of his toes got swollen rapidly and the painful redness spread upward to his knee. As the wind blew across, all kinds of puddles went ding-dong.[9] He felt it hard to pull his leg out of the marsh. In loneliness, he heard the terrible footsteps approaching.

"This is but a dream. I am willing to have such a dream!" He cried, afraid of her approaching.

The footsteps stopped beside him. There was nobody around. The footsteps were just his imagination. The imaginary footsteps stopped by his side.

A formless hand touched the wound on his toe. He wanted to dodge it but he was not able to. The frozen hairs on his body stood on end like pins.

The clock on the wall broke down after its last ring. The gears of the clock all flew away like a flock of birds. The distorted rubber tube fastened itself to the dull and dirty wall. On the floor there was a pool of black blood, dense, dank and dead.[10]

December 20, 1984
(Published in No.8, 1986)

1. 残雪的《旷野里》这篇小说，行文怪诞，充满了神秘的内省气息。"在我们每个人觉察不到的黑暗混沌的地方，到底有些什么？那种东西的结构又是如何的？"（http://www.ycwb.com/gb/content/2006-03/17/content_1088512.htm）这篇小说可以说是对传统阅读习惯的挑战，全文梦境与现实、感性与理性、时间与空间错综交织。这给翻译带来了一些困难。有些地方逻辑关系不清，上下文似乎不衔接，这正是原文的写作特点。读者阅读时要多加体会。

2. "'鬼鬼祟祟真可恶！'她莫名其妙地冲口而出。""It's so abominable to sneak about at night!" She blurted out suddenly, with no rhyme or reason. "鬼鬼祟祟"翻译成to sneak about。还可以翻译为lurk and sneak around like a ghost、be furtive in one's movements、act secretively、like a thief in the night、in a very sneaky way等等，为了行文方便，这里简单译为to sneak about。"冲口

而出"译为blurt out。"莫名其妙"可以译为be rather baffling、be in a fog、be unable to understand、be unable to make head or tail of sth.、cannot make anything of it、difficult to guess what it is all about、have neither rhyme nor reason、incomprehensible、inexplicable、totally in the dark、make nothing of it、very mysterious and abstruse、without rhyme or reason，等等。这里译为with no rhyme or reason。

3. "人生中会发生预计不到的转折"翻译为The unexpected always happens. 与原句大致对应，也符合说话的情境。

4. "她不知不觉用了诉苦的口气"译为：She grumbled unconsciously in a tone of complaint. 英语中grunt、murmur、mumble、grumble等词都有低声说、含混不清地说之意，grumble用在这里表示牢骚、咕哝。

5. "神情恍惚"可以译为in a trance, in a daze, in a stupor, to have a roving/wandering eye。

6. "蜡黄着脸"可以译为 a sallow face 或a sallow complexion。形容人的脸色时，要注意颜色词的使用：a rosy face 肤色红润的/ black and blue 青一块紫一块/ yellow skin 黄种人黄皮肤的/ dark skin 长得黑的/ flushed 脸红的/ blush 脸红/ a black writer 黑人作家/ His face turned blue. 他的脸青了。

7. "愚顽不化"，译者用了英语中的 as obstinate as a mule 来翻译。

8. "踩得一个个水洼哀哀叫痛"，这里是拟人的用法，译为：The puddles felt painful and they cried, begging for mercy. 最后的begging for mercy是译者加的，使拟人的效果更加突出。

9. "叮咚作响"，翻译为：... all kinds of puddles went ding-dong. ding-dong 一词已进入英语，可以指水声叮咚，而jingle、tinkle或clatter 多指金属敲击发出的叮叮咚咚的声音。

10. "一滩沉痛的黑血"译为：On the floor there was a pool of black blood, dense, dank and dead. 译者用押头韵的三个词dense, dank and dead来翻译"沉痛"。dense形容浓厚，dank 意为阴湿阴冷，符合原文忧郁阴沉的格调。前一句用了dull and dirty wall, 也是出于同样的考虑。

飞越我的枫杨树故乡

○ 苏童

　　直到五十年代初，我的老家枫杨树一带还铺满了南方少见的罂粟花地。春天的时候，河两岸的原野被猩红色大肆入侵，层层叠叠、气韵非凡，如一片莽莽苍苍的红波浪鼓荡着偏僻的乡村，鼓荡着我的乡亲们生生死死呼出的血腥气息。

　　我的幺叔还在乡下，都说他像一条野狗神出鬼没于老家的柴草垛、罂粟地、干粪堆和肥胖女人中间，不思归家。我常在一千里地之外想起他，想起他坐在枫杨树老家的大红花朵丛里，一个矮小结实黝黑的乡下汉子，面朝西南城市的方向，小脸膛上是又想睡又想笑又想骂的怪异神气，唱着好多乱七八糟的歌谣，其中有一支是呼唤他心爱的狗的。

狗儿狗儿你钻过来
带我到寒窑亲小娘

　　祖父住在城里，老态龙钟了，记忆却很鲜亮。每当黄昏降临，家里便尘土般地飘荡起祖父的一声声喟然长叹。他迟迟不肯睡觉，"明天醒过来说不定就是瞎子了。"于是他睁大了眼睛坐在渐渐黑暗的房间里，宁静、苍劲，像一尊古老的青铜鹰。

　　可以从祖父被回忆放大的瞳孔里看见我的幺叔。祖父把小儿子和一群野狗搅成了一团。从前的幺叔活脱是一个鬼伢子，爱戴顶城里人的遮阳帽，怪模怪样地在罂粟花地里游荡。有一年夏天，他把遮阳帽扔在河里，迷上了一群野狗。于是人们都看见财主家的小少爷终日和野狗厮混在一起，疯疯癫癫，非人非狗，在枫杨树乡村成为稀奇的丑闻。

　　"那畜牲不谙世事，只通狗性。"祖父诅咒幺叔。他说，"别去管他，让他也变成一条狗吧。"想起那鬼伢子我祖父不免黯然神伤。多少个深夜幺叔精神勃发，跟着满地乱窜的野狗，在田埂上跌跌撞撞地跑，他的足迹紧撵着狗的卵石形蹄印，遍布枫杨树乡村的每个角落。有时候幺叔气喘吁吁地闯到乡亲家里去讨水喝，狗便在附近的野地里一声一声地吠着。沿河居住的枫杨树乡亲没有人不认识幺叔的，说起幺叔都觉得他是神鬼投胎，不知他带给枫杨树的是吉是凶。

逢到清明节，家族中人排成一字纵队，浩浩荡荡到祠堂祭祀祖宗时，谁也找不到幺叔的人影。祖父怨气冲天地对祖宗牌位磕头，碰翻了一碟供果，他沙哑着喉咙问："祖宗有灵，到底是野狗勾引了我儿子，还是我儿子勾引了那条野狗？"

祖父绝望地预见幺叔古怪可恶的灵魂将永生野游在外。几十年后祖父昏昏沉沉地坐在城里的屋顶下，把那张枫杨树出产的竹榻磨得油光铮亮，他向家人一遍遍地诉说着，那年洪水到来时幺叔的弃失。他说一条白木大船载满了家中四十口人和财产，快启锚的时候，幺叔和那条野狗一前一后到了岸边。幺叔问，"你们要到哪里去？"没人回答他，但好多双手都去拽他上船，拽半天拽不动，这时发现那鬼伢子的腿上系了圈长绳，和一条大野狗紧紧相连。祖父跳下去解绳子的时候，幺叔鬼喊鬼叫死命挣脱，抓破了他的脸。祖父骂着娘去找大板斧的时候，幺叔惊恐万状地冲那条狗喊了一声，"豹子豹子快逃快逃！"狗果真撒腿跑起来了，一条绳子把幺叔牵绷紧了，那情景像两只小野兽，一前一后冲出了猎人的枪口。祖父仰天悲啸一声，知道那船是该走了，那鬼伢子是该丢了。

"我望得见枫杨树的，只要我的眼睛不瞎，我天天望得见枫杨树。"祖父说，在他寥廓苍凉的心底，足以让红罂粟大片大片地生长，让幺叔和他的狗每时每刻地践踏而过。

幺叔死于一九五六年罂粟花最后的风光岁月里。他的死和一条狗、一个女人还有其他莫名的物事有关。自幺叔死后，罂粟花在枫杨树乡村绝迹，以后那里的黑土长出了晶莹如珍珠的大米，灿烂如黄金的麦子。

多少次我在梦中飞越遥远的枫杨树故乡。我看见自己每天在迫近一条横贯东西的浊黄色的河流。我涉过河流到左岸去。左岸红波浩荡的罂粟花地卷起龙首大风，挟起我闯入模糊的枫杨树故乡。

有一天枫杨树村里白幡招摇，家屋顶上腾起一片灰蒙蒙的烟霭。有许多人影在烟霭里东跑西窜，哭哭啼啼，空气中笼罩着惶惶不可终日的气氛，仿佛重现了多年前河水淹没村庄的景象。我是否隔着千重山万壑水目睹了那场灾难呢？

那一天是我幺叔的黑字忌日。死者幺叔的灵魂没有找到归宿而继续满村晃荡，把宁静的村子闹腾得鸡犬不宁。我的枫杨树乡亲们在罂粟花的熏风中前去童家老屋奔丧的时候，耳朵里真切地听到一种类似丧钟的共鸣声，他们似乎看见幺叔坐在老屋门前的石磨上，一条腿翘在另一条腿上，此起彼伏的大脚掌沾满灰土、草屑和狗粪，五根脚趾张开来大胆地指向天空。他宽厚温和地微笑着，一双爬满疙瘩肉的手臂却凶恶地拽住了老榆树上的钟绳。

死者幺叔敲着他自己的丧钟，那种声音发自天庭或者地心深处，使乡亲们不寒而栗。他们对幺叔又爱又怕，有许多老人和妇女在忌日里悲恸欲绝，对着日月星辰和山水草木轻轻地喊："带他去吧，带他去吧。"

从前在我的枫杨树故乡，每个人自出生后便有一枚楠竹削制的灵牌高置在族公屋里。人死后灵牌焚火而亡，化成吉祥鸟驮死者袅袅升天。在听祖父说起灵牌的故事后，我又知道幺叔是个丢了灵牌的倒霉鬼。可是没人能说清那秘密。有传说是幺叔在村里一直浪荡成性，辱没村规，族公在做了一个怪梦后跑到河边，将怀揣的一块灵牌缠绑了石头坠入河底；还有说枫杨树的疯女人穗子有一天潜入族公屋里，偷走了幺叔的灵牌，一个人钻到野地里点起篝火，疯疯癫癫、哭哭笑笑地烧掉了幺叔的灵牌。对这些传说我祖父一概不信，他用黯然伤神的目光注视着天花板，对我说，"你幺叔自己拿走了灵牌，他把灵牌卖给怕死的乡亲，捏了钱就去喝酒搞女人，肯定是这样的。他十五六岁就会干好多坏事了。"

但是如果我幺叔的灵牌还凝立在族公的屋里，我将飞临遥远的枫杨树故乡，把幺叔之灵带回他从未到过的城市和亲人中间来。

我这个枫杨树人的后裔将进入童家宗祠，见到九十一岁的族公大人。

老族公的屋子盖在向阳的土墩上，不开窗户，单是一个黑漆漆的门洞就将我吸了进去。在一团霉烂阴暗的空气中，我头晕目眩。下意识地去摸灯绳，手胡乱地沿墙探索，突然抓到一捆灰尘蒙蒙的竹签。竹签沉得可怕，我丢了它继续在屋里撞，终于撞到了族公脸上，很疼，像是撞着一棵百年老树。紧接着眼前升起一缕火焰。我的九十一岁的老族公举起了蜡烛。他的屋里没有电灯。我借着烛光看清了老族公神圣超脱的面貌，他赤裸着干瘪苍老的身体，一丝不挂，古朴而苍劲，他的眼睛爆出的是比我更年轻的蓝色的光焰。

你找什么呢？

告诉我幺叔的灵牌在哪里。

不知道什么时候丢啦。灵牌丢了就找不到了。

族公在烛光之上对我慈祥地微笑。而我在竹签堆里不信任地翻来找去。我闻见屋里的罂粟花味越来越浓，看到墙上地上全拥挤着罂粟花晒干后的穗状花串，连老族公自己也幻变成一颗硕大的罂粟花，窒息了宁馨的乡村空气。我找得满头大汗，在竹签堆里看见了所有枫杨树人的名字，其中有祖父和父亲的名字，还有我的，唯独没有幺叔的灵牌。

谁偷了我幺叔的灵牌？

我大声问老族公的时候，看见族公的脸渐渐隐没于黑暗中，他轻轻舒一口气，把手中的蜡烛吹灭了，赶我出门。我茫茫然走下土墩，我将在枫杨树故乡搜寻幺叔最后的踪迹。我将凭着对幺叔穿过的黑胶鞋的敏感，嗅到他混杂了汗臭酒臭的气息。

黑胶鞋生产于我们城市的工厂。祖父在六十大寿那天看见窗外下起滂沱大雨，他忽然想起什么便冒着雨走到街上买了那双黑胶鞋，那胶鞋用油布包了三层辗转千里寄到枫杨树幺叔手上，是祖父一辈子给幺叔的唯一礼物。

听说幺叔第一次穿上黑胶鞋是在七月半的鬼节。鬼节在枫杨树一带不知何时衍变成了烧花节。在老家呆过的长辈每回忆起烧花节的往事，都使我如入仙境。他们说幺叔穿着乌黑发亮的黑胶鞋站在一辆牛车旁。牛车堆满了晒干的罂粟，整装待发。牛的浑身上下被涂满喷香的花生油和罂粟花粉，绚丽夺目地缚在车轩上。幺叔举起了竹鞭，他们说那是他在村里最风光的时候，他一蹁腿上了车坐，大黑胶鞋温柔地敲打了牛腹两下，一车子大鬼小鬼就紧跟幺叔出发了。在晴天碧空下，火捻子燃烧起来，牛车上升腾起一片暗红色的烟雾，在野地里奔驰如流云。在幺叔的身背后，大鬼小鬼在火焰中幻变成花干花蕾花叶，一齐亢奋骚动起来，野地里挤满了尖厉神奇的鬼的声音。人们听见幺叔开心地笑着，在送鬼的火焰未及舔上他后背的时候，幺叔唱歌、呐喊，快活得有如神仙。

每年都是幺叔充当送鬼人，那似乎是他在枫杨树老家唯一愿意干的事情。他们说后来牛看见黑胶鞋就发出悲鸣："牛眼看人大"，我幺叔的那两只黑胶鞋像两座灾难之峰压迫着那些牛的神经。他经常对别人说起走过牛栏时听到牛一齐诅咒他。幺叔不得好死。枫杨树的牛都是这么说的。

那些送鬼的老牛曾经多次出现在我梦中。我看见许多条牛死在幺叔臀下。牲灵们被有毒的花焰熏昏了，被鬼节的气氛刺激而发疯了。有一条公牛最后挣脱了幺叔的羁绊，逃脱花花鬼鬼，最后涉过了枫杨树的河流。我竭力想像那公牛飘飘欲飞的形象，希望它逃脱所有的灾难，我很想让那条公牛也穿上一双巨大的黑胶鞋。

我祖父曾经预测幺叔会死于牛蹄之下。他心里隐隐觉得送给幺叔的黑胶鞋会变成灾物，招来许多嫉恨。一九五六年传来乡下幺叔的死讯，说他死在老家那条河里。死的时候全身赤裸，脚上留有一只黑胶鞋。

一九五六年我刚刚出世，我是一个美丽而安静的婴孩。可是在我的记忆里，清晰地目睹了那个守灵之夜。

月光地里浮起了秋蝉声，老屋的石磨边围着黑压压的守灵人。沉默的人影像山峰般岿然伫立，众多的老人、妇女、孩子和男人们错落有致，围护一颗莲花心——我的死去的幺叔。我听见一个雪白雪白的男孩在敲竹梆，每烧完一炷香就敲六六三十六下，三十六声竹梆渐渐把夜色敲浓了。

我睡在摇篮里，表情欲哭未哭，沉浸在一种纯朴的来自亲情的悲伤中。我第一次看见了溺水而死的幺叔，他浑身发蓝，双目圆睁，躺在老家巨大的石磨旁。灵场离我远隔千里，又似乎设在我的摇篮边上。我小小的生命穿过枫杨树故乡山水人畜的包围之中，颜面潮红，喘息不止。溺死幺叔的河流袒露在我的目光里，河水在月光下嘤嘤作响，左岸望不到边的罂粟花随风起伏摇荡，涌来无限猩红色的欲望。一派生生死死的悲壮气息，弥漫整个世界，我被什么深刻厚重的东西所打动，晃晃悠悠地从摇篮中站起，对着窗外的月亮放声大哭。我祖父和父母兄弟们惊惶地跑来，看见我站在摇篮里哭得如痴如醉，眼睛里有一道纯洁的泪光越来越亮。

我是不是还看见幺叔的精灵从河水中浮起，遍体荧光，从河的左岸漂向右岸？我是不是预见幺叔无法逾越那条湍急浊黄的河流，恐惧地看到了一个死者与世界的和谐统一？

多年来我一直想寻找幺叔溺死时的目击者，疯女人穗子和那条野狗。祖父记得幺叔的水性很好，即使往他脖子上系一块铁秤砣也不会淹死。那么疯女人穗子有什么本事把鳗鱼般的幺叔折腾而死？据枫杨树乡亲们说，他们没有料到幺叔会被河水淹死，后来见疯女人穗子浑身湿漉漉地往岸上爬，手里举着一只乌黑发亮的黑胶鞋，才知道出了事故。人们都在场院上晒花籽，谁也没注意河里的动静。只有幺叔养的野狗把什么都看清楚了，那狗看见河水里长久地溅着水花和一对男女如鱼类光裸的影子，一声不响。谁也没听见狗的叫声。他们说如果那时我飞临枫杨树故乡，俯视到的也将是个寂静无事的正午。可是我依稀觉得幺叔之死是个天地同设的大阴谋。对此我铭记在心。

在枫杨树人为幺叔守灵的三天三夜里，疯女人穗子披麻戴孝地出没于灵场石磨附近。她头发散乱，痴痴呆呆，脸上带着古怪而美丽的神情。她跪在幺叔的遗体旁，温情地凝视死者蓝宝石一样闪亮的面容。穗子的半身埋在满地纸钱里，一阵夜风突如其来吹散纸钱，守灵者看到了她的左脚光着，右脚却穿着我幺叔的黑胶鞋。

另一只黑胶鞋却失踪了。我不知道幺叔脚上那双黑胶鞋是什么时候逃离他的烂泥脚掌各奔东西的。

我听说过疯女人穗子的一些故事。枫杨树一带有不少男人在春天里把穗子挟入罂粟花丛，在野地里半夜媾欢，男人们拍拍穗子丰实的乳房后一溜烟跑回了家，留下穗子独自沉睡于罂粟花的波浪中。清晨下地的人们往往能撞见穗子赤身裸体的睡态。她面朝旭日，双唇微启，身心深处沁入无数晶莹清凉的露珠，远看晨卧罂粟地的穗子，仿佛是一艘无舵之舟在左岸的猩红色花浪里漂泊。我听说疯女人穗子每隔两年就要怀孕一次。产期无人知晓，只说她每每在血包破掉以后爬向河边，婴儿掉进水中，向下游漂去。那些婴孩都极其美丽，啼哭声却如老人一样苍凉而沉郁。

在枫杨树河下游的村庄，有好些顺水而来的孩子慢慢长大，仿佛野黍拔节，灌满原始的浆汁。那些黝黑肮脏的孩子面容生动，四肢敏捷，多次出现在我的梦境中。我恍惚觉得他们酷似我死去的幺叔，他们也许是死者幺叔的精血结晶，随意地播进黑土地生长开花结果。

我将在河边路遇幺叔养的那条野狗。我听见狗的脚步声跟在后面，我闻见它皮毛上的腥臭味越来越浓地扑向我。我把身子蹲下，回头愤怒地注视它。那野狗硕大无比，满脸狡诈，前腿像手一样举起，后腿支起全身分量，做出人的动作。我看见狗的背脊上落满猩红色的罂粟花瓣，连眼睛也被熏烤成两颗玛瑙石。

幺叔生前和野狗亲密无间。狗经常在幺叔沉睡的时候走到他干瘦的肚皮上去引吭高叫。我觉得那条野狗像个淫妇终日厮缠着幺叔，把他拖垮了然后又把他拽入死亡之河。我搬起了一块石头，和那条狗对峙了很久，当我把石头高举过头顶，狗的喉咙深处忧伤地发出一阵悲鸣钻入罂粟花地销声匿迹。

幺叔幺叔快快杀狗
杀掉野狗跟我回家

当我沿河追逐那条野狗时真切地记起了八岁时寄赠幺叔的那些诗句。那一天我神色匆忙，在枫杨树老家像一只没头苍蝇胡乱碰撞。我将看见死者幺叔的亡魂射出白光横亘于前方，引我完成不可兑现的老家之行。

一路上我将看见奇异的风景散落在河的左岸。我祖父年轻时踩踏过的桐油水车吱扭扭转个不息，一个男人和一个女人交股而立，站在祖先留下的水车上，水渠里的水滞留不动，犹如坚冰。在田野的尽头一头黑牛拼命逃跑，半空中云集了大片胡蜂，嗡嗡地追逐黑牛溃烂的犄角，朝河边渐渐归去。当我走到河的左岸，我亲眼看见披麻戴孝的疯女人穗子。她穿着一只黑胶鞋，一步步朝水里走去。当水没过她丰厚隆起的腹部，穗子美丽的脸朝天仰起又猝然抵住锁骨，将头发垂落至水面。她紧紧地揪住那一绺长发，一遍复一遍地在水中漂洗。涟漪初动的水面上冒起好多红色水泡，渐渐地半条河泛出红色。

一切都将是似曾相识，如同我在城里家中所梦见的一般。唯有我的黝黑结实瘦小落泊的幺叔，他的穿黑胶鞋的亡灵来无影去无踪，他是在微笑还是在哭泣？我的幺叔！

一九五六年农历八月初八，我幺叔落葬的前一天，遥远的枫杨树老家的乡亲都在谈论那个丢了灵牌的死者。没有灵牌死者不入宗墓。乡亲们逡巡了全村的家屋和野地，搜索了所有和幺叔厮混过的女人的衣襟，那块楠竹灵牌还是不见踪影。村里乱成了一锅粥。故去的幺叔躺在石磨上，忍耐了他一手制造的骚乱。敲竹梆的守灵男孩三更时突然竹梆落地，大哭大叫。他狂呼幺叔死后开眼，眼睛像春天罂粟花的花苞，花苞里开放着一个女人和一条狗。

人们都说钻进幺叔眼膜的是女人与狗。我祖父也这么说。给幺叔守灵的最后一夜，我祖父隔着千里听到了那男孩的叫喊声，当时他埋着头精心削制一块竹签，削得跟族祖家堂屋里的那堆灵牌一模一样，然后用刀子刻上了幺叔的名字。这一切做完后他笑了几声，又哽咽了几声，后来他慢慢地从一架梯子上往我家楼顶爬去。祖父站在屋顶上俯瞰我们的城市，像巫师般疯疯癫癫，胡言乱语，把楼顶折磨得震荡了好久。那天路过我家楼下的行人都说看见了鬼火，鬼火从我家楼顶上飞泻而下，停在街路上、哔剥燃烧，腾起一尺高的蓝色光焰。鬼火清香无比，在水泥路面上肆无忌惮地唱歌跳舞，燃烧了整整一个黄昏。

把幺叔带回家

前年春天我祖父坐在枫杨树老家带来的竹榻上，渐入弥留之际。已故多年的幺叔这时辗转于老人纷乱的思绪中，祖父欲罢不能，他拼命把我悲痛的脑袋扳至他胸前，悄悄地对我说，

把幺叔带回家

我总将飞越遥远的枫杨树故乡，完成我家三代人的未竟事业。但是从来没有人告诉我，为什么在河的左岸种下这样莽莽苍苍的红罂粟。为什么红罂粟如同人子生生死死，而如今不复存在。当我背负弃世多年的幺叔逃离枫杨树老家，我会重见昔日的罂粟地。那将是个闷热的夜晚，月亮每时每刻地下坠，那

是个滚烫沸腾的月亮，差不多能将我们点燃烧焦。故乡暗红的夜流骚动不息，连同罂粟花的夜潮，包围着深夜的逃亡者。我的脚底踩到了多少灰蛙呀，灰蛙们咕咕大叫，狂乱地跟随我们在田埂上奔跑。

我将听见村子里人声鼎沸，灯光瞬间四起，群狗蜂拥而出，乡亲们追赶着我，要夺下生于斯归于斯的幺叔亡魂。幺叔留下的那条老狗正野游在外，它的修炼成仙的眼睛亮晶晶犹如流星划破夜空，朝我们迅速猛扑来。人声狗声自然之声追逐我，热的月亮往下坠，栖息在死者宁静安详的黑脸膛，我背上驮着的亲人将是一座千年火山。

在我的逃亡之夜里，一个疯女人在远远的地方分娩出又一个婴儿。每个人都将听见那种苍凉沉郁的哭声，哭声中蕴含着枫杨树故乡千年来的人世沧桑。我能在那生命之声中越过左岸狭长的土地越过河流吗？

我们这个城市的屋顶下住着许多从前由农村迁徙而来的家庭。他们每夜鼾声不齐，各人都有自己的心事和梦境。如果你和我一样，从小便会做古怪的梦，你会梦见你的故土、你的家族和亲属。有一条河与生俱来，你仿佛坐在一只竹筏上顺流而下，回首遥望远远的故乡。

（载1987年2月号）

Flying Over My Hometown of Maple and Poplar[1]

○ *Su Tong*

Till the early 1950s, the land in my hometown of Maple and Poplar was covered with poppy flowers which actually were rarely seen in the south. When spring came, the fields on both sides of the river were dyed scarlet. Piles upon piles of red waves clamorously and aggressively pervaded that remote village, surging and dancing in the blood-tinged breaths of the people, going up and down together with people's weal and woe, life and death.[2]

My youngest uncle lived in the village. Like a wild dog, he loved lingering among firewood piles, poppy fields, poudrette heaps and fat women, seldom thinking of going home. Now, a thousand kilometers away, I always thought of my uncle, that short, thickset and dark-skinned countryman, sitting among clusters of red flowers, looking to the southwest where the city lay, wearing an odd expression — sleepy, laughing or cursing — and humming his favorite tunes at random. One of his tunes was for his beloved dog —

Come, come, my dearest dog,
And lead me to kiss her in the cave.

My grandpa lived in the city. Aged as he was, he had a very good memory. Every day, at dusk, his long sighs arose like drifting dust in the air. Reluctant to go to bed, he always said, "I am afraid to become blind when I wake up tomorrow." Opening his eyes wider, he sat in the darkening room, silent, solemn, like an age-old bronze statue of an eagle.

In grandpa's retrospective eyes, in his enlarged pupils filled with memories, I always saw my youngest uncle, together with a pack of wild dogs. My youngest uncle, the smallest son of my grandpa, was really a scamp. When he was a boy, he loved wearing a queer-looking sunhat which only city people liked and idling away his time in poppy fields. One summer, he hurled his sunhat into the river and turned his interest to a pack of wild dogs. He was obsessed with them, and since then, people always saw my uncle, the youngest son of the richest family in the village, fooling around all day long with a pack of wild dogs. Half normal and half crazy, half a man and half a dog, my uncle became the rarest scandal in Maple and Poplar Village.[3]

"That beast is ignorant of our human affairs. He lives in the dogs' world." Grandpa cursed, "Let him be. Sooner or later, he'll become a dog!" At the thought of my youngest uncle, grandpa always felt sad. On so many nights, uncle, in high spirit, enjoyed himself chasing wild dogs in the field, rushing and tumbling over, following the dogs' pebble-like footprints to every corner of the village. Sometimes, he broke into a villager's home, out of breath, asking for some drinking water, and at this time, his dogs would wait for him in the nearby wild field, barking incessantly. The villagers living along the river all knew him. They said that he might be a sprite or a ghost reincarnated into a human figure. Would this mysterious boy bring good or ill luck to the village? They had no idea.

On the Tomb-sweeping Day, all the family members lined up and went to the family ancestral hall to pay their obeisance, but nobody could tell where uncle was. In a fit of rage[4], grandpa accidentally knocked a plate of sacrificial fruit off the altar table when he was kowtowing[5] before the ancestors' memorial tablets. Grandpa cried in a hoarse voice, "Oh, omnipresent ancestors, can you tell me? Is it the wild dog that lures my son or is it my son who lures that wild dog?"

In desperation, grandpa foretold that uncle's weird and abominable soul would wander about for ever. Decades later, under the roof of the house in the city, my aged grandpa, sitting on his bamboo couch which he took with him from my hometown and which had become shiny and lustrous as a result of years of use, told us over and over again about how uncle disappeared in that fateful year when the village was stricken by flood. Grandpa prepared a big boat made of white wood and put the properties onto it. When all the family, about forty people, boarded the boat and were about to set off, uncle and his dog came. "Where are you going?" Uncle asked. Nobody answered him, but they all tried to pull him aboard. However, to their surprise, uncle stood there still. A long rope, with one end fastened to his leg and the other to his wild dog, tightly linked them! Grandpa rushed to uncle in an attempt to untie the rope. Uncle screamed and snarled, struggling hysterically to rid himself of grandpa's hands. Grandpa was scratched in the face … "Shit!" In exasperation, he dished out a stream of curses.[6] Seeing grandpa going back for a big axe, uncle yelled at his dog in terror, "Run! Run! Leopard! " The dog dashed as fast as it could. Connected by the rope, uncle and his dog ran away quickly in tandem like two small beasts, as if they were escaping a hunter's shotgun. Looking at uncle's back, grandpa uttered a long sigh to the sky. "Oh! Heaven! It's time for me to leave my hometown! It's time to lose my smallest son!"

Grandpa always said, "I can see Maple and Poplar Village. As long as I am not blind, I can see it." In his heart, there must be a vast and bleak land where clusters and clusters of red poppies grew and where uncle and his dog kept running around all the time.

Uncle died in 1956 when red poppies ended their glories. His death had something to do with a dog, a woman and some inexplicable affairs. After his death, red poppies died out in the village. Since then, rice as shiny as pearls and wheat as radiant as gold began to grow out of the black soil in my hometown.

For so many times, in my dream, I flew to my hometown. I found myself approaching a muddy yellowish river which ran from west to east. I waded across the river and got to its left bank where luxuriant red poppies were swaying in the big wind. The rising gale rolled me up and carried me to my hometown.[7]

One day, my home was shrouded with gray and gloomy smoke. White cloth strips fluttered everywhere in the village and people kept coming and going, weeping and wailing. The whole village was in turmoil, seized with fear and anxiety, as if the terrible flood-stricken days returned![8] — Could I witness that disaster at such a faraway distance?

That day was the anniversary of uncle's death. It was said that uncle's soul could not find a place to rest itself and it was still wandering in the village, throwing the otherwise peaceful village into chaos.[9] When the villagers hastened to his old house for his funeral, they all heard a sound echoing in the poppy-scented wind, much like the toll of the knell. They felt as if uncle were still alive — sitting in a leisurely manner on the grinding stone in front of his old house, one leg crossing over the other, uncle was smiling at them warmly and amicably, his big dangling foot strewn with dust, grass crumbs and dog's feces and his five toes stretching daringly to the sky. To their astonishment, his hands tightly clutched the rope of the bell hanging on the old elm, the muscles bulging in his arms.

Obviously, uncle was tolling the death knell for himself! Hearing the sound coming from the heaven or the deepest core of the earth, people couldn't help shivering, chills running down their backs. Uncle, the man they loved and feared, had gone! Many old men and women felt extremely grieved and they cried a lot on that day. They prayed softly to the sun, the moon and the stars in the sky, "Take him away." And they shouted gently to the mountain, the river and the trees and grasses on the earth, "Take him away."[10]

In the past, in my hometown there was a custom: Everyone, after he was born, had a bamboo-made memorial tablet which was put in the clan patriarch's room. After his death, people burned the memorial tablet which would change into an auspicious bird and carried his soul to the heaven. Grandpa told me about this custom and that uncle was such an unlucky dog who lost his memorial tablet. Where was it? Nobody knew. It remained a mystery to all the villagers. Some people said that uncle was considered to bring disgrace to his ancestors for he was such an unrestrained and dissipated rake, and that the clan patriarch, having had a weird dream about this prospect, brought uncle's memorial tablet to the riverside, attached it with a heavy stone and sank it into the water. Some people said that it was the crazy woman called Wheat Ears who sneaked into the clan patriarch's room and stole uncle's tablet and that she set a fire in the field later and burned uncle's tablet up amid much laughing and weeping lunacy. Grandpa didn't believe these stories in the least. Looking up at the ceiling, he said to me in a sad tone, "It was your uncle himself who took the tablet away and sold it to someone who was afraid of death. He spent the money drinking and flirting with women. Things must be like this! At the age of 15 or 16, your uncle began to do bad things."

However, if uncle's tablet was still in the clan patriarch's room, how I wished I could fly to my hometown and bring his soul to the city where he had never been and where his relatives lived!

As a descendant, I would go to the Tong Family Ancestral Hall and see my 91-year-old clan patriarch —

The house of the clan patriarch was situated on a mound, facing south. The window was always closed. The gaping doorway of pitch-black mystery seemed to suck me in. In the dark room, the air was damp and stale, which made me dizzy. Subconsciously, I fumbled for the lamp cord on the wall. As my hand was groping on the wall in the darkness, all of a sudden, I caught a bundle of bamboo sticks, which was terribly heavy and covered with dust. I threw it away and continued feeling my way. Finally, I bumped onto the clan patriarch's face! As if knocking onto a one-hundred-year-old tree, I felt painful. Immediately, a flickering light arose in front of my eyes. It was my 91-year-old clan patriarch who lit the candle. There was no electric lamp in his room. In the flickering candle light, I saw his holy and unworldly face and his stark-naked and withered body with primitive vigor and simplicity. His eyes glowed with blue flames, which look younger and more energetic than mine.

"What are you looking for?"

"Tell me where is my uncle's memorial tablet?"

"It is lost, and we cannot find it."[11]

He smiled at me amiably in the flickering light. Not believing his words, I rummaged among those bamboo sticks. A pervasive odor of poppy flowers hit my nostrils and I saw the walls and the floor strewn with sundried poppies, among which the old clan patriarch looked like a big poppy blossom. At that moment, I felt the peaceful and serene air in the village suddenly became stagnant. After a while, sweat streamed down my cheeks. On those bamboo sticks I found my grandpa's name and my father's and all the other villagers' names, and I even found my own name on a bamboo stick. But uncle's tablet, indeed, disappeared.

"Who on earth stole uncle's tablet?"

I couldn't help but raise my voice and asked. The old patriarch uttered a sigh softly, blew out his candle and shooed me out, his face gradually vanishing into the darkness. In a daze, I walked down the mound, making up my mind to search for and find out uncle's last trace in Maple and Poplar Village. Following the familiar smell of his black rubber shoes, I could sensitively trace uncle's alcoholic breath mixed with his stinky sweat.

Uncle's black rubber shoes were produced in a factory in our city. On grandpa's 60-year-old birthday, it was raining heavily. Looking out of the window, grandpa suddenly thought of something and hastened out in the rain. He bought a pair of black rubber shoes, wrapped it with three layers of oilcloth and mailed it to uncle who was thousands of kilometers away in the small village. The shoes were the only gift grandpa had given to uncle.

The day when uncle first wore his new rubber shoes was the 15th day of the 7th month in the lunar calendar, "the Ghosts' Day" in the traditional Chinese custom. Nobody knew since when the Ghosts' Day became the Flower-burning Day in my hometown. Until now, the moment I heard some elders talking about the Flower-burning Day in my hometown, I immediately fell into a dream fairyland. Wearing his shiny black rubber shoes, standing by the oxcart which was loaded with piles and piles of sundried poppy flowers, uncle looked elated and complacent. The ox was coated with fragrant peanut oil and poppy pollen and tied with the cart in colorful splendor. Flinging a bamboo whip, uncle jumped onto the cart from sideways. He gently kicked the ox's abdomen and the oxcart loaded with all the "ghosts" set off. That day was said to be the most pleasant day for uncle. Under the clear blue sky, after the kindling was lit, rolls and waves of dark red streaks rose from the oxcart and ran in the wild field like scudding clouds. Behind uncle's back, in the flames, all the ghosts transformed themselves into petals, buds and leaves, whirling and crying in the wind. The wild field was choked with the piercing and mysterious

147

wails of the ghosts. Uncle laughed with ecstasy and excitement. Before the flames licked his back, he sang and shouted, as happy as a king.[12]

Every year, on the Ghosts' Day, it was my uncle who drove the oxcart and sent ghosts away. It seemed that this was the only thing he felt like doing. Later, it was said that at the sight of uncle's black rubber shoes oxen would bellow with sorrow. In oxen's eyes, uncle was a giant, whose shoes, like two overwhelming disastrous mountains, pressed upon their nerves, making them agitated and exhausted. From time to time, uncle told people that he always heard oxen cursing him in a chorus when he walked before the pen. "He would not end well!" All the oxen in Maple and Poplar Village swore behind his back.

Those oxen came into my dreams for many times. I saw quite a lot of oxen die under uncle's hips. They were either choked to death by smokes and flames of those poisonous flowers or became mad under the stimulation of that frenzied atmosphere. An ox wriggled out of uncle's control, escaped the flowers and ghosts and waded across the river. I went all out to imagine its flying image, hoping that it could free itself from all the disasters. I also hoped that the ox could wear a big pair of black rubber shoes, too.

Grandpa once predicted that uncle might die under the ox hoofs. Perhaps in his heart he vaguely sensed that the black rubber shoes might one day bring disaster as well as envy and hate to uncle. Uncle died in 1956. He died in the river in my hometown, totally naked, with only one black rubber shoe on his foot.

I was born in 1956. I, the beautiful and tranquil baby boy, experienced the night when people watched over uncle's body before burial.

The chirping of cicadas pervaded that moonlit night. A dark mass of people gathered around the grinding stone of the old house. Elders, men, women and children all stood there, silent, still and well-arranged. They stood around and guarded their "lotus flower" in the center — my uncle. I heard a boy with snow-white skin beating a bamboo clapper. Between two burnings of incense, that boy gave 36 beats, in which the night darkened more and more.

I was lying in my cradle, holding in my tears and immersing myself in a plain and affectionate grief for my uncle. For the first time I saw my uncle. He was lying beside the big grinding stone, his body turning blue all over and his eyes opening wide. He was drowned to death. The mourning hall was far from me but I felt as if it were by my cradle. I felt I was running through the mountain, the river and the crowd of people of my hometown, red-faced and out of breath. Finally, I got to the river where uncle drowned. The water was gurgling in the moonlight and on the left bank of the river an endless field of scarlet poppy flowers was waving in the wind, in which the scarlet human desires were welling up and surging violently. The whole world was permeated with the sad but solemn breaths of life and death. Overwhelmed and touched by something heavy and profound, I stood up from my cradle, crying at the moon outside the window. Grandpa, my parents and my brothers rushed to me. Seeing that I was so infatuated with my crying and that a beam of pure bright light was glistening in my eyes, they were dazed, indeed.

Did I see my uncle's transparent and glittering soul rising from the water? Did I see his soul drifting from the left bank to the right? Did I foresee that my uncle couldn't cross that turbulent yellow river? Did I prefigure with dread the harmonious union of uncle's death and the whole world?

For years I had been longing for finding out the crazy woman Wheat Ears and that big wild dog who witnessed uncle's death. Grandpa once told me that uncle was a good swimmer and that it was impossible for him to be drowned even if an iron weight was tied to his neck. Then, what spell did that crazy woman put on my eel-like uncle and made him die? The villagers had never thought uncle might be drowned and only when they saw Wheat Ears struggling to move her soaked body onto the bank with a black rubber shoe in her hand did they realize something terrible happened. At that time, people were busy drying their flower seeds in the sun and nobody paid attention to what had happened in the river. Only his dog saw everything clearly — the naked bodies of a man and a woman like fish in the splashes of water. Nobody heard the dog barking. If I had flown over the river at that time, I would have seen nothing special but a silent and peaceful noon. However, something always haunted my heart — I felt that uncle died of a conspiracy set by Heaven and Earth.

During those three days and nights when people kept guard over uncle's corpse, that crazy woman lingered around the mourning place. She wore a white mourning dress and her hair was disheveled and her look numb and absent. Kneeling down beside uncle's body, with half of her body buried into piles of paper money, she kept looking at uncle's face which glittered like a sapphire. The expression on her face was so weird, gentle and beautiful. A gust of wind came and the paper money was scattered away, revealing her feet. Her left foot was bare and her right foot was wearing uncle's black rubber shoe.

Where was the other shoe? I couldn't imagine how and when that pair of black rubber shoes escaped his muddy feet and got separated.

I heard some stories about Wheat Ears. In spring, many a man from Maple and Poplar Village dragged her into groves of poppy flowers at midnight. After copulating with her, the man patted her on the ample breasts and ran away like a rabbit, leaving her alone in the waves of flowers. At dawn, when people went to work in the field, they often saw her lying alone in the poppy field. Totally naked, facing the rising sun, opening her lips a little, the glistening morning dews all over her body, she slept silently like a small rudderless boat adrift on the scarlet waves. People said she got pregnant every two years. As to when she gave birth to her babies, nobody knew. They only knew that when the delivery drew near, she would pull herself to the river where her mature baby fell into the water and floated to the lower reaches of the river. Those babies were extremely beautiful but their cries were as bleak and gloomy as those of aged men.

In the villages along the lower reaches of the river, her kids grew up fast like the jointing of grains which were full of primitive vigor and vitality. Those dark-skinned kids with dirty and lively faces and agile and strong limbs appeared in my dreams from time to time. They resembled my youngest uncle so much! They were the quintessence of uncle's blood — the seeds cast at random and the fruits tenaciously growing up in the black soil of my hometown.

I would confront that wild dog on the roadside. It followed me closely and its strong stinky smell agitated me. I crouched and turned around, looking at it furiously. It was quite big and had a cunning look. It held up its forelegs and let its hind legs support its whole body — a human's posture. Its back was strewn with scarlet poppy petals and its eyes, set off by the redness, changed into two bright agates.

This dog was uncle's bosom friend. When uncle was asleep, it always walked onto his abdomen, barking and singing. Like a lustful woman, it clung to uncle day in and day out, exhausting him and pulling him into the river of death. Holding a stone over my head, I glared at the dog for a while. When I was about to throw the stone at it, the dog wailed and disappeared into the poppy field.

Uncle, uncle, come to kill the dog,
And follow me to go back home.

As I was chasing the dog along the river, I clearly remembered the poem I made for my youngest uncle when I was eight. I was in such a hurry like a cat on hot bricks.[13] I knew that I would see a flash of white light emitting from uncle's soul, which would lead me to go back to my hometown and fulfill my mission which could never be fulfilled.

On my way to my hometown, I knew I would come across the peculiar scenes scattered on the left bank of the river — the waterwheel which my grandpa once used in his youthful days were squeaking and spinning; a man and a woman were standing side by side, with one's thigh crossing another's, on the age-old waterwheel; the water was as stagnant as ice; and on the other end of the field a black ox was running for its life and swarms of wasps in mid-air were buzzing around the ox's festering horn. As I walked to the left bank, I saw with my own eyes that crazy woman Wheat Ears. Wearing a white mourning dress and a black rubber shoe, she walked into the river. As the water reached her plump and protruding abdomen, she raised her beautiful face, looking at the sky. Then, all of a sudden, she lowered her head until her chin reached her collarbone and let her hair loose on the surface of the water. Clutching a wisp of hair, she washed it over and over again in the water. Red bubbles appeared on the ripples, and gradually half of the river became reddish.

Alas! All these were so familiar to me, for they had appeared in my dreams for several times! But my youngest uncle, that dark-skinned, strong and thin man, down and out, in a black rubber shoe, approached me without casting a shadow and left without a trace. Was he smiling or crying? Where were you, my youngest uncle?

On the 8th day of the 8th month in the lunar calendar in 1956, the day before my youngest uncle was buried, all the people in my hometown were worried, for uncle had no memorial tablet. Without it the dead was not allowed to be buried in his family cemetery. They searched all the indoor and outdoor spaces in the village and the blouses of all the women who once had affairs with uncle. But to their dismay, it was nowhere to be found. The whole village fell into a mess. Uncle lay quiet on the grinding stone. He had to bear the chaos he himself had made. At midnight, the bamboo clapper suddenly slipped off the boy's hand and fell onto the ground. The boy screamed and cried off his head, claiming that he saw uncle's eyes open, which looked much like two poppy buds in which there were a woman and a dog!

Only women and dogs could go into uncle's eyes. People all said so, and so did my grandpa. The last night when people kept guard over uncle's corpse, my grandpa, a thousand kilometers away in the city, was making a bamboo tablet. He heard the boy's scream. He cut and chopped attentively, in an attempt to make a tablet identical to uncle's lost one. He carefully and elaborately engraved uncle's name on the tablet. After all these done, grandpa smiled and choked. Along a ladder, he slowly climbed onto the top of our building. Looking at the city underneath, grandpa murmured and mumbled like a crazy old man. In his rambling[14], the building under his feet shivered for a long time. The passers-by under the building later said that they saw will-o'-the-wisp falling down from the top of the building and that it burned pit-a-pat on the road with blue flames almost a foot tall. The ghostly fire was fragrant and it sang and danced on the concrete road for the whole dusk.

Bring your uncle back home.

The year before last, in spring, lying on the bamboo couch, my grandpa was dying. Uncle became more and more distinct in grandpa's mind. He could never forget his smallest son. He took great efforts to embrace my head, which was filled with grief, and whispered to me.

Bring your uncle back home!

One day, I would fly over my hometown and fulfill the mission of three generations. Nobody had ever told me why so many scarlet poppies were grown on the left bank of the river and why they disappeared with my deceased relatives. That day when I returned to my hometown to take my youngest uncle away, I might see the luxuriant poppy field again. That must be a hot night. The boiling moon would fall down at any moment on that night and it might burn and sear us. The dark red restless night and the scarlet waves of poppy flowers would wrap and protect us fugitives, and grey frogs under my feet croaked, closely following me and dashing rampantly on the field ridges with me.

The whole village would be in a chaos, with all the lights on and all the dogs barking. The villagers would chase me, trying to grab uncle's soul from my back. Anyway, uncle was born and grew up in Maple and Poplar Village. Though the old wild dog left by uncle was wandering outside, its glistening immortal eyes, like meteors across the darkness of the sky, would plunge toward me. The clamorous sound of men and dogs and all the other sound in nature would run after me. The boiling moon would fall and finally rest on the dark face of my deceased uncle. I would carry my uncle on my back, who was actually a thousand-year-old volcano.

On that night, a crazy woman would give birth to a baby at a remote place. Everyone could hear its bleak and glum cries, which might embody all the vicissitudes of life in Maple and Poplar Village. In that sound of rampant life, could I run through that long narrow strip of land on the left bank and transcend that river?

In the city where I lived, there were many families which had moved here from countryside. At night, they snored and dreamed of their own dreams. If you, like me, also had weird dreams from your childhood, you must have dreamed of your hometown, your clan and your relatives there. To every one of us, there was a river in company with us from our birth. Drifting down that river on a bamboo raft, as long as you cast a backward glance, invariably, you would see your hometown in the distance.

(Published in No.2, 1987)

1. 苏童以独具风格的"枫杨树村"系列小说而引起文坛瞩目。这篇优秀的短篇小说《飞越我的枫杨树故乡》展示了一个凄美艳丽、意象纷飞的艺术世界。这篇小说至少有三个特点，给翻译带来一定难度。第一，它并非按部就班按照时间顺序进行叙述，而是叙述、回忆、想像交织在一起，把一个个故事或事件拆散，置于时空倒错的框架中，读者因而失去了故事逻辑的依凭。译文全部采用了过去时态，时间的先后顺序、逻辑关系，只有靠读者去体会了，这也正是原文的写作风格。第二，整个小说充满了凄美的、花团锦簇的意象：莽莽苍苍的枫杨树、猩红的罂粟花、灰蒙蒙的灵牌、乌黑发亮的胶鞋、浩浩荡荡的大风、浊黄的河流、狂吠的野狗、飞逝长鸣的公牛、燃烧的干花、精灵般美丽而苍老的婴孩、迷人的疯女人穗子、老朽如幽灵的族公等，这些意象把读者带入一个色彩斑斓、荡人心魄的世界。这些意象必须忠实翻译，这些意象所蕴含的特殊意义和文化内涵，要体现在整个译文中。第三，作者诡异绮丽的诗性语言给翻译带来难度，也给译者的创造性发挥提供了很大空间。

2. "春天的时候，河两岸的原野被猩红色大肆入侵，层层叠叠、气韵非凡，如一片莽莽苍苍的红波浪鼓荡着偏僻的乡村，鼓荡着我的乡亲们生生死死呼出的血腥气息。"从篇首这句上，可以看出小说的特点：意象丰富、诗性语言、色彩斑斓。译者对原句进行了拆解，拆解出一些主要元素：原野、猩红色、入侵、层叠、红波浪、偏僻的乡村、生生死死、血腥、气息。然后运用英语重新组句，在译句中体现出这些元素。Piles upon piles of red waves clamorously and aggressively pervaded that remote village, surging and dancing in the blood-tinged breaths of the people, going up and down together with people's weal and woe, life and death.

3. 这一段人物描写，栩栩如生，一个放荡不羁的青年形象跃然纸上。其中，怪模怪样、迷上、厮混、疯疯癫癫、非人非狗、丑闻，都是这段中的关键词，翻译时应体会这些词的风格特点。译文为：When he was a boy, he loved wearing a queer-looking sunhat which only city people liked and idling away his time in poppy fields. One summer, he hurled his sunhat into the river and turned his interest to a pack of wild dogs. He was obsessed with them, and

since then, people always saw my uncle, the youngest son of the richest family in the village, fooling around all day long with a pack of wild dogs. Half normal and half crazy, half a man and half a dog, my uncle became the rarest scandal in Maple and Poplar Village. 译者有意选择了一些具有贬义的词汇来翻译。例如：fool around 闲耍、虚度、鬼混。

4. a fit of 指突然一阵怨气、激情、咳嗽等，in a fit of rage 就是"怨气冲天"。

5. 中国的一些词汇已经进入到英语中，例如：kowtow 磕头 / kang 炕 / maotai 茅台 / litchi 荔枝 / gongfu 中国功夫 / hutong 胡同 / tofu 豆腐 / guanxi 关系，等等。

6. "……幺叔鬼喊鬼叫死命挣脱，抓破了他的脸。祖父骂着娘……"，从这句中"鬼喊鬼叫"、"骂着娘"，可以想像当时混乱的场面。译文：Uncle screamed and snarled, struggling hysterically to rid himself of grandpa's hands. Grandpa was scratched in the face … "Shit!" In exasperation, he dished out a stream of curses. scream 是尖叫，snarl 是狂吼，struggle 是挣扎，三个押头韵的动词连用，有声音效果，也有撕扯的动作感；dish out 大量给予、分发，a stream of curses 一连串骂人话。

7. 这段是作者的想像。全文幻想、现实、过去的回忆全都交织在一起，译者都采用了过去时，这给读者的阅读带来一定挑战。

8. "有一天枫杨树村里白幡招摇，家屋顶上腾起一片灰蒙蒙的烟霭。有许多人影在烟霭里东跑西窜，哭哭啼啼，空气中笼罩着惶惶不可终日的气氛……"小说的基调在此处趋于阴郁，译者选用了 shroud、weep and wail、seized with fear and anxiety 来突出当时混乱和阴暗的局面：One day, my home was shrouded with gray and gloomy smoke. White cloth strips fluttered everywhere in the village and people kept coming and going, weeping and wailing. The whole village was in turmoil, seized with fear and anxiety …

9. "……把宁静的村子闹腾得鸡犬不宁。"译为：… throwing the otherwise peaceful village into chaos. "鸡犬不宁"有多种翻译方法，比如：stir… into a tempest、throw… into chaos/ disorder/ turmoil、even the fouls and dogs are not left in peace、wreak havoc with 等。

10. "对着日月星辰和山水草木轻轻地喊：'带他去吧，带他去吧。'"They

prayed softly to the sun, the moon and the stars in the sky, "Take him away." And they shouted gently to the mountain, the river and the trees and grasses on the earth, "Take him away." 译者把原句拆成两句翻译，即对着日月星辰祈祷，对着山川草木哭喊，说了两遍"带他去吧"，是为了加强语气。

11. 原文此处对话并未加引号，这是作者的一种写作风格，译文为了方便阅读起见，加上了引号。

12. "……幺叔唱歌、呐喊，快活得有如神仙。"译为：… he sang and shouted, as happy as a king. as happy as a king 非常快乐。

13. "那一天我神色匆忙，在枫杨树老家像一只没头苍蝇胡乱碰撞。"没头苍蝇，指慌乱的状态，译文处理为：I was in such a hurry like a cat on hot bricks. 英文谚语a cat on hot bricks 相当于中文的"热锅上的蚂蚁"，形容慌乱、着急。

14. 此处以murmur, mumble, ramble 翻译"疯疯癫癫，胡言乱语"。murmur 低声嘀咕/ mumble 含糊，咕哝/ ramble 东拉西扯，长篇大论。

黄瑶

◎ 林斤澜

　　"浩劫"过去以后，有的机关做得干净，把漫漫十年里的"交代"、"检查"、"认罪书"、"思想汇报"，还有造反派弄的"审讯记录"、"旁证材料"……全从档案里清理出来，装在特大号牛皮纸口袋里，交给本人，任凭自由处理，一般是一烧了之。黄瑶拿回家去时，她的男人多一份儿心，悄悄藏过一边，只说是烧毁了。过了七八年，却派上了正经用场，交给精神病医生。据说，对治疗黄瑶的癔症，大有好处。下边是医生抄摘出来的部分，稍分次序，略加连贯。

　　黄瑶是个美人，五官细致整齐，不过女人们说她是冷面孔。冷面孔的意思是和男人对面走过，不会多看她一眼。男人们反映：没法儿，她老垂下眼皮，和她说话，她的眼睛顶多只瞧在人家胸口上。

　　什么"司令部"、"指挥部"，什么"兵团"，连七长八短的造反组织（出来一个"千钧棒"，跟着就有一个"紧箍咒"），都没有把黄瑶看在眼里。后来有头有脸儿的是共产党都成了叛徒，沾国民党的都是特务，革命还要继续，清理到海外关系，才把黄瑶揪出来。

　　不知道从什么时候起，黄瑶脖子上总有一条纱巾，春秋正好合适。冬天披在领子里，外边再围一条大围巾，也还说得过去。夏天起点风，蒙在脸上挡沙土，就显得勉强些。大太阳时候散披在肩膀上，叫人瞧着纳闷儿——这是哪一路毛病？和海外哪一条勾着？拿它怎么上纲上线？

人家和她说话，她会嗖的扯下来拿在手里。"嗖的"本来是动作飞快，为的叫人眼皮子来不及眨，瞧不真。可是一回"嗖"两回"嗖"，反倒显眼了。人眼里或愣或疑或恼，总之，眼不是眼了。

人家的眼神稍稍一变，她的两手就把纱巾绞来绞去……慢着，不是说她从不抬起眼皮看人吗？顶多只盯到人家胸口上吗？怎么看得见别人的眼神呢？看得见的，仿佛是时下新兴的热门话题儿：特异功能。只要人家的疑心或是恼心或是狠心或是不规矩心胖大了，眼色也随着古怪了。人家多半知道自己的心机，不知道眼神会泄密。可是黄瑶连眼皮也没抬，就会把纱巾越绞越紧，会紧到麻花似的捆住两个手腕子，把自己捆一个贼似的。

黄瑶老家在南方海边，是个侨乡。海外的亲属见过面的，上数能数到叔公，下数论辈分都有外甥孙了。北方的造反派没有见过这阵势，倒想也到海外"外调外调"，顺便也看看垂死的糜烂生活。可惜世界革命大约是过两年再说了，眼下还只可关门打狗。

因此，黄瑶落进了"无头公案"，比走资派还难斗倒斗臭。对她，只能打"心理战术"。

有一个造反派是个矬壮小伙，长一双孩子气的大眼睛。有天他审问黄瑶，灵机一动，一伸手，把那条纱巾抓了过来……

十几年后，才让医生分析出来，这个小动作非同小可，后头的坎坷都由这里起，差一点废掉小伙一双眼，送掉黄瑶一条命。

不过当时，矬壮小伙不禁微微一笑。他看见把纱巾一抓过来，黄瑶冷不丁一个哆嗦，眼睛由人家胸口收回去，盯在自己胸口上了，跟闭上了一样。那出名的冷面孔也黄了，跟黄杨木雕的傻菩萨似的。

小伙心里笑道：开局打得不错，这心理战有打头。脑子里闪闪着想像力的光芒：纱巾犄角上缝着什么？图案上有密码？浸过药水？是个暗号？

小伙走到黄瑶跟前，差不多是胸脯贴胸脯。小伙命令黄瑶抬起眼皮，瞧着他的眼睛。小伙矬壮，为了眼睛对上眼睛，踮起了脚儿来……看起来好像小伙把自己当做一部测谎机，不对，那是外国东西，非资即修。小伙子采用的是施公案彭公案里的国粹……忽然，嗖的，猫扑老鼠，鹰抓兔子，黄瑶两手跟两爪一般飞起落下，落在小伙两眼上。小伙一个激灵，一挣，一扭，转过了身体。黄瑶的两个爪子，还由小伙脑后包抄紧抠。小伙大吼一声，往前一拱，屁股一撅，把黄瑶背在背上，两手一托，打开两爪，腰背一闪，这小伙壮实，把黄瑶"趴蹋"摔在地上了。

大家闻声围上来一看，只见小伙上半张脸，一片的血"糊垃"。赶紧送医院，却用不着抢救。当时小伙和人家眼对眼、鼻子碰鼻子，黄瑶两爪上来不能直扑，只能迂回，就这刹那时间，小伙挤紧了上下眼皮，保住了孩子气的大眼睛。脸上不过是皮伤，抹点红药水紫药水打个大花脸就算完了。

黄瑶当然是现行反革命，铐上手铐——铁麻花，下了大狱。

矬壮小伙的大花脸上孩子气大眼睛睁圆了，说：这下可看见了黄瑶的眼神，好像，好像，黑色素沉淀了，干巴了，像两泡铁砂子，沉沉的，毛糙糙的，没有亮光……说到这里，小伙不知道他那孩子气眼睛也沉淀也毛糙起来，还只顾说别人，说：一句话，不像人的眼神。

若干年后，黄瑶从监狱里放出来，她有悔罪的表现。其中有一条是：常要求把她的手铐上。哪个犯人不怕手铐？那是刑具。绿林好汉把手铐叫做手镯子，可是没有一个要求戴上手镯玩玩的。

审讯记录里也有医生有兴趣的东西。

黄瑶六七岁时，家里日子不好过，爸爸妈妈到海外投奔叔公去，把黄瑶交给亲婆。南方叫做"亲"的，就是"干亲"。北方爽直，用"干"字，好比说干妈干爹。"干亲"本来不"亲"，南方偏叫它"亲"。"亲娘""亲爷""亲婆"。

亲婆有孙子孙女，和黄瑶上下岁儿。好比一块糕半张饼，黄瑶伸手要拿，亲婆的眼神一沉，黄瑶知道是留给孙子孙女的了。后来刚走到水壶茶碗跟前，亲婆在身后五尺地，黄瑶也会后脑勺看见那眼神沉下来了，就缩住脚步。在房檐下过家家，黄瑶稍稍不让，也会看见屋里的眼神。在院子里跳猴皮筋，正热闹着，也会忽然看见不知哪里来的沉重的眼神，扭头往家跑，亲婆正把一捆菜扔到地上，黄瑶赶紧搬盆洗菜。做梦憋着尿，也会叫那双眼神惊醒，起来坐马桶去。

那眼神好沉好沉，好像两兜铁砂子，不透亮，又毛糙。

等到上了小学，和一个山里来的小男孩同桌，只要黄瑶凑过去说句话，小男孩会嗖的抓本书挡住半边脸。黄瑶要是伸手抓书，小男孩就赶紧往一边闪，跌在地上两回，挨老师说还是这样。

慢慢地熟了，黄瑶盘问道：

"你们山里人怕女孩子？"

"不怕。"

"那你怕我？我可怕？我脏？我臭？"

小男孩连连摇头，吞吞吐吐，还是忍不住说道：

"你这个名字是谁给起的？"

"爸爸。"

"怎么起这么个名字，啊呀！"

"这名字好。我爸爸说，瑶是玉，黄色的玉比黄金还好看呢！"

小男孩说出了一种动物，是黄瑶本来做梦也梦不着的，谁知当天晚上就在梦里出现了。第二天第三天又央告又细细盘问小男孩，这个山里来的男孩也鬼，越说越神。

山里有种东西叫黄猺（两个小孩都不理会"猺"跟"瑶"偏旁不一样），狼也怕，猿猴也怕，连老虎都怕这东西。这东西一叫起来，离得远点的，抹头就跑。离得近的吓傻了，四条腿就跟钉子似的钉在地上了。

黄猺有多大？大不过狸猫，小的才比松鼠长点儿，就算全身是力气也才这么点儿。可是那两个前爪跟锥子似的还带钩，这东西就有一手本事，一上来，先不先，抠眼珠子。

这东西没有单个儿的，一把两把（一把是六个，两把一打）成群地跑，一包围上来，防得了前头防不了后头，窜上一个抠掉眼珠子，瞎了，就都扑过来开膛了。

这东西跑得飞快，能钻缝，树缝地缝腿缝过来过去，穿梭似的。能上树，能跳能蹦，就是不能飞。这东西要会飞，老鹰的眼珠子也保不住，树林子全得瞎了。

黄瑶胆战心惊，问道：

"你认识，不，你见过黄猺吗？"

小男孩绕弯子说他们家有条黑狗，带它进山去，只要是人吃什么，也给它吃什么，人吃多少，它也吃多少。它就会没命的钻树林子，不怕累，不怕摔，不怕死。把野兔、野鸡、野猪给人轰出来。有天，在个山坳里，黑狗张大了嘴，舌头掉出来挂着不动，四条腿跟四条木头棍儿似的插到地里去了，打它踢它也不走。我们心想：闹黄猺了吧？钻到林子里一看，刷拉拉，五六个，东奔西窜，眨眼间，不见了。

"你们不怕抠眼珠子？"黄瑶的声儿都哆嗦了。

"不怕，这东西偏偏怕人。"

"它怎么怕人？"

"抠眼珠子这一招是跟人学的。"

这句话把黄瑶吓得出不来声儿。过两天，才盘问道：

"怎么是跟人学的？真还有人教它？为什么教这一招呢？"

159

"我听我爷爷说的。"

"你爷爷怎么说的？说呀，爷爷怎么说？"

说得溜溜的小男孩，到这儿也"卡壳"了。光说：

"我爷爷说：人最坏。"

过些时候黄瑶还盘问：

"你亲眼看见过黄猁——那东西抠——抠眼珠子吗？"

"我看见过一只瞎眼猿猴，叫抠了，没死。还能上树，可是从这树蹦到那树，得咬着别的猿猴尾巴。"

"别的猿猴叫咬吗？"

"怕是它爸爸妈妈。"

"可怜。两个瞎眼窝？两个黑窟窿？"

"不，还有眼珠子在里头，不过没有亮光，像两砣铁……"

黄瑶再也不盘问了，手心里都冒冷汗。

这以后，站在亲婆跟前，会嗖的把两手背到背后，十个手指头交叉上，又紧了，有时候还冒冷汗。可也没有发生过什么举动，平安无事。

黄瑶照常长大，照常结婚、工作、和海外的父母通信。信是平安家信，身体健康啦，生活如常啦，工作愉快啦，变来变去说平安两个字。不过每封信都变得重复了，也写不满两张纸。不能通信的年头，也不特别想念。逢年时节，也给亲婆捎点礼物去。只是生就了一副冷面孔，眼皮爱下垂，觉得世界上最难看的是眼睛。这东西好好的也会一变，那变出来的眼色就不是色了。垂下眼皮，眼不见为净。

"浩劫"中间，不知不觉间，小时候的"特异功能"又回到身上。不用说身背后，就是隔着窗、隔着走廊、隔着袼褙似的大字报，都能看见盯过来、斜插过来、瞄准过来的眼睛，都黑沉沉，毛毛糙糙，没有亮光，好像两兜铁砂子。

有天夜里惊醒，看见一只瞎眼猿猴在树梗上爬，后边五六只小猴子一只咬着一只的尾巴，全是瞎的，眼窝里全是两兜铁砂子。这个景象叫人又心酸又害怕又"嗝厌"。

那个山里小男孩也只说过一只瞎猴，没有说过一串瞎猴咬着尾巴。随着，在一串瞎猴藏身的树上树下，又添上窜来跳去认不真的黄猁。这些景象起先好像小时候看见过，后来变做是活现在眼前的事实。

黄瑶见着人，又仿佛站在亲婆跟前，把两手背在背后，十指交叉，又紧——可是年月不同了，不行了，又不紧了。这才改用纱巾，绞住手腕，绞成麻花……

　　矬壮小伙打完心理战，看见女红卫兵把条纱巾掖在领子里头（不兴散披在外边），他总忍不住抓过来，抓到手又好像烫着他，立刻扔掉。仿佛怪人，女的不爱理他了。

　　"浩劫"过去，黄瑶自由了，海外关系转过来吃香了。黄瑶也还是写写平安家信，把字写得芽豆般大，好摆满两张纸。

　　当然也不免风吹草动，报纸上、广播上、小道上出现"打击"啦，"整顿"啦，"清查"啦，"清污"啦……其实有的是好事，有的要坏也坏不到哪里去。黄瑶都会刷拉一下掉下眼皮，冷面孔冻冰。

　　有天夜里，她男人看见她在被窝里，把条纱巾绞住手腕子睡觉。问问，说是不知道是梦不是梦，总看见一串瞎眼猿猴，还有一串串铁砂子眼神。生怕糊里糊涂里，把贴身睡着的男人，当做那踮起脚来和她贴身站着的矬壮小伙，做出黄猺的那一招来。

　　她男人也思想开放了，竟想到这种事情，是可以去找精神病医生的。因为这里边有些麻烦，好比说把自己的手腕绞上纱巾，明是把自己当做黄猺了吧。可是黄猺只在眼前窜来窜去，长什么样，多大个儿都没有看清楚过。常常出现在眼前的，倒是瞎眼猿猴，那铁砂子眼窝，一只咬着一只的尾巴。叫人又心酸又可怕又"嗝厌"，没有一点解气、报仇的痛快。那铁砂子眼神又不单在猿猴那里，亲婆那里，矬壮小伙那里，大道小道上这个人那个人那里都会出现，黄瑶自己也有过，矬壮小伙踮起脚来看见的，就是这种眼神，难道说她自己又是猿猴又是黄猺？她从小就有瞎眼猿猴的害怕。又生怕自己的两只手做了黄猺！……像这些景象，书记一般解释不了。到了医生那里，一口诊断做癔症，看起来是有把握治疗的吧。

　　　　　　　　　　　　　　　　　　　　　　　　　（载1987年2月号）

Huang Yao

○ *Lin Jinlan*

After the "great havoc" (the Cultural Revolution 1966-1976), some government departments were considerate enough to rearrange their personnel archives made during the ten years. Those "confession letters", "self-criticisms", "reports of thoughts" written by "suspects" as well as "records of trials" and "circumstantial evidences" concocted by "rebels" were all sorted out and put into large-sized kraft-paper bags to be returned to the intended individuals.[1] The person who got his own "bag" could dispose of it at will. Generally, they chose to burn it right away — let the past be buried in ashes. But when Huang Yao brought her "bag" home, instead of burning it, her husband secretly hid it away, believing that these things would come in handy one day. Seven or eight years later, those things in the paper bag indeed came into use. Her husband gave the paper bag to a psychiatrist, who said that it was really useful in treating Huang Yao's hysteria. The psychiatrist selected some materials, made extracts and roughly put them in order so that the passages read coherent. The following was his extracts:

Huang Yao was a beauty. Her facial features were exquisite and well-arranged, but many women said her face was so cold that no man would like to cast one more look at it. Quite a lot of men said: "She always looks downward when I have a talk with her, and in most cases, she just keeps her eyes on my chest!"

At first, "the Command", "the Headquarters", "the Corps" and all the other "revolutionary" organizations (in "the Cultural Revolution") didn't take Huang Yao seriously. Later, all the high-level cadres were denigrated as either "traitors", if they were communist party members, or "spies", if they had any connection whatsoever with the Kuomintang, and as the "revolution" went on, Huang Yao was ferreted out in the end — she had overseas relations!

Nobody knew from what time Huang Yao began to wear a silk scarf. It never left her neck. In spring and in autumn, she wore it; in winter, she tuck it into her collar and put a big and thick shawl outside; in summer, she covered her face with it to block wind and dirt, which actually made her appear quite odd; and under the strong sunlight, she usually spread it on her shoulder. People felt curious: "What's wrong with this woman? What kind of relation does she have with the foreign contacts? What on earth does her scarf allude to?"

When someone had a talk with her, she, invariably, whooshed her scarf off and held it tightly in her hands for fear that he might see it clearly. However, her strange and repeated whoosh-it-off action, on the contrary, drew more attention and made people curious, baffled and even irritated.[2]

Seeing people turning unhappy, she kept twisting her scarf in her hands — since she always looked downward and kept her eyes at most on people's chest, how could she know people turned unhappy? Indeed, she knew it. She could see it with her "supernatural ability", a term in vogue nowadays. In fact, one's eyes always told a tale of his inner feelings or thoughts.[3] When a person's doubt, hatred, resolution or evil intention began to swell in his heart, his eyes changed, but in most cases, he didn't realize it. Hence, Huang Yao could see people's mind without lifting her eyes. When she saw they became unhappy, she did nothing but keep twisting and tweaking her scarf around her wrists as if she were binding a thief.[4]

Her hometown in south China was famous for a lot of extensive connections with overseas Chinese communities. She had seen quite a lot of her overseas relatives, from her granduncle to her cousin's grandson. The revolutionaries from the north had never met such a "problematic" woman with such extensive foreign connections and had never known what foreign countries were like. Secretly, they even longed for an opportunity to go abroad and experience that so-called "decadent and dissolute" life. Yet, to their disappointment, such an opportunity was too faraway to reach — the war for a new world might have to wait another a couple of years. Therefore, what they could do now was to shut the door and beat the dog — they'd better block their enemies' retreat and destroy them.[5]

To them, Huang Yao was a mystery case without clues and she was much harder to be knocked down or overthrown than those capitalist-roaders! Therefore, to such a woman, the revolutionaries had to resort to some "psychological tactics", which might take effect on her. Once, in an interrogation, a stout young man with a pair of childish eyes, on an impulse, grabbed her scarf…

This action was by no means a small matter! It almost cost the young man his eyes and Huang Yao her life! More than 10 years later, the doctor analyzed this incident and arrived at the conclusion that it led to Huang Yao's later tribulations and hardships.

Anyway, at that time, that young man didn't know the serious impact of his impulsive action. He was complacent with his behavior. Huang Yao shivered a great deal, shifting her eyes from his chest to her own chest. Her eyes looked as if they were closed and her well-known cold face, at that moment, turned yellow like the color of the bodhisattva carved with boxwood.

Seeing her expression, the young man turned excited. A good start! The psywar was effective! His brain was lit up by flashes of imaginative sparkles: "What is sewn on the corner of her scarf? Are there any ciphers hidden in the pattern? Has the scarf been submerged in a potent solution? Are there any secret signals?"

He walked close to her, so close that his chest almost touched upon hers. He ordered her to raise her eyes and look him in the eye. To keep their eyes on the same level, he had to stand on his tiptoe. At this moment, he thought himself a lie-detector. No! That was something belonging to either capitalism or revisionism in the foreign countries. He actually was using a method, a Chinese national essence, which the ancient wise judges Shi and Peng once employed to settle their lawsuits. All of a sudden, Huang Yao's two hands stretched out and went for his eyes! Like a cat jumping at a mouse or an eagle making at a rabbit, she intended to clutch his eyes with her fingers. Greatly frightened, the young man broke free from her hands with a sudden jerk and turned around in a scuffle. Then, she clawed his head from behind. Abruptly, he let out a hoarse cry, bent forward, stuck up his buttocks and carried her onto his back; then, he got hold of Huang Yao with his firm hands and, with a thrust of his torso, hurled her overhead onto the ground with a big plop![6]

People around quickly came. They sent the young man to hospital in a hurry. His life was not in danger but the upper part of his face was seriously scratched into a blurry sheet of blood. As the young man and Huang Yao stood face to face with each other, she couldn't paw at his eyes directly but tried to attack by flanking, and luckily, he, at that crucial moment, shut his eyelids tightly in time so that his childish eyes were saved, though his face was bruised. Some red and purple liquid medicine and bandages were applied to his scratched face. That's all.

Nevertheless, Huang Yao was accused of being an active counterrevolutionary and was handcuffed and put into prison.

Later, the young man, opening his childish eyes even wider, told others in an excited tone, "Finally, I see her eyes! It seems that... that too much melanin is deposited in her eyes, which are very dry and withered like two pits of iron sand, heavy, rough and lackluster..." As he tried to search for the words to describe his feelings about Huang Yao's eyes, his eyes turned dim and gruff, too. "In a word, those were not a human being's eyes." He concluded in the end.

Huang Yao was released several years later. The reason was that, as they said, she had a contrite heart. One of her repenting behaviors was that she always required to have herself cuffed. Were there any criminals unafraid of handcuffs, the instrument of torture? Brazen outlaws called handcuffs "bracelets", but none of them felt like wearing such bracelets.

In her interrogation records, something appealed to doctors' interest —

At the age of six or seven, Huang Yao was sent to her grandma, for her family was poor and her parents had to go abroad and live with their overseas relatives. Actually, that was Huang Yao's adoptive grandma. In the north, people simply used "adoptive mother", "adoptive father", "adoptive grandpa" and "adoptive grandma", but in the southern areas, people called them "mother", "father", "grandpa" and "grandma". In fact, they had no blood relations.[7]

Huang Yao's adoptive grandma had her own grandchildren, who were about the same age as Huang Yao. Naturally, the old woman treated Huang Yao and her own grandchildren differently. When Huang Yao stretched out her hands, asking for a cake or a half pancake, the grandma's eyes froze. Huang Yao at once understood that the food was saved for the grandma's own children. When Huang Yao ran to a water jug or a tea pot for some drinking water, the grandma's eyes froze. Huang Yao at once sensed it and stopped short. When Huang Yao played a make-believe game under the eaves, she must give way to the grandma's children, otherwise, the grandma's eyes froze. When Huang Yao was skipping over a chain of rubber bands in the yard, in high spirit, she abruptly saw that pair of frozen eyes. She turned at once and ran back home. Seeing the grandma throw a bunch of vegetables onto the ground, Huang Yao hurried to fetch a basin and began to wash them. At midnight, when Huang Yao wanted a pee, she was always woken up by those frozen eyes. She at once sat up and went to the toilet.

The eyes were heavy, so heavy that they looked like two bags of tough and gruff iron sand.

In the primary school, Huang Yao's desk-mate was a little boy from the mountainous countryside. As long as she got close to him, intending to say a few words to him, the boy quickly took a book up from the desk and blocked his face. As she tried to grab for the book, the little boy quickly dodged aside, even knocking himself down twice. He continued doing so, though he was criticized by their teacher repeatedly.

Later, as they got on familiar terms with each other, Huang Yao couldn't help asking him,

"Why? Are you afraid of girls?"

"No."

"Then you are afraid of me? I am so terrifying? I am dirty? Or I stink?"

He kept shaking his head, speaking in a halting way,

"Who gave you such a name?"

"My dad."

"Aya! Why did he give you such a name?"

"It's a good name. Huang Yao means yellow jade, which looks more beautiful than gold! My father said so."

Then, the boy muttered and mumbled a name of an animal, which Huang Yao had never seen even in her dream! But that night it appeared in her dream. The next morning, she asked him about it and pleaded him to tell her more about it. As he talked with more and more gusto, she came more and more under his spell.

He told her:[8]

In our mountain, there is a kind of animal named *"huang yao"* (*Martes flavigula*, a kind of dark brown weasel).[9] *Huang yao* is so fierce that wolves, apes and even tigers are scared of it! When a *huang yao* roars, the animals far away from it will turn tail at once and flee for life, and those close to it will be so terrified that they cannot move a step as if their four legs were nailed into the ground.

How big is it? The biggest one is like a leopard cat and the smallest is just a little longer than a squirrel. And even the strongest of them is no bigger than such a size. Its two front hooked paws, as sharp as stabbers, contribute a lot to its ferocity. When a *huang yao* makes an attack, the first action is to jump up and dig out the eyeballs of its enemy. Of course, it never takes actions alone. Usually, one or two groups (a group of six) make assaults together. As they circle their enemy, one of them makes at it first by taking off its eyeballs, and then the rest of them rush forward, splitting their prey and tearing its guts out.

A *huang yao* runs very fast. It is good at running through all sorts of cracks and seams. Neither cracks between trees nor chinks on earth nor the seams between two legs can put it off. It can go through them with great ease. Besides, it can climb up tall trees, jump and leap — if only it could fly! Thank God! If it could fly, even eagles would lose their eyes and maybe all the creatures in the forest would become blind!

Hearing the boy talking about the horrible animal, Huang Yao trembled with fear. She asked,

"Have you known... oh, no, have you seen it before?"

The boy didn't reply her directly. He told her:

My family once kept a big black dog. When we went hunting in the mountain, we always brought it with us. It ate what we ate, even to the exact amount. In return, the dog spared no effort to help us chase and drive hares, pheasants and boars out of the woods, regardless of hardship or death. But one day, it was found stiff and dumbfounded, opening its mouth wide with its big tongue hanging outside. Its four legs, like four wooden sticks thrusting into the earth, stayed motionless, and even a heavy kick couldn't make them move. It must have had an encounter with *huang yao*! Then, we ran into the woods to have a look. As we had expected, five or six *huang yao* were running and jumping here and there but instantly they scattered and disappeared.

"Aren't you afraid? Your eyes might be dug out!" Huang Yao asked with a shivering voice.

"No. This animal fears nothing but human beings."

"It is afraid of human beings?"

"Because it learned its unique skill of digging out eyeballs from human beings."

Huang Yao was overwhelmed and greatly shocked, feeling so fearful that she couldn't utter a single word. After two days, she collected herself and continued to ask the boy,

"How did a *huang yao* learn its skill from human beings? Was it likely that a man went to teach it how to dig out eyeballs? And why did he teach it such a cruel skill?"

"I just heard of it from my grandpa."

"What did your grandpa say? Tell me, please. What did your grandpa tell you?"

The boy who had been eloquent and talkative stopped abruptly. He only told her,

"My grandpa told me that human beings are the worst animal."

After a while, Huang Yao continued her questions,

"Have you seen with your own eyes *huang yao* … that thing digging out … eyeballs?"

"I've seen an ape whose eyeballs were dug out. Fortunately, it didn't die but it was blind and had to bite another ape's tail so that it could jump from this tree to that. "

"How come the other apes allowed it to bite their tails?"

"I guess they might be its parents."

"Deplorable, indeed! Two blind eyes. Two black hollow holes?"

"No. The eyeballs were inside the sockets, but they showed no light like two lumps of iron…"

She stopped asking questions, her two hands full of cold sweat.

Since then, when she stood in front of her grandma, Huang Yao, consciously or unconsciously, tightly clasped her hands and put them behind her back, and sometimes she even shed cold sweat. Actually, nothing abnormal happened. She was safe and sound.

Like other girls, Huang Yao grew up, got married and began to work. She kept writing to her parents abroad. Such routine greetings as "Wish you healthy", "I am well and good", "Wish you smooth with your work" and such words as "safe" repeatedly appeared in her letters. By and by, her letters got repetitive and lasted no more than two pieces of paper. In those years when correspondence was blocked, she, indeed, didn't have that particular profound yearnings for her parents. On New Year's Day or other festivals, she also sent some presents to her grandma. It seemed as if she were born with a cold face. She always drooped down her eyelids, believing that eyes were the ugliest thing in the world and that eyes were capricious and once they changed their colors they were no longer eyes. Thus, drooping down her eyelids might be her deliberate choice — out of sight, out of mind.

In the years filled with "great havoc" (the Cultural Revolution 1966-1976), she seemed to recover her "supernatural ability" which was developed in her childhood. The evil eyes behind her back, beyond the windows, at the other end of the corridor, and even behind the handwritten big-font posters of criticism and denuniciation — she could always feel those evil eyes staring at her, squinting at her, or shooting darts at her. Those were frozen, rough, lusterless eyes like two bags of iron sand.

One night, she was woken up with a start. In her dream, she saw a blind ape crawling on a branch and following it were five or six little apes, each biting the tail of the one before it. They were all blind, with two eye sockets of iron sand. The scene made her scared, sad and sick![10]

Her desk-mate had seen only one blind ape, and he had never seen such a chain of apes, biting one another's tail. While the chain of blind apes jumped on and off, that terrible animal *huang yao* appeared, following the apes, jumping from one branch to another. She felt she had seen this scene when she was small and now it became a reality in front of her eyes.

From then on, when she saw someone, she felt as if she were standing in front of her grandma, and habitually she felt like putting her hands behind her back and clasping her fingers. However, the situation was actually different and the person in front of her was not her grandma; therefore, she, no longer clutching her hands, began to twist her scarf on and on until it became a twisted rope…

After the stout young man finished his psywar against Huang Yao, whenever he saw a female "red guard" who tucked her scarf into the collar (it was not popular to let it outside), he always couldn't help but stretch out his hand and grab for it.

Once he got it, as if burned by it, he immediately threw it away. Since he behaved so strangely, his female colleagues were all unwilling to go near him.

After the "great havoc", Huang Yao finally regained freedom, and her overseas relations, as time went by, turned out to be one of her advantages. As before, she wrote letters to her parents, and she wrote the words big enough like beans so as to cover two pages easily.

Of course, foreboding catchwords hinting at unwanted developments such as "attacks", "readjustments", "check and verification", and "clean-up movement" sometimes popped up on newspapers or on radio. In truth, some of them were good news, and even the bad news was not nearly as bad as the events in those ten years. Huang Yao responded to all of these with her invariable action: She drooped down her eyelids and froze her face at once.

One night, her husband found her lying under her quilt with her wrists tied tightly by that scarf. Out of curiosity, he asked her about it. She told him that a chain of blind apes and pairs of dark eye sockets of iron sand always appeared in front of her eyes and that she herself didn't know whether it was her dream or a reality, and that she was afraid she, in confusion, might do something terrible to him as what she had done to that stout young man.

Her husband was open-minded and thought he'd better resort to a psychiatrist, but there was something perturbing and confusing: She tied her own wrists with her scarf, which indicated that she took herself as that terrible animal *huang yao*, though she never saw clearly how big it was and what it looked like. In truth, it was those blind apes with their eye sockets of iron sand and their biting one another's tail that constantly appeared in front of her eyes and made her scared, depressed and sick! The apes were so deplorable, never venting their hatred or depression and never making revenge! The darkened eye sockets of iron sand were possessed not only by those apes, but also by her grandma, that stout young man and many people on the streets. And she even felt her own eyes were also darkened and filled with iron sand, and she was sure that what the young man saw, when he stood on his tiptoes face to face with her, was just this kind of eyes. Did this mean that she was also a blind ape? From her childhood, she was afraid of blind apes, and now she was afraid that her hands would do something as a *huang yao* did!... Therefore, people found it hard to explain her behavior. The doctor confidently diagnosed her case as hysteria. It seemed that the doctor had a cure for her.

(Published in No.2, 1987)

注 释

1. "浩劫"、"交代"、"检查"、"认罪书"、"思想汇报",还有"审讯记录"、"旁证材料"以及下文中的"司令部"、"指挥部"、"兵团"等等,这些都是中国特定时期的用词,翻译时要注意,要加上引号以提示读者这是一些特殊用词,而且必要时可以给予文内或文外注释,帮助读者理解。例如,这里的"浩劫",译者加了注释"(the Cultural Revolution 1966–1976)"。

2. "'嗖的'本来是动作飞快,为的叫人眼皮子来不及眨,瞧不真。可是一回'嗖'两回'嗖',反倒显眼了。"whoosh意为飞快地移动或飞快移动时发出的声音,既是动词又是名词,用在这里比较合适: … her strange and repeated whoosh-it-off action, on the contrary, drew more attention …

3. to tell a tale说明了问题,揭露了内情,泄露了秘密。例如: The lines on his face tell a tale of years of toiling and scheming …

4. "就会把纱巾越绞越紧",翻译为keep twisting and tweaking …,这里twist与tweak两个词都有"拧、绞"的意思,tweak还有苦恼的意思,两个词押头韵,可以比较好地表达"越绞越紧像麻花"这个动作。

5. "眼下还只可关门打狗"。"关门打狗"是汉语中非常生动的表达,译文尽量保留原文形象,为了便于读者理解,译者在破折号后进行了补充说明。对于一些意象或者成语的翻译,在不影响上下行文流畅的情况下,这不失为一个好的办法,可以保留原文形象和语言特色,又可以通过补充部分帮助读者理解。Therefore, what they could do now was to shut the door and beat the dog — they'd better block their enemies' retreat and destroy them.

6. 这一段的翻译,关键是选择好动词,把当时剑拔弩张的情景表现出来。例如译文中stretch out、go for、jump at、make at、clutch、break free、claw、bend forward、stick up、hurl等动词的使用,可以比较好地描述出人物的动作,以烘托出当时的紧张气氛。

7. "南方叫做'亲'的,就是'干亲'。北方爽直,用'干'字,好比说干妈干爹。'干亲'本来不'亲',南方偏叫它'亲'。'亲娘''亲爷''亲婆'。"根据原文的意思,译文没有拘泥于原句的结构和排列,而是重新组织句子,把意思传达出来。Actually, that was Huang Yao's adoptive grandma.

In the north, people simply used "adoptive mother", "adoptive father", "adoptive grandpa" and "adoptive grandma", but in the southern areas, people called them "mother", "father", "grandpa" and "grandma". In fact, they had no blood relations.

8. 山里小男孩的大段叙述，原文没有使用标示直接引语的引号，这是作者的一种写作风格。译文在此处尊重原文，也未加引号，并采用了现在时态。

9. 黄猺是一种动物，身体大小似家猫，头的背面和侧面、四肢和尾巴都呈棕黑色，肩部黄色，腹部黄灰色，吃松鼠、蜜蜂等，皮毛可以制衣服。黄猺与故事主人公黄瑶在汉语中发音完全相同，所以才会有这样的故事情节。因此，在译文中，译者用了拼音*huang yao*来翻译这种动物：In our mountain, there is a kind of animal named *"huang yao"* (*Martes flavigula*, a kind of dark brown weasel).

10. "这个景象叫人又心酸又害怕又'嗝厌'"。"嗝厌"为方言，是讨厌、不舒服的意思。The scene made her scared, sad and sick! 三个词押头晕，把心酸、害怕、不舒服的意思表达出来。

曲胡

◎ 刘庆邦

这地方，胡琴有四种，板胡、曲胡、坠胡、二胡。瞎祥拉的是曲胡。

一只放倒的六棱木筒，用桐油喂过，一端绷上蟒皮，往上立一根深色细木琴杆，杆首雕出诸葛武侯顶冠模样，两侧装上调弦的钮子，这就是曲胡了。曲胡拉起来声音宏大、高亢，但不叫，透着真实的敦厚。

曲胡是给曲剧伴奏的，瞎祥却从未登过戏台，可见他琴技平平。他是胎里瞎，从未见过天日。爹娘送他投师学艺，想让他有一技在身，将来好有碗饭吃。不想世上有的技艺不是下了苦功就能学到的，琴弦不知锯断多少，琴杆被指头磨出槽坑，琴声竟不能入世，拉不出日月星辰、苦辣酸甜来。后来，二老相继过世，念过大学的哥哥在外得了新欢，跟嫂子分手不再回家，家道日渐衰落清苦。这时再听瞎祥的琴声，竟有些不同凡响了。秋叶飘零的夜晚，月白如霜。琴声悠悠扬扬传来，如泣如诉，使好多善良的农人痴痴呆呆，嗟叹不已。大雪封门时，村落静得如死去一般。辛劳一年的人们闲下心来，正要把往事回想，琴声驾着雪朵过来了，悄悄往心里去。不知不觉中，人们记起往人往事，心绪就跑到很远很远的地方去了。有的妇人凭这琴音沟通了心境，想起先前的一个男人，沉醉在一种神情恍惚的境界，把悲欢离合的感情升华。也有人不胜琴力，冒了大雪，循声去瞎祥家里看究竟，见瞎祥弓如腾蛇，指似飞鸟，操琴正酣，且有两道清泪顺鼻窝流下，有些吃惊，就喊："祥，祥，你疯了！拉弦归拉弦，你哭啥？"

祥停了手，马上直脸对来人作笑模样，说："我没哭。"抬手摸到脸上果真有泪，又说："我是迎风流泪。"遂松弦合了弓子，和来人说话，从落雪说到小麦，又卜到来年收成。

晴了天，地里还陷脚，无活可做，到瞎祥这里消闲的人更多。来人先不说话，挤眉弄眼示意别人也缄了口，却蹑手蹑脚过去，一下搂了祥的后腰。祥是做惯了这游戏的，凭他惊人的记忆和细腻的感觉，早就知道搂他腰的人是谁了，他偏不道破，只张三李四地混猜。有时搂他的明明是小伙子，他却说出一个姑娘的名字，直惹得人憋不住笑，他也笑，并承认自己输了，说出输的理由，是怪别人，不怪他，因为搂他的人高了，胖了，皮肉细了。他这种怪人的办法谁都愿意接受一回。

小孩子也喜欢他，愿意跟他玩。小孩子的游戏就是重复，不厌其烦地重复。成人跟小孩子们玩不起，太乏味儿，太累。祥却从不让小孩子们失望。一个在家受了屈、脸上还有泪痕的小女孩，眨着一双星子样的眼睛问祥："扁豆什么样儿？"

"扁扁的。"

"绿豆呢？"

"绿绿的。"

"毛豆呢？"

"毛毛的。"

祥的回答似乎都对，让人驳不倒。可架不住小女孩的问题多呀，她问到猪狗猫，鸡鸭兔，还问到太阳、云彩和墙头上的一盆凤仙花，看见什么就问什么。祥呢？以此类推，有问必答，猪，"猪猪的"；狗，"狗狗的"……太阳，"太太的"……小女孩听出了破绽，笑得待好滚在地上。祥也乐得原地直转："怎么样？难不倒我吧！"

祥突然静下来朝一处听着时，那一处必定悄悄立着一位中年妇女。这妇人年轻时节应当是美人，端庄娴静处不会随着岁月流逝就消失了，从余剩风姿还可以想像得出。这是祥的嫂子。因为有了一个儿子，她离婚不离家。祥的眼睛是秕谷，嫂子的目光关照到弟弟时是毫不避讳的。目光在那无须白脸上滞留的结果，嫂子便有一个念头产生——看来人是不能十全十美的，这样一个男子，送子娘娘偏偏忘了点睛，若再添一双星眼，那该如何！

嫂子以为祥没有眼就看不见她，错了，祥是个盲目不盲心的，目盲了，心更明些，明亮的心子使身体各部都可作眼睛来使，有时比有眼睛的人还"看"得真些。

"嫂，推磨吗？"

嫂靠门不动，微微含笑，心说："你怎么知道是我？要不是你嫂呢？"

祥又叫几声不应，觉得应该跟嫂子开一个玩笑了："嫂，你笑啥，你当我看不见你吗，你的眉毛左边跳了右边跳！"

"你多能，你看见我笑了？！"这样说着，又掺进好多的笑，不承认是不行了。

推磨是他俩的事。一张木制圆磨盘，上面放两扇叠起的石磨，下扇起轴，上扇开洞，轴置入洞中，推动上扇转起来，粮食就变成面面儿，雨一般纷纷落下。祥推磨是很来劲的。嫂让他"慢点慢点，不要慌"，意思怕他累着。他塌着腰，偏要往快里推。嫂只得给他讲一个故事，说她娘家时喂过一条狗，是白狗，白狗耳朵特别灵，鼻子特别尖……故事没讲完，祥喜得又是拍胯，又是跺脚，样子很张狂，说嫂子真坏，嫂子要是再坏，就不喊嫂子了，喊她小名凤儿。他给嫂子说一个谜，让嫂子猜：肯吃嘴儿，拉巴腿儿；推小车儿，卖棒槌儿……

推完磨，祥兴头不减，移码调弦，借了胡琴深厚绵长好嗓子，舒舒徐徐，送柔抽丝，把抚慰的情感抒发。三月春风户外飘，柳条摆动，麦苗起伏，塘边的桃花花蕊微微颤动，托春风捎去缕缕清香。

戏班子的琴师村头过，耳朵张了两张，不由驻了足，说声"这是心弦"，进村找到祥，问他可愿入戏班子。祥只是笑。

嫂子早在一旁站着，说："二弟，你去吧。要得欢，跳戏班，你去吧。"

"好，我去。"嘴角漾一点笑。

"去了好。"

琴师日日坐戏台子，却看不破戏台子以外的戏，料定要领走一位新琴师了。祥换了认真神气，说在家清静惯了，生受不起那般作死作活的热闹，抹了师傅的一番美意了。

嫂的儿子成婚时，哥哥携新嫂子回来了。那城里女人的派头是要压倒一切的，及至见了离婚不离家的那位，不免吃了一惊，气焰矮了不少。男人原称家中无妻，骗她入了窠臼，先占后娶，此为一嫌；结婚后，百般耕种，养不下一个孩子，又生一隙。这两口子过得很苦，本要离婚的。眼下心中升起的醋意使她反了常态，在男人跟前嗲声嗲气，撒不尽的娇，卖不完的乖。先前嫁到这家的那位不知底里，眼不见还罢，如今见那夺去她位置的女人轻薄得没有四两，而欺心男人却看她有千斤重，不免有些不平，意气舒展不开。且想到娘家祖传三代医师，救死扶伤，也算是有造化有脸面的人家，自己算什么，人不人，鬼不鬼，怎的就该这般命苦。想痛痛快快哭一场，看见人来客去，双喜红烛，又不敢哭，只强作笑颜，支撑门面。

体念到嫂子苦处的只有一个，是那个没眼睛的人。过道门楼下有一间耳房，耳房是祥的卧室，他不声不响地坐在卧室床边，自认是个多余的。有道喜的人记起他来，说这大喜日子，正该响琴助兴，要他奏一曲"喜鹊登枝"或"百鸟朝凤"。他说松香没了，奏不成。多事的人把琴摘下看过，化香涩弓的地方果然光光的。哥酒足饭饱过来，问他："怎么样？"哥是做了官的，问话的口气难免有一点官方意味，没头没脑。祥说："怎么样呢？"也是一句问。

嫂子盛了好菜，拿了热馍，把筷子递到他手里，让他吃。他说："我不吃，我吃不下。"

嫂说："饿死，也没人可怜你！"

祥直头静耳，作了一个沉思，才慢慢吃饭。刚吃了一口，又说："嫂，你想开点儿。"

嫂没有吭声。

这家的儿子是个木人，脑迟心笨，闷得敲不响。娶回的儿媳却灵透，满眼是水儿。那水儿有风起波，无风映月。儿子多年全然不知不晓的那件事，她到这家不久就觉察到三五分了。夏夜里，人们饭后到塘边歇凉，摇蒲扇，数星星，听一种不可寻的小虫冥冥地唤唱，和白条鱼跃出水面噗通一响。如果这些还不能使人觉得凉爽，祥的琴声会让人忘记热夜一切。如万事万物的一切过程，他奏出的曲调先疏后密，由缓到急，急到一个高峰，又跌下来，趋于平缓，而后归入寂静。比方说，春雨落下来是一滴一滴丁冬，入了溪流，便连成潺潺，汇成江河呢，必定奔腾，咆哮，而后自然是溶入大海，归于万古。有心的儿媳看见，琴声入了"东海"时，穿白市布夏衫在暗柳下单独坐着的那位，便悄悄起身，到过道下那间耳房里去了。好多次都是这样。儿媳还没过了好奇年龄，乐意把自己那点小聪明加以证实，她把那缓急缓的曲调在心里做了个记号，待优美曲调又到那个记号时，她作小孩子游戏，在耳房背人处藏了一个猫猫。藏猫猫的结果使她受了不小的惊吓。事情过去半日，所见所闻愈加清晰，撞得她心头跳荡不止。这媳妇算是胸中有些泾渭的，她没有张扬，且明白这事非同小可，若是外人知道了，于他二人不好，于自己脸上也没多少光彩。

从夏到秋，儿媳妇未免多藏了几次猫猫，每次仍然脸烧心跳。她不会做诗，也不懂音乐，只知那点秘密事情不无动人处，叫人总忘不下，从中领略到除自己以外人生的新意味，生出莫名的快乐和忧愁。那事情拿音乐作前奏，和音乐连起来，难免不笼罩上一些音乐气氛。或者那事情本身就是一个音乐过程。不能不让人生一点歆羡。与此同时，她对自己那一份夜间的事有些懒散，男人全无男儿作为，名分下的事情怯手怯脚，得着了，恨不能一口吃尽，潦草完事，就忘了她的存在。她开始拒绝男人，男人木木讷讷，竟无怨言。她可怜自己没遇上一个好男人，有时说漏了嘴："你还不如一个瞎子！"男人不知哪儿不如瞎子。

一片树叶，一朵花儿，一种音响，或一个符号，若赋予一种叫人心跳的内容，久而久之，这些东西就是心跳的同义语了。后来这家的儿媳再听到那做了记号的曲调，不必再当猫，就心跳，继而迷乱，仿佛手脚也无处安置了。说来还只能算她一时糊涂，一次，曲胡又作让人心跳的美妙召唤时，她知道婆婆为某一件事走得远些，召唤是听不到了，神差鬼使，她竟走到过道下小耳房里去了。

祥挂了曲胡，坐在床边静等，一种不应有的崭新的脚步声和呼吸骇得他脸色陡变，随即问了一声："谁？"声音是严厉拒人的，被怀疑为贼的人才遭到这样问。

站在他面前伸手可触的人不动，不吭，呼吸想均匀而更不均匀一些。

祥往床尾挪了挪，身上开始抖。他攥成拳头，把身子倾下来压在双腿上，抖还是止不住。他只得借助于胡琴。苍白颤抖的手哪适于调琴呢，"嘣！"琴弦断了一股。断了的丝弦卷曲上来，拘挛着，发出幽幽的余音……

当晚，墙上挂曲胡的橛子派了一个新用场，多挂了一个人的脖子。

祥走了，曲胡还留着。曲胡换了一个地方，挂到嫂子床头的墙上去了。

曲胡断了的一股弦再没接上，可曲胡还响。响声只有嫂子才听得见。那曲调先疏后密，由缓到急，急到一个高峰，又跌下来，趋于平缓，而后归于寂静。比方说……

终于有一天，嫂子也取了与祥同样方式走了。

曲胡也不见了。嫂子有一点遗嘱，让儿媳把曲胡放进她棺材里。

1987年2月22日完成于北京静安里

（载1987年8月号）

Quhu

○ *Liu Qingbang*

There are four types of *huqin* in this place: *banhu*, *quhu*, *zhuihu* and *erhu*. What Xiang played was *quhu*. (*Huqin* is a family of bowed string instruments, more specifically, a spike fiddle popularly used in traditional Chinese music.)[1]

Quhu is essentially a hexagonal wooden box with the opening at the bottom, which is previously submerged in tung oil for quite a time to serve as the resonator body or sound body. The box is covered with python skin on the front side and connected with a long and thin dark-colored pole, at the top of which is an exquisite carving of Zhuge Liang's hat (Zhuge Liang, 181–234, a chancellor of the state of Shu Han during the Three Kingdoms period, recognized as the greatest, the wisest and the most accomplished strategist, often portrayed as wearing a round brimmed hat). On both sides of the pole there are fixed some pegs used for setting and adjusting the strings. The sound of *quhu* is not harsh or sharp; instead, it is loud and sonorous with a real profundity.[2]

Quhu is played as an accompaniment to *Quju* (a local opera popular mainly in Henan Province). Xiang was a player with moderate ability, which perhaps could account for the fact that he had never played it on the stage. He was born blind and had never seen the sky and the sun. When he was very young, he was apprenticed to a *quhu* player. His parents hoped that he could grasp a skill so that he could make a living in the future. Nevertheless, his parents didn't know that not all the skills could be obtained through toil and moil. Years of sweat and pain didn't bear fruit: The torn strings and worn poles as a result of his years of practice didn't make him a good player.[3] Later, Xiang's parents died. His brother, who had attended college, divorced his wife and no longer came back home, for he had his new love in the city. As a result, the family was in reduced circumstances. Xiang's playing, nevertheless, went by and by above the ordinary. On an autumn night when the withered leaves were being chased here and there by the wind under the pale moon, his tune, as if weeping and complaining, sounded melodious and touched people's hearts and made them sigh and grieve in a trance. In winter, when the snow fell thick and fast and the whole village turned deathly silent, when the villagers, after many days' hard work, could finally sit down and have a rest, letting their minds wander in the past, Xiang's music rode on the snowflakes and stealthily drifted into their hearts.[4] In tune with Xiang's music, people were carried back to the past. Their hearts flew to a far and farther place. Some women indulged themselves in the overwhelming yearnings for their former lovers or intoxicated themselves in the joys and sorrows of those heartbreaking partings and meetings. Some people, enchanted by his music, were seized with an eager curiosity to go to Xiang's home and have a look at him. No sooner had they got there than they were startled: Xiang was totally absorbed in playing his *quhu*, his back bending forward, his fingers, like birds, fluttering and dancing on the strings, and hot tears trickling down his cheeks. "Xiang, Xiang. What's the matter? Why are you crying?"

He stopped playing and smiled at them, "No, I didn't cry." As he raised his hand and touched the tears on his face, he added in a hurry, "Oh, my eyes always shed tears in the wind." Then, he put his *quhu* aside and began to talk with them about the snow, the wheat and the harvest next year.

When the sky cleared up and the earth in the fields was still too soft to bear a man's feet, villagers like to idle away their time in Xiang's home. One tiptoed into Xiang's room, winking and making gestures to others for fear that they might say something and reveal his presence, and all of a sudden, he hugged Xiang's waist from behind. Accustomed to this sort of playful games, Xiang was always able to guess out who it was, depending on his remarkable memory and his delicate sensitivity. However, to please his guests, he didn't lay bare the answer in a hurry; instead, he named Tom, Dick and Harry at random.[5] Sometimes, it was a guy that hugged him, but he deliberately shouted out a girl's name, which made people burst into laughter. He laughed, too, admitting that he failed and pointing out the reason why he lost the game. It's not my fault! It's yours! You grow taller, plumper and your skin feels smoother! People were very much willing to accept his "blames" in such a way.

Kids liked him, too. They enjoyed playing with him. Unlike most adults, who always felt bored and tired when playing the same games with kids again and again, Xiang never turned kids down. A little girl with tears all over her face, who had been under her parents' reproaches, ran to Xiang and asked, blinking her starry eyes, "What's a flat bean like?"

"It's flat."

"What about a green pea?"

"It's green."

"A hairy soybean?"

"It's hairy."

Xiang answered the little girl affirmatively. However, the little girl had too many questions: What is a pig like? A dog? A cat? Even the sun, the clouds and a flower on top of a wall made the little girl curious. She asked him questions about whatever she saw, and Xiang answered all of her questions patiently, "A Pig is piggish and a dog is doggish and ... the sun ... the sun is sunlike ..." Finding his answers so interesting, the girl laughed and almost rolled on the ground. Xiang also felt funny and happy, "See? You can't beat me!"[6]

When there was nobody around and the ambience became quiet, invariably, Xiang could hear a woman standing quietly nearby. This middle-aged woman must have been beautiful when she was young, for a woman's grace and decorum would never lapse with the passage of time. She still retained her graceful bearing. He could sense it. She was his sister-in-law, his brother's ex-wife. She didn't leave the family for the sake of her son, though she was divorced. When her eyes lingered on Xiang's handsome, beardless face, her eyes went bold with no shame or scruples at all. An idea always occurred to her: Indeed, man cannot be perfect. God even forgot to give him eyes! If only he had a pair of bright eyes!

She thought he was blind and that he couldn't see her, but in fact, she was wrong. His eyes were blind but his heart brighter. Guided by his heart, every part on his body was his eye, so he could see more clearly than those who were not blind.

"Sister, you want me to grind the grain?"

Leaning against the door, she smiled, saying to herself, "How can you know it's me? What if I am not your sister-in-law?"

He called again but got no response. He thought he'd better play a joke on her, "Sister, why are you smiling? You don't think I can see you? I can! I can see your eyebrows twitching, the left one first, then the right!"

"Look at you! You are so capable! You see I am smiling?!" As she said so, she couldn't help smiling. Obviously, he was right.

They did mill-running together. On a wooden round mill, two millstones were stacked, and the upper one had a hole. A stick ran through the hole and worked as an axis. As the upper millstone wheeled, grain was ground into powder and fell down continuously. When they ran the mill, Xiang always went all out. Thinking that he was too tired, she said to him, "Take it easy. Take it easy. Don't be in such a hurry." However, on hearing her words, he, bending his back, pushed even harder. Then, she told him a story. Her family once kept a dog, a white dog whose senses of hearing and smelling were quite acute … Before she finished, Xiang was beside himself with joy, slapping his hips, stamping his feet and putting on an air of excitement and ecstasy. "Sister, you are so bad! I won't call you sister any longer. I'll call your nickname, Phoenix." After that, he told her a riddle and asked her to guess: Fond of eating and walking, it always pushes its small cart, selling wooden clubs … What is it?

After grinding the grain, Xiang was still in high spirit. He took out his *quhu*, adjusted the strings, and began to play. The tender and soothing melodies, imbued with his emotions and affections, permeated the entire room and flew over to the dancing willows, the rippling wheat and the pond beside which the peach blossoms swayed and constantly sent fresh fragrance to the spring wind.

A player in the local theatrical troupe passed by the village and heard it. He stopped and said to himself, "This is the music from the heart." Then, he went to Xiang and asked him if he'd like to join the theatrical troupe. Xiang smiled and said nothing.

The sister-in-law urged, "Brother, you'd better join it. You can give full play to your skills there."

"All right. I'll go." A trace of smile crept up the corner of his mouth.

"Good!"

The player in the theatrical troupe had been playing on the stage for years, but now he couldn't see through the play in front of his eyes. As he was about to bring Xiang back to his troupe, Xiang, abruptly, turned serious and said that he was used to the leisurely life at home and couldn't cope with a clamorous and bustling environment. Xiang made a few polite and regretful remarks to that player.[7]

When Xiang's nephew, the son of his brother, was about to marry, his brother came back with his new wife to attend the wedding. The woman from the city looked overwhelmingly haughty, but the moment she saw her husband's ex-wife, she was startled and her swollen arrogance lessened a great deal. As a matter of fact, the new couple had been bearing grudge against each other. Before they got married, he coaxed her into marrying him, saying that he had no wife at home; after they got married, however hard they tried, she couldn't get pregnant and give birth to a child. Their life got bitter and both of them wanted a divorce. However, now, seeing her husband's ex-wife, the woman was filled with jealousy. She suddenly changed her attitude to her husband, speaking in a honeyed voice and behaving like a spoiled child in front of him. Seeing the woman who had grabbed her place acting in such a frivolous way, the ex-wife turned fretful, and to add more oil to the fire, her ex-husband even took such a worthless woman as his dearest treasure! She felt angry and depressed! She herself was born in a respected family with three generations of doctors who took healing the wounded and rescuing the dying as their duties and who worked well enough to gain fame and prestige for their family, and the thought made her feel even more frustrated! Look at me! What kind of life I am living? How miserable I am! She sighed, hoping to find a place to cry aloud to her heart's content. But in front of so many guests, on such a happy occasion, she couldn't shed a drop of tear; instead, she must force a smile to play her part properly.[8]

Only one person knew her bitterness — that blind man, Xiang, who was silently sitting on his bed in his side room under the gateway. On such an occasion bustling with noise, activity and excitement, he considered himself an unwanted person. At this time, some guests, who came to give their congratulations, thought of him and advised him to play his *quhu* so as to add more happiness to the jolly atmosphere. They asked him to play *Magpies on the Branches* or *Birds Paying Homage to the Phoenix*, but he refused, saying that he couldn't play them without colophony. Some nosy parkers took his *quhu*, had a look at it and found it really in lack of colophony. After a while, Xiang's brother, who had wined and dined to his fill, came and asked Xiang in a more or less bureaucratic tone, "Hey, bro, how are you?" Unable to make head or tail of his question, Xiang answered with a question, too, "How are you?"

His sister-in-law came with tasty dishes and steamed bread. Handing him chopsticks, she asked him to eat. He said, "No, I've no appetite." She said, "Then, you'd better starve to death! Nobody will show pity on you!"

He lowered his head, as if pondering over something. After a while, he began to eat. After just one mouthful, he said, "Sister, you'd better take it easy. Don't be mad at them."

She kept silent.

Her son was slow-minded, numb and dull, while her daughter-in-law, on the contrary, was quite smart and quick, with a pair of eyes sparkling like shimmering water, which rippled in the wind and reflected moon at night. Shortly after she came to this family, she knew something about which her husband, who had been living here for so many years, didn't have the faintest idea. On the summer nights, after supper, people always went to the pond to cool themselves down. They waved their fans, counted the stars, listened to the crickets' chirping and watched the silvery fish jumping up and flopping into the water. To add more fun, Xiang also played there and his music helped drive all the heat away. Like the developing course of all the things on earth, his tune was at first sporadic, scattered and slow, and then it became urgent, anxious and fast-paced; when the tune mounted to a height, it abruptly and sharply fell down; after a while it began to run smoothly and gently, and in the end, it died out in silence. The spring rain, likewise, had the same developing course: At first, it cling-clanged one drop after another into a stream; the stream gurgled and flew into a river; and the river roared and billowed into the great immortal sea.[9] When Xiang was playing, she, his sister-in-law, in a white cotton shirt, sat alone under the willows, listening to his tune attentively. When the tune flowed into the "East Sea", she stood up and quietly walked toward that small side room. For several times, the clever daughter-in-law saw it. She felt curious and anxious to prove her wild guesses. So, the daughter-in-law bore in mind Xiang's slow-quick-slow tune and secretly made a mark in her heart, and when she heard his tune turning to that mark again, she played a hide-and-seek game — she hid herself in some unnoticed place near the side room. She was really taken aback! After a half day, the scene and the sound still lingered in her mind, making her heart beat violently. She was smart and sensible and she didn't tell others what she saw. Telling a tale would lead to the destruction of Xiang and his sister-in-law. She knew it. Besides, she herself might lose face and be considered a disgraceful woman.

However, as if tempted, from summer to autumn, the daughter-in-law played her game many times. Each time, her face blushed and her heart kept beating violently. If only she were able to create poetry or music! She was touched by their "secret thing", so touched that she was obsessed with it even in the daytime. She felt she began to understand and taste something new and fresh in life and an inexpressible feeling of joy or sorrow always welled up in her heart. The "secret thing" began with music and therefore was enveloped in a musical atmosphere. Perhaps it was music itself. Jealousy gradually arose in her heart. By and by, she had less interest in her own "thing" at night, for her man was so timid, not masculine at all. When he did "it", he did it in a rash with no patience, but after he was satisfied, he left her aside, as if she didn't exist at all. Therefore, she began to refuse him on the bed, but to her surprise, he was so numb that he even had no complaint! She couldn't help but start to pity herself, and sometimes she blurted out, "You are no better than a blind man!" At a loss, her husband was left in the dark.

When a meaning powerful enough to set a person's heart throbbing was attached to a leaf, a flower, a sound or a signal, the concrete thing became a synonym of heartthrob. Later, when the daughter-in-law heard the tune which she had marked in mind, she, invariably, felt her heart throbbing wildly, and in the wake of it, she was stupefied and bewildered, not knowing where to put her hands and feet. Once, her brain misted over for a moment. Beckoned by the melodious tune, perhaps at the behest of some supernatural powers, she even walked direct to the side room! In fact, that day, her mother-in-law wasn't home and couldn't hear Xiang's playing at all.

Putting his *quhu* aside, Xiang sat quietly on his bed, listening and waiting. As the footsteps closed, his face suddenly turned pale. The strange steps and breaths at once threw him into panic. "Who's it?" He asked in a rigorous and sharp tone, which was commonly used on a thief.

The one standing right in front of him remained still and silent, and her attempt at steadying her breaths only resulted in the contrary.

Xiang moved his body toward the other end of the bed. His body, all of a sudden, began to tremble. Clenching his fists, he bent forward, trying to put the weight of his whole body on his two legs. However, all his efforts were in vain. Extending his two arms, he turned to his *quhu* for help, but as his shivering and pale hands touched it, one string broke with a "bang". The broken string curled up, its sound lingering in the air …

On that night, the wooden peg on the wall, which was used to hang a *quhu*, was put to a new use — a man hanged himself on it.

Xiang was dead. His *quhu* changed its place. It was hung on the wall beside his sister-in-law's bed.

The broken string was not mended, but Xiang's *quhu* still produced sound, which could only be heard by his sister-in-law. At first, the tune was sporadic, scattered and slow, and then it became urgent, anxious and fast-paced; when the tune mounted to a height, it abruptly and sharply fell down; after a while it began to run smoothly and gently, and in the end, it died out in silence …

One day, his sister-in-law died in the same way as Xiang did.

And that *quhu* disappeared. She made a last will that her daughter-in-law should put that *quhu* into her coffin.

> Jing'an Alley, Beijing
> February 22, 1987
> (Published in No.8, 1987)

 注 释

1. 胡琴是中国特有的民族乐器，包括很多种类。译者在译文中做了适当的注释，以利读者理解，帮助读者了解中国文化。下文中的 "杆首雕出诸葛武侯

顶冠模样"，译者对诸葛亮以及诸葛亮的帽子也做了注释。

2. "曲胡拉起来声音宏大、高亢，但不叫，透着真实的敦厚。"这句话的关键词是"宏大"、"高亢"、"不叫"、"真实的敦厚"。"不叫"就是不刺耳，"真实的敦厚"指声音不造作、深沉、厚重。The sound of *quhu* was not harsh or sharp; instead, it was loud and sonorous with a real profundity.

3. "不想世上有的技艺不是下了苦功就能学到的，琴弦不知锯断多少，琴杆被指头磨出槽坑，琴声竟不能入世，拉不出日月星辰、苦辣酸甜来。"这句比较难翻译，尤其是后半部分，"琴声竟不能入世，拉不出日月星辰、苦辣酸甜来"。汉语讲究铺排，比如我们常说锅碗瓢盆、花鸟鱼虫、日月星辰，等等，这里的"拉不出日月星辰、苦辣酸甜来"就是指"拉不出个滋味来"，"琴拉得不是出神入化"，"拉琴拉得一般"。这里，译者为了行文流畅，组句方便，弱化了后半句的翻译。Nevertheless, his parents didn't know that not all the skills could be obtained through toil and moil. Years of sweat and pain didn't bear fruit: The torn strings and worn poles as a result of his years of practice didn't make him a good player.

4. 这一段中，"家道衰落清苦"、"不同凡响"、"秋叶飘零"、"月白如霜"、"如泣如诉"、"痴痴呆呆"、"嗟叹不已"、"大雪封门"、这些文学色彩较浓的词汇，在汉译英中都是困难，但却是必须传达的东西。试译如下：As a result, the family was in reduced circumstances. Xiang's playing, nevertheless, went by and by above the ordinary. On the autumn night when the withered leaves were being chased here and there by the wind under the pale moon, his tune, as if weeping and complaining, sounded melodious and touched people's hearts and made them sigh and grieve in a trance. In winter, when the snow fell thick and fast and the whole village turned deathly silent, when the villagers, after many days' hard work, could finally sit down and have a rest, letting their minds wander in the past, Xiang's music rode on the snowflakes and stealthily drifted into their hearts.

5. "……他偏不道破，只张三李四地混猜。" ... he didn't lay bare the answer in a hurry; instead, he named Tom, Dick and Harry at random. Tom, Dick and Harry 是英文中的惯用表达，表示"张三李四、某某人"。

6. 以上这段中是主人公取了每个词中的一个字，运用汉语的叠字，逗小孩子说的话，例如：扁豆是扁扁的、绿豆是绿绿的、毛豆是毛毛的、猪是猪猪的、狗是狗狗的、太阳是太太的。在翻译时，译者处理为：A flat bean is flat;

a green pea is green; a hairy soybean is hairy, a pig is piggish; a dog is doggish; a sun is sunlike. 符合原文的写作特点。

7. 汉译英时，要十分注意人称代词。这里的琴师和瞎祥都是男人，人称代词都是 he，分清人称代词的指代，避免歧义非常重要。

8. "自己算什么，人不人，鬼不鬼，怎的就该这般命苦。想痛痛快快哭一场，看见人来客去，双喜红烛，又不敢哭，只强作笑颜，支撑门面。" 汉语的特点是小句多，四个字或六个字即可为一小句，流散铺排，主语随时变化，靠读者意会即可。而英语是形合语言，主语必须清楚，句子内部和句子之间的逻辑关系必须清楚，所以上面这句译为：Look at me! What kind of life I am living? How miserable I am! She sighed, hoping to find a place to cry aloud to her heart's content. But in front of so many guests, on such a happy occasion, she couldn't shed a drop of tear; instead, she must force a smile to play her part properly.

9. "如万事万物的一切过程，他奏出的曲调先疏后密，由缓到急，急到一个高峰，又跌下来，趋于平缓，而后归入寂静。比方说，春雨落下来是一滴一滴丁冬，入了溪流，便连成潺潺，汇成江河呢，必定奔腾，咆哮，而后自然是溶入大海，归于万古。"
这是全文很重要的一段，重复出现两次。既是描写音乐，也是描写万事万物的发展过程，更是描写人的情感发展过程。注意斜体字的翻译：Like the developing course of all the things on earth, his tune was at first *sporadic, scattered and slow,* and then it became *urgent, anxious and fast-paced;* when the tune mounted to a height, it *abruptly and sharply* fell down; after a while it began to run *smoothly and gently,* and in the end, it *died out in silence.* The spring rain, likewise, had the same developing course: At first, it *cling-clanged* one drop after another into a stream; the stream *gurgled* and flew into river; and the river *roared and billowed* into the great *immortal* sea.

干沟

◎ 杨争光

　　没人来这条沟，虽然离村子不远，可没人来。沟里一满是梢林，就是那号不成材的树，叫不出名字，它们长在沟坡上。这会儿，它们没有叶子，成了干巴巴的枝条，勾着，挽着，缠着。站在山包子上，才能看见沟有多长，可站在沟口，就感到不吉利，就感到走进去会出不来，会干死在里面。

　　他进沟的时候就这么想过。那时，他刚拔了几根鼻毛，鼻子里有些空空荡荡。他捏了捏鼻头，朝沟里看了一眼。听不见什么声音。有时候能听见狼叫唤，就叫那么几声，很远，听不出在哪一块。

　　天快亮了。

　　他感到有些冷，他知道天快亮了。天快亮的时候就有些冷。月亮像吊死鬼，在山包子上边忽忽悠悠，他能看见它。他听见那些枝条碰在他的脸上，划拉着，像划拉石头一样，一点也不动心。他用手拨它们。他想它们会把他绊倒，绊倒就起不来了。

　　他们得一会儿才能来。他想他赶天亮还能睡一觉。他拨开一个空隙，顺坡躺下来。他把手垫在头底下，看了一会儿月亮。月亮好像变得亮了些。他看着它，就睡着了。

　　"走。"他说。他看着拉能的后脑勺。拉能是他妹。他看见拉能转过脸，眼向上翻着看他。他们去地质队看电影，他看见拉能坐在塄坎上，一个地质队的人抱着她。地质队有这号人，他们抱这里的女人，他们给她们钱什么的，给

186

她们尼龙袜子。他们的女人在城里，所以他们抱这里的女人。他们在山里找石头，他们说找出他们说的那种石头，这里的人就会发财。他们就是这么一群恬不知耻找石头的人。

他看见地质队那个人在拉能身上摸。拉能眼睛看着电影，不动身子，让那个人摸。后来，她也摸他。拉能不看电影了。

他一直没看电影，因为他一直想着罗子山那个人。上午，他来他们家了。拉能正做饭，他看见拉能给罗子山那个人笑了一下。

他没吃饭，他出去了，他感到肚子里钻了个苍蝇。他到麻贵家窑里和麻贵打赌。麻贵让他吃冻豆腐，麻贵说他吃完就不问他要钱。他看着麻贵得意的脸，恨不得咬麻贵一口。他没吭声，他蹲在麻贵家灶窝里一口一口吃。他听见冰渣渣在他的牙齿上咯噜咯噜响。他感到牙里边像钻了许多虫子，舌头一层一层脱皮。他感到他把舌头上脱的皮一块吃到肚子里了。开始的时候，麻贵看着他笑，后来不笑了，麻贵脸上的皮也像挨了冷冻，和冻豆腐一个样子。他吃完了，吃了三斤。他想他千万不敢抹嘴，他想他一抹，嘴就会掉下来。他从麻贵家窑里出来，在沟底里跑了几个来回。后来，他跑到山包子上，在那里打滚，一直滚到天麻黑。他看见有人去地质队那里看电影，拉能也去了。他想他也去看。

"走。"他对拉能说。

拉能站起来，拍拍屁股上的土。他看见地质队那个人翻眼看他，他听见那人骂了一声：

"他妈的。"

他们骂人就这么：他妈的。

他们朝回走。他们听见有人在黑咕忧里动弹，在那里咬嘴。这地方兴找相好，不相识也能找，拉着辫子一拽就成。这地方民风纯正，女人不怕坏人。这地方没坏人。

"罗子山那人来了。"他说。

"嗯。"拉能说。

"我看见了。"

"嗯。"

"那人看着日脏。"

"嗯。"

"嗯，嗯！"他说。

"你要跟他？"他说。

"嗯。"

"我知道你要跟他。"

他出气的声音很大。他感到鼻眼里有些痒。有几根鼻毛长得太长了，他想他得把它们拔下来。

他们朝回走。那时候，电影还没完。那时候，他没想会出什么事。

大大睡了，听出气的声音就知道他睡了。他是个瞎眼。他们妈一死，他就瞎了眼。大大挨着炕墙，他们在另一头。他们家就一个窑。

"你甭跟罗子山那人。"他说。

"你甭跟。"他说。

拉能不说话。他们听见窗子上的麻纸不停响，没有风，可麻纸不停响。噼啪，噼啪。

"我不让你跟他。"他说。

"我跟他。"拉能说。

"他看着日脏。"他说。

"他说他们那里有麦子面。"拉能说。

"你跟他，你和地质队的人就好不成了。"

"我没跟地质队的人好。"

"他摸你。"他说。

"哥。"拉能叫了一声。他听见她叫了一声。她一叫，他心里就有些高兴。

"你也摸他。"他说。

"哥！"

"我看见了。"他说。他听见拉能拉棉被子，拉能把头往被子里埋。

"他一摸我，我就想摸他了。"拉能说。

"我不嫌你摸。"他说，"你甭跟罗子山那人，我不想让你跟他。"

"我跟他，我都想好了，我给他说了，我都想好了。"拉能说。

"你跟他，你就毁了。"他说。

"我想不来。"

"我知道你想不来。"

"我想不来。"

"我说你要毁了。"

"我可没想。"

他听见拉能睡着了。大大在炕那头翻身，大大出气的声音很粗。大大睡觉咬牙，像牛嚼草一样。有时候就紧咬一阵，像怀着仇恨。

他醒过来，听见有人说话。有人在他头顶上什么地方说话。他听出是他们村上的。

"也不盖上，抬出来也不盖上。"一个说。

"没见过女人的身子，我还没见过。"另一个说。

"都看哩，他娘的都看哩。"

"没流多少血，日怪，身子光光的。"

"就是眉眼难看。人死了就眉眼难看。"

"没，我看做什么。"

"没看你知道。"

"我没看。看你说的。"

拉能把一只胳膊甩过来，甩在他的肚子上。拉能胳膊上有什么味，他很熟悉，一闻见，他就难过，就不自在。他感到他的喉咙里干得厉害。他想把拉能的胳膊放到被窝里，他想放到被窝里他就会好受一些。可他没放，他把拉能的胳膊拉到他脖子底下。拉能醒了。拉能叫唤了一声：

"哥。"

他听见拉能叫他，他不说话，他抱着她的胳膊，他跪在拉能跟前。他感到他想干什么。

"哥，你是畜牲。"拉能说。拉能用手背挡着脸，她哭了。

"哥，你是畜牲。"她说。

他跪在那里，看着拉能。他感到有什么东西正从他的眼睛里爬出来。

他不想用那把刀，可没有更好的东西，他就拿了它，就是拉能切菜用的那把。这是拉能不会知道的。他感到刀很凉。窗上的麻纸一下一下响，没有风，可它一下一下响。

噼啪。噼啪。

"我不想了，"他给拉能说，"我再也不想了。我没办法。拉能你不敢怪我。要不我就是畜牲了。"他说。

他给她盖好被子。被子很烂，有一股呛鼻的汗臭味。他把被子一直盖到她脖子那里，他用手在那里摸了摸。

她被冰凉的刀激了一下，打了一个颤。这是她想不到的。她猛地伸开胳膊，朝他搂过来。他感到身子里有一股力量涌到他的手上，他朝下一压，她就把他抱住了。他感到她抱得很紧。他听见她呻唤了一声。

"拉能，你可不能怪我。"他说。

他把烂棉被往上拥，一会儿，就听见被子里有一种声音，他知道是她脖子里流出来的东西正往被子里边渗。

拉能就呻唤了一声。他记得她就呻唤了那么一声。

"大大。大大。"

他站在炕墙跟前，看着大大。他感到鼻眼里痒把它们拔了。

"嗯！"

他听见那几根鼻毛从肉里出来了，声音很响。那时候天还没亮，没什么响动，所以他听见拔鼻毛的声音很响。

"你甭找我。"他对大大说。

"看你，我一个瞎眼。"大大翻个身，他不停地咬牙。

"他肯定跑了。他钻在这里边做什么。"

那两个人坐着不走。他们坐在他头顶上什么地方，在那里说话。

"我看不一定。"另一个说。

"我尿些，我出来就想尿，都看拉能的光身子，就忘了。"

"你尿，尿么。"

他听见尿尿的声音从上边传下来。他感到喉咙里很难受。

"这沟里有些怕人，"尿尿的说，"我看这沟里有些怕人。"

"沟有什么怕？"

"你不怕？你想想。"

"我看他不会藏在这里边。"

"说不准。"

"我可不想让他把我弄死。你想，他突然出来，就会把我们弄死。"

"你听。"

"是野兔，肯定是野兔。"

他听见他们拨树枝，一会儿就听不见了。他想喊他们，把他们喊回来。是他们村上的，那两个人。他想他们还会来，说不定什么时候会来。

他想错了，后来他就知道他想错了。许多天后，他爬到那两个人说话的地方，那里有一块大石头。他想他们就是在石头上说话的。

他靠着那块石头，他感到他再也没力气爬了。他张着眼窝，想找见那个人尿尿的地方，没找见。他就这么靠着石头，一动不动。后来，他听见两只老鸦落在他的头跟前，翅膀扫着他的脸。他感到它们啄他的眼窝，啄得很重。后来，它们飞走了，他想它们很得意。他感到眼眶里往外流什么东西。那时候，太阳很红，虽然是冬天，太阳还是很红，半天功夫，他的眼眶干了，变成了两个圆坑。

(载1988年6月号)

The Dry Ravine

○ *Yang Zhengguang*

Nobody came to this ravine, though it was not far from the village. Nobody was willing to come. It was fraught with trees which couldn't be used as timber. Nobody knew the name of these trees which grew on the slope of the ravine, bare of leaves now and with only a few naked shafts and limbs, twisting, enwinding and intertwining one another.[1] Standing on top of the hill, one could see how long the ravine was, but at the mouth of the ravine, one couldn't help but be overwhelmed with timidity. The ravine looked ominous and one might die in it — one might be dried to death in it.[2]

He thought the same way when he was about to enter the ravine. He had just pulled off some nostril hair and standing at the ravine mouth, he felt his nose empty. Pinching his nose, he looked down to the ravine. No other sound could be heard, except a few howls of wolves coming occasionally from afar. It was hard to tell where the sound came from.

It was nearly dawn.

He felt a little cold. He knew it was cold at dawn. The moon, like a hanging ghost, was swaying and flickering there on the hill.[3] He could see it. He heard the branches rustling and scraping his face, as if they were scraping a stone, with no mercy at all. Instinctively, he removed the branches for fear that he might trip over them. Once he stumbled and fell down to the ground, he could no longer stand up. He knew it.

They would come in a while. He thought he could have a nap before daybreak. He cleared the branches away and lay down on an open space on the slope of the hill. With his hands under his head, he looked up at the moon, which appeared bigger and brighter. Staring at it, he fell into slumber.

"Leave!" He ordered, glaring at the back of her head. She was Laneng, his little sister. Laneng turned her face and looked at him with her eyes turning upward. When they were watching a film in the geological outpost, he saw a man holding Laneng in his arms. He knew the men in the geological outpost. They often held local women in their arms and in return they gave those women money or nylon socks. Their wives lived in the city, so they resorted to the women here? These men came here to look for rocks and stones and they said that they could make everyone in this place endlessly rich if they found the stones they wanted. Indeed, they were stone-seekers, dead to all feelings of shame.[4]

He saw that man caressing Laneng's body. Laneng was all eyes and ears to the film, motionless, letting his hand wander freely on her body. Later, she turned her eyes off the screen and began to caress the man, too.

He had no mood in seeing the film, for the man from Luozishan Mountain kept haunting his mind. In the morning, the man from Luozishan Mountain came to his home when his sister Laneng was cooking. He saw Laneng smile at that man.

He didn't have lunch and went out, feeling a fly buzzing in his stomach. He went to Magui's home. They made a bet that if he could eat up the frozen beancurd Magui would let him go free of charge. Looking at Magui's complacent face, he felt an impulse to plunge forward and give the man a bite! He didn't say anything. Squatting by the kitchen stove he began to eat the beancurd. The broken pieces of ice creaked and squeaked between his teeth,[5] and he felt that quite a number of bugs were worming into his tongue and making it peel off layer by layer, and that he was chewing and swallowing the beancurd together with those scraps of peeled skin. At the beginning, Magui chuckled, but after a while, Magui's face turned serious and numb like the frozen beancurd. Altogether he ate up one and a half kilograms of beancurd! He didn't dare to wipe his mouth for fear that it might fall to the ground. After he left Magui's home, he ran to and fro at the bottom of the ravine for some time. Then, he ran upward to the hill where he rolled and rolled till it was late and the sky became dark. Noticing that some people were walking toward the geological outpost for the film and that Laneng was among them, he decided to go, too.

"Let's leave." He shouted to Laneng.

Standing up, Laneng patted the dirt off her hips. He saw that man glaring at him in disappointment and heard the man cursing "Damn it".

Damn it! People in the geological outpost always cursed in such a way.

On their way home, they heard people moving and kissing in the darkness. It was popular for men and women here to find intimate lovers even if they didn't know each other. Simply by pulling a girl's plait, a man could find a lover. The people here were simple and unspoiled. Women were not afraid to meet indecent guys, for they thought there were no indecent guys here.

"The man from Luozishan came." He said.

"Er." Laneng answered.

"I have seen him."

"Er."

"He looks lousy.[6]"

"Er."

"Er, er!" He turned a little angry.

"You want to go with him?" He asked.

"Er."

"I know you'll go with him."

He gasped, feeling an itch in his nostrils. A few pieces of nostril hair grew too long and he felt like pulling them off as soon as possible.

The film was not finished. On their way home, he didn't expect what would happen later.

Their father had gone to sleep. From his heavy breath, they knew the old man had fallen asleep. After their mother died, their father became blind. The old man slept on one side of the kang by the wall and Laneng and him on the other side.[7] Their home was actually a small cave.

"Don't go with that man." He picked up the topic again.

"Don't go with him." He emphasized.

Laneng kept silent. The paper on the window frames was pitter-pattering. There was no wind but the paper went pit-a-pat.

"I don't allow you to go with him." He said.

"I'll go with him." Laneng insisted.

"He makes me sick." He said.

"There is wheat flour in his place!" Laneng said.

"But if you go with him, you can't fall in love with the man in the geological outpost."

"I haven't fallen in love with any man in the geological outpost."

"I saw that man having his hands all over your body!" He said.

"Brother!" Laneng groaned at him. Hearing her calling, he felt warm in his heart.

"You have your hands all over him, too."

"Bro!"

"I saw you touching each other." He continued. He heard Laneng pulling up the quilt and burying her head under it.

"He touched me, so I also wanted to touch him." Laneng said in the quilt.

"I don't care if you touched him," He said, "but don't fall in love with that man from Luozishan. I don't want to see you go with him."

"I like him. I've thought it over and I've told him that I've thought it over." Laneng replied.

"You are ruining yourself!"

"I don't think too much."

"I know you don't think too much."

"I don't."

"You are ruining yourself."

"I don't think so."

After a while, Laneng went to sleep. Their father turned over on the other end of the kang, giving out a loud breath. In his sleep, father always ground his teeth like an ox chewing grass, and sometimes he clenched his teeth tightly as if holding deep hatred against somebody.

He woke up and heard some people speaking. Their voices drifted to his ears from somewhere over his head. They were the villagers.

"Her body was not covered when carried out." One said.

"I've never seen a woman's naked body." The other said.

"Damn! They all came to look at her body."

"It was odd that she didn't shed much blood. Her body was clean."

"Her face was ugly. A dead person's face must be ugly."

"No. I didn't look at her."

"If not, how do you know her face was ugly?"

"I didn't."

Laneng swung her arm out of the quilt and put it on his abdomen. Some familiar odor on her arm hit his nostrils. He felt uneasy all over his body, especially in his throat which instantly turned dry and hot. He thought he should put her arm into the quilt and then, he might feel better. But he didn't. Instead, he put her arm under his chin. She was awakened.

"Brother." She called softly.

He kept silent. Holding her arm, he knelt down in front of her, feeling a desire to do something.

"Brother, you are a beast." Laneng said. Covering her face with her hands, she began to cry.

"Brother, you are really a beast." She said.

Kneeling down there, looking at his sister, he felt something was crawling out of his eyes.

He didn't want to use that knife which Laneng often used in cooking, but he couldn't find a better one. Laneng would never know he would use it. In his hand, it felt very cold. The paper on the window kept making noise, even if there was no wind at all.

Pit-a-pat, pit-a-pat.

"I have no way out," he begged. "Forgive me, Laneng. I have no way out. I have to do it, otherwise, I am really a beast."

He covered her with the quilt, which was worn-out and had a pungent smell of stinky sweat. He pulled the quilt up to her neck and fumbled for her neck with his hand.

Startled at the touch of the ice-cold knife, she shivered. It was out of her expectation. All of a sudden, she extended her arms to him. A fit of strength gushed out of his body and flowed to his hand.[8] He pressed her and she embraced him. He felt her hugging him so tightly. He heard her heaving a groan of despair.

"Forgive me, Laneng." He murmured.

He covered her with the tattered quilt. After a while, he heard a sound. He knew something was streaming out of her neck.

Laneng uttered a groan. Only one groan, he remembered.

"Dad, dad."

Standing in front of the kang, he looked at his father. Feeling an itch in his nostrils, he pulled the hair out.

"Whizz!"

Several pieces of nostril hair came out and he even heard the sound, loud indeed. Before the dawn, he was shrouded by a deathly silence except for that sound.[9]

"Don't blame it on me." He said to his father.

"Look at you! I am blind." The old man turned over, grinding his teeth without end.

"He must have fled. What can he do here?"

The two men kept chattering, sitting somewhere near him.

"I don't think so." The other one said.

"At that time, I came out for a piss. When I looked at Laneng's naked body, I even forgot to piss."

"A piss, now?"

He heard one of them passing water ahead. He felt uncomfortable in his throat.

"It's scary here." The pissing man said, "I think it is terribly scary here."

"What are you scared of?"

"Aren't you scared? Watch out for him!"

"It's unlikely for him to hide himself here."

"Hard to say."

"I don't want to die in his hand. If he jumps on us, he will kill us."

"Listen!"

"It's a hare, for sure."

He heard them removing those branches, and after a while, the sound faded away. He wanted to call them back. They must be living in his village and they will come back sometime, he thought.

He was wrong. Later, he knew he was wrong. They didn't come back. After several days, he climbed onto the big rock where the two men chattered.

Leaning against the rock, he felt listless and worn out. With a great effort, he opened his eyes, trying to find out the place where the man pissed, but he didn't find it. So he could do nothing but lean against the rock. Later, he heard two ravens stop before his head, their wings fluttering and touching his face. He knew they were pecking his eyes with greed and zest. And then, they flew away; complacent and contented they must be, he thought. Something flowed out of his eyes. The sun was red. Although it was winter, the sun was bloody red. Soon, his eye sockets turned dry and became two round pits.

(Published in No.6, 1988)

1. "沟里一满是梢林，就是那号不成材的树，叫不出名字，它们长在沟坡上。这会儿，它们没有叶子，成了干巴巴的枝条，勾着，挽着，缠着。"汉语的句子，逗号隔开的小分句很多，译者需要按照句子间的逻辑关系，把它们重新组织成符合英文规范的句子。It was fraught with trees which couldn't be used as timber. Nobody knew the name of these trees which grew on the slope of the ravine, bare of leaves now and with only a few naked shafts and limbs, twisting, enwinding and intertwining one another. be fraught with充满，后面经常跟稍有贬义的词。bare和naked两个词，为的是突出其干巴巴、光秃秃。twist 扭动、弯曲, enwind 缠绕, intertwine 勾在一起，这三个词意思相近，但也不尽相同，放在这里翻译"勾着，挽着，缠着"，勾勒出枝干缠绕的状态。

2. "……可站在沟口，就感到不吉利，就感到走进去会出不来，会干死在里面。" … but at the mouth of the ravine, one couldn't help but be overwhelmed with timidity. The ravine looked ominous and one might die in it — one might

196

be dried to death in it. 为了突出效果，译者加入了one couldn't help but be overwhelmed with timidity。

3. "月亮像吊死鬼，在山包子上边忽忽悠悠……""忽忽悠悠"，晃动的意思，也有时隐时现、时亮时灭的感觉，所以此处翻译为：The moon, like a hanging ghost, was swaying and flickering there on the hill.

4. "他们就是这么一群恬不知耻找石头的人。""恬不知耻"可以翻译为be devoid of all senses of shame, not feel ashamed, be shameless。这里翻译成：Indeed, they were stone-seekers, dead to all feelings of shame. be dead to意思是对……无感觉；be dead to all feelings of shame语气更重一些。

5. "他听见冰渣渣在他的牙齿上咯噜咯噜响。"译为：The broken pieces of ice creaked and squeaked between his teeth…。creak嘎吱声，squeak尖叫声、吱吱声，这两个词用在这里翻译"咯噜咯噜响"，比较合适而且押韵。下文有类似的拟声词："他们听见窗子上的麻纸不停响，没有风，可麻纸不停响。噼啪，噼啪。"The paper on the window frames was *pitter-pattering*. There was no wind but the paper went *pit-a-pat*. "他感到鼻眼里痒把它们拔了。'嘣!'"Feeling an itch in his nostrils, he pulled the hair out. *Whizz!* 拟声词可以生动的描摹声音，最好不要省去不译。

6. "那人看着日脏。"He looks lousy. 在这篇小说中，人物的语言具有地方特色，选用俚语lousy一词翻译，正好可以体现原文风格。lousy意思是"多虱的、糟糕的、脏的"。

7. 中国人的"炕"，英文翻译为kang。kang这个单词已进入英语。从汉语进入英语的词很多，注意积累，例如：kaoliang 高粱 / gingko 银杏 / longan 龙眼 / ginseng 人参 / typhoon 台风 / shanghai 拐骗 / yen 瘾 / Tao 道家学说中神秘的"道"。

8. a fit of 突发一阵(咳嗽、怒气、激情)，一阵阵、阵发。例如：a fit of yawning / a fit of jealousy / a fit of coughing / a fit of anger / a fit of dizziness / a fit of thunder 等等。

9. "他听见那几根鼻毛从肉里出来了，声音很响。那时候天还没亮，没什么响动，所以他听见拔鼻毛的声音很响。"Several pieces of nostril hair were pulled off and he even heard the sound, loud indeed. Before the dawn, he was shrouded by a deathly silence except for that sound. shroud 裹尸布、覆盖，用这个单词是为了渲染气氛。

太白山记（节选）

◎ 贾平凹

寡　妇

一入冬就邪法儿地冷。石块都裂了，酥如糟糕。人不敢在屋外尿，出尿成冰棍儿撑在地上。太白山的男人耐不过女人，冬天里就死去许多。

孩子，睡吧睡吧，一睡着全当死了，把什么苦愁都忘了。那爹就是睡着了吗？不要说爹。

娘将一颗瘪枣塞进三岁孩子的口里，自己睡去，孩子嚼完瘪枣，馋兴未尽又吮了半晌的指头，拿眼在黑暗里瞧娘头顶上的一圈火焰，随即亦瞧见灯芯一般的一点火焰在屋梁上移动，认得那是一只小鼠，倏忽间听到一类声音，像是牛犁水田，又像是猫舔浆糊。后来就感觉到炕上有什么在蠕动。孩子看了看，竟是爹在娘的身上。爹和娘打架了！爹疯牛一般，一条一块的肌肉在背上隆起，急不可耐，牙在娘的嘴上啃，脸上啃；可怜的娘兀自闭眼，头发零乱，浑身痉挛。

孩子嫌爹太狠，要帮娘，拿拳头打爹的头，爹的头一下子就不动了。爹被打死了吗？孩子吓慌了，呆坐起定眼静看，后来就放下心，爹的头是死了，屁股还在活着。遂不管他们事体，安然复睡。

天明起来，炕上睡着娘，娘把被角搂在怀里。却没见了爹。临夜，孩子又看见了爹。爹依旧在和娘打架。孩子亦不再帮娘，欣赏被头外边露出的娘的脚和爹的脚在蹭在磨在蹬，十分有趣。天明了炕下竟又只是娘的一双鞋和他的一双鞋。

又一个晚上，娘与孩子坐上炕的时候，孩子问爹今夜还来吗？娘说爹不会来，永远也不会来了。娘骗人，你以为我没有看见爹每夜来打你吗？娘抱住了孩子，疑惑万状，遂面若土色，浑身直抖。他们守捱到半夜，却无动静，娘肯定了孩子在说梦话，于门窗上多加了横杠蒙头睡去。孩子不信爹不来的，等娘睡熟，仍睁着眼睛。果然爹又出现在炕上。爹一定是要和儿子捉迷藏了，赤着

198

身子贴墙往娘那边挪。爹，这样会冷着身子的！因为爹的头上没有火焰。但爹不说话，腮帮子鼓鼓的。爹在被人抬着装进一口棺木中时口里是塞了两个核桃的。爹，那核桃还没吃吗？爹还是不说话，继续朝娘挪去。孩子就生气了，恨恨爹，继而又埋怨娘，怎么还要骗我说爹永远不会回来呢？孩子想让爹叫出声来，让娘惊醒而感到骗人的难堪，便手在炕头摸，摸出个东西向爹掷去。掷出去的竟是砖枕头，恰砸在爹身子中间的那个硬挺的东西上。娘醒过来。娘，我打着爹了。爹在哪儿？灯点亮了，却没有爹，但孩子发现爹贴在墙上的那个地方上，有一个光溜的木橛。你这孩子，钉一个木橛吓娘！娘在被窝里换下待洗的裤衩，挂在那木橛上。木橛潮潮的，娘说天要变了，木橛上也潮露水。

翌日，娘携着孩子往山坡上的坟丘去焚纸，发现坟丘塌开一个洞。惊骇入洞，棺木早已开启，爹在里边睡得好好的，但身子中间的那个东西齐根没有了。

孩子在与同伴玩耍时，将爹打娘的事说了出来。数年后，娘想改嫁，人都说她年轻，说她漂亮，人却都不娶她。

挖参人

有人家出外挖药，均能收获到参，变卖高价，家境富裕竟为方圆数十里首户。但做人吝啬，唯恐露富，平日新衣着内破衫罩外，吃好饭好菜，必掩门窗，饭后令家人揩嘴剔牙方准出去，见人就长吁短叹，一味哭穷。

此一夏又挖得许多参，蒸晾干后，装一烂篓中往山下城中出售，临走却在院门框上安一镜。妇人不解，他说这是照贼镜，贼见镜则退，如狼怕鞭竹鬼怕明火。妇人奚落他疑神疑鬼，多此一举，他正色说咱无害人之意却要有防人之心，人是识不破的肉疙瘩，穷了笑你穷，富了恨你富，我这一走，肯定有人要生贼欲，这院子里的井是偷不去的，那茅房是没人偷的，除此之外样样留神，那些未晾干的参越发藏好，可全记住？妇人说记住了。他说那你说一遍。妇人说井是偷不去的，茅房没人偷，把未晾干的参藏好。他说除了参，家里一个柴棒也要留神，记住了我就去了。妇人把他推出门，他走得一步一回头。

妇人在家里果然四门不出。太阳亮光光的，照在门框上的镜子，一圆片的白光射到门外很远的地方，直落场外的水池，水池再把圆片的白光反射到屋子来。妇人守着圆片光在屋中坐地，直待太阳坠落天黑，前后门关严睡去。睡去一夜无事，却耽心门框上的镜子被贼偷了，没有照贼的东西，贼就会来吗？翌日开门第一宗事，就去瞧镜子，镜子还在。

镜子里却有了图影。图影正是自家的房子，一小偷就出现在檐下的晾席上偷参，丈夫与小偷搏斗。小偷个头小，身法却灵活，总是从丈夫的胯下溜脱。丈夫气得嗷嗷叫，抄一根磨棍照小偷头上打，小偷一闪，棍打在捶布面上，小偷夺门跑了。妇人先是瞧着，吓得出了一身汗，待小偷要跑，叫道我去追，拔脚跨步，一跤摔倒在门槛，看时四周并不见小偷。觉得奇怪，抬头看镜子，镜子里什么也没有了，一个圆白片子。

又一日开门看镜子，镜子里又有了图影。一人黑布蒙面在翻院墙，动作轻盈如猫。刚跌进院，一人却扑来，正是丈夫。蒙面人并不逃走，反倒一拳击倒丈夫，丈夫就满口鲜血倒在地上。蒙面人入室翻箱倒柜，将所有新衣新裤一绳捆了负在背上，再卸下屋柱上的一吊腊肉，又踢倒堂桌，用镢挖桌下的砖地，挖出一个铁匣，从匣中大把大把掏钱票塞在怀里。妇人看着镜子，心想丈夫几时把钱埋在地下她竟不知？再看时，蒙面人已走出堂屋，丈夫还躺在地上起不来，眼看蒙面人又要跃墙出去了，丈夫却倏忽冲去，双手在蒙面人的交裆里抓，抓住一嘟噜肉了，使劲捏，蒙面人跌倒地上，动弹不得。丈夫将衣物夺了，将腊肉夺了，将怀中的钱票掏了，再警告蒙面人还敢不敢再来偷？蒙面人磕头求饶，丈夫却要留一件东西，拿了剪刀一铰，铰下蒙面人的一只耳朵。遂扯着蒙面人的腿拉出来，把门关了，那只耳朵还在地上跳着动。妇人瞧得心花怒放，没想丈夫这般英武，待喊时，镜子里的一切图影倏忽消失。

以后的多日，妇人总见镜子里有自家的房子，并未有小偷出现，而丈夫却始终坐在房前，威严如一头狮子。妇人不明白这是一面什么镜子如此神奇？既然丈夫在门框上装了这宝物，家里是不会出现什么事故的，心就宽松起来，有好多天已不守坐，兀自出门砍柴，下河淘米。家里果真未有失盗。

一日，开门后又来看镜子，镜子里又有了图影。一人从院门里进来，见了丈夫拱拳恭问，笑脸嘻嘻，且从衣袋取一壶酒邀丈夫共饮。丈夫先狐疑，后笑容可掬，同来人坐院中吃酒。吃到酣处，忽听屋内有柜盖响动，回头看时，一人提了鼓囊囊包袱已立于台阶，一边将包袱中的参抖抖，一边给丈夫做鬼脸，遂一个正身冲出门走了。丈夫大惊，再看时屋后檐处一个窟窿，明白这两贼诡秘，一人从门前来以酒拖住自己，一人趁机从后屋檐入室行窃。急伸手抓那吃酒贼，贼反手将一碗酒泼在丈夫眼上，又一刀捅向丈夫的肚子，转身遁去。丈夫倒在那里，肠子白花花流出来，急拿酒碗装了肠子反扣伤处，用腰带系紧，追至门口，再一次栽倒地上。

妇人骇得面如土色。再要看丈夫是死是活，镜子里却复一片空白。

三日后，山下有人急急来向妇人报丧，说是挖参人卖了参，原本好端端的，却怀揣着一沓钱票死在城中的旅馆床上。

（载1989年8月号）

The Stories of the Taibai Mountain
(Excerpts)

⬤ *Jia Pingwa*

The Widow

The winter came. It was terribly cold, so cold that stones cracked like crisp pastries.[1] People dared not piss outside for the urine would freeze at once and become an icy stick standing erect on the ground. Unlike women, men in the Taibai Mountain couldn't stand the coldness and quite a many died in winter.

Go to sleep, son. After you fall asleep, you'll forget everything unhappy. Has my dad fallen asleep? Don't mention him.[2]

The mother crammed a wizened date into her three-year-old boy's mouth and went to sleep. The boy gnawed at it bit by bit, and after he ate it up, he still felt greedy for food. He had to suck his own fingers for a while. In the darkness, finger in mouth, the boy cast a look at his mother. Over her head, there was a halo of fire, and on the beam a tiny spark of fire, like a lamp-wick, was moving and flickering: It was a mouse, perhaps. All of a sudden, he heard a strange sound — when an ox was plowing in the paddy field or a cat was licking a jar of paste, they produced such kind of sound. Then, he felt something worming and squirming beside him.[3] Watching closely, he saw his father's body, wriggling and wrenching, on his mother's. They were fighting! Like a rampaging bull, his father was in a hurry to attack his mother, gnawing her lips and cheeks, the muscles on his back bunching out into knots. His pitiable mother, closing her eyes tightly, her hair in a mess, was shivering all over with his movement.[4]

Dad is too bad! I'd better help mom. The boy thought. Extending his arm, he gave his father a punch in the head. His father stopped moving. Is dad dead? In panic, the boy sat up, watched his father closely and felt relieved. His father's head was dead and motionless but his buttocks were still alive and kicking[5]. Then, no longer interested in their movement, the child turned around and went to sleep.

When the dawn came, the child found his mother still sleeping, holding a corner of her quilt in her arms, but his father disappeared. The next night, the same thing occurred. His mother and father wriggled and fought again. This time, he didn't help his mother; instead, he had fun in looking at their feet rubbing and kicking and moving outside the quilt. He felt curious and interested. However, when the dawn came, under the bed, he only saw his mother's shoes and his own.

The other night, as the boy and his mother went to bed, the boy asked: Mom, will dad come tonight? No. Your dad won't ever come. Mom, you are lying! I see you two fight every night! Hearing the boy's words, the mother's face turned pale at once and her body began to tremble all over. Holding the boy in her arms, she felt perplexed and terrified. Both of them stayed up till midnight. He must be talking in his sleep! The mother convinced herself. That night, she added a bolt to the door and went to sleep. The boy was not convinced though, and when his mother fell asleep he opened his eyes, waiting for his father. As he expected, his father came again! As if playing hide-and-seek with him, his father moved his naked body to his mother's side. Dad, don't you feel cold? The boy asked, for there was not a halo of fire above his father's head. His father, with cheeks bulging, didn't answer him. The boy remembered that when his father was put into the coffin people crammed two walnuts into his mouth. Dad, dad, you haven't eaten those two walnuts? His father still kept silent and continued moving toward his mother. The boy turned angry. He began to complain about his father and blame his mother. Why do you fool me by saying that dad won't ever come? He wanted his father to produce some sound, so that his mother could be woken up and feel embarrassed and ashamed of her cheating behavior. He fumbled on the bed and touched something. Without hesitation, he picked it up and threw it at his father — it turned out to be the brick pillow and hit smack on something erect in the middle part of his father's body. His mother woke up. Mom, I hit my dad. Where is your dad? His mother lit the lamp. His father disappeared again! The boy found a bare wooden peg on the wall where his father had just leant. Don't frighten me with that peg, son! His mother took off her underpants under the quilt and hung it on that wooden peg. The peg became damp. His mother said the weather was going to change and therefore the peg became wet with dew.[6]

The next morning, his mother brought him to his father's grave on the mountain slope. To their surprise, there was a hole in the mound! Both of them were shocked and terrified. They entered the mount through the hole and found the coffin open! The dead man was lying quietly in the coffin, but that thing in the middle part of his body disappeared!

Later, when he played with his friends, the boy told them how his father fought his mother at night. Years later, his mother wanted to remarry but nobody was willing to marry her, though they all admitted that she was still young and beautiful.

The Ginseng Digger[7]

In the Taibai Mountain there was this family. The husband often went into the mountain to gather medical herbs and each time he was fortunate enough to discover ginsengs. He dug them out and sold them at a high price. By and by, his family became the richest far and near in the village. However, he was a mean person and always afraid of showing his riches. He always ordered his family to dress themselves up in rags. When they had a good meal he always closed the door and all the windows, and after the meal he never forgot to tell his family to pick their teeth and wipe their oily lips before going out. When he met his neighbors he heaved short and long sighs so as to leave on them an impression that his family was indeed in reduced circumstances.[8]

This summer, as before, he dug out many ginsengs in the mountain. He steamed them and dried them up in the air, and after all these procedures, he put them in a basket and planned to sell them on the market in the town at the foot of the mountain. Before he left, he placed a mirror on the top of his door frame. Seeing his queer behavior, his wife got confused. Then, he told her that it was a thief-detector and that seeing the mirror thieves wouldn't dare to enter the house just as wolves ran away from firecrackers and ghosts were afraid of bright light from a fire. His wife teased him and thought he was too suspicious and had too many unnecessary worries! Why take the trouble to do that? She asked. He turned serious at once. We harbor no ill intentions against others but should never relax vigilance against evil-doers. People's hearts are unfathomable and it's hard to tell what's going on in their minds. If you are poor, they mock at you; but if you are rich they inevitably hold grudge against you.[9] After I leave, I am sure someone will cast greedy eyes on our house. Except the well and the latrine in our yard which nobody can steal, you must keep close watch on all the other things in our house, especially those ginsengs undried. You must bear in mind my words! His wife nodded obediently. OK, repeat what I said! She repeated: The well cannot be stolen; the latrine cannot be stolen; and stow away the ginsengs undried. He hastened to add: Not only ginsengs but also all the other things! You must keep an eye on everything, even a piece of firewood! Now I am leaving. Growing a little impatient, his wife pushed him out. He walked away, casting backward glances from time to time, misgivings still lurking in his mind.[10]

Since he left, his wife stayed at home all day long. The sun shone onto the mirror and a round beam of bright white light shot far onto the surface of the pond outside the yard. And the water surface reflected the white light back to the room. She sat in the room, accompanied by the white light, till sunset. After it got dark outside, she bolted the front and back doors and went to bed. When the dawn came, the first thing she did in a hurry was to look at that mirror for fear that it might have been stolen. Without the mirror, will thieves come? She wondered. The mirror was there.

But she saw something in the mirror — in her yard, a thief was stealing ginsengs on the sun-drying mat under the eaves; her husband rushed to fight the thief who was small but agile in action; seeing the abhorrent thief slipping under his legs, her husband turned furious; shouting in exasperation, her husband picked up a thick stick and tried to hit the thief in the head; the thief dodged nimbly and the stick fell on a piece of pounding cloth; and in the end, the thief ran out of the yard. The scene in the mirror indeed frightened her! Cold sweat broke out all over her body. As the thief was about to escape, she shouted: I'll catch him! But to her dismay, she fell upon the doorsill. Seeing around, she found nobody was there. Greatly puzzled, she raised her head and looked at the mirror. It was just a round white disc hanging on the door frame. Nothing was in it!

Another day, she saw the images in the mirror again. A man whose face was covered by a piece of black cloth jumped over the wall like a nimble cat. As he just set foot on the ground, a man plunged at him. It was her husband! Instead of fleeing away, the masked thief dealt a punch on her husband. Her husband fell onto the ground, blood all over his mouth. The masked thief broke into the room and rummaged through chests and cupboards. He tied up all the new clothes into a bundle and carried it on his back, grabbed a preserved ham off a hook, kicked down the table, dug out an iron box from the brick floor under the table, took out the money from the box and crammed it into his coat. As she looked, she couldn't help but wonder when her husband put aside so much money under the brick floor. At this time, the masked thief was hurrying out of the room. Her husband lay there still. As the masked thief was about to jump over the wall and escape, her husband, all of a sudden, sprang up and dashed to him. He clutched something fleshy in the masked thief's pants and pinched it with all his force. The masked thief fell to the ground and couldn't move. Her husband took back the clothes, the preserved ham and the money, and warned the thief: Dare you come again? The masked thief cried for mercy. Her husband cut off one of the masked thief's ears with scissors, pulled him by his leg, threw him out of the yard and shut the door. Looking at the ear which was still bouncing on the ground, she was elated with satisfaction. You are so brave, honey! As she opened her mouth, all the things in the mirror disappeared at once![11]

In the following days, she always saw the images in the mirror: Her husband was sitting in front of their house, as awe-inspiring as a lion. She had no idea why the mirror had such a mysterious and magical power. Since her husband put it there, it must be very useful. With that thought in mind, she felt a great relief. She went out to cut firewood or wash rice by the river, no longer staying at home all day long. Nothing bad happened to her house.

One day, when she opened the door in the morning, she saw the images again in the mirror: A man walked into the yard. At the sight of her husband, he smiled and greeted her husband in a very deferential manner. He took out a pot of wine and sincerely invited her husband to have a drink. Her husband was alert and bewildered at first, but after a while, he accepted the invitation and they began to drink together in the yard. While drinking excitedly, her husband heard some noise in the room — someone was moving his cabinets and chests. After a short while, a man holding a bulging package appeared on the stairs. The man jerked the package full of ginsengs, made a grimace at her husband and rushed out. Greatly shocked, her husband looked at the house closely. There was a big hole on the back eaves! He came to realize that the two thieves must work hand in glove. One invited him to drink so as to confuse him and the other took the opportunity to steal into the room through that hole. Recovering from his astonishment, her husband intended to catch the one who was drinking with him, but to his surprise, that man splashed a bowl of wine onto her husband's eyes and stabbed him in the stomach. Her husband fell onto ground, his guts flowing out. Putting a bowl onto his stomach to prevent his guts from going out any more and fastening his stomach with a belt, her husband stood up and tried to chase the man who had already fled away. But at the door of the yard, her husband fell down again.

Her face turned ghastly pale as she saw all these.[12] When she recovered from her shock and fixed her eyes upon the mirror, trying to see whether her husband was dead, all disappeared.

Three days later, someone from the town hurried to her with the bad news of her husband's death. He sold all his ginsengs and all was well, yet he was later found dead on the hotel bed, a pile of money in his bosom.

(Published in No.8, 1989)

1. "一入冬就邪法儿地冷。""邪法儿"属于方言，即"非常"之意，此句译为：The winter came. It was terribly cold, so cold that stones cracked like crisp pastries. 译文用terribly cold, so cold that …来强调"邪法儿地冷"。

2. 《寡妇》这篇小说，总的来说是以第三人称的视角讲述的，但是主人公"母亲"和"孩子"的对话全都穿插在叙述中，没有直接引语的引号提示。为了与原文风格对应，译文中对话部分也全都没有引号，对话穿插在故事的讲述中。小说的叙述采用过去时态，人物的对话则采用说话时相应的时态。

3. "后来就感觉到炕上有什么在蠕动。"Then, he felt something worming and squirming beside him. worm 像虫子一样爬行，squirm 蠕动、扭动身体。

4. 以上这段是"孩子"的所见所闻，写得隐晦、含蓄，译文要把这种风格表现出来。

5. alive and kicking 这是一个固定短语：活着、活跃、活蹦乱跳。

6. 以上这段，在故事的叙述中，穿插着母亲与孩子的对话，穿插着孩子的所见和回忆。原文为口语化的句子，叙述比较琐碎。翻译时，要注意时态的变化，便于读者理解哪里是故事的讲述(过去时态)，哪里是人物的对话或心理活动(相应的时态)。同时，注意人物的语气，孩子的话要符合儿童的语言特点。另外，译文没有在整合句子上太下功夫，这是为了保持原文的叙述特点。

7. 《挖参人》这篇小说，同样也是第三人称叙述，其中也是穿插了大量人物对话，没有直接引语的引号提示，译文也没有用引号，读者可以从人称和时态的变化上判断出哪里是对话，哪里是故事的叙述部分。

8. "……见人就长吁短叹，一味哭穷。"When he met his neighbors he heaved short and long sighs so as to leave on them an impression that his family was indeed in reduced circumstances. 此处用的in reduced circumstances 意为家道中落、家境贫寒等。

9. "……咱无害人之意却要有防人之心，人是识不破的肉疙瘩，穷了笑你穷，富了恨你富……"We harbor no ill intentions against others but should

never relax vigilance against evil-doers. People's hearts are unfathomable and it's hard to tell what's going on in their minds. If you are poor, they mock at you; but if you are rich they inevitably hold grudge against you. 这里"害人之意"、"防人之心"等中国人常用的词，可以选择英语中合适的词组传达其意。

10. "他走得一步一回头。"一步一回头，既有动作，也有不放心的意思。He walked away, casting backward glances from time to time, misgivings still lurking in his mind. 后半句是译者加上的。misgiving 是"忧虑、顾虑、恐惧"，lurk 是"潜在、潜伏"之意。

11. 丈夫与蒙面人搏斗的场面，最重要的是动作的描写，所以这段中，所有动词的使用尽量做到准确、生动。

12. "面如土色"表示脸色因害怕惊惧而苍白、没有血色，译为ghastly pale。

小说（节选）

◎ 汪曾祺

明白官
（出《聊斋志异》）

《聊斋志异·郭安》记的是真人真事，不是鬼狐故事，没有任何夸张想像，艺术加工。

孙五粒有个男佣人。——孙五粒原名孙秠，后改名柏龄，字五粒。孙之獬之子，孙琰龄之兄，明崇祯六年举人，清顺治三年进士。历任工科、刑科给事中，礼部都给事中，太仆寺少卿，迁鸿胪寺卿，转通政使司左通政使。孙家一门显宦，又是淄川人，和蒲松龄是小同乡。在淄川，一提起孙五粒，是没有人不知道的，因此蒲松龄对他无须介绍。但是外地的后代的人就不知孙五粒是谁了，所以不得不噜苏几句。——这个男佣人独宿一室，恍恍惚惚被人摄了去。到了一处宫殿，一看，上面坐的是阎罗王。阎罗看了看这男佣人，说："错了！要拿的不是此人。"于是下令把他送回去。回来后，这男佣人害怕得不得了，不敢再一个人住在这间屋子里，就换了个地方，住到别处去了。

另外一个佣人，叫郭安，正没有地方住，一看这儿有空屋子空床，"行！这儿不错！"就睡下了。大概是带了几杯酒，一睡，睡得很实。

又一个佣人，叫李禄。这李禄和那被阎王错勾过的男佣人一向有仇，早就想把这小子宰了。

这天晚上，拿了一把快刀，到了空屋里，一看，门没有闩，一摸，没错！咔嚓一刀！谁知道杀的不是仇人，是郭安。

郭安的父亲知道儿子被人杀了，告到当官。

当时的知县是陈其善。

陈其善是辽东人，贡士。顺治四年任淄川县知县。顺治九年，调进京，为拾遗。那么陈其善审理此案当在顺治四—九年之间，即1647–1652，距现在差不多三百三十年。

陈其善升堂。

原告被告上堂，陈其善对双方各问了几句话。李禄供认不讳，是他杀了郭安。陈其善沉吟了一会，说："你不是存心杀他，是误杀。没事了，下去吧。"郭安的父亲不干了，哭着喊着："就这样了结啦？我的儿子就白死啦？我这多半辈子就这一个儿子，他死了，我靠谁呀？"——"哦，你没有儿子了？这么办，叫李禄当你的儿子。"郭安的父亲说："我干嘛要他当我的儿子呀？——我不要，不要！"——"不要不行！退堂！"

蒲松龄说：这事儿奇不奇在孙五粒的男佣人见鬼，而奇在陈其善的断案。

（汪曾祺按：孙五粒这时想必不在淄川老家。要不然，家里奴仆之间出了这样的事，他总得过问过问。）

济南府西部有一个县，有一个人杀了人，被杀的那人的老婆告到县里。县太爷大怒，出签拿人，把凶犯拘到，拍桌大骂："人家好好的夫妻，你咋竟然叫人家守了寡呢！现在，就把你配了她，叫你老婆也守寡！"提起朱笔，就把这两人判成了夫妻。

济南府西县令是进士出身。蒲松龄曰："此等明决，皆是甲榜所为，他途不能也。"——这样的英明的判决，只有进士出身的官才作得出，非"正途"出身的县长，是没有这个水平的。

不过，陈其善是贡生，不算"正途"，他判案子也这个样子。蒲松龄最后赞叹道："何途无才！"不论由什么途径而做了官的，哪儿没有人才呀！

1991年7月4日

牛飞
（据《聊斋志异》）

彭二挣买了一头黄牛。牛挺健壮，彭二挣越看越喜欢。夜里，彭二挣做了个梦，梦见牛长翅膀飞了。他觉得这梦不好，要找人详这个梦。

村里有仨老头，有学问，有经验，凡事无所不知，人称"三老"。彭二挣找到三老，三老正在丝瓜架底下抽烟说古。三老是：甲、乙、丙。

彭二挣说了他做了这样一个梦。

甲说："牛怎么会飞呢？这是不可能的事！"

乙说："这也难说。比如说，你那牛要是得了瘟，死了，或者它跑了，被人偷了，你那买牛的钱不是白扔了？这不就是飞了？"

丙是思想最深刻的半大老头，他没十分注意听彭二挣说他的梦，只是慢悠悠地说："啊，你有一头牛？……"

彭二挣越想越嘀咕，决定把牛卖了。他把牛牵到牛市上，豁着赔了本，贱价卖了。卖牛得的钱，包在手巾里，怕丢了，把手巾缠在胳臂上，往回走。

走到半路，看见路旁豆棵里有一只鹰，正在吃一只兔子，已经吃了一半，剩下半只，这鹰正在用钩子嘴叼兔子内脏吃，吃得津津有味。彭二挣轻手轻脚走过去，一伸手，把鹰抓住了。这鹰很乖驯，瞪着两只黄眼珠子，看着彭二挣，既不鸹人，也没有怎么挣蹦。

彭二挣心想：这鹰要是卖了，能得不少钱，这可是飞来的外财。他把胳臂上的手巾解下来，用手巾一头把鹰腿拴紧，架在左胳臂上，手巾、钱，还在胳臂上缠着。怕鹰挣开手巾扣，便老是用右手把着鹰。没想到，飞来一只牛虻，在二挣颈子后面猛叮了一口，彭二挣伸右手拍牛虻，拍了一手血。就在这功夫，鹰带着手巾飞了。

彭二挣耷拉着脑袋往回走，在丝瓜棚下又遇见了三老，他把事情的经过，前前后后，跟三老一说。

三老甲说："谁让你相信梦！你要不信梦，就没事。"

乙说："这是天意。不过，虽然这是注定了的，但也是咎由自取。你要是不贪图外财，不捉那只鹰，鹰怎么会飞了呢？牛不会飞，而鹰会飞。鹰之飞，即牛之飞也。"

半大老头丙曰：

"世上本无所谓牛不牛，自然也即无所谓飞不飞。无所谓，无所谓。"

1991年7月8日

（载1992年1月号）

New Literary Sketches

(Excerpts)

⊙ Wang Zengqi

The Wise Officials
(Based on *Strange Tales from a Lonely Studio*)

Instead of a ghost story, *Strange Tales from a Lonely Studio — Guo An* was a true story involving real people and events, with no imaginative exaggeration or artistic embellishment at all.

Sun Wuli had a manservant. — *Sun Wuli successfully passed the imperial examination at the provincial level in the sixth year under the reign of Emperor Chongzhen of the Ming Dynasty (1633) as well as the highest imperial examination in the third year under the reign of Emperor Shunzhi of the Qing Dynasty (1646), and took various important government positions successively.[1] The Sun family, as a result, was rich and influential. He shared the same hometown with Pu Songling (the author of Strange Tales from a Lonely Studio)[2]. In their hometown Zichuan, Sun Wuli was well-known, so Pu Songling didn't say too much about Sun in his book. However, the descendants living outside Zichuan might not know about Sun, and I have to say a few words about him here.* — One day, this manservant was alone in his room. In a daze, he felt he was brought away by someone to a palace. Looking up, he saw the King of Hell sitting there. The King of Hell took a look at him and said, "It's wrong! He's not wanted here." Then, the servant was sent back. After he came back, he was so frightened that he didn't dare to live in the room alone and quickly moved out.

Another manservant Guo An, who was looking for a place to live in, saw the empty room with great delight, "OK! It's good to live here!" He moved in. At night, he quickly fell asleep. Perhaps he had had some wine and he slept soundly.

Li Lu, still another manservant, wanted to kill that manservant who was sent

211

back by the King of Hell, due to years of grudge and hatred.

As the night fell, holding a sharp knife, Li Lu felt his way into the room.[3] The door wasn't bolted. He came into the dark room. Chop! He didn't know that he killed the wrong person — Guo An.

Guo An's father learnt that his son was killed and went to the yamen to lodge a charge.

The county magistrate Chen Qishan opened a court session.

Chen Qishan's hometown was in the east of Liaoning. He had also passed the imperial examination and in the fourth year under the reign of Emperor Shunzhi of the Qing Dynasty (1647) he was appointed the county magistrate of Zichuan. In the ninth year under the reign of Emperor Shunzhi of the Qing Dynasty (1652) he was transferred to the capital and appointed a junior advisory position. Namely, the time when Chen Qishan dealt with this case was between 1647 and 1652, approximately 330 years ago.

The court trial started —

The plaintiff and the defendant were brought to the court. Chen asked both of them several questions. Li Lu admitted that he killed Guo An. Chen kept silent for a while and said to Li, "You didn't kill Guo An on purpose. You killed him by accident. OK, you may go." Guo An's father felt wronged and cried, "How can you end the case in such a haste? This is injustice for my dead son. I have only one son and he met such an untimely end! And in the future whom can I rely on?" "Oh, indeed, you lost your son," said the magistrate, "You may as well take Li Lu as your son." "How can I take him as my son! No, no!" "It is a must! The case is closed!"

— Pu Songling said: The absurdity of the case lies not in the trip to Hell of Sun Wuli's manservant but in Chen Qishan's way to settle the lawsuit.

(*The author's note: I think at this time Sun Wuli was not home, otherwise he would come up to say something. After all, this case involved his servants.*)

In a county west of Jinan Prefecture, a man was murdered. His wife filed a suit. After listening to the woman's sobbing complaint, the county magistrate got furious and had the murderer caught and brought to the court at once. Pointing at the murderer, the magistrate bawled out, "How dare you ruin such a good couple's life! As it is you who made this pitiable woman a widow, you'd better marry her and let your own wife become a widow!" Holding up his red brush-pen, he passed a sentence that the murderer and the woman were to be husband and wife.

— This magistrate had also successfully passed the imperial examination. "Only a government official of such honorable origin could make such a wise judgment." Pu Songling commented. — Magistrates without such "honorable origin" could never have such good sense of judgement. However, Chen Qishan had no such "honorable origin" but he was still capable

enough to make the proficient and wise judgment. No wonder Pu Songling couldn't help exclaiming in admiration, "There are so many ways to become a wise and capable official!"[4]

— July 4, 1991

The Flying Ox
(Based on *Strange Tales from a Lonely Studio*)

Peng Erzheng bought an ox. The ox was very strong, and Peng was happy with that. One night, he had a dream: His ox grew wings and flew away. He suspected that this dream was not auspicious, so he wanted to find someone to help interpret his weird dream.

In the village, there lived three aged and knowledgeable men, who were called "the Three Elders". Peng Erzheng decided to turn to them for help. When the Three Elders A, B and C were smoking and chatting under the gourd trellis, Peng walked to them.

He told them his dream.

Elder A said, "How can an ox fly? Stuff and nonsense!"

Elder B said, "It's hard to say. If one's ox catches some disease and dies, or if it is stolen, the money spent on it is wasted, which means the ox is flying away. Am I right?"

Elder C, who was actually not that old but had the most profound thoughts among the three, said slowly, "Ah, you have an ox? ..." Obviously, he hadn't listened to Peng attentively.

Peng Erzheng got more confused and the more he thought about his dream, the more uneasy he became. In the end, he decided to sell the ox. He led it to the market and sold it at a low price. For fear of losing the money, he wrapped it in a towel and tied the towel around his arm. After all these done, he hastened home.

On his way, he saw a hawk eating a rabbit at the roadside. It had finished half of the rabbit and was happily gnawing at the entrails with its hooked beak. Peng tiptoed toward it. Extending his arm, he caught the hawk easily. The hawk was quite docile and didn't peck at his hand or struggle at all. Its yellowish eyes just kept staring at him.

"If I sell it, I may get a tidy sum of money, which is really an unexpected gain!"[5] He said to himself. Then, he untied the towel from his arm and fastened the hawk's leg with one end of the towel. Thus, the hawk and the money were both fixed by the towel. He held the hawk firmly with his right hand lest it should break loose and fly away. As he was elated with his arrangement, all of a sudden, a gadfly stopped on

213

the back of his neck and gave him a fierce sting. He at once held up his right hand in an attempt to pat it, only to find some blood on his palm. Right at this moment, the hawk escaped and flew away with his towel and money.

With a drooping head, Peng Erzheng shuffled his way back in great depression. On his way, he saw the Three Elders again. He told them what had happened to him in detail.

Elder A said, "Why do you believe in a dream! If not, everything is OK."

Elder B said, "This is Heaven's will. However, although it was destined to be like this, you still had your own fault. If you had not been greedy, if you had not caught that hawk, things would not have been like that. You know, an ox cannot fly but a hawk can. The hawk flies away, which means your ox flies away."

Elder C said, "In this world it doesn't matter whether an ox is an ox, let alone it flies or not. It doesn't matter. Nothing matters."[6]

July 8, 1991
(Published in No. 1, 1992)

1. "明崇祯六年举人，清顺治三年进士。历任工科、刑科给事中，礼部都给事中，太仆寺少卿，迁鸿胪寺卿，转通政使司左通政使。"小说题目叫《明白官》，这些官都是通过了正式的科举考试才拥有了一定官职的，但是判案却是如此草率可笑，明白官实则不明白。小说的讽刺意味即在于此。译者对"举人"、"进士"都进行了翻译，目的是为了让读者了解人物的出身背景，这直接关系到小说的讽刺意义。但是对于中国古代特有的复杂的官职名，译者没有逐一翻译，而是简单处理为took various important government positions。

全句译为He successfully passed the imperial examination at the provincial level in the sixth year under the reign of Emperor Chongzhen of the Ming Dynasty (1633) as well as the highest imperial examination in the third year under the reign of Emperor Shunzhi of the Qing Dynasty (1646), and took various important government positions successively.

中国是一个历史悠久的国家，中国的官制有特殊性，官职称谓也很复杂。在翻译官职称谓时，主要采用以下几种方法。一是意译："州县官儿虽小，事情却大" A district magistrate may not rank too high yet he has a lot of work to do...（杨宪益、戴乃迭译《红楼梦》）二是直译："有六宫都太监夏老爷来降旨。" His Excellency Xia, Chief Eunuch of the Six Palaces, has come with a Decree from the Emperor! (杨宪益、戴乃迭译《红楼梦》）三是释义翻译："不过几年，升了兵部侍郎，兵部尚书。" ... in another few years, becoming Vice-Minister of Civil Affairs and Minister of War. (杨宪益、戴乃迭译《红楼梦》）四是音译加意译："当下安插既定，谁知保龄侯史鼎又迁委了外任大员，不日要带了家眷去上任。" Barely had the newcomers settled in than Shi Ding, Marquis of Baoling, was transferred to a provincial governorship. In a few days he would be taking his family to his new post. (卢红梅《华夏文化与汉英翻译》21–35页）

2. 对《聊斋志异》作者蒲松龄应该加以简单的注释。小说结尾还有蒲松龄的批注，所以这里一定要加以说明。

3. feel one's way 摸索前进。英语里有好多这样的表达，生动形象。例如：worm one's way / snake one's way / fight one's way / elbow one's way / grope one's way，等等。

4. "蒲松龄最后赞叹道：'何途无才！'不论由什么途径而做了官的，哪儿没有人才呀！" "何途无才" 的后面，是对这四个字的白话文解释。译文直接译出 "何途无才"，后面就省去不译了。No wonder Pu Songling couldn't help exclaiming in admiration, "There are so many ways to become a wise and capable official!"

5. "……能得不少钱，这可是飞来的外财。" I may get a tidy sum of money, which is really an unexpected gain! 译文中 a tidy sum 相当巨大的款项，相当一笔钱；an unexpected gain 发横财，意外的收获。

6. "世上本无所谓牛不牛，自然也即无所谓飞不飞。无所谓，无所谓。" In this world it doesn't matter whether an ox is an ox, let alone it flies or not. It doesn't matter. Nothing matters. whether 后面的句子里，动词是肯定形式还是否定形式，意思都是一样的。

寂静

◎ 李锐

　　从浓密的林子里一走出来，他就看见那棵山核桃树了。耀眼的太阳底下，黑绿的核桃叶一闪一闪的，又高又厚的树冠好像一个安详饱满的大草垛，让你觉得这漫山遍野的草木都是它生出来的，都是它的儿女。看见这棵老树，最后的一点担心也没有了，心里头一下子变得又踏实又宽敞。隔着浓浓的草香味儿和一道静静的山水，还能看见老核桃树身后那些坍塌的断墙。密匝匝的蒿草和荆棘从里到外紧紧地逼着它们，石头的断墙七零八落地在荆棘和蒿草中挣扎着，高举着自己眼看就要被淹没的身体。那道清亮的山水从绿墙一样的林木里抽出来，又隐没在绿墙的缝隙和根须之间。如果不是偶尔有落在水面上的树叶漂过，你就看不出它在流。长年没人走，过水的踏石早就看不见了。他弯下身去打算解开鞋带，脱下球鞋和袜子。等到拉开一只绳扣又停住了，嘴角上露出一丝自嘲的微笑，随后，他在浓浓的草香味儿里直起腰来，就那么穿着球鞋踩进清澈的山水里，随着泛起的泥沙和青苔，一个冷战从脚心一下子沁凉地穿透了身体。他停下来深深地吸了一口气，听见汨汨的流水声被远远地闷在枝叶后边。接着，又听见有只啄木鸟在树干上敲打起来，的的的、的的的……把身边的寂静敲打得又辽远，又空阔。他不由得在心里感慨，这地方真清净呀……然后，又感慨，这地方真是清净呀……

　　趟着清水和青草，过河，上坡，沿着几乎被野草埋没的小路，走过两条石头垒的地塄，再上坡，一只山鸡拖着长长的花尾巴扑愣愣地从脚下飞向河对岸，消失在自己刚刚经过的林子里。快走近老核桃树的时候，又有几只野兔闪着白白的屁股窜进草丛里。看见兔子们那份没有必要的慌张，他由衷地笑起来，看把你们吓的，跑啥呀跑，我又没带枪，我又不是豹子，我又不是当官的，我又不想吃你们……对着兔子们说完这些话，他转回身去，顺着山谷把视线放到很远很远的地方。在那儿，黑绿的林子罩在浅浅的山岚里，变成了蒙蒙的灰蓝色。七年前，因为祈雨引起来的那场山火烧毁了下面老林沟里的林子。七年过去了，还是能看见被火烧过的痕迹，大树都没有了，焦黑的山体会突然从低矮的枝叶间暴露出来。雨倒是真祈来了，可那场大火烧死了二罚和毛妮儿，那场大火还把荞麦、臭蛋和张老师送进了监狱。如果没有那场大火，就没有后来这六年的官司。现在，开发公司种香菇的塑料棚子都被捣毁了、割破了，两边动手打了架，公安局来抓了人，可也再没有人往山上种树了，农户们攥着那张叫乡政府废了的合同，谁也说不清乱流河乡政府会不会把过了火的林子再卖一遍。那些焦黑的石头成了村民们心头上的伤疤，压得人六七年喘不过气来。空荡荡的山谷里只有这些空荡荡的灰蓝的雾气。很少看见有鸟飞起来。乌鸦和喜鹊们都吃了拌了农药的种子，山上山下的庄稼人都给种子拌农药，年年拌，年年吃，吃得一只乌鸦和喜鹊也没剩下，多少年了都看不见它们了。现在每年到播种的时候，地里只剩下牛和人，原来满地追着飞的鸟们一只也没有了。豁开的犁沟里黄灿灿的种子撒下去，回头一看空空荡荡的，一只鸟也没有，大太阳底下就剩下受苦的牛和受苦的人。伴着汗珠子掉到地上的只有影子，牛影子和人影子。谁也说不清，那么多飞来飞去唧唧喳喳的鸟们最后都飞到哪儿去了。总不能都吃了农药，都毒死了吧？天底下总有不拌农药的地方吧？总有个让人活的地方吧？虽说天下乌鸦一般黑，可天下的老百姓也总得想办法活呀？总不能因为乌鸦黑老百姓就都得死绝了吧？你乱流河的乌鸦黑，还有县里，县里乌鸦黑还有省里，省里乌鸦黑还有北京，北京乌鸦黑还有联合国，联合国乌鸦黑还有如来佛、还有老天爷，总得找个说理的地方……这么想着，他脸上又露出来自嘲的微笑，你一大清早离开五人坪，急急慌慌赶了二十里山路，来到南背的大山上，找到这个叫七里半的荒村子，找到这棵老核桃树，哪是为了说理呀？离开家门的时候就是担心一件事情，就是猜不准老核桃树到底还在不在了，猜不准它到底是死了还是被人砍了。老核桃树要是不在了，事情就不好办了，自己这二十里的山路就白走了。这些日子只要往炕上一躺，心里就翻腾以前的事情，一件一桩记得清清楚楚的。三十年前，自己从部队上复员回来和春香订了婚，动工盖新房的时候，就是在南背的大山上找到了三根大梁的木材。有一回上山砍树，自己穿了部队上发的黑塑料凉鞋、白丝光袜子，可塑料鞋底在羊胡子草上滑得站不住，差点把自己摔死在山坡上。舅舅一边给自己包伤口，一边在耳朵边上骂，就烧死你个龟孙吧就！进山剁树也要穿上洋鞋洋袜子，五人坪就装不下你个狗日的啦！一伙年轻人围在自己身边唧唧咕咕笑得乱晃。三根大梁是全村的壮劳力分了三次才抬回来的。每一次抬着大梁往回走，都要在七里半歇脚吃干粮。每次歇脚吃干粮都是在这棵老核桃树底下乘凉。老核桃树下面有一盘石碾，碾砣不知叫谁抬走了，只留下空空的碾盘，大伙就坐在碾盘上吃干粮。绿注注的青核桃压了满枝满树。谁也说不清楚这棵山核桃树在这儿站了多少年了。坐在树荫里乘凉，满鼻子都是山核桃树好闻的清香。现在，那股迷人的清香味儿正随着一阵山风从背后飘过来，把他和他的视线深深地包裹在无比的安详和温柔当中。

18岁参军，21岁复员，在一个叫旅顺的地方守着大海站了三年岗，然后，又回到五人坪。汽车、火车、轮船、飞机都看见了。电灯、电话、动物园、百货大楼、花花绿绿的城里人，还有说不出有多么奇怪的电影，说不出有多么大的大海，也都看见了。看见了这一切再回到五人坪，就好像神仙下凡，就好像做梦一样，不知道五人坪和大海到底谁是假的。现在隔了三十年的时间，隔着那一场大火，隔着老核桃树迷人的清香味儿，回想一辈子，回想这六年的官司，只觉得太快，快得就像一场梦……脸上的皮肤被太阳晒得疼起来，很快地，他从自己恍惚的回忆中醒过神来，深深地叹了一口气，松弛的脸上流露出说不出的苍老和疲惫。有一道汗水沿着额角流下来，无力地困顿在交错的皱纹里。他再一次地感慨起来，你要是没有上访过，你就不知道什么叫个累，真累，从心里头累……接着，又感慨，你要是没有上访过，你就不知道乌鸦有多黑，你就不知道什么叫拿人不当人，你就不知道为啥人连个畜生也不如，你就不知道为啥人脸能变得比石头板子还冷还硬……感慨了一番，他又在心里宽慰自己，你真是想不开呀你，事到如今你还想这些烦心的事，你都走了二十里山路，你都过了河，上了坡，你都站在老核桃树跟前，你都快看见那个碾盘了你……三十年的媳妇熬成婆，三十年的大道走成河呀……三十年和春香过日子，过出来三个儿女，两个孙子，过出来满脑袋的白头发……如今总算是熬到老核桃树跟前了，你还是心烦，你还是想不开，你这不是自己找罪受吗……这么想着，又有自嘲的微笑在那些苍老疲惫的皱纹里舒展开来。老核桃树安稳地站在夏天耀眼的阳光里，把说不出的安详和温柔弥漫到山谷里，弥漫到他苍老疲惫的脸上。

他在满地的蒿草里趟出一条路来，没腿高的草地上就像是被人刨出了一条沟，倒伏下去的蒿草叶子露出了白色的后背，像是给草地镶了一道银白的细贝。接着，视线里就出现了那个碾盘。最初的一刻他有点发愣，没看出来碾盘上厚厚地铺了一层什么黑东西，可马上他就认出来，那是剥下来的核桃皮。看来还有别人记着这棵核桃树呢，这是有人捡了落在地上的核桃，把烂黑了的青核桃皮留在碾盘上了。他随手撅了几棵蒿草当扫帚把核桃皮扫下去，把空碾盘打扫得干干净净的。从现在起，七里半村的这张空碾盘归自己一个人享用。

他把肩上背的挂包取下来，舒舒服服地盘腿坐在碾盘上，就像是坐在自己家的炕头上。然后，从上衣兜里摸出烟盒来看看，行，还有半盒烟卷呢，足够抽的。他又摸出火柴，从从容容地点燃了香烟，从从容容地吸了一口，然后，又从从容容吸了一口。到底是有一把岁数了，到底不是当年抬大梁的时候了，二十里的山路走得人还真是有点乏了。现在，浑身的筋骨借着烟劲儿松下来，他微微地闭上了眼睛，让自己停留在短暂的陶醉之中。轻起的山风摇动了头顶的树叶，摇乱了远处的青草和阳光，山野间一阵细语婆娑。

出了事情以后，乡亲们都说，满金，你参过军，见过大世面，又识字懂得政策，你给咱们当这个上访代表吧。定好三十年不变的合同，他们凭啥说变就变？凭啥就把大伙的山地卖给开发公司种香菇？于是，他没有多想就答应下来，当了五人坪村的上访代表，他用自己那辆三个轮子的农用车，拉着古老峪、矮人坪、东沟、南柳的上访代表，怀里装着五村村民画押签名的状子，开始了永辈子没完没了的上访。一直到农用车散了架，家里的牛羊都卖了，也还是没有结果。等到儿子追到北京来的时候，春香已经死了两天了。儿子说他妈就是舍不得东西，吃了几口酸了的剩菜，人就拉肚子拉毁了。上访六年，吃苦，受罪，吃想不到的苦，受想不到的罪，他都觉得那是应当的，那都能忍住。你一个老百姓，不脱十八层皮你能告倒了当官的？可他万万没有想到老伴儿会死，万万没有想到自己不在家的时候春香一个人走了，更万万没有想到老伴儿死了怎么会让自己这么难活，难活得就像把心肝五脏都放进了热油锅。赶回家来和孩子们一起埋了春香，他就觉得自己像是被抽了筋一样的劳累，劳累得连吃口饭喝口水的力气也没有。他一天到晚瞪着眼睛睡不着，不想说话，也不想吃饭，他觉得自己一定得做件什么事情心里才踏实。他觉得自己就想和老伴说句话，可身边的老伴儿就是没有啦，你悔断了肠子也看不见她啦……一直到今天早上鸡叫三遍的时候，他才终于想明白了自己要做的事情。

等到终于过足了烟瘾，他把烟头摁在碾盘上，数了数，正好是三根，行，够本儿了，事事不过三，再抽就是糟蹋东西。他打开挂包，取出一身新衣服，一双方口黑布鞋，脱下身上的旧衣服，换上新衣新鞋，抻抻衣角，裤腿。不错，都是春香的针脚，又贴身又舒服。他把一块石头搬到碾盘上，拍拍手上的土。然后，从挂包里取出那条捆麦子用的麻绳，绳头上打捆用的枣木的杈钩磨得又红又亮，记不清楚使了多少年了。然后，他站到了碾盘上，把又软又滑的绳子朝头顶一根树杈甩过去。然后，把挽好的绳套拉到自己脸跟前。站在碾盘上视线高了许多，他抬起头来又看了一遍远处的山谷，在心里安慰自己，矮人坪的拐叔是上吊死的，南柳村的小五保是上吊死的，青石涧的瘤拐赵老师是上吊死的，乱流河的人不想活了都喜欢上吊，我和他们一样。接着，他又安慰自己，我比他们强，我有这棵老核桃树……现在没有乌鸦了，一只也没有了，我在这儿上吊不用怕被乌鸦啄了眼睛……等我死了，乱流河的人肯定要论讲几天，叫不出自己名字的人就会说，在七里半上吊死的那个老汉是五人坪的上访代表。

三天以后，有人发现了尸体。正像他自己希望的那样，在老核桃树好闻的清香味儿里，他的眼睛完好无损。

2003年6月29日写，7月2日改于太原

Silence

● *Li Rui*

Out of the dense groves, he saw that old hickory tree standing on the mountain. The dark green leaves were sparkling in the dazzling sunlight and its canopy was so tall and thick, much like a peaceful and well-piled haystack. At the sight of it, he got a profound feeling that all the grasses and trees in the mountain were born by it and that all of them were its children. The last trace of worry and anxiety disappeared in his heart. He felt greatly relieved and at ease. Beyond the fragrant grasses and the tranquil water, he saw the broken walls behind that old hickory tree. The stone walls were broken already and the stones and rubbles scattered here and there among clusters of tall grasses and thorns. Nevertheless, the stones were struggling to raise themselves a little bit so that they wouldn't be totally submerged by the invading grasses. A strip of clear water came out of the luxuriant trees which were closely-knitted like a green wall and vanished into the seams among the entangling roots of the trees. But for the leaves which occasionally fell onto the surface of the water, he would never know the water was flowing. The stepping stones in the water disappeared, and obviously this place had been deserted for a long time. He bent down in an attempt to untie his shoes and take off his socks, but as he undid one shoelace he stopped and a smile of self-mockery surfaced on his face. Now, what's the point of taking them off? He stood up, and in the fresh aroma of green grasses, he stepped into the water with his shoes on. Hardly had the mud, the sand and the lichen in the water been stirred up when a cool sensation sent chills all over his body. He stopped to take a deep breath. The gurgling of the water sounded distant and muffled under a thick cover of branches and leaves.[1] A woodpecker broke the silence of the woods, beat, beat, beat, which made the woods more serene and sedate, hollow and spacious. He sighed: What a tranquil place! After a while, he couldn't help sighing again: How peaceful it is here![2]

He waded across the brook, stepped on the green grasses, climbed up the slope of the mountain, walked along the small path covered with wild grasses, treaded on the field ridges made of two lines of stones and went up another slope again. Finally, he approached that old hickory tree. A pheasant with a colorful long tail fluttered to the opposite side of the brook and disappeared into the woods he had just passed. Several hares scurried into the grasses, their white buttocks flashing across his eyes. He grinned, wondering why the hares got so nervous. Look at you! Am I so scary? Why are you escaping? I have no gun and I am not a leopard. And I am not an official and I don't want to eat you …[3] He said to the hares. Turning around, he cast a look at the far, far distance alongside the valley. Over there, the dark green forests were enclosed by a light layer of clouds and mists and the whole valley was dimmed with grayish blue. Seven years ago, their rain-praying ceremony caused a big fire which burned down the trees in the valley. And now, he still could see what the terrible fire left — no big trees grew there and between those low grasses and groves the burnt black rocks were revealed. After their prayer, the rain finally came but two villagers Erfa and Maoni died in that big fire and Buckwheat, Bad Egg and Mr. Zhang the teacher were put into prison. Had it not been the fire, he wouldn't be involved in the six-year-long lawsuit. The Development Company's vinyl house for growing mushrooms was destroyed. The two sides quarreled, clashed and even fought with each other, and some of them were brought away by the police. Now, nobody planted trees in the mountain. Holding the contract made void by the township government, the farmers didn't know what to do. The township government might sell the fire-ravaged forest again! They guessed but nobody could tell it for sure. Those burnt black rocks became the scars in the villagers' heart, embittering them to the point of breathlessness for years! Now the valley in the grayish mist appeared empty and deserted with few birds and little sound. The farmers here all blended their seeds with farm chemicals while crows and magpies all ate those seeds. Thus, day by day, year by year, no birds flew in the valley. For several years, birds were rarely seen here. Now, when the seeding season came, only oxen and people were seen in the fields. There was no longer the scene of birds briskly chasing behind. Where the plough went, the field was scored. And after they sowed the seeds into the field, turning back, they could only see the flat earth with no trace of a bird. Under the big scorching sun, only the hardworking oxen and the suffering farmers were left, their sweat dripping into the earth and their shadows swaying on the field. No one could tell where the birds went, which used to be chirping and flying here and there. Did all of them eat the farm chemicals? Were all of them poisoned to death? There must be a place where seeds were not mixed with

chemicals? There must be a place where people could survive? All crows under the
sun were black, but people had to survive one way or another! People were unlikely
to die out just because there were too many black crows. The crows here were all
black, but what about those in the county? In the province? In our capital Beijing?
If crows in Beijing were black, what about those in the United Nations? If crows
there were still black, people could go to Buddha or God. There must be a place
where crows were not black.[4] There must be a place where people could reason
things out. Thinking of this, he smiled with self-mockery again. He said to himself:
You left the Terrace of Five People at dawn, hurried for more than 10 kilometers
to reach the southern side of the mountain and finally found this deserted village
called Seven and a Half *Li* and the old hickory tree. You took such great efforts
to come here not for reasoning with somebody! Before he left his home, what
worried him was whether the old hickory tree was still here. He was afraid that it
had died or been chopped down. In that case, he would come here in vain! These
days, hardly had he lain on bed when the past memories came back to him, which
kept rolling and surging in his mind. Thirty years ago, after demobilization, he
left the army, came back home and got engaged to Chunxiang. To build the new
house for wedding, he needed three logs of timber as crossbeams, and he found
them on the southern side of the mountain. Once, he went on the mountain to cut
wood, wearing the black plastic sandals and white silk socks issued by the army, and
he slipped and almost dropped to his death. While dressing his wound, his uncle
scolded him beside his ears: You bastard really have a swollen head![5] How can you
wear such shoes and socks to chop wood in the mountain! You are so capable that
our village can't even accommodate you![6] Hearing his uncle's words, a cluster of
young people chattered and laughed their heads off.[7] The three logs he found were
carried back by the strongest young men in his village in three times. Each time they
would rest at Seven and a Half *Li*, eating something and cooling themselves down
under the old hickory tree. There was a stone roller under the tree. The upper part
of the roller was gone but the grinding base remained. Then, under the hickory tree
laden with green walnuts, the young men sat on the grinding base, eating the food
they brought. Heaven knew how many years the hickory tree had been standing
here. In its shade, enveloped by its intoxicating fragrance, they felt quite cozy. Now,
the enchanting fragrance, again, drifted to him and wrapped him and his sight in
serenity and sedateness.

At the age of 18, he joined the army, and after serving in the army for three
years in a place called Lüshun, which was a seaside city in northeast China, he

demobilized at the age of 21. Thereafter, he returned to his hometown, the Terrace of Five People. He had seen buses, trains, ships and planes; he had seen electric lamps, telephones, zoos, department stores and cutely dressed people in the city; he had seen the films which were incredibly strange to him and the sea which was inexpressibly vast. He had seen all he could. Now, he came back to the Terrace of Five People, as if a fairy maiden left the heaven and came to the earth. As if in a dream, he couldn't tell which was fake, the Terrace of Five People or the sea? Now, after thirty years, after that fire, standing in the aroma of the hickory tree again, he couldn't help but draw a sigh for the passage of time. Recalling his life and the six-year-long lawsuit, he felt as if he were in a dream … Feeling his face burnt by the strong sunlight, he instantly came back from his wandering memory. He uttered a long sigh, senescence and fatigue appearing on his sagging face. A drop of sweat streamed down his forehead and listlessly interweaved with his wrinkles. He said to himself with a sigh again: If you don't go for an appeal to the higher authorities for help, you will never know how tiresome it is! Now, he felt really tired, exhausted from the bottom of his heart … He continued to utter a deep long sigh: If you don't experience an appeal to the higher authorities for help, you will never know how black the crows are, and you will never experience the feeling of being belittled! And you will never know why human beings are less decent than animals and you will never know why human faces can be colder and harder than stones … He sighed and sighed and after a while he tried to console himself. Don't take such things to heart any longer! What's the point of thinking about these frustrating things? Now you have walked over 10 kilometers in the mountain, you have crossed the brook, and you have climbed up the slope. Now you have found the old hickory tree and you'll see that grinding base in a minute … Thirty years! Thirty years may turn a young wife into an old granny, a road into a river! In these thirty years, Chunxiang and you have brought up three children and now you have two grandsons. Your hair has gone white … Finally, you are standing under the hickory tree again! Why do you still feel upset? What's the point of being haunted by the past memories? Why are you finding troubles for yourself?[8] Thinking of these, he smiled, the self-mockery spreading among his aged and wearied wrinkles.

He beat a path through the grasses which were tall enough to reach his knees. The grassland under his feet was thus cleaved apart and the grasses on both sides lay down in opposite directions, revealing their white undersides. It seemed as if the grassland had a silver-inlaid pearl frame. Soon, that grinding base came into his view. He stared blankly at it, wondering what it was covered with, and after a short while, he realized they were walnut peels. Obviously, someone else also kept this hickory tree in mind and might have come here to have a look at it; they picked up the walnuts on the ground and left the walnut peels, which had gone black and rotten, on the grinding base. He pulled up a cluster of long grass and broomed the peels off. From now on, the grinding base, which was clean and clear, only belonged to him.

Taking off the bag from his shoulder, he sat cross-legged on the grinding base as if sitting on the bed in his home. Fumbling out a packet of cigarettes from his coat pocket, he became cheery. Good! There is half a packet left. Enough! Taking out a match, he lit a cigarette in a leisurely manner. He smoked a mouthful, and then, another. After all, he was aged. His youthful vigor was gone, never to return! After such a long walk, he felt really tired. Now, he felt all his limbs and bones relaxed, and closing his eyes he intoxicated himself in this transient happiness. The gentle wind shook the leaves above his head and stirred the green grasses in the distance as well as the sunlight. The whisper of rustling leaves spread throughout the mountain. It was a feast for all senses, indeed.

After the conflict, the villagers came to him. Manjin, you were a soldier and saw the world, besides, you are literate and know about policies. You'd better represent us to make an appeal to the government for help. We've made a contract with the government, which ensures that we own the land for thirty years, and how can they go back on it so quickly? Why do they sell our land to the Development Company to grow mushrooms? He agreed to their proposal without hesitation and became the representative of the Terrace of Five People. Since then, carrying the representatives from the nearby villages of the Old Valley, the Midgets' Terrace, the Eastern Ravine and the Southern Willows on his worn-out farm vehicle, holding the pepition paper signed by the people in all the five villages, he started his endless journey of appeals. His vehicle finally broke down on the way and he sold all his cattle and sheep for money, but still, he didn't achieve any result. When his son hurried to Beijing to tell him the bad news, his wife had been dead for two days. His wife was too thrifty! She was reluctant to get rid of the food which had gone bad and sour; after trying a few morsels, unfortunately she suffered from severe diarrhea and died. To him, it was a bolt from the blue. Six years! He had been appealing to the government for six years, in which he suffered so much! He suffered unimaginable hardships and tortures, but he felt he could bear all of them, for he knew it must take a common civilian quite a lot to sue and defeat the government officials.[9] However, he had never expected that his wife died so early! He had never thought that his wife departed alone when he was not home. He had never thought that he could be so sad at her death, so sad as if all his internal organs were thrown into a wok of boiling oil. He hurried home and buried her with the help of his children. He was worn and torn, as if all his muscles were drawn out. He felt so exhausted that he even had no strength to eat or drink. Opening his eyes wider, he just sat there, unwilling to speak or eat. He must do something to relieve himself. He wanted to say a word to her but she was no longer there. He felt guilty and regretful ... At dawn, when the roosters crowed the third time, he came to know what he felt like doing.

When he smoked to his heart's content, he pressed the butt on the grinding base. He counted the butts on the base and said to himself: Altogether three. OK! Enough! Don't do anything more than three times. One more cigarette will be a waste ... Opening his bag he took out a new suit and a pair of black cotton shoes. He put the new clothes on and stretched the corners of the coat and the bottoms of the trouser legs. Good! The clothes bore his wife's stitchwork and fit him perfectly. He felt cozy. He carried a big stone onto the grinding base, clapped the dust off his hands, and took a rope out of his bag. The rope had been used to bundle the wheat and on one of its ends there was a hook made of date wood. He couldn't remember how many years he had used it and now due to years of rubbing the hook was smooth and bright, giving off a red luster. Then, he stood on the grinding base, slung the soft and slippery rope up to the branch above his head and pulled the noose down to his face. Now, standing higher, he could see the scenery farther ahead. He consoled himself: Uncle Crutch in the Midgets' Terrace hanged himself to death, so did Old Childless Chap in the Southern Willows and Mr. Zhao the teacher in the Green Stone Valley. People here who don't feel liking living all choose to die in this way, and now I'll do it as they did. He continued to comfort himself: I am better than them. At least, I have this old hickory tree as my company ... now there are no crows and my eyes will not be pecked by crows after I die ... they will be talking about me for several days after my death, and people who don't know my name will say that the old man who hanged himself in Seven and a Half *Li* is a representative of the Terrace of Five People appealing for help from a higher authority.

Three days later, his body was found. As he had expected, in the aroma of the old hickory tree, his eyes remained intact.

Written on June 29, 2003
Revised on July 2 in Taiyuan

注 释

1. "流水声被远远地闷在枝叶后边"，声音悠远、沉闷，译为sounded distant and muffled。

2. 小说的主人公一再慨叹树林的宁静，这里先后用了serene、sedate、tranquil、peaceful，一方面帮助渲染宁静的氛围，另一方面换词用，可以增加些文采。

3. 小说中主人公的独白或心理活动，都用了现在时或者相应的时态。全文叙述用的是过去时态。

4. 中国有成语"天下乌鸦一般黑"，可以翻译为 All crows under the sun are black. / Crows are black the world over. / Evil people are bad all over the world. 译文保持了原文"乌鸦"的形象，没有把这里"乌鸦"的内涵直接说出来：people who are corrupted，这符合小说人物的语言风格，相信读者可以通过上下文的阅读理解"乌鸦"这一形象在此处的含义。汉语中还有这样的习语："乌鸦的翅膀遮不住太阳的光芒。"The wings of a crow cannot block off the radiance of the sun. "乌鸦嘴" crow's beak — a mouth from which inauspicious remarks are uttered. "你这张乌鸦嘴！"What improper remarks you've made! 英语中还有一个有关乌鸦的词raven，这个词常用来形容"乌黑"，比如：raven hair 乌黑的头发。

5. "舅舅一边给自己包伤口，一边在耳朵边上骂，就烧死你个龟孙吧就！"While dressing his wound, his uncle scolded him beside his ears: You bastard really have a swollen head! "龟孙"是不雅的骂人话。You bastard really have a swollen head! 可以表达舅舅当时的情绪和语言特点。

6. accommodate 容纳，使适应、顺应。

7. "一伙年轻人围在自己身边唧唧咕咕笑得乱晃。" a cluster of young people chattered and laughed their heads off. 译文中用了表示"狂笑"的俗语to laugh one's head off。

8. 以上一大段都是小说主人公的自言自语，属于心理活动。翻译时，一是注意适当的时态，二是注意口语的表达习惯，译文应该符合这样一个人物的语言特点、心理状态、教育背景等。

9. "你一个老百姓，不脱十八层皮你能告倒了当官的？""脱十八层皮"表示费了很大周折，经历了很多困难。译文在这里做了弱化处理：... it must take a common civilian quite a lot to sue and defeat the government officials.

227

在街上行走

● 范小青

　　收旧货的那个人，戴着一副眼镜，穿得也比较干净，看上去像个知识分子，大家这么说的时候，他总是笑笑，然后说，我什么知识分子，我小学毕业，初中只念了半年。

　　他脾气温和，举止也文雅，他总是将收来的旧货，认真地分门别类，然后小心地捆扎好，地下如果留下了杂物，他会借一把笤帚来，顺手替人家打扫一下，然后就把旧货扛出来，搁在停在门外的黄鱼车上，搁得平平整整，他说，放整齐了，可以多放一点货。

　　开始的时候他只是收旧货，然后将收来的旧货卖到废品收购站，慢慢地，时间长了，他也知道有些旧货可以不卖到收购站，它们虽然是旧货，但还不是废品，可以不到废品站去论斤论两，可以找一点其他的买主，比如一些开在小街上的旧书店，当他带着些旧书进去的时候，老板的眼睛亮起来，精神也振奋了，这时候灰暗的小书店里，就会发出一点光彩来，还有一些晚上沿街摆旧书摊的人，对有些尚有价值的旧杂志和旧书，也一样愿意按本论价，不过他们的眼光，肯定不如书店的老板，他们开的价格，也是相当低的，当然，这总比按斤论价要强一些，做过几次交易以后，他就学乖了一点，当然后来他又更乖了一点，因为有一次他亲眼看见摆书摊的人一转手，就赚了钱，所以以后他就自己来摆地摊，白天收旧货，晚上设摊，这样他抢了原来摆书摊的人的饭碗，那个人很生气，他自己也觉得这样不大好，就挪到另一个地方，但是晚上摆摊的事情是风雨飘摇，朝不保夕的，因为经常有城管的人或者其他执法的人来查处，常常偷鸡不着蚀把米，给罚了钱。碰到风声紧的时候，干脆就不敢摆出去了。或者是在雨季，夜里总是阴雨绵绵，摊子摆出去，是得不偿失的，书刊被淋湿了，也不会有人在雨夜里去街头买旧书旧杂志的，在这样的时候，他就在自己租住的小屋里，整理那些收购来的旧货，他没有电视，也不订报纸，漫长的雨夜，他可以看看旧书旧杂志。

还有一些是学生用过的旧课本、旧作业本，他有兴致的时候，也会翻开作业本看看，看到学生做的练习题和老师批的分数，还有一个学生写道：某某是王八蛋，老师也没有批出来，估计是最后本子用完了不再交上去的时候才写的，他不知道这个"某某"是这个学生的同学还是他的老师，他想如果是老师的话，就很好笑了，他将课本和练习本精心地挑出来，留给自己的孩子，他们以后都用得着的，他这么想着，后来有一天，他收购到一大堆旧笔记本，这是一个人写的日记，他起先也没有怎么在意，因为他觉得这对他的孩子以后读书没什么用的，他将这些旧笔记本置到另一边，因为它们不能当旧书旧杂志卖，只能到废品收购站将它们称了。

可是第二天他来到废品收购站的时候，收购站的秤坏了，正在修理，他就坐在一边等待修理，他那时候没事可做，就把手边的旧笔记本抽出一本来翻一翻，浏览一下，看了其中的一段日记，但是看了看后，他想，这叫什么日记，他有些不以为然，便不想看了，他将笔记本重新塞好，就坐在那里看修秤，后来秤修好了，他却有些疑虑，这么快就修好了，你的秤准不准啊？他问道，收购员说，不准你不要来卖好了。其实他平时也是经常遭到别人的质问的，怀疑的口气和他自己今天说话的口气是一样的，所以他也体会收购员的心情，也没有计较，就将一捆捆扎着的笔记本提到秤上，一秤，九斤，收购员说，喂，这只能算你废纸啊，他有些不服气，这怎么是废纸呢，这一本一本的，应该算是书吧，收购员说，你懂不懂什么叫书啊，他觉得收购员今天火气特别大，但是让他把笔记本当废纸卖，他觉得亏了，我不卖了，他说，收购员就一屁股坐下来，说，不卖拉倒。

他将这些废品重新又置到黄鱼车上，他可以再换一家废品收购站试试，要是运气好，说不定有人会当旧书收购他的，他的黄鱼车经过红绿灯的时候，躲躲闪闪地避进一条小街，因为有个交警站在那里，像他这样的黄鱼车，虽然是有牌照的，但上下班时间规定是不许走大路的，他平时也是知道的，但今天因为卖旧货不太顺利，这时候他有点分心，就走到交警的眼皮底下来了，幸好正是高峰时间，交警正在忙着，没有来得及注意到他，他就拐到小街上去了。小街上有一个旧书店，刚刚开门，店主就看到一个收旧货的人骑着黄鱼车过来了，店主看了看他的脸，似熟非熟，但店主还是微笑了一下，说，师傅，今天早嘛，今天有什么货？

他摇了摇头，就是一些笔记本，他说。

笔记本吗，店主说，什么笔记本？

好像是一个人的日记，他说。

他是有些无精打采的，但是店主的精神却渐渐地起来了，日记？他问道，写的什么日记呢？什么呀，他说，就是一些流水账，早上几点起来，起来了洗脸刷牙也要写，水太凉牙有点不舒服的感觉也要写，坐马桶坐多长时间也要写，早饭吃的什么也要写，早饭以后喝茶，是什么茶，哪里买来的，多少钱一斤，都写在上面，然后是什么，是来了一个送信的，送来一封信，他看了这封信，后来，有一个什么人也要看，他不给看，那个人生气了，反正，就是这些琐碎的事情。

店主有一种天生的职业的敏感，他的鼻子已经嗅到了历史的气息，他已经不再矜持，甚至有点急迫地说，能让我看看吗？

他就从一扎笔记本中抽出一本给店主看，他说，本来我已经到收购站了，他要当废纸收，我说这不是一张一张的，这是一本一本的，应该算是旧书，他不肯，我也不肯，又带出来了，再去试试其他收购站。

店主的心思早已经不在他身上了，他只是应付着他，是吗，啊啊，这么应付了两句，店主已经看过了一段日记，他知道笔记本里的内容，至少是六七十年前的生活了，店主决定把它们买下来。

他惊讶地看着店主将一叠钱交到他的手上，这是给我的吗，他差一点问，但毕竟没有问出来，当然是给他的，当然是因为这一扎笔记本，肯定店主喜欢这些笔记本，或者这些笔记本可以卖出更好的价钱，但他并不贪心，废品站的人，只肯给他几斤废纸的钱，现在他拿到这么多，他已经够满足了，至于店主可能会转手卖出多少，他无法想像，他也不再去想像，他知道那不是他的事情，他不懂这里边的规矩，也不懂行情，那钱不该他赚，所以他拿了店主付给他的钱，就可以走了。

但是店主转手的事情，并不是那么容易的，这些日记没头没脑，既没有写日记这个人的姓名和其他情况，他在日记中偶尔提到一些人名，都不是什么有名的人，也无从考查起的，如果是名人的话，那就好办多了，时间再长，也总会有人知道的，后来店主又看出来，这些日记，是这个人许多日记中的一部分，是1936年至1939年这三年中的日记，那么这个人到底记过多少年的日记，从他的三年的日记中也可以看出，他是记了很长很长时间的日记，而且从1939年往后，还会继续记下去的，那么他的更多的日记在哪里呢，等等，都是待解的谜。

店主花了很大的精力去考证，去寻找些什么，甚至还跑到外地去，但一直没有结果，后来店主重新又想起了收旧货卖笔记本的这个人，店主有一种如梦初醒的感觉，他说，我这真是守着和尚找和尚，指着赵洲问赵洲，舍近而求远了，于是他哪里也不去了，就守在店里等待收旧货的人再次出现。

不断有收旧货的人上门来问他收不收旧书，但是他始终没有等到卖笔记本给他的那个人。有时候他已经看到他进来了，但是经过一番盘问，才又知道这个人不是他要等的那个人，还有一次，他看到一个卖旧货的来了，他坚信这就是他要等的那个人，他还记得他的身形和基本的长相，他问他，师傅，你来过这里卖旧书吧。但是那个师傅摇了摇头，说，我没有来过，今天是头一回。

以至于后来他连那个人的长相都已经淡忘了，甚至模糊了，他一会记得他是瘦瘦高高的，一会又记得他是矮矮胖胖的。

晚报上，有一天登了一条寻人启事，寻找一个收旧货的外地人。登启事的这家人家，老保姆将不应该卖掉的笔记本卖掉了，是被一个外地口音收旧货的人收去的，现在他们寻找这个人，希望能够追回不应该卖掉的东西。

有不少人看到了这条启事，但是与他们无关，他们并没有往心上去。店主那天也看了晚报，但是寻人启事是夹在报纸中缝里的，他没有注意到，后来偶尔听人说起，但是谁也不记得那是哪一天的晚报，也记不清到底说的什么事，只记得是有人卖了不应该卖的东西，想找回来。店主想再去找那张晚报也找不到了，过了期的报纸，被收旧货的收走了，卖到废品收购站，然后又运到造纸厂，打成纸浆，再又变成新的纸头出来了。

现在卖错东西的事情多得很，有人将存折藏在旧鞋里，鞋被卖掉了，存折还到哪里去找啊，也有人把金银首饰放在旧衣服的口袋里，或者把情书夹在废纸里，这都是最怕丢失的东西，但是最怕丢失的又恰恰丢失了，而且都是很难再找回来的，所以，大家常说，有些东西，失去了就永远失去了。

店主的念头后来也渐渐地淡下去了，但他知道，这仍然是他的一桩心事。后来他生了病，不久就去世了，临终前，他还是把这桩心事交待给了自己的孩子，他希望孩子继续开旧书店，他说，只要书店仍然开着，就会有希望，那个人会回来的。

但是他的孩子觉得开旧书店没有意思，辛辛苦苦，又不能赚钱，他的女朋友也和他有一样的想法，他们商量了一阵，不久以后，他便将旧书店关闭了，开了个服装店，这是听他女朋友的主意开的，他们一起到浙江去进货，回来后就一起守在店里卖服装。后来他们渐渐地熟了，来来去去的路线熟了，事情该怎么做也都知道了，和那边批发市场里的批发商也认识了，有了交往，所以，有时候店里人手紧的时候，就不必两个人一起去进货了，而是他一个人去，也有的时候他有事情走不开，就他的女朋友一个人去。

但是服装店的生意也不好做，做了半年，一结账，除去开销，也没有多少盈余的，他的女朋友说，这样做到猴年马月我们才能结婚。他们坚持了一年，他的女朋友就走了，她说这个地方发展不起来，她要到浙江那边去发展。

女朋友走了以后，他也不再开服装店了，他将店面转租给别人做房产中介，他坐收房租，比父亲在的时候日子还好过。

做房产中介的人，是个喜欢交朋友的人，所以他的眼线耳目比较多，这是做中介最重要也是最基本的一个条件，许多人都在有意无意中为他提供线索，这个人的朋友搬家了，老房子要出租，那个人的亲戚买了新房子，老房子要出手还新房子的贷款，或者谁家来了个外地亲戚，家里住不下，要租房子，等等等等，这其中有许多线索是有价值的，在别人听来，只是一般的家长里短聊聊天，或者最多只是一个普通的消息而已，而到了房产中介人那里，一般的聊天，普通的消息，就变成了利润。

他租了这个店面以后，很快又和街上的左邻右舍建立了良好的关系，闲着的时候，总是在说话聊天，别人也知道他这一套，他们说，我们说话是白说，嚼白蛆，他不一样，他说话能够来钱的。当然，话虽这么说，但他那一套，他们看得见，学却是学不会的，有一次他只是听到一个人说某某街某某号有两室一厅，其他什么情况也不知道，但是过了三天以后，他就拿到了下家的定金，又过了十来天，他就转手赚了两万。

其实不仅仅是说说话就能挣钱，他还要用脑子，他还要有水平，他还要有相当的思想境界，水平和思想境界从哪里来呢，锻炼出来，还有，可以从书上学来，所以他是很喜欢读书的，不管什么书，他拿到手都要看，开卷有益，书中自有黄金屋，他觉得古人说的话很有道理。有一次他读到一个人的日记，这是正式出版的日记，一套有几十本，这个写日记的人，他并不知道是谁，因为他不是个名人，他的日记也是在他去世以后，他的小辈为了了却心愿，凑钱替他出的，在小辈写的后记里，说了这样一件遗憾的事，就是这些日记，是他们的爷爷二十岁至四十岁的日记，四十岁以后，爷爷就再也没有写过日记，遗憾的是，其中缺少了三年的内容，1936年至1939年的日记，被当年伺候爷爷的老保姆当废品卖了，小辈曾经费了很大的周折，但始终没有找到，所以现在出版出来的日记，是不完整不齐全的日记。

他心里也替他惋惜着，他也曾想像过，那个遗失了的三年，这位老人的生活中曾经发生了什么，或者什么也没有发生，他还想像，这丢失的三年日记，现在到底在哪里。

他做梦也没有想到，这三年的日记，就在他的公司里边的那间小屋里，有一扇小门，拿一把大铁锁锁着，那是房主封闭隔开的，据房主说，是他的父亲留下的一些遗物，是一些旧书，留着也没有用，丢又舍不得丢，放在家里又放不下，反而使整洁的房间变得杂乱，所以在店堂靠里的角落，隔出一小间，存放着。

因为隔掉这一小间，他收的房租就要少收一些，从前他的女朋友曾经劝他不要隔，可以使店堂的面积大一点，多派点用场，但是他想了半天，最后还是隔出来了。

这些日子，这条老街上原先的店面都纷纷地在改换门庭，过不多久，就是旧貌换新颜了，街也兴旺热闹起来，收旧货的人有一次经过，都认不出来了，他还在房产中介公司门口站了一会，也没有想起这就从前的旧书店。他毕竟不是这个城市的人，而且这个城市这样的老街小巷很多，在他看起来，这一条和那一条也都差不多，他只是感叹，怎么旧书店越来越难找，越来越少了，因为这个问题直接牵涉到他的利益。

但是后来发生的这些事情，收旧货的人并不知道。那一次他得到一笔意外的收获，非常高兴，他十分庆幸自己在各种艰苦的工作中确定了做收旧货的工作，现在他更坚定了自己的信心，收旧货的工作，说不定哪天就会有一种意外的收获。当然，他不会傻傻地坐等意外好运的到来，他仍然每天辛辛苦苦地挨家挨户上门收旧货，再送到废品站去卖掉，有时候一天只能赚很少的钱，有时候还分文无收，或者被人骗了，还要倒贴掉一点，比如有一回收了一箱旧铜丝，送到废品站时，才发现只有面上是一团铜丝，下面的都是泥巴砖块，他就白白地贴了一百多元给骗子，但是不管怎么说，他始终坚信自己的钱会积少成多的，有了这样的信念，他就能够不辞劳苦，日复一日地行走在这个城市的大街小巷。

有一天他骑着黄鱼车在街上经过，有一个人挡住了他，问他有没有收过一叠旧笔记本，他觉得这个人有点奇怪，他告诉他，他几乎天天收到笔记本，有小孩的练习本，也有人家家庭的记账本，甚至还有好多年前的记账本，上面写着，山芋粉两斤，共一角，他当时还觉得奇怪，城里人怎么也吃山芋粉，而且城里的山芋粉怎么这么便宜，后来他才发现，那是二十几年前的记账本。那个问他话的人，后来就失望地走了。

在以后的漫长的日子里，在一些无事可做的雨夜，他偶尔也会想到这个人，这个寻找旧笔记本的人，是谁呢？他肯定不是来寻找小孩的练习本的，这样他就依稀回忆起有关日记本的一些事情，但是更多的情节记不起来了，他只记得是有一些日记本，他还读过其中的一段，写的什么，忘记了，拿到哪里去卖了？也忘记了，反正，不是废品收购站，就是街头的书摊，或者旧书店，这些日记本是从哪里收购来的，那是一个什么样的人家，在哪条街巷里，他记不得了，这个人为什么要把笔记本卖掉，是有意卖掉的，还是无意卖掉的，如果是弄错了，他一定很后悔，日记是不能随便给人家看的，他虽然是个乡下人，但这个道理他懂，难怪那个寻找笔记本的人，一脸的焦急，如果他是记的和从前的女朋友的事情，流失出去，万一给现在的女朋友看见了，那就麻烦了。

想着想着，他睡着了。

他从遥远的贫困的家乡来到这里，他也干过其他的一些活，后来觉得还是收旧货比较适合他，他就干定了这一行，慢慢地，有耐心地积累着资金、等积得多一些了，他就到邮局去汇款，他的老婆和两个孩子在家里等着他汇钱回去，他的老婆将他寄回去的钱藏起来，准备以后造房子用，两个孩子以后还要念书呢，他希望他们都能考上大学。

到邮局汇过款后，他怀揣着收据往回走的时候，经过洗头房，他就进去了，珠珠也知道他这几天该来了，他来的时候，珠珠说，来啦，如果她正闲着，她就会站起来说，走吧，如果她手里有客人在洗头，她就说，你等一等。

他总觉得珠珠对他和对别人不一样，有一些特殊的感情，珠珠却不这样想，珠珠说，哪里呀，我对他们都是一样的。

只是那一回有些不同，因为卖了日记本，他发了一笔财，提前来了，那天珠珠看到他进来，奇怪地说，咦，你前天才来过嘛。

不过这件事情也和记着日记的笔记本一样，他已经记不清了。

（载2004年3月号）

Walking on the Street[1]

Fan Xiaoqing

The man who came to collect the second-hand goods looked like an intellectual, for he always wore a pair of glasses and dressed himself neat and tidy. At people's polite compliments, he always smiled gently and said: "An intellectual? I studied in high school for only half a year and I am just a primary school graduate."

He was mild-tempered, always behaving himself in good manners. After collecting the second-hand goods from a household, he put them in the yard, carefully sorted them out and tied them up in different bundles methodically. If he found odds and ends left he would borrow a broom and clear the yard for the family. Then, he carried his bundles out of the yard and put them in order on his cart outside the gate. "I'd better put them in order so as to make room for more goods." He often said so.

At the beginning, he sold the goods he collected to the salvage station, and by and by, he came to know that some second-hand goods were actually not wastes and that except selling them by weight he could turn to other means for a better price. For instance, some small bookstores dealing in second-hand books were one of his better choices. Whenever he brought the old books he collected into a bookstore, the storekeeper's eyes suddenly lit up, and the small store turned alive from the daily monotony. Besides, he noticed that some vendors came out at dusk and set up book stalls along the streets, and they were willing to pay a relatively good price for his old books and magazines which, in their eyes, were valuable and worthwhile. Of course, the vendors' appreciative ability was not as good as that of the storekeepers and compared with the storekeepers' price, theirs was lower, but he was contented. After all, this was much better than selling them as waste paper by weight. After several deals, he learned much and more.[2] Once, he saw a vendor selling the books just bought from him at a much higher price. Simply by reselling them, the vendor made more money! Then, he decided to set up a stall and sell books by himself. Since then, in the daytime, he went out to collect goods and at dusk he sold them at his stall. The vendor who made money by selling second-hand books was angry with him, so he moved his stall to another place. After all, grabbing for others' business was not good. Selling books at the stall was a precarious job and he couldn't know at dawn what might happen by dusk, for city inspectors or law enforcement officials might appear at any moment. For several times, he was fined for his barely legal business — as the saying went, he went for wool and came home shorn.[3] When the situation got tense, he had no guts to go out to set up his stall.

In the rainy season, a drizzle often began at dusk. Selling books at that time might bring little gain and great loss — the books and magazines would get wet, besides, nobody came to buy old books and magazines on a rainy night! Therefore, on those long nights, he had to stay in his small rented room. Since he had no TV and hadn't subscribed to newspapers, he whiled away his time by sorting out the goods or reading those old books and magazines he collected.

Among the goods he collected, some were students' textbooks and notebooks. Sometimes, when he was in a good mood, he opened them and read those exercises and teachers' grading marks. A student wrote on his notebook, "so-and-so is a jerk", but his teacher didn't even notice it! Perhaps the student wrote it after the notebook was filled up and no longer needed to be handed in. He didn't know if this "so-and-so" was a student or a teacher, and he felt the whole thing would be hilarious if this "so-and-so" was the teacher. More often than not, he sorted out some textbooks and notebooks and put them aside on the consideration that his own children might be in need of them one day. Once, he collected a big pile of notebooks, which were someone's diaries. At first, he didn't take them to heart, thinking that these were useless to his children. Since these diaries couldn't be sold as old books or magazines, he had to put them aside and prepared to sell them by weight to the salvage station.

The next day, he went to the salvage station, only to find something wrong with their scale. He had to wait aside while they were repairing it. With nothing to do, he took up a diary at hand and read a passage in it. "Is this a diary?" He thought in disapproval. He crammed the notebook back to the pile and began to look at them repairing the scale. They finished quickly. He was doubtful. "So quickly? Is your scale accurate?" He asked. One of the staff gave him a gruff reply, "Don't sell your stuff to us if you don't believe us!" As a matter of fact, he was often questioned by people in the same skeptical tone, so he didn't make a fuss over the man's impoliteness. He put the bundle of the diaries on the scale. The man said bluntly to him, "Nine *jin*! Hey, guy, we count these as waste paper! You know that, right?" He turned a little unhappy and replied, "How can you say these are waste paper? Look! They are books." The man talked back in a contemptuous tone, "Do you know what a book is?" This guy must get out of the bed from the wrong side![4] He thought. Feeling himself suffering losses, he said: "OK, I won't sell them." The man plopped down into his chair at once: "Up to you!"[5]

He put the bundle back to his cart and left. He wanted to try other salvage stations where these diaries might be sold as second-hand books. As he was about to reach a crossroad, he pulled his cart into a small alley lest the policeman under the traffic lights might see his cart which, though licensed, was not allowed to go on the main street in the rush hour. He knew the rules but today, perhaps due to the setback just now, he was distracted and didn't realize it until he rode his cart close to the policeman. Luckily, it was the rush hour and the policeman, busy in directing traffic, didn't notice him, so he was just in time to turn his cart and sidle into a small alley.

In the alley, there was a second-hand bookstore, which had just opened in the morning. Seeing the cart and that somewhat familiar face, the storekeeper smiled and greeted him, "Hi! So early today. What stuff do you have?"

"Only some notebooks." Shaking his head, he answered.

"Notebooks? What kind of notebooks?"

"Someone's diaries."

He replied listlessly while the storekeeper's spirit was bucking up. "Diaries? What was written?"

"What was written? Just some day-to-day account: Someone got up in the morning, washed his face, brushed his teeth, and he felt quite uncomfortable for the water was too cold. And then he went to the toilet. Oh! See, even the time of toilet was recorded. And what he ate at breakfast, what kind of tea he drank after breakfast and where he bought the tea and how much it was and so on and so forth. And later, a mailman came with a letter. And then, another man came and wanted to have a look at it, but he wouldn't let him. Then, that man got angry. You see? All these daily trivial matters!"

The storekeeper, with his inborn professional sensitivity, smelled something historical. "Can I have a look at them?" No longer hiding his interest, the storekeeper asked in a pressing tone.

He drew one notebook from the tightly-bundled stack and handed it to the storekeeper. "I have been to a salvage station, but they say these are waste paper! I tell them these are not pieces of paper but notebooks which should be counted as books. They disagree. So I want to try some other salvage stations."

Intent on reading the notebook, the storekeeper just hemmed and hawed. It was really a diary which recorded someone's life sixty or seventy years ago. The storekeeper decided to buy all of these notebooks.

Taking a wad of money from the storekeeper's hand, he felt surprised! "To me?" He nearly blurted out. He held back his inquiry and thought: "Of course, he pays me the money for that bundle of notebooks. The storekeeper must be fond of those diaries or perhaps he can sell them for a better price." He was not greedy. He was contented. This was much better than selling them as waste paper by weight to the salvage station! As to how much the storekeeper would earn by reselling them, he couldn't imagine and as a matter of fact he was unwilling to think about it, for he knew it was none of his business. He didn't know the ropes in this circle and some money didn't belong to him.[6] He knew it. Hence, taking the money, he left quickly.

To the storekeeper, it was no easy job to resell these diaries, for there was neither the diary-keeper's name nor any other related account. Some people's names, indeed, were related in the diaries but since they were not well-known the storekeeper could not trace them. If they were well-known, things would be much easier, for they must be remembered or recorded no matter how long had passed. Later, the storekeeper found that these diaries were only a section, recording the diary-keeper's life from 1936 to 1939. Then, for how many years did this person keep writing diaries? From his diaries in three years, the storekeeper guessed that the person must have kept writing diaries for a long, long time, and must have continued writing after 1939. However, where were the rest of these diaries? So many questions lingered in the storekeeper's mind and remained a mystery.

The storekeeper spent much time and energy trying to discover something and he even went to other cities to make investigations; however, to his disappointment, he found nothing valuable. Later, he thought of the man who sold him the diaries. As if wakening from a dream, he sighed: "How silly I am! I am looking for a horse while riding on it — I am seeking far and neglecting what lay close at hand!"[7] Since then, he waited in his store instead of looking around elsewhere.

Second-hand dealers constantly came to his door, but the one he was waiting for never showed up. Sometimes, he felt he saw that man, but after some inquiries, he knew he made a mistake. Once, a man selling second-hand goods came and at the very sight of his face and figure, the storekeeper recognized him — this man must be the person he was waiting for! The storekeeper asked in a hurry: "Have you come here before? Was it you who sold me a bundle of diaries?" The man shook his

238

head: "I've never been here and this is my first time at your place."

As time went by, he gradually forgot the appearance of the man who sold him the diaries. Sometimes tall and slender and sometimes short and stumpy, now visible and then invisible, that man kept haunting the storekeeper's vague memory.

One day, a notice appeared in the evening newspaper. The notice said that a family's old housekeeper mistakenly sold a bundle of notebooks to a second-hand dealer who had a non-local accent, and that the family now wanted to find the dealer in order to retrieve the notebooks.

Quite a lot of people saw the notice but it was none of their business, so none of them took it to heart. The storekeeper, on that day, actually read the evening newspaper, but he didn't see the notice, because it was placed in the central joint of the newspaper. Later, occasionally, he heard people talking about it, but none of them remembered the date of the newspaper and what the notice said exactly. They just told him that someone sold something which shouldn't be sold and wanted to have it back. The storekeeper went all out to find that old newspaper but all his efforts were in vain. The old newspaper disappeared! It might be sold as second-hand goods, sent to a salvage station and transported to a paper-making factory where it might change into paper pulp and become a new paper again!

Nowadays, such things happened a lot. Someone hid his bankbook in one of his old shoes and by mistake he sold his shoes, so his bankbook was gone. Where could he find it? Some hid their gold or silver jewelry in the pockets of their old clothes, and some put their love letters among waste paper. People always lost things which they cherished very much in this way and once their priceless things were lost they couldn't find them. No wonder people often said, "Once you lost something you lost it forever."

The idea to find the man gradually faded away, but the storekeeper knew it was a load on his mind. Later, he fell ill and was dying. On his deathbed, he called in his son and told him to continue managing the bookstore. He exhorted that the man he was waiting for would turn up one day as long as the bookstore opened.

However, the son thought that running a bookstore was too tiresome and couldn't bring in much money. He talked it over with his girlfriend and she agreed with him. Soon, he closed the bookstore and on his girlfriend's suggestion he opened a new shop selling clothes. They went to Zhejiang together to purchase clothes at a lower price and came back to sell them in their shop. By and by, both of them were familiar with the purchasing routes and the business procedures, and they made acquaintance with wholesalers there and established good relations with them. Later, when they were busy or their shop was short of hands, he or his girlfriend took the trip and made the purchase alone.

It was not easy to run a clothes shop. After half a year, they worked out the accounts and found that apart from spending there was little money left. His girlfriend complained a lot: "In this way, when on earth can we earn enough money to get married?" After a year, his girlfriend left with a good-bye remark that she would go to Zhejiang to seek further development.

After she left, he closed his shop and rented the house to a real estate agency. Living on the rent, he led a much comfortable life, more comfortable than that of his father running a bookstore.

The man who ran the real estate agency was very sociable as he had many eyes and ears to keep himself well-informed.[8] Of course, this was one of the most important qualities for a real estate agent. Many people, intentionally or unintentionally, provided him with various information, such as who had moved to a new home and wanted to let out the old home, who had relatives in need of selling the old home so as to buy a new one on a loan, or who had relatives calling in but had no room for accommodation, and so on and so forth. To most people, these were just household affairs or street gossips, but to him, daily chatters or mundane news meant money or profits.

Soon, he established good relations with his neighbors. When he was not busy, he whiled away his time chatting with them. People in the neighborhood knew his purpose, and they said: "To us, chatting is chatting, but to him, chatting with people makes money..." Obviously, his neighbors saw how smart he was but couldn't emulate. For example, once, he heard of an apartment with two bedrooms and one living room in a certain place, and after three days, he got the down payment from the one who wanted to buy it, and after approximately ten days the apartment changed hands and he earned twenty thousand.

In truth, he made money not only by chatting with his neighbors but also by using his brains. Besides, he had great abilities in working and thinking, which contributed a lot to his success. Where did his great abilities in working and thinking come from? From his experience and from books. He liked reading very much, and he read whatever at hand. As the old saying goes, books furnish everything that is needed in one's life.[9] He thought it really made sense.

Once, he read an anthology of someone's diaries, which was published in volumes and consisted of tens of books. The author was not well-known and after his death, in memory of him, his children and grandchildren jointly funded the publication of his diaries. In the postscript, his grandchildren wrote about one regrettable thing: Their grandpa kept writing diaries from the age of 20 to 40 and these diaries recorded his life in those twenty years. After 40, their grandpa no longer wrote diaries. But it was such a pity that they couldn't find his diaries from 1936 to 1939, for the old housekeeper, by mistake, sold them as waste paper. During the past years they spared no efforts in finding the lost diaries but all their endeavors were in vain. Therefore, the anthology of diaries was actually incomplete.

He felt pity for the diary-keeper. He imagined what happened in those three years. What changes took place in the old man's life? Perhaps nothing special happened? Where were the lost diaries?

Never had he dreamed that the lost diaries were stored in a small compartment in his agency! The compartment had a small door with a big iron lock. The house owner once said that his father left him some old books and that he begrudged to throw them away though they were useless to him. Believing that the heap of old books would make the house messy and crowded, the house owner partitioned off a corner of the hall and made a small compartment to hold these books.

Because of the small compartment, the hall appeared smaller and the house owner had to let out his house at a lower price. At first, the house owner's girlfriend disagreed and urged him not to make the partition so that the hall could be larger and they could get more money. The house owner considered her suggestion but in the end he insisted on his decision.

These days, the stores along this old street took on a new look and along with these changes the street turned noisy and bustling. One day, the man who collected second-hand goods and once came here to sell the diaries walked past the street again, but he almost couldn't recognize it. Stopping at the door of the real estate agency for a while, he didn't recognize it to be that old bookstore. After all, he was not born in this city and the old streets and alleys in this city looked almost the same in his eyes. "Why are the bookstores fewer and fewer?" He sighed. To him, this problem had a lot to do with his income.

Of course, he didn't know what happened after he sold the diaries. That day, after he sold the diaries and got the money, he left the bookstore in ecstasy, thinking that he was so lucky to find such a profitable job. He made up his mind to continue collecting second-hand goods, hoping that one day he might, again, get a lucky fluke. Of course, he didn't sit at home all day long, waiting for the stroke of luck;[10] instead, he continued toiling and moiling every day, collecting old things from door to door and selling them to the salvage stations. Sometimes, he earned only a little, and sometimes he earned nothing at all. Sometimes, he even got swindled and lost money. For instance, he once collected a crate of old copper wires and not until he sent it to the salvage station did he find that under a surface layer of copper wires were mud clumps and broken bricks — in that case he lost more than one hundred yuan. Anyway, he still believed that penny and penny laid up would be many.[11] Such a faith sustained him to work hard, day by day, as he walked through each and every street and alley of this city.

One day, as he rode his cart across a street, a man stopped him and asked whether he had collected a bundle of old notebooks. He felt that the man had asked a strange question and replied that he collected notebooks every day, such as children's exercise books, family account books and even notebooks with family accounts years ago. For example, on one account book there was such a record: ten cents for one kilo of sweet potato powder. At the sight of it, he became quite curious: The city-dwellers also ate sweet potato powder? How could it be so cheap? Later, he found out that it was a record twenty years ago. Hearing his words, the inquiring man walked away in disappointment.

In the following days, on rainy nights when he had nothing to do, he thought of the inquiring man occasionally. Who was he? Why did he look for the old notebooks? It was unlikely that he came just for children's exercise books. While guessing, he vaguely recalled the diaries to his mind. However, a long time had passed, and he didn't remember the details. He only remembered that he collected some old diaries and he even read one passage in one diary. As to what was written, he totally forgot. Where did I sell them? Either the salvage station or the book stalls along the streets, or second-hand bookstores. Where did I collect them? What kind of family was it? Which alley did the family live in? He couldn't remember. Why did the family sell the diaries? Did the family sell them intentionally or unintentionally? If they sold them by mistake, they must be regretful and worried. Although he came from the countryside, he knew that diaries were a person's secret. No wonder the man looking for the diaries looked that anxious and harassed! If the diary-keeper noted down something about his ex-girlfriend, it would be terrible if the diaries were lost or seen by his present girlfriend.

While thinking of these, he fell asleep.

His hometown was a faraway poverty-stricken area, and since he came to this city he did all he could. He found his calling in collecting old things, so he insisted on doing it for quite a long time. Year in and year out he saved his money with patience and when the money got more he went to the post office. His wife and two children were waiting for his money at home. His wife stowed the money for future use in either building a house or supporting their children to go on studying. He hoped both of his children could go to university.

He remitted the money in the post office and walked back with the receipt tucked in his pocket. Passing the barber's, he went in. Pearl must know he would come. Each time when he dropped by, she would greet him with a "Hi". If she was not busy, she would stand up and said to him, "Follow me." And if she had her hands full, she would console him, "Wait a moment."

He could feel Pearl's special feelings for him, but Pearl didn't admit it. She said, "No, I treat all of my guests the same way."

But that particular time was different. After he sold the diaries and earned a tidy sum of money, he went to the barber's. Seeing him come earlier than before, Pearl felt strange and asked, "You came the day before yesterday!"

All these things, together with those old diaries, were gradually fading away in his memory.

(Published in No. 3, 2004)

1. 这篇小说写了好几段故事，故事的主人公也在不断变化：收旧货的人、店主、店主的儿子、租房的人，最后又返回到收旧货的人。读者阅读时要注意，主人公在改变，人称代词he的指代对象不同。另外，全文的对话大多没有采取直接引语的形式，人物对话直接穿插在故事的叙述中。为了方便阅读，译文中的对话都加上了引号。

2. 有些汉语的表达很有特点，比如"做过几次交易以后，他就学乖了一点，当然后来他又更乖了一点"，即一天比一天学得多，一天比一天有进步的意思。After several deals, he learned much and more. 形容词或副词的原形与比较级连用，有"一次比一次更……"的意思。例如：他的喊声很大，而且一声比一声高。His voice became loud and louder.

3. "风雨飘摇"、"朝不保夕"、"偷鸡不着蚀把米"这些都是汉语成语或俗语，在翻译时，为了更好地传播中国文化，可以保留原语中的形象。有时需要适当加注，补充说明；有时就要采用符合译入语表达习惯的方法翻译。这里就是采用了后一种方法："风雨飘摇，朝不保夕"译为：... he couldn't know at dawn what might happen by dusk. "偷鸡不着蚀把米"译为：... he went for wool and came home shorn ...

4. get out of the bed from the wrong side 指某人心情不好，情绪欠佳，从早上

一睁眼就火气很大。

5. "收购员就一屁股坐下来，说，不卖拉倒。"这句中的"一屁股坐下来"形象生动，既有动作，又有"扑通"坐下去的声音。"不卖拉倒"是口语化的表达，表达收购员不高兴的语气。The man plopped down into his chair at once: "Up to you!" 其中plop为"扑通声、扑通一声坠落"之意。

6. "他不懂这里边的规矩"，翻译成：He didn't know the ropes in this circle. 译文中使用的短语to know the ropes 是知道内情、熟悉内情、知道诀窍等意思。

7. "我这真是守着和尚找和尚，指着赵洲问赵洲，舍近而求远了……"How silly I am! I am looking for a horse while riding on it — I am seeking far and neglecting what lay close at hand! "守着和尚找和尚，指着赵洲问赵洲"都是有典故的，可以不译为"和尚"、"赵洲"，把"骑马找马"的意思翻译出来就好，这样利于读者理解，不影响行文流畅。

8. "眼线耳目比较多"译为many eyes and ears，在英语中是有这样的表达的，读者可以看懂，且比较生动。

9. "书中自有黄金屋，书中自有颜如玉"，这是中国古人对勤奋读书和考取功名的认识。读书考取功名是当时人生的一条绝佳出路，考取功名后，才能得到财富和美女。译文简单处理为：As the old saying goes, books furnish everything that is needed in one's life.

10. "那一次他得到一笔意外的收获，非常高兴……"、"坐等意外好运的到来……"分别翻译为a lucky fluke（意外的收获，侥幸成功），the stroke of luck（撞大运）。

11. "他始终坚信自己的钱会积少成多的"翻译成：Anyway, he still believed that penny and penny laid up would be many. 符合英语表达习惯。"积土成山""积水成川""积少成多"还可以表达为：Heaped-up earth makes a mountain; accumulated water makes a river — many a little makes a mickle; accumulate/amass little by little; many a little makes a mickle.

捏了一把汗

○ 李红旗

明天就要立冬了，我的玉米秆子还在地里直愣愣地竖着，风一吹，就会哗啦哗啦响。田野一望无际，假如站在我那片玉米秆子之外去看的话。站在我的地里，只能看见死掉的玉米。

我现在一下子就看到了整片田野，四面八方都是。甚至可以望见田野之外的另一片田野。

田野并不真的是一望无际的，但却总让人想到一望无际或者别的什么形容这些大东西的话。

我把锄头的木柄杵在腋下，站在这样的田野上，简直无聊至极。

一架飞机在天上轻轻地飞，像睡着了一样。要不是它那条缓缓拖出来的白尾巴提醒，我也许会以为那是一只被拍死在天上的大蚊子。

天真大。在天底下呆久了，人的心情就会不知不觉地沉重起来。就算你本来有一副好心情。

我没有什么好心情。我的心情很一般。

盛可以刚走。他跟我聊了一会儿天，还给我烟抽，我手头的这支便是盛可以给的。我耳朵上还夹着一支。

我烟瘾很大。

盛可以总让我想到年轻时的自己。那额头，那脚步，那心不在焉的身影都仿佛在向别人表示：这是一个一出生就活腻味了的人。

我今年已经四十岁了，俗话说，四十不惑。我对这句俗话感到十分迷惑，说真的。

盛可以刚刚十八，他得下多大的力气才能活到我这把年纪呢。

您也许已经看出来了，我的思绪很乱。我突然想起了初次跟盛可以建立友谊时的情景。那是一个冬天，天气冷得让人难以置信，我蜷着身子坐在炉子旁边，情绪十分的低落。每当气温下降到摄氏零度以下的时候，我就会感到压抑、伤感，常常莫名其妙地流眼泪。我不能理解气候。这也许是我压抑、伤感的原因。

不知道为什么，那一年的冬天我尤其喜欢流泪。

泪水滴在炉子上，一下一下地蒸发了。我对这件事情有点着迷。这时候，门外响起了咯吱咯吱的脚步声，很快我的门就被推开了。

"红旗，孩子他爹死了！"

我抬起盈满泪水的双眼看了看说话的女人。王春兰一只脚踩在我的屋子里，另一只脚依然留在屋外，脸上的鼻涕比眼泪要多得多。我还没明白怎么回事，她就扑到了我的怀里，鼻子在我的肩头蹭呀蹭的。好多年以前，王春兰就这么哭过，那时候她还是处女呢，当年我也真是不懂事，她哭得那么厉害，我还是狠心脱光了她的衣裳。我又能怎样呢？假如不那么做，她也许会一个人偷偷哭上好几天，还要恨我一辈子。我不了解女人。这些年来，我不断地脱下她们的衣裳，又给她们穿起来，结果呢，我越来越不了解她们了。

这也许是我压抑、伤感的原因。

我想着当年王春兰趴在我的肩头哭泣。盛可以就站在不远处怯生生地看着我们。他是跟母亲一起来的。我以前真是粗心，居然没有发现这孩子跟我是那么的相像。

刹那间，我对盛可以产生了好感。

王春兰再也没有说什么，她呆在我的怀里继续一抽一抽地哭，但我知道那是装出来的。

红旗，孩子他爹死了！我知道这是什么意思——往后，她一旦性欲上来，随时都会推开我的门，要是我不答应，她就会趴在我的身上不起来，让我备受良心的折磨。

"好了，"我拍拍王春兰的肩，告诉她，"我依你。"

说完，我的眼睛再一次湿润了起来。

接下来，我们当着孩子的面干了不该干的事情。我很清楚，不这么办，王春兰是不会罢休的。

后来王春兰终于走了，我请她把孩子留下来陪我多玩一会儿。

"我很寂寞。"我对王春兰说。

她十分愉快地答应了我。

"孩子，你长大了想干什么呢？"

"像你一样。"

我忍不住苦笑了起来，"孩子，你对我了解多少？"

"我知道的可多了，"盛可以不像刚进门时那么不知所措了，他扬了扬胳膊，快活地说："有那么多人恨你，我希望做一个人人都恨我的人。"

"我怎么不知道呢，你是听谁说起这件事情来的？"

"我爸爸活着的时候，就非常恨你，经常跟一伙男人聚在一起一边喝酒一边说你的坏话，说一会儿就叹一会儿气，最后总有一个家伙喝得不省人事，摇摇晃晃地站起来说要去杀你。"

"然后呢？"

"然后其余的人就会拉住那个喝醉的家伙。"

看到我迷惑不解的样子，盛可以又补充道："他们有时候会将那个喝醉的家伙暴打一顿，有时候一起抱着那个喝醉的家伙痛哭，更多的时候是先把他暴打一顿，再抱着他痛哭。"

"原来是这样呀。"我看着盛可以，若有所思地点了点头。

盛可以的话让我想起了另一个寒冷的冬天，真是不巧，我记得那天也是刚刚下过一场大雪。你们可以想见，当我一大清早睁开眼看见这个白茫茫的世界时，心里是多么的压抑、伤感。但是，人不能总沉浸在自己的情绪中，躺在床上抽了两支烟后，我就出门去找一个女人。我跟她有个约定。

可是，我遇到麻烦了。她的丈夫正与她躺在他们的床上，他也在抽着一支烟，看上去很愉快的样子(我有必要说明一下，她丈夫的烟瘾也挺大的)。假如这件事情发生在今天，我一定会扭开头去走开。可那时候我年轻呀，做事冲动得不行(我知道，他们背地里都叫我愣头青)。我不假思索地让她的丈夫从床上下来。他问我为什么，我也没有回答他(熟悉我的人都知道，我不爱跟人说话)。他当时的样子为难极了，涨红着脸，就像受了侮辱似的。我不得不把他从床上拖下来，他哭得再伤心都没有用。

一点都不骗你，我有一副铁石心肠。

那天早晨，我做了曾答应他老婆的事情。过程中她的丈夫一次又一次地从地上爬起来试图把我拉下床去，我都制止了他。我做事情一向是这样。你们可能不知道，当她丈夫最后一次跌到地上时还吐了血。简直令人心碎。

唉，不说这些了。想起那时候，心里还真是怪不好受的。

247

我出神地看着大片大片的田野，思绪在静静地翻滚。飞机依然在我头顶的天空上飞着，依然像睡着了一样，但是白尾巴却拖得更长了。其实，就算它一直动也不动地呆在天上，甚至连白尾巴也不拖出来，我也知道那是一架飞机，而不是什么拍死在天上的大蚊子。人总是这样，一旦情绪低落下来，就会变得像个诗人，说些不该说的话。

　　我对飞机了解得不多。

　　我也不想去了解，你们不要逼我。

　　我又想到了一些关于盛可以的事情。他曾对我说，他想做一个像我一样的人。我并没有当真，我觉得他还是个孩子。时间不久我就把这件事情给忘了。

　　后来，我断断续续从一些女人的口中知道了一些消息。她们的丈夫开始恨盛可以，但他们对我也恨得更厉害了。那些女人说，盛可以总对她们的丈夫说是我派他去跟他们的妻子睡觉的。正如我听到其他消息时的表现一样，每次听到这样的消息，我也只是苦笑。我心想：这孩子真是有他的一套。

　　时间过得真是快啊，一转眼的工夫地里的麦子就熟了。那一天，布谷鸟在天上叫，而我呢，理所当然地要在地里收割那些成熟的小麦。突然，盛可以来到了我的身边。

　　"旗哥，你最近过得怎样？"盛可以向我递来一支烟。

　　我停下手中的活，看了看盛可以。好些日子不见，他长高了，还留起了小胡子，我差一点没认出他来。

　　"正常。"我对盛可以说。

　　"正常就好。"盛可以说。他说话的样子让我觉得我的生活是装在他心里的一块大石头，知道我正常，那块石头就落了地。

　　盛可以没再说什么。大概半分钟之后，一只布谷鸟从他的头顶飞过，匆匆忙忙地叫了一声。盛可以把两只手掌拢到嘴边，对着布谷鸟飞走的方向也叫了两声。他学得挺像的。那只布谷鸟回头看了他一眼，但是并没有往回飞的意思。它很快地回过头去，继续朝前方飞远了。

　　盛可以坚持陪我抽完那支烟，忍不住向我告辞。他是一个游手好闲的人。

　　"旗哥，我再到别处去转转。"

　　"嗯，去吧，别忘了代我向你妈问好。"

　　那一年的秋天，我结了婚。我对以前的生活感到厌倦了。我想跟过去的自己一刀两断。我妻子也很支持我这么做。当我把自己的想法向她说了之后，她哭了，流着眼泪亲了我的脖子和嘴。

我结婚的那天，盛可以给我送来两瓶酒。到了半夜，我们俩都喝醉了。正房的大厅被我们吐得满地都是，我老婆一个人睡在侧房，我不知道她睡着了没有。她一定对我感到很失望。

　　天快亮的时候，我搂着盛可以说："可以，人活一辈子真苦啊！"

　　盛可以不住地点头，却没有说话。过了一会儿，他突然对我说："旗哥，你跟孙红霞搞过没有？"

　　那天我的确喝多了，以至于盛可以问了三遍我才明白他的意思。我一边摇头，一边不由自主地溜到了桌子底下。

　　"真是出人意料，"盛可以说，"孙红霞还挺诚实的。"

　　"嗯。"我又想吐，可是胃里没有一点可吐的东西。

　　"你该跟她搞一下，挺愉快的。"

　　我不知道盛可以什么时候走的，等我清醒过来的时候，发现自己躺在床上，屋子外面的阳光非常好，我老婆正在喂阳光下的鸡。

　　"啊……啊……啊……"我伸了个长长的懒腰。

　　"你醒了。"我妻子在院子里问我。

　　"啊……啊……啊……"我又伸了个长长的懒腰，这才问我妻子："嗯，我睡了多久？"

　　"都快两天了。"

　　我吃了一惊。

　　一从床上爬起来，我就去了孙红霞的家里。

　　接下来的事情，我不说你们也猜得到。正如我遇到的大多数女人一样，孙红霞也十分喜欢在跟从没一块儿睡过觉的人睡完觉后哭泣。我一遍遍地抚摸她，问她是不是我的行为给她造成了很大的伤害。她也不说话，就知道哭。在我的经验里，真的是很多女人都有这个习惯。但是那一次不知道怎么回事，看着孙红霞的样子，我的心里突然产生了异样的感觉，就仿佛感到了愧疚。当时我就知道，我再也不会快乐了。

　　从孙红霞家出来，我碰上了她的丈夫，他跟我打招呼：

　　"旗哥，您好，再坐会儿吧。"

　　我不知道该对他说些什么。我觉得自己就像一只老鼠似的溜走了。

　　后来，盛可以出了事。一个刚刚下过雪的早晨（又是这样的早晨，真是没有一点办法），我正在睡觉，我老婆就躺在我的旁边。下了一整夜的雪让我的心情变得极端沉重，即使在梦里也是这样。

我的门一下子被打开了，就像被踹开了一样。在此之前，还从没有人敢这么干。我从梦中惊醒，心想，是谁这么大胆呀？

　　结果我看到了什么呢？我看到了一条血淋淋的胳膊搭在我的门槛上，伸在前面的手不停地抓挠我家的地面。真是惨不忍睹。

　　"旗哥，救我！"一个疲惫的声音在那条胳膊的后面悲伤地呼唤。

　　我的妻子简直惊呆了。

　　我披上大衣来到了盛可以的身边，"可以，你怎么了？"我不安地问道。

　　"我被人打了。"

　　我觉得帮助盛可以是我的义务。我把他抱到屋里，将炉火烧旺，我妻子甚至把我们的被子裹到了盛可以的身上。

　　"慢慢说，不要着急，我会替你做主的。"

　　经过盛可以断断续续的叙述，我渐渐明白了这件事情。那一阵子，盛可以有点搞昏了头，居然跑到乡里胡搞去了。他总觉得自己已经混出来了。他带着这样的心态跑到别人家里想快活快活。人家家里的丈夫很不喜欢他这样做。

　　盛可以执意要搞，人家的丈夫铁了心一般死活不依他。

　　结果呢？当然是闹僵了。

　　人家把他活活打了一顿，还差一点割掉了他的鸡巴。

　　"还差一点割掉了我的鸡巴。"盛可以裹着我家的被子坐在地上亲口对我说。

　　听了他的话，我心里咯噔就是那么一下。

　　我不知道该怎么对他说。我搞不清盛可以想让我怎么处理这件事情。

　　"他或许希望我陪他去那户人家讨个说法吧。"我在心里暗自琢磨。

　　我想的一点都没错，盛可以果真就是这个意思。

　　后来，我妻子为我们准备了丰盛的午餐，还把菜刀磨得锃亮锃亮的让我们带上。我们没有喝酒，盛可以本打算喝的，我没有同意。他一向比较尊重我的意见，至少当着我的面是这个样子的。

　　事情并没有我妻子准备的那么糟糕。那户人家的丈夫见到我非常客气，拉着我的手一遍又一遍地捏弄着，就像见到久别的亲人似的。

　　"旗哥，原来是你的兄弟呀。"他又拉过盛可以的手用同样的语气说："你怎么不早说呢！"

　　后来，他说要请我们喝酒，我很愉快地答应了他。酒过三巡，盛可以把一个刚刚倒空的酒瓶子砸到了人家的头上。我并不支持他那么做，可我拿他没有一点办法。

回去的路上，盛可以对我说："旗哥，你对我真好。"

我苦笑了一下。当时我想，这也许正是我压抑、伤感的原因。

明天就要立冬了，我的玉米秆子还在地里直愣愣地竖着，风一吹，就会哗啦哗啦响。刚才我正打算用我的锄头将那些玉米秆子一株一株地掘出来。这是一件很无奈的事情。盛可以突然出现在我的面前。他穿着一身新衣服，脖子上还系着一条鲜艳的领带。也许是因为这身装束的缘故，盛可以看上去比较害羞。像往常一样，他向我递来一支烟。

"旗哥，有个事儿我不知道该不该对你讲。"

"讲嘛。"

"刚才我把嫂子干了。"

听了这句话，我的心里咯噔就来了那么一下。一点都不夸张，我几乎说不出话来了。

"旗哥，你不会怪我吧？"盛可以有些紧张地说。

"怎么会呢，你不用放在心上。"

"说实话，旗哥，干的时候我倒没觉得有什么，挺快乐的，可是一旦干完了，心里就隐隐地有些不安，感到好像做了对不起你的事情似的。"

"你真会搞笑，可以，你怎么突然间变得这么幼稚呢！"

"旗哥，你真的不怪我吗？"

"好了，好了，婆婆妈妈的真像个农民，我可不喜欢你变成这个样子。"为了消除盛可以的疑虑，我努力咧开我的大嘴，笑得皮开肉绽。我想我从没有这么开心过，以后也不大可能再做出如此开心的表情了。

"那好，旗哥，既然这样，我先走了。"盛可以又递给我一支烟。刚才的那支我还没有抽完，但我依然接了过来。我把它夹在我的耳朵上。

"等会儿再抽它。"我在心里对自己说。

盛可以慢慢走远了，他的背影渐渐恢复了往昔的神采。

"这孩子有了良心，"我自言自语道，"往后恐怕要吃苦头了。"

盛可以真的走远了，仿佛走出了良心的阴影，走到了我力所不能及的高处。但是，一想起他方才的话语和表情，我还是暗暗为他捏了一把汗。

On Edge[1]

○ *Li Hongqi*

Tomorrow was the Beginning of Winter[2]. My corn stalks were still in the patch, standing erect and rustling in the wind. Seen from the place outside my corn patch, the vast fields stretched as far as the eye could see. However, standing in my patch, I could see nothing but the corn stalks which had withered and died away.

At the moment, stretches of fields surrounded me on all sides and I could even see the fields farther beyond.

In truth, fields could not be really endless but people liked using such words as "endless" or "boundless" to describe them.

The hoe handle under my armpit, I stood on the field, feeling extremely bored.

A plane was flying overhead, so gently as if it were asleep. But for the white trail it left I would consider it a big mosquito swatted dead in the sky.

The sky was so big. Under the big sky, one's heart might unconsciously grow heavy, even if he had a good mood at first.

I had no good mood. My mood was just so-so.

Sheng Keyi had just left. He chatted with me just now and even gave me cigarettes — I was smoking one now and put the other on my ear.

I smoked like a chimney.

At the sight of Sheng Keyi, I always thought of my youthful days. His forehead, his gait and his absent-mindedness made it clear that he was a man who had been tired of living since he was born.

I was forty years old. "Man is free of confusion at the age of forty." To be frank, I was quite confused with this old saying.[3]

Sheng Keyi was only eighteen. How much effort would he take to reach my age?

You might have noticed that my mind was in turmoil. I suddenly thought of the day when I established friendship with Sheng Keyi. That was an incredibly cold day in winter. I huddled myself by the stove, downcast and depressed a great deal. Each time the temperature fell below zero, I felt sad and dejected, and even shed tears with no reason. I couldn't understand climate, indeed. Perhaps this was the reason why I always felt depressed.

That winter, I always shed tears. I didn't know why.

Drops of tears fell on the stove and disappeared into vapor right away. I was a little bit fascinated. At this time, I heard footsteps crunching close to my door.[4] Soon, the door was flung open.

"Hongqi, my husband died!"

Raising my tearful eyes, I saw Wang Chunlan. With one foot stepping in and the other still outside, she appeared sad, with much more snot than tears hanging on her face. Before I made any response, she plunged herself into my arms and rubbed her nose on my shoulder. Several years ago, she cried in my face like this. At that time, she was quite young, a virgin. That time, she cried so hard that I could do nothing but strip her naked. What else could I do at that moment? If I hadn't done so, she would have cried continuously for several days and she would have hated me for the rest of her life. In fact, I didn't understand women. During these years, I always took off their clothes and then helped them put their clothes back on, only to find that I didn't understand them more and more.

Maybe, this was why I always felt depressed.

That year, when Wang Chunlan was crying in my arms, Sheng Keyi stood close to us, looking at us quietly and timidly. He came with his mother. How careless I was! He resembled me so much! But I didn't notice it at that time.

At that moment, all of a sudden, I grew well-disposed toward him.

Resting in my arms, Wang Chunlan continued sobbing. It was but a show. I knew her.

"Hongqi, my husband died!" — I knew what she meant: From now on, once she had a sexual urge she would come to me at any time. If I didn't agree, she would crawl onto my body and harass my soul.

"OK." I patted her on the shoulder and told her, "I'll comply with you."

My eyes turned wet again.

Then, we did "that". I knew if I didn't do it she would not let me go. In fact, we shouldn't do it in Sheng Keyi's presence.

When she was about to leave, I asked her to place her child in my care for a while.

"I am lonely." I said to her.

She agreed in a pleasant mood.

"Boy, what will you do when you grow up?"

"I want to be a man like you."

"How much do you know about me?" I said and smiled bitterly.

"A lot." The child, no longer feeling uneasy, became relaxed a bit. He waved his arm and said to me, "I know that a lot of people hate you, and I hope I can be a man hated by everyone."

"How come I am hated? I don't know it! How do you know it?"

"My dad, when he was alive, hated you very much. He always spoke ill of you when drinking with his friends. While cursing you, he kept sighing and groaning, and in the end, there was always one who, dead drunk, stood up shakily to say that he wanted to kill you."

"And then?"

"And then, the rest of the gang would stop that drunkard."

Seeing me confused, Sheng Keyi added, "Sometimes, they beat up that drunkard and sometimes, they hugged together crying aloud, and in most cases they beat him up first and cried together afterward."

"Oh, I see." Looking at Sheng Keyi, I nodded thoughtfully.

His words reminded me of another cold winter. That day, as luck would have it,[5] a heavy snow just stopped. You could imagine how I felt when I opened my eyes and saw the white world around me. How depressing! How gloomy! Lying on bed, I smoked two cigarettes. Realizing that I shouldn't indulge myself in such a bad mood for too long, I decided to go out. I had a date with a woman.

To my disappointment, as I got to the woman's home, her husband was there. They were lying on bed and to pour oil on the flames, her husband was enjoying a cigarette! He looked quite happy. (Her husband was a heavy smoker, too.) If I confronted such a situation today, I would turn and leave at once. But at that time I was too young to control myself. (They called me Hothead behind my back,[6] for I always did things on an impulse.) Without hesitation, I ordered her husband to get off the bed. He asked me why. I didn't answer him. (People who were familiar with me all knew that I didn't like talking too much.) He looked awkward, his face turning red, as if he were severely humiliated by somebody. I already ran out my patience and tugged him off the bed. It was no use crying in front of me.

True, my heart was as hard as nether millstone.

That morning, I did the thing I promised that woman to do. Her husband, over and over again, climbed up, trying to pull me off the bed. Of course, I stopped his attempt. I always did things in my way. The last time her husband fell onto the floor, he spat blood. How heartbreaking!

I didn't want to mention it! Recalling the past brought a sting of uneasiness in my mind.

Now, stretches of fields extended in front of my eyes. Gazing at them, I fell into a trance, the train of my thoughts wandering and winding its way quietly and wildly. That plane was still flying above my head as gently as if it were asleep, and the only change was that its white trail grew longer. In fact, even if it stopped in the sky, motionless and soundless, with no trail left, I knew it was not a big mosquito swapped dead in the sky but a plane. People always did things like me — once feeling upset, they tended to be sentimental and say something rather baffling as a poet did.

I didn't know much about planes.

I really didn't want to know much about planes. You'd better not make me.

I thought of Sheng Keyi again. He once told me that he wanted to be a man like me. I didn't take his words seriously at first, since he was just a kid. Afterward, I totally forgot his words.

Later, from some women's mouths, I got the news about Sheng Keyi. Those women's husbands hated him much and detested me more, for he always told them that it was I who sent him to sleep with their wives. Each time I heard such news, as usual, I smiled bitterly, thinking that he really had his way![7]

How time flew! Soon the wheat grew mature. One day, as cuckoos were chirping in the sky, I went to the field to reap the wheat. All at once, Sheng Keyi came to me.

"Brother Qi, how are you doing these days?" Handing me a cigarette, he asked.

Stopping my work, I took a look at him. We hadn't seen each other for some time. He grew taller and had a beard now. I almost couldn't recognize him.

"Normal." I replied.

"Good to be normal." He said. Hearing my words, he seemed relieved as if my living condition was a heavy stone in his heart.

He didn't say more. Half a minute later, a cuckoo flew over his head, cooing in a hurry at him. He cupped his hands on his mouth and called at the cuckoo with a perfectly mimicked chirping sound. The cuckoo turned its head to cast a look at him but showed no intention of coming back. Quickly it turned ahead and flew away.

Sheng Keyi insisted on accompanying me for a while. After I finished that cigarette, he couldn't wait to say goodbye to me. He was an idler interested in loafing and wandering about.

"Bro, I'll go to other places to have a look."

"Er. Up to you. Send my regards to your mom."

That year, in autumn, I got married. I was tired of my previous life and wanted a new start. My wife supported my resolution. When she heard me talking about my plans, she cried and kissed me on my neck and lips.

On the day I got married, Sheng Keyi sent me two bottles of liquor. We drank till midnight. Both of us got dead drunk and vomitted all over the main room. My wife slept in the side room that night. I didn't know whether she went to sleep or not. She must be disappointed with me.

At daybreak, I held Sheng Keyi in my arms and said to him, "Keyi, how hard life can be!"

He nodded his consent but didn't say a word. After a while, he asked me abruptly, "Bro, have you slept with Sun Hongxia?"

As I was thoroughly drunk, I didn't hear him clearly. Not until he repeated his question three times did I understand what he was talking about. In response, I shook my head but couldn't control myself from slipping under the table.

"Unbelievable!" Sheng Keyi said. "So she told the truth after all."

"Er." I wanted to vomit but nothing was left in my stomach.

"You'd better get it on with her. You'll feel good."

I didn't know when he left my home. When I woke up, I found myself lying on my bed. It was sunny outside and my wife was feeding chickens under the sunlight.

"Ah… ah… ah…" I stretched my body and yawned.

"Awake?" My wife asked me in the yard.

"Ah… ah… ah…" I gave my body a stretch again. "How long have I slept?"

"Nearly two days."

I felt surprised.

After I got out of the bed, I immediately went to Sun Hongxia's.

You could guess what happened later. Like most women I met, Sun Hongxia was fond of shedding tears after sleeping with a man whom she had never slept with before. I caressed her again and again and asked if I had hurt her. She said nothing but cried. My experience told me that most women had this habit. However, I didn't know what was wrong with me that time. Looking at Sun Hongxia, I suddenly had this strange feeling in my heart. I felt guilty and I knew I wouldn't be happy from that moment on.

On my way home, I met Sun Hongxia's husband. He greeted me,

"Hi, Brother Qi, how are you? Come to my home for a visit."

I didn't know what to say to him, so I slipped away like a mouse.

Sheng Keyi got himself into trouble in the end. A heavy snow kept falling for the whole night and at dawn it stopped. (Such a morning again!) I was sleeping on bed and my wife lay beside me. A whole night's snow had given me a heavy heart, even in my dreams.

All at once, the door was pushed open as if it were kicked hard by someone outside. Nobody dared to do so. I woke up in surprise, wondering who had the guts.

What did I see? An arm with blood all over on my doorsill and a hand keeping scratching the floor! It was too horrible!

"Bro, help!" An exhausted voice wailed desperately behind that arm.

My wife was flabbergasted.

Putting on my coat, I walked to Sheng Keyi, "What happened?" I asked in a disturbed tone.

"I was beaten up."

It was my duty to help him. I held him into the room and turned up the stove fire to make him warm. My wife even wrapped him with our quilt.

"Take it easy. Don't worry. I'll back you up."

He told me the whole thing in sporadic gasps and gradually I came to know what had happened to him: During that period, Sheng Keyi slept with too many women. He felt he was somebody and deserved to have pleasures with other men's wives. He even wanted to have sex with a woman in the town. Of course, the woman's husband didn't allow him to do so.

But he insisted. The woman's husband refused resolutely.

The result? Sheng Keyi and that man had a fight.

The woman's husband gave him a good beating and in great fury that man nearly cut off Sheng Keyi's dick.

"He even wanted to cut off my dick!" Sheng Keyi cried in my quilt.

As I heard his words, my heart thumped hard.

I didn't know what I should say to him, nor did I know what he wanted me to do.

"Perhaps he wanted me to give a lesson to that man?" I guessed.

I was right. He really wanted me to do so.

After serving us a square meal, my wife sharpened a knife and urged us to take it. We didn't drink liquor. Sheng Keyi had intended to have a drink but I stopped him. He respected my opinion, especially in my presence.

Things didn't go so bad as my wife had expected. The woman's husband was very polite and modest to me, holding my hand as if I were his kinsman after a long separation.

"Brother Qi, I didn't know he was your buddy!" The man held Sheng Keyi's hand and said, "Why not tell me earlier!"

Then, he invited us to have a drink. I agreed with pleasure. After we had filled and emptied our glasses three times, Sheng Keyi abruptly stood up and smashed an empty bottle onto that man's head. I didn't think he was right, but I tried in vain to stop him.

On our way back, Sheng Keyi said to me, "Bro, you are so kind to me."

I smiled bitterly, thinking that it might be the reason why I always felt depressed.

Tomorrow was the Beginning of Winter. My corn stalks were still in the patch, standing erect and rustling in the wind. When I was about to dig out the corn stalks one by one with my hoe, which was rather a tiresome job, Sheng Keyi suddenly appeared in front of me, wearing new clothes all over and a bright-colored tie. In such clothes, he looked a little timid. As usual, he handed me a cigarette.

"Bro, I don't know whether I should tell you…"

"What?"

"Just now I slept with your wife."

My heart thumped violently. I was not exaggerating — I felt so surprised that I couldn't even utter a word.

"Bro, you will not put blame on me, right?" Sheng Keyi asked nervously.

"Of course, no. Don't take it to heart."

"To be frank, bro, when I took your wife I felt happy, nothing special in my heart, but after it, I had this uneasy feeling as if I had done something wrong to you."

"Are you kidding? You become so naïve!"

"Bro, you really are not angry with me?"

"Why! You are nagging like a peasant! I don't like such womanish talk!"[8] To eradicate his doubts, I tried my best to open my mouth wider, grinning from ear to ear. I had never been so happy and I believed I would not have such a happy expression in the future.

"OK, bro. I'll go." He passed me one more cigarette. I took it and put it on my ear. The one he gave me just now was still between my lips.

"I'll smoke this one in a while." I said to myself.

Sheng Keyi walked away, brimming with vigor and vitality again.[9]

"He has a conscience now." I muttered, "I'm afraid he'll know pains and hurts in the future."

Indeed, Sheng Keyi walked away as if he would walk out of dark shadows and to a height I couldn't reach. However, at the very thought of what he just said and how he said it, I was on edge.

1. 小说标题为《捏了一把汗》，译为On Edge，意思是紧张、紧张不安、烦躁。"捏一把汗"可以翻译为：one's palm is wet with perspiration、be breathless with anxiety、be seized with fear、extremely nervous、be on edge、be keyed up，等等。用On Edge这样一个短语作标题，比较简单醒目。这篇小说的翻译有两点要注意：一是全文以第一人称视角进行叙述，短句较多，具有口语化风格，翻译时，语言要符合人物的社会地位和教育背景，符合人物的语言特点；二是叙述采用了插叙、倒叙的写作手法，"我"对过去一些事情的回忆交织出现，因全文都采用的是过去时态，为了便于读者理解，运用段落之间的空行帮助读者理清时间关系。

2. 立冬，是中国二十四节气(The 24 Solar Terms)之一，可译为the Beginning of Winter，或Winter Begins。其他节气例如：谷雨Grain Rain/ 白露White Dews/ 惊蛰Insects Awaken/ 春分Vernal Equinox/ 大暑Great Heat。

3. 中国有"三十而立，四十不惑，五十知天命，六十耳顺，七十从心所欲不逾矩"的说法，"四十不惑"可以翻译为Life begins at forty或者Man should be wise at forty。此处译为：Man is free of confusion at the age of forty，与后面一句I was quite confused with this old saying呼应，具有讽刺效果。

4. "门外响起了咯吱咯吱的脚步声"。I heard the footsteps crunching close to my door. 译文中的crunch既是动词也是描摹声音的拟声词，意思是嘎吱嘎吱作响，在这里用作动词。

5. "……另一个寒冷的冬天，真是不巧，我记得……"。"真是不巧"，或者"真巧"、"真走运"或者"真不幸"都可以翻译成as luck would have it，这是一个英语中常用的句型，意思是fortunately 或者unfortunately。

6. "他们背地里都叫我愣头青"。"背地里"可以翻译为behind one's back或者secretly。比较难译的是"愣头青",指做事不用脑子、匆忙鲁莽的人。译文为：They called me Hothead behind my back, for I always did things on an impulse. 这里所用的hothead意思是急性子的人、鲁莽的人,首字母大写表示这里作为一个名字,后半句for I always did things on an impulse是译者所加,帮助进一步解释Hothead。

7. "这孩子真是有他的一套。"这是口语化的表达,意思是真能耐、真随心所欲、真有办法的意思。译为：I smiled bitterly, thinking that he really had his way! have one's way意思是想怎样就怎样、随心所欲、自主行事。

8. "婆婆妈妈的真像个农民,我可不喜欢你变成这个样子！"You are nagging like a peasant! I don't like such womanish talk!"婆婆妈妈"意思是womanish talk。

9. "他的背影渐渐恢复了往昔的神采。"… brimming with vigor and vitality again. brim with 充满、洋溢着；vigor and vitality 活力、精力。

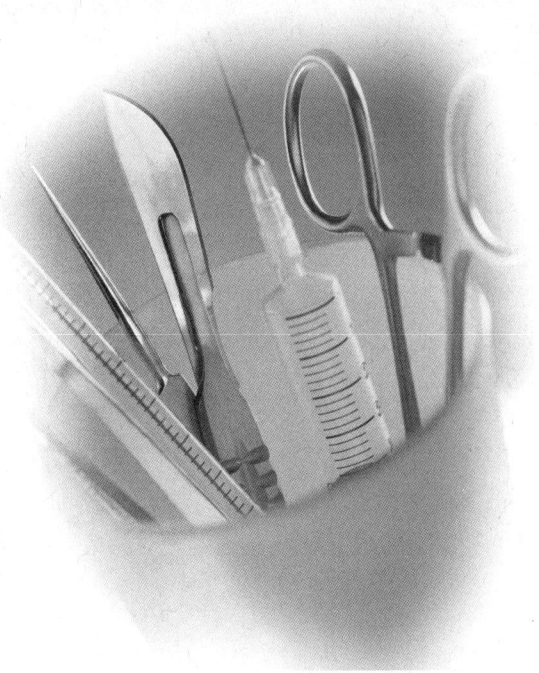

剪刀

○ 郭文斌

你得想办法给我看病，女人说。

知道，男人说，我这就给你叫医生去。

你再别哄我了，我再不想吃那些牛饲料(中药面)了。

那我怎么给你看？

你别给我装聋作哑，你给我把病看好，那些钱我能给你挣回来。

我知道，给你看病的钱，你早就挣回来了。

你把头抬起来，让我看看你的眼睛，我就知道你心里是怎么想的。

男人没有把头抬起来，男人蹲在地上编竹席，两条竹篾在手指间跳跃，像是两条飞鱼。

你得再想想别的办法，靠你打席，就算有十个我，早都死过手了，你听见没有？

听见着呢。

你白天上哪里去了，我让娃娃把村子的肠肠肚肚都找到了，就是找不见个你，如果你烦我，你现在就动手，把我阴治了算了。

你声音小点，娃娃刚睡着，明天还要去学校呢。

女人像是被什么吓了一下似的，侧过脸去看两个孩子，看着看着，眼泪就下来了，就再不说话。

男人把一顶席子打完，侍候女人吃药，女人不吃。我知道，你盼着我死，我就成全了你。

你可千万别吓我,我的胆小。说着,左手把女人的嘴捏开,右手把半杯汤药灌进女人嘴里。一边给女人用毛巾擦嘴,一边说,你就别嚷了,老实给你说吧,我没钱给你看,你知道,医院那鬼地方,是个专门吃钱的地方,上次我们才住了几天?七天,知道吗?就五千。不就动一刀子吗?就五千,五千,我们两个躺下吃,能吃五年,为啥要把这么多钱给医院呢?

男人这样说时,女人的神情反倒好了一些。她帮男人脱下汗褂,脱下臭气冲天的袜子,揭起被子,把男人让进被窝,然后在男人背上挠。男人说,向上,向左,再向左,好。再说你要想开些,你都五十的人了,动上一刀子,再活上五年,花上五千元,值得吗?

男人的腰上就挨了一掐,又一掐。

富贵娘四十五就死了,吉祥娘也没有活到四十,和他们比起来,你都算高寿了,再活,还是这么个样儿,还能活出个啥名堂来?还能活成个黄花闺女?还能跟一次男人?还能上台唱戏?显然不行么。不行就凑合着,能多赚一年是一年,一天是一天,省着那些钱,我给你买吃,买穿,供给儿子上学,你总不愿意看着儿子失学吧,如果你是因为舍不得我,我们现在就说好,下辈子还睡一个炕,咋样?

想得美,下辈子我跟牛跟马也不跟你。

那我就做牛做马。

女人说,你真要气死我吗,那我现在就死给你看。

女人就真死了。

男人忙从箱子里取出老衣给妻子穿。

不想妻子一把把男人打开。女人一看男人手里是一个枕巾,知道上了男人的当,说,把你想得美,我才不死呢,我还要活二十年,活到儿子上大学,上完大学娶媳妇,娶了媳妇生孙子,生了孙子过满月,把你老B干气死,你总不至于把我活埋吧,把我掐死吧,给我灌老鼠药吧,往头顶钉钉子吧?

那也说不定,如果等急了也说不定。

如果你真这样做了,还算一个孝子呢。

你以为我就不敢?如果我今天把你弄死,明天就可以出丧,后天就可以出葬,七天烧一期,十四天烧二期,二十一天烧三期,二十八天烧四期……七期之后,我就能出门了,我再不必每天给你倒尿壶,不必给你喂那些"牛饲料",不必听你烦人的唠叨,你知道你的唠叨有多烦吗?能把鸡烦得不下蛋,把猪烦得不吃食,把牛烦得脱毛,把虱子烦得不咬人……

往出滚,男人的腰上就真挨了一重掐,又一重掐。男人感觉出妻子真的生气了，就有些后悔。这样拌嘴是他们夫妻几十年的家常菜，可现在妻子病犯了，自己是不该这么损的，但他就是想说，他觉得只有这样说上一通才能轻松一下，要不他都快要支撑不住了。

我知道你为啥盼着我死，你以为我不知道？

男人提着的心就放了下来，女人接他的茬，就说明她没有把他的话放到心里去，这让男人再度轻松一下的念头又冒出来。我就是要让你知道，一过七期，我就可以出门了，说不定还有黄花闺女看上我，不是说男人五十一朵花吗？

我知道你老B簧胀了，你舍不得钱给我看病，原来就是省着买尻子。你也不怕把你老B挣死？

男人嗨嗨嗨笑，一边说，也没听说谁干那事给挣死了。

女人说，就算挣不死，就算有黄花闺女给你干，就算换上一百个，也就是那么二分地，还能是银尻子不成？还能是金尻子不成？还会是双眼皮不成？还会长舌头不成？还会开花不成？一次还得一百元。咳，咳咳。女人咳嗽。

男人在女人背上拍着。女人接着说，给别人一次你就舍得一百元，老娘呢？我们结婚都二十八年了。二十八年啊，你把老娘干了多少次？你也不算算？一月少算四次，一年就是四十八次，结婚三十年了，算算，多少？至少一千次吧。你得给我多少钱？少说也得一百万吧。我动十次手术都够了。还不算刚结婚那几月，一晚上不停地拱，像个饿了几辈子的猪。那时你是怎么说的？

男人笑得把一根烟都捏成了沫沫子，说，你算得好，真是好，把这么简单的一件事，闭上眼睛都能做的事，我们竟然干了一千次。其实你算保守了，两千次都冒过了。两千次，就这么一件事，就和你一个人，就那么两下子，竟然做了两千次，你说傻冒不傻冒，寡味不寡味？再说干来干去，干了个啥结果呢？

这话把女人给惹笑了。

男人说，你叫我掏五千元把你治好，就是为了再干这个，我才不干呢。

我还真想再和你好好干一次呢。那事长人精神呢。干上一次，第二天干啥都是有劲头的。

还劲头呢，腰都伸不起来，就那一锅烟工夫的美，剩下的时间都是后悔。

儿子突然从被窝里把头伸出来，说，娘你刚才算错了，不是一百万，是十万，我爹应该给你十万。

原来儿子还醒着，夫妻俩就觉得把人丢大了，一时面面相觑。

男人就索性给儿子说，你说有这十万是给你娘动手术呢，还是留着给你娶媳妇呢？

儿子说给我娘动手术。

为啥？

我不想和我媳妇干，干了腰都伸不起来。

女人睡了，可男人却无论如何睡不着。上前天，他去北集把一头猪卖了三百元；前天，他去南集把几根准备盖房用的檩条卖了六百元。昨天，他去东集把老黄牛卖了一千元，但离动手术需要的钱还差着一大截。这可怎么办呢？我总不能抢银行吧，总不能去偷人吧。如果是女人，我还可以卖身，如果是过去，我还可以卖水，而现在呢？上次动手术时，他把能借的亲戚邻居都借到了，这次实在是再也开不了口了，即便是两个出嫁的女儿。再说他们都在农村，还得过日子啊，总不能把嘴封起来给娘看病吧。但妻子的病是不能再耽误了。看来只有卖口粮了。

就在这时，女人把男人搂进怀里。温存了一会儿，女人说，我想通了，你就把这五千元省下，供儿子上学，给儿子娶媳妇。

男人说，这才像个当母亲的。

女人说，上次动手术时欠的账还有多少？

男人说那早还清了。

女人说你别骗我，我全知道。就像你说的，我就这样试着活，能活几天算几天，说不定老天爷一眨眼，还好起来呢。

男人说，那也说不定，世上的奇事多着呢。

女人说，你得早些给你察访着找一个可心的，万一我这病好不了，好歹给你父子有个动锅动灶的。

男人说，对，我就按你说的办，要找，就找个和你一样的。女人说你就不想换个口味？

男人说我就觉得你顺口。女人说顺口你就再吃一次。

男人看了看儿子的被窝，轻声说，等你好了，我还像刚结婚时那样吃你。

天快亮时，男人醒来，发现女人坐在炕头梳头。男人惊异，女人今天的精神怎么如此好，平常下个地都十分困难的。接着，男人又发现女人给他将火炉生着了，这是女人几十年不变的功课。女人病了后，男人就自己生，却总是不得手，把个屋子弄得烟熏火燎的。几十年了，男人的火总是女人生。都成了习惯了。女人不像别人家的女人，早早地就将男人赶起来干活，自己却窝在被筒里睡懒觉。女人喜欢在男人还在炕上睡着时起床干活，喜欢男人从被窝里散发出来的带着汗腥味的梦的气息。女人从不主动将男人叫醒。农闲时节，等女人将早上要干的活干完，如果男人还睡着，她就上炕偎在男人身边做针线。有时不防就被男人搬倒，拉进被窝里，女人就将一双冻得冰凉的手伸在男人那个地方，把男人的火焰凉下去。其实女人也想，但女人疼男人。女人想，日子长着

264

呢，不要将男人三下两下刮干。男人就将女人的两只手抓住，一边握着，一边寻找话头和女人拌嘴。农忙时，女人将火生着时，男人也就起来了。等男人喝完茶，女人已经将牛套好了。天还没亮，露水尚未散去，但有女人和牛伴着，男人就不觉得天有多黑，地有多湿。

女人病后，这事就颠倒过来，每天早上都是男人早早起来，给女人生火炖药，给儿子收拾吃喝。现在女人起来给他生火，倒让他觉得不习惯的。端起茶杯，手上像是有什么东西在蹿，心里有种说不出的感觉。

女人将一把剪刀拿在男人面前，让男人一边喝茶，一边磨一下。

男人问女人磨剪刀干啥。

女人说她想做点针线。

男人说你就歇着吧，都做了一辈子针线了，又不在乎这两天。

女人说你以为是我给你表现干活？我是想做针线改个心慌，这样窝在炕上，都要把人闷死了。

男人就找磨石磨。

男人磨剪刀时，女人问男人今天干啥去。

男人说去集上。

女人说天天去集上干啥。

男人说眼看就要开春了，想买些菜籽。

女人说，也真到买菜籽的时候了。

男人说，大夫说你这病要多吃菜。

女人说，大夫还说什么了？

男人说，大夫还说，今年的气候潮湿，说不定你能躲过那一刀子。

女人说，是吗，如果能躲过那一刀子，也真把天叫喘了。说着把床头糖盒里的白糖全倒到男人茶杯里。

男人吃惊地看着女人说，那是给你喝药的，你怎么？

女人用勺子把糖搅化，双手递给男人说，你看你的嘴皮干的，都要成十八瓣桃花了，到了集上，还有谁家的女人看得上啊。

男人的心里就潮了一下，说，也好，今天再给你买些红糖，大夫说，红糖补血。

女人说，难得你有这份孝心，买就买些吧，买着备一些也好。说着打开地柜，拿出小铝锅，在炉子上打鸡蛋。

男人见女人一次打了两个鸡蛋，说，今天有胃口了？

女人说，今天有胃口了。

男人说，只要有胃口了就好。

女人说，开春了，鸡也到下蛋的时候了。

男人就再没有说什么，继续哧哧哧地磨剪刀。

炉火正着到旺处，鸡蛋不一会就打好了。女人盛在碗里，却端到男人面前。

男人说，你今天怎么了，你知道我不吃鸡蛋。

女人说，就学着吃一次吧。女人知道，男人是舍不得吃，刚结婚那几年，男人一次能够吃八个鸡蛋。

男人说，我最近胃里满，一点都不想吃，你就吃了吧。

女人说，正是春乏的时候，你把身子掉倒了，我们娘们子靠谁去啊，谁给我挣钱治病啊。

说着，从男人手里拿过剪刀，把毛巾递给男人，让男人擦了手。男人端起茶杯，失神地看了看，喝了一口，显得有些不忍心。

女人已经端着鸡蛋碗等着了，看架势是不看着他吃下去决不罢休。男人只好接过去，吃了一个，将另一个放下了。

女人说，赶快吃了我洗碗。

男人说，如果你不吃，就留给得富和得贵吧。女人看了看还在熟睡的两个儿子，说，就剩一个鸡蛋，他们两个谁吃？再说，他们吃的时间还长着呢，你就吃了吧。男人的眼睛就湿了。就端起碗，几下刨到口里。

男人把茶杯里的茶喝完，背上席出门。

女人送男人到大门口。天还没有亮透，背着席的男人看上去隐隐约约的。男人都到门口了，女人叫了一声三亿儿。男人一惊，三亿儿是他的小名，已经好多年没有人叫过了。按当地的习俗，男人有了孩子后，人们称呼男人都是用儿子的名字，包括自己的女人。女人今天却怪怪地叫了一声。男人心里一惊，回头看女人。男人想，女人肯定有啥心事。女人果然走上前来，一下子抓住他，拚命地亲。搞得男人一阵慌乱。结婚这么多年，他们还没有这样站着亲热过，这让他觉得有些生，有些难以适应。

男人觉得，女人都快要把他的骨头啃出来了。

路上，男人想，她这是怎么了？是病好转了，还是因为打春了？

男人出门后，女人就奔到厨房里打饼子，女人一口气打了七七四十九个大饼。

打啊，打啊，直打得瓷白瓷白的饼子整整摆了一面板。

看着眼前热气腾腾晃人眼扎人心的饼子，女人想，等他们父子把这四十九个大饼吃完，也就出了七期了。

女人是在儿子放学之前动手的，用的就是那把剪刀。

The Scissors[1]

● *Guo Wenbin*

You must manage to have my disease treated and cured. The woman said.

Yeah, I know. I'll send for a doctor. The man responded.

You are fooling me again. I don't want to eat that cattle feedstuff thing (Chinese herbal medicine powder) any longer.

Then, how can you recover if you don't take medicine?

Don't play deaf and dumb.[2] If I am well, I can make up for the money you spent on me.

I know. I know. You've earned a lot.

Raise your head and let me see your eyes! I want to know what you are thinking about.

The man didn't raise his head. He was squatting on the ground and weaving a mat. Two slices of bamboo splits were dancing among his fingers like two flying fish.

Think of some other ways. You can't support a family by making mats. Ten wives would die in your hand. Do you hear me?

I am listening.

Where were you in the daytime? I asked the kids to look for you all over the village. They didn't find you. If you don't want to come back to see me, you'd better kill me now.

Lower your voice. The kids just went to sleep. They'll go to school tomorrow.

Alerted, she turned her face and looked at their two kids. Tears gushed out of her eyes. She stopped nagging.

Having finished a mat, he stood up and attended to her in taking the medicine. She didn't want to take it. I know, you expect me to die sooner. I'll satisfy your wish.

Don't frighten me. I am chicken-hearted.[3] He said. Opening her mouth with his left hand, he fed into her mouth half a cup of decoction.

Wiping her mouth with a towel, he said: Do not nag any longer. To tell you the truth, I have no money to treat your disease. You know, that damned hospital simply devours money! Last time, how many days did we stay in the hospital? Seven days. Seven days in hospital cost us five thousand! Do you know? Just one operation. Five thousand! The money is enough for us to live an idle life for five years in which we don't need to work a single day. Why do we send so much money to the hospital?

Hearing his words, instead of getting angry, she felt better. She helped him take off his clothes and stinky socks. Lifting her quilt, she let him in. She began to scratch his back for him. He instructed: Up … left … left … here … OK … besides, you'd better not take it too much to heart. You are over fifty years old and after an operation you can live another five years at the most. Is it worthwhile to spend five thousand for just five years' life?

She gave him a pinch on the waist. And another pinch followed.

Wealthy's mother died at the age of forty-five and Lucky's mother died at the age of forty. Compared with them, you live a long life. Every day is the same! Can you lead a different life? Can you become a young girl again? Can you fall in love with another man? Can you act on the stage again? Of course, no! So, make do with the remaining days. If you live out another year, good! If you live out another day, OK! See? I'll buy you good food to eat and pay for our kids' tuition with the money we can spare by not doing the operation. You are unwilling to see our kids drop out of school, aren't you? If you loathe to part with me, let's make a deal now — we'll sleep on the same bed in the other life[4], OK?

You are flattering yourself! In the other life, I'd rather marry an ox or a horse than marry you!

OK. I'll become an ox or a horse in the other life.

You really want to irritate me to death? Now I die in front of you!

She pretended to be dead.

He, in a hurry, took out a "shroud" from the trunk.

As he was about to cover her with it, she pushed him aside. Seeing that he was holding a pillow cover, she came to know she was tricked. You are daydreaming![5] I won't die. She continued. I'll live another twenty years till our sons go to university, till they get married, till their wives give birth and till our grandsons are a month old and we hold a celebration for them. Piss you off! You won't go so far as to bury me alive or choke me to death or force me to take rat poison or pound nails into my head, will you?

Perhaps I will if I am impatient with you.

You will be dutiful to me if you really do it.

You think I won't dare to do it? If you die today, I'll hold a funeral procession tomorrow and bury you the day after tomorrow. And, as the custom goes[6], after seven days, I'll burn paper for you, and after another seven days, I'll burn paper for you again… and after three sevens, after four sevens … after seven sevens (forty-nine days) my task will be over and I can go out any time. I won't need to pour the urine pot for you, I won't need to feed you with those "cattle feedstuff", and I won't need to listen to your nags. You know how irksome when you are nagging! Hearing your nags, hens aren't able to lay eggs, pigs have no appetite to eat, cattle shed hair, and in a fret even lice give up biting …

Get out! She pinched his waist heavily. Seeing that she turned exasperated, he felt regretful.

Such quarrel between them was a routine, a common occurrence in their life. But now, she was sick! He thought he shouldn't say such nasty words to her, but he really wanted to speak to her in such a way. Only in this way could he feel a little bit relaxed from the pressure. He felt he himself was going to break down.

I know why you expect me to die. You don't think I know it?

Hearing her picking up the thread of conversation, he felt relieved. He knew she hadn't taken his nasty words seriously. Feeling like releasing more depression from his heart, he continued: I just want you to know that forty-nine days after your death I can go out freely and at that time maybe a young girl will fall in love with me! You know, a man at the age of fifty is still a flower in women's eyes.

I know your dick is swelling! You grudge spending money for my treatment, but would rather splurge money for pussies! Aren't you afraid of exhausting your dick to death?

I've never heard of a man who exhausts his dick to death. He tittered and talked back.

Even if your dick doesn't feel exhausted, even if you can find a young virgin to sleep with, even if there are a hundred girls waiting to sleep with you, what's the difference? They are the same! Are their pussies made of silver? Or gold? Do their pussies have double-fold eyelids? Or tongues sticking out? Are there any flowers? Besides, they cost money! One hundred yuan for a go! She began to cough.[7]

He patted her softly on the back. She continued gabbing: One hundred yuan each time. You are so generous! Then think about me! We've been married for twenty-eight years. How many times have we made love in these twenty-eight years? Can you count the number? Four times a month at least. Altogether forty-eight times a year. Roughly speaking, in more than twenty-eight years we did it at least a thousand times. Then, how much should you pay me? At least a million, enough for ten operations. My calculation doesn't take into account the number in the first months of our marriage, when you humped on my body incessantly every night like a pig starved for generations! What did you say at that time? Do you remember?

He laughed so heartily that he nipped the cigarette in his hand into dust. Great! You are good at calculating! I've never thought we have done such a simple thing a thousand times! In fact, your calculation is not precise. We've done it more than two thousand times. I can't imagine I've done such a simple thing which anyone can do with closed eyes for at least two thousand times! Two thousand times. Only with you! How silly! How boring! Doing such a monotonous thing for so many times! How ridiculous!

She giggled.

You want me to spend five thousand curing you, so that we can continue doing that? No. I don't want it. He said.

In fact, I do hope I can do it with you again! It is invigorating. After doing it, I am full of zing the next day.[8]

Full of zing? You know, after doing it, I am so tired that I can't even stand erect! The thrill lasts a moment and the regret lasts long.

One of their sons, all of a sudden, jutted his head out of the quilt and said, "Ma, just now you calculated wrong. Father should pay you one hundred thousand, not a million."

The son was awake all the time! Both of them **felt** embarrassed.

After a while, regardless of the embarrassment, he put the question to his son directly: If we had a hundred thousand, should we spend it on your mother's operation or save it for your marriage?

Operation. The son answered.

Why?

Because in the future I don't want to do that thing with my wife. I may be too tired to stand erect.

She fell asleep, but he couldn't. Three days ago, in the northern market, he sold the pig for three hundred yuan, and the day before yesterday in the southern market he sold a few sandalwood beams, which he had saved to build a house, for six hundred. And yesterday, he sold his old ox for a thousand in the eastern market. But the sum was far from enough for the operation. What could he do? He was so worried! I can't rob a bank. I can't steal others' money. If I were a woman, I might sell my body to earn some money. If I lived in the past I could sell water on the street. But, but what can I do now? He said to himself. In fact, he borrowed money from all his neighbors and relatives and did all he could do to raise the money for her previous operation, but now he couldn't open his mouth to borrow money again, even from his two married daughters. Both of them lived in the countryside and they were not rich, either. He couldn't force them to tighten their belt to help him survive the financial pinch. But the treatment of his wife's illness couldn't be delayed. Now, he had no other means but to sell the family's hoard of grains.

While he was thinking, she turned to him and held him in her arms in a very tender manner. I've come round. Spare five thousand to pay our kids' tuition and prepare for their marriages. She said.

This is what a mother should do. He said.

How much money do you owe for my last operation?

I've already paid off the debt.

You are lying. I know. As you said, I won't go to the hospital. It doesn't matter how many days I can live out. Perhaps, one day, God opens his eyes and shows pity on me, then, I am likely to recover and live a long life. She said.

Maybe. Mysterious things happen every day. He agreed.

However, you'd better make preparations earlier. Find a good woman. In case I die one day, she can replace me. At least, she can cook for you and our kids.

Yeah. You are right. I'll find a woman like you. She couldn't help but ask: Don't you want a change?

No. You are tasty. He said. Then, taste me again, now! She urged.

I'll taste you when you are well. I'll taste you the way I did when we just got married. Keeping an eye on their sons, he said softly and gently to her.

It was nearly dawn. He woke up and found her sitting on the edge of the bed and combing her hair quietly. He was surprised! How could she have such a good spirit today? After she fell ill, it was hard for her to get out of the bed. Today she even lit the stove for him. During the past years, it was she who lit the stove every morning. In fact, he had got used to letting her light the stove. Now, she was seriously ill and he had to take over the job, but he was so clumsy that he often filled the entire room with smoke. Unlike other women in the village, who woke up their husbands early in the morning and urged them to go to work in the fields while they themselves slept snugly on bed till late hours, she liked getting up early and busying herself doing all the housework while he was sleeping. She enjoyed his sweaty and dreamy smell coming out of the quilt. She never woke him up. In the slack season in farming, after she finished her work in the morning, she always sat beside him and did her sewing. Sometimes, he woke up and drew her under his quilt. She put her cold hands on his private "place" so as to cool down his fire of sexual desire. As a matter of fact, she liked it but as she loved him, she believed that they had a long way to go and that she didn't want to exhaust him. At this time, he always held both of her hands and quibbled with her over some trivial matters. When the busy farming season came, he got up when she was lighting the stove. After he drank some tea, she had the ploughing ox ready for him. It was still dark and foggy outside, but with her and the ox at his side, he never minded how dark the sky remained and how thickly the ground was covered with dew.

However, after she fell ill, it was his turn to do all the work she once did. Every morning, it was he who got up early, lit the stove, decocted herbal medicine for her, and prepared breakfast for their sons. Today, to his surprise, she got up so early and even helped light the stove. He felt curious and a little unaccustomed to all these. Holding the tea cup, he felt something shivering in his hand. An inexpressible feeling welled up in his heart.[9]

Handing him a pair of scissors, she asked him to sharpen it while drinking the tea.

What are you going to do with the scissors? He asked.

Do some sewing.

You'd better take more rest. You've been sewing all your life. Why not stop doing it for a day or two?

You think I am doing it for you? No. Staying on bed for days like this, I really feel bored.

He tried to find a whetstone.

What are you going to do today? She asked him.

Go to the market.

Why do you go there every day?

Spring is coming. I want to buy some vegetable seeds.

Yeah. It's time to buy vegetable seeds. She said.

The doctor said you'd better eat more vegetables.

What else did the doctor say? She asked.

He also said that the climate is humid this year and that perhaps you don't need an operation.

Really? God bless me so much if I can escape the operation. As she said so, she picked up the sugar box from the bedside and poured all the remaining sugar into his cup.

Why? The sugar is saved for you when you take the bitter medicine. He said in surprise.

She stirred the sugar with a spoon and passed the cup to him with both of her hands. Your lips have gone dry! They crack like the petals of a peach flower! Which woman would like to take a look at you in the market! She said.

He felt his heart melting. All right. Today I'll buy some brown sugar for you. The doctor said brown sugar can enrich the blood.

You are so nice to me. OK. Buy some for me. As she said so, she opened the cabinet, took out a small pot and put it on the stove. Then she began to crack some eggs.

Seeing her cooking two eggs, he was curious. Have a good appetite today?

Yeah.

Good!

The spring is coming and our hens are going to lay eggs.

He made no response and began to sharpen the scissors on the whetstone.

The fire in the stove was burning and after a while the eggs were ready. She put them into a bowl and held it to him.

What's the matter with you today? You know I don't eat eggs. He asked.

Have a try. She knew he begrudged eating them. When they got married, he could eat eight at one meal.

Recently, I feel full in my stomach. I have no appetite. You eat them. He said.

In this busy season, people always feel tired. If you fall ill, whom can we rely on? Who can earn money for us? She urged.

Taking the scissors from his hand, she passed him a towel and asked him to wipe his hands with it. He took the cup, had a dejected look at the eggs in it and ventured a taste. Obviously, he begrudged eating them up at once.

She held the bowl in front of him. It seemed that she had made up her mind to see him eat the eggs. He had to take the bowl and ate one egg, leaving the other to her.

Eat them up. I'll wash the bowl. She said.

If you don't want to eat it, leave it to our sons. He advised. She cast a look at their two sons still sound asleep. There is only one egg. They can eat eggs later. You eat it now. His eyes turned moist. Holding the bowl, he swallowed the egg quickly.

He drank the tea up, put the mats on his back and left.

She sent him to the gate. It was nearly dawn. In the dim twilight, he looked vague from behind. As he got to the gate she suddenly shouted out his nickname. He was surprised. For quite a many years nobody called him by his nickname. As the local custom went, when a man had his own kid, he was to be called the father of his kid and his wife the mother. Now, he felt strange on hearing her calling him by his nickname. He turned his head. Maybe she had something to tell him? She rushed toward him, caught him by the neck, and kissed him over and over. It made him uneasy and even a little flurried. They had been married for years but they had never made out like this. He felt awkward standing outside and kissing each other in such a passionate way.

He felt she almost gnawed into his bones.

What's wrong with her? Does she turn well? Does she have a sexual urge? On his way, he kept wondering.

After he left, she walked directly to the kitchen. She made forty-nine big pies.

She didn't stop working until forty-nine white pies covered the whole kneading board.

Looking at the dazzling white and steaming hot pies in front of her, she felt her heart pricked.[10] When they eat up these pies, forty-nine days will have passed. She said to herself.

Before their sons came home from school, she finished her life with that pair of scissors.

注 释

1. 这篇小说有两个突出特点。一是故事的讲述和主人公的对话穿插在一起，对话部分没有引号。在翻译时，为了再现原文风格，对于所有对话部分，译者也没有加引号。故事的讲述用的是过去时，对话部分用的是符合说话人讲述时间的相应时态。二是人物对话朴实直白，口语化的语言风格非常突出。故事主人公是一对生活在农村的夫妻，小说基本由夫妻俩私下里的对话构成，所以语言很口语化、很亲近、很私密，有些对话甚至都是"脏话"，毫不避讳，毫不委婉。翻译时，译者注意到了文风对应，在选词和语气上符合说话人的语言特点。

2. "你别给我装聋作哑。" Don't play deaf and dumb. "装聋作哑"可以译为to pretend to be ignorant, to pretend to be deaf-mute，但都不如to play deaf and dumb来得更口语化，更符合说话人的语气。

3. "你可千万别吓我，我的胆小。" Don't frighten me. I am chicken-hearted. "胆小"可以译为shy, timid, cowardly，但都不如chicken-hearted更符合丈夫的语气。

4. 下辈子、来生、来世，译为the other life。今生今世，可译为this life或this lifetime。

5. "想得美，下辈子我跟牛跟马也不跟你。""把你想得美，我才不死呢……"两次出现"想得美"，这是口语化的表达，根据上下文，前者译为You are flattering yourself! 后者译为You are daydreaming! 翻译不要拘泥于原文字句，应根据上下文，选择最合适的表达。

6. "七天烧一期，十四天烧二期，二十一天烧三期，二十八天烧四期……七期之后，我就能出门了……"这是中国特有的丧葬文化，为了便于读者理解，译者加入了as the custom goes...。

7. 上面这一大段是夫妻俩在床上的私密对话，对于有些身体部位的用词、有关两性关系的用词，都说得直来直去，毫不避讳。译者也刻意没有用委婉语，而是选择了一些粗俗的单词如dick, pussy等，这更符合原文风格，符合说话人的语气。

8. "干上一次，第二天干啥都是有劲头的。"After doing it, I am full of zing the next day. 这里用的zing是非正式用语，意思是兴趣、激动、兴奋、活力、生气、热情。full of zing用在这里既体现口语特点，又比较恰当。

9. "心里有种说不出的感觉"An inexpressible feeling welled up in his heart. 动词短语well up 涌出，涌现，油然而生。

10. "看着眼前热气腾腾晃人眼扎人心的饼子……"Looking at the dazzling white and steaming hot pies in front of her, she felt her heart pricked. 热气腾腾、晃眼、扎心，这些词正是烘托主人公心情的关键词，不能省略。

总统的遗言

◎ 何员外

1

从他当上总统的那一天起，就注定了他要为这个战乱已久的国家操劳一生。

他没有和他的前任、前任的前任、前任的前任的前任一样，在就职演说之后举行酒会，而是举行了一个记者招待会。

招待会现场是一个大屏幕，他站在大屏幕前直接宣布政府军之外的武装均为非法武装。

大屏幕上是热带雨林中的一栋别墅。

这栋别墅属于众多反政府军中的一个的大本营，在全国观众的注视下，大屏幕上的别墅被一颗从天而降的导弹轰成了废墟。

如此凶恶的行径让同样凶恶的反政府军不寒而栗，一些胆小的反政府军开始投降，被整编入政府军。

本以为他会将反政府军拆散收编，但他却没这么做。反而让他们成为一支名义上隶属于政府，但却独立存在的军队。他说既然他们投诚，就要相信他们。

意识形态上的分歧被信任两字盖过，昔日的反政府军，成为真正的政府军，悉数听任总统差遣。

这是这个国家从来没有过的事情。

罂粟种植一直是这个国家赖以生存的命脉，毒品出口国是这个国家带给国际社会的最大印象。

以往历任总统一直都想方设法让国民种植别的替代作物以改善本国在国际上的形象，但收效甚微，多年来习惯了播种后就不需要管理的罂粟种植业者实在不习惯每天耕作的生活。

他没有沿袭这些做法，而是积极与发达国家沟通，安排各大制药企业收购罂粟，这样在不改变种植者习惯的情况下，将原本用于制造毒品的罂粟用于制造药品，一下子让这个国家从一个幕后施暴者的形象改变成悬壶济世的形象。

国家日益强大，一些顽抗的反政府武装也日渐衰落，逐渐，他们的活动也从公开转入了地下，他们也不再叫非法武装，而只能叫"恐怖分子"。

2

当他们是反政府武装的时候，他们是为了能够实现自己的政见而动用武力；当他们成为恐怖分子的时候，往往早已忘记了初衷，渐渐战斗已经成为生存的唯一意义。

建国日，总统参加了花车游行活动。

全国人民都在电视里观看总统向大家招手的镜头。

这么多年了，总统头发已经花白，但却精神依旧。

电视里传来枪声，总统倒在血泊中。

那天电视转播最后一个镜头是总统费力地对助手说了三个数字：119。

之后所有的转播信号都没了。

当晚电视信号恢复时，播音员用沉痛的声音向全国人民宣布，总统遇刺，当场身亡。

整个国家又陷入了混乱之中。

一周之内，有三十八个组织声称对总统遇刺事件负责。有的恐怖组织还特地改名为"119"，因为总统的遗言就是"119"。

因为在他们看来，总统是这个国家有史以来最伟大的总统，刺杀总统的组织也理所当然是最伟大的组织，怎么看都是一件很长脸的事情。

但又过了一周，警方却宣布抓住了凶手。

凶手声称不代表任何组织，只代表个人，于是他成了那个恐怖分子觉得最牛逼的人。

凶手被处决了，最牛逼的人没了。

3

全国人民都听到了总统的遗言。

有人揣测，"119"是核手提箱的密码……

但随后官方出来辟谣，说本国是没有核武器的。

有人说，总统之所以能完成大业全靠来自海外的大量资金援助，"119"是他在海外银行账户的密码……

但随后官方又出来辟谣，说总统一直坚持不让他国插手本国内政，决不会接受经济援助的。

119到底指的是什么？

民间已经炸开了锅，所有人都通过电视转播听到了总统的遗言，所有人都觉得自己的判断才是总统遗言真正的意思。

当所有的猜测被否决时，大家不禁失望地想，119，不就是我们国家的医疗急救电话吗？莫非……总统只是想让助手拨打119？

抑或是他说的119只是当时旁边的国防军119医院？

没人能够知道了……

当所有的人都失望的时候，总统的遗言也变成了一个笑话……他的潜台词是：我觉得我还可以抢救一下……

总的来说，大家对总统很失望，觉得总统是不能贪生怕死的，总统应该说一些大义凛然的话然后死去才是符合大家审美情趣的。

4

当总统的遗言逐渐被大家遗忘的时候，几辆装甲车开进了国防军119医院，一群荷枪实弹的士兵将几个沉重的大箱子搬上了装甲车，开走了。

有目击者声称带队的是总统年轻有为的儿子。

也有消息灵通人士声称，总统藏在119医院里的宝藏被找到了。

很多人惋惜，自己明明听到了总统的遗言，却从没想过指的是这个，否则，哪怕搬一箱走，此生也衣食无忧了。

几年后，这个国家又结束了战乱状态，一位年轻的总统统治了这个国家。

在他的统治下，反政府武装纷纷投诚，据说他发掘了宝藏，跟他一起发财比跟他对着干要好很多……

在他的统治下，恐怖组织也逐渐瓦解了，是啊，这么多年了，恐怖分子也会老去的……

老总统遇刺的忌日，例行会讲话之后，年轻的总统在自己的办公室里，把一本《孙子兵法》放回了箱子里，那箱子赫然就是当年从119医院搬出来的，坐倒在沙发里，想，当年父亲的遗言到底是什么意思呢？

The President's Last Words

○ *He Yuanwai*

I

Since the day he became the president, he was destined to a lifetime of toil and moil for this chaotic country inflicted by incessant warfare.

Unlike the former president or other previous presidents[1], after his inaugural speech, he held a press conference instead of a grand banquet.

A big screen was hung in the front of the meeting hall. Standing in front of the screen, he announced directly that except the government armed forces all the other forces were illegal.

A villa in the tropical rainforest was shown on the screen.

The villa was the headquarters of one of the anti-government armed forces. Now under the watchful eyes of the people of the entire nation, the villa was blasted into smithereens by a missile plunging down from the sky.

The fierce anti-government forces shuddered at this fiercer show of force. Some of them surrendered and were reorganized into the government armed forces.

People had thought that the new president would dismantle those former anti-government forces. However, to their surprise, instead of separating them, he transformed the anti-government forces into an independent force nominally affiliated to the government. Since they came over to our side, we'd better trust them. He said.

Thus, the ideological divergences were wiped out under his trust, and the former anti-government forces now became a government force under his command.

This had never happened in this country.

The country had been relying on poppy-growing for survival and development. Export of drugs was the biggest impression it left to the whole world.

The previous presidents all encouraged the people to grow some other things so as to change the country's image in the world. However, the poppy growers had got used to their leisurely life and didn't want a change. After all, instead of daily soil tillage, poppy-growing only needed seeding.

The new president didn't follow the previous presidents' practice. He engaged in active communication with developed countries and negotiated an arrangement for big pharmaceutical companies to purchase the poppies for medical use. In this way, the poppy growers in his country went on with their traditional lifestyle, and on the other hand, his country's image changed from a back-alley bully to a benevolent savior providing the world with much-needed medicine.[2]

As the country got stronger, those dogged anti-government forces declined gradually and turned from public actions to covert operations. They were no longer called "anti-government forces". They became "terrorists".

II

The anti-government forces previously resorted to violence in order to advocate and practice their political views, yet, after they became terrorists, they forgot their original mission and their only raison d'être turned out to be fighting with the government.

On the National Day, the president took part in the parade on a decorated vehicle.

On the television screen, he waved his hand to his people.

After these years, his hair turned gray but he remained vigorous.

All of a sudden, the television audience heard a gunshot. Their president fell in a pool of blood.

With all his might, the president said to his assistant, "119." That was the last scene in the television that day.

Thereafter, all the television signals broke off.

In the evening, when the signals came again, the announcer, in a sad tone, said to the people all over the country: Our president was assassinated and died on the spot.[3]

The entire country was tossed into chaos again.

Within a week, thirty-eight organizations claimed that they were responsible for the assassination and some of the terrorist organizations even changed their name into "119", for it was the president's last words.

To them, the president was the greatest in the history of their country and the organization which made the assassination must also be the greatest and deserved to be proud.

After a week, the police announced that they caught the assassin.

The assassin claimed that his action was not instigated by any organization. He, consequently, became the most respectable man in terrorists' eyes.[4]

The assassin was sentenced to death at last. The most respectable man in terrorism disappeared in this world.

III

The people all over the country heard the president's last words.

Some people assumed that "119" was the password of his nuclear suitcase …[5]

The authorities denied the rumor by announcing that there were no nuclear weapons in the country.

Others guessed that "119" might be the password of his savings account in a foreign bank and that the president might have received a large amount of fund to help him develop the country …

The authorities denied the rumor again and proclaimed that the president had never accepted any financial aid from other countries. As a matter of fact, for years, the president insisted that other countries shouldn't interfere with the internal affairs of his country.

Then, what did "119" stand for?

Various conjectures arose. All the people heard the president's last words and all of them thought themselves smart enough to figure out the meaning of his last words.

After all the guesses and assumptions were denied, people began to make wild speculations: Now that 119 was the number of our medical emergency call, did our president just … just want his assistant to dial the number to seek help?

Or he just referred to the No.119 Army Hospital nearby?

Nobody knew …

People began to feel disappointed at the president's last words. They even made fun of his words: Perhaps he just meant that he didn't want to die and was asking for medical aid …

All in all, they were disappointed. A president shouldn't cling to life and fear death like a coward. In order to live up to the people's expectations of a worthy president, he should say something heroic and awe-inspiring.[6]

IV

As time went by, people gradually forgot the president's last words. One day, several armored vehicles came into the No.119 Army Hospital. A group of fully armed soldiers got off, put some heavy trunks onto the vehicles and left quickly.

The team was led by the president's young and capable son, according to a witness.

Some well-informed people said that the president's treasure hidden in the hospital was finally discovered.

What a surprise! Quite a lot of people felt regretful. They heard the president's last words but didn't expect that the president had hidden a hoard of treasure there! If they had known it earlier, they would come to take the treasure away. Just one trunk of the treasure would suffice to ensure a wealthy and comfortable life.

After several years, the scourge of war finally ended in the country and a young president took the chair.

It was said that this young president dug out untold treasure. The anti-government forces gave in one after another, as they believed that sharing in big fortunes with their wealthy young president was much better than fighting him …

Under his rule, the terrorist organizations all broke apart. After all, even the toughest terrorists grew old with time …

On the anniversary of the death of the former president, after delivering the commemorative speech, the young president came back to his office. He put a copy of *Sun Tzu's Art of War* (an influential ancient Chinese book on military strategy, written by the famous Chinese strategist Sun Tzu in the 6th century BC)[7] back to the trunk which was taken from the No.119 Army Hospital years ago, sank into the couch and fell into contemplation: Father, what's the meaning of your last words?

1. "他没有和他的前任、前任的前任、前任的前任的前任一样……" 这里 "前任" 可以翻译出来，但是 "前任的前任、前任的前任的前任"，就不 好翻译了，译者简单处理为：Unlike the former president or other previous presidents… 以符合英语的表达习惯。

2. "一下子让这个国家从一个幕后施暴者的形象改变成悬壶济世的形象。" … his country's image changed from a back-alley bully to a benevolent savior providing the world with much-needed medicine. 难点是"悬壶济世",了解其意后,译为a benevolent savior providing the world with much-needed medicine。

3. "总统遇刺,当场身亡。" Our president was assassinated and died on the spot. "当场"可以翻译为on the spot,或者then and there。如果是"当场"抓住捕获某人,还可以翻译为red-handed。

4. "于是他成了那个恐怖分子觉得最牛逼的人"。"最牛逼的人",译为the most respectable man。俚语"牛逼"还可以译为awesome、cool、superb等,要根据文体特点,选择褒义或贬义词来翻译。

5. "揣测"这里译为assume,意思是武断地认为、没有根据地猜测。英语中表示"猜测、预测"意思的词很多,例如presume、guess、surmise、forecast等,注意区分,正确使用。

6. "大义凛然"可以译为with a strong sense of righteousness、fearless of death for a just cause、awe-inspiring righteousness、heroically、stand firm for the cause of justice,等等,这里简单译为heroic and awe-inspiring。

7. 翻译《孙子兵法》时,应该给出相关信息,帮助读者理解,也起到传播中国文化的目的:*Sun Tzu's Art of War* (an influential ancient Chinese book on military strategy, written by the famous Chinese strategist Sun Tzu in the 6th century BC)。

驼粪

◎ 石舒清

　　那时节，我就是七岁多一些。记下的事情像是牢实得很，一辈子都忘不掉。

　　先说个骆驼的事。

　　那时候，村子里常过骆驼，是脚夫哥们赶的。有骆驼队，有骡马队，你的一个姑太爷就是顺德客的骡子踢坏的。那骡子说是个头高得很，膘也好，胯子上肥得苍蝇都趴不住，能驮三四百斤走长路，已经有一口袋麦子驮着了，你姑太爷和顺德客又抬了一口袋往它背上架，它大概看出你姑太爷是个生人，不顺眼，胯子一拧，就给了你姑太爷一蹶子，正踢到眼眶骨上，糊涂了一天一夜，从山背后请了一个老中医守着看，也没有救下他的命。都是常来常往的老朋友嘛，你姑太爷个子碎（小的意思），人是一个大肚量人，把羊皮羊毛发给顺德客，几年不见面，几年后把钱再拿来都是可以的。顺德客难过得很，后悔得很。但说到底是牲口踢坏的，又不是人踢坏的。顺德客留下两个骡子，你姑太爷家没要。这个不要是对的。顺德客呦着骡子哭着走了，听说是改了线，再没有打你姑太爷的庄子里走过。

　　脚夫们有打陕西来的，有打宝鸡、平凉一带来的，也有四川来的。

　　叫我忘不掉的是骆驼队。

不知道为啥，骆驼队都是夜里过，白天是见不着一个的。有时节灯还没有吹，在窗台上亮着，你祖太太就凑在灯跟前补这个缝那个，实际上你祖太太的眼睛已经看不着了，是黑摸着补呢，她先是找到破的地方，拿手一遍一遍地摸着熟悉着，然后把破的地方捏紧，针脚跟紧着补过去。针脚有些粗，有些歪扭，大样子还是看得过去的。那时节你祖太太已经是九十多岁的人了，刚刚吃过饭，刚刚把碗放下，刚刚用手把嘴擦过，你问她，你老人家吃了没有呢？说没有。说你刚刚把碗放下，碗都没有洗，咋能说没有吃呢？她说，我吃了么？我记着我没有吃。然后眯着眼睛像是想了一阵子，有些委屈埋怨地说，你们哪个给我吃呢，你们都是各人顾各人吃。你要是再端来一碗饭呢，老人是真吃呢。但是再不敢端了。实际上她是吃了嘛，她心里没数，我们心里是有数的。就是忘不了做针线。针鼻关在哪边都看不出来了，还做。一做针线，眼睛往上的皱纹就多起来，一个把一个挤得不行，两个眼睛里还流水，不是眼泪，就是水，把老人家的脸泡得像一个烂果子。你祖太太是咱们家里寿数最高的人，庄里有些年龄大的人说，她老人家活了九十九岁，还有的说过了一百岁。你祖太太做的最后一个针线活就是你的尿布子，拿一些布片片子往一起弄。说个不该说的话呢，她常摸你妈的肚子，摸着说，活嘛也活过了，福嘛也享过了——也不知道她享的是啥福。要是重孙孙下来，看上一眼，她就走，再不活在世上丢人现眼了。可是把你的尿布子没弄完，老人家就无常了，过了一个多月你才养下，这个我给你讲过吧。

我就记得你祖太太凑着煤油灯做针线的时节，能听到骆驼队过村子的声音。骆驼都是有铃子的。当唧，当唧，还不像是这么个声音，是咋的个声音呢，我想办法给你说一说，这个我记得牢实得很，就像昨儿夜里还听过一样，我给你咋说呢？唉，秃嘴笨舌的，没办法说出来。就是叫人忘不下，想起来人的心都要忍不住颤了，像是要化掉呢。一阵阵听起来远得很，像在天边边呢，像紧贴着豆子大的星星走呢，一阵阵又响起来，像离着街门不远了，狗也咬起来了，就像是在咬这些铃声。狗的声音听起来像蔫萝卜。但是听得出来，狗没有办法咬那些声音，它们咬不上，一声一声都咬在了旁边，空处，那些声音像是一点子也不怕，一点子都不乱，有时候简直是没有了，费了劲去听，听得耳朵胀，听得人像是从深崖里掉下去，掉不到个实处，没有底底子，听得人像是一个空壳壳子，心都像不跳了，还是听不到它们的声音。但是不知咋弄了一下，又听到了，像个绣花针的针尖尖一样，在你的眼前头，一下一下地清楚着，但总还是有些不清楚。像是太清楚了，人会受不了。不知道你祖太太听到这声音没有，也没细问过。还有个要说的，就是一想起这些驼铃时，就会也想起窗台

286

上的灯盏来，那灯盏黑呼呼的，有一个人的拳头大，火苗儿就像随手掐下的一截韭菜叶子。在驼队经过的时候，这一截韭菜叶子也不长一下，也不短一下，也不动一下，就那么端端正正一动不动地站着。像是和远处的声音有着一种啥关系。那时节觉得，就是贴在灯盏跟前，鼓劲吹这灯，也吹不死它。还有你祖太太，对着窗前的灯盏背坐着，背影子那么大，黑呼呼的，头低下去只叫人看到个脑勺子，看起来也像是一个还没有点着的大灯盏。这一些子给我留下的印象真是太深了，一想起来心就不由得跟上走了，像是我的魂丢在那里了，不想嘛还罢了，想起来就觉得只有美美地哭一场才能舒服。

有时候灯吹了，人睡下了，还能听到那声音，不远不近的，不紧不慢的。灯一吹，像是把它能听得更清楚了。但是听起来像是结了冰打了霜一样，叫人觉得冷清得很，无缘无故地伤心得很。狗还在有心无意地咬着。这里一声那里一声的，风吹散的野蒿子一样。脚夫哥们都是冬天过。跟驼铃子的声音比较，狗叫声听起来还算是暖和的，汪的咬一声，它们喷出嘴来的雾气像是都能看见。现在村子里的狗不多了。那时节狼多，常跑到村子里来叼羊，狗就也是不少的。现在想那时节狗叫的声音，就像是夜里的一些火把。只要灯亮着，狗叫着，骆驼队不紧不慢地由村子里走过去，人心里就是很安宁很踏实的，像是没有啥害怕的了。还有一个奇怪的情况，灯亮着时还觉不来，灯一吹，睁着眼睛，听着像有又像没有的驼铃声，再睡上一阵阵，就会觉得不但是驼队在慢慢地走在黑夜里，睡在炕上的人也像是一晃一晃地向哪里去，说不清是往前走还是向后退，像是黑沉沉晕呼呼的说不来个方向，又像是原地旋转着，就像是睡在大大的磨盘上。这么着一摇一晃，再加上个旋转，人就一点一点的忘了自己的胳膊腿子，睡着了。

我记着骆驼队没有在村子里住过。在我的印象里驼队是一直走着的，没停过。实际上跟路边的人家要过水，干粮啥的。咱家住得偏，过了那么多年驼队，脚夫哥也没有到门上来过。出门人是很大胆的，但也是很胆小的，听说他们跟路边的人家买东西换东西时，街门里都不进去的，就在街门外头规矩地等着，一拿到手里，道个谢就走。他们出手是大方的，你拿一碗黄米就能换值几碗黄米的东西。但是你不能一见便宜就收不住闸，背出一麻袋黄米来跟人家交换。脚夫哥一次最多只换一小盆黄米，多了人家是不要的。村里人也清楚便宜得一点一点地沾，不能一下子沾尽，于是就按脚夫哥的来，脚夫哥说换多少，就换多少，脚夫哥顺手给什么，就拿什么，总之闭着眼睛也不会吃亏的。都在这世上活，无论主人客人，各自都有着各自的规矩的。

但是也有破规矩的。也难免，骆驼队过了多少，再好的糜地里也出个火穗呢。常出事不好，但一件事情都不叫出也不可能。这事情说来没有发生在咱们村子里，发生在哪里呢？发生在水淌清。那时节无论是咱们村子，无论是水淌清，都小得很，咱们村子是两个队，相对还大些，水淌清就只有十几户人家。说是两个村子邻居着，但看起来要比现在远老多。

一天夜里就发生了个事情。

路边上一户人家的儿媳妇脑子一热，跟上脚夫哥跑了。具体是谁家我就不说了吧。说了也不妨事，就是那个那个谁家。那个女人本身是有些个俊，本身就不大看得上自己的男人，脚夫哥在街门上站过几回，两个眉来眼去地沟通上了，就叼了个机会跟上跑了。

这个女人错就错在跑了就不该再回来。但是她回来了。回来也不能再回水淌清呀。她端端儿回到水淌清来了。大概过了个一月半月吧，她就跳到水窖里去了，怀里还抱着她的个女儿。都淹死了。都夸着说这个媳妇子野是野，但还算是仁义的，把女儿抱着淹死了，把儿子给婆家留下了。

两个庄子离得近嘛，我们一伙子娃娃还跑去看了呢。屋子里又黑又窄狭，紧挨着门槛停着母女两个人的尸体。那时节的记性就是好，我还记得用一条补满了补钉的红单子盖着，一揭开来，先看到大人；再揭得开些，就看到睡在她胳膊边的碎女子。

就听到人们议论说，要是能捉到那个脚夫哥，就在这两个尸体前头把头用老刀子割掉了，就算是美死了。

但绝大多数脚夫哥都还是好的，都规规矩矩本本分分地呦自己的骆驼。要都像那个不负责任地乱领女人的脚夫哥，他们出门在外，无亲无故的，势必要被村里人捉住，一个个宰掉。听说脚夫哥们在这一点上规矩是很大的，比如已经混熟的人家，一天夜里又到他门上，发现女主人出来，男主人不在时，脚夫哥就会匆匆告一个别，到另外一家去换取自己需要的东西。和村里人再熟悉，他们也不会在村子里过夜。据说他们都是在荒野里过夜，就算下大雪也是这样。据见过的人讲，大雪天，他们找一个僻背的地方，让骆驼一字儿排开，挨紧着卧下来，然后每个人把骆驼头跟前的雪清去，清出够一个人睡的地方，然后在每个骆驼脖子里吊一个草料袋子，夜里，人就睡在骆驼的脖子下面，一边听骆驼吃草料，一边在骆驼的脖子边上望着天空扯闲话，只要把腿脚和头顾缠好，是不很受罪的。

实际上骆驼的脖子比几个棉被都要厚的。

我已经七岁多了，得帮家里做点子活计了，我最爱干的就是拾粪。

那时节每家都有几个拾粪权权的。

拾粪最好是赶早儿，星星还没落净，但又能看清地上时，最好。太早了看不着粪，太迟了粪叫别人拾去了。说起来，拾粪的时节嘛，冬天最好。冬天是有些个冷，可是呢冬天的粪容易冻住，冻住就容易拾。上去先来给一脚，踢得动了，权子一端，就整个的端起来了，又轻省又方便又一点也不浪费。不像别的时节，看着一泡粪大得很，但一点点捞到背斗里得老半天。牛粪驴粪的倒罢了，遇上狗粪人屎，还臭得很。冬天的粪就没有臭味。

但我最爱拾的还是骆驼粪。不要看骆驼比牛还大，巴下的粪却不大，而且不像牛那样稀嗨嗨的给你拉一大滩，骆驼粪是一个个圆蛋儿，比核桃大不了多少。

骆驼夜里走过村子去了，我们赶早儿去拾骆驼粪，抢着拾。实际上拾骆驼粪用权子倒不得劲，你用权子一拾核桃就知道了。干脆我们就用手去拾。拾回来我们先玩，然后再给家里烧水填炕用。那时候是有不少关于骆驼粪的玩法的，现在像是忘掉了。细细想还能想得起来吧。

我一直都觉得我自小儿就见过骆驼的，今儿给你讲这些，一细想，才觉得那时节我不能说是见过了骆驼，我只是见过骆驼粪，听过它们脖子底下的铃声。

说起来我第一次亲眼见骆驼已经到了十五六岁，那时节你爷爷在银川劳改，我骑自行车给他老人家去送吃的，路过中卫，第一次见到了骆驼，说个老实话，我有些意外，觉得它们不像。

Father's Stories: Camel Dung[1]

⊙ *Shi Shuqing*

At that time, I was only a little over seven. Yet, those things that I remember from that time have dwelt so firmly in my mind that I can hardly forget them for the rest of my life.

Now let me tell a story about camels.

At that time, camels often passed by our village in caravans driven by porters from different places. In addition to camels, there were also caravans of mules and horses. One of your great grand-uncles was kicked to death by a mule owned by a porter from Shunde. It was said that the mule was very fat and strong, so fat that even a fly couldn't stand steady on its slippery hips and so strong that it could take a long walk with a load of up to two hundred kilos. That day, as your great grand-uncle and that porter from Shunde were about to put one more sack onto its back, the mule suddenly turned angry. Perhaps because it was not familiar with your great grand-uncle, it swung its hips and kicked him smack on the eye socket. Your great grand-uncle fell into a coma right away. An old doctor was sent for from behind the mountain and attended him for a day and a night, but your great grand-uncle died all the same. Despite of his small build, your great grand-uncle was a man of great generosity. He trusted the porter from Shunde with his parchments and fleeces, and allowed the porter to go out selling the goods for years before finally coming back to balance the account. Naturally, the porter from Shunde was very sad upon your great grand-uncle's death. He cried a lot as he felt guilty and regretful. Nevertheless, it was, after all, not he but his mule that did the dreadful thing, so your great grand-uncle's family didn't put too much blame on him. He wanted to offer two mules as compensation, but they refused. It was right not to take the mules. Then, that porter drove his mules and cried all his way down the mountain. Since then, he changed his route and no longer passed by our village.

The porters came from Shaanxi, and some from Baoji and Pingliang, and some from Sichuan.[2]

The most deep-rooted in my mind is the memory of those camel caravans.

Camel caravans passed by our village mainly at night. I seldom saw one camel caravan in the daytime. At night, before the lamp on the windowsill was blown off, your great grandma always kept herself close to it and did some sewing under its dim light. Actually, she was blind. She fumbled for the frayed part in the clothes first, and touched and felt it with her fingers over and over to get herself familiar with it; then, she nipped the frayed part with her fingers and quickly ran her needle through. Her stitches were long and rough but passable in general.[3] She was over ninety at that time. Right after she finished her dinner, put down her bowl and wiped her mouth, we would ask her: "Did you have your dinner?" She always answered: "No." We said: "You just put down your bowl which hasn't been washed and how come you say you didn't have your dinner?" She answered: "Really? Did I? I didn't have it." At this moment, she always narrowed her eyes and thought about it in a serious manner. After a while, she complained with much grievance: "Indeed, I didn't have dinner; each of you had yours, but nobody saw to me." If we gave her one more bowl, she would eat it up. Of course, none of us dared to do so. As a matter of fact, she indeed had her dinner. She was too old to remember it. To her, the only thing she never forgot was her sewing work. Where was the needle eye? She couldn't see it at all, but she did her sewing all the same. When she picked up her needle, more wrinkles, one overlaying the other, piled up in her forehead and much water flowed out of her eyes, so much that her face was almost soaked into a rotten fruit. In our family, she lived the longest. Some people in our village said she lived to ninety-nine, and some said she lived to a hundred. Her last sewing work was your napkin, which was pieced together with several strips of cloth. At that time, she often put her hand on your mother's abdomen and said: "I've lived a long life and enjoyed a lot." — What did she enjoy? Who knows? — "If you can give birth to my great grandson and let me have a look at it, I am contented and I'll go."[4] But before she finished sewing your napkin, she passed away. A month later, you were born. Did I talk of this before?

I remember that when your great grandma did her sewing in the dim light, I always heard the camel caravans passing by our village. Each camel had bells under its neck and as they moved those bells produced some sound — clang-clang — no, not like this. How do I put it? The sound was deeply imprinted in my mind as if I heard it last night. How do I describe the sound? Ah! You see, my stupid tongue! In a word, I cannot forget the sound! At the very thought of it, I feel my heart shivering, as if it were going to melt away. Sometimes, the sound of the camel bells was so far, far away in the sky as if it were keeping pace with those scudding pea-like stars, and sometimes, it was so close, close to the path in front of my house. The dogs kept barking, which sounded like withered turnips, and running about in an attempt to catch and bite the sound of camel bells. However, they could just have a bite on the rim or the blank of it. Chased by dogs, that sound was not scared or flurried at all! Sometimes, the sound was so vague that I almost couldn't hear it, even though I pricked my ears and listened with all my strength. I tried all my best to trace it, but, to my disappointment, it disappeared! I felt as if I were falling into an unfathomable abyss endlessly or I were just a hollow shell whose heart was too exhausted to beat. All of a sudden, it reappeared. Like an embroidery needle, it was right in front of me, clear but not clear enough. You know, people cannot bear things too clear and concrete. I don't know whether your great grandma heard that sound. I never asked her about it. Oh, one more thing: at the thought of the sound, I always think of that lamp on the windowsill. The lamp itself was black, as big as a fist, and its flame was much like a section of a leek nipped at random. When a camel caravan passed, the leek-like flame remained as usual, neither becoming long nor turning short. The flame kept calm and didn't flicker at all, as if it had some special intimate relation with the sound outside. At that time, I always had a strange feeling that even if I stood near the lamp and blew it hard I couldn't blow it out. Your great grandma sat with her back toward the lamp, leaving her big and dark shadow on the wall. She lowered her head and I could only see the back of her head, which looked much like an unlit big lamp. These past memories have been lingering in my mind for so long that whenever I think of them my heart roves away with them to that remote village. I am afraid my soul was left there and perhaps that's why I always feel like crying while thinking of the past. If only I could cry to my heart's content![5]

Sometimes, after we blew out the lamp and went to bed, that sound still lingered, now distant, now close, now fast, now slow.[6] In the darkness, it became more distinct. But on hearing it, I felt cold, frozen with forlornness and sullenness, and for no reason I couldn't help shedding tears. Dogs barked off and on, running here and there like wild weeds scattering in the wind. Porters often came in the cold winter, and the dogs' barks added warmth to that cold and lonely sound of the camel bells. When the dogs opened their mouths, I almost could see the white steam they puffed in the air. There are just a few dogs now, but at that time, there were quite a lot of dogs in our village. Besides, there were many wolves which often came to our village to pilfer sheep. Now, when I recall the past, I find the dogs' barks, like torches, warm enough to liven up the dark cold nights.[7] Provided the light was on, the dogs kept barking and the camel caravans were strolling past our village, people felt at ease as if nothing terrible would happen to them. There was one more strange thing: When the light was off, opening eyes wider in the darkness, I could trace the sporadic sound of the camel bells; after a while, when I was about to fall asleep, I felt not only the camel caravans moving but also myself moving together. It was hard to tell to which direction I was moving ... Forward or backward? Or I was just swirling where I was as if I were lying on a big millstone? Swaying and swirling, I gradually forgot my arms and legs and fell into a sound sleep. However, when the light was on, I didn't have such a strange feeling.[8]

The camel caravans never stayed in the village overnight. It seemed to me that they kept hurrying on with their journey and never stopped for a moment. In fact, they took a rest by the roadside and asked for some water or food. Since my home was a little far from their route, they never came to my door. Those porters were brave in their journey, but they were at the same time timid. When they asked for something from or exchanged something with the villagers, they just stood politely outside the gate of the yard and never ventured a step inside. Hardly had they got what they wanted when they said thanks and left quickly.[9] They were very generous: With a bowl of yellow rice we could get from them what was actually worth more than several bowls. Of course, we'd better not be too greedy. If we took out a whole sack of yellow rice to make an exchange with them, they would decline. Each time, they accepted a small basin of yellow rice at most. We all knew their rules and we knew we'd better gain our benefits little by little and not take advantage of their generosity too much. Thus, when the porters came, we followed their requirements and took whatever they gave us with pleasure. We knew that we were unlikely to suffer losses in trading with them. You know, living in this world, everyone should act out their roles by the rules.

Nevertheless, someone indeed violated the rules. It was inevitable. There were too many camel caravans coming and going through our village, and it was unlikely that nothing happened. You know, even the best-protected field might catch a sparkle. It didn't happen in our village. Where then? Clear Water Wade, a small village next to ours. Both of the villages were very small at that time. Our village was larger than Clear Water Wade, where only several families lived. Though we were next to each other, we were far away from each other than it looked.

It happened one night.

A villager's wife eloped with a porter. Whose wife? I'd better not say it. Oh well, it doesn't matter to say his name. She was a Mr. John Smith's wife. She was good-looking. She didn't like her husband.[10] The porter went to her door for several times and they made goo-goo eyes at each other and then they eloped.[11]

But she made a big mistake. She shouldn't come back! Even if she wanted to come back, she shouldn't come back to Clear Water Wade! About one month after she came back, she was found in the water cave, holding her daughter in her arms. Both of them died. She was not loyal to her husband, but she had conscience at least, leaving their son alive to her husband. The villagers all said so.

Since the two villages were next to each other, we went to have a look. The room was dark and small, and close to the doorsill lay two dead bodies. Until now, that scene is clear in my mind: They were covered with a red sheet with patches all over and when we uncovered it we saw the woman first and then her little girl.

The villagers said it would be wonderful if they could find that porter and cut off his head in front of the two dead bodies.

In fact, most porters were good and well-behaved. Essentially a bunch of travelers without local connections, if they did something irresponsible as that eloping porter did, they would be caught by the villagers and killed one by one. It was said that the porters actually had strict rules in this respect; for instance, if one went to a familiar house, only to find the hostess at home, he would say goodbye quickly and go to another house. They never stayed in a village overnight, no matter how familiar they were with the villagers; instead, they slept, rain or shine, in the wilderness outside the village. Someone told me that on snowy nights they let their camels lie down in a line, cleared a space in front of each camel's head, a space enough for a man to lie down, hung a bag of fodder around each camel's neck, and each lay down. While listening to their camels eating the fodder and looking up at the sky, they chatted with one another. As long as their feet, legs and heads were warmly covered, they didn't suffer a lot.

As a matter of fact, a camel's neck is much thicker than several quilts.

At that time, I was already seven years old and was supposed to do some work for the family. The job I liked the best was collecting dung.

Every household had some stick forks for use in collecting dung.

To collect dung, I had to get up early. The best time was when the stars were still twinkling in the sky and the earth was sufficiently visible. If I went out earlier, it was so dark that I couldn't see the dung on the ground clearly, but if I went out later, the dung might be picked clean. Besides, winter was the most suitable season. It was cold indeed but the stubs of dung were frozen and easy to be forked up. I just needed to give it a kick and fork it up. It was effortless and convenient; besides, no dung was wasted. However, things were different in other seasons, when it would take me quite a long time to put a pile of dung into my basket. If I was lucky, I picked ox or donkey dung, but if it came from a dog or a man, I had to endure its stink.[12] However, in winter, any dung had no smell.

What I liked the most was camel dung. Camels were bigger than oxen, but their dung was smaller in pile and less watery than oxen's, and each piece of camel dung was a small round ball, no bigger than a walnut.

At dawn, we got up early to collect camel dung. The forks were not convenient. Have you picked up a walnut with a fork? Then, we picked them up with our hands. After we got home, we played with the dung balls first and then put them into fire as fuels. We had various ways to play with the dung balls, but now I cannot remember them. Perhaps I can recall some of them if I think about them more intently.

I thought that I saw camels when I was a little boy, but now when I am telling you my childhood story I come to realize that actually I didn't see them at that time; instead, I just saw their dung and heard the bells jingling under their necks.

When I was fifteen or sixteen, finally I saw camels with my own eyes. At that time, your grandpa was sent to Yinchuan to do his time in reform through labor, and I delivered food to him by bike; as I passed Zhongwei, I saw camels. That was my first time to see them. Frankly speaking, they were unlike what I had expected. I felt they were unlike camels.

1. 小说以主人公"我"之口娓娓道来，为第一人称视角。全文仿佛是一个老人在对一个孩子讲述自己童年的经历和感受，所以口语化风格明显。译文在用词方面，尽量体现口语风格。因为是口头讲述，在时态上，过去时态与现在时态并用。

2. "脚夫们有打陕西来的，有打宝鸡、平凉一带来的，也有四川来的。"宝鸡事实上是陕西的一个城市。译文就是按照原文直接翻译的，没有体现出陕西与宝鸡的关系，这样更符合人物的说话特点。

3. "……是黑摸着补呢，她先是找到破的地方，拿手一遍一遍地摸着熟悉着，然后把破的地方捏紧，针脚跟紧着补过去。针脚有些粗，有些歪扭，大样子还是看得过去的。"这一小段非常生动地描写了眼睛看不见东西的祖太太缝补衣服的动作，动词用得非常生动，翻译时，动词的选择是难点。She fumbled for the frayed part in the clothes first, and touched and felt it with her fingers over and over to get herself familiar with it; then, she nipped the frayed part with her fingers and quickly ran her needle through. Her stitches were long and rough but passable in general.

4. "说个不该说的话呢，她常摸你妈的肚子，摸着说，活嘛也活过了，福嘛也享过了——也不知道她享的是啥福。要是重孙孙下来，看上一眼，她就走，再不活在世上丢人现眼了。"从这一段中，可以看出小说的口语化风格。译文把祖太太的话处理成了直接引语，这样更生动些。另外，译文语言尽量符合农村老太太的说话特点。At that time, she often put her hand on your mother's abdomen and said: "I've lived a long life and enjoyed a lot." — What did she enjoy? Who knows? — "If you can give birth to my great grandson and let me have a look at it, I am contented and I'll go."

5. "想起来就觉得只有美美地哭一场才能舒服。"If only I could cry to my heart's content! 译文使用的if only...句型，意为"要是……就好了！"可以表达原文的语气和意义。to one's heart's content意思是尽情地、尽兴地。

6. now … now … 时而……时而……，相当于sometimes … sometimes…

7. 以上一大段都是对声音的描述，运用了拟人、比喻等修辞手法，并且通过狗、灯盏等具体实物的衬托，把看不见摸不着的声音以及这种声音带给自己的说不清道不明的感受描述得具体而实在。关于声音的描写是全文的高潮，也是翻译的难点。翻译时尽量忠实原文，不要省略。

8. 以上一段，"只要灯亮着，狗叫着，骆驼队不紧不慢地由村子里走过去，人心里就是很安宁很踏实的……人就一点一点的忘了自己的胳膊腿子，睡着了。"汉语主语缺省的特点很明显，全文既然是讲自己的童年回忆，译者在翻译这段时，添加主语I。

9. "一拿到手里，道个谢就走。""一……就……"可以用hardly... when... / no sooner... than / scarcely... when...。注意时态：hardly 引导的句子里一般用过去完成时，when引导的句子里用一般过去时，表示出两个动作的先后时间关系。有时为了强调，可以把hardly提到句首。Hardly had they got what they wanted when they said thanks and left quickly.

10. 从以上这一小段译文中，可以看出，简单句较多，语言显得琐碎、絮叨。这符合口语的表达习惯，符合人物的身份。

11. "两个眉来眼去地沟通上了，就叼了个机会跟上跑了。" The porter went to her door for several times and they made goo-goo eyes at each other and then they eloped. "眉来眼去"可以翻译成：cast sheep's eyes at each other、make eyes at each other、exchange amorous glances、throw the eyes at somebody、flirt with each other等等。这里译者用了make goo-goo eyes at each other。goo-goo为俚语，意为：勾引人的、着迷的，有贬义。

12. 臭味stink。关于气味或者味道的词，在翻译时要准确，平时要注意积累。比如：bitter 苦的/bland 清淡无味的/earthy 泥土气的/fishy 鱼腥的/fruity 有水果香的/musty 有霉味的/perfumed 有香味的/pungent 刺鼻的/scented 芳香的/stale 霉臭的/sugary 甜的/sweaty 汗味的/vinegary 有酸味的/garlic 大蒜味的，等等。

小沙弥陶陶

◎ 宗璞

　　小沙弥陶陶从麦积山来。麦积山在中国甘肃境内。山形如麦垛，山壁上石洞相连，有着丰富的极生动的泥塑、石刻。第一百几十号洞中有一个小沙弥，和真人一般大小，袈裟似在飘动，眉清目秀，口角边有一缕笑意，十分淡远温厚，人们誉为东方的微笑。

　　不知是什么年月，人们在洞中发现一块土坯，便把它当作垃圾，扔在一辆破车里，运到很远的地方，又换了一辆更破的车，运到更远的地方。经过长途颠簸，土坯裂开了，一块块掉落，到它躺在一片旷野上时，已经出现了一个漂亮的小沙弥，一尺来高，眉清目秀，嘴角上带着那东方的微笑，和那洞窟中的小沙弥一模一样。他不是复制品，而是原稿，凝聚着塑者最初的心血。他在长途颠簸后显露了本来面目，却不幸折断了左臂。几只小鹿走过来，看见小沙弥，觉得他真是漂亮，它们用草做成一个筐，把他和他的断臂装进去。两只小鹿衔着筐慢慢走，走了不知多少天，经过了各样的山谷和林木，来到一座森林。小鹿们商量了一阵，郑重地推选了两只小鹿仍旧衔着他，走进森林。林中很阴暗，弯曲的路拐来拐去，后来到了一片开阔的草地。草地上开着星星点点的野花，从这里可以看见高得无比的天空。草地当中有一棵大树，非松非柏，非杨非柳，气象很是威严。小鹿恭敬地把他放在树下，把他的断臂摆好，便离开了。不知过了多少天，树上飘下几片叶子，落在小沙弥的身上，有一片正好覆盖了他的断臂。这样又不知过了多少天，一只野兔从树下跑过，它拍了拍小沙弥，说："别睡了，到外面去看看好不好？"

　　小沙弥忽然醒了。他坐起身又站起身，活动着手臂、腿脚，断臂已经长好了。他对野兔说："你好！"野兔的长耳朵向前弯了一下，那是打招呼。小沙弥跟着它走到草地边，转回身仰望那棵大树，看了好一会儿，又跟着野兔走，走过森林中弯曲的路，出了林子，野兔不见了。小鹿们在灌木丛中玩耍，这已是原来那些鹿的后代了。一只鹿请小沙弥坐在自己的背上，大家一起在旷野上遨游。它们有时慢慢走，东张西望，有时跑得很快，小沙弥也没有跌下来。又不知逛了多久，它们把小沙弥放在一个小村边，自己跑走了。一个村民看见这个小沙弥，"这样好看的小泥人。"他说，便捡起了他，拿到市场上去卖。一位雕塑家从那里过，看见小沙弥，不觉吃了一惊，这不是那"东方的微笑"吗？他拿起他研究了一番。他把一件新外衣送给村民，那是他买来抵御西北的寒风的。村民还要他头上的帽子，他立刻同意。他把小沙弥装在一个玻璃匣子里，经过长途旅行，一直送到一个人家的客厅。

这个人家在一条河边，河水缓缓地流，流过两岸的树木草丛。那里春天开满了浅紫色的二月兰，夏天是一片浓绿；秋天的落叶给了河岸金黄的颜色，冬天则是晶莹的白雪。河水也流过这一栋小小的房屋，房屋是粉红色的，前后有许多花。里面住着一个母亲和她的两个女儿，大女儿十五岁，小女儿十三岁。

雕塑家把玻璃匣子放在桌上，他一打开，两姊妹就欢呼起来："这是我们的朋友！"她们说，"你看他正在微笑。"于是雕塑家介绍了东方的微笑。他说："你看这微笑，给人以宁静和安慰，必须有慈悲心才会有这样的微笑。"妈妈也讲了他那飘飘然的服饰，说他是佛门中的小沙弥。她从事的工作是服装设计，自然看得清楚。

"我要叫他陶陶。"妹妹说。陶这个字和土有关又和快乐有关。"这真是个好名字。"大家说。小沙弥向他们转动眼睛，可是谁也没有注意。

小沙弥陶陶在这家的客厅里住了下来，或者说站了下来，站在放艺术品的多宝格里。这是一个温暖的家庭。他最爱听小女儿放学回家一路喊着"妈妈"跑进屋里，最爱看大女儿帮助妈妈换鞋。妈妈伏案太久，脚有些肿。还有妈妈在餐桌上为孩子们分食物时，那慈爱得几乎有些虔诚的目光。她们常一起唱歌，陶陶不知道她们唱的是什么，只觉得和谐悦耳，像春天的轻风细雨，像一个繁星闪烁的夜。雕塑家是唯一的听众。

陶陶也喜欢听两姊妹的讨论。她们坐在客厅里，在他站的那个格子下面，低声热烈地讨论。姐姐说："我要把世界画下来。"她拿着两张画稿，一张是花园里的丁香。她只画了两个斜枝，枝条把发亮的小花朵送进画面，小白花在一张浅绿色的纸上面好像鼓出来似的，引得人想去摸一摸。另一张画的是她们家门前的那条不大不小的河，远处的桥在垂柳的掩映中，河岸边系着两只很小的小船，好像应该给陶陶坐。它们互相依偎着。妹妹很为这两条小船感动，她说："我来造船吧！造许多许多船，让它们顺着这条河一直漂到海里。每一个海浪上都坐着一个小娃娃，他们可以到甲板上来跳舞。你说好吗？陶陶。"她忽然向陶陶发问。陶陶有些受宠若惊，想点点头却没有动。

妹妹果然画了一条大船，船舷上挂满了发亮的浪花，像那点点丁香。浪花上真的站着几个小娃娃，他们互相招手，好像彼此在问："你要上哪里去？"

陶陶觉得非常快乐。他情愿这样站着、听着、看着、守望着，不管时间流到了哪里。

有一天，姐姐从学校回来，在花园里采了一把丁香花。预备插在瓶里，她走到桌前举着丁香花，忽然叫道："我看不见了！"丁香花落在桌上，也落在地上。妈妈跑过来问发生了什么事，姐姐只是说："我看不见了，我看不见了。"显然，她的眼睛出了毛病。

姐姐得了一种急性眼疾，两眼同时失明，本来在少女面前的一个光明灿烂的世界变成一片黑暗。花在哪里？河在哪里？黑暗像一口深不可测的井，而且盖着沉重的井盖，谁也掀不动。这不只是姐姐一个人的黑暗，它也遮蔽了妈妈和妹妹的生活。这个家落入了凄惨的境地。她们千方百计想挽救姐姐的眼睛，可是无效。晚上母女三人坐在一起哭，陶陶很想对他们说："不要哭，哭了更伤害眼睛。"他还没有说出这句话，自己先流下了眼泪。他的裙裳上立刻有一道湿痕，他是最不能哭的，水会立即把他融化。

经过多方寻医问药，不见疗效，这是一种无法医治的眼疾。姐姐只能在黑暗中过日子，而且一天比一天衰弱。"我不愿意！"她对着太阳喊，又对着月亮喊，"我不愿意！"

陶陶受不了这样的日子，下了决心，要去帮助姐姐。他从格子里飘了下来，走出屋子，在花园里定了定神。他想到的办法是去找那棵树，那棵给他精神和灵气的树，但是怎样去呢？他呆呆地站在屋角。

又一个清晨，他听见屋里彼此问答，像在找什么东西。妹妹在喊："陶陶！你在哪儿啊？你怎么不见了？"姐姐站在台阶上，大声说："我虽然看不见你，我可以摸到你。你怎么一点儿都没有了？"妹妹牵着姐姐走下台阶，绕到屋后去寻找。陶陶感到温暖又酸楚，不管用什么办法，他必须立刻出发，去找那棵大树。他沿着河岸跑，他的步子太小了，跑了很久，才到那座桥。过了桥又走了很久，面前是一座山。他抬头向上看再向上看，这样高的山怎样才能翻越！好不容易爬到半山，看见一片云歇在一块大石旁。云说："你是陶陶？我能帮助你吗？"陶陶说："你能帮助我到那片旷野上去么？我要去找那棵树。""你上来吧！"云说，"小心，坐好了。"陶陶坐在这一片云上，好像在一堆棉絮中。不过，云的形状是不规则的。一时这边凸出来，那边凹进去，一时那边凸出来，这边凹进去。陶陶必须随时移动座位，免得掉下去。云说："你很聪明，很能掌握平衡。"他们很快到了那片旷野，看见了那座大树林。云停在树顶上，让陶陶下来。它说它不能再低飞，否则会化成水。陶陶在树顶上走了一阵，找不到那棵树，这里是一片树木的海洋，可是他找不到那棵特殊的树。他懊恼地滑下树来，在森林边转了好久，没有发现可以走进去的路。几只野兔跳过来，把长耳朵向前弯了一下。又有几只鹿从草原上跑过来看热闹。陶陶说："你们都是我的老朋友。我能进去到那棵大树跟前么？"鹿们和兔们商量了一阵，派出一只鹿和一只兔领着陶陶进了森林。他们在弯曲的小路上，走呀，走呀，终于在夜里来到那棵大树下。那棵大树发着光，把这一片草地照得很亮。陶陶对大树说："我知道你会帮助受难的人。我在这里等，好么？"他定定地站在树下，举着双手，他是不怕累的。一天没有动静，两天没有动静，到了第三天，鹿和兔说它们太饿了，真想吃点东西，可它们不敢动这里的草和花。忽然一阵音乐，在音乐声中飘下了两片叶子，落在陶陶手上。陶陶大喜，双手捧着这两片叶子，随着兔和鹿走出了树林。兔坐在鹿背上，向那茂密的灌木丛跑去了。陶陶很希望再遇见那片云，可眼前却是万里无云的晴空。不管怎样还是得往前走，陶陶告别了树林。他不需要吃喝，也不需要休息，日夜兼程，不浪费一点时间。这一天，他爬上一座山坡，忽然看见天边停着片片白云，有一片云正向他飘来。陶陶挥舞着那两片叶子，云停在他面前，这是一片解事的云，它让陶陶坐上去，并且客气地说："随便坐，不用紧张。"它果然不像变形虫，而是像一只真正的船。在万里晴空中平稳地飘着。他们很快来到离大河最近的那座山上，陶陶下了"船"，云很快不见了踪影。陶陶跑呀，跑呀，跑过了桥，一直跑进小屋。屋里空无一人，他到花园寻找，在丁香树下找到一座小小的坟墓，上面堆满了鲜花，一小块石片上写着姐姐的名字。他把那两片叶子放在坟上，叶子很快便枯萎了。"我来晚了，我来晚了。"他伤心地回到格子里站着。傍晚，妈妈和妹妹回来了。妹妹看见他时，将他抱起，端详了一阵，递给妈妈。妈妈摸摸他的衣服，轻轻叹了一口气，仍将他放在格子里。妹妹沉默多了，妈妈衰老多了。小沙弥的心很痛，很痛。

雕塑家来了，也拿着陶陶端详。他们都不问陶陶到哪里去了。从他们的谈话里，陶陶知道雕塑家曾想再做一个小沙弥，可是他没有动手，他知道自己做不出来。他对妈妈说："我可以做出一个泥俑，但我不能给他一颗心。"

母亲和妹妹不再唱歌了，雕塑家说："唱一唱吧，那样也许会好受些。"陶陶很赞成，可是小屋里还是没有歌声。

日子平静地过了两年，妹妹十五岁了。妈妈邀请了一些女孩来为她过生日，她们准备唱一个快乐的歌。妹妹穿着白纱衣裙走进客厅的刹那，突然叫了一声："我看不见了！"就像两年前姐姐那样。谁能安慰一个盲人？当她眼前是一片漆黑的时候，没有办法的。朋友们散去了，只留下妈妈牵着妹妹的手。船在哪里？海在哪里？它们永远消失在黑暗中了吗？妹妹并不喊叫，把妈妈的手贴在自己脸上。

"我对上天只有一个乞求。"妈妈呜咽道，"让我替我的女儿做盲人。"

她们都知道，盲人还不是最坏的结局。

妹妹做了一个梦，梦见一座森林，树木长得很密。她觉得自己进不去，可还是向前走。树木向两旁分开了，让出一条弯曲的小路。她走到一片奇怪的草地，草地上变幻着山和海，中央有一棵大树，轮廓模糊，但是有一种威严的气象。她想，这是自己眼睛有毛病的缘故。她又向前走，大树就向后退，很快混入森林中，不再显现。乌何有之树，妹妹给它起了一个名字。忽然树林都不见了，只看见陶陶在旷野上跑。她大声叫时，陶陶也不见了，只有黑暗。妈妈听见叫声，想是妹妹梦魇了，过来抚慰，妹妹说："我看见了乌何有之树。"但愿你能看见，妈妈在心里叹息。

陶陶不能耽误一点时间，又一次出发了。这一次，他走得更快，有一个听不见的鼓点在催着他。他又跑又跳，过了桥，回头望了望那粉红色的小屋，继续向前跑，一直爬到那座山半腰。在那块大岩石旁又歇着一片云，这是一片彩色的云，它很娇懒。它说："你就是陶陶？告诉你，我可飞不了那么远。"陶陶拱手又鞠躬一直向它微笑。云沉默了一阵，说："你上来吧。"这片云好像挂满彩色璎珞的小船。陶陶尽量缩小自己已经很小的身躯，生怕碰坏了什么，可是他们飞到那片旷野时，璎珞还是少了一半。陶陶感到很抱歉，云并不抱怨，悄然飞走了。陶陶很顺利地进入了森林。来到树下，大树没让他多等，很快给了两片叶子。陶陶两手举着叶子，像举着两面旗帜。他在森林外寻找那片云，又是晴空万里。陶陶焦急地向天空乞求，诉说他必须争取时间。一阵强劲的风来，把他卷到半空。"你怕么？"风问，"你随时会掉下去粉身碎骨。"陶陶摇头。他只有一个念头，不要迟到，别的都不在话下。他们很快就到了那座山坡。风把他稳稳地放下，自己向另一个方向吹去。陶陶看见停在天边的云，像许多花朵。一朵云飘过来了，越近越大，有几层花瓣，真像一朵硕大花。陶陶爬进去，坐在中间。云一面飞，花瓣一面转动，转动的方向不同，有的向前转，有的向后转。陶陶和云商量，说花瓣要是都向一个方向转动，会飞得更快一些。云不理他。云飞得并不慢，又飞了一会儿，就把他放在那座山的一块岩石上。陶陶鞠躬致谢，跑下山去。

这时已是秋天，树叶有红有黄，颜色绚丽。有的树叶子已经落尽，光秃秃的树枝，显出好看的线条。陶陶拼命地跑，他到了河的这一边，已经看到了那粉红色的小屋。人们出出进进，有人在说："没想到这次发作这么快。"陶陶不假思索地跳进水里，他没有时间走那座桥。在汹涌的河水中，他不久便失去了双腿，他努力用一只手把两片叶子举得高高的，露在水面上。手臂也被起伏的水花打湿了，一点点消瘦。他拼命游向岸边，终于靠近了岸，河水不断地流过他的身躯，陶陶没有了，只剩下那只手臂碎作几块泥土，簇拥着那两片鲜亮的绿叶。

房间里，妹妹低声呻吟，她的生命在一点点消逝。她用力低声问妈妈："陶陶在哪里？"妈妈茫然地走出门来，一眼就看见了河边的那两片叶子。"秋天的绿叶！"妈妈心里一惊，弯腰拾起他们，放在妹妹的眼睛上，每只眼睛放一片。

妹妹没有死。她又看见了这光明灿烂的世界，但她再也看不见小沙弥陶陶。

2006年3月22日稿
2006年4月5日定稿

303

Taotao the Novice Monk[1]

○ Zong Pu

The novice monk named Taotao was from the Wheat Stack Mountain in Gansu Province, China. The mountain looked like a stack of wheat, hence its name. On the walls of the mountain, there were many grottoes abounding in vivid clay sculptures and stone inscriptions. In a grotto whose number ranked over one hundred, there was a statue of a novice monk. His gown was carved so vividly that it looked as if it were swaying in the wind. As tall as a real person and with delicate brows and eyes, the novice monk looked composed, kind and gentle. The smile on his lips was particularly enchanting and thus called "Smile of the East".

Long time ago, people found an adobe in a cave. They thought it was useless and threw it into a shabby cart. The cart carried it to a faraway place where it was thrown into another shabbier cart and moved to a farther place. After such a long journey on the bumpy roads, the adobe cracked and its outer cover began to peel off. In the end, when it was thrown onto a wilderness, the outer cover totally broke off and a beautiful novice monk inside was revealed. He was about half a meter tall, and had beautiful brows and eyes and that unique "Smile of the East". He looked like a miniature copy of the novice monk in the grotto. As a matter of fact, he was not a replica but the original which embodied the painstaking effort of his creator. After the long and hard journey, he showed his true form. But, unfortunately, his left arm broke up. Some deer came and seeing him so beautiful they weaved a basket with grass and put him as well as his broken arm into it. Two deer held the basket and walked slowly forward. The drove of deer walked on and on, and nobody knew how many days had passed. Through all kinds of valleys and groves of trees, one day, they came to a forest. The deer had a discussion and finally two capable deer were selected to continue carrying him into the forest. Through the dark and damp clusters and groves of trees and over many winding and zigzagging paths, they finally came to an open grassland dotted with beautiful wildflowers. There, the sky appeared too high to be fathomable. A big tree stood in the middle of the grassland.

It was neither a pine nor a cypress, neither a poplar nor a willow, and it exuded an awe-inspiring aura. The two deer meticulously and reverently put him under the tree, set his broken arm right in position and left quietly. Many days passed. Several leaves drifted down on his body and his broken arm happened to be covered by a leaf. More days passed. One day, a hare ran over to the tree. Seeing him lying under the tree, it patted him softly and said, "Wake up! Shall we go out to have a look together?"

All at once, the novice monk woke up. He sat up, looked about and stood up. Stretching his limbs, he found his broken arm already healed! He greeted the hare with a "Hi", and that lovely hare curled its long ears to show its greetings in return. The novice monk followed the hare and walked away. As they were about to walk out of the grassland, he turned his head and looked at that big tree for quite a while, then he continued his trip with the hare. They passed the winding path and in the end walked out of the forest. At this time, the hare suddenly disappeared. He saw many deer frolicking in the groves. Oh! They were the descendants of those deer who once saved him! A deer invited the novice monk to sit on its back and they roved and played on the wilderness in high spirit. Sometimes, they slowed down, gazing around, and sometimes, they ran and chased each other in brisk steps. The novice monk sat steady on the deer's back, feeling himself on top of the world.[2] Nobody knew how much time passed. One day, the deer put the novice monk by a village and they left. A villager happened to see him. "What a beautiful clay figurine!" He picked him up and took him to the market. A sculptor saw him. Isn't it the "smile of the East" on his face? Feeling surprised, the sculptor took him up and studied him closely. He traded his new overcoat, which he had bought to live out the winter, for the novice monk. But the villager want more. The sculptor agreed and gave his hat to the villager. The deal done, he put the novice monk into a glass box and after a long trip sent him to a family's sitting room.

The family lived by a river, where the water flowed slowly between grass-lined banks. In spring, the light purple flowers were in riot blossom; in summer, the land was covered with dense green grasses, groves and trees; in autumn, both sides of banks were dyed golden yellow; and in winter, snow glistened with silvery light. The river ran past a small rose-pink house, around which there were many flowers in blossom.[3] A mother and her two daughters lived in this house. One daughter was 15 years old, and the other 13.

The sculptor put the glass box on the table. The moment he opened it, the two girls at once exclaimed with happiness, "This is our friend!" They shouted, "Look! He is smiling at us." The sculptor then introduced the clay figurine's "Smile of the East" to the two girls. He told them, "Look at his smile! It is tranquil and consolatory. Only the one who has a kind, compassionate and charitable heart can have such a smile." The clay figurine's gown fascinated the mother, and from a fashion designer's point of view, she made a judgment that he was a novice monk.

"I'll call him Taotao." The little sister said. The word "Tao" was associated with both "clay" and "happiness". "What a good name!" They all nodded with consent. The novice monk winked at them but none of them noticed it.

Since then, Taotao settled down in this family. Exactly speaking, he stood in the cabinet as a work of art. This was a warm family. Every day, he enjoyed hearing the younger girl call "Mum" after school and was moved to see the elder girl change shoes for her mother, because their mother bent over her desk too long and her feet got swollen. When the mother ate with her two daughters at table, and when she divided food for them, he was even more touched by her passionate and even reverent eyes. More often than not, they sang songs together. Though Taotao didn't know what they were singing, he found their songs melodious and quite pleasant to the ear, like soft breezes, refreshing drizzles in spring or the night sky bejeweled with twinkling stars.[4] The sculptor was their only audience.

Taotao was also fond of hearing the girls talking with each other. From time to time, the two sisters sat below where he stood and had a heated discussion in high spirit. The elder sister said, "One day, I'll draw a picture of the whole world." Taotao was fascinated by the two pictures in her hand. On one picture, several glistening lilacs were blooming on two crooked branches. At the sight of it, Taotao felt like putting his hand on those small white flowers which seemed to come alive on that light green paper. On the other picture, the river in front of their house, the bridge and the drooping willows, which set each other off in the distance, and the two small boats mooring side by side by the river all attracted him so much! The two small boats leaned against each other. Perhaps they were prepared for Taotao? The younger sister was moved and said, "Let me make boats. I'll make many many boats and let them float down the river into the sea. And on each wave there sits a doll and when the dolls see my boats they will come on board and dance together. What do you think, Taotao?" She suddenly threw such a question to Taotao. Overwhelmed by flattery and honor,[5] Taotao was eager to nod his agreement, but he didn't move.

Later, the younger sister drew a big boat, on the side of which hung many waves, glittering and shining like lilacs. And on each wave stood a doll, and they waved to each other, greeted each other and asked, "Where are you going?"

Taotao was intoxicated. How he wished he could stand here for ever, listening, watching and keeping guard for these two sisters, no matter how time flew, no matter where time flowed![6]

One day, the elder sister came home from school, holding a bunch of lilacs she had plucked in the garden. As she was about to put it into a vase, she suddenly cried, "I can't see!" The lilacs fell onto the table and the floor. Her mother rushed to her, "What happened?" The girl cried, "I can't see! I can't!" Obviously, there was something wrong with her eyes.

Suffering a kind of acute eye disease, she became blind in both eyes. The bright colorful world suddenly turned into a hole of total darkness. Where were the flowers? Where was the river? The terrible darkness, like an unfathomable deep well covered with a lid which was too heavy to be lifted, drove her desperate. It darkened not only her life but also her mother's and her younger sister's lives. The whole family was cast into a melancholy and miserable abyss. They tried ways and means but all their efforts were in vain.[7] When the night fell, the mother and her two daughters sat together, weeping in desperation. Seeing this, Taotao really wanted to tell them, "Don't cry. Too much crying will hurt your eyes." Before he uttered a word, his tears streamed down and left a wet streak on his gown. He was not supposed to cry, for his body couldn't be exposed to water, or it would melt.

They went from one hospital to another, trying to find some effective ways to cure her eyes, but to their dismay, all their endeavors fell flat.[8] And at last, the miserable girl had to live her life in darkness. Like a withering flower, she turned weaker and weaker. "What shall I do?" She shouted at the sun in the day, and in the evening, she yelled at the moon, "What shall I do?"

Taotao couldn't bear hearing her plaintive wails. He made up his mind to help her. He flew down from the cabinet and walked out of the house. He composed himself in the garden and tried to collect his thoughts.[9] He thought of that tree, the miraculous tree which cured his wound and helped him restore his vigor and vitality. "Where is it? And how can I find it?" He stood there in a daze.

It was dawning again. Taotao heard the mother and the girls speaking in an anxious tone, as if they had lost something. The younger sister shouted, "Taotao, where are you? Why can't I find you?" The elder sister stood on the stairs and called, "I can't see you now, but I can feel you. But... but where are you, Taotao?" The younger girl led her elder sister's hand and they walked downstairs together. They went to the back of the house to look for him. Taotao felt his heart warm and moved. Somehow or other, he must start out right now. He must find that magical tree! He ran along the bank of the river, but as he was too short and his steps too small, it took him quite a long time to reach the bridge. Down the bridge, he continued running, lowering his head and exerting all his efforts. After a long time, as he raised his head he saw a big mountain standing in front of him. "How can I climb over such a gigantic mountain?" When he reached halfway of the mountain, he saw a cloud resting beside a huge rock. The cloud asked, "You are Taotao? Can I help you?" He answered in a haste, "Could you help me to the wilderness ahead? I am looking for a tree over there." "Come onto me." The cloud said, "Be careful. Sit steady." Taotao climbed onto the cloud and got himself seated. Like a pile of cotton, the cloud had an irregular shape and an uneven surface. Due to its convexes and concaves, Taotao had to adjust his seating from time to time so as not to fall down from it. The cloud praised, "You are smart! You keep your balance very well." Soon, they arrived at the wilderness. He saw that forest again! The cloud stopped at the top of a tree. It said that it couldn't fly lower, or it would melt into water. Taotao got off the cloud and lingered on the top of the trees for a while. To his disappointment, he couldn't find that magical tree! Facing such a sea of trees he felt dazzled and confused. In desperation he slipped down to the ground. He wandered in the forest for quite a long time but still he couldn't find the way. At this time, some hares jumped up and ran to him, curling their long ears to greet him, and some deer also came, joining the hares and looking at him up and down curiously. Taotao said, "We have been friends all along. Can you help me find the tree that I am looking for?" The deer and the hares had a discussion. They sent a deer and a hare to accompany him into the forest. Then, the party set off. Along the winding path, they walked on and on and finally they arrived at the magical tree at midnight. In great excitement, Taotao rushed to it. The tree was glowing with mysterious light, shining over the grassland beneath. "I know you are willing to help those in trouble. Can you help me? I'll wait for your help here, OK?" Standing erect, holding up his hands, he waited and waited. One day passed, two days passed and on the third day, the deer and the hare told him that they really wanted to leave because they were very hungry and that they didn't dare to eat the grass and the flowers here. Suddenly, he heard a waft of music in the air, and in the music two leaves drifted down to his hands. Taotao was overjoyed! Holding the leaves carefully, he followed the deer and the hare and went out of the forest. The deer carried the hare on its back and they ran away into the dense groves. On his way back, he really hoped to see that cloud again, but it was a sunny and clear day, and there was no cloud at all. Anyway, he must go on his way. He didn't need to eat, drink, or rest. He pressed forward day and night, for fear of wasting a little time. One day, he climbed onto a hill and all at once he saw some white clouds were taking a rest in the sky. Seeing one of them floating to him, he at once held up his leaves and waved to it. The cloud stopped in front of him and said to him kindly, "Come! Suit yourself. Sit anywhere you want."

What an understanding cloud! Unlike the previous cloud which always changed its shape, this cloud was more like a ship, adrift steadily in the air. Soon, they arrived at the mountain nearest to the river. Taotao got off the "ship", which quickly vanished without a trace, and began to run in a hurry. He ran and ran and ran, and after passing the bridge, he finally reached the small house. Excitedly he ran into it, only to find nobody inside. He turned at once and ran to the garden. Under the lilac tree he saw a small tomb covered with flowers. On a small tombstone he found the girl's name. Oh, the elder sister had died! He was too late! In grief, he put the two leaves on the tomb. Instantly, they withered and faded away. "I am late! I am late!" He cried sadly, fraught with regret. After some time, he returned to stand in the cabinet. At dusk, the mother and the younger girl came back. Seeing him back, the younger sister held him up, watched him closely and handed him to her mother. Touching on his gown, the mother sighed and put him back to the cabinet. The girl was no longer happy and her mother aged a lot! The novice monk felt a piercing pain in his heart.

The sculptor came. He looked at Taotao for a good while.[10] None of them asked Taotao where he had been. Taotao later knew that the sculptor intended to make another novice monk statue, but he didn't do it. He said to the mother, "I can make a statue but I can never give him a heart."

The mother and the girl no longer sang songs. The sculptor suggested, "Sing a song, and you'll feel better." Taotao agreed with him. Yet, the room stayed silent.

After two years, the younger girl was fifteen years old. The mother invited some girls home to celebrate her daughter's birthday. The guests planned to sing a happy song for the girl. When the girl, in white gown, stepped into the sitting room to receive her birthday blessings, she suddenly cried, "I can't see!" The terrible cries reminded them of her elder sister! Now, the younger sister was also blind! Who could console a blind girl when she faced a totally dark world? Her friends left one after another, leaving her mother and her alone in the sitting room, hand in hand. Where were the boats? Where was the sea? Did all of them disappear forever in the darkness? The little girl, instead of shouting in desperation, put her mother's hand on her face.

"Oh, God! I have only one wish — do not let my daughter go blind. Let me go blind!" The mother sobbed.

Both of them knew that being blind was not the worst thing to happen.

The girl had a dream. In her dream she saw a forest. At first, she thought she couldn't enter such luxuriant foliage of trees and groves, but as she walked forward, the trees ahead parted and gave way for her. Along the winding path she came to a strange grassland where the mirage of mountain and sea loomed. In the center of the grassland stood a tall tree, which was not clearly outlined but exuded an awe-inspiring aura. She was dazed at such a scene and thought that it must be her eye problems that led to such an illusory vision. Then, she continued walking forward. As she went forward, that tree moved backward and soon merged into the forest. "The Tree of Nowhere" — she gave it a name. All of a sudden, the whole forest disappeared. She saw Taotao running on the wilderness. When she shouted after him, Taotao also disappeared. Before her, there was nothing left but the total darkness. The mother heard her crying and came to wake her up. It was a nightmare. The girl said, "Mom, I saw the Tree of Nowhere." The mother said to herself, sighing with sorrow, "How I hope you can see something."

Taotao started out again. This time he told himself he couldn't waste a little time. He must be faster. As if driven by a drum beating after him, he ran and ran and ran. After passing the bridge, he turned and cast an affectionate look at that rose-pink small house. Then, he continued forward. About the halfway up the mountain, he saw a cloud resting by the rock. It was a colorful cloud full of finicky airs. "Are you Taotao?" It asked, "To tell you the truth, I can't carry you so far away." Taotao made an obeisance to the cloud by cupping one hand in the other before his chest, bowed to it, and kept smiling at it. The cloud was moved by Taotao's sincerity and finally it said, "All right. Come and climb onto me." Like a small boat nicely decorated with colorful jades and pearls, the cloud looked too delicate to bear much weight. Taotao tried his best to huddle his petite body, for fear of breaking or damaging its decorations. Nevertheless, after they flew past the wilderness, the jades and pearls had been reduced by half. Taotao felt sorry for it, but the cloud flew away with no complaint in the least. Taotao went into the forest and found that magical tree. He didn't wait long before the tree shed two leaves for him. Holding up the two leaves in his hands as if holding two flags, he ran out of the forest. He wanted to ask for the cloud's help again, but there was no cloud in the sky. He anxiously pleaded to the sky that he couldn't waste time any more. A gust of wind came to his help. The wind rolled him up in the air. "Are you scared?" The wind asked, "You may fall down anytime. In that case, you may break into pieces." Taotao shook his head resolutely. He had only one hope in mind: "Don't be late! Saving the girl's life is more important than anything else." Soon, the wind brought him to the mountain. Putting him down, the wind went away. Taotao saw a cloud, which looked like a flower with many layers of petals. As it drew near, it became larger. Indeed, it was like a huge multi-layered flower. Taotao climbed onto it and they began to fly. As the cloud flew in the sky, one layer of petals turned in one direction and the other layer turned in an opposite direction. Taotao advised the cloud that all its petals had better turn in the same direction so that it could fly faster, but the cloud simply ignored him. In fact, they were already flying at a considerable speed. After a while, they reached a rock on the mountain. Taotao bowed to the cloud gratefully and ran down the mountain.

Now, it was autumn. The leaves had turned red or yellow and some had fallen off the branches. With naked shafts and limbs, the trees showed off their lovely figures.[11] Taotao desperately rushed to the river. He could see people coming and going before that rose-pink house. "It's really beyond our expectation that her disease develops so quickly!" Taotao could hear people murmuring to one another. He had no time to think more and he had no time to take that bridge. At once he jumped into the turbulent water. His legs soon melted and disappeared. He went all out to hold the two leaves with one hand high above the surface of the water. His arms were soaked in the splashes and became thinner and thinner. Finally, he drew close to the bank. However, with his body scoured by the water, Taotao was gone and what remained of him was his hand, now reduced to several earthy lumps, in whose embrace the two leaves appeared greener and fresher.

In the room, the girl was groaning. She was on the verge of death. "Where is Taotao?" She whispered to her mother. The mother walked out of the room in a daze and suddenly saw the two leaves glistening on the riverside. "Green leaves in autumn?" Startled, the mother walked toward the riverbank. She picked them up and brought them back. She put them on the girl's eyes, one leaf on each eye.

The girl survived. She saw the splendid world again. But since then, she never saw the novice monk Taotao.

Written on March 22, 2006
Finished on April 5, 2006

1. 这是一个童话小故事。文笔清新、自然、简洁，可以作为儿童读物。为了与原文风格对应，译文也尽量做到文风简洁。

2. "它们有时慢慢走，东张西望，有时跑得很快，小沙弥也没有跌下来。" Sometimes, they slowed down, gazing around, and sometimes, they ran and chased each other in brisk steps. The novice monk sat steady on the deer's

back, feeling himself on top of the world. 后半句feeling himself on top of the world是译者加上的，以表达陶陶当时高兴的心情。on top of the world 幸福到极点、心满意足。

3. "这个人家在一条河边，河水缓缓地流，流过两岸的树木草丛。那里春天开满了浅紫色的二月兰，夏天是一片浓绿；秋天的落叶给了河岸金黄的颜色，冬天则是晶莹的白雪。河水也流过这一栋小小的房屋，房屋是粉红色的，前后有许多花。"像这种童话小故事，里面经常有梦境般的景色描写，而且颜色词用得非常多，翻译不能省略，因为这些颜色词对景物描写、情感的表达以及气氛的烘托有着至关重要的作用。The family lived by a river, where the water flowed slowly between grass-lined banks. In spring, the light purple flowers were in riot blossom; in summer, the land was covered with dense green grasses, groves and trees; in autumn, both sides of banks were dyed golden yellow; and in winter, snow glistened with silvery light. The river ran past a small rose-pink house, around which there were many flowers in blossom.

4. "陶陶不知道她们唱的是什么，只觉得和谐悦耳，像春天的轻风细雨，像一个繁星闪烁的夜。"童话小故事的语言特点就是擅用比喻、拟人的修辞手法，使故事更具有童趣、更生动。这是翻译的重点，可以在忠实的基础上加以适当创造。Though Taotao didn't know what they were singing, he found their songs melodious and quite pleasant to the ear, like soft breezes, refreshing drizzles in spring or the night sky bejeweled with twinkling stars.

5. "受宠若惊"可以译为be overwhelmed by an unexpected favor、be overwhelmed by a special favor、be overwhelmed by a superior's favor、be overwhelmed by flattery and honor、feel overwhelmingly flattered、receive a favor with awed excitement等。

6. "他情愿这样站着、听着、看着、守望着，不管时间流到了哪里。"这里"情愿"译者没有译为would rather或者be willing to do。为了表达陶陶的心愿和心情，译者处理为：How he wished he could stand here for ever, listening, watching and keeping guard for these two sisters, no matter how time flew, no matter where time flowed! 后面的两个no matter…也是为了烘托主人公的心情。

7. They tried ways and means, 他们想尽了一切办法。means方法、方式、手段，注意这个词，单复数同形。再比如species、series、headquarters、

312

crossroads等都是单复数同形的。

8. "经过多方寻医问药，不见疗效……" They went from one hospital to another, trying to find some effective ways to cure her eyes, but to their dismay, all their endeavors fell flat. 此处用了短语fall flat完全失败，未产生预期效果。

9. "……在花园里定了定神。" He composed himself in the garden and tried to collect his thoughts. compose oneself 让自己镇静下来，collect one's thoughts 集中思想、整理思路。

10. "也拿着陶陶端详。" He looked at Taotao for a good while. 端详就是仔细地看，这里译者通过短语for a good while来体现"端详"的意思。a good while 好长时间。

11. "光秃秃的树枝，显出好看的线条。" With naked shafts and limbs, the trees showed off their lovely figures. show off 有"使突出"的意思，"光秃秃的树枝"译为naked shafts and limbs，比较形象，与后面的lovely figures一起构成拟人效果。

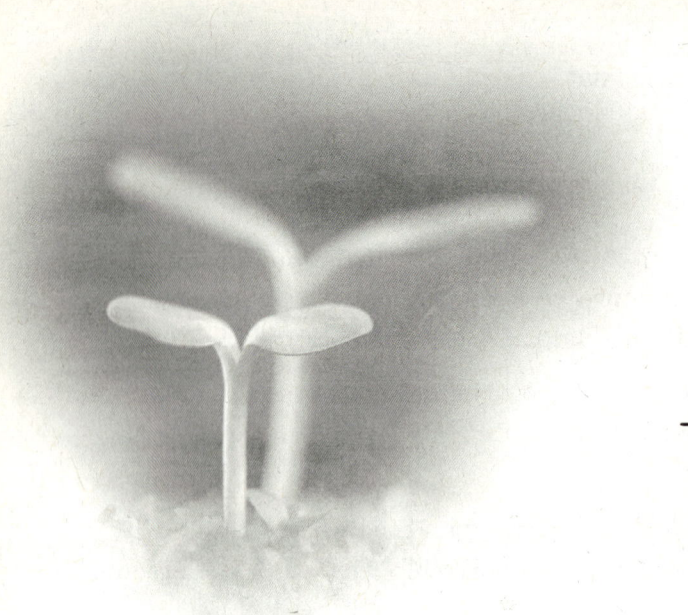

转

世

 龙仁青

一

　　米扎拿着望远镜，从帐篷门口往前面舒缓的草原望了望，便猛地站起来，气呼呼从羊毛卡垫上捡起"大哥大"大声呼道："喂，你是死人吗？你没看见咱们两家的羊群合群了吗，啊？！"

　　"噢，是吗？米扎，我正在打游戏机呢！""大哥大"那头传来克克的声音，"好，我这就去看看。"

　　米扎哼了一声，复又把"大哥大"扔在了卡垫上。这时，帐篷左角的一件硕大的羊皮袄蠕动了几下，一只大花猫便从羊皮袄上跳了下来，随之，一张苍老并且丑陋的面孔从皮袄中探出来，艰难地翘着下巴说："怎么啦，我的心肝，你说羊群合群了？"

　　"是的，阿妈索吉。"

　　"那你咋不去分群呢？"

　　"我已经给克克说了，他已经去了，阿妈索吉。"

　　"哦——"那张苍老的面孔在羊皮袄顶上停顿了片刻，又缩了回去，羊皮袄也随之蠕动了几下，便不再有动静了，却有一句话从羊皮袄缝里传了出来："唉，你还是不像固杰巴登，要是他，早就暴跳如雷了。"

　　米扎听见这话，朝羊皮袄看了一眼，他看见那只大花猫又卧在羊皮袄上。

二

邮递员本巴跌了七次跤，迷了三次路之后，终于找到了次达部落。他吃力地推着摩托车，往部落里最近的帐篷行走时，碰上了克克。

"喂，打问一下。"克克就要和他擦肩而过时，他忽然说，"你知道这里有个叫米扎的人吗？"

"哪个米扎，我们这里一共有六个叫米扎的。"

"就是……"本巴想了想说，"他可能在省城有认识的人，省城有人写信给他。"

"省城里有认识的人？"

"是的。"

"……不知道。"克克转着眼珠想了又想后说，"不过你看见那群羊了吗？那是我和米扎家的——合群了。"

本巴朝克克指示的方向看了看说："你认识一个叫米扎的？"

"当然，昨晚我们还在一起喝酒呢！"

"……"

三

米扎从克克家出来，天已经黑了，他跨上马，吐着酒气，一边五音不全地哼唱着刚才他在克克家唱过的一支酒曲，一边在马背上摇头晃脑地打着拍子。"阿香洛洛，阿香洛——洛——"他不断重复着，任凭老马驮他走去。

老马识途，不紧不慢地往家里走着。一只山雀忽然从草丛中扑棱一声飞了出来，老马一惊，响亮地打着响鼻，便飞跑起来。刚才，米扎从克克家出来时，忘了给马备上鞍子，这会儿，他在马背上滑来滑去，老马却越跑越快，不太会骑马的米扎只好闭上眼睛，默默在心里祈祷着："要跌就跌在一块比较软的地方吧，要跌就跌在一块比较软的地方吧！"果然，米扎就从马背上飞了出去，只听"扑通"一声，他被摔进了路边的一个水洼里。米扎从水洼里爬起来，用手擦去脸上的水，说："这也太软了！"

米扎回到家里，不想却着凉感冒了，第二天一早，米扎给克克打了电话："我感冒了，克克。"

"是吗？吃药了吗？"

"刚吃过一粒'康泰克'。"米扎说，"克克，今天我不能放羊了，你就替我放一天羊吧。"

"好，那当然。"克克说。

对米扎的要求，克克总是有求必应，唯命是从，因为在他看来，米扎就是固杰巴登。

四

次达部落和琼达部落隔河相望，琅曲河在两个部落之间弯弯曲曲地伸向东南，它便成了两个部落间的草山分界线。据说早在先祖时候，双方就有先约，凡是有牛羊吃了别家的草山，这牛羊便可被受侵犯的部落宰杀吃肉。但牛羊总归是畜物，不知禁令，不懂人类有这么多的规矩，因此时常便有啃吃人家青草的事件发生，两个部落便也就闹起了草山纠纷。这草山纠纷愈演愈烈，特别是那条可以宰杀他家牛羊的破烂规矩使部落的人们甚是放肆。哪个部落想吃肉了，便到对方草场上偷来几只牛羊宰杀，然后又以侵犯了草山为借口，掩盖事实，便安然无恙。

一晚，趁天黑不见五指之时，琼达部落十几个壮汉打马冲到次达部落的草场，将草原上未被牧人收去的牛羊尽数赶走，共计七十三头(只)。

一位知情的牧民连夜赶到固杰巴登家，向他禀报实情，并将前因后果绘声描述了一番。

"欺人太甚！"固杰巴登听了，狠狠地把茶碗摔在地上，那茶碗顿时成了两半。

"怎么办？"前来禀报的牧民问。

"走！"固杰巴登拿了叉子枪，冲出帐篷，跨上了大马。

五

"唉呀，你连马都骑不好……"当米扎又一次从马背上摔下来后，阿妈索吉眼睛中的那一丝光芒熄灭了，她看着眼前这个肩宽体胖而又笨笨拙拙的小家伙，叹声道："咱这次达部落是咋啦，自打固杰巴登以后，就没出过一条像样的汉子……"说着便眼望远方，不声不响了。"阿妈索吉，给我讲讲固杰巴登的故事好吗？"看着阿妈索吉此时的样子，米扎怯生生地说。

"唉，固杰巴登，固杰巴登可不是你这熊样儿，他胆大力大，并且视死如归！"

"视死如归？"

"对呵，难道你连这都不知道？"阿妈索吉看米扎摇了摇头，便滔滔不绝讲了起来："有一次，雄狮大王格萨尔去四方降服妖魔鬼怪，就把守护花花岭国和保护珠姆的事情交给了固杰巴登他们，而就在这个时候，霍尔国白帐王听信了黑乌鸦的谗言，偷袭花花岭国，想把珠姆抢去做妃子，为了花花岭国的安宁，为了珠姆，固杰巴登过世了。"

"阿妈索吉，你说的不是固杰巴登的故事，是岭国大将嘉察夏根的故事。"

"固杰巴登就是嘉察夏根，是嘉察夏根转世！"阿妈索吉坚决地说。

米扎愣愣地看着阿妈索吉，半晌后，他忽然说："阿妈索吉我可以做固杰巴登的转世吗？"

"你？！"阿妈索吉大吃一惊，忽地跳了起来。

后来，阿妈索吉对部落里的人说：米扎是固杰巴登转世，后来，部落里的人们对阿妈索吉说：米扎是固杰巴登转世。

六

米扎吃了"康泰克"，又按着药盒上的说明，连喝了几碗开水，便沉沉地睡了过去，并做起了美梦：他骑着一匹高头大马，雄赳赳赶着琼达部落的大群牛羊，正在偷渡琅曲河，阿妈索吉笑笑地立在河岸上等着他，手里还拿了一本写着烫金大字的聘书，米扎甚至看见了那聘书里的一串黑字：聘米扎为固杰巴登之转世。

大群牛羊下了河，那畜物踩水溅起的水花，老高老高，"哗哗"之声也不绝于耳，米扎便被这水声惊醒。原来，他身边的"大哥大"正在叮铃铃作响，打断了他的美梦。

米扎气呼呼地拿起"大哥大"。

"米扎，感冒好些了吗？"是克克的声音。

"关你屁事！"

"哦，米扎，你怎么啦？"

"关你屁事！"

"大哥大"半天无话，片刻后又说："米扎，我是说，我把咱们两家的羊群分开了。"

"那你还不去看着羊群！"米扎说完，就要挂断"大哥大"时，他清晰地听见克克叫了他一声固杰巴登。

七

固杰巴登带着他的人马，一路浩浩荡荡开进了琼达部落，几十顶跑掉了人的黑帐篷在他们的铁蹄下成了碎布条。随后，他们赶着琼达部落的一大群牛羊，向次达部落返回，不一会儿，就到了琅曲河边。

"过河！"固杰巴登挥动着叉子枪，打马往前跑去，正在这时，就听到身后一声枪响，固杰巴登的坐骑随之翻了个跟头，人便从马背上飞了出去。这一突如其来的事件使众人目瞪口呆，一个个傻坐在马背上不知所措。

固杰巴登弓身躺在地上，痛苦地抽搐着。有人这才回过神来，赶紧下马想把固杰巴登扶起来，却看见一团血糊糊的肠子堆在地上，在河水的寒光下冒着热气——固杰巴登身上的那支叉子枪，把两个用羚羊角做成的叉子深深刺进了他的肚皮。

"固杰巴登！"首先跳下马的那位牧人大叫一声。

"固杰巴登！"众牧人也大叫，悲恸之声响遍琅曲河畔。

八

"伙计，有你一封信！"本巴把摩托车撑立在地上，向在帐篷门口晒太阳的米扎扬了扬手。

"我的信？"

"是的，从省城来的。"本巴说，"如果不识汉字，我可以帮你念念。"

"那你就念念吧。"米扎说。

本巴打开了信。信上除了米扎的名字是用钢笔填上去的外，其他都是印刷的铅字："米扎先生：全省藏族摇滚歌手大奖赛将在5月4日举行，请你届时参加，并带上自己参赛歌曲的乐谱。"

"米扎，你还是歌手？真了不起。"本巴说，"不过，今天已经是6月9号了，真遗憾。"说着把信交给了米扎。米扎看着信，想起自己喝醉酒时爱唱的那首"阿香洛洛"放声大笑起来。

The Reincarnation

○ *Long Renqing*

I

At the door of the tent, Mizha looked at the vast grassland ahead through his binocle. He suddenly rose up with fury. Picking up the mobile phone from the woolen cushion, he shouted, "Hello? Are you dead? Can't you see our herds of sheep merge together? Can't you?!"

"Oh, really? Mizha, I am playing a video game!" Keke's voice came from the other end of the line. "All right. I'll go and have a look at it."

Mizha grunted with dissatisfaction and hurled his mobile phone back to the cushion.[1] At this time, a huge sheepskin coat in the left corner of the tent moved and a big cat jumped out of it. Whereat, an ugly face mummified with age came out of the coat.[2] The old woman lifted her chin with some difficulty and asked, "My dear, what's wrong? Your sheep merged with the other's?"

"Yes, Granny Suoji."

"Why not go and separate them?"

"I've told Keke and he'll go, Granny."

"Oh —" The old face remained on top of the coat awhile and shrank back. The sheepskin coat moved slightly and became motionless again. A voice came from within, "Ah! After all, you are not Gujie Badeng. If he met such a thing, he would leap up in a thundering rage."[3]

Hearing the words, Mizha cast a look at the sheepskin coat. That big cat was lying on it again.

II

After tumbling down for seven times and losing his way for three times, the postman Benba finally found the tribe of Cida. He walked his motorcycle laboriously to the nearest tent. On his way, he met Keke.

"Hi, excuse me." As Keke passed by, he blurted out, "Do you know a man named

Mizha?"

"Which Mizha? There are six Mizhas here."

"It's ..." Benba thought a while and said, "He might know someone in the provincial capital. Here is a letter for him from the provincial capital."

"He knows someone in the provincial capital?"

"Yah."

"... I don't know." Keke gave it a second thought with his eyes rolling and said to the postman, "Do you see that herd of sheep? They are mine and Mizha's. They've merged."

Looking at the direction Keke pointed at, Benba said, "So you know one called Mizha?"

"Of course. We drank together last night!"

"..."

III

Coming out of Keke's home, Mizha climbed onto his horse. It was nearly dark. As he rode his horse home, he hummed a happy drinking song which he sang at Keke's just now. Rocking back and forth to his improvised beat, he sang a rather bad tune. "Ah-xiang-luoluo. Ah-xiang-luoluo —" He hummed in refrain, not caring about where his old horse went.

The old horse knew the way. Carrying its master, it trotted home in a leisurely manner. All of a sudden, a titmouse fluttered out of the groves.[4] Taking fright, the old horse snorted and began to gallop. When Mizha left Keke's home, he forgot to put a saddle onto the horse. Now, he slipped to and fro on the horseback as the old horse ran faster and faster. Mizha, who was not a good rider, had to close his eyes and pray, "It'll be better to fall onto a soft place. It'll be better to fall onto a soft place!" As he expected, he finally flew off the horseback and flopped into a puddle on the roadside.[5] Climbing out of the puddle, he wiped the water and mud off his face and said, "This is too ... too soft!"

After he got home, he fell ill from a cold. The next morning, he called Keke, "Keke, I've caught a cold."

"Have you? Did you take some medicine?"

"I just took a tablet of Contac." Mizha continued, "Keke, I am afraid I cannot graze sheep today. Would you please help me graze my sheep?"

"Yeah, of course." Keke replied.

Keke was willing to satisfy all Mizha's demands. He was happy to be at Mizha's bidding,[6] for, in his eyes, Mizha was Gujie Badeng.

IV

The two tribes of Cida and Qiongda were located opposite to each other as they were separated by Langqu River which snaked its way to the southeast. Therefore, the river served as the borderline of the two tribes. It was said that from as early as the primitive age their ancestors reached an agreement that cattle or sheep which crossed the line and ate the other side's grass were allowed to be slaughtered by the "invaded" tribe. However, animals were animals and didn't know about agreements or prohibitions, and they really didn't understand why human beings had so many rules. As a result, they often crossed the "borderline" to feed on the grass of the opposite side. Eventually, the two tribes clashed. As more and more conflicts occurred, people of the two tribes grew more audacious under the protection of the outdated tradition handed down from their ancestors. If they wanted to eat meat, they stole some cattle or sheep from the opposite side of the river. After they ate the meat, they covered up the theft and absolved themselves by saying that these cattle or sheep invaded their own grassland. Thus, they got away with it every time.[7]

One night, it was pitch-dark. A dozen able-bodied men from Qiongda rode their horses to the grazing ground of Cida and took away what was left of the day's pasturing herds — altogether 73 cattle and sheep.

A herdsman in the know hurried to Gujie Badeng's home at night and told him what had happened.[8]

"That's going too far!"[9] Hearing the descriptive account, Gujie Badeng got furious. He hurled his teacup onto the ground, and the cup broke into two pieces at once.

"What can we do?" The herdsman asked.

"Follow me!" Gujie Badeng took out his harpoon, rushed out of the tent and climbed onto his horse.

V

"Ah! You can't even ride a horse well ..." As Mizha fell off the horse again, the last glow in Granny Suoji's eyes went out. Seeing this flabby and clumsy lad, she sighed, "What's wrong with our Cida Tribe? After Gujie Badeng, no man as good as him has appeared ..." Looking afar, she fell into silence.

"Granny Suoji, can you tell me something about Gujie Badeng?" Mizha requested in a timid tone.

"Gujie Badeng? He was not like you! On the contrary, he had great strength and bravery, and he had the guts to face death with a smile!"[10]

"Face death with a smile?"

"Yeah! Don't you understand it?!" Granny Suoji asked in surprise. Seeing Mizha shaking his head, she began to spout on and on, "Once, the Lion King Gesar was about to go on an expedition to vanquish demons and monsters. Before he left he entrusted his warriors led by Gujie Badeng with the task of guarding the Kingdom of Flowery Ridge and protecting Princess Zhumu. At this time, the King of White Tent of Huo'er, confused by the black crow's slanderous talk, made a sneak attack at the Kingdom of Flowery Ridge in an attempt to grab Princess Zhumu away and make her his concubine. In protecting the Kingdom of Flowery Ridge and Princess Zhumu, Gujie Badeng sacrificed his life."

"Oh, granny, this is the story of Jiacha Xiagen, the general of the Kingdom of Flowery Ridge, not Gujie Badeng's."

"Gujie Badeng is Jiacha Xiagen. He was the reincarnation of Jiacha Xiagen!" Granny Suoji said resolutely.

Mizha stared at her in a trance. After a while, he suddenly asked, "Then, granny, can I be the reincarnation of Gujie Badeng?"

"You?" Granny Suoji jumped up with astonishment.

Later, she told the people in the tribe that Mizha was the reincarnation of Gujie Badeng. And later, people said to granny Suoji that Mizha was indeed the reincarnation of Gujie Badeng.

VI

After Mizha took one pill of Contac and drank several bowls of water as instructed on the medicine package, he fell into a sound sleep. He had a great dream: Riding on a tall horse, he was driving a large herd of Qiongda's cattle and sheep to cross Langqu River stealthily. Granny Suoji was waiting for him at the bank with a smile and holding an appointment letter on which the gilded characters looked exceptionally striking: We appoint Mizha as the reincarnation of Gujie Badeng.

As the crowd of cattle and sheep were driven into the water, the water splashed in all directions. The noisy splashes awoke Mizha. Ah! It was his mobile phone ringing that cut short his wonderful dream.

Exasperated, he took up the phone.

"Mizha, are you well?" It was Keke's voice.

"None of your business!"

"Oh, Mizha, what's wrong?"

"None of your business!"

For a moment, the other end of the line kept silent. After a while, Keke said, "Mizha, I am telling you that I've separated our sheep."

"Then, see to them now!" As he was about to hang up, he clearly heard Keke call him "Gujie Badeng".

VII

Gujie Badeng led his men to Qiongda to take revenge. People there had fled, and Gujie Badeng and his men ripped tens of tents into pieces. Then, they drove a big herd of cattle and sheep back home. Soon, they reached Langqu River.

"Cross the river!" Waving the harpoon in his hand, Gujie Badeng called out his command. As he rode his horse forward, a sudden gunshot boomed from behind his back. The startled horse turned a somersault and Gujie Badeng was thrown off. All his men were greatly shocked and sat on horseback dumbfounded.

Gujie Badeng doubled his body and kept twitching on the ground. It took some time before his men could respond to the sudden accident. Someone got off the horse and held Gujie Badeng up. A lump of his intestines piled on the ground, steaming in the cold air — the two spears made of antelope horns on his harpoon had thrust into his abdomen.

"Gujie Badeng!" The herdsman who was the first to dismount cried out loud.

"Gujie Badeng!" All the herdsmen began to shout. Soon Langqu River was fraught with their throbbing wails.[11]

VIII

"Hi, buddy. Here is a letter for you!" The postman Benba stopped his motorcycle and waved to Mizha, who was enjoying the sun at the door of his tent.

"My letter?"

"Yes. Your letter from the provincial capital." Benba said. "If you can't read Mandarin, I can read it to you."

"OK, thanks."

Benba opened the letter. Mizha's name was written by pen, but all the other words were printed. "Mr. Mizha, the Provincial Rock-and-Roll Singing Contest for Tibetans is going to be held on May 4th and we sincerely invite you to take part in the contest. Please take the music score with you to the contest."

"Mizha, you are a Tibetan singer? Great!" Benba exclaimed. "But today is June 9th. It is really a pity!" He handed the letter to Mizha. Looking at the letter and thinking about his "Ah-xiang-luoluo" which he loved singing when drunk, Mizha burst into a hearty laughter ...

1. "米扎哼了一声，复又把'大哥大'扔在了卡垫上。""哼了一声"是指小说主人公当时生气的样子，"大哥大"是对手机的俗称，流行于手提电话刚刚面世那几年。Mizha grunted with dissatisfaction and hurled his mobile phone back to the cushion. "哼了一声"译为grunted with dissatisfaction，grunt有抱怨、哼哼之意。hurl意思是狠狠地摔或扔，英语里cast、throw、toss、discard都有扔掉的意思，但用法和搭配不尽相同。"大哥大"直接译为mobile phone。

2. "一张苍老并且丑陋的面孔从皮袄中探出来……"An ugly face mummified with age came out of the coat. mummify使成木乃伊状、干瘪、使干瘪。mummified with age，译者用这个短语翻译"苍老"，即由于岁月流逝，脸已经干瘪。

3. "要是他，早就暴跳如雷了。"一是注意虚拟语气的使用；二是"暴跳如雷"的翻译，可以译为stamp with rage、be in a frenzy of rage、be in a thundering rage、fly into a rage、leap up furiously、stamp frantically in anger，等等。译文为：If he met such a thing, he would leap up in a thundering rage.

4. "一只山雀忽然从草丛中扑棱一声飞了出来。"All of a sudden, a titmouse fluttered out of the groves. 这里的flutter是一个非常生动的动词，既有"扇着翅膀飞"的意思，也有"受惊"的含义，所以这里译者没有用fly，因为flutter既有动作又有声音，更为生动。

5. "只听'扑通'一声，他被摔进了路边的一个水洼里。"... and flopped into a puddle on the roadside. flop意思是笨拙地落下、沉重地落下、失败、扑通一声，用在这里既表动作又有声音。

6. "克克总是有求必应，唯命是从……"此句中"有求必应，唯命是从"可以译为be absolutely obedient、be at somebody's beck and call、be at somebody's disposal、be at somebody's service、be guided entirely by the orders of ...、do everything as one is told、follow the dictates of others、listen to and attend to somebody's every order等等。这里译为：He was happy to be at Mizha's bidding. at one's bidding 遵照某人指示，听命于某人。

7. "安然无恙"，意译为get away with it，即闯祸后扬长而去，不受惩罚。

8. in the know 知情的、熟悉内情的。

9. "欺人太甚！"翻译为：That's going too far! too far 过火、过头、过分。

10. "视死如归"可以译为take death calmly、look death calmly in the face、face death unflinchingly、look upon death as going home、willingly to walk to one's death、death is only a homecoming，等等。这里译为face death with a smile，比较简单，符合当时的情境和人物的语言特点。

11. "众牧人也大叫，悲恸之声响遍琅曲河畔。"All the herdsmen began to shout. Soon Langqu River was fraught with their throbbing wails. throb 抽搐，跳动，throbbing 抽动的、震颤的，wail 哀号。英语中cry（哭喊）、wail（哀号）、weep（默默流泪）、sob（抽泣）、blubber（苦恼）都有"哭"的意思，注意区分辨别。

门卫之死

○ 孙颙

　　每天早晨，泛着黑色光泽的轿车，准时而恭敬地前来迎接年轻的院长。

　　上车后，韦的脑袋习惯地靠在软背上，右肩紧挨车门，让明媚的阳光涂抹在棱角分明的脸上。他打量着窗外滚滚的车流和脚步匆匆的上班族，偶尔难免产生滑稽的幻觉，怀疑坐在轿车沙发上的，是否真是那个姓韦的穷学生？真是那个来历不明的被众人鄙视的男孩？噢，仅仅是十几年前，他还经常几天也吃不到一顿荤菜，看见同学碗里油光闪亮的红烧肉，馋得偷偷咽口水……

　　车子照例驶进医院的后门。让韦觉得更滑稽甚至不自在的，是那位比他年长二十几岁的门卫，总是抢前几步，轻轻打开车门，还张开右手挡住车门框，好像生怕院长碰疼了脑瓜。那样的时刻，很容易让人产生错觉，以为自个确实是了不起的大人物。韦毕竟还不习惯。有一回，他忍不住对门卫说："朱师傅，我自己会开门。"韦不知道门卫的姓名，只晓得他是街道介绍的临时工，旁人唤他朱师傅，韦也就这样称呼。

　　亮晃晃的晨光下，朱的脸显得黑瘦，皱纹深深地刻写在额头和两颊。他不知所措笑着，倒也不慌乱，仅仅是有些儿窘迫，慢慢退后，讷讷地应着："是，是。"那谦恭却并不卑微的神情，忽然让韦生出几分好感。凭直觉，韦感到做门卫的朱属于有点文化的人。韦的好感，也许来自本身的经历，当他还完全属于底层时，他的精神底线就是如此，面对必须迎合的对象，谦恭是必要的，却不能显出寒酸和卑微。

　　那天以后，车子到后门时，朱师傅就不再迎上来开门，只是迅速走出门卫室，笔直地站立在门右侧，微笑着行注目礼，表示对院长的尊重，韦也就礼节性地朝他点头笑笑。后来，细心的韦感到了诧异，原因是两次半夜被召唤到医院解决紧急病例，竟又在门口见到了黑瘦的朱。院长便叫来办公室主任兼后勤处长的李查问，朱师傅到底值什么班头。李尴尬地笑笑："哦哦，他是二十四小时连班……"

韦瞪圆了双目："二十四小时？这不违反劳动法？"

主任慌了："有个门卫回乡了，是朱师傅再三请求，他的孩子读大学，学费贵，他顶班多挣点……"

韦听罢没有吱声。他突然想起，从小，家里最困难的时候，是开学要交费的那些日子。那年头，学费不像眼下这般贵，却已经够他摆小摊的母亲伤神，到处借，到处求，只要能说上话的亲戚邻居，老着脸皮求援，韦自己也拾废纸去卖，凑点零钱。妈说，今后就指望韦，一定要读出头……

主任见院长阴沉着脸不回答，赶紧知趣地说："噢，我懂我懂，违反劳动法不得了，我立刻找人换班。"

韦叹了口气，犹豫着说："不忙吧，你先把门卫室的空调检查一下，冬天了，值班很辛苦。"一脸纳闷的主任，显然没猜透领导的心思，只得连连应着往门外退去。韦暗想，他莫非收了朱的什么好处吧？平时，这位主任一口一个规定神圣不可侵犯，还倚老卖老地用来劝诫新院长，这次为何如此通融？难道仅仅是同情朱师傅？韦不太相信。每次捐援助款，韦总愿在标准之上多捐点。母亲在世时说过，咱们日子好了，要帮帮穷的，过去我们也是靠人帮的。李主任却劝韦少捐，还嬉皮笑脸地说："你院长捐多了，让下属难啊，捐少不好，捐多不舍得，嘿嘿。"

今天早晨，院长的车开进后门时，意外地发现，门卫换人了，一张胖胖的陌生面孔代替了见惯的黑瘦的朱。韦想，朱顶不住连班，终于去休息了。

韦决定，在适当的时候，向李主任提出，可以在互助金里给朱一点帮助，如果他付不了孩子学费的话。韦猜想，李的第一反应，肯定说互助金借给临时工不合规定啊。韦应该马上给他顶回去："二十四小时连班合什么规定？"

韦至今不知道父亲是谁，他完全靠摆补衣小摊的母亲抚养。他记得，小时候在山村到处疯跑，识字是母亲教的，母亲是插队到那里的知青，也是破落的小学校里惟一的老师。和小朋友吵架，人家骂他野种。他哭着回家向母亲要父亲。母亲不回答，轻轻地呜咽。他懂事，从此不再问。有一天，母亲突然郑重地和六七岁的他商量，要带他返城。他记得清楚，母亲说："外公外婆老了，要人照顾。到城里生活也苦，要过好日子，全指望你读书争气！"他似懂非懂，但是明白了一个道理，母亲和他，甚至外公外婆的希望，全压在他身上了。他比任何学生用功。所以，他考上了重点医学院，毕业后又奋斗十年，成为最年轻的脑外科主任，直到当上院长。

善良的母亲播在韦心里的种子发芽了。韦真心觉得，自己成功以后，能给其他穷孩子一点帮助，生活显得更加实在。在都市的繁华和喧闹中，那是他与穷困的山区童年的一丝牵连。此刻，他对朱和朱的孩子产生了强烈的同情。

韦刚坐定，李主任慌张地跑进来："不好了，出大事了，朱师傅脑溢血……"

韦的脑袋哄地一声也跟着充血了："什么时候？"

"大概是半夜吧，准确说不上，其他值班人发现时他已经昏迷了。"李的声音嘶哑着，显出些怯懦："不得了，要是劳动部门查起来，追问让他连班的责任，不得了！"

韦瞪他一眼："先不管这个。救人要紧，是动手术还是保守疗法？"

李答："正在读片。看样子，没手术不行。不过，他没有医保，按规定，要家属先交四五万，他家肯定没那钱。"

又是规定！韦想发火，但是不得不忍住。前两天在全院大会上，作为院长的他，刚强调过严格管理的重要性。是啊，规定面前，他院长也不能随心所欲。人家会说，像朱那样的穷人多着，你单为他破例？韦听院里老人说过，以前是先抢救再说，哪有没钱不手术的？！也不知什么时候搞的这些规定！韦抬头看见桌上的一只信封。那是星期天到其他医院抢救重病号开刀的报酬。他把信封交给李："我捐给朱师傅。你去想办法，需要的话，尽快手术！"

李恍然大悟："对，对，发动大家捐款，你院长带头，好办，好办。"

这次，李没有说捐多捐少的话，拿了那信封，赶紧往外跑。韦想，他不能不卖力。人命关天，查起来，批准连班的李逃不脱责任。

上午，韦被上级领导叫去讨论医院的改革。中午，刚端起碗，又听说有个检查组在医院，只好跑过去寒暄几句。还没应酬完，就有电话追来，是本地最高级的医院紧急求援，要他参加一项重要而艰难的手术。韦早已经习惯了，最困难的脑外科手术才会找他，看重的是他的年龄。资历高的权威虽然不少，三十五六岁的脑外科专家，他是头一份。这活儿，年龄也是关键啊，站几个小时的手术，体力不支的话，难免出错。作为一个大医院的领导，他天天疲于应付，常常忙得成了来不及思考的机器。

救火似的忙了一整天，傍晚，太阳消失在城市的高楼背后时，韦疲乏地回到自己的医院，在下车时又见到了新门卫胖胖的脸。韦这才突然想起了朱师傅，不知他的手术是否进行得顺利？

走上二楼，通往院长室的走廊已经没有了白天的喧哗。下班了，科室的人回家了。走廊的尽头，还有个工人在拖地板，从背影看出，那是个上年纪的女工。韦皱皱眉头。他想，需要提醒李主任，今后用临时工，尽量还是用年轻点的。

韦经过办公室，见屋里亮着灯。探头一看，不是李，只有一位新来的大学生坐在桌前看书，小伙子见到院长，赶紧起立。韦摆摆手，示意不必客气。他还是不习惯被人过分尊重，那样，反倒唤醒他的少年时代痛苦的记忆。因为穷，小学中学，他经常处于被人瞧不起的窘迫的境地，比方说，交不起春游的钱，交不出班费……

院长室的门被打开了，在宁静的小楼里，锁和门铰被启动的声音十分清晰。黑洞洞的屋子呈现在韦的面前，同时扑面而来的，还有那股熟悉的混杂着消毒水的气息。韦站立片刻，才去开灯。在灯亮的刹那，他惊讶地发觉，在走廊上打扫的女工已经默默走到自己的背后，他正感到诧异，那有点年纪的女人，竟然跪了下去，随后是呜咽的声音，在寂静的小楼里断续地飘散开来："韦院长，你是好人，我们老朱也是好人，你千万救救他……"

韦醒悟过来，打扫走廊的，原来是朱师傅的妻子。他赶紧招呼女人起身，把她让进屋子。他望着那张和朱一样黑瘦的脸，不解地问："还没有动手术吗？"

一问，女人更哭得紧了，"你们都是好人啊，你带头捐钱，院里很多人捐了，我把家里的钱全挖出来，李主任说还缺一二万，他做不了主啊……"

韦的血又呼的往脑门上冲。他疏忽了，应该明确关照李，不管钱多少，先动手术，救人如救火，这时间拖得起吗？

他冲出房门，对着院办的门想喊李，忽然记起，那儿只有个年轻人，李可能下班了，只好把值班的年轻人叫过来问。果然如此，因为缺一万多，李说不符合规定，手术还等着，人是在急诊间。

韦板起脸差点说了粗话，他妈的什么规定，想到那规定还是自己签发的，只得忍住了火说："马上准备手术吧，你去通知，手术间那里下班走了的，马上叫回来！"韦见年轻人还没反应过来，狠狠加上一句："你告诉李主任，钱不够，下个月扣我工资，再不够，还有下下个月的工资！"

女人见院长发火，胆怯地说："李主任他们全是好人，全捐钱了，只怪我们家太穷啊。老朱本来不会那样穷，也是读书人，就是太好心，救别人，反倒吃官司了，弄到这地步。"

韦打发年轻人去通知手术，并且明确说，这手术他自己主刀。

韦喝了口水，静静神，对女人说："你到医务处签个字，就休息一下等着，手术总要两三小时。"

女人千谢万谢，刚要退出，韦又问："你刚才讲朱师傅救人吃官司是怎么回事？"

女人道："是三十几年前的事情。他在山区插队落户，有个女知青被坏人在路上糟蹋了，作孽啊，二十岁的姑娘，啥也不懂，到显形了，想做也做不掉，就不想活了。老朱可怜她，就劝那姑娘养下孩子，他认了，就说是他的种。孩子和姑娘的命是保住了，老朱倒霉栽进去了，说正要抓破坏上山下乡的典型，便送他去劳教，苦头吃了多少年啊，一辈子全毁啦……"

韦听到这里，身子一阵惊颤，手中的瓷杯掉到地上，打了个粉碎，带着茶叶沫子的水流，在打蜡地板上四处漫延开去。

女人慌张地说："啊，院长，你辛苦一天了，我不该这样唠叨，对不起！实在对不起！"

韦见女人已经趴在地上收拾，赶紧说："没关系，我自己不小心。"待女人收拾完，要离开房间时，韦仿佛不经心地问了一句，朱当年是在哪里插队落户。当听清和母亲不在一个地区后，他才暗暗松了口气。

院长靠在沙发上，合拢双眼，让自己的心安静片刻，这才起身，换上白大褂，去手术间，准备亲自做这个手术。

刚走进手术准备室，又冒出两段插曲。先是麻醉医师犹豫着说没信心用药，他觉得病人的时间拖得太久，各种指标均显示危险，怕麻药下去就出问题。韦听了麻醉医师的话，拿起病历细看，沉吟着尚未来得及答话，李主任匆匆赶到了。他把院长叫到一边，低声劝道，这手术太危险，让其他人主刀吧。韦认真地看他一眼，从李忐忑的表情中，明白此话也是一片好心。担心手术失败会毁坏院长名声。韦何尝不明白做朱的手术的风险！不过，动手术，也许是惟一向垂危中的朱表达心意的办法。社会曾经亏待过这个好心人，临危，他应该受到救助。

韦清楚地回忆起母亲最后的时刻。在研究生论文答辩结束后，他才获得母亲病危的消息。母亲坚持要等儿子通过答辩后才通知他。韦连夜坐火车赶回老家，母亲已经在弥留之际。枯瘦的脸，了无生气，勉力睁眼看着儿子，怔怔地流泪，已经一句话也说不上来。后来，他问姨妈，母亲清醒时讲过点什么，姨妈说，母亲要她转告韦，如果有出头的日子，要多多帮助其他的穷人，人要知恩报恩，他们母子没有好心人的接济，也活不到今天。当院长之后，韦天天忙得难以招架，渐渐很少回忆去世多年的母亲，此时此刻，母亲临终深深盯住他的眼神，清晰地浮现出来。她摆小摊二十年，苦了一辈子，独自抚养韦成人，但没来得及享受儿子的孝顺。她在生命的尾端向儿子提出的要求，当然是韦无法忘怀的。

韦缓慢但是响亮地说："这个手术是我决定的，出问题我承担责任。哪怕只有万分之一的希望，我们搏一次！"

两个小时之后，韦脸色严峻地走出了手术室。他的身后，疲惫的助手和护士们无声地尾随着。突然，绝望的哭泣打破了冰冷的寂静，那是等候在手术室外的女人难以抑制的哀伤。

韦在手术室内的最后一个动作，是摘去医生的白帽，向停止了生命的朱师傅深深地鞠了一躬。他内心说："对不起，我没有办法了！"他尽了全力。作为年轻一代的脑外科专家，他聚精会神，一丝不苟，手术还是失败了，无情地失败了！也许，早几小时开始手术，还有挽回生命的机会。现在，后悔已经无济于事。

朱是在韦的眼皮底下，在他主持的手术中安静地离开了人世。作为声名显赫的新秀，这是倒霉的纪录。韦在决定手术之前，明白失败的概率远远大于成功的可能。韦只是觉得，他必须有所行动。朱在倒下后一直处于昏迷状态，不知道围绕他发生的这些情况，当然也不会明白韦的复杂心情。

韦离开众人，回到院长室所在的宁静的小楼，他走进自己的办公室，没有开灯，于黑暗中走进去，慢慢走着，最后伫立在窗前。夜色晴朗，漫天星斗在黑暗的天幕上闪烁，一片云彩缓缓移动着，时而遮盖了通往星空的视线。他回忆起遥远的山区的遥远的童年，那里没有城市华丽的一切，不过，那里的夜空却更加澄净明亮。

朱死了，韦觉得自己的灵魂也好像死了一回。

也许，他还可以重生。

在韦的面前，尚有长长的路要走，母亲的临终嘱托，够他做一辈子了！

The Death of the Gatekeeper

○ *Sun Yong*

Every morning, a black shining car stopped at the gate on time, respectfully waiting for him, the young president of the hospital.

After he got into the car, he had a habit of leaning his head against the soft backrest and his right shoulder against the door so that his well-chiseled face could be bathed in the warm and bright sunlight. Looking at the bustling people and vehicles coming and going outside, he from time to time had an absurd illusion: "Am I that poor student named Wei? Am I that boy of dubious origin, often belittled by his peers?" Oh, several years ago, he, a poor student, often couldn't afford a meat dish for several days and, looking at the shiny pork braised in brown sauce in his classmates' bowls, he could only swallow his saliva …[1]

As usual, the car went into the hospital from the back gate. The gatekeeper, more than 20 years older than Wei, rushed forward, gently opened the car door and considerately put his right hand on the upper frame of the door lest Wei's head should bump onto it. The gatekeeper's lavish hospitality always made Wei uneasy and even gave him a false impression that he was somebody, some great VIP. Indeed, Wei wasn't used to being treated in such a deferential and meticulous manner. Once, he couldn't help but tell the gatekeeper directly, "Old Zhu, I can open the door myself." Wei didn't know the gatekeeper's name. He only knew that the gatekeeper was a temporary worker recommended by a neighborhood committee. People all called him "Old Zhu", so Wei followed suit and addressed him "Old Zhu".[2]

In the morning glow, Old Zhu's face looked dark and lean, with wrinkles all over his forehead and cheeks. Hearing Wei's words, Old Zhu gave a confused smile. It seemed that he was not flurried but a little bit embarrassed. Stepping back slowly, he said, "Oh, yes, yes." His courteous but still dignified manner left a good impression on Wei. By intuition, Wei thought Old Zhu must have had some schooling. His favorable impression towards Old Zhu perhaps came from his own experience. He knew that a person at the bottom rung of the society had to be very courteous to cater to others but shouldn't appear too shabby and humble.

Later, when Wei's car got to the back gate, Old Zhu no longer rushed forward to open the car door. Instead, he hurried out of his room and stood upright on the right side of the gate, smiling and saluting with his eyes. In return, Wei nodded politely to him. By and by, Wei found that Old Zhu was always on duty. He was surprised! Wei was called to the hospital at midnight to treat emergency cases twice and he saw Old Zhu at the gate twice! Feeling curious, he called in the office director Li, who was also in charge of the general service of the hospital, and asked him about it. Li hummed and hawed with an embarrassed smile,[3] "Oh, oh, Old Zhu was on duty for 24 hours every day …"

"24 hours? Doesn't it violate the Labor Law?" Wei opened his eyes wider.

Li replied in a flurry, "The other gatekeeper went back home. It was Old Zhu himself who begged us over and over to let him stay on duty for more time so that he could earn more money. His child is in a university and he needs money to pay the tuition …"

Wei didn't say a word. He became lost in recollection: From his childhood, when the new semester came, his family confronted the greatest difficulty in the whole year. Although the tuition was not that high by today's standards, his mother, who earned a meager income by running a stall on the street, got worried very much and had to borrow money here and there. She had to beg each and every acquaintance and relative she knew and asked for their help; by doing so she cast aside all the considerations of her own face or dignity.[4] Wei also went out to collect waste paper and sold them for some money. It was so difficult scratching up money for his tuition! At that time, his mother often said to him: "You are my only hope, son. Study hard, and you'll stand up with your head high in the future …"

Seeing Wei's sullen face, Li hastened to respond with a knowing smile, "Oh, I see, I see. This is a serious matter. I'll find someone to replace Old Zhu at once."

Wei uttered a sigh and said hesitantly, "Take your time. You'd better go to the guard room and have the air-conditioner checked first. It's winter and it must be very cold there."

Li, perplexed at his inability to read his superior's mind, nodded his consent and left. Wei felt curious: "Li always stresses the importance of various rules which, in his eyes, are sacred and inviolable, and he, presuming on his years of service in the hospital, always imposes his ideas on me. What's going on with him today? Has he accepted some benefit from Old Zhu? Why does he bend his rules so easily this time? He has pity on Old Zhu? Is it possible?"[5] — Wei thought of the days when they made donations. Each time, Wei always donated more than what was required. When his mother was alive, she always told him, "It is depending on others' help that we lived through our hardships. Now our life gets better and we should help the people in need." However, more often than not, Li came and dissuaded him with a sly smile, "President, You donate so much! You put us underlings in an embarrassing situation — it's not good to donate less, but we begrudge donating more."[6]

This morning, when his car got to the back gate, Wei found a fat face in the place of that dark lean one. Old Zhu must be tired and taking a rest now, Wei said to himself.

Wei decided to raise a suggestion to Li at a proper time, advising him to give Old Zhu a little more share of the mutual fund to help him pay the tuition. "Giving out the mutual fund to a temporary worker doesn't conform to our regulations." This must be Li's first response, Wei guessed. In that case, he would retort at once, "Does working continuously for 24 hours comply with our regulations?"

Up to now, Wei didn't know who his father was. He was brought up by his mother alone who earned a living by making or sewing clothes for people. He spent his childhood in a mountain village and it was his mother who taught him knowledge. His mother was a high school graduate sent to live and work in the countryside, and at that time, she was the only teacher in that shabby primary school. He remembered that when he was small he was always called a bastard. As he cried all the way back home and asked for a father, his mother kept silent and wept softly. Later, when he grew up a little, he no longer mentioned it to his mother. One day, his mother engaged him in a serious talk about going back to the city, "Your grandparents are aged and in need of our help and care. Let's move to the city and live with them. The life there will also be hard. If you want to have a good life in the future, you must study hard from now on!" He was only six or seven years old and he couldn't quite understand his mother's words, but he understood clearly that his mother and his grandparents put all their hopes on him. Since then, he studied harder than any other classmates. He successfully passed the entrance examination of a key medical university, and after graduation he continued working hard for ten years. Later, he became the youngest director of the Department of Cerebral Surgery in his hospital, and he continued struggling all his way forward. Finally, he became the president of the hospital.

The seeds his good-natured mother had sown in his heart began to sprout. Now he finally held his head high, and he really wanted to give a hand to those

334

children in poverty. In helping them he found his life fulfilling and meaningful. In the bustling hubbub of the city, this was the only way connecting him with his childhood life. Now, he had a strong sympathetic feeling toward Old Zhu and his child.

As Wei settled himself into the seat, Li rushed in nervously, "Oh, something terrible happened! Old Zhu just suffered a cerebral haemorrhage ..."

Feeling his brain also suffused with blood all at once, Wei asked, "When?"

"Maybe at midnight. Who knows? He was found in a coma." Li said in a hoarse voice. He continued, appearing a little scared, "What shall we do? If the labor department comes and makes an investigation, what shall we do? He works overtime!"

Wei glared at Li and said, "No time to think of that! We'd better save his life first! What is good for him now, an operation or a conservative treatment?"

Li answered, "Doctors are checking his X-ray film now. It seems that an operation is necessary. But he has no medical insurance. According to the regulations, his family must pay 40 to 50 thousand yuan in advance. I am afraid he cannot afford it."

Regulations again! Wei was irritated but he had to hold in his anger. Several days ago, in a meeting, as the head of the hospital, he reiterated the importance of strict management according to regulations. Yes, nobody could do as he pleased, even if he was the head of the hospital. His subordinates might say, "There are too many poor people like Old Zhu, and why do you make an exception just for him?" The veteran employees in the hospital told him, "In the past, we always saved a patient's life first and operations were done as quickly as possible no matter whether those patients had money or not!" Now, where did these regulations come from! Wei cast a look at the envelope on the table. Last Sunday, he was asked to do an operation in another hospital and the money in the envelope was the payment. Without hesitation, he picked the envelope up and handed it to Li, "Here is some money. You manage it. If needed, the operation should be done as soon as possible!"

Li suddenly saw the light,[7] "Oh, I see. OK! Let me organize a donation for him among our staff. OK! Let me do it."

As to how much money everyone should donate, Li gave no comment this time. Clutching the envelope, he went out in a hurry. It was a matter of life and death and Li must go all out to solve it. Otherwise, he couldn't evade the responsibility. After all, it was he who permitted Old Zhu to work overtime.

In the morning, Wei had a discussion with his superiors about the reform in the hospital. In the afternoon, as he was about to have his lunch, he got the news that an inspection group came to visit the hospital, so he had to hurry there, exchanging a few polite words of greetings with them.[8] During their talk, a telephone call came for him. It was an emergency call from the city's best hospital requesting his presence in an important and difficult operation. Wei had got used to this tempo of life. He knew it must be the hardest operation and that they asked for his help because he was young and capable. There were quite a few cerebral surgery specialists with seniority and authority but none of them were so young as him. He was only 35 years old. An operation sometimes took several hours and an old doctor might not have enough physical endurance to finish it without error. As a leader of a big hospital, he busied himself every day working like a machine, with no time to think about other things.

As if fighting a fire, Wei was kept extremely busy for the whole day. At dusk, when the sun disappeared behind the skyscrapers, he trudged back to his hospital with great fatigue. As he got off the car and saw the fat face of the new gatekeeper, he suddenly thought of Old Zhu. Did everything go on smoothly with his operation? He thought.

On the second floor, the hallway leading to his office was silent. People had gone back home. At the other end of the hallway, someone was mopping the floor. It must be an aged female worker. He could judge it from behind. Knitting his brows, he thought it was really necessary to advise Li to hire young people to do the temping job.

As he walked past a room, he found its light still on. He thought Li was there, but to his surprise, it was a university graduate who was reading a book at the table. Seeing him, the young man stood up at once. Wei gestured him to sit down. Being flattered or over-respected always reminded him of his painful past. When he was in primary school and high school, poverty always brought him to an awkward situation: He was looked down upon for he couldn't hand in the class fees or afford a spring outing …

The lock and hinge creaked in the silent building.[9] On opening the door, he was at once greeted by the darkness together with that familiar disinfectant smell. After standing at the door for a while, he came into the room. The moment he turned on the light, he found that the woman who mopped the hallway floor just now was standing right behind him! To his surprise, she all of a sudden knelt down in front of him and began to cry. Her sobbing words resounded off and on in the quiet building, "President Wei, you are a good man and my husband Old Zhu is also a good man. Please save him. Please! I beg you …"

She was Old Zhu's wife! He invited her into his room. Looking at her face, which was as dark and thin as Old Zhu's, he asked in perplexity, "Didn't he have an operation?"

On hearing his words, the woman cried louder, "All of you are kind-hearted. Many people in the hospital have made donations and I have taken out all of our savings. But Director Li told me we are still short of 10 or 20 thousand. He had no idea …"

Wei felt his blood gushing onto his forehead. He forgot to tell Li that they must do the operation no matter how much money it would take. The priority was to save Old Zhu's life! How could they put off the rescue like this?!

He rushed out of his office. As he was about to call in Li, he suddenly realized it was off-duty time and Li must have left. He called in that young man on duty and asked him about the details. As he reckoned, for the lack of 10 thousand yuan, the operation was not done in time and Old Zhu was still in the emergency room. Director Li said that the regulations came first and nobody could break them.

Wei straightened his face and some dirty words almost slipped out of his mouth. What damned regulations! Considering that the regulations were signed by himself, he had to curb his fury and said to the young man, "Get ready to do the operation at once! You call those off-duty doctors back right away!" Seeing the young man still standing there, he added forcefully, "Tell Director Li, if the money is not enough, use my salary next month to cover it. If it still isn't enough, go on using my salary!"

Seeing him flare up, the woman said in a low and timid voice, "Director Li and all the others are indeed very nice to us. They all donated money for us. It's our own fault. We are too poor! You know, my husband is also well-educated, but the problem is that he is too kind-hearted. He saved a person's life but was sued and punished, otherwise we wouldn't be so poor, so down and out!"[10]

Wei asked the young man to notify relevant doctors to get ready for the operation, stressing affirmatively that he himself would be the chief-operator.

He drank a little water, composed himself and turned to the woman, "Now, you go to the medical office to leave your signature and go home to have a rest. The operation will take two or three hours."

The woman thanked him over and over and as she was about to leave, Wei asked, "Just now you mentioned that Old Zhu saved someone but was sued?"

"It happened more than 30 years ago when he was sent to the countryside to live and work in a production commune. A girl, also a high school graduate sent to the countryside, was raped by some bad guy. She was just about 20 years old. So innocent! When her swelling belly started to betray her, it was too late to make an abortion. She fell into desperation and wanted to commit suicide. My husband pitied her so much that he persuaded her to give birth to her baby and that he would like to take the baby as his own. So the girl and her child were protected safe and sound but my husband fell on hard luck. He was charged with ruining the good image of the high school graduates sent to live and work in the countryside and was sentenced to years of re-education through labor. He had suffered many hard years and his whole life got ruined ..."

In great shock, Wei began to tremble, the porcelain cup in his hand falling onto the ground. The water with tea leaves flowed out of the broken cup and scattered all over the floor.

The woman hurried to apologize, "Oh, sorry! You've been busy for the whole day. I shouldn't gab so much to disturb you. Sorry! I am so sorry!"

Seeing her bending over the floor to clean up, Wei said, "It doesn't matter. I was careless and I should be sorry." She quickly cleared the floor and before she left he asked her in a haphazard way, "Where did your husband work in the countryside during those years?" After he heard the answer, he felt utterly relieved. Old Zhu didn't work in the place where Wei's mother once worked.

Sinking into the couch, closing his eyes, he tried to compose himself. After a while, he stood up, put on his white uniform and walked to the operation room. He was going to do the operation himself.

Two episodes popped up as he just entered the preparatory room for operation. The anesthesiologist turned hesitant and said that it was risky to apply anaesthesia, for the operation had been delayed too long and the patient was in great danger. Wei took up the medical record and read it carefully. At this time, Li came in, pulled him aside and whispered: "It's risky to do this operation! Let someone else do it." Looking at Li's anxious face, he knew Li was well-intended. An unsuccessful operation would spoil his reputation! He knew it. However, doing an operation by himself might be the only way for him to express his heartfelt sincerity to Old Zhu. The society owed a lot to this kind-hearted man, who was now dying and deserved some help.

The scene of his mother's last moment was deeply engraved in his mind. He was not informed of his mother's critical condition until he passed his postgraduate thesis defense. It was his mother who insisted on withholding the knowledge of her condition from him until he secured his postgraduate degree. By the time he hurried back home by the night train, his mother was dying. On her deathbed, his mother, lean and faint, took great efforts to open her eyes. She stared at her beloved son and couldn't utter a single word, as tears streamed down her withered hollow cheeks. Later, he asked his aunt about what his mother said when she was conscious. "Your mother let me tell you: In the future if you are capable, you should try your best to help those poor people. Without others' help, we couldn't live till now. You should know how to repay an obligation with gratitude." After he became the president of the hospital, he was too busy to recall the old days and his mother. At this moment, his mother's eyes clearly appeared in front of him again. She set up a small stall on the street and toiled and moiled to bring him up. For more than 20 years she had such a hard life! She left in such a hurry that she had not enjoyed her filial son's success. He could never forget that last will of hers, passed on to her beloved son at the last moment of her life.

Thinking of these, Wei said slowly but resolutely, "It is I who made the decision. If anything goes wrong, I will shoulder all the responsibilities. We must fight even for a one-in-a-million opportunity!"

Two hours later, he stepped out of the operation room, cold-faced and glum. Following him were a group of assistants and nurses, exhausted and silent. All of a sudden, a desperate cry broke the cold silence. Old Zhu's wife who had been waiting outside the operation room could no longer control her grief.

The last action that Wei made in the operation room was taking off his white skullcap and bowing to Old Zhu whose heart had stopped beating. He said to him silently, "I am sorry. I have tried my best!" As a young and excellent expert in cerebral surgery, he had tried his best. He had been very careful and attentive, but still couldn't save Old Zhu's life. The operation failed mercilessly! Old Zhu's life would likely be saved if the operation had been done earlier, but now, it was too late for everything, even for regrets.

Old Zhu passed away quietly in Wei's operation. For a brilliant young doctor, this failure was a hapless record in his career. Before the operation, he had estimated that the operation would more likely turn out a failure than a success, but he insisted on doing the operation as he felt that he must do something for Old Zhu. Old Zhu was in a coma, oblivious of what happened around him, let alone Wei's complicated feelings.

Leaving the operation room and the crowd of people, Wei returned to his office. He didn't turn on the light. In darkness he felt his way to the window. The stars were twinkling on the dark clear sky and a cloud drifting slowly sometimes blocked his view. In retrospect, he thought of that faraway countryside village where he spent his childhood, where the splendid city life seemed nonexistent and where the sky looked purer and clearer.

Old Zhu died and Wei felt his soul died too with the gatekeeper.

Or perhaps, he could be reborn through redemption?

To Wei, there was a long way to go. One thing was for sure — his mother's last words would guide him all his life!

1. "红烧肉" pork braised in brown sauce。中餐菜名的翻译方法很多，有时主要翻译其烹调方法，有时翻译菜的主要成分，有时采用字面翻译再加上注释的手段。例如：鸭黄焗南瓜braised pumpkin with salted egg yolk/ 芋头蒸排骨steamed spare ribs with taro/ 杏仁鸡丁chicken cubes with almond/ 芙蓉虾仁shrimps with egg-white/ 叫花鸡beggar's chicken (chicken toasted in lotus leaf and earth mud, invented by two beggars in the Qing Dynasty)/ 东坡肉Dongpo's favorite braised pork (invented by Su Dongpo, a famous poet in the Song Dynasty)。在小说的行文中，简单处理就好了。

2. 英语中master 的意思为：主人、户主、统治者、技艺高超的艺术家和音乐家等、大师、名家、能带学徒的工匠能手、男教师、(放在名字前)少爷、硕士，等等。很多情况下，master也不能用作称谓。小说人物朱师傅只是一个门卫，不宜译为Master Zhu。译者译为Old Zhu。"在言语交际中，不同的称谓，反映了交际双方的年龄性别、亲疏关系、角色身份、社会地位、情感好恶乃至说话场合等情况。"(包惠南、包昂)汉语称谓非常复杂，英译时一定要注意文化差异。例如："低声的叫：老程！老程！老程是王家的车夫。"(老舍《骆驼祥子》)译文为 "Old Cheng!" He called softly. "Old Cheng!" Old Cheng was the Wangs' rickshaw man.(施晓菁译)(卢红梅《华夏文化与汉英翻译》48页)

3. hum and haw 吞吞吐吐，支支吾吾，也作hem and haw。关于"说"可以根据上下文使用不同的动词来翻译，这对刻画人物的形象、描述人物心理有重要作用。例如：state 正式陈述/chat 闲谈聊天/chatter 喋喋不休/gossip 背后议论/announce 宣布/declare 宣布/scream 尖叫着说/relate 叙述/utter 发出声音/prattle 小孩般天真地谈话/narrate 讲述/babble 空谈唠叨/allege 断言声称/assert 坚持认为/affirm 肯定地说。

4. "老着脸皮求援……"。这里，"老着脸皮"翻译成 thick-faced, cheeky, shameless 不妥。译者处理为… cast aside all the considerations of her own face or dignity。下文中的 "一定要读出头……"，译文为：Study hard, and

you'll stand up with your head high in the future … 其中，to stand up with one's head high意为扬眉吐气。

5. "韦暗想，他莫非收了朱的什么好处吧？平时，这位主任一口一个规定神圣不可侵犯，还倚老卖老地用来劝诫新院长，这次为何如此通融？难道仅仅是同情朱师傅？" Li always stresses the importance of various rules which, in his eyes, are sacred and inviolable, and he, presuming on his years of service in the hospital, always imposes his ideas on me. What's going on with him today? Has he accepted some benefit from Old Zhu? Why does he bend his rules so easily this time? He has pity on Old Zhu? Is it possible? 这是一段主人公的心理活动，翻译时一是加上了引号，使之成为直接引语；二要注意口语特点，不要太复杂太书面；三是几个难点的翻译，比如"神圣不可侵犯"、"倚老卖老"、"通融"，分别译为：sacred and inviolable、presume on his years of service、bend his rules so easily。presume on 意思是：不正当地利用、滥用。

6. "……还嬉皮笑脸地说：'你院长捐多了，让下属难啊，捐少不好，捐多不舍得，嘿嘿。'"。Li came and dissuaded him with a sly smile, "President, You donate so much! You put us underlings in an embarrassing situation — it's not good to donate less, but we begrudge donating more." "嬉皮笑脸" 可以译为to behave in a noisy, gay and boisterous manner或者to grin cheekily，但是用在这里不合适，所以简单译为with a sly smile。

7. "恍然大悟" 可以译为see light suddenly、a light breaks in upon somebody、be suddenly enlightened、be wide awake等等。这里译为… suddenly see the light…

8. "寒暄几句" 译为exchange a few polite words of greetings。

9. "在宁静的小楼里，锁和门铰被启动的声音十分清晰。" The lock and hinge creaked in the silent building. creak 拟声词、动词，(门)嘎吱作响。

10. "……弄到这地步。" … otherwise we wouldn't be so poor, so down and out! 这里的down and out 意思是穷困潦倒，境遇非常不好。

马车夫

○ 阿来

    通常的乡村图景中，马车与马车夫都是古老的意象。但在机村，情形并不是如此。

    车的关键是轮子。但在机村不可考的漫长历史上，轮子是有的，但可能是没有宽阔大道的缘故吧，很有历史的轮子只与宗教相关。手摇的、水冲的，甚至被风吹动的轮子里面，填满了整卷整卷写满简短、不断重复的祝诵的经文。还有一种轮子固定不动，装置在寺院最高的顶上，金光闪闪。

    一直到了五十年代，外面是柔韧的黑色橡胶，里面由坚固的钢圈形成支撑，用于使物体移动的轮子才来到了机村。最不可思议的是，在轮子里外之间的那个空间，只是充满了经过压缩的空气——橡胶与钢结合时，产生了一种特别的魔法，使虚无缥缈的空气也变得无比坚硬了。

    从古到今，轮子就是奇妙的东西。就说那些经轮吧，不管是用什么方式推动，一旦转动起来，大的经轮隆隆作响仿佛雷霆滚过，小的经轮嗡嗡出声仿佛蜜蜂飞翔。就这样，里面那些经文，不是一字一字、一句一句读诵出来，轮子转动一周，里面全部的经文就被整体地呈现一次，同时，也被上天的什么神灵笼统地领受了。

    就是说，轮子转动的时候，上天的神就已经听见了。那么多的字符紧巴巴地挤在一起，嗡一声就飞上天去，神都能逐字听见，仅此一点，也可知其神通绝非一般。

但是，人没有听见。踯躅于尘世中的人感觉早已被区隔，只能领受一字一字、一词一词的祝诵了。谁也听不见那么多轮子嗡然一声转动起来一瞬之间释放出来的字符与声音。依照佛在佛经中所说，正是这种浩大无边的无声之声才能称之为"大声音"，只有大声音才能上达天庭。而辗转于尘世中的人们早已失去了天听，他们只能听到轮子转动的声音。

所以，当轮子以车辆部件的形式出现时，人们感到了一种很新鲜的刺激，轮子提供的价值不再过于缥缈虚无了。当第一辆马车由崭新的车轮支撑着出现在人们眼中，还不等它运动起来，人们就意会到一种能够更快、更多地运送物品的运载工具已经出现了。

这个工具叫做"车"。

古歌里出现过这个词。古歌里车的驭手是战神。

现在，车出现在凡世，凡夫们谁又能成为它的驾驭者？因为这车与马相关，所有人立即就想到了最好的骑手。

骑手的形象与通常的想像大相径庭。这个人身材瘦小，脸上还布满了天花留下的斑斑印迹。但他就是机村最好的骑手。机村人认为，这样的人用马眼看去，会有非常特别的地方。怎么样的特别法呢？人生不出马眼，所以无从知道。这跟各种轮子的诵经声凡人的耳朵不得听闻大概是相同的道理。

试驾马车那一天，麻子一副事不关己的模样。人们扎成一圈，看村里的男子汉们费尽力气想把青鬃马塞进两根车辕之间，用那些复杂的绊索使它就范。这时，麻子骑着一匹马徘徊在热闹的圈子外边。这个人骑在马上，就跟长在马背一样自在稳当。折腾了很长时间，他们也没有能给青鬃马套上那些复杂的绊索。青鬃马又踢又咬，让好几个想当车夫的冒失鬼受了点小伤。

人们这才把眼光转向了勒马站在圈子之外的麻子。

在众人的注视下，他脸上那些麻坑一个个红了。他抬腿下了马背，慢慢走到青鬃马跟前。他说："吁——"青鬃马竖起的尾巴就慢慢垂下了。他伸出手，轻拍一下青鬃马的脖子，挠了挠正呼出滚烫气息的鼻翼，牲口就安静下来了。这个家伙，脸上带着沉溺进了某种奇异梦境的浅浅笑容，开始嘀嘀咕咕地对马说话。马就定了身站在两根结实的车辕中间，任随麻子给他套上肩轭和复杂的绊索。中辕驾好了，两匹边辕也驾好了。

人群安静下来。

麻子牵着青鬃马迈开了最初的两步。这两步，只是把套在马身上那些复杂的绊索绷紧了。麻子又领着三匹马迈出了小小的一步。这回，马车的车轮缓缓地转动了一点。但是，当麻子停下了步子，轮子又转回到了原来的地方。

"走啊，麻子！"人们着急了。

麻子笑了，细眼里放出锐利的亮光，他连着走了几步。轮子就转了大半圈。轮箍和轮轴互相摩擦，发出了旋转着的轮子必然会发出的声音：

——叽——

像一只鸟有点胆怯又有点兴奋地要初试啼声，刚叫出半声就停住了。

马也竖起了耳朵，谛听身后那陌生的声音。

他又引领着马迈开了步子。

三匹马，青鬃马居中，两匹黑马分行两边，牵引着马车继续向前。转动的车轮终于发出了完整的声音：

——叽——吭！

前半声小心翼翼，后半声理直气壮。

那声音如此令人振奋，三匹马不再要驭手引领，就伸长脖颈，耸起肩胛，奋力前行了。轮子连贯地转动，那声音也就响成了一串：

——叽——吭！

——叽——吭！——叽——吭！——叽——吭！

麻子从车头前闪开，在车侧紧跑几步，腾身而起，安坐在了驭手座上，取过竖在车辕上的鞭子，凌空一抽，马车就窜出了广场，向着村外的大道飞驰起来。

从此，一直蜗行于机村的时间也像给装上了飞快旋转的车轮，转眼之间就快得像是射出的箭矢一样了。

这不，马车开动那一天的情景好像还在眼前，那些年里，麻子一脸坑洼里得意的红光还在闪烁，马车又要成为淘汰的事物了。因为拖拉机出现了。拖拉机不但比马车多出了四只轮子，更重要的是，一台机器代替了马匹。拖拉机手得意地拍拍机器，对围观的人说："四十匹马力。什么意思，就是相当于四十匹马。"

人群里发出一声赞叹。

拖拉机手还说："你们去问问麻子，他能不能把四十匹马一起套在马车前面？"

其实，拖拉机手早就看见麻子勒着手里的缰绳，骑在他心爱的青鬃马上，呆在人圈外面，那情形，颇像是第一次给马车套马时的情形。但他故意要把这话让麻子听见。麻子也不得不承认，拖拉机手确实够格在自己面前威风。不要说那机器里憋着四十匹马的劲头，光看那红光闪闪的夺目油漆，看那比马车轮大上两三倍的轮子，他心里就有些可怜自己那矮小的马车了。

拖拉机电门一开，机器的确就像憋着很大劲头一样怒吼起来。它高竖在车身前的烟筒里突突地喷射一股股浓烟。那得意劲就像这些年里麻子坐在行驶的马车上，手摇着鞭子，嘴里叼着烟头喷着一口口青烟时样子。看着力大无穷的拖拉机发动起来，麻子知道马车这个新事物在机村还没有运行十年，就已经是被淘汰的旧物了。

麻子转过身细心地套好了他的马车。他要驾着马车让所有想坐他马车的孩子们都坐上来，在路上去跑上一趟。过去，可不是随便哪个人都能坐上他的马车。他是一个不太喜欢孩子与女人的家伙。加上那时能坐马车也是一种身份的象征，所以很多人特别是很多孩子都没有坐过他的马车。但他驾着马车在村里转了两三圈，马车上还是空空荡荡的。那些平常只能爬到停着的马车上蹭蹭屁股的孩子们，这会儿都一溜烟地跟着拖拉机跑了。拖拉机正在人们面前尽情地展示它巨大的能耐。村外的田野里，拖拉机手指挥着人们摘掉了挂在车头后面的车厢，从车厢里卸下一挂有六只铁铧的犁头。熄了一会儿火的拖拉机又突突地喷出了烟圈，拖着那幅犁头在地里开了几个来回，就干下来两头牛拉一套犁要一天才能干完的活路了。村里人跟在拖拉机后面，发出了阵阵惊叹。只有麻子坐在村中空荡荡的广场上，点燃了他的烟斗。

过去，他是太看重，太爱惜他的马车了。要早知道这马车并不会使用百年千年，就要"退出历史舞台"，那他真的就用不着这么珍重了。明白了一点时世进步道理的他，铁了心要让孩子们坐坐他的马车。第一天拖拉机从外面开回来时，天已经黑了。第二天一早，他就把马套上了。人们还是围着拖拉机热热闹闹。他勒着上了套的马，一动不动地端坐在马车之上。人们一直围着拖拉机转了两三个钟头，才有人意识到他和马车就在旁边。

"看，麻子还套着马车呢！"

"嗨，麻子，你不晓得马车再也没有用处了吗？"

"麻子，你没看见拖拉机吗？"

麻子也不搭腔，他坐在车辕上，点燃了烟斗。

这时，拖拉机发动起来了，昨天就已经预告过了，拖拉机要装上自己拉来的那个巨大的铁铲，一铲子下去，够十几个人干上整整一天。

拖拉机的吸引力真是太大了，麻子想补偿一下村里孩子们，让他们坐一趟马车的心愿都不能实现了。他卸了马，把马轭和那些复杂的绊索收好，骑着青鬃马上山去了。这一上山，就再也没有下山。还是生产队的干部上山去看他。领导说："麻子还是下山吧，马已经没有什么用处了。"

他反问："马怎么就没有用处了？"

"有拖拉机了，有汽车了。"

"那这些马怎么办？"算上拉过马车的马，生产队一共有十多匹马。"不是还要人放着吗？那就是我了。"

第一个马车夫成了机村最后的牧马人了。机村人对于那些马，对于麻子都是有感情的。他们专门划出一片牧场，还相帮着在一处泉眼旁边的大树下盖起了一座小屋，那就是牧马人的居所了。时间加快了节奏飞快向前。新人新事不断涌现。同时，牧马人这样的人物就带一点悲情，隐没于这样的山间了。隔一段时间，麻子从山上下来，领一点粮，买一点盐，看到一个人，他那些僵死的麻子之间那些活泛的肌肉上浮起一点笑意，细眼里闪烁着锐利的光，就算是打过招呼了。当马车被风吹雨淋显出一副破败之相的时候，他赶着他的马群下山了。每匹马背上都驮上了一些木料。他给马车搭了一个遮风挡雨的窝棚。

机村终于在短短时间里，把马车和马车夫变成了一个过去，属于过去的形象。这个形象，不在记忆深处，马车还停在广场边一个角落里，连拉过马车的马都在，由马车夫自己精心地看护着。马和马车夫住在山上划定的那一小块牧场上，游走在现实开始消失，记忆开始生动的那个边缘。

拖拉机的漆水还很鲜亮，那些马就开始老去了。一匹马到了二十岁左右，就相当于人的六七十岁，所以马是不如人经老的。第一匹马快要咽气的时候，睁着一双水汪汪的大眼。麻子坐在马头旁边，看见马眼中映出晚霞烧红西天，当彤红的霞光消失，星星一颗颗跳上天幕时，他听见马的喉咙里像马车上的绊索断掉一样的声响，然后，马的眼睛闭上了，把满天的星星和整个世界关在了它脑子的外边。麻子没有抬头看天，麻子就地挖了一个深坑，半夜里，坑挖好了。他坐下来，抽起了烟斗。尽管身边闪烁着这明明灭灭的光芒，马的眼睛再没有睁开。他熄灭了烟斗，听见在这清冷的夜里，树上草上所起的浓重露水，正一颗颗顺着那些叶脉勾画的路线上滴落在地上，融入了深厚而温暖的土里。深厚的土融入了黑夜，比黑夜更幽暗，那些湿漉漉的叶片却颤动着微微的光亮。

他又抽了一斗烟，然后，起身把马尸掀进了深坑，天亮的时候，他已经把地面平整好了。薄雾散尽，红日破空而出，那些伫立在寒夜中的马又开始走动，掀动着鼻翼发出轻轻的嘶鸣。

麻子下山去向生产队报告这匹马的死讯。

"你用什么证明马真的死了？"

他遇到了这样一个从来没有想到的问题。

"埋了？马是集体财产，你凭什么随便处置？皮子，肉，都可以变成钱！"

　　他当然不能说是凭一个骑手，一个车夫对马的疼爱。他却因此受了这么深重的委屈。但他什么都不说，就转身上山去了。其实，领导的意思是要先报告了再埋掉。但领导不会直接把这意思说出来，领导也是机村人，不会真拿一匹死马的皮子去买几个小钱。但领导不说几句狠话，人家都不会以为他像个领导。但麻子这个死心眼却深受委屈，一小半是为了自己，一多半还是为了死去的马和将死的马。从此，再有马死去，他也不下山来报告。除了有好心人悄悄上山给他送些日常用度，他自己再也不肯下山来了。

　　这也是一种宿命，在机器成为了新生与强大的象征物时，马、马车成了注定退出历史舞台的那些力量的符号，而麻子自己，不知不觉间，就成功扮演了最后骑手与马车夫，最后一个牧马人的形象。他还活着呆在牧场上，就已经成为一个传说。

　　从村子里望上去，总能看到马匹们四散在牧场上的隐约影子。那些影子一年年减少，十年不到，就只剩下三匹马了。最后的那一年冬天，雪下得特别大。一入冬就大雪不断。马找不到吃的，又有两匹马倒下了。那一天，麻子为马车搭建的窝棚被雪压塌了。当年最年轻力壮的青鬃马跑下山来，在广场上咴咴嘶鸣。

　　全村人都知道，麻子死了。青鬃马是报告消息来了。人们上山去，发现他果然已经死去了。他安坐在棚屋里，细细的眼睛仍然隙着一道小缝，但里面已经没有了锥子一样锐利的光。

　　草草处理完麻子的后事，人们再去理会青鬃马时，它却不见了踪迹。直到冬去春来，在夏天，村里有人声称在某处山野里碰见了它。它死了还是活着？活着？它在饮水还是吃草？答案就有些离奇了：它快得像一道光一样，没有看清楚就过去了。那你怎么知道就是青鬃马？我也不知道，但我就是知道。就这样，神秘的青鬃马在人们口中又活了好多个年头，到了文化大革命运动一来，反封建迷信的声势那么浩大，那匹变成传说的马，也就慢慢被人们忘记了。

The Horse-carriage Driver

○ *A Lai*

A horse-carriage and its driver were the ancient images in a typical scene of the countryside. However, in Ji Village, things were different.

The key part of a carriage was its wheels. In the long history of Ji Village — nobody knew how long it was — there were wheels but they were not associated with roads, perhaps because there were no wide roads in the village. The wheels here were only related with religion. Wheels rotated by hand, by falling water and by wind were all filled with rolls and rolls of laconic and repeated scriptures. There was another kind of wheels in the village, which were fixed on top of the temples, glittering in the sun.

The wheel covered in pliable black rubber and supported with a steel ring inside, which could help an object move, didn't appear in Ji Village until the 1950s. The space between the inner and outer parts of the wheel was infused with condensed air and under the integrated work of rubber and steel the insubstantial air suddenly turned firm and solid. What wonderful magic!

Wheels had been the most marvelous tool from the ancient times. For instance, the scripture wheels, rotated by whatever means, always possessed some mysterious power. As long as they began to run, the big ones rumbled as if rolls of thunders were passing by and the small ones buzzed as if swarms of bees were flying overhead.[1] The scripture text inside was presented not word by word or sentence by sentence, but in its entirety as the wheel made a complete revolution. Deities, in the meantime, could hear all the words in the scripture text and sense people's pieties and worships.

Namely, as a scripture wheel was revolving, deities in the heaven could hear all the content of the scripture. The words tightly packed in the scripture text zoomed onto the heaven all at once and then deities heard every word in the scripture. Wheels had such an extraordinary supernatural power!

However, human beings didn't have the omnipotence of deities. The senses

348

of people wandering in this mundane world were dulled and confined; as a result, people could only hear the prayers chanted syllable by syllable or word by word, and none of them was able to hear the entirety of all the meanings and sounds released from a scripture wheel in the twinkling of an eye. In light of Buddha's words in the Buddhist scripture, the immense soundless sound was indeed the "grand sound", and only the "grand sound" could reach heaven. Human beings had lost the ability to hear it, so they could only hear wheels turning and rumbling.

Consequently, when wheels appeared as a part of a vehicle, people felt curious and excited. The value of wheels was no longer imaginary or intangible.[2] When the first horse-carriage with brand-new wheels appeared in Ji Village, before it began to move, people had realized that they now had a new kind of transportation, which ran faster and could carry more goods.

This tool was called "carriage".

The word "carriage" had appeared in the ancient songs, in which the person who drove the carriage was called "War God".

Now, the carriage descended into the earthly human world. Who could drive it? Since carriages had something to do with horses, people at once thought of the horseman, the best horseman among them.

Then, the horseman came. He was entirely different from what people had imagined him to be: He looked thin and small and his face was besprinkled with pockmarks left by smallpox. Anyway, he was the best horseman in Ji Village. Villagers all deemed that he must have something special in horses' eyes. What specialty did he possess? They had no idea, for they had no horses' eyes, just the same way as the ordinary people couldn't hear the entirety of a scripture while a scripture wheel was revolving.

On the day when the carriage was first put to use, all the villagers came. That horseman with a pockmarked face looked indifferent as if all these were none of his business. While several strong men were taking great efforts and trying all means to harness the blue-hair horse between the two shafts of the carriage, the pockmarked man on his horse was lingering outside the crowd. As if grown on the horseback, he sat steady and looked quite at ease. After a long time, people still couldn't harness the horse into place. The horse kept kicking and biting, and a few rash and imprudent men were bruised in the process.

In the end, the villagers turned their eyes to the pockmarked man outside the crowd.

Under people's eyes, the pock-pits on his face turned red one after another. Getting off his horse, he slowly walked to the blue-hair horse. "YU ..." He uttered a sound to console it. Hearing his voice, the horse's erect tail drooped down slowly. He patted the horse on the neck and lightly scratched the outside of its nostrils which were continuously exhaling hot breaths. Soon, the horse calmed down. Then, with a smile on his face, this guy, henceforth called Pockmark, began to whisper to it, as if he were absorbed in some fantasies. Under his spell, the horse stood obediently between two shafts and Pockmark quickly and neatly harnessed it with the yoke and those complicated reins. After a short while, the blue-hair horse in the middle and the other two black horses on both sides were all harnessed into place.[3]

The crowd became silent.

Led by Pockmark, the blue-hair horse started its initial two steps. The ropes on its body became taut. He insisted on driving the troika forward. As they moved a step, the wheels began to revolve a little; however, when Pockmark stopped, the wheels turned back to where they had been.

"Go on, Pockmark! Go on!" People turned anxious.

He smiled, an acute ray of light shooting out of his narrow eyes. He moved a few steps, and following him the wheels turned more than half a circle. Hubs and axles rubbed each other and produced a sound which any revolving wheels would inevitably produce.

— Creak —

Like a new-born bird trying to utter its first chirps, the sound was a little timid and a little excited, but it stopped abruptly.

The horses also cocked their ears, listening attentively to the strange sound behind them.

Pockmark continued to drive the troika forward.

And the three horses — the blue-hair horse in the middle and the other two black horses on both sides — pulled the carriage forward. The turning wheels, in the end, uttered a complete sound —

— Creak — Rattle —![4]

The first part sounded meticulous and the latter courageous and confident.[5]

The sound was so stimulating that the three horses, no longer under the urge of Pockmark, stretched out their necks, straightened their backs and strove to go forward. The wheels began to revolve continuously and produced a consecutive chain of sound —

— Creak — Rattle —!

— Creak — Rattle —! — Creak — Rattle —! — Creak — Rattle —!

Pockmark dodged aside and ran beside the carriage. After a few steps, he jumped up and sat on the driver's seat on the carriage. He took the whip off the shaft and cracked it loudly in the air. At the sound of the whip, the carriage scurried out of the small square and rushed toward the road outside the village.

Since then, the time in Ji Village, as if furnished with wheels, passed by as quickly as a flying arrow.

While the scene of the horse-carriage was still lingering in people's minds and the complacence was still glowing on Pockmark's face, horse-carriages went outdated. A new kind of vehicle turned up — the tractor. It had four more wheels than a horse-carriage and more importantly, it replaced horses with an engine. The tractor driver tapped the engine and told the people around in an elated tone, "Forty horsepowers. Do you know what it means? It means it has the power of forty horses."

Admiration arose in the crowd.

The driver continued, "You can ask Pockmark. Is he able to harness forty horses in front of a carriage?"

In fact, the tractor driver said this on purpose. He saw Pockmark holding the rein and sitting on his beloved blue-hair horse outside the crowd just as what he used to do years ago when he harnessed the first horse-carriage. Pockmark had to admit that the tractor driver did have the right to put on airs in front of him. The tractor had the power of forty horses! Besides, the shining red paint on its body and the imposing wheels twice to three times bigger dwarfed his horse-carriage. A pitiful sense arose in his heart. How deplorable his horse-carriage was![6]

As soon as it was switched on, the tractor began to roar, as if it finally found a way to let out its suppressed vigor and vitality. The chimney on its body puffed dense smokes and looked as complacent as Pockmark once was when he sat on his horse-carriage, holding the whip, having a pipe between his teeth and puffing mouthfuls of blue smoke. Looking at the powerful tractor, Pockmark knew that the horse-carriage, having been used for no more than ten years, would have to retire.

Pockmark turned and carefully got his carriage ready. For so many years, children had been eager to sit on his carriage and run on the road. Now, he wanted to satisfy them. As a matter of fact, he was not fond of children and women. In the past, he was fastidious about who had the privilege to sit on his carriage for in his heart riding on a carriage symbolized a high status; as a result, many villagers, especially children, had never been allowed to sit on his carriage. The moment those children barely rubbed their hips on his parked carriage, he would mercilessly drive them away at once. But now, after running two or three circles in the village, his carriage was still empty. All the children were running after the tractor and no one showed interest in his horse-carriage. Now, in the field outside the village, the tractor was manifesting its gigantic power. Under the instruction of the driver, people unhooked the van and took out a plough with six iron plowshares from it. The engine stalled for a moment and soon it restarted, puffing out smokes again. Dragging the plough, the tractor ran to the fro in the field, and after several rounds, it completed the work which would take two oxen with a set of plough a whole day to finish. Running after the tractor, the villagers gasped in admiration. On the empty square in the village, Pockmark sat alone. He lit his pipe and fell into contemplation.

In the past, he valued his carriage too much! He treasured it too much! If he had known that his carriage was not likely to be used for hundreds and thousands of years and had to "step off the stage of history", he would not have been cherishing it in such a meticulous manner! Indeed, man should keep pace with the times. Realizing this, he resolved to let children ride his horse-carriage. On the first day, when the tractor came back, it was dark; on the second day, he got his carriage ready in the early morning, but to his disappointment, people still followed the tractor with great zest. In disappointment, he sat on his carriage, still and silent. After two or three hours, finally, some people took notice of him.

"Look! Pockmark and his horse-carriage!"

"Oh, Pockmark, don't you know your horse-carriage is useless?"

"Oh, Pockmark, you don't see that tractor?"

Keeping silent, he just sat on the carriage shaft and lit his pipe.

At this moment, the tractor was being started. People knew its power the day before: Equipped with that huge plough, it could do the work which would take a dozen people a whole day to complete.

The tractor was so attractive to the villagers that it even didn't give Pockmark an opportunity to make up for the children who had never ridden his horse-carriage. In disappointment, He put the yoke and those complicated reins aside and rode his blue-hair horse up the mountain. Since then, he had never come down. The cadre of the production commune once went onto the mountain and said to him, "Pockmark, go down the mountain. Your horses are useless."

He retorted, "Useless? Why?"

"We have tractors, and trucks!"

"Then how do we deal with our horses?" Their production commune had more than ten horses altogether, including the ones used for the horse-carriage. "They need to be taken care of, don't they? I'll be the one for the job."

Thus, the first horse-carriage driver became the last horse tender in Ji Village.

Still bearing affectionate feelings to him and his horses, the villagers lined out a special pasture for his horses and built a hut under a tree beside a spring for him. How time flew! As life proceeded in an accelerated pace, new things appeared pell-mell.[7] Old-timers like him, more or less in detached sadness, were gradually forgotten. Once in a while, Pockmark got down the mountain to fetch some grains and buy a little salt. When he saw someone, he signaled his greetings with a faint smile, acute light glittering in his narrow eyes. When he found his carriage weather-beaten and dilapidated, he drove a herd of horses down the mountain with a load of timber on each horse's back. He built a shed with these timber planks to shelter his carriage from rains and winds.

Thus, within a short period of time, the horse-carriage and its driver were out of date. Both of them became the images belonging to the past. Nevertheless, these images were not deeply buried in people's memory but still alive around them. The carriage was parked at a corner of the village square, and the horses and the driver were living in a pasture specially reserved for them, all lingering on the borderline where reality started disappearing and memory started livening up.

While the coat of paint on the tractor was still fresh and bright, those horses got aged. Compared with a man's life, a horse's life was much shorter. A horse at the age of 20, equivalent to a man at the age of 60 or 70, was approaching the end of its life. When the first horse was dying, Pockmark sat right beside its head. The scarlet glows of sunset burned in its eyes but by and by the red clouds and glows faded away. As the stars began to jump onto the sky one after another, he heard a hoarse sound coming out of its throat as if a rope on the horse-carriage suddenly snapped. Then, the horse closed its eyes, shutting the starry sky and the whole world outside.[8] Pockmark didn't look up at the sky; instead, he began to dig a pit beside him. At midnight, he finished his work. He sat down, lit his pipe and began to smoke. The light around him was glittering and twinkling as before, but his horse's eyes closed for ever. He put the pipe out. On such a cold and quiet night, he could hear thick dews rolling along the veins of the leaves and dripping into the fertile warm earth which integrated itself into the endless night. In the darkness, those wet leaves shivered and shimmered.[9]

After smoking one more pipe, he lifted the dead horse and pushed it into the pit. At daybreak, he had leveled the earth off. The rising red sun drove the thin fog away and the horses, after such a cold night, began to move about, snorting and whinnying.[10]

Pockmark got down the mountain to report the horse's death.

"How can you prove that the horse is really dead?"

He was thrown a question he had never thought of before.

"What? You've buried it? It is our collective property, and how can you deal with it at will? Its skin and its meat can be sold for money!"

Of course, he couldn't say that he did it because as a horseman and a carriage driver he loved his horse as his own life. Feeling wronged seriously, he didn't say a word and left. The head of the production commune actually meant that Pockmark should report first before burying the horse. The leader was also from Ji Village and was not so mean as to sell a horse's skin for a little money. However, as a leader, if he didn't say something tough and strict, he felt himself unlike a leader. So what the head did was actually understandable, but Pockmark, one-track-minded and as stubborn as a mule, felt wronged and grieved, not so much for himself as for the dead horse and those which were going to die in the future.[11] Since then, he never went down the mountain to give reports for his dead horses. Luckily, some warm-hearted people sometimes went onto the mountain stealthily and sent him the daily necessities. Indeed, he was unwilling to come down the mountain.

Maybe this was a sort of predestination. While machines became the symbols of novelty and power, horses and horse-carriages became the signs of those which were doomed to withdraw from the stage of history. Pockmark, unknowingly, played the role of the last horseman, the last carriage-driver and the last herdsman on this stage successfully. He had already been considered a legend before his death.

Looking up to the mountain, villagers could always see horses lingering here and there on the pasture. However, they became fewer and fewer, and in less than ten years, only three horses were left. That winter, an extremely heavy snow kept falling. As the horses couldn't find food, two died. One day, the shed which Pockmark built to protect the carriage suddenly collapsed. The blue-hair horse, once the youngest and the strongest, rushed down the mountain and neighed continuously on the small square of the village.

All the villagers knew that Pockmark must have died and that the horse came to tell them about it. Climbing onto the mountain, they found him sitting peacefully in his shabby hut, dead. His narrow eyes were not completely closed but from the small seams under his eyelids there was no sharp light shooting out.

After his funeral, which was arranged and done hastily, people tried to take care of that blue-hair horse, only to find it gone without a trace. One year passed. When summer came, someone said he had seen it in a mountain. Alive or dead? Still alive? Was it drinking water or eating grasses? The answer was quite a fantastic one: "It ran as fast as a flash of light, so fast that I had no time to see it clearly." "Then, how do you know it is that horse?" "I don't know but I am sure it is!" So, this mysterious horse lived several years longer in people's imagination. Later, with the advent of the Cultural Revolution and the fervent denunciation of feudalist traditions and superstitions, the blue-hair horse, the legend in the village, was gradually forgotten.

1. "……一旦转动起来，大的经轮隆隆作响仿佛雷霆滚过，小的经轮嗡嗡出声仿佛蜜蜂飞翔。"这里，有比喻的修辞手法"仿佛雷霆"、"仿佛蜜蜂"，有动作"滚过"、"飞翔"，有描摹声音的"隆隆作响"、"嗡嗡出声"，翻译为：As long as they began to run, the big ones rumbled as if rolls of thunders were passing by and the small ones buzzed as if swarms of bees were flying overhead. 选择恰当的动词和拟声词对翻译的成功具有至关重要的作用。

2. "轮子提供的价值不再过于缥缈虚无了。"The value of wheels was no longer imaginary or intangible. 这里"虚无缥缈"译成imaginary or intangible，指轮子的价值以前是存在于想像中的，现在是看得见摸得着的了。

3. 这是马车夫首次套马的过程，翻译时，动词的选择要恰当、生动。

4. "——叽——吭！"马车车轮转动发出的声音。creak可以指门嘎吱作响，rattle指迅速而嘎嘎作响地移动，这里译者选用这两个词来描写轮箍和轮轴摩擦发出的声音以及车轮开始转动发出的声音。

5. "前半声小心翼翼，后半声理直气壮。"这是对声音的拟人。The first part sounded meticulous and the latter courageous and confident.

6. "不要说那机器里憋着四十匹马的劲头。光看那红光闪闪的夺目油漆，看那比马车轮大上两三倍的轮子，他心里就有些可怜自己那矮小的马车了。"The tractor had the power of forty horses! Besides, the shining red paint on its body and the imposing wheels twice to three times bigger dwarfed his horse-carriage. A pitiful sense arose in his heart. How deplorable his horse-carriage was! imposing 庄严的、威仪的，dwarf (使) 显得矮小，使相形见绌。

7. "新人新事不断涌现。"… new things appeared pell-mell. pell-mell是形容词也是副词，意思是：凌乱的、匆忙的、一个接一个的。

355

8. As the stars began to jump onto the sky one after another, he heard a hoarse sound coming out of its throat as if a rope on the horse-carriage suddenly snapped. Then, the horse closed its eyes, shutting the starry sky and the whole world outside. 这里描写马临死的情景，注意动词用法。snap发出尖厉声音地突然断裂。

9. "……那些湿漉漉的叶片却颤动着微微的光亮。" In the darkness, those wet leaves shivered and shimmered. shiver 颤动，shimmer 发出微光。两个词押头韵。

10. "薄雾散尽，红日破空而出，那些伫立在寒夜中的马又开始走动，掀动着鼻翼发出轻轻的嘶鸣。" The rising red sun drove the thin fog away and the horses, after such a cold night, began to move about, snorting and whinnying. 译文没有拘泥于原句的句式结构，而是重新组句，把原文中的几个意象"薄雾"、"红日"、"寒夜"、"马"、"嘶鸣"表现出来。马的嘶鸣声可以翻译为whinny或者neigh。

11. "但麻子这个死心眼却深受委屈，一小半是为了自己，一多半还是为了死去的马和将死的马。" … Pockmark, one-track-minded and as stubborn as a mule, felt wronged and grieved, not so much for himself as for the dead horse and those which were going to die in the future. "死心眼"译成了：one-track-minded 一根筋的、思想僵化的，as stubborn as a mule 固执的。

厨房

◎ 王安忆

我还记得那间厨房里的地板，这是整幢房子里最肥沃的地方。奇怪的是，应该肥沃的，房子前面，朝南的小院子却是枯瘦的。灰白的地皮，掘不到两公分，就是破砖烂瓦碎石头，它们拱着地皮，使得嶙峋不平。除了一些车前籽和狗尾巴草，它再长不出什么。昆虫呢，只有一种，瓦灰色的干瘪的西瓜虫。小院子反是这里最贫瘠的地方。而厨房，却很丰饶。地板最初一定是上过漆色的，此时全叫油腻糊住。要是几家合力用碱水刷洗过，它暂时地呈现出一种惨白，结果是，更深而彻底地吸进油腻。再刷碱水，再吸油腻，这就合了油漆的原理和工序，地板完全成了油腻的颜色，一种肥沃的灰黑，它简直要长出东西来了！它果然是长出了些东西。在墙根——假如能够挪开煤气灶、菜橱、桌子以及瓶瓶罐罐，露出墙根，就可看见那里长着一种黑色的植物，它的名字叫作"霉"。这里的动物品种就多了，老鼠、蟑螂、壁虎、蜘蛛、蚰蜒、蚂蚁，也有西瓜虫，但这里的西瓜虫比前面院子里的要肥硕和丰润，它们湿漉漉的；有不定期来到的猫，那都是野猫，过着居无定所的生活，时而来，时而走；还有人看见过一只黄鼠狼，神秘地露了一下面，就再看不见了。厨房就像一个动物园。它们彼此相克，比如猫吃老鼠，壁虎和蜘蛛吃虫子，可这就是生物链啊！总的来说，厨房里的生态十分活跃。在某个季节，气候特别干爽，空气又十分明澈，午后三时左右，太阳从后门照进厨房，这一刻，厨房里往往没有人。烧晚饭的时候没到，小孩子又没有放学，阳光一下子将厨房照亮。地板呈现出一种油色，黄蜡蜡的，缝是油黑的，地板面上的木纹和裂隙也是油黑，上面有一只三条腿的板凳，是本木的白。厨房突然鲜丽起来，几乎是夺目的。光线稍一转移，那些爽利的线条和块面又毛出一层绒头，变得有些绰约，因而生动起来。然后，噪声起来。

我再也无从知道那个奶妈是何方人氏，姓甚名谁，即使在小孩子的年龄来看，她也是年轻的。她身个结实匀称，面色红润，梳一对黑亮亮的辫子，直垂到腰间。她的衣裤是一种鲜艳的毛蓝，搭襻布鞋。除了奶那个女婴，她还要搭伴着做一些杂事。我总是看见她背着门，面朝里，在砧板上切菜。无论切什么，她都会从刀下拾起一块填进嘴里，同时回身张望一眼，是以为有人看她吗？这种习惯不知源于怎么样的生活经历，也无从考起了。她所哺乳的那个女婴通常是睡在一个木头小床，四面围着栅栏的小床被她挟在胳膊底下，随身带着。下午，小孩子们都放学回家，壅塞在弄堂里的时候，她就将小床停放在后门口，自然就会有小孩子过来看她，逗她，甚至大胆地将她抱出木床，走来走去。就好像是一个换工，她借给全弄堂的小孩子一个大玩具，全弄堂的孩子则负起照护女婴的责任。免不了会有摔着女婴的，婴儿没怎么哭，那孩子先吓得哭起来。其实没有人会责备她，或是他，在多子女的年代里，孩子都是这么摔摔掼掼长起来的。

　　是记忆模糊了，还是事实如此，那奶妈在印象中是颟顸的。时间久远的人和事都有一种颟顸的表情，就像从旧胶片上放映出来的老电影，反映迟钝，有个时间差。那奶妈拥着女婴而坐，听凭她拱着她的乳房吸吮奶水。看不出来她对这女婴的态度，是有些亲，还是相反，憎恨她吸去了本该是她孩子的奶水。但她显然不会是有着强烈感情的女人，她只是年轻，这样的年轻，身心里总会积蓄和汹涌着一种能量，这就使她的沉默有了重力。担任这家主要家务，包括监管她的，是女婴的祖母。照理已经是多年媳妇熬成婆的年纪了，可是上面的婆婆还健在，媳妇们呢，都是现代的独立的女性，有自己的收入，所以，这祖母就一直屈抑着，也是沉默的。但这祖母却有着意想不到的幽默感，这表现在，当人们说话，她适时发出会心的微笑。这微笑流露出的还不止是幽默，还有一种秉性，敦厚的秉性，这让她能够消受别人的智慧。她说是东家，实际要比奶妈辛苦，买菜，收拾，烧饭，洗衣，而奶妈大部分时间是坐着，哺乳怀里的女婴。等家务暂告段落，有一时的空闲，祖母也终于坐定下来，就坐在奶妈身边。她的神情，即便隔了岁月，依然是比奶妈灵敏，灵敏于各种感受，这是由阅历决定的。于是，她的身型就有了些微的轮廓，破开岁月的氤氲。而奶妈是一片空洞，这空洞将在某个时候变得深邃，以后会谈到这一点。

　　这一老一少，一主一仆并排坐在小凳子上，听谁说话呢？听那个帮佣的女人说话。这个女人是厨房里的精英，她只要开言，大人小孩必听无疑。从现在往那时候推溯，她其实了不到三十，至多三十，可在那个时代，却是一个成熟的年龄。她的见识呀，简直丰富得没法说，虽然一点也无从考证，可就她说话的威仪来看，没什么可说的！她的脸很清晰，在整个混沌的景象中，唯有这张脸，是以肯定的线条勾勒的，也因此变得平面，而其他的印象倒是有一些立体的效果，比如奶妈，因为有影调。也因为此，她变得尖锐了。她的眼睛，有着明显的双睑，鼻子有些窄，鼻梁这里因为常常是收紧的，就有了一道竖纹，嘴唇是单薄的，因而使笔触更加锋利。她单身未婚，对于一个帮佣的人，这似乎有些过于摩登了，可是在她，这又理所当然，有哪个男人敢娶她呢！在她们的阶层里，那种传统的婚配，不外是乡下老家的男人，或者杨树浦的也是同乡人的工人，显然不适合她。那么，找一个职员，可是谁听说过职员的太太是帮佣的？于是，不结婚也罢。由于是她，完全有权力过这么一种特殊的人生。她所服侍的东家是一对没有儿女的夫妇，这就像配好了的，她也不必和小孩子交道。小孩子总是不洁的，屎啊尿啊，还有乳臭啊！就像那个奶妈，她的身上永远散发出这些气味，而这个女人，冰清玉洁。她的用物，我说是"她"的用物，而不是她东家的，都是单独分出来。碗是镶金边的，筷子镶的是银箔。她是怀着怎样的心情积攒起她的财物，在这拥挤、油腻，而且嘈杂的厨房里，要收藏它们，不那么容易。它们实在太精致了，而公用厨房是粗砺的，什么事没有，地板上撬起来的铁钉子都会绊你一个大跟头，就像地里的老树根。她的碗具上的金边银片，还有温润的细瓷，波光粼粼穿行在时间的黑暗隧道。

因为她，这间厨房里会有一些贵客造访，那多是隔壁门牌号码里的主妇，总是向她请教某种菜肴如何制作，某种衣物如何洗涤，甚至于，还有一个主妇，很信任地将小孩子交到她手里，请她刮痧。要知道，她其实并没有生养孩子的经验，大概唯其因此，才下得了手。只见她将小孩子翻倒，挂在膝上，这时，不易觉察地，她的身子向后仰了仰，为了避开小孩子身上汗、尿、乳、还有眼泪交织成又发了酵的酸臭味。然后，她很镇定地将一枚分币在一碗水里蘸蘸，就像刮鱼鳞一般在小孩子的背上刮去。由这些交道生出了交情，邻家主妇们就有时候并不为什么事，而是专门过来与她闲话。她们使这间厨房蓬荜生辉。

完全是与她相对而设地，厨房里另一位成员，也是帮佣的女人，质地特别柔软。你甚至会惊异，这样柔软的质地如何还能在这一片混沌中占位，似乎轮廓的每一条边线都有危险被吞噬淹没，而它却依然存在着。这说明它的韧劲，颇有弹性。这是以圆为单位而组合的占位，有些像太极，含而不露，用的是内功。她是记忆中最昏晦的一块，许多暧昧从她这里生出。她从很年轻的时候就守寡，已经度过长久的没有男人的日子，可是奇怪的是，她比那个年轻健硕，奶汁像是从熟透的浆果里迸流着的奶妈，更具有情欲的气息，这也就是暧昧所在。这柔软的质地同时还是湿润的，就有些幽微的光悄然挥洒出来，这里亮一点，那里亮一点。她在厨房所占据的位置是后窗侧边，后窗底下是一具水斗，光线就斜着照亮了她的侧面。由于窗玻璃上蒙了油垢，像结了一层乳胶般的霜，光也是暧昧的。这一个存在于记忆中的位置最微妙了，它不像那一个精英女佣的清晰和锐利，它浑圆的形状很容易和周边环境混为一谈，于是就有了一种游动的不确定的性质，可它就是不消失。很像是水银，打散了，碎成蔺粉，一旦聚拢一起，又是完整的一颗，一丁点不缺。那精英女佣是焊得很牢的一个整体，这却是由细枝末节合成，就变得很是黏腻缠绵。

方才说的，厨房里露过一回面的黄鼠狼，就是被她看见。她大惊失色，随后流下眼泪。在她们的乡俗看来，黄鼠狼是不吉祥的动物，谁看见谁就遭厄运。所以，她不让人们提起她看见黄鼠狼这件事。可偏偏有些调皮的孩子，冷不防冲她喊一声"黄鼠狼来了"，她愠怒的表情并不让人骇怕，这就是她和那一位帮佣的女人不同之处，那一位不怒而威。小孩子其实对事物的质地最了解，他们代表人类的本能，所以他们就选中这一个来欺负。小孩子并不为她吓退，继续玩着这个残酷的游戏，还扮演着黄鼠狼从她跟前蹿过，这一回喊的是"我是黄鼠狼"！结果，她笑了。她的笑，不是像那位女婴的祖母，出于幽默感和谦逊，而是好脾气，甚至是有一些轻浮的脾性，这使她的原则性受了损。她的这种质地就是好变通，因为密度不够。关于黄鼠狼的信仰就这么瓦解了。尽管她没有将她的有神论贯彻到底，可她的宿命感依然笼罩了这一间厨房。我为什么要强调这一间厨房，那是因为，在厨房的前面，还有楼上，各个居室里，过着和社会主流世界观相合的生活，就像是社会的正面。而厨房，则是在社会的边缘，甚至有一些负面的意思，这里流淌着思想的暗流。谈到宿命论，就要扯出这幢房子之外的一个女人，一个老女人，她有时候会来到我们的厨房。

我们的厨房是敞开的，任何人都可以进来，这也是和正式居室不同的地方。每一种制度，无论多么严密都会有疏漏的空隙，厨房就是这样的空隙。这老女人不晓得住在哪一幢房子里，她可能都不是我们弄堂里的人，而来自另一条弄堂。也不知道她是怎么摸到了我们这里，因她来到这里并不是专对着某一个人，好像她看中的就是我们这个地方。她每一次来，总是坐在一张小矮凳。这张小矮凳的榫松动了，一不小心就会夹了肉，我们就管它叫"夹屁股矮凳"。这里的物件都有名字，另一张板凳叫"阿跷"，因为只有三条腿。相反，人倒未必有名字了，小孩子往往叫"阿大""阿二""阿三"，这么依次排下去，奶妈就叫奶妈，保姆则是"三号阿姨""二楼阿姨""小花园阿姨"，以所服务的东家的居住地为标号。这从某种程度上体现了厨房里的自然观，世上万物，都是有生命的，生命都是平等的。

老女人坐在"夹屁股矮凳"上，身子就靠着门，这扇门就和地板一样破损和油腻，我不记得它曾经关上过，它总是推到墙上，敞开着。老女人就像瘫倒似地靠着门，身子还在继续往下滑，终于奇迹般地没有滑到地板上。她抱怨她每天夜里听到鬼叫，鬼叫扰得她一夜无眠。这话说得无比森然，忌讳黄鼠狼的女人同样忌讳这老女人，每一回她离去，都要在她身后吐唾沫，说她带来了死气——这就对了，我为什么怀疑她来自另一条弄堂，那就是她携带的气息不是我们弄堂的气息，别看我们的厨房有着阴晦的气氛，可这是朗朗乾坤里的阴晦，就像光投下来的同时也投下了影子。虽然如此忌讳老女人，但当老女人再度来到时，厨房的门还是向她敞开，那宿命的女人依然是听众之一，她照例不能将原则贯彻到底。

老女人来到的时候，最兴奋的是小孩子。我们挤作一团，听她描绘鬼叫。女人们想将我们驱赶出去，因为小孩子耳朵干净，最听不得这种事情。可是，她们赶不走我们，我们坚决不被赶走。赶不走的另一个原因是，我们都怕走过老女人身边，而她就坐在门口。我们爱听她的鬼话，却惧怕走近她，在我们看来，她和那打扰她的鬼，就是一家人。倘若我们没听懂她的话，她的口音很古怪，又总是连哭带诉，我们向大人们要求证实，鬼叫究竟是如何叫法，那么，所有的人，勿管有神论无神论全都变了脸，斥道：谁听见鬼叫了？谁听见鬼叫谁就要死！老女人不知道什么时候不再来了，可是，也没有她的死讯传来。对于这个人，厨房的全体人员都噤声不提，她就此退出了厨房的社交圈。

这些阴惨的色彩，并没有使厨房变得恐怖，相反，它在某一方面，更加强了凝聚力。因为神秘、未可知、惊惧而越团越紧，身体挤着身体，由此产生出一股子相濡以沫的气氛，增添了这里的温湿度。这种温湿度特别适合小的物种，一些渺小的情感也在这里滋生滋长着。比如说，受委屈的小孩子通常是在这里哭泣。与兄弟口角；受了母亲的责打；或是弄堂里遭到欺压，弄堂是个强食弱肉的社会；再有，同学间的诬陷和背叛，等等，诸如此类的冤情，翻是翻不过来了，总要有个地方诉说吧！那么，就到这里来！这里的人阅历都很深，而且是在最底层，用她们的眼睛看，那么点芝麻绿豆，算得上什么呢？哭一会儿，再重整旗鼓，回到弄堂，学校，抑或同胞兄弟的社会里，人生总是要面对的。吃偏食和私食也是在这里，多子女的家庭，爱是有偏颇的，要是在主仆之间，这却是类似私情一般了。人总是有偏疼的一个，那么就叫到厨房来，从碗橱的角落里，拿出私藏下的半只咸蛋，两片夹心肉，一个鸡腿，或者面糊里调了白糖，用肥肉膘开一只油锅，煎一张甜饼。此时此刻，声音和动作都是细小而且轻悄的，蹑着手脚，以防被家中其他孩子看见。在这机密的气氛里，生出贴己之心。一大一小，一个坐，一个立，也不说什么，偶尔对一下眼睛，便有无限的柔情交流。小孩子不被首肯的宾客也是在这里接待，这里纲纪松懈，小孩子倒有了人权。他们谈一些玻璃弹子或者香烟刮片的交易；磋商玩意儿的技艺；搬弄口舌——上海弄堂里的流言实在是从嫩到熟，从熟到衰，收割后的老茬子地里再播下种，这时节，还是些流言的芽儿呢！他们挤在这里，也不怕炒锅里溅出来的油花烫了，水斗底下的积水湿了鞋，女人们则将他们驱来赶去。就像动物趋光趋热的本能，暮色降临，他们还不想分手，弄堂里暗沉沉的，他们便奔这里来了。这一盏蒙了灰和油腻的电灯，投下的光，简直就是人间的暖意，藏污纳垢，却结结实实。这些小萝卜头。小小的，薄薄的，几乎透得光，就像皮影戏里驴皮做的人儿，交互错踪，一会儿叠起，一会儿散开。

有多少小孩子从这里流淌过去，留下凸凸凹凹的印记，然后又弥合起来。这些小巧玲珑的凹痕，以及迅速的弥合，使空间呈现出活跃变化的形态。他们的小身子和小悲欢，虽然是小小的体积，分量又轻，可是具有穿透力，或者说渗透力，从漫漫时光滴漏进来，给记忆镀上亮闪闪的斑点。他们的正史都记录在前面的和爸爸妈妈共处的居室里，还有弄口的小学校，在这背阴的脱离了社会辖制的厨房里，写下的是野史，逸闻轶事，不上台面，可是谁知道呢？也许这也是重要的，那些杂七杂八的怪力乱神的鬼话，那些伤心的泪水，鬼鬼祟祟吃到嘴里的偏食，也是一种知识呢，填补着正统教育的盲区。每一个时代里的正统都有着它的狭隘性，需要一些旁门左道开拓视野。

从这里走过的孩子形形色色，来自社会各阶层。有一些穿着体面，肤如凝脂，根本和这厨房的环境不合契，可他们也来到这里。另一个极端是，破衣烂衫，面露菜瓜色，眼睛躲避着灶上锅里的吃食，是为抗拒诱惑，和这厨房也不大合契。他们带来了平等的色彩，使这厨房变成大同世界。事实上，厨房是一个中等社会，它的生活水准是温饱略有剩余。小孩子没什么绝色的，但总归平头整脸；衣着平庸，尚可算得上整齐；吃的呢，绝不会饿着，只是有些馋；家里有些规矩，却还不至于完全丧失自由。他们，就是厨房的小主人。

那个宁波籍的小男孩子，他的橄榄形的头颅，时常拓开着记忆的空间，出自老练的手笔，凌空一划，再一收。这种头型是经过多少千年的进化，就像是一种美丽的陶罐，记录了人类文明的历史。他是一个有历史感的小男孩子，他的头型，口音，还有衣服上时常散发出的某一种食物的气味，都透露出悠久的遗传。他有着非凡的急智，他机敏的呀，不像人，而像一种动物，不同的是，这机敏于他是表现在语言上，这就是文明了。他能够立刻抓住对方说话里的漏洞，作出反应，称得上"静若处子，动若脱兔"。我们每个人，都逃不过他的洞察，然后被他的语言剥开伪装——假如说小孩子也有伪装的话。像他这样，乳臭未干，并没经什么世事，只能用天赋来解释，而天赋其实是历史的积淀。他的手，那纤长的十指，也是文明进化的果实，制作起游戏的工具，简直就是天工开物，弹弓，弹丸，三角和四角的刮片，蝈蝈笼，铁环，俗称"贱骨头"的陀螺。这双手对小动物的爱抚也很温柔，我说的小动物就是厨房地板缝里的那些居民，虫子啊什么的，还有来去不定的野猫。他的手在野猫的胸脯上轻轻挠一挠，对生灵很有经验的样子。和他的温柔成为匹对的是他有同等程度的残酷，他生生把一条蚯蚓掐成两段，放在手掌心上看它们各自扭动，变成两条蚯蚓。西瓜虫也是生生地掰开来，看它小小的白肚腹里有什么。这温柔和残酷也来自原始遗传，都可追溯到上古，物种之间有着另一种强弱优劣的排序，经过漫长的演变，一种胜出的生物与一种败出的生物又一次邂逅，彼此认不得对方，又觉似曾相识。这是小孩子中的历史动物，还有一类完全没有历史的产物，那就是我。

回望过去，我几乎看不见自己的面目，这就是没有来历的人的浅近的性质，还没有脱离主观性，成为客观的存在。不像那男孩，他的存在不可质疑，一下子揳进记忆之中，拔也拔不出来。我的印记是游离的，一会儿浮现出来，一会儿泯灭在混沌里。我还来不及在凿开时间隧道，于是就无法在空间里伫留，这就是时间和空间相互的依附作用。具体到现场，我好像是被那历史男孩一口一口吞噬的，他无情地讥消我的口音，这是一种没有乡音的口音。我从小说普通话，一种基于北方语系，然后由政治生活再造，为适合传播删节与简化韵和声的语言。为了学习上海话，我又损失了普通话的标准，屡次在上海话那个短促的入声上绊倒，终于生出口吃的毛病。然后我又在厨房这个五方杂居的地方吸纳各地乡音，帮佣女人的扬州话，无锡话，奶妈的不知什么地方的话，甚至包括那男孩的宁波话，我吸纳的都是各路乡音的糟粕，因为我根本不懂得什么是好话，什么是孬话。不纯良的语言，就成了我这个新移民的羞耻的徽记。作为一个小孩子，我最大的缺陷是玩不来弄堂游戏，造房子，跳皮筋，捉人，"老狼老狼几点了"……全是以优胜劣汰的方式进行，我一上来就出局，只得站在一边看，然后回到厨房呆着。所以，厨房里也染了小孩子我的寂寞，还有屈辱。这屈辱也是他，历史男孩给予的，他取笑我的挫折，我的挫折作了他的笑料。我的悲伤，滴水穿岩一般从时光里渗漏过来，转眼间消除了痕迹。没有历史的拖尾，它转瞬即逝。我只得依靠一种媒介，文字，来辅助它留下印记，让主观变成客观。

在历史男孩和我中间，还有一个过渡性的人物，我称之为近代女孩。她的形态比我们俩都光鲜，这就是这城市的近代色彩。她不像男孩那么枝蔓繁多，牵丝攀藤，也不像我，单薄，孱弱，而且形状不定，一切有待塑造，她线条流利，表面光洁，附着一些织物，犹如蝉翼，从她轮廓周边派生出来。她比我和男孩更物质化，这些物质性的因素帮助撑开了空间，使她获得可观的占位。于是，她的人，包括肉身，都有了另一种工业化材质的质地，哪一种材质？珐琅瓷，发出人工的光泽。是记忆上的一片螺钿，打磨得光滑透亮。她也是游戏高手，她的游戏是另一路的，不像历史男孩那么具有草根气，而是带了都会的声色，所以叫她近代女孩嘛！比如，挑十字绣，在一块网格细麻纱上，穿了花线的针在每四个一组的格子里对挑一个十字，一个十字又一个十字组成图案。她煞有介事地一针一针挑着，就像一个淑女，一个住在租界上，因为身处异族人中缺少婚姻机会，贻误了青春的外国淑女。她的玩意儿也带着工业革命的空气，比如双股的牛皮筋上，穿着一列机制线团的木头线轴，可以增添牛皮筋的弹性，随着双脚的舞蹈上下翻飞。再则，她会唱"小弟弟小妹妹让开点，敲碎了玻璃老价钿"……幸好有了她，我和男孩才不至于出现断裂，而是有了衔接。我们三个人，接成了历史的链条，就像小女孩子用树叶的茎给自己做的项链——我们将一片树叶，捋得只剩下一条茎，然后万般小心地折成一小段，一小段，段和段之间由拉出的细丝串着，如同蛛丝，在空中摇曳，一不小心就断了。这就是我们身上的历史痕迹。

在我们三个之外，自然还有许多其他的小孩，也穿行在厨房里，可是由于缺少主要事迹，多少是模糊了，成为记忆的碎屑，弥漫在空气里，改变着光影和色彩。所以，他们的存在也是必要的。其实他们也并不是那么没性格，只是被我们这三个遮蔽了。他们不像我们三个那么有含意，这含意在当时不觉得，走过了漫长的时间，渐渐地凸现起来，这是记忆的选择。当然不那么公平，可是就像常言道：历史是胜利者的历史，记忆也是，谁的记忆谁有发言权，谁让是我来记忆这一切呢？那些沙粒似的小孩子，他们的形状只得湮灭在大人物的阴影之下了。可他们还是摇曳着气流，在某种程度上，修改与描画着他人记忆的图景。

而我必须要说一说那两个小孩子，一个是姐姐，一个是弟弟。他们是某一家的小客人，时常前来造访，而我们彼此都没有留心对方。当时间进行到某一个点上，也就是通常说的契机的意思，我们和他们忽然地彼此注意。是一个寒假，天气阴冷，已经不适合做弄堂里的游戏，我们都蜷缩在厨房里。朝北的厨房，又潮湿，谈不上有多少暖和，可是认识新朋友使彼此激动，亲密的感情一分钟一分钟地递进着。转眼过了中午，主人家留了饭，又过了下午，主人家也留了饭，夜晚降临，主人家继而留了宿。第二天，众人又在厨房聚首。只有公用厨房，我们这些来自各个家庭的小孩子才可以聚会。来自另外的街区，另外的学校，以及另外的不为我们熟悉的生活里的孩子，他们，严格地说，只是他们中的一个，那个姐姐，她身上异样的气质，强烈地吸引了我们。我们眼界很窄，没什么见识，他们，或者说是她，是我们从未接触过的一种类型。

我应该把她放在哪一个历史阶段上呢？上古，近代，或者如我，来不及创造历史。好像都不对，都不适合她，她兀自立于历史之外。也许，原因只是，她不属于我所认识的历史，而是来自另一个历史。每一个街区，每一种生活，甚至每一种房子的结构里，都有着自己的完整的历史，每一种历史的体现都不相同，各有各的生动性。她也是有光泽的，但不是珐琅瓷，而是真正的贝类。真正的贝类在于它其实不像人工打磨的那么有亮度，也不够鲜丽，而是有一些暗。但组织密度更高，于是有了深度和厚度。她就是这么样散发着幽暗的光，这光仿佛来自一个活跃的源头，使她有一种流动的性质。她就像舟筏，被记忆载着，穿越时光而来。她习惯用一块头巾裹着头，头巾沿了发际向两边去，在下颌交叉，再绕到颈后，打一个结实的活结。透过围巾的形状，可看出她纤巧的头颅，头颅上梳得很光的头发和编得很紧的发辫。她就这样裹着头巾，手插在棉袄口袋里。她的裹在红格子棉袄里的身子，骨骼匀称。她直直地站在我们中间，与我们说话。她的脸色和身姿，一点没有寒冷的样子，不像她的弟弟，嘴唇青白，瑟缩在煤气灶旁边。倘若煤气灶上正好在烧煮东西，他就将手伸过去取暖，很快又被燎着，赶紧缩一下。这是一个孱弱的男孩，她却很健康，不仅她不感到冷，而且令别人也热烘烘的。这是一种格外结实的体质，内分泌平衡。我们热情地看着她，怀着欣赏和羡慕，不放过她的一举一动。而且很奇怪的，我们女孩比他们男孩更受她的吸引，在这个年龄阶段，女性气质更为同性所敏感，男孩还没有开蒙呢！

一天过去了，我们还不想放她走，又过了一天，下一天，依然没走。显然她在我们中间也如鱼得水，脸色越来越红润，神气越来越飞扬。在此同时，她的弟弟却日益萎缩，苍白和虚弱。他就像一个雪人，在炉火边上消融下去，他的人都小了一圈。主人家终于发出逐客令，女孩子只当耳旁风，她的镇定也是少见的。就在此时，寒流来临，风在弄堂里激荡，暴冷使我们更加兴奋，好像有什么不平凡的事情要发生了，连她弟弟的眼睑下面也生出红晕，渐渐蔓延了整个脸颊。最后，事情的结束是，姐弟俩的父母来到，将他们带走了。此时，弟弟已在高热中，其实他从一开始就病了，却没有人发觉，注意力都在姐姐身上。在魅力四射的姐姐的阴影下生活，他必须要有隐忍的性格。谁知道呢，在他弱小的身体里，正进行着一场什么样的抵抗。他几乎要消失了踪迹，他无声无息地，没有一点响动，要不是后来发生的事情，他就算完全地退出记忆。后来发生的事情是，他死了，不是在这一场病中，也不是在他身历的无数病中，这一个多病的孩子，很平静地死于无病无灾之中。儿童猝死至今还是一个谜，没有谜底。他的死，在人们的记忆中砸开一个窟窿，边缘迸裂，犹如金石相撞。

　　这是小孩子里的死者，大人呢？你们不会猜到，大人中的死者是那个最年轻结实的奶妈。颟顸的她，就这样夯进记忆，形成一个凹坑。这就是死亡的永恒性，死者就此停滞在时光中，占领了空间。要是依那帮佣的女人的宿命论来说，厨房这地方不干净，出现过黄鼠狼，还有老女人来抱怨鬼叫扰了她睡眠。然而，这又说明厨房是有渊源的地方。有渊源的地方，总是生生息息，于是，万象生罗。所以，我说它肥沃，那油腻泡软了的地板，什么长不出来！

　　有几次，房管所木工来修地板，他们拆去腐朽的木板，钻进地板下面，敲打修理龙骨。里面黑沉沉的，堆积着漏进地板缝的陈年旧物，筷子，勺子，发卡，顶针，肥皂头，白菜头，肉骨头，这就是厨房的地质层。再后来，连龙骨也朽烂了，房管所彻底拆除地板，推来碎石，铺上了水泥。厨房里的木质的膏腴的霉气味换上了水泥的凉森气，别小看气味了，气味改变了这间厨房的属性，它不再是柔软的肉感的属性，而是冷和硬。这就像是一种蜕，从此，小孩子都长大。大人呢，趋向老，然后，是死亡，不是那样不期然的夭折，而是寿终正寝。

2007年5月18日　上海

The Public Kitchen[1]

○ Wang Anyi

I still remember the floor of the public kitchen, the most fertile place in the whole house. The yard facing south in front of the house should have been the most fertile place, but strangely enough, it was poor and barren. A dig of no more than two centimeters under the grayish white surface of the earth might reveal a layer of decaying stones and broken bricks, which humped upward and made the ground rough and uneven. Except plantains and foxtail grasses nothing grew in this yard. Only one type of bugs lived here: the gray and withered wood lice. Compared with the poor yard, the kitchen was warm and fertile. The floor must have been given a good coat of paint at the beginning but now it was totally pasted with greasy and oily dirt. If scrubbed with soda water, it turned deplorably pale and the more terrible consequence was that it absorbed more oily things! The more it was scrubbed with soda water, the more dirt and grease it absorbed. Then, more soda water, more dirt and grease — this actually complied with the necessary rules and procedures of applying paints. By and by, the kitchen floor turned out a rich grayish black. It was every inch greasy and oily and something was likely to grow out of it![2] Indeed, something grew out of it. At the foot of the walls — if the gas cookers, the cupboards, the tables and the odds and ends on the tables were removed — a black plant ran rampant, which was called "mould". Besides, many species of creatures dwelled here, such as mice, cockroaches, lizards, spiders, house centipedes, ants and wood lice. Unlike those in the yard, the wood lice in the kitchen were bigger and fatter and their bodies were moist with luster. The wild cats with no fixed residence, more often than not, paid a visit here at irregular intervals. Besides, a yellow weasel once put in a mysterious appearance here and never showed up thereafter. Much like a zoo, the kitchen followed the natural law of mutual production and destruction:[3] Cats ate mice while lizards and spiders ate worms and bugs. This was the biological food chain! In a word, the ecology was quite active here. In certain months when the climate was dry and the air clear, after three o'clock in the afternoon, the sunlight shone into the kitchen from the back door. At this time, the school was not over and it was not the time to prepare for supper. The kitchen was tranquil. The glaring sunlight beamed in and the kitchen turned very bright. The yellowish floor with an oily luster, the black seams pasted in greasy filth, the glossy black textures and cracks of the floor, and a three-legged stool in an unpolished wooden white, all added a special charm to the kitchen, which appeared fresh, bright and almost dazzling. After some time, as the rays of sunlight shifted, the clear-cut lines and spots on the floor became blurred with soft edges and the kitchen turned lively and animated. Soon, the kitchen bustled with noise and activity.[4]

I didn't know the wet nurse's name and hometown. With a strong and well-proportioned figure, a rosy face and a pair of raven-black plaits long enough to reach her waist, she looked quite young, even in a child's eyes. She always dressed herself up in bright blue clothes and a pair of cotton shoes with button loops. In this house, she breast-fed that baby and also did some odd jobs. I always saw her chopping food in the kitchen, with her back to the door. Whatever she was chopping, she always took up a piece and quickly threw it into her mouth; at the same time, she turned around and cast a vigilant look outside. Perhaps she was afraid that someone was looking at her? Perhaps her habit came from her personal experience? Who knew! The little girl baby she was nursing was put in a wooden crib with bars on all four sides. Holding it under her arm, she brought it with her wherever she went. In the afternoon, as the kids came back from school, she put the crib at the back door in the alley. Then, the kids would come to play with the baby and even took it out of the crib, holding it in their arms and walking around in the alley. It seemed that the wet nurse lent a big toy to all the kids, who were supposed to take care of it and play with it on shifts. Of course, it was inevitable that sometimes a kid couldn't hold the baby steady and let it drop. On this occasion, before the baby uttered a cry that kid was so scared that he immediately burst into wails.[5] As a matter of fact, nobody would put blame on him. In an age that encouraged childbirths, children were not much pampered at all.[6]

In my memory, the wet nurse was muddle-headed.[7] Is it my memory that got blurred after so many years? Or was she indeed like this? I didn't know. People or things we bear in our minds for too long tend to wear a muddle-headed expression,[8] just like old movies played from worn-out films — unresponsive and laggy. I always saw the wet nurse sitting there alone, holding the baby in her arms and letting it suck her breasts. It was hard for me to tell her attitude towards the baby. Did she love it? Or, on the contrary, did she hate it for sucking up all her milk which would otherwise be saved for her own child? Obviously, she was not the emotional or sensational type, but she was young, so young that she must have accumulated surges of energy in her body. Therefore, her silence weighed a lot. The one who took charge of supervising the wet nurse was the baby's grandma, who did most of the housework. The old woman was supposed to enjoy considerable standing in her family, yet her own mother-in-law was alive and surpassed her in seniority. The daughters-in-law in the family were no longer young and they earned their own money independently. Their mother-in-law, the baby's grandma, therefore, kept silent in the family. However, this old woman had an amazing sense of humor. When people were talking, she always gave an understanding smile, which revealed not only her sense of humor but also her personality, her kind and accommodating personality enabling her to appreciate others' wisdom.[9] Although nominally the master of the household, she did more work than the wet nurse. Such house chores as buying food, cleaning, cooking and washing were all within her duty, while the wet nurse, in most of her time, just sat there, feeding the baby in her arms. When the grandma was free, she sat beside the wet nurse. Her eyes, though much older than the wet nurse's, were still keen and sensitive. Perhaps it was her rich personal experience that contributed to her acute sensitivity. As a result, though years have slipped by, the old woman has remained distinct and impressive in my memory. In contrast, the wet nurse appears hollow, without content. Nevertheless, her hollowness would turn into profundity sometime in the future. I will talk about it later.[10]

The old grandma and the young wet nurse sat side by side on their stools. They listened to whom speaking? The maidservant, who was regarded as the "elite" of the kitchen. As long as she opened her mouth, adults and children all felt an urge to listen to her attentively. She was young, aged 30 at most, which, nevertheless, was considered a quite mature age at that time. She was very experienced and well-informed, although that statement was of course hard to put to verification. When she talked, her manner was, to be frank, beyond words! Her well-chiseled face was highlighted in affirmative lines and as a result appeared flat and hard in the vague picture of my mind, while others, for example, the wet nurse who was always accompanied by a shadow behind her, took on some stereo-effect in my memory. This maidservant's double-fold eyelids, her narrow nose, the vertical wrinkle on her usually tautened nose bridge, and her thin lips added a sharpness to her clear-cut face.[11] She was single — a status that sounded a little too modern for a maidservant. However, it was, in truth, inevitable and reasonable. Who dared to marry her! In her class, she was supposed to marry a man in her hometown in the countryside or a worker in Yangshupu (an industrial district of Shanghai), also originating from her hometown, but obviously such men didn't deserve her. What if a clerk in the city? How could a clerk's wife be a maidservant? So she remained single. Actually, she was absolutely capable of leading a different life. She served a couple who had no kids, which was perfect for her, for she didn't need to see to the kids, who were untidy and smelly in her eyes! Feces, urine and the smell of milk! That wet nurse always gave off such sickly smell! This woman was different. She was pure as jade and clean as ice. All her things — I mean her belongings, not her master's — were all stashed separately in a meticulous manner. Her bowl had golden rims and her chopsticks had silver foils. I really can't imagine what elaborate feeling she cherished in her heart and how she collected and protected her things in such a crowded, dingy and noisy public kitchen. Her things were so delicate! The public kitchen was so inelegant! The iron nails on the floor, like stumps on the field, might trip you up anytime! The golden rims, the silver foils as well as the warm and humid fine porcelain of her bowl go through the dark tunnel of time and are still shimmering in my memory now.[12]

Because of her, some distinguished guests often came to pay a visit. Most of them were the housewives in the neighborhood, who came to consult her about how to make a dish or how to wash a particular sort of clothes. Once, a woman even asked her to scrape the skin of her kid (as a medical treatment). Perhaps it was just because she had no kid that she had the merciless heart to do it. She put the kid on her knees. Instinctively, she inclined backward to escape the child's sour fermented smell mingled with sweat, urine, milk and tears. Then, she took out a coin, dipped it into water, and began to scrape the kid's back with it as if she were scaling a fish. By and by, she went on well with the women in the neighborhood and they often came to chat with her. Their constant visits added glitters to this humble kitchen.

As if designed to be a contrast to her, another maidservant in this kitchen was quite gentle. I often wonder how such a soft-textured soul could survive the chaotic and greasy environment! It seemed that each and every fiber of her texture was facing the danger of being ruined, but it survived, which was a convincing manifestation of its tenacity and flexibility. She had her way of living, like the Chinese Taiji with a focus on the exercise of the internal force and the implicit quality.[13] She is the vaguest part in my memory and a lot of obscurities have something to do with her. She had been a widow since she was very young, but strangely enough, after living alone for so many years, she looked still sexy and desirable. Perhaps that could account for her obscurity and dubiousness. She even possessed more sensual charm than that young and voluptuous wet nurse whose breasts, like over-ripe berries, kept flowing out milk. Besides, her soft texture was moist, from which sparks of light sprinkled here and there.[14] She took up the place beside the back window, under which there was a sink. Through the window the sunlight shone onto her aslant. As the window was covered with a layer of oily dirt like emulsified frost, the sunlight became vague and misty — so did she. Unlike that "elite" maidservant, whose keenness and acuteness were quite impressive, this woman appears indistinct in my memory. Her image is not clear-cut; instead, it is integrated into its surroundings. It flows in all directions with uncertainty but never disappears. It shares the similar feature with mercury: If a body of mercury is broken into pieces, all the pieces will soon gather and become a whole, intact and complete. That capable and acute maidservant was a well-welded whole piece while this one was glued together with broken pieces; as a result, she was fragile and imbued with tender sentiments.[15]

It was she who saw the weasel which I mentioned above. At the sight of it, she was greatly frightened and turned pale, tears streaming down her cheeks. According to the customs in her hometown in the countryside, weasels were ominous animals associated with bad luck. Hence, she told others not to reveal that she had seen a weasel. However, some naughty kids, just for fun, often caught her off guard and shouted at her, "Here comes the weasel!" They were not afraid of her sullen and angry expression at all. Unlike her, that "elite" maidservant always looked stern and severe even if she wasn't angry. In truth, children knew the nature of everything and they themselves represented the basic instincts of human beings. They chose this gentle woman to make fun of and continued their cruel game over and over again, never being scared away by her anger. Some of them even played a weasel and kept leaping to and fro in front of her, shouting loudly, "I am a weasel! I am a weasel!" Looking at those naughty children, she smiled. Unlike that grandma whose smiles were out of humor and generosity, her smile originated from her good temper, which even made her appear a little frivolous. She seemed to be a woman in lack of principles. With the absence of firmness and density, her soft texture made her flexible and accommodating. Her belief about weasels easily collapsed. Although she didn't follow her belief persistently, her sense of foreordination kept haunting the kitchen. Why do I talk about this kitchen all the time? Because people living in the rooms in front of the kitchen and the rooms upstairs were leading a life in conformity with the prevailing and accepted values, which stood for the positive side of the society. But this kitchen was the margin of the society, carrying, more or less, some negative connotations, where the undercurrents of thoughts were flowing stealthily and rampantly. Speaking of foreordination, I have to relate another person, an old woman who occasionally paid a visit here.

Our public kitchen was open to anyone. That was quite different from other rooms of any formal residence. Each system, no matter how rigorous it is, has its omissions and the public kitchen in this house was such an omission. This old woman was unlikely to live in our residential lane. Heaven knew where she lived! Perhaps in another residential lane? Who knew! Nobody knew how she felt her way to our kitchen. She came here not for a particular person; instead, she seemed to take a fancy to the kitchen itself. Each time she came, she invariably sat on that stool, which almost broke down and often nipped a careless sitter's buttocks. Everything here had its name. We called that stool "Buttocks Pincher", and the other stool "Up-holder", for it had only three legs and the one who sat on it must keep its fourth leg up. However, not all the people here had their names. Children were called "Kid One", "Kid Two", "Kid Three" and so on; the wet nurse was called "Wet Nurse"; and all the maidservants working in this house were called "Aunt No.3", "Aunt on the Second Floor", "Aunt in the Garden" and so forth. Obviously, they were named after the place they were in the service of. To some extent, the philosophy of nature was revealed in this kitchen: All the things in nature are infused with life and they should be treated equally.

Each time she came to our kitchen, she always sat on the "Buttocks Pincher", leaning against the kitchen door, which was as greasy and dilapidated as the floor. In my memory, the kitchen door had never been closed and it clung to the wall and kept open all the time. The old woman, limp and listless, rested her back against the door and it seemed that she was too feeble to sit straight. Her body kept sliding downward and mysteriously she didn't slip onto the floor. She complained incessantly that she heard a ghost's howl, which greatly perturbed her and made her sleepless night after night. What she said sounded horrible! She was as horrible as the weasel in the eyes of that soft-textured maidservant, who always spit at the old woman's back as soon as the old woman left, saying that the old woman brought bad luck of death. She was right. Why do I suspect the old woman came from another residential lane? Because the bad luck of death she brought didn't belong to our residential lane. Sure, our kitchen was dirty and dark but it was dirty and dark under the bright sunlight just as the sun gave us the light along with its shadow. Though the old woman was such a nuisance here, the door of the kitchen was always open to her and that good-tempered maidservant believing in foreordination was always one of her faithful listeners. Indeed, she was a person in lack of principles.

When the old woman came, the most excited among her audience were us children! We huddled together and listened to her ghost stories. The women working in the kitchen wanted to drive us out, as they believed that children's ears were too clean to hear such things. However, they failed. We refused to be driven out; besides, we were afraid of walking past the old woman who sat right at the door. Indeed, we loved listening to her ghost stories but feared to get close to her. In our eyes, she and the ghost who always came to disturb her at night were one family. Her strange accent and her complaints accompanied by cries and wails were so much appealing to us, though we couldn't understand her all the time. Sometimes when we asked adults about what a ghost's howl was like, they all turned serious at once, whatever belief they held, and yelled at us: "Who on earth has heard a ghost howling? Whoever has heard it is doomed to death!" Later, the old woman no longer came and we didn't get the news of her death, either. All the people in the kitchen held their tongue, not mentioning her in the least. From then on, this old woman retired from the social network of our kitchen.

Tainted with these gloomy colors, the kitchen, instead of becoming ghastful, got more cohesive and lively. Thanks to the mysterious, unknowable and horrible forces, people in the kitchen grew more and more intimate to one another. They came to each other for mutual help and relief in time of hardships, which constantly added warmth and humidity to the kitchen. Such an environment was beneficial to the growth of those tiny species and meanwhile did good to the cultivation of people's insignificant feelings and emotions. For instance, the kids who felt wronged always came here. The kids having a quarrel with their brothers, blamed and beaten by their parents, bullied in the residential lane — the residential lane was a jungle where the weak fell prey to the strong — or framed up or ill-treated by their classmates all came here. After all, they had to find a place to complain and cry to vent their grievances![16] People here were experienced from their lives in the bottom of the society, and they saw things and made judgment with their own eyes: "What's the point of crying over such trivial matters? OK, cry for a moment, then, go back to your neighborhood, your school or your brothers. And you'd better pluck up your courage and face your problems." — They often consoled the kids in this way. Besides, special treats and secret favors always took place here. In a family, the parents had their favorite kids; likewise, in this kitchen, the maidservants also had their favorite masters, not unlike the case in an extramarital affair. When the lucky kid was called secretly into the kitchen, such foods as half a salty egg, two slices of meat, a chicken leg, a bowl of sugared flour porridge and a sweet pancake fried in fat oil, carefully stashed in the recesses of the cabinets, were produced for the preferred one. At this moment, they spoke or behaved meticulously and lightly, for fear that other kids might hear or see them. Thereupon, intimate relations were built. One sat there and the other stood. They didn't talk much but as their eyes occasionally met both of them felt a stream of infinite tenderness. In addition, the kitchen also provided a venue for kids to entertain their guests, who would otherwise be frowned upon in their own families. Under no strict disciplines, little kids enjoyed more human rights here: They made the deals of glass balls or cigarette packs; they consulted one another about the techniques of playing with various things; they talked stuff and nonsense freely. As a matter of fact, the gossips popular in Shanghai's alleys went around from puberty to maturity and from maturity to decline, and began afresh as the seeds of a grown plant was cast into the field. Now, what the kids talked about was just the sprouting period of the gossips! They huddled here, never caring about the sprays of hot oil coming out of the frying pans or the water seeped from the bottom of the sink, which almost soaked their shoes. They were driven here and there by the women in the kitchen, but like animals prone to a warm and bright place, they were reluctant to leave even at sunset when the lane turned dim and dark. To them, the lamp covered with dirt and oil shedding vague light was simply the hearth of the world. In this congested kitchen, filthy but real and solid, the shadows of these little potatoes,[17] small, thin and almost transparent, much like little puppets made of donkey skins in a shadow play, sometimes overlapped and folded and sometimes parted and scattered...

A stream of children stopped by and left their traces here. Their delicate traces put the kitchen in a state of constant activity and change. Their little bodies and their trivial joys and sorrows were tiny in size and light in weight, but they had an incredible penetrating force to slowly leak through the net of time and leave in our memory some gilded spots which have kept sparkling until today.[18] The children's formal histories were recorded in the front rooms where they lived with their parents and the primary school at the entrance of the lane. However, in this dim kitchen off the social constraints, they left their privately compiled histories and their anecdotes, which could not be placed aboveboard but perhaps were more important to their future life. Who knew? The stuff and nonsense, the hole-and-corner affairs, the ghost stories, the sad tears, and the delicious food they ate as a secretive favor might be a sort of knowledge which could make up for their formal education.[19] In every age, the orthodox education has its limitations and children need some heterodox ways to help enlarge their horizons.

Children of different backgrounds and stratums came here. Some dressed decently and looked delicate, who in reality were not compatible with the environment here, and some, in rags, wearing a sallow complexion and always trying their best to avoid the sight of the food on the kitchen range so as to resist the temptation, were also incompatible with the atmosphere of the kitchen. However, due to their presence, the kitchen became a utopia characteristic of equality and harmony. The kitchen was a moderately developed society, where everyone could have adequate food and clothing with a slight surplus. Children coming here were not very beautiful but good-looking; their clothes were ordinary but tidy; they ate their fill at home but the food here all the same made their mouths water; they were restrained by family rules but not totally deprived of freedom. These children were the small masters of the kitchen.

That little boy from Ningbo had an olive-shaped head, in which the space of memory must be broadened from time to time. As if drawn by an experienced painter — first a swipe in the air, then an abrupt backstroke — his head must have gone through a thousand years' evolution, much like an unearthed porcelain jar with beautiful patterns which recorded the history of human civilization. He was a boy with a sense of history. His head, his accent and his clothes which always gave off a smell of certain food told a tale of his age-old heredity.[20] He was extraordinarily smart, too smart to be human. His dexterity made him more like an animal, and the only difference was that his dexterity was shown in his language, which was the manifestation of human civilization. Indeed, he was as quiet as a maiden when at rest and as nimble as an escaping hare when in action.[21] While speaking or discussing with someone, he was able to perceive the loophole of the other party instantly and uncover the disguise at once — if children also had disguises. To such a little boy, still wet in his ears, his talent must be endowed by nature — that was the only explanation for his unusual smartness. In truth, a person's endowment comes from his historical deposits. He had a pair of deft hands with long and slender fingers, which likewise must be the outcome of human civilization. When he made such tools of game as slingshots, pellets, triangular or oblong blades, cricket cages, iron rings and the spinning-tops which we called "rotter", we were greatly amazed at his hands' adroitness. Besides, when he touched those small creatures — the inhabitants in the seams of the kitchen floor such as bugs and worms, and those peripatetic wild cats — his hands were extremely delicate and tender. As he lightly scratched a cat's chest, he looked experienced and gentle. Nevertheless, his tenderness was only matched by his brutality — he tore a living earthworm apart and put the two parts on his palm, looking at them twisting and struggling before turning into two earthworms; he tore a wood louse apart, too, because he was curious about what was inside its white belly. His tenderness and brutality came from the primitive heredity, which could be traced back to the ancient times when the species formed their hierarchy according to their abilities: The strong defeated the weak, and after a very long time the triumphant one might come across the defeated one again. Both of them had a feeling of déjà vu but they couldn't recognize each other.[22] Obviously, this boy was a result of history. There were another kind of results totally devoid of history — me.

Looking back, I almost can't see my own face clearly — that is typical of those who had no history, who didn't break away from subjectivity and actually didn't come into objective existence at all. Unlike that boy with an affirmative and definite existence which went into people's memory at once and could never be pulled out, my traces were drifting, wandering and sometimes disappearing into the oblivion of time. As I hadn't dug out a time tunnel, I wasn't able to stay in the space either. This is the mutual dependence between time and space. In the case of the kitchen at that time, I seemed to be swallowed little by little by that boy with history. He mercilessly poked fun at my accent, which actually carried no accent of any locality. From my childhood, I had been speaking mandarin, a language based on the dialects of northern areas in China, reconstructed in accordance with the political needs and abridged and simplified for the purpose of wide spreading. However, in order to learn the Shanghai dialect, I had to sacrifice my standard mandarin and for so many times I tumbled upon that short and awkward "entering intonation" in the Shanghai dialect. In the end, I became a stutterer. Then, in this kitchen where people from different places gathered, I absorbed accents of various places: those maidservants' Yangzhou dialect and Wuxi dialect, the wet nurse's dialect whose origin I didn't know at all, and even that boy's Ningbo dialect. I accepted the dross of all these dialects, for I had no idea about which was good and which was bad. As a result, my mixed accent became a disgraceful mark on me, a new immigrant here. As a child, I had a biggest defect: I was not good at such children's games as "building a house", rubber-band skipping, run-and-seek and "Old wolf, old wolf, what time is it?" All these games were done in light of the rule of survival of the fittest. Shortly after I entered the game, I was knocked out. I had to stand aside, looking at them playing happily and excitedly, and then returned to the kitchen in dejection. Therefore, the kitchen was tainted with my childhood loneliness and humiliation. My humiliation came from him, that boy with history, who always mocked at my setbacks and took my frustrations as a laughing stock. How sad I was! Such sadness ran through my childhood years and, without the burden of history, it might disappear instantly without a trace like water dripping through a rock. I resort to my pen to note it down so that it, no longer subjective, could leave its objective stamp in my memory.

Another child played a role of a transition between the boy with history and me without history, whom I called "the modern girl". She looked fresher and brighter than us, bearing the color of a modern city. She was neither like the boys who had rough, disorderly and entwined lines, nor like me who was thin, frail and subject to further moulding. She was cleanly shaped with smooth lines and the fabric on her body was as thin as a cicada's wing, which wrapped her body and rimmed her outline. She was more on the materialistic side than the boy and me, which helped her obtain a relatively good position here. She and her body featured a texture of industrialization. What texture? Enamel with a man-made luster. She was a well-polished mother-of-pearl in my memory, very smooth and brilliant. Besides, she was good at playing games, but her games were different from those the boy with history always played. They were not so crude and rustic; on the contrary, hers had a metropolitan appeal. That's why I called her the modern girl! For instance, she liked making cross-stitches on a linen cloth. One cross-stitch was embroidered on four checks, and a complete pattern was made up of many crosses. As she did it, she put on such a serious air that she looked like a foreign fair lady, who had passed her prime as a result of living among alien people and lost the opportunity to get married. In addition, her belongings always took on a look of an industrial revolution. For instance, she put her bifilar rubber band through a machine-made reel of thread, which added elasticity to the rubber band, and as she skipped over the rubber band, the reel danced up and down with her feet. Besides, she could sing "Little sisters and brothers, get out my way please, or you'll break my valuable glasses"… Thanks to her, there was no missing link between the boy with history and me, and we three children were jointed into a chain, like the necklace that girls made with the leaves' stems. We sometimes pulled a leaf off a tree and rubbed it till only a stem was left. Then, we meticulously folded it into several short sections which were still connected by the clinging fiber. The stem wavering in the air, frail like a thread of a spider-web, was likely to break at any moment. That was the historical trace left on us.

Barring us three, of course there were other children coming and going in this kitchen, but their stories didn't leave me a deep impression. They were the crumbs of my memory permeating the air and changing the shadows and colors of light. In fact, they were not bland and their existence had some meaning, but they were overshadowed by us three whose meaning wasn't given too much thought at that time but as time went by whose particular connotation became more and more clearly manifested. This is the choice of memory. Doesn't it sound a little unfair? As the saying goes, the winner writes the history. The same is true with memory: A person decides what stays in his or her memory. In my memory, the other children's forms were as tiny as sand and they almost disappeared against the shadows of the more important ones. Nevertheless, they remained, with their breaths flowing here and there, and to some extent helped to revise and depict the past scenes in people's memories.

I must relate those two kids among them — a girl and her little brother. They were the frequent guests of a family, but we didn't take too much notice of them. As the time got to a point, which many people often called the turning point, we began to pay attention to them, and vice versa. In the winter vacation, it was gloomy and cold. We couldn't play games in the lane, so we gathered in the kitchen. The north-facing kitchen was also cold and damp, but we were excited to make new friends here and our relations got closer and closer minute by minute. At noon, they were invited to have lunch with that family and in the evening they were invited to have supper. And as the night fell they were invited to sleep there. The next day, the bunch of kids were reunited in the kitchen. Only in this public kitchen could we get together. Among the children from other blocks, other schools, or other lives which we were not familiar with, only one, to be exact, that girl, attracted us strongly. Her unusual temperament was new to us who were not informed or experienced. We had never seen her type.

Which historical stage should I put her in? The ancient age? The modern times? Or, like me, she hadn't created her own history? All these seemed improper. Perhaps she stood alone outside any history. Or perhaps she didn't belong to any history that I knew. Perhaps she came from other histories which I had no idea of. As is known, every block, every sort of life and even every house has its complete history, which embodies its own distinctive features in a variety of vividness. She had her luster, not of enamel but of genuine seashells. The luster of seashells was not as fresh or bright as that of enamels carefully polished by human hands. It was dimmer. However, the structure of genuine seashells was densely organized and had its unique profundity. She was such a seashell with a particular luster which came from some unknown source and reflected a state of constant flux. Like a small raft, she ran through the river of time and always emerged in my memory.

She always wore a scarf, which ran along her hairline on both sides of the face, crossed under her chin, went after her neck and formed a tight slipknot there. The scarf set off the contours of her delicate head, smooth hair and tight plaits. She had a well-proportioned figure and wore a cotton-padded coat with the pattern of red checks. When she had a talk with us, she always stood straight among us, with her hands in her pockets. Her complexion and her posture showed no sign of feeling cold, while her little brother felt so cold that he huddled beside the gas stove, his lips turning blue and pale. If something was cooking on the stove, he might reach for it to warm himself, only to jerk his hand back when stung by the flame. This was a frail boy. In contrast, she was strong, healthy, resistent to cold, and she even radiated light and heat. Her body obviously had a balanced endocrine system and looked extraordinarily strong. We observed her each and every action in an appreciative and envious manner. Strangely, we girls were more attracted by her, perhaps because girls were more sensitive to her femininity. Boys were utterly ignorant at that age.

One day passed quickly. We didn't let her leave. The second day passed and she didn't leave, either. Obviously, she got along well with us, and like a fish getting into water, she was happy to be together with us. Her face turned more and more ruddy and her mood better and better. But her little brother was withering. He was pale and faint and like a snowman beside a stove he was thawing and shrinking. Finally, the two were ordered to leave. Turning a deaf ear to it, the girl showed her unusual calmness. Right at this time, a cold wave came. The wind howled and surged in the lane, which made us more excited as if something rare and unusual were going to happen! A cloud of redness even appeared under the weak boy's eyes and slowly spread to his whole face. In the end, their parents came and brought them away. Their story rang down the curtain.[23] At this time, the boy was in a high fever. In fact, he was ill at the beginning but none of us paid attention to him. Living in the shade of his charming sister, he had to endure. Nobody knew what strenuous struggles he had made within his tiny body. But for the later event, he would have vanished silently and totally seceded from our memory. The later event was that he died. He didn't die of his disease at that time or his later series of diseases but died abruptly and quietly with no reason. The sudden death of the boy has remained a mystery till now. As if metals collided with stones, the death of such a feeble child pounded out a big hole with broken edges in our memories.

What about the adults in the kitchen? You might not guess out. That wet nurse, most young and strong but muddle-headed, died, also leaving a big hole in our memories. The dead stayed permanently in their time and space, which best demonstrated the eternity of death. In the words of that maidservant who believed in foreordination, this kitchen was not clean and auspicious for a weasel once appeared and the old woman often came to complain about ghosts. But seen from another perspective, the kitchen was a place of rich origins, where all kinds of creatures bred and reproductions ran in endless cycles. Hence, I would like to consider it a fertile place. Out of its floor soaked in oil, anything could grow!

Later, workers sent by the housing management office came to repair the floor. As they took the rotten boards off and tried to mend the under-floor supports, they found age-old odds and ends underneath, such as chopsticks, spoons, hairpins, thumbstalls, pieces of soaps, cabbage stumps and bones, which constituted the geological stratum of the ground in the kitchen. Thereafter, the under-floor supports completely broke down and workers had to remove the original floor and paved the kitchen ground with gravel and a layer of cement. Finally, the moldy smell was replaced by the cold concrete odor. You'd better not make light of the function of smells! The new smell changed the kitchen. Its feel turned from soft and fleshy to cold and hard. The kitchen experienced its metamorphosis. Since then, children grew up while adults aged and proceeded toward death. They had natural deaths, not the untimely ones, indeed.

May 18, 2007　Shanghai

1. 《厨房》是王安忆短篇小说的代表作。在这篇小说中，时间是凝固的，空间缓慢变迁，缺少戏剧冲突，通篇都是对记忆中的厨房的景物、厨房中的细枝末节的琐事以及厨房中的人物的描写。描述细致缜密，语言朦胧隐晦，意象丰富，浓墨重彩，多种修辞手法并用。翻译的困难在于：一、原文中有些可意会而不可言传的、模糊朦胧的文字，在具体、逻辑的英语语言中是否可以正确体现；二、原文所创造的整体氛围或意境，译文是否可以再现，译文读者是否可以感受到。

2. It was every inch greasy and oily and something was likely to grow out of it! every inch彻彻底底地、完全地。这个短语简单生动，例如：He is every inch a man. 他绝对是个爷们。

3. … the natural law of mutual production and destruction. 相生相克的自然法则。

4. "然后，噪声起来。"这里指到了晚饭时间，厨房不再安静，人们开始忙碌起来。Soon, the kitchen bustled with noise and activity.

5. On this occasion, before the baby uttered a cry that kid was so scared that he immediately burst into wails. wail是哀号、大声嚎的意思，burst into wails 指小孩子犯了错，怕大人说，心里害怕，于是放声哭嚎起来。sob或weep用在这里都不合适。

6. "在多子女的年代里，孩子都是这么摔摔掼掼长起来的。" In an age that

encouraged childbirths, children were not much pampered at all. 在那个年代，一家养育多个孩子，家长对孩子不是特别娇宠，孩子也不是那么娇气。pamper 纵容、娇宠、娇惯。

7. "颠顸"意思是糊里糊涂的、笨拙的、木木的，所以翻译成muddle-headed。

8. "时间久远的事"此处补全原文省略的部分，译为people or things we bear in our minds for too long.

9. "……当人们说话，她适时发出会心的微笑。这微笑流露出的还不止是幽默，还有一种秉性，敦厚的秉性，这让她能够消受别人的智慧。"这句中有几个翻译难点："会心的"、"秉性"、"敦厚的秉性"、"能够消受"，在翻译时要注意作者的语气，把这些关键点用合适的英文表达出来。When people were talking, she always gave an understanding smile, which revealed not only her sense of humor but also her personality, her kind and accommodating personality enabling her to appreciate others' wisdom. accommodating 通融的、具有调节性的、包容的。

10. "她的神情，即便隔了岁月，依然是比奶妈灵敏，灵敏于各种感受，这是由阅历决定的。于是，她的身型就有了些微的轮廓，破开岁月的氤氲。而奶妈是一片空洞，这空洞将在某个时候变得深邃，以后会谈到这一点。"全文像"身型有了些微的轮廓"、"破开岁月的氤氲"、"空洞"、"变得深邃"这样的表达很多。汉语的朦胧性、诗性给译者的创造性提供了很大空间，译者需要根据自己的理解，转换成合适的、符合逻辑的英文表达。

11. "她的脸很清晰，在整个混沌的景象中，唯有这张脸，是以肯定的线条构勒的，也因此变得平面，而其他的印象倒是有一些立体的效果，比如奶妈，因为有影调。也因为此，她变得尖锐了。她的眼睛，有着明显的双睑，鼻子有些窄，鼻梁这里因为常常是收紧的，就有了一道竖纹，嘴唇是单薄的，因而使笔触更加锋利。"这是一段人物形象的描写，仿佛素描画一样，简单几笔勾勒出一个活灵活现的形象。

12. "她的碗具上的金边银片，还有温润的细瓷，波光粼粼穿行在时间的黑暗隧道。"The golden rims, the silver foils as well as the warm and humid fine porcelain of her bowl go through the dark tunnel of time and are still shimmering in my memory now. 注意原句修辞手法的运用。

13. "你甚至会惊异，这样柔软的质地如何还能在这一片混沌中占位，似乎轮廓的每一条边线都有危险被吞噬淹没，而它却依然存在着。这说明它的韧劲，颇有弹性。这是以圆为单位而组合的占位，有些像太极，含而不露，用的是内功。"这几句是对一个人物的描写，写得含蓄优美，用"圆"、"太极"、"含而不露"、"内功"、"韧性"、"弹性"等等写一个人的形象和性格。注意译文中的斜体字。I often wondered how such a soft-textured soul could survive the *chaotic and greasy* environment! It seemed that *each and every* fiber of her texture was facing the danger of being ruined, but it survived, which was a convincing manifestation of its *tenacity and flexibility*. She had her way of living, like the Chinese Taiji with a focus on the exercise *of the internal force* and *the implicit quality*. 原文就很含蓄，译文应该与原文风格对应，也不能太直白。

14. "这柔软的质地同时还是湿润的，就有些幽微的光悄然挥洒出来，这里亮一点，那里亮一点。"原句写得含蓄、可意会而不可言传，表达的是一个女佣在"我"记忆中留下的印记。Besides, her soft texture was moist, from which sparks of light sprinkled here and there.

15. "那精英女佣是焊得很牢的一个整体，这却是由细枝末节合成，就变得很是黏腻缠绵。"That capable and acute maidservant was a well-welded whole piece while this one was glued together with broken pieces; as a result, she was fragile and imbued with tender sentiments. "黏腻缠绵"译为imbued with tender sentiments。

16. "诸如此类的冤情，翻是翻不过来了，总要有个地方诉说吧！"After all, they had to find a place to complain and cry to vent their grievances! vent one's grievances 诉说冤情，发泄不满。

17. "小萝卜头"翻译成了small potato，即小孩子、小人物、不重要的人。potato 在英语中可以指某一种人，例如：big potato 大人物；sweet potato 甜美的人儿：The daughter of our respected Salt Commissioner Lin is also a sweet potato. She is the sweetest sweet potato of them all. (David Hawkes,《红楼梦》英译本)

18. "他们的小身子和小悲欢，虽然是小小的体积，分量又轻，可是具有穿透力，或者说渗透力，从漫漫时光滴漏进来，给记忆镀上亮闪闪的斑点。"描述中有比喻，有拟人，经常把一些看不见说不清的感受或感情用具体实在的"客观对应物"体现。翻译的时候，要尽力保留原文的意象和修辞，因为这也正是原文最突出的特点。Their little bodies and their trivial joys and sorrows were tiny in size and light in weight, but they had an incredible penetrating force, which slowly leak through the net of time and leave in our memory some gilded spots which have kept sparkling until today.

19. "那些杂七杂八的怪力乱神的鬼话，那些伤心的泪水，鬼鬼祟祟吃到嘴里的偏食，也是一种知识呢，填补着正统教育的盲区。" The stuff and nonsense, the hole-and-corner affairs, the ghost stories, the sad tears, and the delicious food they ate as a secretive favor might be a sort of knowledge which could make up for their formal education. stuff and nonsense 胡说八道，hole-and-corner affair 偷偷摸摸、鬼鬼祟祟的事情。

20. "他是一个有历史感的小男孩子，他的头型，口音，还有衣服上时常散发出的某一种食物的气味，都透露出悠久的遗传。" He was a boy with a sense of history. His head, his accent and his clothes which always gave off a smell of certain food told a tale of his age-old heredity. to tell a tale of... 说明了问题、揭露了实情。

21. 中国成语"静若处子，动若脱兔"直译为 as quiet as a maiden when at rest and as nimble as an escaping hare when in action。

22. "彼此认不得对方，又觉似曾相识。" Both of them had a feeling of déjà vu but they couldn't recognize each other. déjà vu 似曾相识，此词来自法语。

草丛
中

◎ 司 屠

　　透过草丛，陈张村的陈法根窥视着一个女人的背部，主要是屁股。刚才他收工回家，在树林间穿行，不曾想到前方会有这样一对屁股等着他。在他正要自草丛间走出时他看到了它。他便仿佛干了什么见不得人的事，随即蜷缩身子，往后躲了一躲。就此他潜伏了下来。此处位于树林的边缘，草丛很高，应该可以将他的身子隐没在该女子的视线之外，一旦她转过身来朝草丛中看的话。

　　必须承认，前方是一对不错的屁股。由于女人背向着陈法根在地上挖掘，因而它朝着草丛翘起，不时地连同腿部四面摆动。如同所有的屁股，它被从中间一分为二，但和陈法根老婆的屁股明显不同的是，它更大更圆而更紧绷，使得短裤的形状凸现无遗。即将落山的阳光笼罩其上，更增其光彩。从而使得陈法根很想把他的手放在那上面，一边各一只。这对于一双摸惯了扁平的屁股的手而言，将会是何等新鲜的感受啊！

　　那么她的奶子呢？应该也有着一对翘翘的奶子，但这仅是一种设想。如果要证实事实确实如此，方法如下：一个是陈法根横向绕到山的对面去，也就是位于该女人的正面。但，一旦他绕到那里，她无须走掉，只须将身子转一下，他岂不是白跑一趟。何况对面可潜伏之处与该女子的奶子之间不像他此刻与她的屁股那么近，即便到时她依然保持着原状，也有可能因为距离的关系使得陈

384

法根不能获得准确的看法。因此，陈法根寄希望于该女子自己转过身来，从而使她的奶子面向着他的藏身之处。这么一来，他便可心满意足地下山了。可是她却久久不转过身来。一如既往、坚定不移地在他眼前晃荡着她的屁股。这他妈的算什么意思！此种情形，终于使得陈法根忍无可忍。他告诉自己，如果她再不转过身来让他看到，他只好冲出去看了。

光阴荏苒，四十年后，陈法根仰卧在床上，回首往事，上述情景历历在目。他记得他数完三下，便从草丛间钻出。他的速度很快，同时确保了悄无声息。他很满意自己有如此上佳的表现。这一念头闪过，他已到她身后。尚未等她回过身来，他便一个俯冲，将她从背后按倒在地。他将绕在她裤腰上的绳子扯掉，扒下她的裤子，使她的屁股部分裸露，从中他还发现了一颗痣。但在当时，这对他来说是远远不够的。于是，他一手按住她的头，使其不能回头，另一只手在脚的帮助下将她的裤子包括短裤也脱了下来。虽说在此过程中，他遭遇了一番有力的挣扎，但他还是比较顺利地进入了她。在那一瞬间，她的身体终于松弛了下来。

他默默地搞着，而她则被他默默地搞着。

完事之后，陈法根迅速提起裤子，兔子一般跑回到了草丛中。即便此女于此时坐起身子，茫然四顾，最多也只能看到他的背影。而她是谁，他却很清楚，虽说自始至终他都没有看到她的脸，但他知道她是外村张屠夫的女儿张菊花，因为这块地是张屠夫的。听说张屠夫的女儿不久就要结婚了。

虽然这些年来陈法根曾不止一次观察过张菊花的奶子（可惜是隔着衣服，果然其圆无比），可那次在他搞张菊花时，他却没有看到，甚至都忘了摸上一把。想到这里，便有微笑自陈法根的老脸上显现。他叹了一口气，干咳着示意老婆靠近。

咳，咳，你把张菊花给我叫来。

张菊花？都什么时候了，叫张菊花？

我叫你叫，你就去给我叫。

如果条件允许，陈法根此时便会伸出手去，给他老婆一个耳光。但现在的情况是，他连说话的力气也不太有了。陈法根老了，快要死了。

陈法根本想叫张菊花的儿子不妨也一道来，但这也确实太唐突了。即便是对于一个将死之人，也显得有些过分。这些年来，陈法根一直关注着张菊花儿子的成长，尤其是在他小时候，陈法根待他如同己出。根据日期推算，他确实有可能是陈法根种下的。况且他一点也不像张菊花的老公。陈法根觉得像他，越看越像。年青时，他曾旁敲侧击和张菊花谈及此事，但看不出张菊花有什么特别的表情。她掩藏得很好。在这之前及之后，他曾不止一次对她进行过试探。有时，他真想干脆就向她挑明了事。一次，当他经过那块地时，张菊花正好也在。他便故意加快步伐进入草丛。虽说他没有回头，但可以感觉到张菊花停了手中的活，将身体的全部重量置于锄柄之上，若有所思地目送他远去。

有时候，陈法根也不能不怀疑，张菊花当时可能是故意让他得手。当她在草丛外摇曳她的屁股时，很有可能她已经发觉她身后潜伏着一个男人。要不然，她为什么老是使她的屁股冲着他的方向呢？她只须调个向，使她的奶子面向着草丛，不就什么事都没了。

不管怎么说，陈法根和他老婆都应该感谢张菊花，如果不是因为他总是将他老婆当作是张菊花，这些年里，他老婆就不可能在他身上获得这么多的欢乐，而他也很有可能早就对此事丧失了兴趣。试想一下，你将和同一个女人干上三十年之久，岂不乏味之至！

张菊花在陈法根老婆的带领下走了进来。陈法根示意众人退下。亲戚们磨蹭再三，最后只剩陈法根老婆一人徘徊不去。张菊花则站在门边，带着几乎是哀求的神情看着陈法根的老婆。陈法根不发一言以此来表达他对他老婆不执行他意图的愤怒，直至他老婆慑于他往日的威严、无能为继走出门去。于是，陈法根的手指在席子上点了两下，示意张菊花近前。

两分钟后，张菊花骂骂咧咧穿过客堂，在跨越陈家的门槛时差一点绊倒在地。张菊花一个趔趄出得门去。

你家法根死昏头了，说什么乱七八糟的，真是的。

等到疑惑不解的陈法根的老婆和亲戚们急不可耐地涌入室内，他们发觉陈法根已经死了。他的眼睛向着房梁张着，一副死不瞑目的样子。

那么，在死之前，陈法根会想些什么呢？如下：张菊花之所以不承认她被强奸，可能性有二，一个是她被强奸过，但不愿承认。这种可能性的确不小。但对于一个将死之人，她又何苦如此。所谓天知地知，你知我知。陈法根一死，便只有张菊花知了。她应该不必担忧对他承认了此事。难道说她并没有被强奸，难道说那只是他陈法根年青时做的一个梦之类，或者是他陈法根强奸的是另一个女人，这后一种可能也不是没有，毕竟到人家的地头掘点土豆是一件稀松平常的事。若是此种情况，他陈法根偷偷地爱慕着张菊花达四十年之久，岂不是有些莫名其妙了。

　　陈法根感觉到了自己的笑。他拍拍屁股，从地上站起身来。此时，太阳几乎已完全落下山去，该女子扛着一篮土豆离开了地。陈法根自草丛中走出，仿佛他正好走出草丛。由于他故意弄出了一点声响，使得前者回过头来，嫣然一笑。如他所料，她就是张菊花。

In the Grass

○ *Si Tu*

Through dense clusters of grass, Chen Fagen, who lived in Chen-Zhang Village, was peeping at a woman's back,[1] especially her buttocks. Just now, Fagen, after working in the field for the whole day, was on his way home, and as he walked through the woods, out of his expectation, he found a pair of buttocks waiting for him ahead. As if he had done something underhand, he quickly huddled his body and hid himself in the grass. His hiding place was at the edge of the woods, where the grass grew so tall that he was unlikely to be found even if she turned round and looked to his direction.

That was a pair of splendid buttocks, indeed. Bending down, the woman was digging something, with her buttocks up toward him. With the movement of her legs, that pair of buttocks wriggled and moved back and forth. Like all the buttocks, hers also had two parts, separated in the middle, but different from his wife's, this pair was bigger, rounder and firmer, which made the shape of her underpants visible; in addition, the glow of the setting sun added irresistible charm to it. At this moment, Chen Fagen really had an impulse to put both of his hands on her buttocks, one hand on the left part and the other on the right. To his hands, which were used to the small and flat buttocks for years, it must be a fresh and exciting experience![2]

What about her breasts? They must be ample and firm, too! Of course, this was just his imagination. To prove it, one way would work: He could walk around to the opposite side to see the woman's front. However, he was afraid to make the efforts in vain — she might turn back without even moving away. Besides, the distance between his new hiding place and her breasts was not as close as that between him and her buttocks now. Even if she maintained her posture, far away from her, he would find it difficult to make the right judgment. Therefore, he had to put all his hope on the woman herself. He expected her to turn around and let her breasts face him directly. Then, he would have a close look and could go down the mountain

388

with satisfaction. But instead of turning round, she persisted in her position and posture, wriggling her buttocks in a dogged manner. What on earth did she mean![3] Chen Fagen could no longer bear it! Secretly he made up his mind. "If she doesn't turn around, I'll go for her!"

How time flew! Forty years later, Chen Fagen lay on his bed and what happened on that day came back clearly to him: After counting one, two, three, he dashed out of grass quickly and silently. He was satisfied with his excellent performance. In a flash, he was behind her. There was no time for her to make any response. He threw himself at her and brought her to the ground from behind. He untied the rope around her waist and yanked off her pants. On her exposed buttocks, he saw a mole. This was far from enough. Pressing her head with one hand, he took off her underpants with the other hand, with the help of his feet. During this process, he confronted a fit of forceful struggle. Nevertheless, he succeeded in entering her at last. She paralyzed at that moment, giving up all her resistance.

He did it to her silently, and she stood it through silently.

After it was done, he stood up, quickly tied his pants and escaped into the grass like a rabbit. Even if she sat up in time, she had no time to see clearly who he was. At most she could have a view of his back. But he knew her, though he didn't see her face throughout the process. He was sure she was the daughter of Zhang, a butcher living in another village, for the land here belonged to the Zhang family. He heard that Zhang's daughter named Zhang Juhua was going to get married.

All these years, Chen Fagen was interested in her breasts and more than once he fixed his eyes on her ample bosom (under her clothes, they seemed round and firm). However, when he made love to her, he was in such a hurry that he even forgot to have a look at them and touch them! At the thought of this, a complicated feeling welled up in his heart and a smile appeared on his aged face. He sighed and coughed, motioning his wife to come near.

"Ask Zhang Juhua to come here."

"Zhang Juhua? Why? Why do you want to see her? "

"Do as I tell you!"[4]

If possible, he would slap his wife in the face.[5] But now, the situation was different: He barely had enough strength to speak. He was aged, dying.

He thought it would be better to ask Zhang Juhua to bring her boy to his bedside, but on a second thought, he gave up the idea which was too impudent.

Though he was dying, he didn't dare to go too far.[6] During all these years, he had been caring for her son, especially when the boy was small. He treated the boy as his own child, for the boy presumably was his progeny. The boy didn't look like her husband in the least! Instead, he found the boy's resemblance to him even more pronounced with every secret comparison. When he was young, Chen fagen once chatted with Zhang Juhua and made oblique references of her son, but she remained her usual self and didn't appear to be flurried at all. Maybe she was trying to cover up the fact. Thinking of this, he tried to speak to her meticulously for several times. Sometimes, he really wished to lay the cards on the table![7] Once, he happened to find Zhuang Juhua working in that place again, and he sped up into the grass on purpose. Although he didn't turn his head, he could feel that she stopped working, leaning on the hoe and staring at him thoughtfully as he went away.

Sometimes, Chen Fagen couldn't help conjecturing that she deliberately made him have sex with her, and that when she wiggled her buttocks in the grass she might have already discovered him behind her. Otherwise, why did she keep her buttocks to him all the time? In fact, if she had turned around and let her breasts face him, nothing would have happened.

Anyway, both Chen Fagen and his wife felt grateful to Zhang Juhua. Year in and year out, when he made love to his wife he always imagined that he was having sex with Chen Juhua, and as a result, his wife indeed got a great deal of sensual pleasure from him and his imagination. How boring it was to make love to the same woman for more than 30 years! Without his imagination, perhaps he lost interest in sex long long ago!

Led by his wife, Zhang Juhua came in. He gestured the people around to leave the room. They dilly-dallied and went out,[8] except his wife who lingered there, unwilling to leave. Standing by the door, Zhang Juhua cast an imploring glance at his wife, and he kept silent to show his dissatisfaction and even fury to his wife's disobedience. Finally, his wife succumbed to his residual awe and left the room. Chen Fagen tapped the bed with his two fingers, signaling Zhang Juhua to come close.

Two minutes later, Zhuang Juhua burst out, swearing and cursing all her way. As she walked to the doorsill she stumbled and almost fell over herself.

"Chen Fagen has lost his mind! What nonsense he is talking about! What's wrong with your husband?" Zhang Juhua said before she staggered away.

Totally at a loss, his wife and relatives rushed into the room, only to find him dead. His eyes were wide open, staring at the ceiling. It seemed that he died with everlasting regret.[9]

Then, in his final moments, what did Chen Fagen think about? Perhaps the following: Why didn't she admit she was raped by him? There were two possibilities: First, she was raped indeed but she was unwilling to admit it. It was really possible! But to him, a dying man, what was the point of denying the fact? After Chen Fagen died, only she knew it. Nobody else would know it except Heaven and Earth. She shouldn't be so worried! The second possibility: She was not raped at all. What Chen Fagen kept in mind all his life was but a youthful fantasy. Or the woman he raped was someone else? After all, stealing some potatoes from the neighbor's land was not unusual in those years. If the latter surmise held water, wasn't it ridiculous for him to yearn for the wrong woman for forty years?

He smiled. He knew he was smiling. He patted the dirt off his pants and stood up. At this moment, the sun had already set and the woman was about to leave the land, carrying a basket of potatoes on her shoulder. Chen Fagen pretended that he happened to walk past the grass. He made some sound intentionally. She turned her head and beamed at him.[10] As he expected, she was Zhang Juhua.

注 释

1. peep at 偷看。英语中表示看的短语很多，在翻译时要灵活使用，例如：ogle at/ peer at/ glance at/ glimpse at/ gaze at/ stare at/ glare at/ fix one's eyes on/ pore over/ clap one's eyes on/ leer at等等。

2. "必须承认，前方是一对不错的屁股。由于女人背向着陈法根在地上挖掘，因而它朝着草丛翘起，不时地连同腿部四面摆动。如同所有的屁股，它被从中间一分为二，但和陈法根老婆的屁股明显不同的是，它更大更圆而更紧绷，使得短裤的形状凸现无遗。即将落山的阳光笼罩其上，更增其光彩。从而使得陈法根很想把他的手放在那上面，一边各一只。这对于一双摸惯了扁平的屁股的手而言，将会是何等新鲜的感受啊！"从以上这段，可见这篇小说的语言风格：直白、平实、大胆、幽默。翻译时应尽量注意选用风格比较对等的单词和短语。

3. "一如既往、坚定不移地在他眼前晃荡着她的屁股。这他妈的算什么意思！" But instead of turning round, she persisted in her position and posture, wriggling her buttocks in a dogged manner. What on earth does she mean! "坚定不移地"可以用 pertinacious、persistent、stubborn、obstinate等。这里用的是in a dogged manner。

4. 原文对话没有用引号，译文照顾到英语行文习惯用了引号。

5. If possible, he would slap his wife in the face. "耳光"可以翻译为a slap on the face或者a box on the ear, "打某人耳光"可译为slap one's face或者box one's ear。

6. He thought it would be better to ask Zhang Juhua to bring her son to his bedside, but on a second thought, he gave up the idea which was too impudent. Though he was dying, he didn't dare to go too far. on a second thought 或on second thoughts 转念一想，impudent 鲁莽、唐突，go far / go too far 太过分、过火。

7. "有时，他真想干脆就向她挑明了事。" Sometimes, he really wished to lay the cards on the table! "挑明"可以翻译为bring … into the open或者lay bare …。这里译为lay the cards on the table 摊牌。

8. dilly-dally 磨蹭，磨磨蹭蹭。

9. His eyes were open, staring at the ceiling. It seemed that he died with everlasting regret. 成语"死不瞑目"意译为die with everlasting regret。

10. "嫣然一笑"可以翻译为：give a pleasant smile、give a sweet smile、give a charming smile、smile gently, 等等。这里译为beam at。beam有"微笑"、"灿烂的笑"、"发出光和热"的意思。明媚的一笑，仿佛照亮了陈法根的一生。

耳朵环

◎ 郁 俊

　　辗转经过几户中上人家，小刘就出了名，被人相中去上海做住家阿姨。介绍的亲朋当然话得花好桃好，人口哪样爽清，哪样笃定，就一个台湾老太；生活何等轻松，又是场伙大，家境富贵，给的薪水是上海行情。小刘你乡俗就是家家有女人行走城里，这个差事，倘被你的乡邻听到，怕她们不眼红？你厂里夜班做得瞌眬颠倒，南京城东的那户日本人又下流下作，还不如索性走得长远些，横竖小孩子大了，有你男人管教，不用再操闲心。那个台湾老太住的场伙，只怕有我们前年去拧螺丝的厂房那般大，又是闹市，上海静安寺南京路啊。小刘听了，嘱咐了家里，当夜打两个包，坐长途车一路闻着臭袜子味道进了上海。司机老鬼，掐算得分秒不差，车进站时天方亮，驾驶座上方的小电视机里《江湖情》正好给字幕，已经走调的片尾曲还没听完，周润发万梓良都只留下一个影，她已经站在了水门汀地面上，小雨滚圆，一只坑一只坑砸给人看。她拿出手机给家里打电话，推敲了一下怎么说，冲口第一句却是，钟哥，车站是乱得不能再乱。

　　长途汽车站在新客站贴隔壁，过恒丰路桥已是静安区，小刘捏紧写有台湾女人地址电话的纸片，看迎面是新闸路，几栋鎏金的大门面买卖立在那里，都是多层的夜总会，写着中国和日本的字。她原本在足疗城桑拿房做过大锅菜厨子，点点头，晓得上海钞票多，流出来，这种场伙比南京的看来还要吓人。

　　小刘从出租车窗里张望出去，阴雨天也是人潮滚涌，仿佛大难临头，没有见一个人立停下来，她只好想自己的心事。出租车一路又堵又赶，停顿得她有些嗝酸，想摁键开窗，司机已经停了车问：刷不刷卡，到了。

　　闹市边，总有可以取静的所在，而小马路的门牌，好像完全错乱。小刘在奇偶数字间苦挣了好久，想还是找人打听问讯，看街边拥摊自重的皮匠，人物倒很和气，指点如此这般迭样伊样，"香特莉"糕饼隔壁派出所对过，一幢矮下去的洋房就是，号码钉在朝里的一面，看不见的，1949年以后重编，老住户只认以前的号码。小刘听了，死死记住转几个弯怎么怎么走，想上海人是笨，东南西北也问不清爽，一棵一棵数着梧桐树走过有花纹的上街沿，偶尔拿不定主意，看到两块紧靠着的方砖，是一脚踩在缝隙里呢，还是地角四方踏到砖中间。人家窗口散出腥香的蓝烟，正在油氽爆腌带鱼块；另有一户却不是厨房，一个男人哑壳喉咙在训小人，不多歇都静默了，只剩弄堂很深的所在，有人在洗牌。

待小刘碰开金宅的门，金老太迎了出来，上下看她，恰似人干样地一束，讲很急的台湾官话，只有少数字小刘要想一想，才明白。她突然觉得自己好比扮台湾苦戏，《青青河边草》或是旁的，置身其中，总要弄副拆污面孔出来才像。高抬腿轻落步，金宅的台阶不升反降，自地平挖下去半人多深，小刘想这倘是落暴雨，怕不是一层都尽淹了？金老太拍下门边的小白方块，走廊两边伸出的老灯，跳几下，纷纷模糊地给出一点亮。原来进门就横着走廊，面对面装嵌八块长方镜子，外框厚厚地砌了玫瑰葡萄西番莲之类，还有没卵的小天使，一旦顾盼着经过，就是百千亿万个化身形影不离地跟随，望进深处去，不免能听到影子间相互碰撞的轻微脆响和回声。

走廊尽头站着高大的另一个女人（显得金老太越发矮小得不成体统），她穿着很不体面，板起面孔来笑，又迎上来寒暄，原来是管清扫的江北严阿姨，每天早上还负责买菜顺路带过来，竖长横阔一张大脸，话听来倒还伶俐，只是不停嘴地说。小刘原本晕车就没醒，再给这两个女人瞎七搭八说到头胀，只好将就着随她们边啰嗦边引路，灯自然是随走随关。窗户窄小，上面花花绿绿敷演着西洋神仙典故，每个南房间因了这点花窗，都有几块尘扬舞蹈的彩色应和残照。

严阿姨说此地不比上海名宅枕流公寓，那边的走廊是那样弯的，这边的是这样弯的，指手画脚。账还不曾讲清爽，小刘已到自己的房间，一橱一榻，角落散堆着几袋子杂物，正对床放了台油汀，显见得是新买的。正好到了下午准点，严阿姨收好唇舌下班走了，金老太去瞌盹一个半个钟点，留下小刘自己端正行李。她先空床板上坐一坐，环顾这房间还颇周旋得过来，格局也正，松了一口气，站起来，理包之前，掏出手机看短信。

住家的阿姨，每户大同小异就这点日课，有小孩子的加一层繁难。金宅的人口太少，小刘又不是新开豆腐店，轧苗头似乎应付得来。晚饭时金老太夸奖小刘很会烧菜,招呼她同桌吃。她原本想在厨房里东窜西窜找点因头假忙,有钱人都要他们自己想像的那份干净,不过看老太一个人对着大空桌子,有点不忍,磨蹭了一会儿,想想还是爽爽气气装碗饭,坐在边上陪吃。

金老太饭后,讲究啜一口滚茶,弄茶手段的是闽俗,先细细考究小刘出身来历,末了变成了痛说家史。照金老太讲把小刘听的的说法,她守寡太早,新婚不久就怀胎做了产妇娘,生养一个男宝宝尚不满月,做电器生意的男人一场急病断送在卫生署台北医院手术台上,连医生都措手不及,小毛头名字也只好她自取。金氏娘家一脉,多少年来修桥铺路,斋僧敬佛,是个虔诚的大施主,小孩子借了这点祖荫,居然百伶百俐,卖相又好。她看看时局,学古人收拾了自家门庭,钞票暂时不缺,关门来教养这个孩子,从此指望也都在孩子身上。三姑六婆来劝她宽解一些,活动活动心思,看她崖岸高峻,渐渐生了畏惧心,不敢再攀附撩拨。孩子读书很要上进,亡夫留在上海的买卖更见发展,那97、98两个年头,钱着实好赚,她顺理成章移居静安,寻常要好的生意圈内朋友,往往住虹桥古北,她偶尔也去名都城会会联合利华的董事太太,趟数数得过来,唯有和在坎布里奇读书的儿子天天通电话,雷打不动。小刘你问厂?厂么早就开到苏州去啦,上海郊区的地皮太贵了,不对,上海哪里还有郊区?茶罢,金老太收紧面皮说,我要休息了,小刘,没事你不必过来。

夜上海,别样无啥新鲜,唯有不论阴晴,总是亮如白昼,看不清星星。小刘梳洗过,回到自己的房间,遭遇簌齐崭新的被头,身心俱软,窝在床上不想动了。天花板上的大饼灯突然坏掉,请了个白衣工人来修,那人个子不甚高,却能强摁小刘倒地,伸腿蹬在小刘胸上,再踮起脚来取灯炮。白衣工人发力一够,小刘不免痛彻心肺,皱眉醒来,觉得胸闷得不行,要找痰盂呕酸水,肋骨确实像被踏碎了一般脆痛,强忍着撑起来坐,气尚不得喘足两口,眼前尤残留电工肥腻的恶脸,却听得走廊那边,金老太房里的异动。

那是一种渐高的喘息,起初以为发自喉间肋上,后来竟能寻根去丹田,声音由低渐高,终于响得肆无忌惮,又似乎是在独白,仔细分辨,里面说了很多内容,简直是高密度的声音粉末,抑扬顿挫……这么多孤苦的夜;迅速皱缩的身体和意志;渴望哪怕一点点的温暖和可以望见的绝望将来;在隐秘的传说间与自己发出相同喘息的数不清的过客……各种动作和姿态显现出来,渐渐的声音越发响亮欣快,戏里面唱得落这句狠心话,叫十年久旱的禾苗逢甘霖,点点滴在芯。似乎每个午夜都只有用这样的手法,她的生命才可以有那么一小口润泽,能过得下去。撕扯和飞升的喊叫终于来了,小刘在门外,双腿发软隐隐等待着大概也就是这个时刻，终于她发觉周围和事先一样，又静若太初，只留下自己心动过速的闷响。

凌晨四点三十分，台湾官话飘飘然穿过镜廊，送到和小刘同样渴睡的枕头毛巾上：小……刘……小刘睁眼，披衣裳着拖鞋踢哩踏拉奔到金老太的房门口，镜子里这点影子惊慌失措看着自己的主人眼黑隆肿急冲过去，一边消隐一边议论纷纷，阿大啊，阿二啊，哪能每趟都是这个样子……金老太着灰绒困衣，端着一只骨瓷杯，对小刘说哎呀抱歉，我早上起来有个好习惯，必要喝一杯开水，润肠通便，上了年纪手指头上没螺把握不住，倾在床上了，麻烦你替我洗一洗，机洗就好，天气预报今天多云，应该有太阳。小刘答应"嗯"，伸手到床上摸摸位置，把盖被的被套拆下来，用床单一包，抱着这大卷就往外走，偏着头，不免闻了一下。严阿姨准八点来上班了，提着一袋子素食，说老太婆常年吃素，也不是一点不碰荤腥，只是不知道什么时候就会随便抽本《护生画集》就桌子上的荤菜对厨子讲报应循环，上次那个厨子听得汗毛凛凛面皮都变了颜色，所以小刘，你能常常做点素吃点素么？小刘说这个倒还不妨。严阿姨回头看花园里，百卉凋零，月季却仍有的开，铁质的户外衣架上大片的好看颜色，问小刘：洗过被单了？拉小刘立在壁角落大讲账，原来的几个阿姨是怎么走的？我说把你听，统统是洗被单洗走的，老太婆也不知道怎么搞的，三天两头往床上撒尿，然后就说打翻了水，让阿姨去洗，所以都做不长。有个阿姨做得最长，我还奇怪，辣里晓得原来她生鼻窦炎，没得知觉。

小刘终究也没做长，下午四点的火车，她一点半等着人家开了门，穿过马路走进东方典当的分号，进门，开言：先生你好。我看见你们这里黑黑的，还以为不开门。我是做阿姨的，住家保姆。我和我们主人，就住在那边，南京路和这条小马路的交界，不远。我要不是心脏不好，走过来，十分钟也不要的。

我来是给你看这个东西，值不值钱。我不太晓得你们这里的规矩，我妈说以前的典当是穷人也可以进去的，破衣服也能调钞票。老早的东西值钱，特别是吃的和着的。这副耳朵环，是我们家的老太太，送给我的，她说她没有耳洞，是她在什么外国宣扬佛事的时候，那边的太太给的。她看我有耳洞，就给了我。你看，就在这个盒子里。我虽然不是睁眼瞎，这种英文不懂。

典当里的二掌柜细细打量过盒子，开始拿正眼看她。

The Earrings

Yu Jun

After she worked for several well-off families, Xiao Liu gained quite a reputation far and near. Now, she was recommended to work as a housemaid for a family in Shanghai. Of course, that family was described and praised in superlative terms: There was only one old granny from Taiwan in that family; the life there must be very easy and comfortable; the house was spacious; and the salary was competitive. "Xiao Liu," they persuaded her, "I know there is a custom in your hometown that women always go out to work in the cities so as to earn more money to support the family, so, take it! If your neighbors know you get such a good job, I am afraid they must be green-eyed at you! The night-shift job at the factory was too exhausting and that Japanese family in the east of Nanjing was mean and nasty, so this time you might as well work in a farther and better place.[1] Besides, your kid has grown up and you can leave him to your husband. You cannot imagine how big the granny's house is! It is as big as the workshop where we turned screws the year before last. It is located on Nanjing Road, you know? The downtown area, the busiest shopping district in Shanghai!" That night, Xiao Liu said it to her family, packed her luggage and left home. Sitting on a long-distance bus in the unpleasant smell of stinky socks all the way, she arrived in Shanghai at dawn the next day. The bus driver was good at calculating. When the bus stopped at the station, it was exactly daybreak and the Hong Kong movie *Rich and Famous* playing on the bus's small overhead TV was scrolling its credits. Before the out-of-tune end song was over, she had set her foot on the cement platform and totally forgotten the heroic characters of Yun-fat Chow and Alex Man. It was raining. The raindrops made small and round holes on the watery ground as if displaying their majestic strength to people. She took out her mobile phone and made a call to her family. After weighing the words for a while, she blurted out to her husband: "Honey, I'm at the station — what a total mess here!"[2]

The long-distance bus station was next to the new Shanghai railway station. Holding the slip of paper with the old granny's address and phone number, Xiao Liu crossed Hengfeng Bridge and came to Jing'an District. She looked ahead and saw Xinzha Road where several buildings attracted her attention. With splendidly gilded frames and decorations, these night clubs looked resplendent and magnificent. The Chinese or Japanese characters on them looked eye-catching and inviting. She once worked as a cook in a foot-massage and sauna parlor and she knew the city dwellers had much money. Shanghai people had more! She nodded with admiration. The scene in front of her eyes now was more imposing than what she once saw in Nanjing.

Sitting in the taxi, she looked out of the window. Floods of people were surging and rolling in all directions even on such a rainy day! Nobody stopped or slowed down his steps as if a terrible disaster were around the corner. She withdrew her eyesight and began to ponder over things in her own mind. The taxi sometimes slowed down or jerked to a stop due to traffic jams and sometimes sped up crazily like a lunatic, which made her dizzy and woozy.[3] As she was about to press the button to roll down the window, the driver pulled the car over. "Here we are. Cash or credit card?" The driver turned to ask her.

There must be some tranquil places concealed in the noisy downtown area. The small road here was such a quiet place. But the house numbers confused her completely. Struggling with those odd and even numbers for quite a while, she finally decided to ask for help. She went to a cobbler working at a stall by the road. The amicable and warm-hearted cobbler gave her directions patiently: "Next to Chantilly Bakery there is a police station and on the opposite side of the police station there is a Western-style house which is the place you are looking for, but the doorplate nailed on the wall faces inward, so you cannot see it. The house numbers here were actually reset in 1949 but people living here just use the old numbers." She listened attentively, trying her best to memorize all the turns and routes she was going to take. "How stupid those Shanghai people are! They don't even know east, west, south and north!" She said to herself. Counting the numbers of plane trees all the way, she wandered on the sidewalk paved by flower-patterned bricks. Occasionally, she got befuddled. She was hard put to know where she should put her foot,[4] the seam between two pavement tiles or the center of one square tile? Wisps of blue smoke drifted from one window and curled up slowly in the air: someone must be frying salted hairtail fish; a stern voice came from another window: a father was giving his disobedient son a good telling-off in a husky voice. As she pricked up her ears, all the other sound faded away except the vague sound deep in the alley: some people were shuffling mahjong pieces. The alley was tranquil, indeed.

Finally, she found the old granny's house. She knocked on the door and after a while the owner, Granny Jin, came out. She looked at Xiao Liu up and down and greeted her in the Taiwan dialect. She spoke so fast that Xiao Liu couldn't catch all of her words. At this moment, Xiao Liu suddenly felt herself quite pitiable, much like the ill-fated heroine in the Taiwan TV drama *Green Grasses*. Granny Jin might expect to see a housemaid with a dirty and miserable face! Instead of the ascending high stairs commonly seen in those wealthy households, the stairs in this house were going downward to about half a man's depth. "How can she build her house like this? If it rains hard, the house will be flooded!" Xiao Liu thought as she followed Granny Jin and entered the house. Beside the door there was a white square button. Granny Jin pressed it lightly and the lamps along the corridor flickered and went on. In the dim light, Xiao Liu saw eight oblong mirrors hanging face to face on both sides of walls in the corridor. The frames of the mirrors were decorated with such brickworks as roses, grapes and passionflowers, as well as winged Cupids without genitals. When walking through the corridor and looking around, one would find millions of her own shadows and reflections in the mirrors momentarily following her and even hear these shadows and reflections clashing and clattering after her.[5]

At the end of the corridor stood another woman in bad clothes who was quite tall and strong. Compared with her, Granny Jin looked terribly small.[6] She was Aunt Yan from northern Jiangsu, who did cleaning work here and also was in charge of buying food in the morning for Granny Jin. Seeing them, Aunt Yan came forward to greet Xiao Liu with clumsy smiles on that big face. Fortunately, Aunt Yan had clear enunciation, but as she rattled on and on[7], Xiao Liu found it hard to cope with these two women. Still dizzy from her taxi ride, Xiao Liu had no other choice but to follow them. They turned off the lamps as they walked. The windows of each room were quite small, on which there were some colorful patterns and figures in the Western fairy tales. Thus, on the walls or floors of the rooms facing south, there were often illuminated colorful patches with grains of dust dancing in the dim light.

Aunt Yan told Xiao Liu that this house was different from the well-known Brookside Apartment, whose corridor turned in that way, while the corridor here turned in this way… Aunt Yan gesticulated as she talked, and before she finished her showoff, they came to the room designated to Xiao Liu. There were a cabinet and a bed inside and bags of odds and ends piled in one corner of the room. An electric heater, which seemed to be newly bought, stood on the opposite of the bed. It was the off-work time, and Aunt Yan finally held her tongue and left. Granny Jin also left for a nap. Xiao Liu was left alone in her room. She sat on the empty bed, looked about and felt relieved. The room was not too narrow and the arrangement was

399

relatively convenient. She stood up and before unpacking her luggage, she took out her mobile phone and had a look at her messages.

The work of a housemaid was pretty much the same in every household. Of course, if a family had a child, things were different. Here, Granny Jin lived alone in this house and Xiao Liu was not a green hand in tending to housework, so everything went on smoothly with her. At dinner, Granny Jin spoke highly of Xiao Liu's cooking skill and happily asked Xiao Liu to sit down and have dinner with her. At the beginning, Xiao Liu wanted to make the pretence of being very busy in the kitchen, doing all the cleaning work. She knew all the wealthy people wanted their houses to be as clean as they would imagine. But seeing Granny Jin alone at the big table, Xiao Liu didn't have the heart to turn her down. She hesitated for a while and in the end she filled a bowl of rice and sat down with the old woman.

After dinner, Granny Jin had a habit of drinking a cup of hot tea, which should be made and served totally in the Fujian style. While drinking the tea, she had a chat with Xiao Liu. At first, she just asked about Xiao Liu's family and some other personal trivialities; then, she spouted on and on about her own life. She became a widow when she was very young. Shortly after she got married, she was pregnant. And right after she gave birth to a son, her husband, who was a businessman in electric appliances, suffered from an acute disease and died on the operation table in Taibei Hospital, too quick for the doctors to even put in their hands. She had to name their son herself. Her parents were well-to-do, and for years they had been building roads and bridges for charity in the earnest observance of Buddhist doctrines. Perhaps blessed and protected by her parents, her little son was very smart and nice-looking. As she wasn't in short of money, she stayed at home looking after her son attentively. She placed all her hope on him. Her relatives came one after another, persuading her to remarry, only to falter at her strong resolution and retreat in the end. Gradually, no one dared to mention it again. During those years, her son studied hard and made rapid progress, and her late husband's business in Shanghai developed quite well and made easy money for her especially in 1997 and 1998. She, then, moved to Jing'an District. As most of her good friends in the business circle lived in Hongqiao and Gubei, where wealthy people and foreigners gathered, she, once in a while, went there to visit them. Occasionally, she went to Mingduhui, one of the best residential communities in Shanghai, to have a chat with the wife of Unilever's chairman of board. She went there just for a limited number of times. Everyday, she must make a call to her son, who was studying in Cambridge, and this daily routine remained unchanged under any circumstances. Her factory was in Suzhou now, for the suburban land in Shanghai was too dear! Did Shanghai have a suburb now? No. After drinking the tea, Granny Jin stopped chattering and said to Xiao Liu with a straight face: I want to have a rest and you must stay out unless called for.

There was nothing special at night in Shanghai, except that the night was always as bright as day, so bright that one could never see stars in the sky. After washing up, Xiao Liu came back to her room, and as her body touched upon the brand-new bedsheets, she felt tired and relaxed. Sinking into the bed, she didn't want to move a muscle. But the pancake-shaped lamp on the ceiling suddenly broke down. She had to get up and send for an electrician. The electrician, who was not very tall and wore a white overall, pushed her down to the floor and stepped on her chest to take down the lamp bulb. He was so heavy and had so much strength that she was pressed hard and felt great pain. As she knitted her brows and wanted to utter a cry, she woke up. It was a dream! Feeling her chest tight and painful as if her ribs were really kicked and tramped upon by someone, she exerted herself to sit up and tried to find a spittoon. She panted and the electrician's fat evil face still lingered in front of her eyes. Right at this moment, she heard some strange sound coming from Granny Jin's room.

It was the sound of breathing or gasping. At the beginning, she thought it came from one's throat, but later, she traced it to the inner recess of one's body. From low to high, the sound went on and on, and at last, it ran riot without scruples at all. It sounded like a soliloquy but upon close observation it was abounding in content, a highly condensed body of accoustic grains in a great variety of cadences... On so many lonely nights, the shrinking body must be longing for, if any, a touch of warmth no matter how meager it was; the withering mind must be expecting the future no matter how bleak it was. She must be full of yearnings for a person who could gasp together with her... in various actions and postures... the sound became louder and brisker. A good rain after a long drought fell onto the flower bud. It seemed that only through such gimmicks at midnight could her life be full and glossy, and only in such releases of emotions could she live out her remaining years. The final scream came in the end, struggling and flying high.[8] Xiao Liu stood outside Granny Jin's door, her legs shivering, as if she were waiting there for this final moment. Soon, everything restored to its former tranquility. Only her heart was beating violently alone outside the door in the darkness.

At four thirty in the early morning, the Taiwan dialect drifted through the mirror-lined corridor to Xiao Liu's pillow which was as sleepy as her — Granny Jin was calling her. Xiao Liu opened her eyes, put on her clothes in a hurry and rushed out. Looking at her in a fluster, her reflections in the mirrors sighed and whispered: "Why are you always in such a flurry…"[9] Granny Jin, in grey pajamas, was waiting for her with a porcelain cup in her hand. "Ah, I am sorry, Xiao Liu! I have a habit of drinking a cup of water in the morning to relax my bowels, but just now I didn't hold the cup firmly and poured some water on the bed. I will trouble you to wash the sheet and the quilt case for me. You can use the washing machine! The weather forecast says it's cloudy today, but I think the sun will come out soon." "OK." Xiao Liu nodded. She reached out her hand to feel the place where it was wet, took off the quilt case and wrapped it with the sheet. Holding a big roll of bedclothes in her arms, she walked out. On the way, she couldn't help but take a smell of it as she tilted her head. At eight o'clock sharp, Aunt Yan arrived with a bag of vegetables. She told Xiao Liu, "Granny Jin eats vegetables all year round but she is not a rigid vegetarian. Occasionally, there is meat on her table, but who knows! She often takes out a pictorial book called *Protection for Living Beings* and rants on about retribution to the cook. Once, the cook was so frightened that her face even turned pale! Xiao Liu, can you cook vegetables?" Xiao Liu answered, "Err, I can." Turning her head, Aunt Yan cast a look at the yard where all the other flowers had withered except roses which were still in bloom. Seeing the colorful bedclothes hanging on the rack outside, Aunt Yan asked, "Xiao Liu, you washed them?" Dragging Xiao Liu to a corner, Aunt Yan confided to her in a nervous tone: "Do you know why all the previous housemaids left? Let me tell you. They left because of washing the bedclothes! Who knows what's wrong with Granny Jin! She always pisses on her bed and then asks the housemaid to wash the bedclothes for her, with an excuse that she carelessly pours water on them. No one could stand it, so they all quit, sooner or later. The one who worked here for the longest period of time had nasal disease. No wonder she worked longer. She lost her sense of smell!"

As Aunt Yan predicted, Xiao Liu didn't work long in that house. She was to take the train home which departed at four in the afternoon. She crossed the road and came to a branch of Oriental Pawnshop. At half past one, it opened. She came into the pawnshop and said: "Hi, sir. It's so dark inside and I thought you weren't open yet. I am a housemaid and live in my master's house which is right there at the junction of Nanjing Road and this small road. It's quite near. But for my heart problem, it'll take me less than 10 minutes to walk here."

"I am here to ask for your help with this thing. I don't know whether it is valuable, neither do I know your rules. My mother once told me that in the past a pawnshop was a place where poor people could come for help, and where rags were worth some money. My mother told me that old things could be pawned for more money, especially things for eating and wearing. Here is a pair of earrings, which my master, an old granny, gave me. She said that she got them from a foreign old lady when she held a Buddhist service abroad. She has no use for the earrings as she has no ear holes. I have ear holes, so she gave them to me. Look! In this box. I can read, but I don't know the English inscriptions at all."

The shopkeeper took the box and looked at it closely. When he raised his head, he looked at her in the eye.[10]

1. "还不如索性走得长远些……" So this time you might as well work in a farther and better place. may as well 表示一种建议，意为"不妨……"，注意与may的区别。may 是情态动词，表示许可，二者意思不同。

2. "乱得不能再乱"简单意译为：What a total mess here! 试比较There is not a messier place than this one!

3. "出租车一路又堵又赶，停顿得她有些嗝酸……" The taxi sometimes slowed down or jerked to a stop due to traffic jams and sometimes sped up crazily like a lunatic, which made her dizzy and woozy. 翻译"又堵又赶"，为了叙述的生动，译者有所发挥。dizzy 头昏眼花的、眩晕的，woozy 糊里糊涂的、轻度恶心的。

4. be hard put to do something 做某事有很大困难，为难，不知所措。

5. "一旦顾盼着经过，就是百千亿万个化身形影不离地跟随，望进深处去，不免能听到影子间相互碰撞的轻微脆响和回声。When walking through the corridor and looking around, one would find millions of her own shadows and reflections in the mirror momentarily following her and even hear these shadows and reflections clashing and clattering after her. 这里，"形影不离"、"轻微脆响"、"碰撞"、"回声"，都是关键词。"形影不离"可以翻译为 follow like a shadow、be always together、be after each other like shadows、inseparable as body and shadow、inseparable like a person and his shadow、keep each other's company all the time、not separated for a moment、stick

403

like glue to等等，这里为了组句方便，用的是momentarily following her。clash 碰撞，clatter 发出咔哒清脆的声音。

6. "显得金老太越发矮小得不成体统。" Compared with her, Granny Jin looked terribly small. 矮小得不像样、不成体统，译文处理为：terribly small。

7. rattle 迅速而嘎嘎作响，喋喋不休地说话。下文中spout on and on 意为滔滔不绝地讲。

8. 这一段是小刘在金老太门外听到的声音的描写，用语十分隐晦，给人留下了想像空间，翻译时要注意体现这一点。

9. 这里用到了三个意义相近的短语：in a hurry 匆匆忙忙地，in a flurry 慌慌张张地，in a fluster 慌乱不安地。

10. "典当里的二掌柜细细打量过盒子，开始拿正眼看她。" The shopkeeper took the box and looked at it closely. When he raised his head, he looked at her in the eye. look somebody in the eye 正视某人，目不转睛地看某人，盯着打量某人。

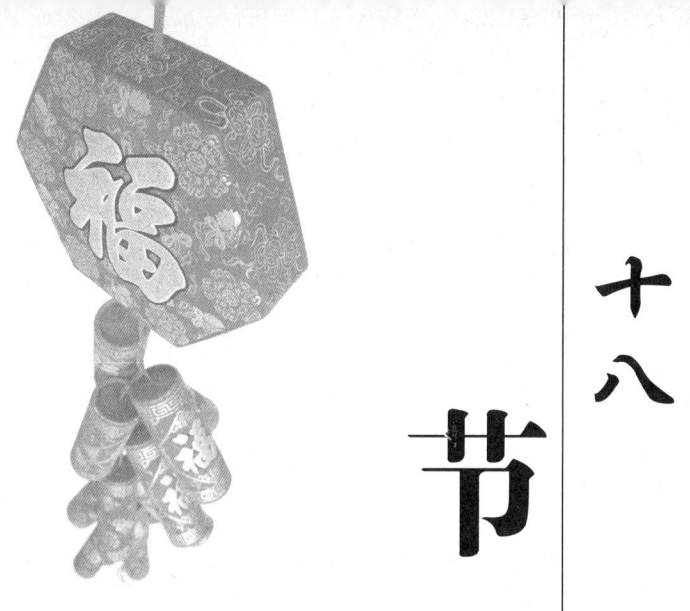

十八节

◎ 林 宕

　　去年这天，姚雪娟碰到了李春荣，当时他们的摊位设在一起。姚雪娟搭帆布顶篷的时候，李春荣已设好了摊。双方都在对方的眼睛里看到了火花。之后李春荣就来帮忙，姚雪娟的公公高德奎也从船上下来，坐着看李春荣忙。看了一阵，说是去看老朋友陈结巴，就走了，这样李春荣忙碌得更欢了。等一切收拾完，姚雪娟把绞干的毛巾递过去，李春荣伸手接的同时，顺便就想亲她，姚雪娟连忙躲开。"是怕你阿公知道？"李春荣拉了一把姚雪娟，她再一次躲开。

　　今年这一天的上午，高德奎同样也是走开了，姚雪娟知道，公公中午肯定回不来了。交流会在重固，离他去的县城有近二十里路，一个来回要两个多小时。近午时分，摊位上就她一个，因此她不准备吃饭，省得走回船上一趟……看着来来往往的人，光顾搪瓷摊位的人还很少。虽然这是河东街"黄金地段"，背面十几米远就是东庙。每年农历八月，这里的"十八节"庙会，人声鼎沸，现在叫城乡物资交流会。苏、浙、沪客商驾着大小各式船只早已经云集此地，四条水路泊满船只，尤其横泾河更是桅樯林立。船上的艳丽女子，也使沉寂的重固集镇风景异常，许多本地年轻男人，甚至中老年男人天天往这里赶，看戏一样看她们。

　　李春荣做着买卖，开始确实也看过那些女人，他经常让一旁的姚雪娟照顾摊位，自己到河东河西去逛荡，确实是仔细看哪个女人的面孔，哪个女人的胸，想跟哪个女人搭讪。可为什么看来看去，"十八节"的女人都没有身边的姚雪娟好。以后他不再走了，稳稳坐在自己摊位里，有时帮姚雪娟张罗搪瓷家什，忘了照顾自己的竹器。因此去年的"十八节"，李春荣没有赚到钱，算上花在看各地夜戏班子及风味小吃上的钱，他是亏了点。但也赚了——认识了刚失去丈夫的姚雪娟。

一般是高德奎先回船吃中饭，然后来替换姚雪娟。这天中午，只见姚雪娟一直坐着。

"你阿公呢？"李春荣问姚雪娟。

"去县医院了。"

"吃饭呢？"

"中午他回不来，我就不吃了。"

李春荣招呼隔壁卖锄头铁搭的老黄，请他代看摊位。

"走，到后街吃豆沙馒头去。"他说。

姚雪娟摇摇头。刚才有顾客来看搪瓷夜壶，李春荣在一边撺掇着，暗地里攥了一下姚雪娟的手……还记得去年同李春荣在夜市上吃的小馄饨，皮薄汤浓，想起来是那么鲜，那夜，他们往回慢慢走，到了一个巷子暗处，记得李春荣有力的一抱，让她真有点激动……只是现在，她还真没想好，不太想跟他去吃东西。"十八节"才开始，现在就让李春荣活络得逞，到了"十八节"结束，不知会发生什么事体。

姚雪娟听任肚子咕咕叫，说："不吃了，我不饿的。"

"还是回船去吃吧。"李春荣说。

"真的不想吃。"

"那等着，我去买。"

"不要不要，"姚雪娟急了，"那……帮我看着吧，我去吃。"

没等他说话，姚雪娟起身走了，在河东街熙熙攘攘的人流里走了一程来到桥堍下。她家的船就泊在"泰安桥"的桥拱附近。桥上人头攒动，晚上行人渐少，公公高德奎就在桥上坐着，倚住桥栏抽烟。桥栏上刻着云纹，望柱上刻有石狮、竹节，桥栏尽头处有抱鼓收尾。拱桥顶的龙门石上刻着暗八仙图案。姚雪娟记得去年"十八节"，一位苏州来的女客商，从这桥上往河里纵身一跳，就在"十八节"收尾前的那一夜里，结束了自己的生命。

饭是一早就烧好了的，三顿饭烧在一起，放在簍箩里，上面遮着毛巾，用一根细绳吊在船舷旁的水面上。

把饭簍箩拿进舱，才想起今天没有备菜，方口瓮里有咸菜，冲了一碗虾米酱油汤，没有吃几口，船摇晃了一下，眼前猛地一暗。

李春荣笑眯眯地站在她的面前。在她愣怔时，李春荣盘腿坐在舱板上，把油纸包着的四个豆沙馒头放在矮腿小桌上。

"你吃吧。"姚雪娟说着，扒拉碗中的饭。

"我吃了，别客气，趁热吃了吧。"

姚雪娟看着桌上的馒头，白得像新刷的墙。

"吃几个馒头怕什么，又不是要调换什么。"李春荣说。

"知道你不是，是我不想吃。"姚雪娟说。

"买来了，你就吃吧。"李春荣抓一个馒头放到姚雪娟碗里。

之后，李春荣又抓了三次。姚雪娟挺怕李春荣还有别的什么动作，但是没有，他的脚也没有从方桌的四条矮腿间伸过来。只是静静地看她嚼嘴里的馒头。她尽量不露出好吃的表情，慢慢地嚼。想到吃，这一点公公是很舍得的，每顿有荤菜，他的筷子只夹素菜……从她嫁过来到现在，高德奎对儿子、儿媳一直很好，丈夫虽不是公公亲生，丈夫有病，她一直没怀上孩子，公公总是乐呵呵的，爽朗，脸色红润，每月都把自己的积蓄补贴给当家的儿媳，丈夫死后，公公与她吃在一起，依旧十分照顾她……今天晓得公公要出门，她懒得做，却让李春荣看到自己吃咸菜酱油汤，她有点难为情。

姚雪娟收拾碗筷。

"看上去你有怨气。"李春荣说。

姚雪娟没吱声，把碗筷、馒头纸归拢到脚旁的篾篮里。想起身去洗，听到李春荣说话，就没有动。

"已经一年过去了，有什么想不开的？"他说。

姚雪娟不知该怎么回答，目光穿过卷帘的船窗，宽阔的河面上，水色清亮，几只长喙水鸟来回飞掠，传来婉转的鸣声。有一对水鸟停在水面上开始交颈。

李春荣动了一下嘴唇，有点结巴。

"……为啥你不改嫁？"

姚雪娟回过脸看李春荣。她的目光让李春荣害怕。

"你阿公是单身，你再不找，有人会说闲话的。"

"什么？"姚雪娟像是没听清李春荣的话。

"怕你名声不好。"

"我已经被人嚼惯舌头，叫我嫁给谁？"姚雪娟低着头说。

李春荣指指自己，姚雪娟没有反应。

李春荣想到高德奎与姚雪娟站在船板上的画面。在他眼里，他们公媳之间像是从不讲话，只有动作上的配合，一个搬东西，一个往摊位上摆放，没有见到他们说笑。

船窗外有一股水气袭来，他们突然无话可说。

姚雪娟有点后悔自己刚才的回答。

"有水气，帘子放了吧？"李春荣说。

姚雪娟点头。李春荣探身把船帘放落，舱内的光线随之暗了好多。

李春荣安静地坐在姚雪娟对面。姚雪娟不知他今天为什么这样，周围没有人，用不着避眼目了，怎么他这样本分。

"你今天蛮老实的。"

说着，她把自己的手放在小方桌上。

"你一直反感我动手动脚嘛。"李春荣说。

"是真的反感，你一直要动。"

"我现在不是不动吗？"

"所以我奇怪。"

"现在反而不想了。"李春荣说，"我要你自愿。"

"以前是不情愿的。"

"你从没自愿过，你的手一直像条白鱼，从我手里滑脱。"

姚雪娟注视李春荣，笑。

"现在不是鱼了，不会滑掉的。"

她的目光落在方桌上，她掌心朝上。现在这段时间，她一直在等待李春荣。

于是李春荣抓住了姚雪娟的手，攥紧她的手腕。肚子挤住小方桌边沿，方桌另一边，也顶在姚雪娟的腹部。姚雪娟想往回抽走。李春荣抓得很紧，站起来，用脚把两人间的方桌拨到一边。姚雪娟也站了起来，想把李春荣从自己的身上推开。李春荣的手是两根老藤，绕在姚雪娟的身上。姚雪娟推李春荣，怎么也推不开。脚下的船左右摇晃得厉害。

"我要叫了，你再不松手。"姚雪娟推搡李春荣。

李春荣终于感觉到无趣，颓然垂下双手，后退，气喘吁吁看着姚雪娟。姚雪娟也看着他，胸脯一起一伏。忽然间，姚雪娟挨过去，身体贴着李春荣，握住李春荣的手。

"夜里八点，到船上来好吗？"姚雪娟说。

李春荣一时没有反应，姚雪娟重复了一遍。

"做什么？"李春荣瓮声瓮气回答。

"想做什么，就给你。"

李春荣吃不准姚雪娟的路数了。感觉她贴近的柔暖的身子，李春荣的呼吸急促起来。暗暗抑制自己，一切留到晚上吧。他想。这时有一丝疑虑袭上心来。那她公公夜里不在船上？

"八点？你阿公呢？"他问。

姚雪娟说："他在桥上抽烟。"

"不是害我吧？他回船来怎么办？"

"不会的。他总在我迷迷糊糊快睡着时才回船的。"

"我不来。"

姚雪娟更紧地贴住了李春荣，李春荣有了反应，经验告诉他，如果他主动，姚雪娟会又一次躲开他的。但此刻他真不想让姚雪娟柔柔暖暖的身子离开他。

"即使他回船上来，怕他什么？他不是你对手。"姚雪娟说。

"我不想跟他斗。"

姚雪娟低下头，空气变得凝重了。

"跟他斗，我就弄翻船。"李春荣说。

姚雪娟不说话，抱着李春荣。

"你落水要紧吗？"他说。

"我会游水。"姚雪娟说。

李春荣看一眼船窗，帘子遮盖得严严实实。他感到一种委屈，他知道姚雪娟面临着选择，牵挂着她的公公。水气从帘子缝里穿过来，很凉爽，让他清醒。"你阿公肯定不会游水。"李春荣自言自语。

"我会的，我会把他拖上岸。"她说。

"我晚上不过来。"李春荣说。

说这话时，莫名的悲哀漫上李春荣的心头。紧贴姚雪娟的身体，他放不开这个女人，就想一直这样抱着她……

傍晚时分，横泾河两岸的一个个水阶上站满了打赤膊洗澡的男子。其中有本地人，也有参加"十八节"物资交流会的各地客商。他们往往跳到河里游几个来回，不着急去看后街各地戏班子的演出，在河里花费好长时间。整个横泾河水浪翻滚，扑腾之声此起彼伏。时不时地响起"哗"的水声，有一条白白的肉身蹿上岸边的水阶，薄暮中，也依稀看到某个浑身精赤的暗影。而附近另一段水阶，是一些中年妇女在洗澡，她们身上的薄布衫，被河水浸湿，紧贴身体，勾出曲线。有几件布衫是淡色，明显映出内里深色的突起和暗影。因为有这样的妇女在河中，薄暮中的河东街、河西街上，就会发出亮光，吸引那些站立着没有下河的闲散男人，目光直溜溜徘徊。总是隔不多久，一名女子在河中尖叫一声，然后看她突然蹿上岸来，像是摆脱水里可怕的蚂蝗或者大条的水蛇。于是他们贪婪地看她，等待她走近来，注意女子身上的薄布衫，甚至注意刚受袭击的某个部位。女子是恼怒的，抹着满脸的水，嘴里狠狠咒骂屈死、杀千刀之类的话，可第二天的傍晚，她们依旧禁不住这样跳入河中，像是忘了昨天的屈辱。

江南的八月，依旧日长。晚上八点左右，笼罩在一层薄暮中的横泾河两岸仍是能见度很高，随时间的推移，一缕缕夜的霾气在四周浮动，像一条条游龙，吞噬白天遗留下来的燥热，喷吐本该属于江南之夜的凉意。泰安桥上，行走的人是越来越少了，倚着桥栏或坐在桥阶上乘凉的人却多了。

桥下，高德奎家的船身激烈晃动起来，一条浑身精湿的躯身挂在木船左侧的船窗上，整船朝左侧大角度倾斜，这躯体猛地一扭，滑入窗内，船迅速恢复了正常。

船内很暗，进入船内的李春荣熟练地爬到里舱。躺在凉席上的姚雪娟，直起腰坐了起来。

"呵呵，他没在，你就想弄翻船？"姚雪娟轻声说。

李春荣穿着短裤，赤裸着黑黝黝的身体在黑暗中泛着一层油光。他抱住姚雪娟，弄湿了姚雪娟的纱衫，姚雪娟没有挣脱，两人朝舱底上的草席倒下。

"不是说不来的吗？"姚雪娟贴着他说。

李春荣没有吱声，只手忙脚乱地动作。被姚雪娟攥紧了他的手。

"不急不急，先躺着讲会话。"姚雪娟低声说。

李春荣还是急，姚雪娟两只手拼命地攥住他。

"不是说要什么，就给我吗？"李春荣说。

"也不能一下子就要呀，躺一会。"姚雪娟近乎哀求了。

李春荣安静下来，搂住姚雪娟的胸口。姚雪娟没有阻止。李春荣无奈地躺着。挺怕还没有做成事，高德奎就回来了，那就很惨，就算能在高德奎发现前顺利溜走。如果成事，即使被高德奎撞上，挨他几下老拳，弄翻了这木船，给他带来什么麻烦，也值得承受。

李春荣不想说话，躺不下去，缓慢压到姚雪娟的身上，姚雪娟没有去抓李春荣的手，只攥住了自己裤带。她竖着耳朵，极力捕捉着引板、船梢头是否突然有脚步声。没有。

这时如果从泰安桥的一侧向下望，会看到高德奎家的木船在轻微地左右晃动，系在岸边船缆石上的缆绳，一伸一缩，牛鼻石发出嗦嗦的声音。

"再躺一会，保证依你。"姚雪娟说。

姚雪娟知道自己不在状态，李春荣也感觉到对方的身体很硬，尽量往一边侧转，她抓住裤腰的手也十分坚定。

"你真会弄人。"李春荣从姚雪娟的身上翻下来。在舱板上摸索自己的短裤，想迅速离开这里。

姚雪娟却扳过他的肩膀，让他重新躺在自己一侧。李春荣想再次坐起来，她就再次扳倒他，抚摩他肩膀，李春荣不动了，朝天躺着，两眼看着黑黝黝的乌毡舱顶。

"你与你阿公好了？"李春荣突然问。

船舷旁有一阵响亮的划水声喧哗，李春荣的心跳到了嗓子口。片刻工夫后，这划水声就远去了。

"没有呀，"姚雪娟说，"别怪我，本来是想和你好的，你来我又怕了……"

"你们都是好人，都对我好。"姚雪娟说。

"我其实很笨，"李春荣说，"本来是不恨你阿公的。"

"不要恨他，恨我好了。"姚雪娟叹了一口气。

她觉得今天有点特别，平时高德奎都在九点左右上船，今天没有。她在八点前看到他在泰安桥栏上抽烟的。

"那怎么办，等不及，我就找别的女人过了。"李春荣说。

"我要想想。"姚雪娟的声音很无力，"我难过，要不要离开这里，离开我公公，我一直不去想，想到了就很烦……"

姚雪娟泪流满面。

"你是哪年嫁到高家的？"李春荣问。

"十八岁就嫁去了，已经十年了，现在再嫁你……我两手空空地走掉？也不甘心的。"

女人呜呜地哭起来。

李春荣说："我不在乎的，只要你答应。"

"我没想好……叫你来，是想今天就决定的，可你来了，我又怕起来……"姚雪娟泪流满面。

两人静了很久，两人的手都松开了，听着水声……

李春荣像是什么都懂了，也像是一直恍惚，无意间，手摸索到自己的短裤，他惊醒似地立刻套上，坚决地坐起身，弯腰从舱底站起走上船梢，这时候，身后的女人竟发出了嚎啕大哭的响声。他很害怕，立刻迅速、慌乱地跃入河中。

高德奎靠着桥栏，看看远处河面上在扑腾着的一些手臂，看着天上，已经有星星在晶亮地闪动。九点钟了，暮色依旧不是很浓厚，朝横泾河的两岸看去，那些还不愿打烊的一个个店家和商贩们的摊位前，点起了盏盏汽油灯和电石灯，河东街和河西街看上去就像两条灯的长龙。泰安桥上行走的人中，也有了提着一只摇晃的彩色灯笼的，样子有点放荡。

高德奎手中的烟燃完了，又掏出一支来，用还没泯灭的烟头当火种。他的手碰到了系在腰带上的荷包。外出时系在腰带上的褐色荷包，并不是放烟叶或者手机，有时，姚雪娟会定定地朝荷包看一眼。每次觉得她在看，高德奎就想，看什么，里面的东西，迟早是你的。

高德奎转着头颈，目光再次落到自己家的木船上。一小时前，他的目光突然像天上的星星一样发亮，嘴角露出一丝不易察觉的微笑。他看到一条精湿的身子滑入他家的船窗内。

"等了几天了啊，终于等到了这一天。"他在心里说。

高德奎没看清那条身子到底是谁。但这对于他已经不重要了。此刻他真切

411

体会了彻底放松下来的心情，就像他独自把十亩稻子一担一担往场地上挑，挑完最后一担体会到的心情。一担担稻子沉重地压在他的胸口，自己只是和姚雪娟有过那一次，然后稻子就沉重地压在他的胸口，他酒醒以后，见姚雪娟不停地擦洗身体，以后他们不再说话了，他明白了，自己挑到场上的稻子，永远也挑不完……

高德奎似乎一直在等待，等待这样一个时刻到来，今晚的情景说明，姚雪娟分明有自己的心意，他叹了一口气，觉得轻松起来，他不必要一直心痛，感到对不起死去的养子。

高德奎一步一步走下泰安桥的石阶，朝陈结巴家走去，他要去那里与陈结巴喝几杯。陈结巴是本地人，住在河东街西梢头，设摊，卖稻绳、草鞋、稻草饭窠。有年"十八节"结束，高德奎把卖剩的搪瓷器具送给了陈结巴，两人关系更好。

土烧酒使高德奎脸上的神情愉快起来。

"今天、好、好像、碰到高兴、事？"陈结巴问。

高德奎没有开口。

"一、一定要说、给我、听、听、听。"陈结巴说。

"以前一直觉得自己坏，做了对不起死鬼儿子的事。"高德奎说。

"现在我不想了，来，老陈，你喝呀。"他说。

"什么什么？"陈结巴说。

"我觉得这样也好，将来，我就和你住养老院去。"

"什么什么？"

河东街上的行人已经少了好多，一些店铺和摊位前的电石灯和汽油灯仍在放射着橘红色的光芒，照亮了地上的石板条，照亮了横泾河的河面。

高德奎走到河沿，走到水阶上，上了自家的船。

除了水声，船上十分安静，高德奎在前舱里点亮了煤油灯，脱掉了上衣，解下腰带，解下了那只荷包。

"我说，我大概是胃病犯了，女医生说，吃药是没用的。"高德奎朝着里舱说。快大半年没开口和姚雪娟讲话了，高德奎起先以为自己会说不利索，也许是酒的原因，还算溜顺。

"既然吃药没用，以后我不再去看了。"高德奎说。

里舱悄无声息，但高德奎感觉到姚雪娟在听。

"我对结巴说，我没有多少日子啦。"高德奎自言自语，拿住荷包他使劲攥了攥，朝里舱扔了过去。

"……前前后后我都想过啦，这几个存折，还有图章，迟早要给你的，明天，你代我去取出来，好好去过日子，当心你自己身体，我拿不出什么了。"

高德奎心里，再次感到卸了稻担般的轻松。

　　"这几年，也就攒了这点，不过别担心我的，结巴也要接我去住的，你自管去好了。"他说。

　　里舱里毫无声息。

　　随后，响起了轻微的，呜呜呜的哭声，伴随河水拍打船舷的声音，像流动着的凉水，像是细雨，逐渐漫上高德奎的心头。哭声持续好长时间才停住。

　　高德奎听到细微、颤抖的声音从里舱传过来。

　　"你过来吧。"

　　高德奎躺在前舱里没有动。

　　"你过来吧。"姚雪娟说。

The Eighteenth Festival

○ *Lin Dang*

On this day last year, Yao Xuejuan met Li Chunrong. Their stalls were located next to each other. When Yao Xuejuan was busy putting up the canvas covering, Li Chunrong had made his stall ready. As she turned and caught his eye, sparks of love burst out. He came to give her a hand. Gao Dekui, her father-in-law, got off the boat and sat aside, looking at Li Chunrong bustling about for her. After a while, Gao Dekui stood up and left with a remark that he wanted to visit his old friend Stammer Chen. Seeing him walking away, Li Chunrong was in full swing.[1] After all work was done, she handed him a wet towel. As he took it, he intended to kiss her, but she dodged aside promptly. "Are you afraid of your father-in-law?" Li Chunrong asked, trying to draw her close, but she stayed away again.

This year, on the same day, her father-in-law left her alone again. The exchange fair was held in Zhonggu and her father-in-law left for the county town twenty *li* away. She knew for sure that he couldn't be back at noon because it would take him more than two hours to simply go there and come back. At noon, at her stall alone, she decided not to have lunch, saving the trouble of walking back to the boat. People were hustling and bustling in the fair but only a few were interested in her enamels,[2] though her stall was set in the "golden area" of Hedong Street, several meters behind which was the famous East Temple. Each year, in the eighth month of the traditional Chinese lunar calendar, the temple fair called "the Eighteenth Festival" was held here, where a sea of people from different places and a hubbub of voices and activities gathered.[3] Now, the temple fair was renamed "the Exchange Fair of Goods and Materials Between City and Countryside". Sellers from Jiangsu, Zhejiang and Shanghai all came here by boat or by ship and the four water-routes were filled with all kinds of vessels, Hengjing River in particular, where a forest of masts and sails fluttered in the wind. Besides, the beautiful women on ships and boats added an irresistible charm to the scenery of Zhonggu. Quite a lot of local young men and even middle-aged men gathered here with great zest in order to have a look at those women as if watching a magnificent play.

At first, Li Chunrong, like most of the men at the fair, also took interest in those women. He often entrusted his stall to Yao Xuejuan and went about ogling at the various women: whose face was beautiful, whose breasts were full and firm and whom he wanted to flirt with … But for some reason or other, he still felt that none of them was as good as Yao Xuejuan. After some time, he no longer went about; instead, he sat by his stall all day long. Sometimes, he went to help her sell enamel wares and forgot about his own business in bamboo wares. As a result, last year, he didn't make money and taking into account his spending on night plays and local snacks he even lost money. However, he thought he indeed made a big fortune — he made acquaintance with Yao Xuejuan who just lost her husband.

Usually, Gao Dekui went to the boat and had lunch there before coming back to take her place at the stall. This noon, Li Chunrong found Yao Xuejuan sitting by her stall all the time.

"Where is your father-in-law?" Li Chunrong asked.

"He has gone to the county hospital."

"Have you had your lunch?"

"He can't come back to replace me and I don't want to eat."

Then, Li Chunrong entrusted their neighbor Lao Huang, the hoe-seller, with the care of their stalls.

"OK, let's go to the backstreet to eat some steamed buns filled with sweet bean paste."[4] He suggested.

She shook her head. Just now, a customer came to buy an enamel chamber pot, and when Li Chunrong egged that person on to buy it,[5] he took the opportunity to touch her hand … Last year, he brought her to the night market where they ate small wontons, and until now, she could clearly remember the thin wonton wrappers and the thick-flavored soup. The wontons tasted so delicious! That night, on their way back, as they walked into a small alley, he suddenly gave her a forceful embrace, which made her heart beat violently. She really felt excited … But now, she was reluctant to go with him. The Eighteenth Festival just began, and if she yielded to his advances now, she couldn't imagine what would happen when the festival ended.

Her stomach was grunting,[6] but she said to him, "I don't want to eat. I am not hungry."

"Then you'd better go back to your boat to eat something," said Li Chunrong.

"Indeed, I don't want to eat."

"I'll buy something for you."

"No, no," she turned impatient. "All right … Please see to my stall and I'll go to eat something."

Before he said a word, she stood up and left. She elbowed her way through crowds of people on Hedong Street. Finally, she came to the Peace Bridge, under the arch of which her boat was mooring. The bridge was thronged with people, who tended to disperse in the evening. She saw her father-in-law sitting and smoking on the bridge, leaning against a balustrade. This bridge had cloud patterns on the balustrades and lions and bamboos on the poles. Drum-shaped bearing stones marked an end to the balustrades and on the upper side of the bridge eight talismans symbolizing the Eight Immortals in traditional Chinese myths were exquisitely and vividly carved.[7] Last year, on this festival, a woman seller from Suzhou jumped off the bridge, ending her life on the night before the end of the Eighteenth Festival.

The three meals for a day had already been cooked in the early morning. Covered by a towel, they were put into a basket, which was hung with a thin string on the board side of the boat.

She took the basket into the cabin. Remembering that there were no cooked vegetables to go with her lunch, she took some pickles out of a square-mouthed jar and poured a bowl of hot water with shrimps and soy sauce. As she just sat down and began to eat, the boat had a sudden jolt. Something suddenly blocked her eyes.

It was Li Chunrong. He stood in front of her with a smile. Before she came to know what happened, he had sat down, crosslegged. He took out four steamed buns filled with sweet bean paste from a greaseproof paper package and put them on the small table.

"You eat them," she said, cramming herself with the rice in the bowl.

"I've had lunch. Eat them while they are hot."

She cast a look at the buns, which was as white as a newly whitewashed wall.

"Why? Just some steamed buns! What are you afraid of? I am not exchanging them for anything." He said.

"Yeah, I know. I have no appetite." She answered.

"I've bought them for you. You'd better eat them." He put a bun into her bowl.

He put the steamed buns into her bowl for another three times. She was really afraid that Li Chunrong might make such petty actions as stretching his feet to her under the table. But he didn't. He just sat there silently, looking at her. She chewed and minced slowly lest he should see her greediness. While eating, she thought of her father-in-law Gao Dekui. He was nice and generous to her and her husband.

The couple had meat in every meal but he only picked up vegetables with his chopsticks… After she got married, her father-in-law was very happy, smiles always appearing on his ruddy face, though her husband, who was actually an adopted son, had some serious illness and consequently couldn't impregnate her. Her father-in-law was good-tempered and open-minded, and every month he used his own money to help her cover the daily expenses of her family. After her husband died, her father-in-law still lived with her, caring for her as considerately as before… Today, she knew her father-in-law couldn't be back at noon, so she didn't make the lunch. Now, eating pickles and soy sauce soup in front of Li Chunrong, she felt sort of embarrassed.

After lunch, she began to tidy up.

"You look unhappy," Li Chunrong observed.

She turned her back on him, putting the bowl, the chopsticks and the bun wrapper into the basket by her feet. As she was about to do the washing-up, she heard him speaking again. She remained there.

"One year has passed. What on earth are you worried about?" He asked.

She was hard put to answer him. Her eyes, through the window of the boat, stopped on the vast field of shimmering water outside, above which several long-billed water-birds were skimming and scudding, chirping their melodious songs. Two birds were winding their necks around each other on the surface of the water.

Li Chunrong's lips shivered a little. He stammered:

"… Why don't you remarry?"

She turned and stared at him. He was taken aback by her look.

"Your father-in-law is single, and if you don't remarry there will be gossips behind you."

"What?" She asked as if she didn't understand what he was talking about.

"I am afraid you may fall into disrepute."

"I've got used to gossips. Besides, whom can I remarry?" She muttered,[8] lowering her head.

He pointed to himself, but she made no response.

A scene popped up in his mind: On the boat, she and her father-in-law Gao Dekui were busy doing things side by side. They were seldom seen talking or laughing to each other. They cooperated with each other only in actions: One carried and moved the goods and the other placed them in order at the stall.

Mist gradually rose up outside the boat. They fell into silence.

She felt a little regretful about what she said just now.

"It is damp. Roll down the curtains?" Li Chunrong asked.

She nodded. He leant over and rolled down the curtains. It became dim in the boat.

He sat quietly opposite her. She didn't know why he was so quiet today. There was nobody around.

"You behave well today." She said.

She put her hand on the table.

"You don't like me touching you."

"Indeed. I don't like you taking liberties with me."

"I don't do it now."

"That's why I feel curious."

"I won't do it, " he continued, "until you are willing."

"I was unwilling."

"Yeah. You were never willing to let me touch you. And your hands, like white fish, always slipped out of mine."

She looked at him and chuckled.

"Now they are not fish and I am sure they won't slip off," she encouraged.

Her sight fell on her own palm on the table. She was waiting for him.

Braced up this time, he instantly grabbed her hand and clutched her wrist tightly, his abdomen pressing against one side of the small table between them. Under his strength, the other side of the table pressed hard against her abdomen, too. She intended to withdraw her hand, but the more she tried, the more tightly he clutched. Finally, he stood up and kicked the small table aside, and together with him, she stood up too. She exerted to push him away, yet his two hands entwined tightly around her body like two strong vines. The boat rocked badly with them.

"Let go of my hand, or I'll shout." She threatened, struggling to push him off her body.

Feeling discouraged, he loosened his embrace and dropped his hands. Taking a step back, he looked at her, panting in disappointment. She looked back at him, her breasts heaving up and down excitedly and nervously. All of a sudden, she returned to his arms, nestling up to him, tenderly holding his hand.

"Come at eight o'clock tonight, OK?" She was inviting him.

Before he made any response, she repeated again.

"Come for what?" He asked in a muffled voice.

"For whatever you want."

He didn't know what she had got in her sleeve.[9] Feeling her tender and soft body, he burned with excitement, his heart beating faster and faster. Trying to cool down, he cautioned himself to leave it to the evening. But after a while, a flicker of doubt popped up:[10] Wouldn't her father-in-law be onboard at that time?

"Eight o'clock? What about your father-in-law? "

"He'll be smoking on the bridge."

"No prank, right? What if he comes back?"

"Impossible. Every night, he doesn't come back until I nearly fall asleep."

"No. I won't come."

She clung to him closer. He turned impulsive again, but his experience told him that if he didn't control himself she would escape again. He really didn't feel like parting with her warm and soft body.

"Even if he comes back, what are you afraid of? He is no match for you."

"I don't want to quarrel or fight with him."

She lowered her head. The air thickened inside the cabin.

"If a fight is inevitable, I'll capsize the boat." Li Chunrong said.

She was silent, holding him tightly.

"Are you afraid of water?" He asked.

"I am able to swim." She answered.

He cast a look at the windows. The curtains were tightly shut. He felt upset at the unpleasant idea that she was facing a choice. She must be worried about her father-in-law. The mist outside, rising up and drifting in through the curtains, refreshed and sobered him a little.

"Your father-in-law cannot swim, I am sure," he mumbled.

"I can and I'll pull him ashore," she said.

"I won't come tonight," he insisted.

Something was gnawing his heart. She snuggled up to him. How he wished to embrace her for ever …

At dusk, the stairs on both sides of the river were full of half-naked men. After a busy day, they were having a bath in the river. Some of them were the locals and some were the sellers who had travelled a long way here for the Eighteenth Festival. They swam several rounds in the river and didn't seem to show an interest in seeing the plays performed by troupes from different places in the backstreet. They frolicked in the water which rolled, foamed, churned and splashed with them.[11] More often than not, in a splash of water a white fleshy body suddenly leapt out onto the stairs on the bank. In the evening twilight, sometimes stark naked men could be vaguely seen in the water. Near the stairs, some middle-aged women were taking a bath, too. Their thin dresses got wet, pressed tightly on their bodies and hugged their curves cleverly.[12] Under their light-colored cotton dresses, some women's private parts vaguely stood out. Thanks to their presence, the streets on both sides of the river glittered at dusk. The men who were taking a leisurely stroll on the streets screwed up their eyes and gazed at those women for quite a long time. Every now and then, a scream was heard before a woman abruptly sprang onto the bank as if she just had a narrow escape from a terrible leech or a water snake. Greedy eyes fell onto her body and her wet dress at once, especially the part assaulted under her dress. Greatly irritated, she wiped the water off her face and began her foul-mouthed outburst.[13] Nevertheless, the next day, when the dusk came, these women bathed in the water again, totally forgetting the humiliations they got the night before.

In August, the day was still long in the south of the Yangtze. Night didn't fall until eight o'clock. In the dim twilight, everything on both sides of the river was considerably distinct. As time went by, wisps of mist finally descended. Like loitering dragons, they devoured the remaining heat and puffed out fresh and cool air to the tranquil night. Fewer people were walking on the Peace Bridge. More people just sat on the stairs of the bridge or leant against the balustrades, enjoying the cool air.

Under the bridge, a boat suddenly rocked violently. A body, wet all over, was hanging on the port side of the boat which consequently inclined a great deal to the left. The body made an exertion and slipped into the boat through the window and the boat soon recovered its usual peacefulness.

It was dark inside. Li Chunrong crept into the inner cabin. Yao Xuejuan sat up straight at once.

"He is not in. You want to turn the boat upside-down?" She chuckled and spoke in a low voice.

In short pants, his dark skin appeared smooth with luster. He held her tightly in his arms and wetted her cotton dress. This time, she didn't struggle. They lay down on the mat.

"You said you wouldn't come," she said, nestling up to him.

He said nothing but ran his hands all over her body. She stopped it.

"Wait! Don't be in such a hurry! Let's lie still and talk," she murmured.

He was so eager. She had to hold down his hands with all her might.

"You said I can do whatever I want," he said.

"Not in such a hurry! Lie down with me for a while," she was nearly begging him.

He quieted himself down a bit, putting his hands on her breasts. She didn't resist. He felt frustrated nonetheless. It would be a big trouble if her father-in-law came back before he did "that" to her. But if he could make love to her, things would be different. Even if her father-in-law saw him and gave him a good beating in a racket that overturned the boat, he believed it was well worth his effort.

He had no mood chatting with her at this precious moment, and he could not idle away his time just lying motionless on the mat. Slowly he climbed onto her. She didn't grasp him by the hand, but clutched her belt tightly while pricking her ears trying to capture the pattering footsteps or any other sound outside the boat. No, there was no sound.

Seen downward from the bridge, the boat was swaying slightly. The mooring rope tied to the stone on the bank strained and loosened from time to time and the stone, which was shaped like a buffalo's nose, produced a rustling sound.

"Lie for a while, and I promise ..." She said.

She knew she was not in the mood. He also felt the stiffening of her body, which was trying to dodge aside. Her hands on her belt were firm and resolute.

"You are playing with me." He sprang from her body and fumbled for his short pants on the cabin floor. He wanted to leave as soon as possible.

However, she pulled him to her by the shoulders and let him lie beside her again. He intended to sit up, but, once more, she dragged him down. With her hand on his shoulders, he lay still and motionless, looking at the black felt ceiling of the cabin.

"Are you in love with your father-in-law?" He asked abruptly.

A sudden sound of water thrashing and splashing came loud from outside, and he had his heart in his mouth.[14] After a short while, the sound faded away.

"No," she said, "I am sorry. I really want to be together with you but now I am scared ..."

"Both of you are nice men and both of you treat me well," she continued.

"It's stupid of me," he told her, "and I don't hate him."

"Don't hate him. It's my fault," she heaved a sigh.

She felt something special tonight. Her father-in-law came back at nine every day, but today he wasn't back on time. She had seen him smoking on the bridge sometime before eight o'clock.

"Then what can I do? I cannot always wait. I'll go for other women," he said.

"Let me think about it," her voice was listless. "I am upset, indeed. I don't know whether I should leave here and leave my father-in-law. Actually, I don't want to think about it. The thought of it worries me ..."

Tears gushed down her cheeks.

"When did you get married?" He asked.

"When I was eighteen, ten years ago. Now if I marry you ... I'll go with you, empty-handed? Let me think."

She burst into tears.

"I don't care. I just want you to say yes."

"Let me think ... As a matter of fact, I want to decide it tonight, but now you are here and I am scared ..." She wept, tears all over her face.

They fell into silence, both listening to the gurgling water outside. They let go of each other's hands ...

Li Chunrong came to understand something, but after a while he felt lost again. As he wavered as if in a trance, his hand touched his short pants. Like waking up with a start, he put on his short pants and sat up in a resolute manner. Bending his back, he walked out of the cabin, leaving her wailing alone inside. The wail filled him with fright, and he jumped into the water at once in panic.

Leaning against the balustrades, Yao Xuejuan's father-in-law Gao Dekui was looking at the arms stroking and paddling on the surface of the water in the distance. Sometimes, he cast a look at the sky where stars twinkled, winking at him. It was nine o'clock. The dusk was gathering but didn't merge into total darkness. The shops and stalls on the two streets alongside the river were still open, and their petrol lamps or carbide lamps lit up the streets. Seen from the point of the bridge, the two streets turned into two long chains of lights. Some people walking on the bridge carried colorful lanterns swinging in their hands — a somewhat dissolute enjoyment.

The cigarette burned out and Gao Dekui lit another one with the remaining butt. His hand touched the small pouch fastened to his belt. The brown pouch held neither tabacco leaves nor his mobile phone. Each time Yao Xuejuan was staring at it, he thought: "Don't worry. It'll be yours sooner or later."

He turned and once again cast a look at his boat underneath. An hour ago, his eyes suddenly lit up like the stars in the sky and a smile crept imperceptibly up the corner of his mouth. He saw with his own eyes a wet-through body slip into his boat.

"Finally this day comes! I've been waiting for it for several days." Gao Dekui said to himself.

He didn't see clearly who it was. It was no longer important to him. Now, he felt totally relieved, as if he had just finished moving all the loads of harvested rice from a ten-acre field. These days, he felt his chest painfully pressed by a heavy load — he made love to Yao Xuejuan, his daughter-in-law! Only once, then the heavy load had been there. When he sobered up from the alcoholic influence, he saw her washing her body again and again. And since then, they no longer spoke to each other and he knew it was unlikely for him to remove the heavy load from his heart for the rest of his life …

It seemed that he was waiting all along. He was waiting for this moment when he could make sure that she had another man in her heart. He heaved a long sigh, feeling relaxed a bit. He no longer needed to be regretful or feel guilty to his dead foster son.

He walked down the bridge step by step and went to Stammer Chen's. He wanted to have a drink with his friend. Stammer Chen was a local resident, living at the west end of Hedong Street, who made a living by selling straw ropes, shoes and pots. They were on familiar terms with each other. One year, after the festival, he gave his remaining enamel wares to Stammer Chen, and by and by they became good friends.

The local liquor soon cheered him up.

"Today, you … you … you are happy?" Stammer Chen asked.

Gao Dekui didn't reply.

"You gotta tell … tell … tell me," Stammer Chen pursued.

"I thought that I was a bad man and that I did something wrong to my dead son," he said. "But now, I no longer think so. Come, Chen! Cheers!"

"What are you talk … talk … talking about?" Stammer Chen was puzzled.

"It's good! In the future, let's live in an old age home."

"What?"

There were fewer people on Hedong street. The lights of the stalls and shops along the street were still on, lighting up the stone slates and the surface of the water.

Gao Dekui walked along the bank, stepped on the stairs and went onto his boat.

Except the gurgling sound of water, nothing else could be heard. He stopped at

423

the front cabin, lit the kerosene lamp, took off the belt and untied the pouch.

"I am afraid there's something wrong with my stomach again. That woman doctor told me it was useless to take medicines." He cast the words at the inner cabin. It was almost half a year since they stopped talking with each other. He thought he would stammer, but he said it rather smoothly, perhaps with the help of the liquor.

"If taking medicine is useless, I won't go to see a doctor," he said.

It was silent inside. He knew she was listening.

"I told Stammer Chen that I don't have much time left," he mumbled. After taking a firm and final grip on his pouch, he threw it into the inner cabin.

"I've thought it over and over again that I should give these bankbooks and this seal to you. Tomorrow, you go to the bank and withdraw the money. In the future, go on with your life and take care of yourself. There's nothing else I can do for you." He felt relieved. The heavy load was finally removed from his chest.

"This is all I've saved these years. Don't worry about me. I can live with Stammer Chen for some time. Just do as you please." He went on, but there was only silence in the inner cabin.

Later, he heard her whimpering and sobbing, and alongside with her cries was the water tapping on the sides of the boat. He felt her tears, like streams of cold water or drizzles of rain, gradually submerge his heart. It was a long time before she stopped weeping.

Then, a soft and shivering voice came from the inner cabin.

"Come in."

He didn't move.

"Come in." Yao Xuejuan said.

1. "……这样李春荣忙碌得更欢了。" Seeing him walking away, Li Chunrong was in full swing. in full swing 活跃、全力进行、全面展开。

2. People were hustling and bustling in the fair but only a few were interested in her enamels… hustle and bustle 熙熙攘攘，可以作动词，也可以作名词，形容人多忙乱。

3. "每年农历八月，这里的'十八节'庙会，人声鼎沸……"Each year, in the eighth month of the traditional Chinese calendar, the temple fair called "the Eighteenth Festival" was held here, where a sea of people from different places and a hubbub of voices and activities gathered. 农历即the traditional Chinese calendar或者the lunar calendar。"人声鼎沸"用a sea of people和a hubbub of voices and activities表达出来。hubbub 嘈杂的说话声、骚动。

4. "豆沙包"译为steamed buns filled with sweet bean paste。中国特色小吃的翻译还是很有意思的，例如：冰糖葫芦 crispy sugar-coated fruit (haws, yam, etc.) on a stick / 驴打滚 glutinous rice rolls with sweet bean flour / 艾窝窝 steamed rice cakes with sweet stuffing / 豆汁 fermented bean drink / 饺子 jiaozi, Chinese dumplings / 油条 deep-fried dough stick / 锅贴 pot sticker / 馒头 steamed bread / 麻花 deep-fried dough twist / 粽子 zongzi, pyramid-shaped sticky rice wrapped in reed leaves / 馄饨 wonton / 元宵 glutinous rice balls for the Lantern Festival in China /火烧 backed wheat cake / 麻团 fried glutinous rice balls with sesame。详细翻译的话，外国人会明白这种小吃的做法和主要成分。但是在小说的翻译中，有时可以简单处理，或者用注解的形式，免得影响行文流畅。

5. egg sb. on to do sth. 煽动、怂恿某人做某事。

6. "肚子咕咕叫。"Her stomach was grunting. grunt呼噜声，（不满等的)嘟哝声，哼哼声，用在这里表示声音，也表示肚子的不满。

7. "桥栏上刻着云纹，望柱上刻有石狮、竹节，桥栏尽头处有抱鼓收尾。拱桥顶的龙门石上刻着暗八仙图案。"This bridge had cloud patterns on the balustrades and lions and bamboos on the poles. Drum-shaped bearing stones marked an end to the balustrades and on the upper side of the bridge eight talismans symbolizing the Eight Immortals in traditional Chinese myths were exquisitely and vividly carved. 这是对拱桥的描写。其中"暗八仙"是一种传统寓意纹样，以八仙手中所持之物(汉钟离持扇，吕洞宾持剑，张果老持鱼鼓，曹国舅持玉版，铁拐李持葫芦，韩湘子持箫，蓝采和持花篮，何仙姑持荷花)组成的纹饰，俗称"暗八仙"。它与"明八仙"纹样同样寓意祝颂长寿之意。

8. mutter 低声嘟囔，小声说话。近义的有mumble, murmur, grumble等。

9. "李春荣吃不准姚雪娟的路数了。" He didn't know what she had got in her sleeve. have sth. in one's sleeve 有好主意、有锦囊妙计。

10. "有一丝疑虑袭上心来。" A flicker of doubt popped up. a flicker of smile 一丝微笑/ a flicker of fear 一丝恐惧 / a flicker of doubt 一丝疑虑 / a flicker of hope 一线希望 / a flicker of surprise 一丝惊讶 / a flicker of flame 一丝火焰。flicker通常指灯火闪烁摇曳，"一丝疑虑"表示怀疑的情绪是闪闪烁烁、似有似无，所以用flicker 比较好。

11. "整个横泾河水浪翻滚，扑腾之声此起彼伏。"原文有动作、有声音、有形态，译者用了四个动词尽力把"翻滚"、"扑腾"、"飞溅"、"此起彼伏"表现出来。They frolicked in the water which rolled, foamed, churned and splashed with them.

12. "她们身上的薄布衫，被河水浸湿，紧贴身体，勾出曲线。" Their thin dresses got wet, pressed tightly on their bodies and hugged their curves cleverly. to hug one's curves cleverly 突出身体的曲线，cleverly 精巧地、巧妙地。

13. "女子是恼怒的，抹着满脸的水，嘴里狠狠咒骂屈死、杀千刀之类的话……" Greatly irritated, she wiped the water off her face and began her foul-mouthed outburst. foul-mouthed 说话下流的、满嘴脏话的，outburst 蒸汽、怒气的突然爆发。

14. "心跳到了嗓子口"译为he had his heart in his mouth，这是一个惯用表达方式，表示紧张、害怕。

暗器

◎ 缪克构

　　面前的盲人词鼓手似乎有点面熟。在我偶然的回神中，我发现他的温州词鼓唱得实在太差，要不是我正沉湎于一件往事之中，我真想跟他说，在我见过的所有的盲人词鼓手中，他是技艺最差的一位。

　　一大片潮湿正将我带入某个雨季之中。由于风向预测错误，满载黄鱼的船最后停靠在一个叫炎亭的地方。我真不知道此地离我家乡盐廒有多远。看着这淅淅沥沥绵延不绝的雨，我担心那些刚刚打上来的弃置于船舱中的黄鱼，肯定会发臭、腐烂，爬出无数的小虫，慢慢地将我吞吃光。全船的人——除了我，还有三个同村人——都感到非常害怕。我是船长，他们都向我建议：还是将这些黄鱼随便卖给附近居民吧，即使只有几个钱，也比落下一身臭气要好。我摇了摇头，炎亭这个地方实在太小了，即使每户人家都到船中挑走一担黄鱼，也不能让船舱空出一半。海神面前我注定发不了财。前一年里，我们没有遇到一次像样的黄鱼汛。这次出海已经一个月，先是在一场莫名其妙的风暴中迷失了方向，然后意外地打到了一舱又大又肥的黄鱼。就在我们归航之际看错风向，一次三十年不遇的低级错误，让我们突然置身异乡。

　　我作出了一个惊人的决定：趁黄鱼还新鲜，请附近居民将它们全部分走，拿回家中，剖片晾起来。"等这些黄鱼都变成了鱼干，我们就收回其中的大部分，留下小部分，作为给村民的酬谢。"那些收购黄鱼干的小贩子们不知道在我家中已经着急地等了多少天了，我却只能在陌生的地方——炎亭，而不是家乡盐廒，冒险做这件事情。

　　我请炎亭村长驼背锡来监督这件事情，有条不紊地让每户人家都从舱中挑走三担黄鱼。做完了这些事情，我请驼背锡到舱里喝酒。

　　驼背锡其实长得很好看——除了背有点驼外。他拍了拍我的肩膀，"船长真是精明呐，要不然这满舱的黄鱼只有等着发臭，然后再次扔到海中去——当然那已经不是黄鱼啦。"

　　我为他斟满了酒，"现在万事俱备，只欠天上出个太阳了。如果事情真正能成，我们是不会亏待村长您的！"

驼背锡嘿嘿一笑，说："你们竟碰上了百年不遇的特大黄鱼汛，真让人纳闷。但你们的船突然停泊在我们炎亭，我倒丝毫也不觉得奇怪。因为几天前，我的瞎子弟弟说，他在夜里听到了黄鱼的喊叫声，有很多很多的黄鱼在叫，自己一宿未睡。过几日，我弟弟就要结婚了，我妻妹要嫁给他。"

对驼背锡这些话，我将信将疑。因此我答应他，明天就到他家喝酒。他的瞎子弟弟竟能在夜里听到黄鱼的叫声……我感到已经有无数条黄鱼正向我游来，仿佛我每撒出一张网，总能网回一根金条。

第二天我没有见到瞎子弟弟，驼背锡说，他喜欢唱温州词鼓，不知跑到什么地方去了。

我见到了驼背锡的妻子。她长得异常的好看，我甚至有点想入非非。要知道，我离家已经有一个多月，在四个男人的天地中，在有风有雨到处是惊险的大海中，我不知已憋闷了多久。我和驼背锡面对面坐在一张圆桌前。驼背锡的妻子先上了几道菜，然后又给我们各人拿了一壶酒。她对我说："这酒不知放了多少年，除非稀客，我们不拿出来招待人的。"

驼背锡给自己倒上了一杯，满屋的香味，我心里暗想：人好，酒更好，真是好酒！可他倒给我的一杯，我却感觉到一点香味都没有，而且舌根发麻——凭我多年品酒的经验，我想，我该带领几个伙伴赶快逃离此地，一场杀身之祸，似乎马上就要来临了。

就在我拔腿想跑之际，突然有一种力量极力告诉我，在这次噩梦一般的出海经历中，我必须为自己留下一点什么。

在驼背锡的妻子转身离开之际，我借口方便一下，绕到了驼背锡的身后。掀起一条长凳将他打晕过去，然后摸进了内房。

让我大吃一惊的是，驼背锡的妻子正在抹澡。她变得更年轻了，回过身来看了我一眼，慌慌张张穿衣服，她行动速度之快让我深感吃惊。我几乎不费什么力气就将她放倒在床上。在整个过程中，她几次想挣脱，并不说话，口中只是咿咿呀呀，像个哑巴。我突然想起了驼背锡的话："过几日，我弟弟就要结婚了，我的妻妹要嫁给他……"

盲人词鼓手终于断断续续将一曲词唱完了。

父亲从记忆的莽原中走回，吩咐母亲上饭。每次请路过的盲人词鼓手唱词，父亲总是这样招待他们：先上黄鱼头，后上白米饭。这在贫困年代中是一场盛宴。父亲用一根火柴梗剔着牙缝，将口中残余的黄鱼肉一一除去。他刚喝过酒，满脸红光，七八成的醉意，十二分的舒坦。在他的对面，盲人词鼓手还在断断续续弹拨着牛皮筋。也许摆在他面前的两个黄鱼头的香味屡屡飘进鼻中，他每句唱腔在坚持了三分钟的正调后一次又一次滑向了食欲的边缘。好在

428

父亲并不在意，在正午的阳光之下，他正细眯着眼睛，看着从檐角垂下的一株瓦花……

父亲想到了什么，开口说道："现在的黄鱼真是越来越少了，每个黄鱼头代表一条黄鱼，但黄鱼头显然要比黄鱼香得多。"

盲人词鼓手并不动筷子，他说："黄鱼是越来越少了，对听得见黄鱼叫声的人来说，是一件喜事。"

父亲一惊，脱口问道："听得见黄鱼的叫声？"

盲人词鼓手说："没有了黄鱼，自然也就听不到它的喊叫声，夜里就睡得踏实了。"

父亲还在喃喃自语："很多年前，也听说过有人能听得见黄鱼的喊叫声，在炎亭……"

说到这里，父亲突然大惊失色，他知道了，为什么这个盲人词鼓手这么面熟，原来长得像极了驼背锡。他明白了盲人词鼓手原来就是驼背锡的瞎子弟弟。可是已经明白得太迟了。

盲人词鼓手说："我听见你的心跳得厉害，皇天不负有心人，我找了这么多年，终于找到你了，我可以为含羞死去的未婚妻报仇了！"

盲人词鼓手双手齐动，剧烈地弹动着牛皮筋。牛皮鼓剥辣辣地爆响，突然裂开，从鼓腹射出几枚锋利无比的暗器，射向我父亲的身体……

母亲一再告诉我：在1983年你的故乡盐廒，到处都晒着你父亲出海打来的黄鱼。黄鱼只买八分钱一斤，只要谁扔下一块钱，一次可以随便拿走多少。那时候，黄鱼都当饭吃，你们兄弟都是吃着你父亲打来的黄鱼长大的。可是黄鱼实在太多了，满村庄晒着大大小小的黄鱼，招惹来你父亲的仇人。他终于将你父亲杀死了。

我仔细算了一下，发现母亲描述的盛景是50年代的事情，可是她却将1983年我父亲的死联系起来，实在太巧妙了。

显然，母亲疯掉已经有好些年了。

The Hidden Darts[1]

⬤ *Miao Kegou*

The blind man, standing in front of me and singing a story to the accompaniment of a drum,[2] looked familiar. Intermittently, I recovered from my train of thought and found this drumbeat lyric singer rather awful.[3] If I were not indulged in the recollection of a past event, I would say to him: "You are the worst singer I've ever seen."

A vast field of humidness brought me back to that rainy season.[4] Because I wrongly forecast the wind direction, our ship, loaded with yellow croaker fish, had to stop at a place called Yanting, perhaps far away from my hometown Yan'ao. Who knew! Seeing the continuous rain pitter-pattering, I was quite worried! Those yellow croaker fish, though newly caught, would stink and perish soon! And the rotten fish would attract innumerable little worms, which might eat me up slowly! All the crew — besides me, there were three men from my village — panicked. As I was the captain, they all suggested to me: "We'd better sell the fish to the local people. Earning a little money is much better than ending up in total losses." I shook my head and said: "Yanting is too small a village, and even if every family takes away a load of fish, altogether they can just empty half of our ship." Perhaps I was doomed to failure in face of the Sea God. Last year, I wasn't on time for the yellow croaker fishing season. This year, we stayed on the sea for a whole month. At first, we got lost in a rather odd storm and later, though we fished a whole ship's hold of yellow croaker fish, on our way home, I unfortunately misjudged the wind direction, which was really a stupid mistake rarely made during my thirty years' career. We were abruptly thrown to such a strange place! I made a daring decision: I asked the villagers nearby to come to divide and take away all the fish still fresh in our ship, and requested them to slice the fish and dry the slices in the air. "When the fish slices are dried out, we'll take back most of them and leave a small portion to you as a reward." I could imagine how anxious the fish dealers in my hometown were to purchase my fish slices. They must have waited for me for quite a few days, but now, I had to take the risk here in Yanting, a completely strange place to me, instead of getting my money in my hometown Yan'ao.

I entrusted this job to Hunchback Xi, the head of Yanting Village. He arranged for each family to take three bundles of fish back home in perfect order. When the job was done, I invited him to a drink.

As a matter of fact, Hunchback Xi was a good-looking man, except for his hunchback of course. He patted me on the shoulder and praised me, "You are really smart! If you didn't do with your fish this way, all your fish would go stinky and have to be thrown back to the sea — no longer yellow croaker fish at that time!"

Filling his cup with wine, I said, "Now everything is ready except the strong sunlight. If things go on smoothly as we planned, I'll give you your due."[5]

He smiled and said, "It is a wonder that you met such a once-in-a-century fish season,[6] but I am not surprised in the least to know that your ship stopped by our village, for several days ago my blind little brother told me that he heard yellow croaker fish crying at night and that the cries of so many fish made him sleepless the whole night. In a few days, my brother will get married. He'll marry my wife's sister."

I didn't know whether I should believe his words or not. I agreed to go to his home to have a drink the next day. How could his blind little brother hear the cries of fish at night?... Anyway, I was filled with hope and almost saw many yellow croaker fish swimming toward me. A net of them was worth a gold bar.

The next day, when I drank in his home, I didn't see his blind brother. Hunchback Xi said that his blind brother liked the Wenzhou drumbeat lyrics very much and might go to sing it somewhere.

However, I saw Hunchback Xi's wife. She was extraordinarily beautiful and some wild whims arose in my mind.[7] I had been away from home for more than a month and in the small world where there were only four men between the hardships and the deep blue sea, I felt suffocated and sullenly bored.[8]

Hunchback Xi and I sat face to face at a round table. His wife served us a few dishes and a bottle of wine for each of us. "This wine has been kept for years, and we only treat a rare visitor with it." She said.

Hunchback Xi filled his cup. The fragrance of the wine pervaded the room at once. "The woman here is good and the wine is even better!" I said to myself. However, from the wine he poured into my cup, I smelled nothing aromatic; instead, my tongue turned a little numb. Years of drinking experience told me that I'd better escape with my men as soon as possible. I could sense a disaster was around the corner.

As I was about to run away, all of a sudden, I felt a strong power urging me to stay. Yes! In this nightmare on the sea I'd better win something for myself!

His wife turned round and left. Saying that I wanted to use the toilet, I stood up and walked quickly behind Hunchback Xi. Before he came to know what happened, I knocked him out with a bench. Then, I felt my way to his bedroom.

To my great surprise, his beautiful wife was toweling her body in the room. At this moment, she looked much younger! She turned her head and saw me. In great surprise she put on her clothes in a hurry. I was amazed by her speedy action and even more shocked by my own. I almost took no effort in overpowering her and putting her down on the bed. During the whole process, she struggled but didn't say a word. She just hummed and groaned like a mute, which suddenly reminded me of Hunchback Xi's words, "In a few days, my brother will get married. He'll marry my wife's sister …"

The blind drumbeat lyric singer finally finished his off-and-on songs.[9]

Father also walked out of the wilderness of his retrospection. He asked mother to serve the meal. Each time father invited a blind lyric singer to perform, he always asked mother to treat the singer with a meal — the heads of yellow croaker fish were served first, then the white steamed rice, which were seen as a lavish feast in those years when most people lived in poverty. Father picked his teeth with a match, removing the fish stuck between his teeth. With the wine working in stomach and his face glowing with redness, he was intoxicated and felt more than contented and comfortable.

That blind singer, sitting opposite father, continued singing, while plucking the strings with one hand. Perhaps because his nostrils were constantly hit by the inviting smell of the fish heads, after three minutes' singing, he went out of tune. Luckily, father didn't care about it. Bathed in the sunshine at noon, father narrowed his eyes to look attentively at a flower drooping down from the corner of the eaves …

He suddenly thought of something and said, "Now there are fewer and fewer yellow croaker fish, and here in the plate each fish head represents a fish. Do you know that the head of a fish tastes much better than the fish itself?"

The blind singer didn't touch the chopsticks. He replied, "Yes, there are fewer and fewer yellow croaker fish but to the person who can hear their cries it is really a good thing."

Stunned, father blurted out, "Hear their cries?"

The blind man answered coldly, "Without yellow croaker fish, there are naturally no cries of them. That means a good sleep at night."

Father muttered, "Many years ago, I heard that someone could hear the cries of yellow croaker fish. At that time, I was in Yanting …"

Father's face suddenly turned pale. He suddenly came to understand why the blind singer looked so familiar! He resembled that Hunchback Xi! He must be Hunchback Xi's brother. But it was too late!

The blind singer said, "I hear your heart beating violently. All things come to those who wait.[10] I've been looking for you for so many years and now I can take revenge for my fiancée who died in humiliation and disgrace!"

The blind singer plucked the strings with both of his hands. The strings quivered violently and the drum thundered in hatred. And all of a sudden, the drum burst with a crack and from within several sharp hidden darts shot out at father …

Mother told me several times: In 1983, slice of the yellow croaker fish that your father harvested from the sea were being sun-dried everywhere in your hometown Yan'ao. At that time, the yellow croaker fish were sold in a very low price, 8 cents for 500g. With one yuan you could buy whatever amount you wanted. Anybody could afford it. You and your brothers grew up eating the yellow croaker fish. There was such a huge supply of yellow croaker fish that the whole village was overflowing with sun-drying fish slices. That drew the attention of your father's enemy, who came to our village and killed your father in the end.

I made a careful calculation. What my described was the scene in the 1950s, while my father died in 1983. How ingenious it was of her to connect these two events together!

Obviously, mother had been mad for many years.

1. 这篇小说前面一部分的"我"是一位出海捕黄鱼的船长，后面一部分的"我"是那位船长的孩子，前后是两个人不同的叙述视角。

2. 温州词鼓，流行于浙江温州及其毗邻地区的一个曲艺品种，俗称"唱词"，是一种有乐器伴奏的边说边唱的表演艺术，过去的艺人多为盲人，所以这里翻译为：singing a story to the accompaniment of a drum。

3. "在我偶然的回神中"译为：Intermittently, I recovered from my train of thought and …。train of thought 思路、一系列的想法，intermittent 间歇的，断断续续的。

4. "一大片潮湿正将我带入某个雨季之中。"这句之后就是"我"在听温州鼓词时的回忆了。下面的回忆都是以第一人称"我"的视角进行叙述的。为了提示读者以下是倒叙，这句用了bring back这个短语：A vast field of humidness brought me back to that rainy season.

5. "如果事情真正能成，我们是不会亏待村长您的。" If things go on smoothly as we planned, I'll give you your due. "给你应得的"译为give you your due.

6. "百年不遇"可译为do not occur even in a hundred years或者 once in a blue moon。这里为了行文方便，用了once-in-a-century作形容词：It is such a wonder that you met such a once-in-a-century fish season …

7. "想入非非"有很多种翻译方法，例如：aim at the moon/ allow one's fancy to run wild/ aspire after the impossible/ be full of whims and fancies/ give loose rein to one's fancy/ give free play to one's imagination/ have bees in the head/ harbor fantastic ideas/ have strange whims or fancies/ let one's imagination run wild/ nourish wild ideas等等。这里处理为some wild whims arose in my mind。

8. "憋闷"指憋气不自由加上烦闷，所以翻译为I felt suffocated and sullenly bored.

9. The blind drumbeat lyric singer finally finished his off-and-on songs. 从这句之后，故事的叙述者"我"换成了刚才那位船长的孩子。

10. "皇天不负有心人。" All things come to those who wait.

苦竹

○ 章　缘

夏日之夜，有如苦竹，竹细节密，顷刻之间，随即天明。

在梦里，她跟他说起这首偶然读到的日本短诗，他们见面时总是聊文学居多。她问，夏日之夜为何有如苦竹？这苦竹是什么样的，一语未毕，他突然凑过脸来，探舌在她眉心之间舔了一下。

她一惊，醒了。天已大亮，梦境还很清晰，还没有被外界干扰，那充满挑逗的一舔，分明还在眉心，湿润舌尖的力道令她惊异、怅惘，既然是梦，为什么没有梦久一点。

下午一点，她敷上净白淡斑面膜，躺在香妃竹榻，空调森森送爽，想起这一节，已经失去那种颠倒魔力，只觉得可笑，这样的春梦竟会是跟他？那么一个拘谨胆小的老男人，从不敢迎看她大胆的眼光，只在她移开目光时才偷瞥一眼。难道我会吃了你？她暗笑，就是要吃，也轮不到你。

四十多岁的她，喜欢看青春洋溢的小伙子，二十左右，五官分明唇红齿白，目光要单纯，态度有点青涩，身材嘛，要结实偏瘦，像山里一棵棵修竹，在晚风斜照中轻轻摇曳，对，就是那种感觉。常常可以看见这样清秀可人的年轻男孩。以前，当她如鲜花初绽时，她没看见，忙着躲避陌生男孩的眼光。那时候，那个保守的年代，她穿着白衬衫和长裙，头发挶在耳后一丝不乱，胸衣外一定要加件小马甲，不能让人看出任何胸衣的样子。岁月匆匆，她跟跄跌入胸衣外穿、肩带外露的年代。

男孩总是看着她，一群女学生放学从那条有男校的路上经过，她感到许多突然亮起的眼睛，一闪一闪。她目不斜视。所以，一直要到这么多年后，她才能看见，好整以暇地打量，一株株顾然而立嫩青如竹的男孩。

对街马路那家理发院，就是那么块宝地，养着数个清秀的男孩。年龄足以当她儿子的7号，头发理得极短，只在前额处留了一络长发，染成金红，青青头皮有了那络红发平添几分妖媚。他擅长吹鬓发，梳子一卷一拉，吹风机首尾并用，热气烘上，吹出一股一拧的复古麻花，把两边两股鬓发在脸旁一拉，弹回，轻触她脸颊。

10号是新来的师傅。那天她从长镜里看到他，坐在一旁等客人，侧脸线条清极俊极，正面看去，脸略窄，眼梢上扬，红唇像刀削般分明。他的眼光接触到她，低头一笑。下回，她指定找他吹头发，在镜里把他看个够。

5号还是个小孩，身形没长全，但双瞳盈盈，十指修长有力。那一回他替她洗了头，松颈按肩，轻拢暗捻抹复挑，她闭眼任他按去，按着按着，他笑，"姐，怎么你肩膀在动？"

"唔？"她睁开眼。

"我手一边按，你肩也跟着动。"

"有吗？"她否认。

有吗？她问自己，刚刚真的应和着他的手势，你进我退我进你退如跳探戈伦巴？她暗暗叹气。

他们每回总甜甜叫她姐，央求她把美发卡再充个几百元，买一份促销中的水疗护发，或是烫发染发等各种高额消费。她或应允或摇头，笃定如山却又忍不住微笑。就像看孩子在面前撒娇要糖，给或不给，全凭她高兴。

她至此完全懂得，老男人为什么喜欢小姑娘。

但是那个老男人，梦里的那个，倒是老成持重，没有多看班上年轻的太太。眼观鼻，鼻观心，他看着桌上那本上海话课本。小区会所开办的上海话课，一班六个太太，年岁相当，孩子都上中学、大学了，陪着先生在上海，家中大小事务有阿姨打点，学上海话打发时间，学三句忘两句。她倒是很认真，从小就喜欢语文，特别喜欢用各种语言卖弄嘴皮，她是唯一返课时能流利读出课文的学生。

休息时间，太太们聊天，她拿书到老师身旁请教"坐"和"做"的发音。老师一看她过来，突显慌乱，颤抖着摸索桌上眼镜，她也诧异，但还是把问题问了。老师严肃示范两字发音区别，她细辨其中差异，在课本上写下：坐，俗，做，卒。她微嘟着嘴，索吻似的，从噘起的红唇送音。嘴唇是她五官里最美丽的一部分，饱满丰润，唇型微翘。

然后，她开始注意到老师从不抬头看大家，但只要轮到她读课文或发言，他便带着一种愣愣的神情，专注地从厚厚的镜片后望过来。她并不是班上最年轻，甚至不是最漂亮的一个。有个成都太太，皮肤白皙，热情爽快，常邀大伙儿到她家吃火锅。

　　每回休息时间，她都去请教老师，但是说话的内容从上海话慢慢变成文学。他是退休的中学老师，年轻的时候也是文艺青年，到现在还固定阅读严肃文学刊物。结婚前，她做过几年编辑，中外文学作品也看了不少，两人有了共同话题，这是其他太太无法介入分享的话题。来上海多年，头一回遇到可以谈文学的男人，向来见到的都是老公生意圈里的人，股票和房地产，设厂或培训，具象而不能抽象。

　　她把一周一次的敷面，移到上海话课前。轻敷脂粉，淡扫蛾眉，不动声色地打扮起来。她的腿仍然纤细修长，她穿塑身有弹性的烟管裤，紧贴合身的牛仔裤，扬长隐短的名牌恤衫和短外套遮住发福的腹和臀。她让5号把青丝护得发亮，10号染成咖啡红，7号吹出妩媚的鬈发，低低束成马尾，用珠圈盘在脑后，或散披肩上。

　　相较起来，对手简直是一成不变，从春天到夏天，他只是脱去那件米色夹克，里头是单色恤衫和起了毛球的西装裤，天气更热，恤衫换成了短袖。中等身材，一张缺乏个性的老实脸，眼睛因为高度近视常带着一种空茫的神情，幸而有股书卷气，不惹人厌，更幸而他不时在镜片后追随蝴蝶般翩翩的她。

　　就跟对5号、7号和10号一样，她也是笃定如山又忍不住微笑，一个要糖吃的老男人，提供了一个继续爱美扮俏的动机。她不想知道他下课后的生活，一周三个小时上课之外的家庭和其他种种。她也在他面前保持神秘，台湾，已经让她有异域情调，再加上住在这种小区的多金暗示，她拥有的是他无缘窥见只能想像的奢华生活。

　　一个月，一或两次，老公会在不加班没有越洋电话开会的晚上，突然坐到看电视或看报的她身旁，她清楚今晚又有任务了。她履行任务前会穿上各种鲜丽或丝或绸的性感内衣，在浴室对镜苦笑。在床上，她紧闭眼睛，随意召唤5号7号或10号。但她从未，从未，召唤过他。如果他看到她穿着这种内衣的模样，肯定吓得面红耳赤，眼镜都要从脸上跌下来吧？但昨天的那个梦，那一舔，却让她怀疑他也许不像她想的那么畏缩胆怯，反而暗藏着一种爆发性的热情，在她猝不及防时，将势如破竹席卷她征服她。

　　无眠的夏夜，火烧火燎，空气胶结黏稠，浸满汗渍的裸身辗转于滚烫的席榻，企望绿竹生凉，企望竹林生风，企望终结这漫漫长夜折腾的天际曙光，但夜风无情，不消暑热却让弱竹颤栗呻吟。老公那断断续续的抽送，浊重的呼吸伴着打嗝放屁，5号的手指，7号的热风，10号的俊脸，繁复交错，一节又一节，一轮又一轮。她从未，从未，在此时召唤他，求他帮忙，求他让她自觉美好，就像白天那样。

她怎能如此分裂，分裂若此？

两点差五分，她在眼皮上抹上最后一笔发光的银色眼影，带上课本往会所款款而去。她喜欢晚几分钟进教室，让他小小担心一下她是不是缺课了。但是教室里只有他和成都太太，看到她进来，两人都松了口气。她挑了远一点的位子坐下，不看他。

过了十分钟，没有别人来。成都太太说了，"大伙儿都出去耍了，肯定是，今天，还上课不？"

他有点犹疑，"你们，要上吗？"

她还是不看他，只望着成都太太，"你上不上？"

成都太太有点抱歉地笑着，"其实我待会儿也有事，本来就要早点走，不过，对老师不好意思吧？"

他好脾气地说："不要紧，下星期再上吧，我，我也有点事。"

成都太太走了，她站起身拿了课本，有点忿忿地对他说："你有什么事？"这是今天头一回正眼瞧他。

"没，没什么，不要紧，你要是想上，我们也可以……"他把眼镜取下又戴上。

她提议在小区走走，天气这么好。这是上海闻名的涉外小区，占地极广，四周高楼中包绿地，树影婆娑鲜花处处，有池塘假山，还有户外泳池白沙滩。他们走过儿童嬉笑追逐的白沙滩，走进池塘边柳阴深处。两人面向池塘而立，塘里有一群锦鲤，色彩斑斓，看到人影，都聚到他们脚前，等待着。

这一路两人都没说话，沉默中，有种说不出的压力和密度。她窃喜于这压力密度，仿佛他们之间的确是有着什么暧昧不明的情愫，这情愫在发酵中，一步一地雷。但他如此生分沉默地跟在一旁，却又让人感到委屈，堵得心头发闷。她终于抵不住了，笑着说："昨天读到一首小诗，挺有意思，却又不太懂。"她才念了诗的上半，他便接着念完。

"原来你知道，那么，这夏日之夜和苦竹，是个什么关系？"一问出口，突然感到眉心被刺了一下，脸色乍变。

"怎么了？"

她举手摸眉心，"不知道是什么，虫还是什么？"

"我看看。"他凑过脸来，跟梦里一模一样。两人脸挨得很近，他的吹气拂到她脸上，他的脸也刹时涨红了，鼻翼紧张地掀动，眼神里有种很陌生的什么。她心跳突然飙速，搽着银亮眼影的眼睛盯着他，红润性感的双唇等着他，命中注定的事她不能负责。但他马上退回去了，垂眼看自己的脚："没，没看到什么。"

"哦，没有吗？"她双手抱胸，把课本紧抱入怀，以免自己把课本扔到他脸上。

"咳，那个苦竹我晓得，"他清清喉咙说，"中看不中吃，满山遍野疯长，密密麻麻一大片，人到里头，就像天黑了一样。"

那天深夜，当老公气喘吁吁压住她时，她试图召唤他。有何不可呢，不过是另一个跟她不搭界的男人。他来了，但只是把眼镜拿下，疲累地揉揉眉心，然后瞪着一双空茫的眼睛说：忍着点，天，就要亮了。

The Bitter Bamboo

○ *Zhang Yuan*

The summer night, like a slender bitter bamboo with dense joints, is beautiful but transient. At dawn, it vanishes with no trace.

In her dream, she related to him this Japanese poem she once read. When they met, they always talked about literature. Why is the summer night like a bitter bamboo? What do the bitter bamboos look like? Before she finished her questions, he, all of a sudden, came close to her, stuck out his tongue and gave her a lick on the place between her eyebrows.

She was taken aback and woke up. It was already bright dawn. The dream kept lingering in her mind, clear, intact and undisturbed by the physical world. His flirtatious lick still stayed between her eyebrows. Tantalized by his moist and forceful tongue, she felt amazed, distracted and at a loss! Why didn't the dream last longer?

At one o'clock in the afternoon, leaning against the bamboo couch, with a film of whitening facial mask on her face, she enjoyed herself in the cool breeze from the air-conditioner. Now, clear-minded, she was no longer infatuated head over heels with that dream. She even found herself ridiculous. With him in that amorous dream? That meticulous and timid old man never dared to meet her eyes directly! Only when she looked away from him did he steal a glance at her. Will I eat you? She sneered secretly. Even if I want to eat somebody, you are not in the list![1]

She was more than forty years old. As a middle-aged woman, she found herself attracted by those young and vigorous men, who were about 20 years old with fine-chiseled faces, red lips and white teeth. Of course, their eyes should be clear and their manners green and pure.[2] As to their stature, she preferred those who were strong and slender, like bamboos swaying gently in the evening glow. Yes! Such young men gave her the very feeling she wanted! Fortunately, she always met such good-looking young males. When she was young, as young as them and as beautiful as a flower, she always tried to avoid boys' eyes. In her youth when the society was more conservative, she always wore a white shirt and a long skirt, and her hair was always neatly combed. She always wore a waistcoat so that nobody could see she wore bras. Alas! How time flew! Before she realized it she had bumbled into a new age when it was fashionable for women to put on underwear as outerwear or at least to reveal the straps of their bras.[3]

At that time, boys always had their eyes on her. When passing by a boy's school with a group of girls, she felt many eyes suddenly brightening up and sparkling around her, but she never dared to turn her head or look sideways. Now, after so many years, she finally took a good look at the boys, who were young, slender and delicate like green bamboos. She looked at them with care and interest.

The barber shop on the opposite side of the street was such a wonderful place where quite a few good-looking young men worked. No.7 was young enough to be her son. He wore his hair neat and short, and a wisp of long hair in front of his forehead was dyed golden red, which added a seductive charm to his blue and pale scalp. He was good at styling the curly hair. Holding a wisp of her hair, he curled it, straightened it and dried and styled it with the two ends of his hair-dryer. In his skillful hands, wisps of twisted hair came into being, which looked attractively classic. The two wisps of the curly hair beside her ears sprang upward when given a pull, caressing her cheeks softly and briskly.[4]

No.10 was new here. The other day, she sat before a long mirror and saw his profile. He was sitting aside and waiting for his guests. That was a comely profile, so delicate and handsome! His face was a bit narrow, the corners of his eyes slanted upward and the clear-cut red lips looked very attractive. When his eyes met hers, he lowered his head, smiling shyly. She smiled in her heart. Next time, she must ask him to style her hair, so that she could observe him closely to her heart's content.

No.5 was still a boy. He wasn't tall and had sparkling eyes and slender fingers. Once, after washing her hair, he massaged her neck and shoulders. Closing her eyes, she enjoyed herself a lot as his forceful fingers touched, kneaded, rubbed and pressed her body in a skillful manner.[5] He grinned and asked, "Madam, why are you moving your shoulders?"

"Oh?" She opened her eyes.

"Yes. Your shoulders are moving with my hands."

"Really?" She intended to deny it.

Is it true? She asked herself. Yes, indeed. Just now, she was moving her body in response to the movement of his hands. She felt she were dancing tango or rumba with him! She sighed to herslf.

Each time she went there, they always called her "Madam" in a sweet tone, urging her to deposit more money into her hairdressing card or persuading her into buying such promoted services as water treatment or such costly services as perming or dyeing. Each time, she either nodded her agreement or shook her head with a smile. She felt as if they were spoiled kids asking for candies from her, and whether to grant them their wishes solely depended on her own mood! She loved such a feeling.

Now she thoroughly understood why old men were interested in young girls.

But he, the man in her dream, appeared reserved and prudent. He didn't cast unnecessary looks at the women (all younger than him) in his class. Instead, his eyes were always fixed on his textbook of the Shanghai dialect. That was a class of the Shanghai dialect in the community club of the residential neighborhoods. She and the other five women were almost in the same age and their children had gone to either high school or university. They came to live in Shanghai with their husbands. Since the housekeepers did all the housework for them, they attended the class to learn a little Shanghai dialect to kill time. As they were far from hardworking, they always forgot what they had learned. She was an exception. She was quite serious with her study in the class. From her childhood, she was interested in languages and liked to show off her talent with different dialects. Now in this class she was the only student to be able to read a text fluently which was taught in a previous lesson.

During the break, while the other students were chatting, she went to consult him, their teacher, about the correct pronunciation of two words. Seeing her coming, he turned nervous, fumbling for his glasses on the desk with a shivering hand. She felt surprised too. In a serious manner, he told her the subtle difference between the two words. She listened carefully and wrote down on her textbook some other words with the similar pronunciations.[6] Pouting her lips as if asking for a kiss, she practiced reading them. The upward corners of her mouth and the red, fresh and ample lips constituted the most attractive feature on her face.

Later, she noticed that he never raised his head or looked at his students directly as he was teaching them. However, when it was her turn to read a text or make a speech, his eyes behind the thick glasses turned attentive and dazed.[7] She was not the youngest in the class, nor the most beautiful. A lady from Chengdu was fair-skinned, warm-hearted and hospitable, always inviting them to her home for a hotpot dinner.

During the break, she always consulted him about some problems. By and by, their topics changed from the Shanghai dialect to literature. She got to know that he was a retired high school teacher, that he was interested in literature when he was young, and that up to now he continued reading literary journals. She had been an editor for several years before she got married and she, too, read quite a number of literary works. Thus, they found their common interest and subject of talk, which other ladies in the class couldn't share. For the first time, she met a man who could talk about literature with her. Since she came to Shanghai several years ago, the people she knew here all worked in the business circle and kept talking about such concrete topics as stocks, real estates, factories, training programs ... As to such abstract topics as literature, they never had a touch upon it.

She began to do the weekly facial mask before the class. After the facial mask, she put on light make-up and dressed herself up. In her spongy underpants and tight jeans, her legs looked long and slender. A designer T-shirt set off her good figure, and her slightly plump abdomen and buttocks were cleverly hidden in her overcoat. She had her hair done in her favorite barber's — No.5 made her black hair shining; No.10 dyed it into brownish red; No.7 curled and styled it into either a ponytail or a coiled bun decorated with a pearl hair-band; and sometimes, she just let her hair loosely droop down on her shoulders.

Compared with her, he was simply unfashionable and almost unchangeable. In spring, every day, he wore a beige jacket, a solid-colored T-shirt and a pair of pants which pilled a lot; when the summer came, he just took off his jacket; and as the weather got hotter, he changed his T-shirt into a short-sleeved one. He was medium-sized and had an ordinary face without any memorable features. Perhaps due to serious myopia, his eyes often looked dull and vacant. Fortunately, thanks to his scholarliness he actually appeared quite likeable, especially when he peered from time to time behind his thick spectacles at her, who was a beautiful butterfly dancing in his eyes.

She knew everything well enough and in her heart she couldn't help but chuckle as she did to No.5, No.7 and No.10 in the barber's. Here, the old man was like a boy extending his hand and asking for candies from her, which gave her a good reason to continue dressing herself up every day. She didn't want to know his personal life after the three-hour weekly class. She kept herself mysterious in front of him: She was from Taiwan, which already rendered her an exotic appeal; besides, she lived in a high-end neighborhood which denoted wealth and fortune. In his eyes, she must be leading a luxurious life which he could only imagine but never had the opportunity to experience.

Every month, once or twice, when her husband didn't need to work overtime or attend a transoceanic telephone conference, he would all of a sudden sat beside her while she was watching TV or reading a newspaper — she knew she had to fulfill her "task" at night. Before going to bed, she, as usual, put on her sexy and bright-colored underwear made of silk or satin. In the bathroom, looking at herself in the mirror, she smiled bitterly. On the bed, she closed her eyes tightly, summoning No.5, No.7 or No.10 at random in her mind, yet she had never summoned him, her Shanghai dialect teacher. Seeing her in such outfit, he must be so embarrassed that his face and his ears would flush all over. Perhaps even his glasses might fall off? But that lick, that dream confused her! Maybe he was not as cowardly and timid as she imagined? Maybe he nursed a gust of enthusiasm and desire which were strong enough to conquer her at once, like a knife splitting bamboos.

The summer night was so hot and endless. The air turned sticky and dense. The naked bodies with sweat all over turned and rolled on the moist and scorching mat. If only the green bamboos could bring some fresh coolness! If only the restless tossing and turning could end soon! However, instead of driving the overbearing heat away, the merciless wind shook the bamboos and made them shiver and groan at night. Her husband's off-and-on movement upon her, together with his heavy breaths, his hiccups and his farts, struck her incessantly. At this time, No.5's slender fingers, No. 7's warm air and No.10's handsome face appeared alternately in front of her eyes over and over again. But she never, never called for his help.

Why? How could she be such![8]

At five to two o'clock, she finished her last stroke of silvery eye shadow. Taking her textbook, she went to the class. She liked being a little late so that he could be a little worried about her. But as she got there, she found only the woman from Chengdu and him in the room. Seeing her coming in, both of them appeared relieved. She picked a seat a little far from them and sat down, without casting him a look.

After ten minutes, nobody else came. The woman from Chengdu said to him, "They must have gone out to play, I am sure. Do we continue our lesson?"

He got hesitant and answered, "What do you think?"

She didn't look at him and turned to the woman from Chengdu, "What about you?"

That woman smiled and said apologetically, "I also have something to do in a while. I had thought to leave earlier, but I feel sorry to our teacher …"

He said in good temper, "Never mind. We can resume our class next week. I … I also have something to do."

The woman from Chengdu left. She stood up and picked up her book from the desk. "You also have something to do?" Looking at him, she asked in a complaining tone. It was her first time to make eye contact with him today.

"No. No. Doesn't matter. If you want to listen, we might as well …" He took off his glasses and put them on.

She suggested having a walk in the neighborhood. The weather was quite good. The neighborhood she lived in was well-known in Shanghai as a favorite of the expatriates. It covered a large area with tall buildings, green grassland, rustling trees, flowers in blossom, rockeries, pond, swimming pool and man-made sand beach, all of which added charm to one another. Crossing the sand beach where children were skipping or frolicking about, they sauntered into the willow grove beside the pond. They stopped there. Seeing them, a school of colorful fancy carps swam to them and gathered beneath, waiting for something.

They kept silent all the way, but in silence she felt something pressing and powerful. She liked this kind of feeling and secretly she felt happy about it. She sensed something growing, fermenting and swelling by and by between them, inexpressible, infatuating and flammable.[9] He just stood beside her quietly, however, and she began to feel wronged and suffocated. Finally, she couldn't bear the silence and said to him, "Yesterday, I read a poem. It's interesting, but I can't fully understand it." She began to recite the poem. As she read halfway, he continued and finished the other half of the poem.

"You know this poem! Then, what's the relation between the summer night and the bitter bamboos?" She asked, suddenly feeling a pricking pain between her eyebrows. Her face turned red.

"What's wrong with you?"

She put her fingers on the place between her eyebrows, "I don't know. Perhaps it's a worm?"

"Let me have a look." He approached her — the situation in her dream happened in reality! Their faces drew near and she could feel his breath. His face turned red abruptly, his nostrils shivered in nervousness, and there were something strange in his eyes. Her heart began to beat violently, her silvery-shadowed eyes were fixed at him, and her sexy red lips opened slightly. She was waiting for him! She didn't want to take the responsibility for what was destined to happen! However, he backed off. "No. There is nothing." Looking at his feet, he said in a low voice.

"No? Nothing there?" She held her book tightly in her arms lest she should hurl it at him in fury.

"Er. I know the bamboos you mentioned," he cleared his throat and continued. "They are pleasant to the eye but not agreeable to the palate. They grow luxuriantly in the mountains and a person may get the feeling that the night has fallen when he goes into them. "

That night, when her husband climbed onto her with heavy breaths again, she summoned him. Why not? He was just a man on the street who had nothing to do with her. In her imagination, he really came. Taking off his glasses, rubbing the place between his eyebrows, he looked at her vacantly. "Be patient. It's nearly dawn." He said.

1. "想起这一节，已经失去那种颠倒魔力，只觉得可笑，这样的春梦竟会是跟他？那么一个拘谨胆小的老男人，从不敢迎看她大胆的眼光，只在她移开目光时才偷瞥一眼。难道我会吃了你？她暗笑，就是要吃，也轮不到你。" Now, clear-minded, she was no longer infatuated head over heels with that dream. She even found herself ridiculous. With him in that amorous dream? That meticulous and timid old man never dared to meet her eyes directly! Only when she looked away from him did he steal a glance at her. Will I eat you? She sneered secretly. Even if I want to eat somebody, you are not in the list! 这几句中，有的是主人公的心里所想，因此用了现在时。注意几个词汇和短语：clear-minded 头脑清醒的，be infatuated with 被冲昏头脑、迷醉，head over heels 神魂颠倒地，meticulous and timid 谨小慎微的、胆小的，meet one's eyes 对视，steal a glance at 偷偷扫一眼，sneer 冷笑，in the list 在名单上。

2. "目光要单纯，态度有点青涩……" Of course, their eyes should be clear and their manners green and pure. "青涩" 翻译成了 green and pure。green 有 "年轻的、稚嫩的、未成熟的、无经验的" 等等意思。英语中的颜色词与汉语颜色词的含义不尽相同，翻译时要注意。例如：in a brown study 出神、默想/

be green-eyed at sb. 嫉妒某人，红眼病/ He is yellow. 他为人胆小怯懦。

3. bumble 跌跌撞撞、笨手笨脚地做、踉跄。注意区分几个相近动词：rumble 发出隆隆声，tumble 摔倒、翻滚、突然坠落，fumble 摸索，stumble 绊脚、出错。

4. 这是一段在理发店做头发的动作描写，要注意一些用词的生动准确。Holding a wisp of her hair, he curled it, straightened it and dried and styled it with the two ends of his hair-dryer. In his skillful hands, wisps of twisted hair came into being, which looked attractively classic. The two wisps of the curly hair beside her ears sprang upward when give a pull, caressing her cheeks softly and briskly.

5. "那一回他替她洗了头，松颈按肩，轻拢暗捻抹复挑，她闭眼任他按去……" Once, after washing her hair, he did massage for her neck and shoulders. Closing her eyes, she enjoyed herself a lot as his forceful fingers touched, kneaded, rubbed and pressed her body in a skillful manner. "轻拢暗捻抹复挑" 用以说明按摩时的各种手法，英译时使用了多个动词。

6. "做、坐、俗、卒"都是汉语中发音相同或相近的字，难以用英语表现，所以省略不译了。

7. "但只要轮到她读课文或发言，他便带着一种愣愣的神情……" "愣愣的"，在这里是既专注又神情恍惚的意思，故译作… when it was her turn to read a text or make a speech, his eyes behind the thick glasses turned attentive and dazed.

8. How could she be such! such 在这里是代词，意为"这样的人，这样"。

9. "这一路两人都没说话，沉默中，有种说不出的压力和密度。她窃喜于这压力密度，仿佛他们之间的确是有着什么暧昧不明的情愫，这情愫在发酵中，一步一地雷。"这是人物的心理描写，激动、紧张、企盼、害怕。They kept silent all the way, but in silence she felt something pressing and powerful. She liked this kind of feeling and secretly she felt happy about it. She sensed something growing, fermenting and swelling by and by between them, inexpressible, infatuating and flammable. 这里的"压力"、"密度"、"暧昧不明"、"窃喜"、"发酵"、"地雷"等词都在译者的译文中以不同形式体现出来。pressing and powerful 有紧迫感（两个单词押头韵），growing, fermenting and swelling 形成、发酵、膨胀，inexpressible, infatuating and flammable 难以言喻、令人头晕、容易爆炸。

鸟飞过

○ 朝　君

　　我们走出河道，向树林里走去。两闸中间有个半岛，半岛四周植满了柳树，柳树在春风中摇曳着，叶片嫩绿嫩绿。我们在这里方便后，柴佑说去里边看看。我说，你不怕杨老师？他说怕什么。我们钻过树林，有一片爽眼的油菜地，油菜已经开展了花，黄黄的油菜花，一眼望不到边。我说，这景色好美呀，柴佑采下一朵闻闻，真香。我也学着采一朵闻闻，一股清香扑鼻。几只蝴蝶在花丛中起舞着，我去扑捉，蝴蝶飞来飞去，非常逗人。柴佑抓着一个小蜜蜂，他说被蜇了一下，捋起胳膊果然一片红。他将蜜蜂掐住，用蜜蜂肚子里的汁涂抹在红肿的地方，那部位很快凸红一片，我建议他找苤苤菜叶敷上止痒，可越是想找，越是发现不了。

　　这样找着，我们突然发现一个坟丘。这时有个女孩忽然惊叫着跑了出来，吓了我们一跳，竟然是纤纤，她见是我们才笑了笑，忙将裤子系好。原来她也正在这里方便。她一脸通红，我们也不好意思起来。我说柴佑被野蜂蜇了。她很关心，柴佑伸出胳膊，纤纤捏住红肿的地方，两个拇指往外挤毒，也许用劲太大，疼得柴佑龇牙咧嘴。她挤出血水，从衣袋里掏出手绢擦干，她说，很快就会好的。这时，有一种响声让纤纤惊奇。她说刚才听到了一种响动，我侧耳听，听到"咕咕"的叫声和"扑扑啦啦"的响动，看看四周，只见一片黄花。日头快顶到正上方了。柴佑说，在这里，响声在这里。我们顺着他手指的地方看，顿时吓住了，那是个坟丘。仔细听，声响确实是在那里发出的，大家都往后撤。纤纤连退几步，偎在柴佑身边。柴佑说不要怕，他去看看。他走近坟丘，仔细听了一刻，叫我过去。我不大敢，他说，大白天的怕啥，我只能走过去。呆了好长时间，他将坟丘尾端的活砖拆开一个缝。顿时，有一个活物从里面飞出来，被他一把抓住，竟是一只鸟。鸟头上长着一撮毛，柴佑说是"一把扇"。他笑着，说这也叫戴胜鸟，它最喜欢和坟在一起，他小时候常跟爹爹在坟丘里捉"一把扇"。"一把扇"被抓着了，扭动几下没有挣脱，无奈地看着柴佑。这鸟真漂亮，也很可怕。见纤纤走过来，柴佑想递给他，纤纤不敢接。

我们走出黄花地，纤纤不高兴了，她的黑色裤上沾满了油菜花的黄粉，我们看看自己的裤子，也沾满了花粉。纤纤急得要哭，说这可怎么办？怎么办？柴佑说，到前面去再说。我们进了一片柳林，慢慢走过坡地，看见了河水在发亮。柴佑说，用河水洗一下裤腿吧。

河水流动着从西边而来，两岸的芦苇长出半人高，绿莹莹的。有的柳树长在苇坑里，倒影在水面上，暖融融的春天，阳光无处不在，我们沿一条小路穿过芦苇丛，来到河边。柴佑将“一把扇”递给我，这个美丽鸟已经没有什么可怕，我接过来仔细瞅着。说实话，我以前见过这种鸟，但是从没有捉住过，现在拿在手中，仿佛掂着一个宠物。纤纤掏出手绢，弯腰在河水里弄湿，擦裤子时不小心差点滑倒，她扶住了柴佑，让他去洗手绢。一群小鱼游过来，向柴佑的手边游去，等柴佑提起手绢，鱼群又纷纷向周围游开。河面泛起层层涟漪。“一把扇”在我手中扭动，挣扎。柴佑脚下一滑，纤纤“啊”的一声，我连忙去抓他们，“一把扇”趁机飞了。我们三个都险些掉进水中，望着远远飞去的鸟，柴佑感到遗憾，他将纤纤裤子擦拭完。纤纤问我们要不要擦。柴佑说腰酸，不擦了。于是我们走出苇丛，沿着河岸的小路慢慢地走着。苇丛里不时有几只小鸟“喳喳”着飞来飞去，忽然飞来两只鹤，落在水边，纤纤说，没想到这里还有这么多鸟。柴佑说有水就有鸟，赶明儿带你去个地方捡鸟蛋。纤纤问去哪儿？柴佑说暂时保密，纤纤便噘起了嘴。

我们快要走出树林时，遇见一个精神病人。他一见纤纤就喊“秀悯哟……”纤纤吓得躲在柴佑身后，柴佑和我将他轰走，然后向工地跑去。同学们让我们去吃油条，油条已经完全凉了。同学们吃过饭都坐在柳林里休息，纤纤吃了一口凉油条又递给我们，她不想吃。我和柴佑都饿坏了，一根接一根吃。纤纤去找女同学玩，我们不大会儿，就将两捆油条吃进肚里，柴佑提着纤纤那一捆让我吃，我摇摇头说吃饱了，然后从水桶里舀了两碗水，一人一碗喝着。柴佑将剩下的油条包好，然后坐在柳树下歇息。

一天的植树劳动几乎就要完工，有人挖出了闸底板的一些石头。就在我们看清这些石头时，发现是一块块石碑。上面刻着不同的文字，我们一块一块念着，多是坟碑。有三个字频繁出现，那就是“清处士”。我们不理解什么意思，历史老师说，清处士就是普通、无官位的清朝富户。你们想想，穷人能立得起碑吗？护闸的老刘也过来了，他回忆说，建大闸当时，全镇的坟头碑和庙院的碑都拉来了。提到庙院的碑，历史老师来了兴趣，一块块地看碑文，让同学们打扫干净，终于他激动地说：“找到了，找到了……西来庵。”原来，学校后面半块清碑的后半截埋在了这里。他将这事告诉了校长，校长没有多大兴趣，让他别这样神经质，一惊一乍的。

晚上我们在农家早早地躺下，同学都很困乏，我也很快睡着了，在冥冥中，我梦见了戴胜鸟，那只美丽鸟向我飞来，飞到跟前，变成一个女人，不是毛兰同学，不是纤纤，像在哪里见过，她一直对我笑着，又变成一只鸟飞走了。我激灵一下，醒了，把柴佑唤醒，告诉他我的梦。他说睡吧，别瞎想了，我可能想女人想疯了，连鸟也变成了女人。我打他，他翻身又睡着了。我闭上眼，回顾坟丘里捉住的"一把扇"，想着想着，身上起了冷汗。

第二天我发高烧，柴佑领我去柴大仙那里拿了药。我没有上课，整整躺了一天。到天黑儿，柴佑告诉我，他刚才去了河闸北边的村庄，他了解到，那个飞出美丽鸟的坟丘里，确实是埋了个女人，是个女知青。据说她在村里住的时间最长，后来跳河死了。当时支书说，她怪可怜的，给她砌了个坟丘。

柴佑说，对呀，我们昨天碰到的那个精神病，听说就是当年的支书。我问，他怎么变神经了？柴佑说，听说是有一天他实在受不了，就发了疯。

A Bird Passing By

○ Zhao Jun

Out of the watercourse, we walked into the woods. Between two sluices there was a small peninsula covered with luxuriant willows whose green leaves and tender branches were swaying in the spring wind. After we passed water, Chai You said that he wanted to have a look inside. "Aren't you afraid of our teacher Yang?" I asked. "What are you afraid of?" He replied. Then we walked into the woods. Our eyes feasted upon a vast expanse of yellow rape flowers which stretched as far as we could see.[1] "How nice!" I exclaimed. Chai You plucked a flower and smelled it. "Fragrant!" Like him, I also plucked one and smelled it. A waft of fresh fragrance greeted my nose.[2] Several butterflies were dancing among groves of flowers, and as I tried catching them they quickly fluttered away. How interesting! Chai You caught a little bee and he said it stung him. A red lump appeared on his arm soon. He pinched the bee's body and applied its succus to the red lump which was swelling up. I suggested using splendens to stop itching, but it was so hard to find.

As we walked about, trying to find the splendens, all of a sudden, a tomb mound came into view. At this moment, a girl screamed and rushed toward us. We were taken aback. It was Xianxian. Seeing us, she smiled shyly and flurried to fasten her pants. Oh, just now, she was passing water here. Her face flushed and we also felt embarrassed. I told her Chai You was stung by a bee. She was worried and wanted to have a look. Chai You extended his arm. As Xianxian pinched that red lump, trying to force out the poison inside, Chai You felt so painful that he couldn't help gremacing a lot. Patiently, she squeezed out the poisonous blood and wiped his wound with her handkerchief. "It'll soon recover." She comforted him. At this time, a strange sound surprised us. Xianxian said she heard the sound just now. I listened closely — "Flip-flop"… "Splitter-splatter"… Looking about, we saw nothing but a field of yellow flowers and the sun overhead. "Here, here, the sound comes from here!" Chai You cried aloud. Following the direction of his hand, we saw a tomb.

We were astonished and scared! The sound indeed came out of it. We stepped backward. Xianxian was so frightened that she leaned against Chai You. "Don't be afraid. Let me have a look at it." Chai You walked close to the tomb and listened attentively. After a while, he called me. I was afraid to approach it. "In such broad daylight, what are you afraid of?"[3] Chai You asked. I had to walk closer. He took a loose brick off the tomb and a crack was revealed. All of a sudden, something fluttered out of the crack. Chai You caught it in time. It was a bird. On its head there was a wisp of hair, which Chai You called a "fan". He smiled and told us that this bird was called a hoopoe and that when he was small his father often took him to catch hoopoes around tomb mounds as these birds liked to make their nests in tombs. The hoopoe in Chai You's hands fluttered and struggled to free itself, but to no avail. At last, it could do nothing but stare at Chai You helplessly. The hoopoe was beautiful but frightening. Chai You wanted to hand the bird to Xianxian who was approaching with interest, but she didn't dare to touch it.

After we walked out of the field of rape flowers, Xianxian turned unhappy, for her pants were stained with yellow pollen. All our pants were stained. "What shall I do? What shall I do?" Xianxian cried. "Go on, and let's think of a way out." Chai You comforted her. We went forward. Through quite a lot of willows and past a slope, we finally saw a river shimmering in the sunlight. "Look! Let's wash our trouser legs there!" Chai You said.

The river gurgled here from the west and on its banks green reeds grew as tall as half a man. Some willows growing out of the reed pits cast their reflections in the water. The warm sunshine was everywhere on such a beautiful spring day. Along a small path we crossed the reeds and came to the riverside. Chai You passed me the hoopoe, which didn't look so frightening now. I looked at it closely. As a matter of fact, I had seen this kind of birds before but never caught one. I held it meticulously in my hands as if holding a pet. Xianxian took out a handkerchief and bent down to wet it in the river. Then she used it to clean her pants. As the riverside was too slippery, she almost fell down. So she held Chai You's arm and asked him to wash her handkerchief. A school of small fish came,[4] lingering around Chai You's hands. As he took the handkerchief out of the water, the fish scattered away, leaving circles of ripples on the surface. The hoopoe kept struggling in my hands. Chai You slipped and almost fell. "Ah!" Xianxian cried. As I extended my hands in a hurry to hold him, the hoopoe broke loose and flew away. All of us nearly slipped into the water. Chai You looked with regret at the hoopoe flying farther and farther. He crouched and helped Xianxian wash her pants. When she intended to help us, Chai You said that his waist ached a lot so he didn't need a cleaning. Then, we three walked out of the reeds. As we were walking slowly on the path along the riverside, several birds chirped and fluttered to and fro around us. Two cranes stopped at the riverside. "I've never expected that there are so many birds here." Xianxian said. "Where there is water, there are birds. Tomorrow let's pick up birds' eggs, OK?" Chai You suggested. "Where?" Xianxian asked. "It's a secret!" Chai You said. Xianxian pouted her lips.

When we were about to walk out of the woods, we met a madman. At the sight of Xianxian, he cried, "Ah, Xiumin ..." Xianxian was frightened and hid herself behind Chai You. We drove the madman away and rushed toward the working field where our classmates gathered. Seeing us back, our classmates offered us fried flour sticks,[5] which had been cold already. They were having a rest under the willows. Xianxian took a bite of the cold fried flour stick and gave it to us, saying that she didn't want it. Chai You and I felt hungry and gobbled down the flour sticks without stop. After a while, we had eaten two bunches of flour sticks. Chai You took Xianxian's bunch and handed it to me. I shook my head and told him I had had my stomach full. I took two bowls of water and gave one to him. Chai You wrapped the flour sticks and sat under the willows.

As our tree-planting day drew to an end, someone dug out some stones under the sluice gate. We found that in these stones there were some old stone plates inscribed with characters. We read those inscriptions and knew that they were tomb tablets. Three characters appeared frequently — "Qing Chu Shi" (a talented man yet to be granted an official position in the Qing Dynasty). I didn't understand it. "Qing Chu Shi" refers to those wealthy people who had no official titles in the Qing Dynasty. Our history teacher told us. Yes. His words sounded reasonable. The poor couldn't afford a tomb tablet. At this moment, Liu, a worker at the sluice gate, came to offer his story. To build the sluice gate, all the tomb tablets and temple tablets were gathered here, Liu told us. On mentioning the tablets in temples, our history teacher became enthusiastic. He asked us to clean every tablet and read them one by one. "I find it! I find it! The Xilai Temple!" He shouted excitedly. Behind our school there was half a tablet and now he found the other half here. He told our schoolmaster his discovery. Our schoolmaster wasn't interested in it at all and told him not to make such a fuss.[6]

In the evening, we stayed in a farmhouse. As we were tired we went to bed early. I fell asleep soon. In my dream I saw that beautiful hoopoe, which flew to me and turned into a woman. She was not my classmate Mao Lan or Xianxian. I felt I had seen her somewhere. She smiled at me and after a while she changed into a bird again and flew away. I woke up with a shudder.[7] I awakened Chai You and told him my dream. "Go to sleep, and don't think more about it." Chai You chuckled. "Perhaps you are in great need of a woman. Even a bird changes into a woman in your dream!" I gave him a couple of hits and he turned around to fall asleep again. Closing my eyes, thinking of the hoopoe we caught in the day, I broke into a cold sweat.

The next day, I had a high fever. Chai You took me to Immortal Chai for some medicine. I didn't go to school and lay on bed for the whole day. At dusk, Chai You came and told me he went to the village north of the sluice gate and learned that a woman was buried in that tomb from which the hoopoe flew out. She was an "educated youth" (usually referring to the high school graduates who were sent to the countryside for reeducation during the Cultural Revolution 1966-1976)[8] and it was said that she lived the longest in the village in her group of "educated youths" and in the end jumped into the river to commit suicide. The head of the village felt pity for her and built a tomb for her.

"Oh, yes! The madman we met yesterday was the head of the village!" Chai You told me. "How did he go crazy?" I asked. "It was said that he could no longer endure all this and lost his mind in the end," Chai You answered.

注 释

1. "有一片爽眼的油菜地，油菜已经开展了花，黄黄的油菜花，一眼望不到边。" Our eyes feasted upon a vast expanse of yellow rape flowers which stretched as far as we could see. one's eyes feast upon … 大饱眼福，as far as we could see 一眼望不到边。

2. "一股清香扑鼻" 翻译成：A waft of fresh fragrance greeted my nose. waft 空中飘来的一阵气味，greet one's nose 使鼻子愉悦。

3. In such broad daylight, what are you afraid of? broad daylight 大白天。

4. a school of small fish 一群小鱼。英语中单位词生动而有特点，例如：a swarm of bees / a pack of wolves / a flock of birds / a herd of cattle / a cluster of ants / a brood of chickens / a litter of puppies，等等。

5. fried flour sticks 油条，fried flour twist 麻花。中国特有的小吃，第一个单词指做法，最后一个单词指形状。

6. "一惊一乍的"这里翻译为make such a fuss. make a fuss 大惊小怪，小题大做。

7. "激灵一下"就是由于恐惧等原因全身哆嗦了一下，所以翻译为：I woke up with a shudder.

8. "知青"是中国的一个有特殊含义的名词，所以在翻译时，译者用括号的形式，加入了文内注释，一来不影响行文流畅，二来对相关文化知识做一个简单介绍。She was an "educated youth" (usually referring to the high school graduates who were sent to the countryside for reeducation during the Cultural Revolution 1966-1976).

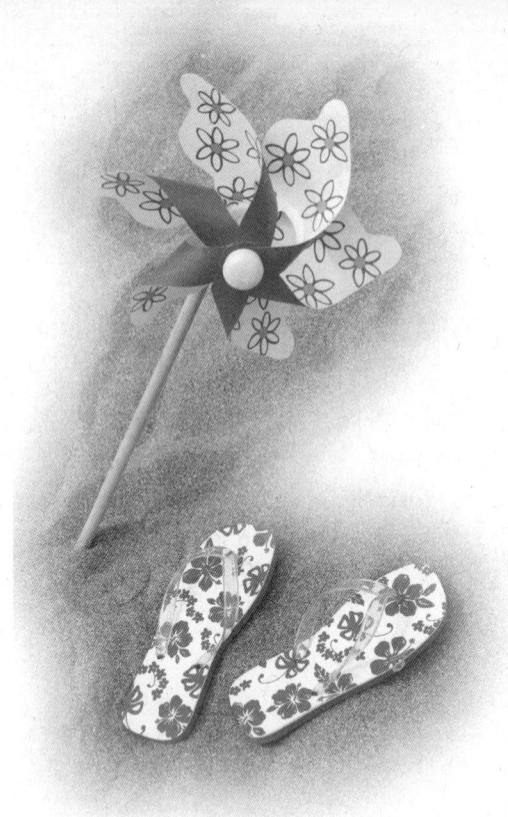

如梦令

● 尹庆全

　　夏天一个中午，小唇在河边捡到一双崭新的红色塑料凉鞋，不知被谁搁在这块栗色的洗衣石上，扣襻一只解开着，另一只扣得好好的，望望四周，寂静的河面空无一人，只有河中间隆起的一块沙洲上立着几只长脚鹭鸶。

　　洗衣石上的凉鞋，火炭一样烫手，小唇把鞋子放到水里浸了浸。

　　谁的鞋呀——

　　小唇喊了几声，清脆的童音像翠鸟在空旷的河面四处飞翔。受到惊扰的长脚鹭鸶展开雪亮的翅膀，长唳一声，掠着水面朝对岸飞去。

　　绕着苏庙车站的是白露河。缓缓流淌的河水下，沉淀着厚厚的沙子和大大小小的卵石。靠站台的岸边是麻石筑起三十多米高的路基，块块石条在河上潮气的浸洇下布满了苔藓。陡斜的石阶伸向河边，站上的人们到河边取水、淘洗衣物、钓鱼都是顺这条石阶下去。对岸是宽阔的河滩，长着柔韧的河柳和一丛丛、一片片的芦苇。站台北头的扳道房附近架着一座石桥，三个桥墩都是用巨块麻石垒砌而成，桥面上是白石栏杆。桥那边是一条漫长的乡间大路。

　　小唇猜测这双鞋是站里某个洗衣服的女人丢在河边的。但他没去车站寻找失主，他掂着鞋爬上路基，往石桥那边走去。

　　透过扳道房的窗户，扳道员老曹远远望见爬上路基的小唇，以为小唇在河里逮了两条红鲤鱼，他甚至望见了拼命甩来甩去的鱼尾。到了跟前，老曹才看清楚小唇提着的两只鞋。

小唇，你手里哪来的鞋？

河边捡的。

老曹仔细看了看鞋子，认出是售票员姚小茹的鞋。

姚小茹有这么一双红塑料凉鞋，而且一个多小时前，老曹还在河边看见过她。

这天早晨，老曹在河边钓鱼，位置在桥墩底下。后半晌天气热起来，几个在河边洗衣服的妇女陆陆续续地走了，老曹也开始收竿。老曹收拾东西的时间也不过几分钟。转身走的时候，发现河边还有一个人，垂着湿漉漉的长发在那里洗头，身边搁着一个盛满衣物的脸盆。当时老曹并没在意是谁，只是想，都快晌午了，这么晒，怎么还有人在河里洗头呢。老曹刚爬上路基，听见河底下传来一个熟悉的声音：

曹师傅，钓到鱼了吗？

老曹听出来是售票员姚小茹的声音。他回头往河下看去，蹲在水边的果然就是姚小茹，清澈的水底倒映着她笑盈盈的脸。老曹说：

是小茹啊，我还当是谁呐。

小唇在河边捡的一定是姚小茹的鞋。老曹就对小唇说：这是姚小茹的凉鞋，售票员姚小茹，你不认识吗？

认识。

那你还把鞋往哪里乱掂？你去站台问问，肯定是她的。

不，我要交给小惠老师。

小唇头也不回地上了石桥。

入夏以来，小惠老师经常做梦。

这会儿小惠老师坐在讲台前面，学生们都趴在座位上午睡。前排的一个女生睡得非常香，嘴角挂着一丝熟睡中的口水。小惠老师的瞌睡也一阵阵袭来。后来实在撑不住了，靠着椅子睡着了。

梦开始很好，她跟谁在一棵刚抽芽的柳树下面亲热……接着柳枝在风中剧烈地飞舞，舞着舞着，柳枝儿变成了血乎乎的小手。小惠老师心惊肉跳地醒了过来，燥燥地、愣愣地瞅门口那棵枝叶浓密的大柳树。就在这时，小唇出现在热浪滚滚的大路尽头，让正愣神儿的小惠老师不由地打了一个寒噤。

小惠老师觉得这双凉鞋是好友姚小茹的。她非常羡慕姚小茹有一双如此漂亮的凉鞋。这双鞋使姚小茹走起路来格外轻盈，身姿格外婉约，她在月台上行走，拖曳着娇柔的水红色光焰，始终在小惠老师的眼中燃烧。

苏庙这块地方，车站、粮库、学校、砖瓦厂，包括苏庙集，没有第二个女人拥有这么耀眼的红凉鞋。也有女人穿红颜色凉鞋，都是又厚又硬的生塑料鞋，没一点光泽，死死板板的，只有姚小茹这双塑料鞋质地特别柔软，透明、水润，款式好看，鞋后跟高出好些。

小惠老师把红凉鞋带进办公室，几个女教师立刻围了上来。高门大嗓的洪老师很快认出了鞋主：姚小茹的鞋吧。

我也看着像。小惠老师说。

洪老师说：准是她的，别人谁也没有这么洋气的鞋。

听说是她爱人从部队寄回来的。另一个女教师说。

在上海买的。小惠老师说。

她爱人不是在东北吗？

小惠老师说：她爱人托人从上海买的。只有外汇商店才卖，专门卖给外国洋女人穿的。

这鞋子真小巧。姚小茹会是这么小的脚？

小惠老师说：她35码鞋，跟我一个号。

小惠老师穿的是一双浅黄色的凉鞋，前头露脚趾头、后头包脚后跟的样式，单独看还可以，跟这双红凉鞋一比，笨头笨脑、土里土气。这还是上次流动售货车来苏庙时，姚小茹帮她抢购的。

洪老师说：小惠，你把鞋换上，让我们观赏观赏！

小惠老师有些不好意思起来，但拗不过她们，只好坐到椅子上，把浅黄色凉鞋脱下，换上红凉鞋。扣椭圆形亮熠熠的金属扣襻时，手指抑止不住地一阵阵颤抖。她在旁人的鼓动下走了两趟，说什么也不肯走了，红着脸把鞋换下，说：穿着真是拿捏人！

下午放学，小唇被叫进了办公室。小惠老师从抽屉拿出那双红凉鞋，递到小唇手里，告诉他，鞋是他拾来的，由他交给失主。失主就是售票员姚小茹。洪老师提醒：最好找张报纸，把鞋包着，别让这孩子路上再掂丢了。

小唇说：不用包，我放书包里！

站台上暑气未消，热气蒸人。一盆水泼在水泥地上，嗤嗤地就干了。值班员老黑连续朝门口泼了四五盆水。

苏庙站台就一幢房子，红瓦灰墙，跟沿线其他小车站一样是幢仿俄式建筑。由南至北，分别是候车室、售票室、站长室、值班室、行包房。售票室又被一道夹墙隔成前后两间，前一间是售票室，朝候车室那边开了一个方方正正的售票口。后一间就是姚小茹的住室，住室的门窗正对着白露河。

仅有的几名旅客这时都在候车室的后门外躲避酷暑。远处的河面，时不时地能吹过来一丝河风。这个京广线上的末等小站，每天只有一对慢车停靠，分别是晚上十点多钟往南的302次和第二天上午九点多钟往北的303次，时常晚点。姚小茹的工作就是给乘这两趟车的旅客售票。

458

姚姐——姚姐……

小唇的喊声出现在站台上，在炽热的空气中显得格外刺耳。

他在售票室门前又喊又敲。里面没有反应，穿过候车室的后门，一边喊一边拍门板，拍窗户玻璃，里面仍然没有动静。他立起脚尖，勉强把脑袋送到窗台上，发现玻璃后面严严实实被一块浅绿色的窗帘遮住了，什么都看不见。

值班员老黑走了过来。

娘的腿，喊什么喊？

我找姚姐，我捡了她的鞋。

不是她的鞋。老黑皱着眉毛说，她不在家。

小唇不信，又去拍窗，说：她在家！老曹中午还在河边见着她了。

老曹？老曹说明天过年！姚小茹昨天就上部队探亲去了，怎么还能在河边？

天快黑的时候，小唇糊里糊涂把鞋掂回了家。

车站上的人很快都知道了小唇捡回一双非常时髦的凉鞋，跟姚小茹常穿的那双一模一样。

晚上乘凉时，扳道员老曹讲到在河边见过姚小茹，还跟她说过话。老黑就嘲笑说：老曹中午肯定是搭讪鬼了，人家姚小茹这会儿恐怕该过山海关了，你还能在河边看见她洗头！

老曹说：昨天姚小茹走，我怎么不晓得。

她昨天是乘302次去的信阳，然后转车去牡丹江。不信问站长去。

老曹说：可能她在信阳误了车，又乘303回来了。不然小唇怎么能捡到她的凉鞋。

根本不是她的鞋。她出门不穿鞋吗？

老曹说：牡丹江多冷你知道吗，那地方夏天零下几度知道吗？姚小茹穿着凉鞋不冻脚吗？

车站货运员秦素贞在一旁笑，她刚去苏庙小学找了赵小惠老师，才洗过澡，坐在一张竹椅上撩拨着湿润的头发，说：你俩争得真笑人！曹师傅一定是看花眼了，小茹才走，曹师傅就惦念上了，见谁都像姚小茹！

老曹说：姚小茹的鞋子会飞？鞋子会自己飞到河边？

秦素贞被老曹问住了。小唇在河边捡到的红凉鞋，像姚小茹的那双。记得姚小茹从粮库回来时，一只鞋帮儿被石棱子划了道印痕，她用牙膏爱惜地擦拭了半天，污渍擦去了，印痕却没能去掉。若说小唇捡的不是她的凉鞋，有一模一样的印痕，未免太巧合了。

可是，昨晚秦素贞亲眼看着姚小茹上的火车。她突然要去东北，临走把房门钥匙让秦素贞转交小惠。秦素贞追问：

小茹！这么急急忙忙，遇了什么急事？

姚小茹在车门口转过身，微笑着摇摇头，举起被灯火涸染得红酥酥的小手，朝秦素贞轻轻地晃了几下。

苏庙车站有三排家属房，对面就是苏庙粮库。高大的仓房在月光下耸立着像一座座山丘。火车在远处轰隆轰隆地响，一道粗粗的光柱子慢慢移过茫茫苍苍的野地，扫到白露河，河水霎时泛起霞霓般的光晕。

老曹不停地嗅着鼻孔。闻到隐隐的茉莉花气息。他知道那气息来自秦素贞身上。他悄声地说：小秦，你肯定洗澡的时候抹了东西。

秦素贞坐的竹椅响了一下：你长的是狗鼻子。

不光是狗鼻子，还是狗眼睛！

老曹听这瓮声瓮气的声腔，把身体端正过来。

老曹女人说：你龟孙口口声声见着人家在河边洗头，还见着人家洗屁股了吧，那人呢？你龟孙藏起来啦？

乘凉的人都笑起来，秦素贞也悄悄跟着笑。

笑个屁！老曹的女人起身就走。

在小唇家，小唇母亲坐在帐子里，把那双塑料凉鞋往脚上套，她脚太厚，硬往里套，勒得直叫唤。小唇爹说：

别把人家姚小茹的鞋撑岔了。

她说：穿着试试就撑岔啦，瞧你心疼的。

小唇的爹腾一下子爬起来，把她掀倒在草席上。小唇的母亲哼哧着，鞋还举在脚上，说：提起姚小茹小妖精，就来劲头，看你急的……小唇，小唇你睡着了没有？

娘，我睡着了。小唇说。

几乎就在同一时刻，身上微微沁着汗粒儿，小惠老师又做了个梦。

她梦见流动售货车又到了苏庙车站，停在车站边道上。人们都向车站涌去，洪老师抱着一块才从售货车上抢购的灯心绒布闯进屋来：小惠，你怎么还睡，快去呀，售货车上有姚小茹穿的红凉鞋！

小惠奔跑起来。头发在风中直直地飞舞，却怎么也跑不快。车站的人群已经散尽，售货车如同遭到洗劫一样，货架上只剩下一块块用来卷布匹的木板，地上狼藉地散落着一些空盒子。

姑娘，你来晚了。什么都没有了。一个声音说。

小惠失望地转身要走，一个声音又说：就剩最后一双鞋了。

小惠打开盒子，里面装的正是一双高脚跟的、有着椭圆形扣襻的红凉鞋。

小惠，穿上吧。这双鞋归你了，试试合不合脚。一个熟悉的声音说。小惠循着声音一看：小茹，怎么是你？

这双鞋归你了。我不在苏庙做售票员了。流动售货车上也挺好，可以去好多好多地方。我这就要走……

车门"轰"一声关闭了，眼前的音影全部消逝，变得一片漆黑。小惠想打开火车的铁门，但沉重的门怎么也拉不动，她想喊叫，但喉咙像被一双手紧扼着怎么都发不出音……小惠老师惊醒过来，发现自己光着脚站在地上，一阵剧烈的轰鸣声来到了耳畔。

是小唇最先发现那两只脚的。

跟许多个早晨一样，那天清晨白露河传来阵阵鹭鸶高亢的叫声。站上的人们都听习惯了，他们每天早晨都是在鹭鸶长一声短一声的鸣叫中苏醒过来。

小唇从家里出来。远处的河滩是鹭鸶聚集活跃的地方，从河柳与芦苇丛中成群结队地起飞，又纷纷落在河边、浅滩、水中突出的巨石及隆起的沙洲上。

走过姚小茹住室的窗户时，发现跟昨天看到的情形不一样，拉得严严实实的浅绿色窗帘，从边沿闪出明显的一条缝隙，露出室内墙壁的颜色。他扒着窗台，透过缝隙朝里边张望，先是瞧见挂在墙上的黄色军用挎包，接着是一条粉红色纱巾，搭在床尾的木撑子上，然后看见了床上露着两只白乎乎的脚。

小唇以为是姚小茹，"姚姐、姚姐"地喊，两只脚没有一点动静，用力拍窗户，两只脚仍然一动不动，小唇有些害怕。

小唇紧紧拉住从河边过来的老曹女人的衣襟，指着姚小茹的窗：有两只脚！我看见了姚姐的脚……

老曹女人说：两只脚？怎么可能。说着俯到窗前，顺窗帘缝隙往里张望，让她一下子慌了神。她退到路边，对一起从河边返回的养路工小齐的女人喊：快过去看看，小姚的床上！

小齐女人被老曹女人吓得缩手缩脚，不敢看，哆嗦着声音说：不可能吧……都讲小茹探亲了嘛？

这时，老曹扛着钓鱼竿走过来，小齐女人慌张地说：快过去看看，老曹，小姚床上到底怎么回事？老曹凑近姚小茹的窗户，仔细一看，头皮顿时一阵阵发麻。姚小茹床上，一动不动的确实是人的两只脚，除了姚小茹，谁的脚能这么小巧白嫩？而且从两脚分开的距离看，床上的两条腿应该叉得很开，姚小茹正常睡着，两腿怎么能叉这么开！

不好了，姚小茹出事啦！

嘭——，小齐女人的脸盆从手中滑落，震碎的白瓷四处飞溅，巨响在清晨寂静的候车室内激烈回荡。

值班员老黑跑过来，以为是哪个捣蛋小孩弄碎了窗玻璃，看见滚在水泥地上的脸盆、散落的衣物和大惊失色的老曹他们，忙问：怎么回事，怎么回事？

小唇哭着说：屋里有两只脚……

老黑大步迈到窗子跟前：两只脚？哪有两只脚，在哪……没有啊。

老曹吼道：还说没有！在床上！

老黑被吼声震蒙了，他又仔细瞅瞅，还是没有。

老曹狐疑着俯近窗缝，刚才还在床上的那两只脚，这会儿真的不见了，正犯着嘀咕，窗帘恍惚一下，小惠老师困倦而又愠怒的面孔出现在玻璃后面……

这年秋天，苏庙车站又调来一名女售票员。附近的村民买票的时候，总爱好奇地朝窗口里面多看几眼，都想瞧瞧车站新来的这名女售票员长什么模样，有没有原先那售票员漂亮。

车站的月台上再也没有出现过姚小茹的身影，音信杳然。人们只能猜测她去了爱人那里，与苏庙不辞而别了。

而小唇从河边捡到的那双红色塑料凉鞋，也一直无人认领。

一天上午，小唇来到河边，手里还是掂着那双红凉鞋。小唇在洗衣石附近把红凉鞋扔进了河里。红凉鞋在水面久久浮着，好几次又漂回到岸边。小唇捡起来，奋力地往河中间扔。红凉鞋终于像鱼儿一样游去了。

The Dreamlike Song

● *Yin Qingquan*

One afternoon on a summer day, Xiaochun saw a pair of red plastic sandals on a brown laundry stone by the river. They were spick-and-span.[1] Who put them here? On the laundry stone where women often washed and rubbed clothes, the sandals lay still, with one buckle undone and the other well done up. Looking around, Xiaochun could see nothing but the tranquil water and several long-legged egrets standing on a protruding sandy islet in the center of the river.

The sandals felt as hot as fire on the scorched stone. He picked them up and dipped them into the water.

"Whose sandals —"

He shouted, his ringing boyish voice spreading far and near, like a kingfisher gliding on the surface of the water. The startled egrets spread their bright white wings, uttered a long whoop, skimmed over the water and fluttered to the opposite side of the river.[2]

The river was called White Dew, which slowly ran around the Sumiao railway station. A thick layer of sands and pebbles of different sizes deposited at the bottom of the river. By the riverbank near the station was the roadbed made of chiseled ashlars, which was as tall as thirty meters. Due to the riverside dampness, the ashlars were covered with green moss. The sheer stone stairs extended downward into the river. Every day, people walked down these stairs to fetch water, wash clothes and do some fishing by the river. On the opposite side of the river was a vast field of riparian beach where groves of supple willows and clusters of reeds grew luxuriantly. To the north of the platform, near the switchman's cabin, there was a stone bridge with white stone balustrades and three piers also made of huge chiseled ashlars. Beyond the bridge, a country road extended as far as the eye could see.

Xiaochun guessed that a woman from the station must have come here to do her laundry and left her sandals on the stone. But instead of going to the station to look for the owner, he walked towards the stone bridge.

Through the window of the switchman's cabin, Lao Cao saw Xiaochun climbing onto the roadbed and carrying two red carps caught from the river. He even seemed to see the carps thrashing their tails in an attempt to free themselves. As Xiaochun got close, Lao Cao came to see that they were not fish but a pair of shoes.

"Xiaochun, where did you get them?"

"I picked them up by the river."

Taking a close look at them, Lao Cao recognized that they were Yao Xiaoru's shoes. Yao Xiaoru was the ticket seller in the station.

Yao Xiaoru wore such a pair of red plastic sandals. About an hour ago, Lao Cao saw her by the river.

This morning, Lao Cao went fishing under the bridge pier. At noon, it grew hot and the women who came to do their laundry left one after another. Lao Cao also drew back his pole and in a few minutes he gathered his things up. As he turned and was about to leave, he found someone washing her hair by the river, with her long, wet hair drooping to the water, beside whom there was a basin filled with clothes. He didn't give it too much thought at first. It is nearly noon and this person is washing her hair under such scorching sun![3] He thought. As he walked upstairs onto the roadbed, a familiar voice came to his ear from behind —

"Lao Cao, have you caught fish?"

It was Yao Xiaoru's voice. He turned his head and looked down. Indeed, it was Yao Xiaoru, squatting by the water. Her smiling face was reflected in the clear water.

"Ah, it is you, Yao Xiaoru!"

So now, he thought the sandals Xiaochun picked up by the river must be Yao Xiaoru's. "These are Yao Xiaoru's sandals! Don't you know her, the ticket seller in the station?" He said to Xiaochun in a definite tone.

"I know her."

"Then, where are you going with them? You'd better go to ask around in the station. They must be hers."

"No. I want to give them to Miss Xiaohui."

Xiaochun walked direct onto the bridge without looking back.

Since the beginning of the summer, Xiaohui, a teacher, always had dreams.

Now, sitting at the teacher's desk in the classroom, Xiaohui felt drowsy again. It was noon and all her students were taking a nap with their heads on their arms.

A girl in the front row slept so soundly that a stream of saliva ran out of her mouth. Pelted by doziness,[4] Xiaohui fell asleep with her back against her chair.

The dream began well: She and someone were making out under a young willow tree which had barely put forth sprouts, until all of a sudden, the willow branches began to dance violently in the wind and as they waved they became many blood-stained hands. She woke up with a start. Staring at the big willow tree thick with leaves at the gate, she felt fretful and distracted. Right at this moment, Xiaochun came into view, who was walking toward her from the other end of the scorched road. A sudden chill shot through her.[5]

Xiaohui also believed the sandals belonged to Yao Xiaoru, her good friend. Yao Xiaoru had such a beautiful pair of sandals! Xiaohui had been envying her so much! With them on, Yao Xiaoru looked exceptionally graceful in her brisk gait, which added irresistible charm to her perfect figure. When Yao Xiaoru walked on the platform, her reddish sandals, as soft and tender as flickering flames, glittered and almost burned Xiaohui's eyes.[6]

In Sumiao, either in the station, in the granary, in the school, in the brick factory, or in the Sumaio fair, nobody else had such wonderful sandals! Some women here also wore red sandals which were made of thick and hard plastics and looked dull with no luster in the least. In contrast, Yao Xiaoru's were soft, transparent, lustrous, stylish and even had higher heels.

When Xiaohui brought the red sandals into her office, other female teachers came up at once. Ms. Hong who always spoke in a loud voice quickly recognized these sandals. "They are Yao Xiaoru's?"

"I think so. " Xiaohui agreed.

"They must be hers! Who else here have such stylish shoes?" Ms. Hong exclaimed.

"I heard that it was her husband who mailed the sandals to her from his military service." Another teacher said.

"The sandals were bought in Shanghai." Xiaohui added.

"Isn't her husband stationed in the Northeast? "

"Her husband asked someone to buy them in Shanghai. You know, only foreign exchange shops sell this kind of shoes, to foreign women only." Xiaohui explained.

"How cute the sandals are! Yao Xiaoru' feet were so small?"

"She wears size 35, same as I." Xiaohui answered.

Xiaohui wore a pair of light yellow sandals which revealed her toes and wrapped her heels. They looked OK but compared with the red sandals, they appeared countrified and rustic.[7] Last time when the travelling sales van came, it was Yao Xiaoru who bought them for her in the shopping rush.

"Xiaohui, put on the red sandals and let's have a look!" Ms. Hong urged.

Feeling embarrassed but unable to turn them down, Xiaohui sat on the chair, took off her yellow sandals and put on the red sandals. When her fingers touched that D-shaped golden metal buckle, they couldn't help shivering. Encouraged by her colleagues around, she walked to and fro in the office. After a short while, she insisted on taking them off, her face blushing. As she took off the sandals, she said in a low voice, "They really pinch!"[8]

In the afternoon, after class, Xiaochun was asked to go to the teacher's office. Xiaohui took the sandals out of the drawer and handed back them to Xiaochun. "It was you who picked them up and you'd better return them to the owner yourself. The sandals belonged to Yao Xiaoru." She said to Xiaochun. Upon Ms. Hong's suggestion, she was also to wrap the sandals with a piece of newspaper lest Xiaochun should lose them on his way home.

"Don't worry. I can put them in my schoolbag!" Xiaochun said.

The whole platform was permeated with unbearable heat. A basin of water splattered on the ground sizzled and dried up instantly.[9] Lao Hei, the operator on duty, had sprinkled four or five basins of water on the ground.

There was only one building in the Sumiao railway station. It was a Russian-style building with red tiles and grey walls, like in all the other small stations along the railway line. The waiting room, the ticket office, the station master's room, the operator's room and the luggage room were aligned in a row from the south to the north. The ticket office was partitioned off into two small sections. The front was the ticket seller's room with a square wicket on the wall facing the waiting-room, and the back was Yao Xiaoru's dorm, whose door and windows faced the White Dew River.

There were just a few passengers on the platform. And now, to escape the heat, they all waited at the back gate outside the waiting room. A wisp of wind, more often than not, came to them across the surface of the water. Sumiao was one of the smallest stations along the Beijing-Guangzhou line and every day only two slow trains stopped here: the southbound No.302 departing at about ten o'clock at night and the northbound No.303 departing at about nine o'clock in the morning. Both of them were often late and couldn't keep up with the schedule. It was Yao Xiaoru's job to sell tickets for the two trains.

"Miss Yao — Miss Yao …"

Xiaochun's voice pierced the sweltering air in the station.

He shouted and knocked at the door of the ticket office. There was no response. He ran through the back gate of the waiting room and tried shouting and patting the door and windows of Yao Xiaoru's dorm, but still got no response. He stood on tiptoe to barely put his head on the window sill and looked inside, but to his disappointment, a light-green curtain tightly blocked his sight. He saw nothing.

Lao Hei, the operator on duty, came to him.

"What on earth are you screaming about?"

"I want to see Miss Yao. I found her shoes."

"These are not hers. She is not in." Lao Hei said with a scowl.

Not quite believing his words, Xiaochun turned and continued knocking at the window, saying, "She must be in the room! Lao Cao saw her by the river at noon!"

"Lao Cao saw her? If Lao Cao says tomorrow is the New Year's Day, do you believe it? Yao Xiaoru left yesterday! She went to visit her husband. How could Lao Cao see her by the river?"

It was nearly dark. Feeling confused, Xiaochun had to go back home with the sandals.

Soon, all the people in the station knew Xiaochun picked up a pair of beautiful and fashionable sandals by the river, which were identical to what Yao Xiaoru often wore.

At dusk, people went out to enjoy the cool breeze. When Lao Cao mentioned that he had seen Yao Xiaoru by the river and had a talk with her, Lao Hei laughed. "Lao Cao, you must have come across a ghost! Now Yao Xiaoru must be passing Shanhaiguan in the Northeast. How could you have seen her washing her hair by the river!"

"She left yesterday? Why don't I know it?" Lao Cao said.

"She took the train No.302 yesterday. After she arrives in Xinyang, she will change to another train bound for Mudanjiang. If you don't believe me, you can ask the head of our station."

"Perhaps she missed her train in Xinyang and came back by No.303? Otherwise, how could Xiaochun have picked up her sandals?" Lao Cao reasoned.

"They are not her sandals at all. Is it likely for her to go out without wearing shoes?" Lao Hei retorted.

"Do you know how cold Mudanjiang is? Even in summer, the centigrade falls below zero there, doesn't it? Doesn't she feel cold in sandals?" Lao Cao said.

Qin Suzhen, the operator in charge of freight transport in the station, chuckled aside. She just visited Xiaohui in Sumiao Primary School. Now, after a bath, she was sitting on a bamboo chair, combing her wet hair with fingers. Hearing the two men's argument, she butted in. "How funny you both are! Lao Cao, you must have been fooled by your own eyes! No sooner had Yao Xiaoru left than you began to miss her and mistook everybody for her!"

"Can Yao Xiaoru's sandals fly? Can they fly to the riverside by themselves?" Lao Cao talked back.

Qin Suzhen couldn't answer him. Indeed, the red sandals resembled Yao Xiaoru's very much. Qin Suzhen remembered clearly that once Xiaoru went to the granary and got one of her sandals scratched by sharp stones. After she came back, she wiped the scratch carefully with toothpaste, but although the smear was removed, the scratch stayed. If these sandals were not hers, how could they have the same scratch! Could such a coincidence exist?

However, last night, Qin Suzhen saw with her own eyes that Yao Xiaoru got on the train. All of a sudden she decided to go to the Northeast to see her husband. Before she left she asked Qin Suzhen to give her doorkey to Xiaohui.

"Why are you in such a hurry? Is there anything urgent?" Qin Suzhen asked Yao Xiaoru on the platform.

Yao Xiaoru turned around at the door of the carriage, smiled at Qin Suzhen and shook her head. She raised her hand which hued to a lovely red in the lights of the station and waved goodbye to Qin Suzhen.

There were three rows of residential houses at the Sumiao railway station. The Sumiao granary was on the opposite side. The big and tall barns, like a chain of hills, stood silently under the moonlight. A train rumbled far away, casting thick beams of light across the vast and dark fields to the White Dew River which, all at once, shimmered with brilliant light halos.

A vague smell of jasmine continuously hit Lao Cao's nostrils. He knew it was from Qin Suzhen. He sidled to her and whispered by her ear —

"Qin, you must have applied something to your body in your bath."

Qin Suzhen's chair creaked. "You must have got a dog's nose."

"Not only a dog's nose but also a dog's eyes!" A woman cut in.

Hearing the thick and rough voice, Lao Cao quickly straightened his body.[10]

It was Lao Cao's wife. "You bastard kept on saying that you saw her washing her hair by the river, and you must have seen her washing her prat, right? Where is she? You son of bitch hid her away?"[11]

People around all burst into laughter. Qin Suzhen sniggered, too.

"Bosh!" Lao Cao's wife stood up and left.

At Xiaochun's home, his mother was trying to put the red sandals on. Her feet were too fleshy and pinched a lot in the sandals.

"Don't stretch them too much. They may be out of shape!" Xiaochun's father said.

"I just want a try. How can I make them out of shape? Your heart aches, eh?"

Hearing her words, Xiaochun's father abruptly sat up and pressed her down on the mat. Xiaochun's mother grumbled, the sandals still on her feet, "A slightest mention of that seductress will turn you on! Look at you! So impatient … Xiaochun, are you asleep?"

"Mom, I am asleep." Xiaochun answered.

Almost at the same time, Xiaohui had another dream as she sweated all over in her troubled sleep.

In her dream, the travelling sales van came again. It stopped at the roadside near the station and a flood of people rushed toward it. Ms. Hong broke into her room, holding a piece of corduroy bought from the van, and shouted at her, "Xiaohui, don't sleep any longer. Be quick! The red sandals like Yao Xiaoru's are for sale!"

Xiaohui began to run excitedly, her hair flying in the wind, but however hard she tried, she couldn't run fast enough. And when she got there, the crowed had dispersed and the van was left alone, as if it had just been ransacked. On the shelves, there were only some empty wooden boards, which had been used as spindles for the cloth. A mess of empty boxes scattered on the ground.

"Miss, you come too late. Nothing is left." A voice came to her ears.

As she turned and was about to leave in disappointment she heard that voice again, "Except a pair of sandals."

She opened the box and to her surprise she saw the high-heeled red sandals with D-shaped golden buckles!

"Xiaohui, put them on. The sandals belong to you now. Try them on and see if they fit you." She heard a familiar voice. Looking up, she saw Yao Xiaoru. "Ah, It's you!"

"They belong to you. I won't sell tickets at the station any longer, and it's good to sell goods on the sales van, as I can go to many places. I am going to leave ..."

As the iron door of the train was closed with a bang, all the things disappeared right away. It was a complete darkness in front of Xiaohui's eyes. She tried to open the door, but she couldn't. She wanted to cry, but her throat was strangled, as if by a pair of forceful hands ... Xiaohui woke up with a start and found herself standing on the ground, bare-footed. A great noise was assaulting her ears.

It was Xiaochun who found those two feet first.

The other morning, as usual, the long-legged egrets sang loudly and sonorously beyond the White Dew River. People had got used to this and they woke up in the egrets' cries and ululations every morning.

Xiaochun walked out of his home. A lot of egrets gathered on the riparian beach in the distance. They were flying here and there in groups over the dense groves of willows and clusters of reeds. After a while, they landed one after another on the riverside, the shoals, the exposed boulders or the sandbars in the river.

While walking past Yao Xiaoru's window, he found something different. The color of the wall was revealed from the side of the light-green curtains, which were otherwise drawn tightly shut. He stood on tiptoe and peeped into the room. First, a military green bag came into his view, then, a pink gauze kerchief on the footboard of the bed, and then, two white feet.

Xiaochun thought Yao Xiaoru was in the room and called, "Miss Yao, Miss Yao!" Those two feet remained motionless. He began to tap the window, but those two feet kept still. Xiaochun began to feel alarmed.

Seeing Lao Cao's wife, who happened to pass by, Xiaochun held fast to her blouse and led her to Xiaoru's window. "Look! There are two feet! I see Miss Yao's feet ..."

"Two feet? How come?" Lao Cao's wife looked closely between the curtains. In a wink of an eye, she turned pale.

She retreated to the roadside and shouted at the wife of Xiao Qi, a railway maintenance worker, who was on her way back from the riverside. "Come! Come over and have a look! Yao Xiaoru is on her bed!"

Xiao Qi's wife was too scared to look into the room. "Is it likely? ... They say she has gone to visit her husband." She muttered in a shivering tone.

At this time, Lao Cao came, carrying his fishing pole on his shoulder. Xiao Qi's wife said to him in a hurry, "Go to have a look! What's wrong with Yao Xiaoru?" Lao

Cao put his face close to the window and looked inside. At the sight of those two feet, he felt his blood freeze at once. He was utterly thrown into panic and confusion.[12] Except Yao Xiaoru, who else had such fair and delicate feet? Judging from the distance between her two feet, he thought her two legs must be wide apart. If she was sleeping, why were her legs so wide apart?

Something terrible must have happened to her!

Flump! Xiao Qi's wife let a laundry basin she was holding slip onto the ground.[13] The broken white enamel fragments flew in all directions. The bang broke the silence of the waiting room and reverberated in the morning air.

Lao Hei who was on duty heard the sound and hurried in, thinking that some naughty boy might have broken a window. When he saw the laundry basin, the clothes scattered about and the people all in a flutter, he asked in a hurry, "What happened? What's wrong?"

"We see two feet in the room …" Xiaochun cried.

Lao Hei strode to the window. "Two feet? Where are they? Where? … I can't see them."

"You can't? On the bed!" Lao Cao roared.

Stunned, Lao Hei looked more closely. Indeed, he saw nothing on the bed.

Bewildered, Lao Cao looked inside again. The two feet on the bed disappeared! As he mumbled to himself in doubt and terror, the curtain jerked and Xiaohui's face appeared behind the window. She looked sleepy and sulky …

In autumn, a new female ticket seller was employed. When the villagers nearby bought tickets, they all cast a curious look at her so as to see whether she was as beautiful as the previous one.

Since then, people never saw Yao Xiaoru on the platform and never heard of any news about her. They all believed that she went to live with her husband and left Sumiao without a goodbye.

The red plastic sandals Xiaochun picked up by the river remained unclaimed.

One morning, Xiaochun went to the riverside. Near the laundry stone, he threw the red sandals into the river. They kept drifting on the surface of the water and for several times they flowed back to the bank, but Xiaochun picked them up and threw them at the center of the river with all his strength. The red sandals, like fish, finally swam away and disappeared.

1. spick-and-span 崭新的，还可以用 span-new、brand-new。

2. "受到惊扰的长脚鹭鸶展开雪亮的翅膀，长唳一声，掠着水面朝对岸飞去。"鸟的动作和声音让人有身临其境的感觉。The startled egrets spread their bright white wings, uttered a long whoop, skimmed over the water and fluttered to the opposite side of the river. 注意动词的选择和使用：be startled 吓了一跳，spread the wings 展开翅膀，whoop长而尖的叫喊声，skim 掠过、擦着水面飞过，flutter 扇着翅膀飞。

3. 这是人物心理活动，所以用了一般现在时。

4. "瞌睡也一阵阵袭来"译为 pelted by doziness。pelt 连续投掷、连续攻击、连续开火，这里用这个词，是为了突出"睡意连续袭来，难以阻挡"的意思。

5. "小惠老师心惊肉跳地醒了过来，燥燥地、愣愣地瞅门口那棵枝叶浓密的大柳树。就在这时，小唇出现在热浪滚滚的大路尽头，让正愣神儿的小惠老师不由地打了一个寒噤。"这句中，"心惊肉跳"、"燥燥地"、"愣愣地"、"热浪滚滚"、"愣神儿"、"寒噤"都是翻译的难点。She woke up with a start. Staring at the big willow tree thick with leaves at the gate, she felt fretful and distracted. Right at this moment, Xiaochun came into view, who was walking toward her from the other end of the scorched road. A sudden chill shot through her. wake up with a start 惊醒，fretful 心烦的、不安的，distracted 心烦意乱的、魂不守舍的，a sudden chill shot through her 打了个寒噤。

6. "这双鞋使姚小茹走起路来格外轻盈，身姿格外婉约，她在月台上行走，拖曳着娇柔的水红色光焰，始终在小惠老师的眼中燃烧。"With them on, Yao Xiaoru looked exceptionally graceful in her brisk gait, which added irresistible charm to her perfect figure. When Yao Xiaoru walked on the platform, her reddish sandals, as soft and tender as flickering flames, glittered and almost burned Xiaohui's eyes. 翻译不必拘泥于原句的句式结构，但要把原句的亮点在译句中体现出来。比如这句中的"轻盈"、"婉约"、"摇曳"、"娇柔"以及比喻的用法，都是翻译时必须展现的。这需要译者积极发挥主观能动性，比如这里酌情处理成 which added irresistible charm to her perfect figure 使她的美好身材更加具有吸引力。

7. "……单独看还可以，跟这双红凉鞋一比，笨头笨脑、土里土气。" They looked OK but compared with the red sandals, they appeared countrified and rustic. countrified 乡下派的、粗俗的，rustic 有村民特点的、不雅的。

8. "穿着真是拿捏人！" 意思就是鞋有些挤脚。They really pinch! pinch 捏，掐，夹，拧；作不及物动词时，可以指(鞋)挤脚。

9. "站台上暑气未消，热气蒸人。一盆水泼在水泥地上，咝咝地就干了。" The whole platform was permeated with unbearable heat. A basin of water splattered on the ground sizzled and dried up instantly. be permeated with 充满、渗透、充盈，sizzle 咝咝响，既是拟声词又是动词。

10. "老曹听这瓮声瓮气的声腔，把身体端正过来。" "瓮声瓮气"的声音是老曹妻子发出的。Hearing the thick and rough voice, Lao Cao quickly straightened his body.

11. "老曹女人说：你龟孙口口声声见着人家在河边洗头，还见着人家洗屁股了吧，那人呢？你龟孙藏起来啦？" 这里有骂人话，翻译时不要避讳，选词要符合说话人的身份和语气。You bastard kept on saying that you saw her washing her hair by the river, and you must also have seen her washing her prat, right? Where is she? You son of bitch hid her away?

12. "头皮顿时一阵阵发麻" … he felt his blood freeze at once. He was utterly thrown into panic and confusion. 译者把 "头皮发麻" 的意思换个说法表达出来。

13. Flump! Xiao Qi's wife let the laundry basin she was holding slip onto the ground. flump 砰的摔下。用这个单词，有声音，有动作。

山猫

◎ 王瑞芸

　　"你这样的人在越南待过……打仗？我是无论如何不能相信的。"我对莱瑞说。

　　莱瑞先眯起眼睛，然后才笑起来。我很熟悉他这个表情。我来美国后，跟他学英文已经有三年了。我们每星期见一次面，两人面对面坐谈两个小时，他的每个表情我都熟悉。而这个表情，表示他要开始讲笑话了。

　　"我在你眼里……至少不是天使吧？"

　　我直直地望着莱瑞——一个七十来岁的美国老人，五短身材，肥厚结实，整整齐齐的花白头发，整整齐齐的花白胡子，全都修理得跟刀切的一样。这样边线整齐的老人容易叫人心生好感，虽然他不笑时显得有些威严，但他常常笑，笑起来慈眉善目，可亲得很。

　　我也笑起来，轻快地说："嘿，我倒喜欢见着个长胡子的天使……不过，你既参加了越战，天使怕做不成吧！"

　　"这也难说，哼，魔鬼，天使……人哪！就是……可是，算了，不如听我说说在越南的事，你只管听着就是……只说当时我在越南，感谢上帝，没有被编进连队，编进连队……了得！背着卡宾枪，子弹袋，再加四到六个像小甜瓜似的炸弹，哈，别忘了，还有水，食物袋……除去这些之外，脚上还得添一双沾了足有五磅湿泥的靴子……那种苦，跟下地狱也差不多了。我的运气好，我的运气好得叫人没法相信。这都得益于我有点技术的缘故……嗯，恐怕，还有点别的什么……我寻思。"

　　"当时，我是个谍报人员，专门负责架设天线，收听密码，并且破译电文。你知道，这在部队里显然是技术骨干了，享受军官待遇。因为那时我已经大学毕业，是个有技术的人，而且是个有特殊技术的人！因此，大学一毕业我就被国家安全局雇用了，可是不出几个月，在越南的美军部队向他们要人时，他们就把我派去了……"

　　"士兵们都叫我长官，其实我并没有军衔，我还是归国家安全局管。在那里我是个特殊的角色，军官们都跟我称兄道弟，知道我是'有背景的人'——
国家安全局！他们总拉我去他们的俱乐部，喝酒，打牌，玩闹……一句话：寻
欢作乐。哪里能缺少寻欢作乐呢？打仗的人，今天不知道明天，你要理解才
是。实在说，他们那帮倒霉鬼都挺喜欢我——对不起，我叫他们倒霉鬼，待会
儿你就能知道……总之他们喜欢我，并不是因为我的'背景'，而是，而是
……我是那样一种家伙……照他们的说法是'按自己的心思糊弄事儿'——那
样一种家伙！哈哈哈。"

"我差不多总待在西贡，哈，在西贡那样的城市，只要常去军官俱乐部，
喝着美国的蓝带啤酒，听着爵士乐，你觉得跟在美国也没差太多，再说，当地
越南人对我们挺好。可就是天太热，湿热湿热的，跟狗吐出来的舌头似的——
哪里像我的家乡蒙大拿，天冷得叫人精神抖擞！可是天热呢……真叫人受不
了。我的头发和胡子都长得特别快，因此我要常理发……我的故事几乎始于理
发，嗯！"

"我常去的一家理发店，是一个小得要命的店，在一条小得要命的街上，
那种小店只会有本地人，恐怕还只是穷人才会光顾吧，美国大兵们才不去呢。
可我这个人哪，就会异想天开，做一些别人不做的事。告诉你吧，幸亏了这脾
性，我今天才可以在这里跟你说话儿……算了……是这样，是一些孩子引我去
的。在我们营地周围总能碰到越南孩子，他们有各种理由来接近我们，捡烟
头啊，向我们要香烟壳啊，当然，更好的，是从我们这里得到糖果。我最乐
意给他们糖了，这谈不上慷慨什么的，我只是喜欢亚洲的小孩子们，那样
的小圆鼻头，蘑菇似地长在那样团团的小盘子脸上……哎啊，我的天！……我
总爱用糖果逗他们，告诉他们，能说上一个英文词的，给一颗硬糖，说一个英
文整句子，给一颗软糖。因此我只要一出营地，就会有一群孩子围上来，七腔
八调地用英文跟我打招呼，莱瑞，早上好，莱瑞，再见，晚上好……莱瑞，去
哪里？……他们就这样，活像一群小狗，围着我汪汪叫。我呢，哈！我就说，
今天啊，完蛋啦，没有糖，我要去理发。理发这个词，他们就听不懂了，我
就用手做成个剪刀，在头顶上移动。孩子们瞧明白了，哗啦一笑全跑开，只留
下一个孩子还在当地站着。那孩子突然就那么孤零零地站在我跟前，窘得要
命，几乎要流出泪来。这下可轮到我不明白了，他站在我跟前做什么？那孩子
正好是不能从我手上得到糖果的那一种，你知道，怕羞得要死的那一种。看他
瘦伶伶的，豆芽似的，窘得连我都要替他出汗。可是呢，他倒也并没有跑回同
伴那里，而是像个受惊的兔子看我一眼，然后开始朝前走。别的孩子都在一
丈开外站着，见那孩子走动起来，就一起朝我哄叫：GO，GO（走，走），TO
HIM（朝着他走），我居然也就听话跟了那孩子走，——我这个人有时候会非常
不听话，哪怕上级的话也可以不听，可有时候又能非常听话，听这群孩子的话
……瞧瞧我这德性！别人看我真正是个没道理的人，可是你记着，我就照这样

475

的'没道理'才活到现在。好，我就跟了那孩子走，结果，一走就走到那家理发店去了，原来那个孩子家里开着理发店……对了，就是这样。"

"那个理发师，他的爸爸，对我非常客气恭敬，显然我肯让他理发，给了他好大的面子，看得出，他替我剃头，刮脸，每个动作中都充满了敬意。在那里，你就是能碰到这样的越南人，他们对你恭恭敬敬，不是装的，是真心的，这看得出来，真心的……你为什么要奇怪，事情毫不奇怪，你心里没事，他们对你就没事，你心里想着他们是敌人，那么，他们就是。何况，我们是在南越，只有北越，对了，就是越共，那才算敌人，可是对于南越人，我们则是朋友甚至救星。你为什么笑，事情就是这样。敌人和朋友，那算个什么呢，你只管听着就是……哼。"

"得，一次，上面给了我们谍报人员一个硬任务：一定要接收到北越的电波信号。谍报科把这事交给我去办，说我是安全局特别派来的，兴许能有技术解决，这可是胡扯——要我的好看嘛。事情再明显不过，在南越架设接收器，很难收到北越清晰的电波信号。若要有效地接收越共的电波信号，唯一的办法只能是把接收器架到越共的地面上才成。这个活儿谁做得了？你又不能公然打进去，占了一个山头，把接收器架起来，那等于是扬铃打鼓地让所有人都知道。你要偷偷潜进去呢，也难。我曾找作战部队的军官商量过，试着请他们派人到北越地面上架设天线。他们倒是肯派一个班给我，可是，待那个班长向我问明了架设天线是在越共的地盘上，他对我简直破口大骂：'操！不去！你这个王八蛋选得真妙！选中越共对我们杀伤最多的死亡之地！你们这些该死的混蛋成天待在屋子里，滴滴答答地拍拍电报，就跟孩子玩跳棋那么轻巧，从早到晚把自己擦得跟一枚新崭崭的钱币一样，有的是大把闲工夫喝啤酒，玩女人……然后伸出一根狗日的手指头在地图上轻轻一点，就打算把我们十来条好汉的命送出去，我操你祖奶奶的！'你别介意我说粗话，当时他就是那么说的，那些玩命的大兵们说话就这样。问题是，他骂得有理，这分明是件送死的事。"

"天！这可怎么办。事情无法解决，华盛顿那边已经对我很不满意，你跟他们解释这一切，不会有人要听，记着，指挥官们永远不听下属的任何解释，他们只对你下命令。"

"我能怎么办呢，我也只能骂娘了。我去理发，烦躁地在椅子上动来动去，害得理发师失手在我的下巴上割开了一个小口子，我跳起来就朝他破口大骂。该死，我可一向没有对越南人逞过凶，我知道，许多美军不把他们放在眼里，可我不是那样的人……理发师看得出来，因此他对我非常恭敬，恭敬得出奇。可我突然开口骂了他，他吓得缩在边上，几乎矮下去半截，他们全家人都给吓呆了，全都缩成一团。看到他们吓成那副熊样，我狼狈起来，知道自己是个货真价实的大混蛋，可我不是故意的，上帝作证，我当时的心情实在糟透了。后来我给了理发师双份的小费，理发师当然明白，我用钱在向他认错了。"

"那个理发师……我得说说，哎，是个典型的越南人，又黄又瘦，那真叫一个瘦啊！可是他的眼睛非常温柔，奇怪得很，羔羊似的那种温柔，这让他那张本来不好看的瘦脸有一种挺中看的表情，好像他心里藏着什么好东西似的。他总对人温和地笑，对门口的脏孩子，或者狗，也那样温和地笑，虽然嘴里总在吆喝他们：去，去，走开。"

"他收下了我的钱，深深地对我鞠躬，他的女人在一边也深深地对我鞠躬，我心里有愧，觉得自己那样地骂人，用几个小钱就补偿了，挺不是个东西。可我看得出钱对他们挺重要，他们喜欢得很，这让我多少安心了。美元啊！谁说美元不是好东西呢……我就照这么想着，哈，突然，这个思路把我引到亮光里去了……我已经走出那条小街，马上又折回去，照直就问理发师：'你说，如果用钱，我可以向越南人买到什么？'他听我这么问，愣了一下，脸突然红了，垂下眼睛，挣扎似地过了好一会儿，才低声回答：'买得到任何东西。军爷。'虽然他声音非常低，但我听得清清楚楚，这对我就足够了。我朝他微微笑了，理发师呢，也朝我微微笑了，他八成已经猜出我的意思了。告诉你，我一直觉得这个理发师是个聪明人，从一开始就这么觉得，这也是我肯一直让他给我理发的原因。你要知道，聪明，跟人的身份没有关系，我在美军部队里，见过多少身居高位的蠢汉哪！……不过，不说这个。只说理发师，他突然开口跟我说了许多，好像是要给自己一个台阶一样：'……瞧，我们是人，我们需要活下来。就说你，军爷，是个美国人，你来越南，干什么，我管不了。可你来理发，就是我的贵客，何况，你的小费给得好，你照顾我，我和我一家都感激你。'他说的时候，他一家人都在一边眼巴巴地看着我。我注意到，他的几个孩子都破衣烂衫，赤着脚……理发师顺着我的眼睛也看看他的孩子，对我说：'不容易啊……军爷，你看得见……这些孩子们，喏，照这样……长大……可这还不算太差呢。你如果往北边去，特别是到乡下，一篮大米能换一个孩子，一个能干活儿的孩子！嗯……兴许还要不了一篮子大米呢，你得相信……'"

"他就照这么唠唠叨叨说下去，虽说他的英文破破烂烂，可我全都能明白他，他也能明白我，我已经完全有数了。跟着，我比划着把架天线的事跟他说了，单刀直入地告诉他我会付个好价钱。我还告诉他，这活儿倒是不难，横竖就是在地上打几个桩，可就是要力气，因为天线架子是个挺重的大家伙，而且要竖在山顶那样的位置上，主要是竖在越共的地面上。理发师听了没费什么事，就对我说：你明天天黑了来一趟吧。他也许并不很明白什么是天线，显然也不明白竖天线是做什么用的，他只想帮我，当然，也能帮他，因为我给钱。"

"第二天，我在理发店里遇到了他介绍给我的人，我一看吓一跳。那是个黑黑的小个头男人，不光皮肤黑，偏还穿了一身黑衣裤，主要是，那个越南汉子的脸是歪的，左边的脸好像被谁抓了一把，皱了起来，估计这一辈子就得照那样皱着了，他的眼睛也因此一大一小。那样眉眼歪斜的黑瘦瘦的家伙，再加上他表情阴沉，一句话不说，看着活像是打地狱里派来的魔鬼。那个黑色的魔鬼不光不说话，甚至也不看人，眼皮一直那么朝下垂着，好像谁都不值得他来瞧上一眼似的，由着理发师弯腰用越南话在他耳朵根前嘀咕，他要么摇头，或者点头，反正一声不吭……我们就照那样谈好了价钱、时间、地点，讲好隔几天我把天线运到他指定的河边上，他用木船来运走，但那个地方离美军的哨站很近，我要负责他的安全，这个是当然。"

"哨站那里我私下跟管事的打了招呼，他们还派了两个人在远处警戒呢。那个黑铁的天线接收器实在非常笨重，平搁在船身上，前后伸出去老远，像一只大螃蟹向两头伸出的大钳子。不过，谢天谢地，它总算没有把船压得进水——那越共弄来的是条小船。我简直想不出他怎么能一个人把这个大家伙运到山上去，单看他为了把船推离岸边，腰弯成了一张细弓，我就想得出这件事情够有多么吃力。我还看得见他因为弯腰，裤管吊上去露出了他的脚踝，因为月亮照亮了水面，我看得清楚那脚踝简直像理发师小儿子的脚踝那样细……我的天，那双细脚踝到现在还晃动在我眼前，倒像是我昨天晚上才见过的一样。我其实一点点都不喜欢这个表情阴沉的黑衣越共，比如那个脸儿黄黄的理发师，倒蛮招人喜欢，可这个黑小的越共，从头到脚没有一点招人喜欢的地方，不只是不喜欢，我简直——我得对你说实话——我简直，简直……就是恨他，虽然他肯为我们做事，可我本能地恨他那张歪斜的脸，恨他阴沉的表情，甚至他在那样的黑夜里，拚了命地推他的船，他费力的喘息声，也一样叫我不喜欢，那声音在黑夜里听来简直像一匹老衰马似的，在每一声后面还带着细哨子似的尾音——嘶，嘶，嘶的，可能他的肺八成都有问题……这些细节我全都记得，一辈子不会忘记……他越是推得吃力，让我越有一种恶意的快感：这个黑色的魔鬼当然不配把钱挣得太容易，那是好一笔钱呢！"

"他那么推着，船终于往前一滑，显然他没有收住力，往前一栽，很响的'咚'一声，声音不像在水里——尽管他终究还是跌到水里去了。我吓了好一跳，本能地伸手去拉他起来，鞋全踩水里了——水挺凉。虽然他被我从水里拉了起来，可一直弯腰站着，手捧着脑袋，一声不出，在嗦嗦地抖，八成脑袋都磕破了，可能在船沿上……我看他那样子……你知道让我想起什么了？想起我在中学时养过的一只狗，德国猎狗，大个头，威风凛凛，让我爱死了。可一次它过街让车撞断了一条腿，当时，那狗就是这么拱起腰站着，疼得嗦嗦地抖，让我心痛得简直要晕倒。打那时候起，我知道，无声地抖，那才叫疼！照这样一想，我的心不由哆嗦了一下……可你也不难知道，我怎么会像当年搂着我心爱的狗一样去把他搂住……根本不可能，不可能的！这是实情。我当时就是能感到他在疼，就觉得必须为他的疼做点什么，后来，我一把脱下了自己的上衣，递了过去。我根本不知道这样做能管什么用，难道是让他用来包扎一下跌伤的地方？让他别冻着？……天知道，反正我就那么做了，也就只能做那么多了。其实，从头到尾，我们两个一直没有说过话，黑地里，什么都朦胧不清。我想到他那原本歪斜的脸，如果再磕破了脑袋，那真够瞧的，幸好天黑不叫我看到，我也不想看到。"

"我递衣服给他，他显然是一愣，但接过去了，什么表示也没有，只是慢慢直起身，大口喘气，喘了一会儿，转身往船上一跳。就在他抽出船篙撑离岸边那一刻，他第一次对我凝神看了看，我当然看不清他脸上有什么表情，只感到他的脸正对着我停了有多半分钟，天知道他在想什么，然后，船就撑走了。"

"谢天谢地，一切都顺顺利利，天线竖起来，竖在一个叫黑寡妇的山上，我一想到黑寡妇和那个黑衣越共，就觉得整个事情不可思议地有趣。因为后来我从理发师那里得知，那个黑衣越共正是个鳏夫，家里一溜四个孩子，还有病歪歪的老人，饿得成天只能喝凉水，那种一篮子米换得到手的孩子大概就出在这样的家里。那笔钱肯定可以让他那个穷家起死回生了吧。反正，任务总算完成，华盛顿方面对我很满意，可是在越南的美军部队却对我颇有非议，有的军官指责我根本是直接用钱去援助越共，把他们养活了来收拾美军。什么话！"

"莱瑞，"我终于忍不住插嘴，向他笑道，"你别说，你这个人可真敢想，那个越共也真敢做，这事情放在我们中国人，绝对行不通，你是通敌，他是叛徒，全是杀头的罪。"

莱瑞也笑，说："这个理我知道……可我的理由是，那个黑衣越共有钱买粮食，应该只会给家人，他为什么要给他的同志买粮，弄得人人知道，他傻啊？！另外，你要了解，我们从越共截获的密码究竟在战争中起了什么作用，还说不准呢，有时候根本会帮倒忙。现在回过头来看我们当年在越南干下的事情，嘿，整个一堆垃圾！死了的全是白送命。我呢，我至少是让那一个班的人没有白送死，我让自己不白送死，我还让那个越共一家活了命，我要接受审判，也只能是上帝来审判，我马上让你知道，这种事唯有上帝才判得公平。"

"这事过去了之后，我看得出，那些真正有脑子的军官，都更瞧得起我，凡喝酒取乐的事必定要拉上我。那时只要没有晚间的任务，每个晚上我们都派对，西贡的酒店我们几乎全去过了……可是到了越战后期，北越南越两边的摩擦越来越厉害，平静的希望是没有了，只有尖锐的对抗和仇恨。危险的袭击甚至发生到西贡的街面上来，我们就不大出门取乐了。通常总是到美军俱乐部里去，把外面的姑娘叫进来，你知道，就像通常那样……"

"一天晚上，我正在俱乐部和军官们打牌，哨兵进来对我说，外头有个人要见我，我对哨兵说，'去，去，别烦我！'我大概是在赢钱，或者是在输钱，谁耐烦在那个时候被人叫出去。见哨兵还磨蹭着不走，我恶声对他说，'儿子，他是什么人，不见，叫他走！'哨兵只好走了，可一会儿又回来了，说，'请长官您好歹出去罢，要打发他走，您去打发，那个家伙简直跟苍蝇一样赶都赶不走，拿枪指着他都不走，他一定要马上见到您。'我问，什么人？哨兵说，是个越南人，我一听，心里起了疑，越南人？嘿，会是谁呢，上次那档事，早就两清了，我如数付了钱。什么人找我呢？我放下牌，就去了。我一站到门外的灯影里，一个黑影子似的人就窜上来，我倒退一步，一眼就看见了那张歪斜着的脸，还是那样的一身黑褂裤。一看见他那副嘴脸，我心里别扭，就粗声问他要干什么？他也不答话，伸手就拉我的胳膊，然后才开口说——说的倒是英文——COME，COME（来）……我还是第一次听到他出声说话，那声音粗，哑，怪腔怪调。虽然他帮过我的忙，可我实在是没法喜欢这个人，而且他居然敢来拉扯我。我挺不高兴当着哨兵被这个越南人拉扯，而且开始警惕起来。我怎么能不警惕呢，想到我和这越共之间的交易，恐怕他已经在他的同志们那里露了馅，现在八成是来找我算账罢。先哄了我跟他走，然后，干掉我，嘿，想得还真美。我对他说，'咄，撒手，你撒手！'那个越共不仅不撒手，反倒更紧地拽着我的胳膊往外拉，在灯下……谢天谢地，幸亏当时在灯下，不然事情就全两样了……灯下，我看得见他的大小眼完全睁大了，里面满满的竟是恐惧和恳求的表情。我心里格登一下，他的表情不知在什么地方打动了我。尽管我的理智告诉我不要理睬他，可是，他眼睛里发了疯似的那种恳求，甚至他那只死攥着不肯松开的手，都让我的身体不由自主地肯跟了他走，好像我的身体接收到的是和脑子不同的电波信号似的……我就那么半推半就地被他拉出去好远。直到凉风一吹，我脑子重新清醒起来，我冷丁一下子站住，厉声喝他住手，扭头就往回走，想不到就我转身的那工夫，他从旁边对我狠命一推，快得像只山猫，我扑地便倒，心里叫苦，坏了！坏了！！我还是着了他的道了，我怎么会蠢到肯跟他走出这么远。我拼命要爬起来，同时往身上摸枪……就在这个时候，哇，眼前强光一闪，一声巨响，我想，自己死定了……过了好大一会，我才觉得自己胳膊腿都在，而且开始感到眼前又热又亮，那时候，我突然明白了那个黑衣歪脸的越共对我做了什么。好家伙，几分钟前我在里头打牌的俱乐部被炸飞了，里面所有的人和那个哨兵全报销啦。上帝啊……等我完全明白过来之后，黑衣越共早已经走得不见了影子。"

莱瑞突然住了口，笑眯眯地，同时也带点儿研究性地瞧着我。我定定地看着他，什么也说不出来了。

2009年于美国加州千橡城

The Lynx[1]

○ *Wang Ruiyun*

"You were in Vietnam … and fought there? I don't believe it." I said to Larry.

Larry narrowed his eyes and smiled. It had been three years since I came to the United States and started to learn English from him. We met once a week and each time we sat face to face, chatting and discussing for two hours. Therefore, I was familiar with each and every expression of his. Now, the expression on his face indicated that he was going to tell a funny story.

"In your eyes … I am no angel. Right?"

Looking at him, a seventy-year old American, thick-set, with graying hair and white moustache both neatly trimmed, I felt kindly toward him.[2] Such a refined and well-groomed old man was likely to leave people a good impression. He looked a bit serious and august when he was not smiling, but he had a habit of smiling. When he smiled, he wore a benevolent and kind countenance, which was lovely and inviting.

I smiled and said to him in a brisk tone, "Ah, I expect to see an angel with moustache … Since you joined the Vietnam War, I am afraid it's hard for you to be an angel."

"It's hard to say. Err, devil, angel … human beings! It's … but … OK, forget it. Let me tell you my story in Vietnam. You just listen to me … When I was in Vietnam, thank God! I wasn't in an army company. If I was in a company … Oh, my goodness! Can you imagine? Carrying a carbine, bags of bullets, four or six grenades like little melons … Oh, don't forget … Water, food packages … Besides, the boots with almost five pounds of wet mud … One must feel he was in the hell! Fortunately, I was lucky, incredibly lucky, perhaps because I had some skills, maybe … I am afraid there were some other reasons …"

"At that time, I was an intelligence agent in charge of setting up wires, listening to the encrypted telegrams and deciphering those secret codes. I was the technical backbone in the army and treated as an officer. I graduated from university and I was a person with professional skills, or say, special skills! One year after my graduation, I was employed by the National Security Council, but just after a few months, the U.S. military forces in Vietnam were in need of people like me, so I was sent there ..."

"Soldiers there all called me officer, but, as a matter of fact, I was not granted any military ranks. I was a member affiliated to the National Security Council. In Vietnam, I was special among those officers, who called me brother and got on well with me. And they all knew I had some sort of special background — the National Security Council! They often brought me to clubs to drink, play cards, fool around ... In a word, we indulged ourselves in pleasure. Of course, pleasure was in urgent need, especially during wartime. In the war, you never know if you can live to the next day. You must understand. To be honest, those unfortunates were fond of me — I am sorry! Why do I call them 'unfortunates'? You'll know it in a while ... All in all, they liked me, not because of my 'background', but, but ... but because I was the type of guys they liked ... In their words, I muddled through 'after my nature' — that type, you know? Ha."

"I spent most of my time in Saigon. You know, in Saigon, lingering in the officers' clubs, drinking the American Blue Ribbon, listening to Jazz, you felt as if you were back home. Besides, the local Vietnamese were kind to us. The only problem was the climate. It was too hot! Hot and wet like a dog's tongue sticking out — totally different from my hometown in Montana where it is so cold that people feel refreshed and greatly braced up![3] But in Saigon, it was unbearably hot ... Indeed, unbearable! As my hair and moustache grew very fast I had to go to the barber's from time to time ... and my story started there. Yes! "

"I often went to an awfully small barber's located on an awfully small street,[4] which perhaps only the locals or the very poor frequented. American soldiers were unlikely to go there! But I was such a man with the wildest fantasies and often did things unusual and impractical ... To tell you the truth, but for my trait I wouldn't live to this day and talk with you now ... Forget it ... It was a group of kids who led me there. Around our camp, there were quite a few Vietnamese kids, who approached us with various intentions: picking cigarette butts, asking for cigarette packages, or getting candies from us. Of course candies would be the best thing they could get from us. I liked giving them candies. It had nothing to do with generosity. I simply liked Asian kids whose little round snub noses grew on their little flat faces like mushrooms ... Oh, my! ... I always gave them candies and played with them, promising to give a hard candy to anyone who could speak an English word and a soft candy to anyone who could speak a complete English sentence. Consequently, as soon as I stepped out of the camp, I was quickly surrounded by children, who vied with one another to greet me in their clumsy English. Hi, Larry! Good morning! Larry, goodbye! Good evening … Hey, Larry, where are you going? … They yelped at me like a brood of puppies. What did I say? Ha! I said: 'Today, oh, damn! I run out of my candies! I must go to the barber's.' They didn't know what 'the barber's' mean, so I moved my hand up and down on my hair, as if it were a pair of scissors. They understood me at once, and they laughed and ran away. Only one boy didn't move. He stood alone in front of me, so embarrassed that tears almost streamed down his cheeks. I felt curious. What was he standing here for? He was not the type who could win my candies. You know? He was that type of kids … Very shy! And timid! He just stood there, lean and weak like a bean sprout, so awkward that even I myself shed sweat for him. Instead of running away to join those kids, like a startled rabbit, he gave me a look and began to walk forward. The other kids, standing afar, saw him moving and shouted in chorus at me. 'Go, go, to him!'[5] I was puzzled and then I followed the boy — I am disobedient sometimes and even ignored my superiors' orders, but sometimes, I am very docile, even to the point of following children's instructions — look at me! Others may think that I am too irrational, but you must know that I live till now just because of my irrationality. OK, let me go on with my story — I followed that boy and arrived at a barber's shop. I came to know that the boy's family ran a barber's … All right, that's it."

"His father, the barber, was very polite to me. Obviously, he was greatly honored to have my presence in his shabby hut. His gratefulness and courtesy were shown in his meticulous service to me. In Vietnam, you often came across such Vietnamese who treated you with politeness and sincerity. Their sincerity was genuine, you could see it, they were genuinely sincere to you … You feel curious? Why? If you were friendly to them, they would be friendly to you. If you considered them your enemy, they were your enemy. Besides, we were in South Vietnam, and only North Vietnam was our enemy. To the people in South Vietnam, we were their friends, even their savior. You are laughing, why? Friend or foe, does that matter? You just listen to me … "

"Once, I was assigned a difficult task: to receive North Vietnam's signals. They asked me to do it, saying that I once worked in the National Security Council and that I must have special skills. Stuff and nonsense! They wanted to make me look bad. Obviously! You know, it was difficult for a device set in South Vietnam to get signals from North Vietnam, and the only effective way was to set the receiver on a place controlled by the Viet Cong. Who had guts to do such a dangerous thing? Of course, we couldn't fight into their turf, seize a hill and set a receiver there. If we could, our receiver would be known to everyone. It was absurd! On the other hand, we could sneak into their controlled area, but that would be difficult too. I had to consult the officers of combat troops, asking them if they could help me set up a receiver in North Vietnam. They agreed and sent a squad to me. However, when the squad leader knew I needed them to go to the Viet Cong-controlled area, he turned furious and yelled at me, 'Shit! I won't go! Why the hell have you chosen such a place, where the Viet Cong killed a lot of our soldiers! You son of bitch stay in your room all day long, tick-tacking on the telegraph as if playing draughts with children, dressing yourself up clean and tidy like a piece of brand-new paper money. You have enough time to drink beers and to flirt with women ... Then, one day, you tap on one spot in the map with your goddamned finger and send us guys to death. Go to hell!'[6] Please don't mind my speaking in such a vulgar and coarse manner. The fact is that the frontline soldiers with their lives at risk indeed spoke like this. His complaint was understandable. It was really a risky job."

"Oh, God! What could I do? I really couldn't find a way out. Those gentleman in Washington were already dissatisfied with me, and if I explained all these hardships to them, nobody would listen! Remember, the commanders were unlikely to listen to their subordinates' explanations. They just issued orders to you and you must get on with your mission."

"What should I do? Nothing but curse profusely to my heart's content.[7] Feeling worried and frustrated, I went to the barber's. Sitting on the chair, I was in such a fidget that the barber, by mistake, left a small cut on my chin. In my bad mood I jumped up and began to throw bad words at him. Damn! I had never been so cruel to the Vietnamese. I knew many American soldiers made light of them, but I was not that kind of person ... That barber knew me well and appeared polite, too polite to be true.[8] However, when I suddenly let loose a torrent of abuses, he was so surprised and frightened that he humped down to almost half of his normal size. His whole family were taken aback and shrank into a terrified huddle. Seeing them so scared out of their wits, I felt embarrassed, knowing that I was wrong. I was really a bastard! But in the name of God, I promise that I didn't do it on purpose. Indeed, at that time, I was in a terribly bad mood! Later, I gave a double tip to the barber, and he understood I was buying myself an apology."

"That barber ... eh, I should say, he was a typical Vietnamese. He was sallow and skinny, even bony! But his eyes were gentle. To my surprise, his eyes were as gentle as those of lambs, which added charm to his uncomely thin face. Seeing his eyes, I got such a strange feeling that he was hiding something immeasurably good in his heart. He always gave an amicable smile to people. He smiled gently to the dirty children and stray dogs at his door. 'Get out, get out!' he shouted at them, though."

"He took my tip and bowed to me deeply. His wife followed him and bowed to me, too. I felt sorry to them, knowing that I was such a bad egg that I used a little money to make up for my mistake.⁹ Money meant a lot to them and they were very pleased and contented to take my money, which made me somewhat relieved. U.S. dollars! Who said dollars were no good ... As I thought about this, I suddenly found myself dawned upon by a thread of light ... I had walked out of that small street already but I turned back to the barber's. 'Can you tell me what I can buy from Vietnamese with money?' Hearing my question, the barber felt surprised, a sudden flush appearing on his cheeks. He looked down at the floor, perhaps struggling for a proper answer, and after a while, he murmured, 'You can buy whatever you want, officer.' Though his voice was quite low, I heard it clearly. It was enough for me. I smiled at him, and he, too, gave me an understanding smile. To tell you the truth, since I came to know him, I thought that he was a smart man, and that was why I kept going to his shop. You know, wisdom has nothing to do with one's status. In the U.S. army, I find a lot of dimwits in high-ranking officers ... Oh, let's not talk about this. That day, the barber talked a lot with me, perhaps because he wanted to get himself out of that awkward situation. 'Look! We are human beings. We must survive. You, the American officer, come to Vietnam. For what? None of our business. But you come to me to have your hair cut, so here, you are my distinguished guest. Besides, you tip me well. You are good to us, and our family must be good to you.' As he was talking, his family all stood aside, looking at us. His kids were all in rags, bare-footed ... Following my eyes, the barber also cast a look at his kids. 'Life is hard! Look! My kids ... my kids grow up in such a condition ... However, things are not so bad here. If you go to the north, especially the countryside, for a basket of rice you can get a child, a child who can do quite a lot of work for you! Err ... maybe a basket is too much. You have to believe ... me.'"

"He babbled on and on with me. I could understand his poor English and I was sure he could understand mine. After some time, I gesticulated to him about the wire-setting mission, telling him in a direct and clear way that I could pay a good price for it. I told him that it was not a very hard job, and that he just needed to set up several poles on the ground. I told him that the device was a heavy thing that needed to be erected on a hilltop in the Viet Cong-controlled area. He understood me soon and told me, 'Come tomorrow evening.' Perhaps he didn't understand what the device was and why we needed to set it up. He just wanted to help me. Of course, I could help him, too. I could give him the money he needed."

"The next day, when I arrived at his shop, he introduced to me a small-sized man, who really startled me a lot. That was a dark-skinned man, in a black coat and black pants. The most striking thing about him was that his face looked askew. The left side of his face shrank and crumpled as if it were scratched by someone, and I thought it would remain that way for the rest of his life. As a result of his deformed face, one of his eyes was much bigger than the other. He wore a gloomy and sullen expression and kept silent all the time. See? Such a guy looked much like a devil sent out from the hell! The dark devil didn't utter a single word, and he even didn't raise his eyes to cast me a look. It seemed that nobody was worth his looks. As the barber bent down and whispered in his ear, he sometimes nodded and sometimes shook his head, but kept silent all the time ... We bargained in this way and reached a deal in the end: We settled the price, the time, the place and so on and I promised that in a few days I would take the device to the place of his choosing and he promised he would carry it into place with his wooden boat. He asked me to ensure his safety, for the place was close to a U.S. sentry outpost. I agreed for sure."

"I talked it over with the sentry outpost and they sent two guards to keep sentry from afar. The receiver device made of cast iron was so heavy and bulky that it jutted well outside the boat, looking like a crab extending its two big pincers. Anyway, thank God! It didn't sink the boat, which that Viet Cong man had brought. I couldn't imagine how he would manage to carry such a big thing uphill! Simply pushing the boat offshore was a laborious task for him, I concluded as I watched him hunching his back into a bow in great strain. When he bent down, his ankles were revealed from his pants. In the moonlight, I saw clearly his ankles, as thin as those of that barber's little boy ... Oh, my! Until now his thin ankles dangle in front of my eyes from time to time, as if I just saw them yesterday. To tell you the truth, not in the least was I interested in this Viet Cong man who always wore a gloomy expression and black clothes. Compared with him, that barber with a sallow face was much lovelier. That small and dark man had not an appealing spot on him, from head to toe. I disliked him so much, and to be frank, I almost harbored hatred toward him. He was willing to take risk in doing this thing for me, but from the bottom of my heart I detested his skewed face, especially his gloomy and cold expression. And even his exhausted gasps were quite revolting! On that dark night, like a weak old horse, he gasped as he tried all his strength to push his boat.

A whistling sound followed each of his heavy breaths … Sizz … sizz … Something must be wrong with his lungs![10] I can remember all the details and I won't forget them for the rest of my life. The more fatigued he became, the happier I was. That was a sort of guilty happiness. This dark devil deserved such a labor, because he could get a tidy sum of money!"

"He pushed and pushed, and finally the boat moved a little. But perhaps he pushed so hard that he tumbled forward and flopped into the water. I was taken by surprise and extended my hand to him instinctively, trying to pull him up. My shoes were both in the water, which felt cold. When pulled out of water he stood still with a bent back and his head in his hands and kept shivering without uttering a sound. His head must have bumped onto the rim of the boat … When I looked at him … Do you know what I was thinking of? … I thought of the dog I kept when I was in high school. It was a German shepherd, big and awesome-looking. I loved it so much! Once, when it was crossing a street, a car sped by and hurt one of its legs. In great pain, it stood up, bent his back and kept shivering. Seeing the pitiable dog, I felt my heart aching so hard that I almost fainted away. Since then, I knew that if one kept shivering without uttering a sound, he must be suffering an unbearable pain! At the thought of this, my heart felt a sting … But you know, at that time, I couldn't hold him in my arms as I did to my beloved dog … Impossible! Impossible at all! At that moment, I knew he was in great pain and I felt like doing something for him. That's the way it was.[11]I took off my coat and handed it to him. Why did I give my coat to him? I didn't know! To dress his wound? Or to make him warm? … Who knows! Anyway, I gave my coat to him, and that's all I could do. As a matter of fact, we didn't speak to each other in the whole process and in the darkness we didn't even see each other clearly. The wound on his head must have added a look of hideousness to his skewed face. Luckily, it was too dark for me to see anything clearly about him. In fact, I didn't want to have a look at his pathetical face in that wretched situation."

"As I handed my coat to him, obviously, he was surprised. He took it without saying a word of gratitude. He stood up slowly, gasped for a while and then jumped onto the boat. The moment he pushed the boat off the bank with a shove of a pole, he, for the first time, fixed his eyes on me. I couldn't make out the expression on his face but I could feel his eyes resting on my face for almost half a minute. Heaven knew what he was thinking about at that moment. Then, he left with his boat."

"Thank God! Everything went on smoothly that day. The device was set up on a hill called 'Black Widow', and at the thought of that ominous name and that small black man, I felt the whole story so mysteriously interesting. Later, from the barber's mouth, I got to know that that small man was truly a widower, who had to raise four children and his sick parents. His family were always starving and perhaps willing to trade one of his children for a basket of rice. I am sure that the money he got from me must have saved the lives of his entire family. Anyway, I finished my mission successfully and the officers in Washington were satisfied. However, the U.S. troops in Vietnam were unhappy. They said that I actually supported the Viet Cong with money so they could survive and continue their struggle against the Americans. Bullshit! "

"Larry," I couldn't help chipping in, "you were bold in thought and that Viet Cong man was bold in action! If this had happened in China, both of you would have been sentenced to death, because you colluded with your enemy and he was a traitor."

Larry smiled and said, "Yah, I know, I know … but my logic goes like this: After that Viet Cong man got the money, he would buy food for his own family only. Was it likely that he bought food for his comrades and let everyone know about his collaboration with me? Was he so stupid? Impossible! Besides, what good were the ciphers we intercepted in our war against the Viet Cong? It was hard to say! Sometimes, those ciphers were more of a hindrance than of a help! Now, I look back at what we did in Vietnam … Crap! Many Americans died in vain. As to me, at least I saved a squad of soldiers, I saved myself, and I saved that Viet Cong man and his entire family! If I must stand trial, I only accept God's judgment, for only He was truly fair and square. I'll let you know it soon."

"I could say that, after that mission, the officers with brains had higher regard for me than before, and when they went to clubs to relax they always take me with them. At that time, provided I had no task at night, I went with them. We had been to all the hotels and clubs in Saigon … Unfortunately in the later stage of the Vietnam War, the clashes between the north and the south grew more intense, and as a result, the peaceful days were gone and only antagonism and hatred remained. Violent assaults occurred even on the streets of Saigon, so we no longer dared to go out often. But the U.S. Army Club was still our favorite hangout. You know, we called girls into the club …"

"One night, while I was playing cards in the club, a guard on sentry came and told me someone was waiting for me outside. I said, 'Get out! Let him go! I am busy now!' At that moment, I was winning money — or perhaps losing money. Anyway, I was in high spirits. Who would bother to leave the table? Seeing the guard still hesitating, I yelled at him in a vicious tone, 'Hey, son, who's that guy? I don't want to see him. Let him go!' The guard left but after a while he came back and said, 'Officer, that guy is really like a troublesome fly! He wants to see you at once! He refuses to be driven away even at gunpoint.' I asked impatiently, 'Who's that guy anyway?' 'It's a Vietnamese.' I felt surprised. A Vietnamese? Could it be him? I paid the money to that guy and our deal was over. If it was not that dark devil, who else wanted to see me? Fraught with doubt, I put down the cards and went out with that guard. No sooner had I set foot on the illuminated spot of the lamp outside the gate than a black figure rushed to me quickly. I stepped back instinctively. Oh! That skewed face and the black clothes! At the very sight of him, I felt uneasy at heart! 'What are you doing here?' I asked in a rough tone. He didn't answer me. Clutching my arm, he opened his mouth — he was speaking English — 'Come, Come!'... For the first time I heard him speaking. His voice was hoarse and queer. He had helped me, but he still disgusted me! Now, he even came to drag me by my arm in front of the guard! I turned angry and meanwhile became alert. I must be alert. Maybe the deal between us had been discovered by his comrades and now he was sent to get even with me.[12] He might coax me to go with him first, and then find a good opportunity to kill me. In your dreams! Thinking of these, I said to him, 'Hey! Let go of me. Let go of my arm!' But he held fast to my arm. The more I struggled, the more tightly he clutched me. Under the lamp — Thank God we were under the lamp, or things would be different — I could see his eyes, one big and one small, both opening wide and filled with panic and imploration. My heart was somewhat touched by his expression, though I knew I should turn my back on him. His eyes begged me like mad and his hands held on to me tightly as hell. So I followed him involuntarily as if my body ignored my mind and followed another set of signals. Half willingly and half reluctantly, I was pulled far and farther from the club. Not until the cold wind blew onto my face did I come to be clear-minded. All of sudden, I stopped and threatened him to let go of my arm. I must be back! As I was turning around, he, like a lynx, gave me a hard push from beside. His action was so fast and so forceful that I fell heavily onto the ground. Oh, my God! I was played into his hands! How could I be so stupid to walk so far away with him! I exerted the last ounce of my energy to stand up and fumbled for my gun ...[13] Right at this moment, a flash of strong light and a tremendous sound of explosion struck me. 'Oh! I am dead!' I said to myself and almost lost my consciousness ... After quite a while, I found my arms and legs intact and felt the air extremely hot and bright in front of my eyes. Collecting my thoughts, I suddenly realized what the Viet Cong man had done for me! The club, where I was playing cards several minutes ago, was blown up and together with it all the officers and that guard at the gate were sent to their Creator! My God … Before I understood what had happened, that Viet Cong man had left without a trace."

Larry stopped his story abruptly and looked at me with a smile, trying to read my mind. Staring back at him, I couldn't say a word.

Thousand Oaks, California, USA, 2009

1. 整个小说是两个人的对话，以一个人为主，完全是口头讲述，具有明显的口语化特点。译文现在时与过去时交织。为了风格对应，译文也多用口语表达。

2. "这样边线整齐的老人容易叫人心生好感……" I felt kindly toward him. Such a refined and well-groomed old man was likely to leave people a good impression. feel kindly toward sb. 对某人有好感，倾向于某人。"边线整齐"指形象整洁，所以译为refined and well-groomed。

3. "哪里像我的家乡蒙大拿，天冷得叫人精神抖擞！" … totally different from my hometown in Montana where it is so cold that people feel refreshed and greatly braced up! brace up 精神振作，精神抖擞。

4. "我常去的一家理发店，是一个小得要命的店，在一条小得要命的街上"。I often went to an awfully small barber's located on an awfully small street. "小得要命"，指非常小，这是很口语的表达，译文用了awfully small。

5. 这是越南孩子说的英语，不标准，不规范。

6. 这是一个军官拒绝执行任务，连骂人带抱怨的话。里面有脏话，注意把语气表现出来。

7. "我能怎么办呢，我也只能骂娘了。" What should I do? Nothing but curse profusely to my heart's content. profuse 毫不吝惜的、慷慨的、挥霍的、浪费的，to one's heart's content 尽情地。

8. "他对我非常恭敬，恭敬得出奇。" (He) appeared polite, too polite to be true. 用 too … to …句型来突出其"恭敬"的难以置信。

9. "挺不是个东西"是个很口语化的表达，此处译为I was such a bad egg. bad egg，口语词，坏家伙，混蛋。good egg，口语词，好人。

10. "他费力的喘息声，也一样叫我不喜欢，那声音在黑夜里听来简直像一匹老衰马似的，在每一声后面还带着细哨子似的尾音——嘶，嘶，嘶的，可能他的肺八成都有问题……" And even his exhausted gasps were quite revolting! On that dark night, like a weak old horse, he gasped as he exerted to push his boat. A whistling sound followed each of his heavy breaths … Sizz … sizz … Something must be wrong with his lungs! 翻译时把原句重新组织，植入关键词。

11. That's the way it was. 就是这样，当时就是这么回事。

12. get even with sb. 向某人报复。

13. "我拼命要爬起来" I exerted the last ounce of my energy to stand up. the last ounce of my energy 最后一点力气。

1956年的债务

○ 铁　凝

父亲临终的时候，托付给万宝山一件事：1956年，父亲很肯定地回忆说，就是万宝山出生那年，他向老同事李玉泽借过钱。父亲说，好像就是你妈去医院生你，家里钱没凑够，我就找当时住对门的李玉泽借了五块钱。后来，也忘了为什么……为什么就是没有把钱还给人家。今年是2009年吧，五十三年了。六娃，无论如何，你要亲手替我把钱还上。

万宝山在兄弟姐妹中排行老六，人称六娃。六娃——万宝山，这个五十三岁的男人站在病床前，看着蜷缩在床上说话再无底气的父亲，不停地点着头。父亲见他点了头，吃力地撑起身子，从枕头底下抽出一个皱皱巴巴的牛皮纸信封托在手掌上说，这里装着该还的钱，当然不能是五块。五块钱按定期存款五十三年算利息，咱就按1956年的定期利息算吧，我记得是百分之五，加起来是五十八块左右。这一阵我天天计算这五块钱的利息，大齐概不会错。

万宝山从父亲手里接过信封，发现信封下方有红色仿宋体"福安市人民医院"字样，不觉在心里感慨：到底是父亲，一辈子精打细算。都病成这样了，也不知在什么时间、用什么办法弄到了医院不花钱的信封。可父亲说话却常常颠三倒四，比如他喜欢把"大概齐"说成"大齐概"，比如他永远把沙发说成"发沙"。这使他的思维看上去仿佛异于常人，同时也掩盖了他的心机。成年之后的万宝山想，父亲其实是有心机的，只是他一生的心机大都放在把家过日子上了，父亲一直掌握着家中的经济大权。万宝山将轻而薄的信封叠了个对折塞进衣兜，他无心核对信封里那连本带息的钱数，都五十三年了，多一分少一厘的真那么重要吗？这时，已经躺上枕头的父亲突然又奋力抬起身子，冲他的六娃张开了两条胳膊。那像是一种乞望，好比儿童对大人撒娇时要大人抱抱。或者那也是一种对托付之事的再次确认：我们爷儿俩抱了，你才算真的答应了我。万宝山对父亲的这种姿态缺乏心理准备，虽然他排行老六，是家中最小的孩子，但他和父亲从来没有这种亲密的身体接触。父亲也从不娇宠他，很可能是他不允许父亲娇宠。从小他就不喜欢父亲，在他印象中，父亲朋友很少，因为他那出了名的吝啬。父亲的吝啬也不时带给年幼的万宝山一些难堪。现在生命垂危的父亲用这种类似外国人的方式要和万宝山拥抱，他顽强地张着胳膊，白发蓬乱，眼球浑黄，面目黧黑，四肢枯瘦，宛若一只凄风中的大鸟，干脆更像是大鸟的标本，万宝山想。紧接着万宝山就被心中的大鸟标本这个比喻吓了一跳，刚才的扭捏才转换成一种不期而至的怜悯——刚才他扭捏了。他想，这拥抱的示意本不属于父亲的风格，但谁能判断一个行将结束的生命会有哪些意外举动呢？他微微弯下身子，小心地抱了一下父亲。父亲是肝癌晚期，这时已经轻若无骨。他还闻见了父亲身上的一股哈喇味儿，如同厨房里陈年的老油。

几天后，父亲去世了。

万宝山很想尽快完成父亲的嘱托。倒不是因为那五块钱的债务，而是父亲在病床上那奋力张开胳膊的姿势。正是那病鸟般的姿势提醒着他，他不愿意父亲死前的那个瞬间总在脑子里盘旋。只有还了钱，那形象才能从他脑子里消失。父亲特别提出要他"亲手"还钱，他理解这是当面归还的意思。那么，他必得亲自去一趟北京了。他向父亲工厂的老同事打听李玉泽在北京的具体地址，厂里很多人都知道。他们把地址写给他，还告诉他，李玉泽退休以后跟儿子住，那地址是儿子家的。

父亲在春天去世，但万宝山执行父亲的遗嘱一直拖到秋天。万宝山成人之后在一所中等卫生学校当水暖工，刚结婚就和父母分开单过。他的小家经济收支大致平衡，偶尔略有盈余。可万宝山出门也要算成本，假若他去还钱的成本超出了他要还的钱数，那他决不贸然行事。秋天了，学校借着新中国六十年大庆的气氛，在国庆节之后分批组织老师和职工去北京参观，这才给了万宝山当面向李玉泽还钱的机会。学校组织的参观是学校花钱，也可以看做这是一次公费旅游——北京公费一日游。

出门之前，万宝山才认真想到了债主李玉泽。其实他并不记得李玉泽，有关李玉泽一家，万宝山都是从大哥那里听说。从前李玉泽和万家住对门，两家都住在纺织厂宿舍。万宝山的父亲在厂办宣传科编厂报，李玉泽是厂里的技术员。在大哥印象里，李玉泽家总是比他们家吃得好，李玉泽的儿子李可心和万宝山的大哥是小学同学，他对万宝山的大哥说，夏天他爸每天都给他买一角西瓜。而万宝山的父亲只会号召万宝山的哥哥们攒牙膏皮卖钱。卖了钱也得上缴父亲，父亲每次返还三分钱，规定一个月吃一根小豆冰棍。后来李玉泽调到北京去了，那一年，万宝山还不到三岁。

但是，关于父亲的借钱不还，万宝山仿佛从记事起就知道。小学一年级的暑假里，他和几个孩子围着宿舍楼门口推冰棍车的奶奶买冰棍。他们都知道，这个卖冰棍的奶奶是可以赊账的，她是厂里工人的家属，认识这些孩子，他们可以先吃冰棍再回家拿钱。万宝山也想先吃冰棍后给钱，旁边一个大点的孩子立即指着他，揭短似的说，"他们家大人借钱不还！"万宝山已经伸出去的手，像被这喊声烫着似的赶紧缩了回来。那时的他还没有能力用"羞愧"来形容自己，却明白地知道，借钱不还会让一个人抬不起头。再大一点，他知道了五块钱在1956年的价值，便愈加意识到问题的严重性。1956年，在外省这个离北京三百公里的城市，父亲一个月挣三十六块钱就能养活全家八口人。虽然日子拮据，但总能将就着过去。

1956年，一个高级寄宿小学学生一个月的伙食费是十二块五毛钱。

1956年，一件斜纹咔叽布中山装是六块三毛钱。

1956年，母亲生了万宝山之后回乡下娘家坐月子，下了长途汽车在县车站小饭馆花一毛钱吃了一碗荷包蛋，那大海碗里足足有十个鸡蛋啊，一分钱硬币大的香油珠子飘了一层，硬是把碗都盖严了。这是母亲百讲不厌的一件往事，而父亲更愿意让她在全家吃饭时开讲，他说，这样就可以不炒菜了，一人举着一个窝头，就着故事里的香油荷包蛋吃。

1956年，五块钱是一个普通中国人家的一笔大钱。父亲从对门借的，对门邻居，正所谓低头不见抬头见，他用了什么办法，能够在长达两年的时间里拒不还钱呢？假如两年之后李玉泽没有搬出对门调去北京，父亲又将如何天天面对债主？这需要铁一样的脸皮钢一样的神经。万宝山在买冰棍赊账遭"揭发"之后问过母亲，母亲双手一拍，一只手的手背啪啪地砸着另一只手的手心说，她一看见对门李家的人，就恨不得有个地缝钻进去。可是，她不掌握钱，她是个没有工作的家庭妇女，花二分钱买火柴都得提前和父亲打招呼。长大一点的万宝山鼓足勇气去问父亲，父亲却不似母亲那么激动，他说，那五块钱啊，第一，我没说不还；第二，李玉泽家只一个独子，比咱家条件好不少，他又不急等这五块钱用；第三，人家李玉泽都从来没催过我还钱，你们着什么急呢！还有第四，父亲说，就在他准备好还钱的时候李玉泽调到北京去了，一下子就隔了一个城市啊……父亲对自己的不还欠债振振有词，但全家人都明白他更像是强词夺理。比如说李玉泽家只一个儿子经济条件好，自己家是六个，仿佛李家的钱活该给他用。母亲有一次曾经抢白他说，知道人家背后都怎样讲吗，讲咱们生得起孩子还不起钱！父亲立刻对答道，是呀，所以六娃之后咱不就打住了么。万宝山想，这倒是真的。母亲的生育打住了，父亲的借钱行为也打住了。据万宝山所知，自从那"著名"的五块钱之后，父亲终生没再向别人借过钱。也许他心里很在乎厂里同事在背后的议论，特别是这议论已经伤及自家孩子的自尊。李玉泽固然没有当面催他还钱，但人们背后的议论最初肯定是来自李家。

父亲的借钱典故随着李玉泽一家的离开渐渐告一段落，他的另一种习性凸显出来，他吝啬。或者换句好听的话，他极端地节约。他嘱咐上街买菜的母亲说，你买茄子，是买一个大的呢还是买两个小的？依我看你要买一个大的。为什么？两个小的会多出一个茄盖儿，占分量。在家里他身体力行，带头喝隔夜的已经馊了的菜汤，吃过期的药片，不许点15瓦以上的灯泡。家里不买手纸，他利用编厂报的职务之便，把那些油印小报带回家来，亲自裁成幼儿巴掌大小做如厕之用。当孩子们抱怨纸面太小擦不干净时，他会耐心给他们讲授方法，这曾经让年幼的万宝山很有一种说不出的别扭。他还锯煤——把一整块蜂窝煤拦腰锯成两块，说这样分两次添煤烧得更透（可能是谬论）。他给煤盖了煤"屋"上了锁，钥匙挂在腰上，他不开锁，你休想取出一粒煤渣，哪怕你正要蒸馒头炒菜，炉中火急待添加新煤。家中的米、面、油更要上锁，每餐饭他都用自备的量具——母亲娘家一个核桃木的木碗量米量面。在万宝山印象里，他的童年和少年时代老是觉得饿，他和哥哥姐姐们从来没有放开肚子吃过饭。他们都在私底下盼着父亲出差，那样说不定就能获得饮食的暂时解放。可是父亲不出差——纺织厂无差可出。

　　2009年秋日的这个早上，万宝山坐在去往北京的城际列车上，衣兜里装着父亲嘱咐他要还的钱。他不吃一口零食，不喝一口需要花钱的水。车厢里的售货车来来回回在他眼前过了几趟，卖"娃哈哈营养快线"饮料的，卖快餐火烧、茶叶蛋的，还有黑瓜子白瓜子，奶油花生口香糖……同车厢的老师们把售货车上那些食品袋扒拉来扒拉去的，他则看得淡然。他只是忽然想到，自己这习性是不是受父亲的影响呢？售货车上那装在食品袋里烤得焦黄的看上去很香的火烧，只是让他想起少年时吃过的唯一一次火烧。那一次，父亲空前绝后地出差了，一走就是十天。省里举行大型职工业余汇演，纺织厂一个名叫《太阳光芒像金梭》的女声小合唱被选中，父亲参与了歌词的创作，因此有机会和演出队一起去省会。但父亲的短暂离家并没有让家人得以放开肚子吃饭，父亲对此早有准备。临走之前他已经把十天的米面提前备好，并不忘刨去自己的那一份，其余的自然又上了锁。母亲在父亲给粮食上锁之前及时申请出小半碗白面，她必须用它打糨糊。万家人是不买鞋的，全家都穿母亲纳底子做成的布鞋。纳底子需要糊袼褙，糊袼褙就要用糨糊。母亲在炉火上打糨糊时万宝山愿意歇在她跟前，他愿意闻那白面和水搅拌在一起，经炉火的熬制散发出的诱人清香。当糨糊打好时，他更会趁母亲不备，伸出食指挖出一坨糨糊迅速送入口中。吞咽完糨糊他还会长时间地嗍食指，他自认为面糊的暖香能在这根食指上存留好几天。每逢这时，母亲又会站在父亲一边劝慰她的六娃，她说你爸锁住米面是为了家里别吃了上顿没下顿，咱们的粮食有定量管着。万宝山知道定量是什么意思，定量之外，你就是有钱也没处去买粮食——何况万家也没有多余的钱，万家从来没有多余的钱。十天后父亲从省里回来了，万宝山盯着父亲手中那个他十分熟悉的、印着一架白色飞机的墨绿色帆布提包（直到2009年腊月父亲住院，这只"飞机"模糊、拉链破损的老提包依然跟随着父亲），他发现提包有点鼓，这让他兴奋，父亲该不会给他们带回了什么好吃的吧。在食品匮乏的年代，很多孩子特别关注外出回家的大人手里的提包。父亲的提包里果然有内容，他带回了八个火烧。

事情是这样的，父亲和纺织厂的演出队乘火车去省城，火车路过一个大站时，车厢里突然有广播说，这个大站的站台食堂专为旅客提供火烧，车上旅客可以凭车票购买，每张车票限购火烧一个。广播里特别强调说："椒盐发面火烧五分钱一个，不要粮票。"坐在火车上的父亲立即注意到了这则广播，他尤其注意了"不要粮票"这句话。在中国的票证时代，不要粮票的火烧几乎等于不要钱白给。这是当时国家对出门旅行的公民的优惠政策，除了在火车站的站台，其他地方几乎没有不要粮票的食品。父亲反应敏捷地开始行动，他挨个问同车的厂里同事一会儿是不是要下车买火烧，几个正忙着打扑克的女工都说不买，她们知道去省会参加汇演是有人管饭的。父亲立即把她们的车票敛到自己手中，一边说着借我用用。说话之间火车进站了，父亲飞速下车，在站台上那个瞬间形成的买火烧的队伍里，他的位置是前三名。父亲借到手七张车票，加上自己的那张，他买回八个火烧。厂里工人对父亲那著名的习性深有所知，现在他突然一下子买了八个火烧，大家忍不住尖刻地当面议论起来：精于算计的万师傅啊，这回可没算准。火烧不要粮票是占了便宜，可你什么时候吃呢？你要把它们放十天吗？回家时早长绿毛了！

父亲还有一个特点就是从不忌讳人们议论他的吝啬，父亲认为这和议论他借钱不还有本质的区别。为此他不仅经常像欣赏自己的优点一样欣赏人们奚落他的吝啬，还会适时做些补充。只见父亲把火烧藏进提包，对大家解释道，我听说在省里参加汇演这十天是统一发餐券的，要是用不完，最后凭餐券还能退给你粮票和钱，一张餐券少说也值四两粮票三毛钱吧。我准备每天吃一个火烧顶一顿饭，省下餐券就可以退成粮票和钱啊。你们有谁想到了！

父亲这构想居然对大家产生了吸引力，有几个工人也跃跃欲试。只是，她们没能如父亲那般手疾眼快抢购到不要粮票的火烧，而到达省会之后，父亲的预谋也没能"得逞"。原因是那次汇演的用餐方式没有采取餐券制，所有参会人员不领餐券了，大家可以随便吃。这是一个让与会者即刻狂欢的优待：随便吃！在那样的岁月里，"随便吃"带给人的惊喜就如同天天有人给你涨工资。在这做梦一般的餐饮狂欢面前，父亲的八个火烧果然如人们的预料，三天后就长毛了。但你不要以为父亲会抛弃它们，他把招待所房间的窗台擦净，将长着绿毛的火烧一字排开，在太阳下晒火烧。晒好一面，他用扫床的小笤帚扫去火烧上的绿毛，把火烧翻个过再晒。十天里，翻晒火烧是出差在外的父亲一个不大不小的乐趣。十天后，他重又把这八个干火烧或者叫火烧干背回了家。后来，父亲的"火烧事件"在厂内广为流传。在宣传科，在车间，在夏天里人们乘凉的家属院，和父亲同去省城的人公开把这事当成故事讲，并且不断添油加醋。每逢这时，作为听众之一的父亲甚至一块儿帮着补充材料，比如用小笤帚扫绿毛这个细节就是父亲本人贡献的。众人因为父亲对"事件"的当场证明而更加开心。

万宝山始终记得父亲带回火烧的那个晚上，那是一个欢乐而奢侈的晚上。晚饭时分，出差归来的父亲先是制止了母亲熬玉米面粥的计划，他说今晚能省下一顿粥了，今晚有干粮。说着，父亲郑重地从提包里捧出八个火烧分给围桌而坐的全家八口人。最后他把属于自己的那个递给万宝山说，六娃最小，吃个双份吧。哥哥姐姐们都看着万宝山笑，母亲阻拦说，还不到出力气的年纪，吃什么双份呢。又把火烧推到父亲眼前。父亲笑笑说，你没看见我胖了呀，开会吃的。这次汇演，不限制饭量，让我们随便吃。说着拿起火烧塞到万宝山手里。万宝山一手攥着一个火烧不撒手地看父亲，他发现父亲是胖了，腮帮子鼓着，脸上泛出油光。让他感到有趣的是，父亲脖子上还带了个西式衬衫的假领子，这个假领子是母亲用几块蓝白方格交织的手绢拼在一起缝成，连带一部分肩膀，肩部以下是空的，腋下有松紧带前后衔接固定在身上。父亲从来不买真衬衫，假衬衫领子也是做"礼服领"之用。刚才进门后他脱掉外衣就忙着给孩子们拿火烧，忘了把假领子摘下来。他带着假领子，假领子下边是补丁叠加的纺织厂自产的灰色针织秋衣。这使他看上去就像一个幼儿园里带着布围嘴的孩子，至少也是一个正在扮演孩子的大人。万宝山冲着带假领子的父亲笑了，他不客气地咬起那难以咬动的火烧，火烧干硬如铁，使牙齿在上面打滑，他还是咬出了这椒盐火烧不一般的香。夜里躺在床上，牙缝里残存的芝麻粒大的碎花椒被他用舌头舔了出来，他舍不得咽下去，小心地含住这喷香的花椒睡得很酣。后来他从旁人那里知道了父亲晒火烧的故事，他像以往听到这类故事一样的恼火，但这次的恼火并没有抵消那天晚上吃火烧的所有美好感觉。

三十几年过去了，万家的孩子都已长大，告别父母各立门户，且都先后离开了生养他们的这个城市。就仿佛他们共同被父亲的吝啬吓怕了，他们心照不宣地拒绝再和父亲近距离地生活。只有万宝山留在离父母不远的地方：他自己的家和父母的房子相隔两条马路。票证时代过去了，生活渐渐好起来。大米白面可以自由购买，人们炒菜也开始舍得放油。但父亲的吝啬却一如既往。他照旧把粮食锁进橱柜，为了便宜，他只去农贸市场采购那些快要孵出小鸡的鸡蛋。上世纪80年代，万宝山给父母买过一对人造革的仿皮沙发，第二天就被父亲卖掉，卖沙发的钱也被他理直气壮揣了起来。他逢人就讲："发沙"，又花钱又占地方。退休以后他时间更多了，他曾经要求万宝山把正在读小学的女儿放在他们身边照顾，被万宝山的爱人坚决拒绝。他无事可做，干脆就独自承担了买菜的任务。说他买菜不如说那是捡菜，每天下午市场快要收摊他才前往，他坦然捡拾着菜贩们遗弃的菜帮、菜叶，弄好了也有完整的收获：一个正在生芽的土豆，或一棵筋络粗大的老芹菜。院子里的老邻居们为此嘲笑他，他们说，老万什么时候捡到一块肉就好了，也改善生活做一顿红烧肉给我们看看。父亲说改善生活还用得着捡肉啊，我今天就改善。邻居们问他怎么改善，父亲自豪地说，他准备做一份红烧芹菜。众人笑起来，父亲却不觉得这是玩笑。吝啬在他，已不是生活所迫，那就像是他人生的一个信仰，或者生命的一个动力，简直须臾不可离开。吝啬在他，也没有什么不光彩，能够做到尽最大可能地不花钱，那才叫光彩。这的确，的确和借钱不还不同，这是一个人给自己找乐儿，碍着谁啦。

　　火车进站，北京到了。万宝山跟随卫生学校的同事们下车走出站台。在学校的安排下，他们参观了天安门广场、鸟巢和水立方。万宝山和同事们一起感叹，到底是首都，到底不一样啊。到底是开过奥运会的首都，到底是六十年大庆刚过的首都，到底是不一样啊。天空湛蓝，鲜花怒放，新楼们如森林一样错落，大街上的人个个神气活现……大家忙着在每一个参观点拍照。万宝山没有照相机，他请一个老师给他在鸟巢拍了一张留念照，就向他们此行的领队——一位副校长请假：他要去一个熟人家办点事。想到在北京打手机是漫游的价码，太贵，他又谎称自己的手机没电了，借用副校长的手机，按照父亲厂里老同事提供的号码给李玉泽打了电话。

　　电话是李玉泽本人接听，万宝山听出那是一个有点耳背的嗓音洪亮的老人。他大声向老人报出父亲的名字，简单说明是代父亲来看望他老人家的。他没在电话里提到还钱也没告之父亲已经去世，他觉得这话应该放在当面。李玉泽显然还记得父亲，五十多年前外省纺织厂那个住对门的邻居。他很痛快地答应万宝山来家中拜访，又详细告诉万宝山乘车的路线。他说儿子今天在家里办个大"趴替"，人多有点乱，不过没关系，他来了可以同他们一块儿喝酒。万宝山没听懂"趴替"这个词，他推断反正和人多、喝酒有关。他挂掉电话，在鸟巢乘地铁10号线，顺利找到了李玉泽的住址，一个名叫绿水庄园的地方。原来这是一片别墅，当万宝山确凿地站在庄园门口，盯着眼前那两扇巨大的、铸有一对鎏金麒麟的黑色铁艺大门，他才又想起父亲厂里老人们的介绍，他们说李玉泽的儿子李可心做的是房地产生意，李玉泽跟着儿子养老，有福了。万宝山正犹豫着不知如何进门，一个身穿藏蓝色制服、肩上缝着金色肩章的门卫从警卫室里跑出来，问他贵姓，他报了姓名，保安客气地说，刚才A8座的业主已经通知我们，对您放行。

　　保安引万宝山进了大门，热心地指给他去往A8座的路径：右转，上那座罗锅桥，下了桥一直向前两百米就是。万宝山机械地按照保安的指示走上那座弧度并不太大但跨度不小的罗锅桥，他看见了桥下的池水，水中的睡莲，环绕水池的大片草坪，喷泉，木椅，一些树种珍贵的树们。他下了桥，走两百米，路过了几幢白房子黄房子，他看见了一幢屋顶覆盖着铁灰色龟背形油毡瓦的红房子，他不知道为什么会特别注意这红房子的龟背形灰瓦，也许是因为他在外国电影里见过它们。一大片修剪整齐的毛茸茸的草坪由房脚处伸展开来，形成一个足有上千平方米的庭院。院门的浅褐色毛石门柱上，镶嵌有"A8"字样的紫铜门牌。万宝山站在门口，隔着院墙——半人高的漆成白色的木栅栏，看见一大片落地窗和一个从落地窗探出的白色大阳台，几位老人正闲坐在那里，晒着秋日里干爽的阳光。在他们当中，应该有一位是李玉泽吧。庭院草坪上有铺着雪白台布的长方形餐台，锃亮的银盘里是各种水果、点心和烤肉——一定是烤肉，因为不远处还有一架烧烤炉，两名头戴雪白高帽的厨师站在炉前忙碌，油烟夹着肉的香气不时飘扬过来。一些男人、女人，一些尖叫着的孩子，他们或坐或站或走来走去，吃着什么，喝着什么，聊着什么。一个五岁左右、留着分头的小男孩跺着脚正冲他的母亲（一定是母亲）大叫：我不喝法国的"依云"，我不喝法国的"依云"，我要刚才那种二十六块钱一瓶的"无量藏泉"，二十六块钱一瓶的矿泉水……

本打算进院的万宝山，站在A8的木栅栏之外背过身去，一阵莫名的瑟缩。他忽然不想让草坪上的人们看见他。他想，这就是刚才他在电话里听见的那个"趴替"吧？虽然他早已知道李玉泽父子的富裕生活，但眼前的场景还是远远超出了他的想像。那孩子要的二十六块钱一瓶的水，还让他立刻想起衣兜里父亲嘱托的那五十八块钱。五十八块钱在这样的院子里，也就刚够买两瓶水的。李玉泽或者李玉泽的儿子会怎样看待一个老邻居的儿子奉还的这五十八块钱呢？以他们今天这生活的气派，难道当真会记得五十三年前被别人借过的五块钱么？万宝山继而对自己有些怨忿起来：他这是干什么，也是五十几岁的人了，不远几百公里，又打电话又问地址，最后煞有介事地向这幢别墅交出一个皱巴巴的轻薄的信封。这简直有点滑稽。一想到滑稽这个词，万宝山决意离开A8。他沿着来时的路，迅速朝着远远的那座罗锅桥走去。他步履轻快，不一小会儿就行至桥下。他拔腿往桥上走，过了桥，就离这庄园的大门口不远了。就在这时，他的腿出了问题：他的腿忽然迈不开步了，他没有办法上桥。他定定神，换一条腿再迈步，不行，他还是走不动。他站在桥下发愣，不相信自己遇见了鬼，不相信这是鬼使神差。片刻，他镇静着自己慢慢调转身向着相反的方向——A8试着迈步，两条腿立刻又听他的使唤了。可当他借着这股劲儿转回身再次上桥，他的腿就再一次地抬不起来了。万宝山僵着身体无助地站在罗锅桥跟前，好像一个正在思考高深问题的哲人。夕阳西下，在桥的两岸开阔的草地上，几个仰着脸放风筝的孩子引起了他的注意。既然他的腿像被施了法术似的不能动弹，他便只好随着孩子们的目光仰望天空。他看见了一些高高飞翔的鸟：燕子，蜈蚣，老鹰……一只红嘴的黑鹰展着双翅飞得最高，威风凛凛地俯视着大地。一个形象忽然在万宝山脑子里复活了：病床上的父亲张开胳膊对他的那个乞望，凄风中的大鸟样的乞望。他仰望着空中的黑鹰，该不是父亲的魂灵正俯视着他吧？他并不迷信，但那一刻他心生畏惧。他就在这样的俯视之下回转身，朝着A8迈步。他的步子顿时就迈开了，原来他的腿没病，他确信自己的腿是两条好腿。

他脚步均匀地再一次朝着A8走，那空中的老鹰依然在他头顶的天空翱翔，似是监督，似是护送。万宝山看看天空，又看看四周。天高气爽，四周无人，在这样的人居超低密度的地方，经常是四周无人。他就破天荒地在这陌生的庄园里，向着天空不好意思地夅了一下他的胳膊，宛若与天上的大鸟打着默契的招呼。他发现，当他勇敢地把胳膊舒展开来的时候，久已潜藏在身体内的什么东西嘎巴巴地奔涌了出来，他那颗发紧的心也略微感觉到了平安。

2010年3月19日

The Debt in 1956

○ *Tie Ning*

On deathbed, his father entrusted him with an important task. "In 1956, the year when you were born, I borrowed money from my colleague Li Yuze," his father recollected affirmatively. "At that time, our family was poor. When your mother was sent to hospital to give birth to you, I had to borrow 5 yuan from Li Yuze, who lived opposite to our door. Later, for this reason or that … I didn't return the money. Now, It is 2009, right? 53 years have passed! Little Six, you must return the money to him with your own hands."

Wan Baoshan, at the age of 53, whose nickname was Six for he was the sixth child in his family, stood in front of his father's bed, listening to his father's exhortation in great grief. Looking at his father, who was huddling on the bed, weak and withered, he kept nodding his head in agreement. The old man took great efforts to prop himself up with an elbow and took out a crumpled envelope made of kraft paper from under his pillow. Holding it on his palm, the old man said in a weak tone: "The money is in this envelope. It's not just 5 yuan. I should return him 5 yuan plus the interest in these 53 years. The bank interest rate for fixed deposit in 1956, I remember, was 5%, so altogether I should return him 58 yuan. These days, I have been calculating the interest of this 5 yuan and *bemay* it's right."

Taking over the envelope from his father's hand, Wan Baoshan saw a line of red characters printed on the lower part of it — People's Hospital in Fu'an City. He couldn't help sighing in his heart. Father never changes! All his life he counts every cent and makes every cent count![1] And now, even in such serious illness, he somehow managed to get a free envelope from the hospital! Though a man of sagacity, father often uttered words that didn't hang together. For instance, he often said *bemay* instead of *maybe* and *faso* instead of *sofa*, which made him appear rather peculiar but masked his shrewdness. After growing up, Wan Baoshan came to know that his father was indeed a very smart man, who, nevertheless, devoted most of his smartness to managing the family affairs. Father had kept a tight hand on the family finances in all his life. Now, Wan Baoshan folded the envelope and tucked it into his pocket as he had no mood to check the money in it. 53 years had passed! Was the exact amount of the money that important? At this moment, Wan's father, who had laid his head on the pillow, all of a sudden, strove to raise himself again. The old man stretched his two arms toward his son with the look of a spoiled kid yearning for his parent's embrace. Maybe, father wanted to get a confirmation of the task in his own way: We hug each other, and that means you promise to fulfill the task I entrust you with. Wan Baoshan was surprised at his father's behavior, which, obviously, was beyond his anticipation. Although the smallest child in his family, he had never made such an intimate physical contact with his father. His father never doted on him, or to be exact, he never allowed his father to dote on him. From his childhood, he didn't like his father, who, in his impression, had been a miserly person with few friends. When he was very young, his father's stinginess often embarrassed him. But now, on deathbed, his father wanted to embrace him like those foreigners did in movies! Extending his arms obstinately, the old man was waiting. With disheveled white hair, yellowish eyeballs, a sickly dark face and lean weak limbs, he looked like an old bird in the wailing wind, or the specimen thereof. The specimen of an old bird! Wan Baoshan was startled by such a simile. Soon, a pitiful and merciful feeling welled up in his heart, replacing his bashfulness — just now, he was bashful. This is not father's style, but who knows what a dying man is likely to do? Wan Baoshan said to himself. He bent forward slightly and hugged his father gently and meticulously. In the late stage of lung cancer, his father was but skin and bone,[2] or perhaps his bones had dissolved already. The old man gave out a stale smell like a bottle of cooking oil left unused for many years in the kitchen.

Several days later, his father passed away.

Wan Baoshan really wanted to complete his father's last will as soon as possible. He was prompted not by that 5 yuan's debt but by his father's strenuous arm-extending posture which was deeply imprinted in his heart and constantly reminded him of his mission. The image of the dying sick bird lingered in his mind and he was clear that only after he returned the money could such an image disappear. His father asked him to return the money "with his own hands", which meant he must go to Beijing to meet Li Yuze in person. Then, he began to ask about Li Yuze's address. Fortunately, many people in the factory knew about it. They wrote him the address and told him Li Yuze had been living with his son after retirement.

His father died in spring, but Wan Baoshan didn't embark on his task until autumn. He was a plumber in an intermediate health school and since he got married he lived separately from his parents. He managed his family well, making the ends meet every month and sometimes saving a little. To him, a trip to Beijing would require careful planning and calculation: If the cost surpassed the money he was going to return, he would definitely not go. Finally, the opportunity presented itself. It was autumn and the 60th National Day came. His school organized a group visit to Beijing for its staff in different batches. Of course, all the expenditures would be covered by the school. To him it was a one-day junket to the capital.

Before he started out, he thought of Li Yuze. In fact, he didn't remember Li Yuze at all and he only heard about the Lis from his big brother: In the past, the two families both lived in the textile factory's dormitories, their doors opposite to each other. His father, working in the publicity department of the factory, was in charge of compiling the factory gazette, and Li Yuze, at that time, was a technician in the factory. Wan Baoshan's big brother and Li's son Li Kexin were schoolmates. According to his big brother, Li's family was richer and Li's children ate better, and in summer Li Yuze bought a portion of watermelon worth 10 cents for his son every day. In contrast, Wan Baoshan's father was stingier, always calling on his sons to collect toothpaste tubes and sell them for a little money. After they handed in the money their father gave each of them three cents as a reward. They were only allowed to buy a bean ice-sucker every month. Later, Li Yuze transferred his job and moved his family to Beijing. That year, Wan Baoshan was only three years old.

When he was small, he knew that his father, more often than not, borrowed money but didn't return it. As a first-year student in the primary school, he liked summer vacation so much! An old granny always came to sell ice-suckers in front of the dormitory building, and he and several kids invariably encircled her, scrambling for ice-suckers in happiness. The old granny was a worker's relative, so she was acquainted with these kids and allowed them to eat first and pay later. Like the other kids, he also wanted to eat first; however, as he just extended his hand to the granny, a child who was a little older than him pointed a finger at his nose and shouted in derision, "His father won't pay for it!" Hearing the harsh words, he jerked back his hand quickly as if it were suddenly burned in fire. From then on, he knew that a person failing to clear a debt would eventually be subject to belittlement. Later, when he grew up a little, he came to know the value of 5 yuan in those years and he was more and more aware of the seriousness of his father's problem. In 1956, his family lived in a city which was 300 kilometers away from Beijing and his father took home a monthly salary of 36 yuan which could support the whole family of eight people. At that time, though they just lived from hand to mouth,[3] life was not too bad.

In 1956, a pupil in a boarding school paid 12.5 yuan per month for his meals.

In 1956, a twilled khaki Chinese tunic suit cost 6.3 yuan.

In 1956, after his mother gave birth to him, she went back to the countryside to recover from the labor. After getting off the long-distance bus, she went into a small restaurant at the county station. A big bowl of poached egg soup cost her only 10 cents. What a big bowl! There were ten eggs in it! Drops of sesame oil — each drop as big as a coin — thickly covered the surface of soup. This was the most impressive experience his mother had had in her life and she often related it to the family later. His father preferred listening to her story when all the family were having dinner, saying that he didn't need to prepare the dishes and that each of them could eat the steamed corn bread while imagining the poached eggs in her story.

In 1956, 5 yuan was really a tidy sum of money for a common family in China. His father borrowed it from Li Yuze who lived opposite to their door. At that time, they, as neighbors, must have met each other regularly or frequently. Wan Baoshan really couldn't imagine how his father managed to hold back the money for two years! If Li Yuze hadn't moved to Beijing two years later, how could his father face Li Yuze every day? His father must have a face as thick as iron and nerves as strong as steel. Wan Baoshan once told his mother about the "ice-sucker incident". "At the sight of the Lis, I am so embarrassed that I really wish I could hide myself under the ground!" Slapping the palm of one hand with the back of the other, his mother said in anxiety. As a full-time housewife, his mother held no financial power in the family, and she even had to ask for his father's permission in advance if she wanted to spend two cents on a box of matches. Wan Baoshan once plucked up enough courage to ask his father about the debt. Unlike his mother, his father answered him in a relaxed and composed tone: "First, I have never said I won't return it; second, Li Yuze has only one son and his family enjoyed much better financial conditions than mine, so he is not in urgent need of that 5 yuan; third, he has never urged me to return the money — I really don't know why you are so worried! Fourth, as I was about to return the money, the Lis moved to Beijing. So faraway! We are living in different cities ..." His father spoke in such a plausible and voluble manner, yet the family all knew he was arguing unreasonably to defend himself.[4] For instance, his father said he had six children while Li Yuze had only one son and Li's family circumstances were better, which, in his father's logic, seemed to justify the use of Li's money indefinitely! Once, his mother reproved his father to the face. "Do you know what they are saying behind us? They speak ill of us! They say we can give birth to children but cannot afford to bring them up!" His father retorted at once: "Yeah, they are right. That's why we don't want to give birth to more children." It was true. After Wan Baoshan, his mother no longer gave birth to children and his father no longer borrowed money from others. Wan Baoshan knew that after that "famous" 5-yuan debt, his father never borrowed money. Taking others' gossips to heart, his father didn't want to hurt his children's feelings? Maybe. Though Li Yuze never urged father to return the money, Wan Baoshan was sure that the gossip must have begun from the Lis.

The Lis' moving to Beijing brought the story of the 5-yuan debt to a temporary close, but a trait of his father became annoyingly noticeable: He was miserly, or in better language, extremely frugal! When his mother went to buy vegetables in the market, his father, invariably, enjoined her: "If you see eggplants, will you buy a big one or two small ones? Listen, you must buy a big one. Why? Two small ones have two pedicels, which are inedible and make up more weight." At home, his father practiced what he preached consistently, taking the lead in eating spoiled overnight soup, taking expired medicines and refusing to use light bulbs of more than 15 watts. He never bought toilet paper for the family; instead, taking advantage of his work in the factory, he brought home the mimeographed gazette and cut the paper into pieces as small as a baby's hand. When the children complained that the "toilet paper" was too small, his father patiently instructed them on how to make best use of it in an effective way. Wan Baoshan, at that time, always felt awkward and fretful at his father's dinginess. Besides, his father always sawed a whole briquette into half, saying that in this way a briquette could burn more sufficiently (a fallacy, perhaps). To protect his briquettes, he even built a "hut" and locked it. Wherever he went, he took the key with him, and if he himself didn't take it off his waist-belt and unlock the hut, nobody could get a grain of coal even when a dish was being cooked and a good fire was needed in the stove. Rice, flour and oil were all locked up and while preparing for each meal, he used his measuring tool, a bowl made of walnut wood brought from Wan's mother's home, to take out the exact amount of rice and flour. In his childhood and his teenage years, Wan Baoshan always felt hungry. In his memory, he and his brothers and sisters had never eaten their fill. In private, they always wished that father could go out to other places on business so that they could get the opportunity to eat freely. But to their disappointment, their father had never been away on business — the textile factory never needed people to go on business in other places.

On an autumn morning in 2009, Wan Baoshan finally got on the train for Beijing, with that enveloped money in his pocket. He ate nothing and drank nothing for they cost money. The mobile sales cart was pushed to and fro through his compartment for several times, carrying quite a lot of delicious snacks, such as "Wahaha Nutri-express Milk", baked wheaten cakes, tea eggs, black melon seeds, white melon seeds, cream peanuts and chewing gum … Seeing those teachers picking and choosing among packages of various colors and sizes, he remained silent and indifferent. An idea suddenly occurred to him: Does my frugality come from my father? Those golden-colored baked wheaten cakes in the sales cart gave off an inviting smell and brought him back to his boyhood days. He ate the baked wheaten cakes only once in his boyhood. At that time, once in a blue moon,[5] his father was sent on a business trip and would be away for ten days. A large-scale workers' performance was going to be held in the province and the show of the textile factory, a semi-chorus called "The Sunshine Glitters Like a Golden Shuttle", was selected. His father had contributed to the writing of the lyrics, so he got the opportunity to go to the provincial capital with the performing troupe. However, his father's brief absence didn't give them the chance to eat to their hearts' content. His father made preparations in advance. Before his departure, he took out the exact amount of rice and flour for ten days' use minus, of course, his own portion. Before he locked up the hoard, his mother, in time, put in for less than a half bowl of flour,[6] with which she was going to make the adhesive paste. The whole family never bought shoes but wore crude cloth shoes hand-made by his mother. The paste was used to make the soles. When his mother prepared the paste on the stove, Wan Baoshan always sat beside her. He liked that wonderful smell as flour and water were mixed and boiled. When the paste was ready, he always watched for a chance to dig out a lump with his forefinger and quickly sent it into his mouth. After swallowing it, he licked his forefinger for quite a long time, believing that the warm and mellow smell would stay on his finger for several days. At this time, his mother always took up the side of his father and consoled him: "Your father hides the grains and locks them up for our own good. You know, our supplies are rationed and if we eat up the grains we won't know where the next meal comes." Wan Baoshan understood it and he knew that barring the rationed grains they couldn't get more, even if they had money. In fact, his family had no extra money — they had never had extra money. Ten days later, his father came back with that familiar dark green canvas bag with a picture of a white plane (a favorite personal item which father always carried with him — he even brought the old bag with him when he was hospitalized in December

506

2009, though the plane picture had turned indistinct and the zippers broken down by that time). Wan Baoshan was excited to find the bag slightly bulging. Perhaps father brings me something good to eat? He thought. In that age when food was insufficient, children took great interest in their parents' bags, especially when their parents came back from a business trip. As he expected, there were eight baked cakes in his father's bag!

This was how it happened: His father went to the provincial capital with the troupe and as the train was about to stop at a big station, it was announced in the train klaxon that the station canteen made baked cakes for the passengers and anyone could buy a cake by showing his or her ticket — one ticket for one cake only. And the announcement emphasized, "Five cents for a sesame baked cake made of leavened dough and spiced salt! No grain coupon needed!" That was definitely an attractive ad, especially the last words — "No grain coupon needed!" In that age when everything was in short supply, coupons were needed everywhere, but here, the cakes could be bought free of coupons, which, to the people at that time, equaled to giving them cakes free of charge! Of course, this preferential policy was only offered to the travelers on business trips, and except the railway station no other places sold food free of coupons. Father immediately took action, asking his colleagues on the train one by one whether they wanted to buy baked cakes. Some of his female colleagues were busy playing cards and told him they didn't want to buy baked cakes. Now that they were going to take part in the grand performance in the provincial capital, they could eat free of charge there! Father quickly collected their tickets, and as the train stopped at that station, he jumped off the train at once and joined the long queue which instantly formed on the platform. Fortunately, he was the third one in the line. Altogether he had eight tickets, so he bought eight baked cakes. The colleagues all knew about his frugality, but this time they couldn't help but make sarcastic comments in his face: "We know you are good at calculation, but perhaps you are wrong this time! Yes, indeed, you don't need to use coupons but you buy so many cakes at one time! Can you eat them up? You want to put them aside for ten days and bring them home? They will go spoiled!"

Father had another distinctive feature: He never cared about being considered a miserly person and he thought there was an essential difference between a miserly person and a person who borrowed money but didn't return it. As a result, when people scoffed at his stinginess, he enjoyed and appreciated their comment as if stinginess was one of his virtues which deserved to be talked about. More often than not, he even made complementary remarks. He put the cakes into his bag, raised his head and explained to them patiently, "I hear that in these ten days they will offer us meal tickets and if we don't run out of them, we can exchange them for grain coupons and money when the event is over. And one meal ticket can be exchange for a four-*liang* grain coupon or thirty cents at least. I plan to eat a cake as a meal every day so as to save the tickets and exchange them for grain coupons and money. Have you thought of this?" Father said with a smile.

Father's idea turned out to be quite appealing! Actually several workers also wanted to have a try, but to their disappointment, they didn't grab enough cakes free of coupons. Nevertheless, when they arrived at their destination, father came to know that his elaborate plan would fall flat.[7] They weren't offered meal tickets; instead, they were allowed to eat as much as they could. All the people were elated with such a great favor: Eat as much as they could, which, in those years, was enough to make people jump up with ecstasy as if they got a pay raise every day. Such a good treatment could only come up in their dreams. As they had expected, father's eight baked cakes grew mouldy after three days. However, instead of throwing them away, father put those mouldy cakes neatly in a line on the window sill. He was going to dry them under the sun. When one side of a cake was dry enough, he brushed the green mould off with a small sheet broom, turned it over and let the other side take in the sunlight. In those ten days, it was a great joy for him to turn the baked cakes over and over again. Finally, all the cakes got dry through and through.[8] Then, he put those cakes, or dried cakes to be exact, into his bag and went back home. Later, his "story of baked cakes" became popular in his factory. It was told in the publicity department, in the workshop, in the residential courtyard where people frequented to enjoy the cool air in summer, and everywhere else. The people who had been to the provincial capital with his father spread the story everywhere and kept adding highly colored details to it.[9] And when they were telling the story with great excitement and gusto, father even helped make some complement. For example, the detail of brushing the green mould off with the small sheet broom was contributed by father himself. The audience were happier in father's presence, for the story was proved true on the spot.

Wan Baoshan cherished the memory of the night when his father brought them eight baked wheaten cakes and they had a happy and lavish supper. That night, as his mother was about to make corn porridge, his father came home. He stopped her, saying that they could save their porridge because there was something else to eat, and took out the cakes in a serious manner. Each one of the family sitting around the table was given one cake but Wan Baoshan had two. His father gave out his own and said that the smallest kid might as well have two cakes. Wan Baoshan's brothers and sisters all looked at him with admiration. "He is too small and has no heavy work to do. What's the point of letting him eat two cakes?" His mother objected. Then, she returned one cake to his father. His father smiled. "Don't you see I am getting fatter? We were offered meals free of charge and we all ate as much as we could." His father put the cake into Wan Baoshan's hands again. Holding fast to the two cakes, one in each hand, Wan Baoshan looked at his father. He found his father had really put on weight, with cheeks getting plumper and glowing with greasy luster. The funniest thing was his father's fake western-style collar, which his mother had made by piecing together several blue and white plaid handkerchiefs. It actually looked like the upper part of a shirt and was fastened to the body by the elastic bands tied together under the armpits. His father never bought a shirt and this fake collar was his "formal attire". Just now, he was busy handing out baked cakes and forgot to take it off. Above his waist, outside his gray stockinet sweater, which were full of patches and made in the textile factory he worked for, that short fake collar gave his father a ridiculous look, like a kid with a bib in the nursery or at least an adult pretending to be that kid. Wan Baoshan grinned at his father, took up the cake and began to eat. It was as hard as iron! He went all out but all his efforts were in vain. His teeth kept sliding on the cake, but he had a taste of its distinctive flavor all the same. At night, on the bed, Wan Baoshan felt a piece of minced prickly ash, as small as sesame, stuck between his teeth. He licked it out but grudged sending it down his throat. Having it in his mouth meticulously, he went to sleep. Later, when he heard others talking of his father's "story of baked cakes", he felt as fretful as before, but the fret didn't cancel out the pleasant feeling he got that night.

Thirty years passed and the children in Wan's family all grew up. One after another, they left their parents and had their own families. Perhaps because they were scared by their father's penny-pinching, all the children made it a tacit rule to stay away from father, except Wan Baoshan, who lived close by — there were only two blocks between his home and his parents'. The days of coupons for fixed rations had gone and people enjoyed better lives. They could buy rice or flour freely and use more oil when cooking dishes. However, father was as miserly as before. He continued locking the grains into cabinets and constantly went to the market to buy unwanted eggs which were about to hatch chickens. In the 1980s, Wan Baoshan once bought a pair of sofas made of artificial leather for his parents, but right the next day, father sold them and put the money aside. He did so with good reason as he said to whoever he met: "*Faso* costs much money and takes up much room!" After retirement, father had more leisure time, so he wanted to live with Wan Baoshan's little daughter who was in a primary school at that time and promised to take good care of her, but Wan Baoshan's wife declined firmly. Now that he had so much free time, he took over the task of buying vegetables every day. In truth, he was picking up rejected vegetables rather than buying them. Every day, in the afternoon when the market was about to close, he arrived in time. Unperturbed and fully at ease, he bent down and picked up the fragments of vegetables which the vendors had discarded here and there on the ground and sometimes, if he was lucky, he made a great discovery: a budding potato or an old celery with rough and hard fibers. People in the neighborhood often made fun of him: "Wan, when will you pick up a piece of meat in the market? In that case, you can stew it with brown sauce and give your family a feast!" On hearing these jeers, father always responded with pleasure: "I can feast them whenever I want. All right, I'll do it today." As his neighbor asked him what dish he wanted to cook for the feast, he answered proudly: "I am going to braise the celery with brown sauce!" On hearing this, the neighbors burst into laughter but father didn't find it funny at all as he really meant to do so. Father's parsimony was not a result of hard life; instead, it had become his faith or his drive of living, which he couldn't part with for a moment. Being penny-pinching, to him, was not shameful at all. On the contrary, trying his utmost to save every penny was indeed glorious. True, being a miser was really different from borrowing money but not returning it. He amused himself in his own way! It was his own happiness, none of others' business!

The train came into the station. Finally, Wan Baoshan arrived in Beijing. Following his colleagues, he went out of the station. According to the arrangement, they visited Tian'anmen Square, the National Stadium nicknamed "Bird's Nest" and the National Natatorium nicknamed "Water Cube".[10] They all cried in exclamation: "The capital is awesome! The Olympic Games has been held here! The celebration of the 60th anniversary of the National Day has been held here! Indeed, our capital Beijing is magnificent!" The flowers were all in blossom under the azure sky and new buildings, tall and low, rose up majestically to the sky. And people all looked proud and lively on the busy streets … At the sight of these, his colleagues began taking pictures here and there in excitement. Wan Baoshan had no camera. Standing before the "Bird's Nest", he asked a teacher to take a picture of him. Then, he went to the leader of their team, a deputy headmaster, and asked for leave, saying that he wanted to go to visit one of his acquaintances in Beijing. Knowing that making a roaming call was expensive, Wan Baoshan lied that his phone was out of battery and called Li Yuze with the deputy headmaster's mobile phone.

It was Li Yuze himself on the other end of the line. He was aged, a little hard of hearing but speaking with a sonorous voice. Wan Baoshan said his father's name and told the old man that he wanted to make a visit on behalf of his father. He didn't say his father had died and that he came here to return the money. He thought he'd better talk about these when they were face to face with each other. Obviously, Li Yuze remembered Wan Baoshan's father, his neighbor in the textile factory 50 years ago. In a happy mood, he told Wan Baoshan the route to his home in detail and that his son was about to throw a big party, in which there would be a whole mess of people and Wan Baoshan was welcome to have a drink with them. A party? Wan Baoshan had no idea what a party meant. It must have something to do with people and drinking, he guessed. After hanging up the phone, Wan Baoshan took the subway line No.10 at the Bird's Nest station. It didn't take him much trouble to find Li Yuze's residence. Wan Baoshan stopped at the gate of a great estate called "Green Water Manor", apparently a neighborhood of villas. Staring at the huge black iron gate with a pair of gilded kylins, he thought of what the old colleagues once told him: Li Yuze's son Li Kexin was doing a real estate business and Li Yuze was leading a very good life in his son's. As he hesitated at the gate, a guard in blue uniform with golden epaulets on both shoulders came out of the gatehouse. After inquiring his name, the guard said politely to him: "Just now, the household in the A8 unit informed us of your visit and asked us to let you in."

The guard ushered him in and showed him the way warmheartedly: "Turn right, go onto that hunchback bridge, and walk straight on for two hundred meters. You won't miss it." Following the guard's instructions almost mechanically, Wan Baoshan walked onto that bridge which arched smoothly but stretched quite long. Looking down from the bridge, he saw green water in the pond, lotus leaves adrift, patches of lawn around the pond, a fountain with wooden benches and quite a lot of trees of rare species. Off the bridge, after walking two hundred meter, passing several white and yellow houses, he finally stopped in front of a red house. He didn't know why he was so much attracted by the grey tortoiseshell pantiles on its roof. Maybe he had seen this kind of tiles in foreign movies? A well-trimmed lawn extended in all directions from the foot of the house and thus formed a yard of more than a thousand square meters. On the light brown columns at the gate of the yard, a purple bronze plate was inlaid, bearing the name "A8". Standing at the gate and looking inside beyond the fence, which was actually a row of white wooden railings, Wan Baoshan saw a very big French window, from which a big white balcony extended, where a few old men, leisurely and cozy, were enjoying the autumn sunshine. Li Yuze must be among them? Wan Baoshan said to himself. In the yard, on the lawn there stood an oblong picnic table covered with snow-white cloth, on which fruits, cakes and meat — it must be barbecued meat, for there was a barbecue nearby — were placed in glistening silver plates. Two chefs in white tall hats were busy working at the barbecue. The inviting smell of the roast continuously assaulted Wan Baoshan's nostrils. A small group of men, women and some yelling kids who were sporting and frolicking in the yard attracted his attention. Sitting at leisure or strolling to and fro, they were eating, drinking and chatting. A five-year-old boy in a parted hair was stamping his feet in anger and shouting at his mother (it should be his mother, anyway): "I don't want French Evian! No! I want to drink 'Tibetan Spring Water'. 26 yuan a bottle. I want that!"...

All of a sudden, Wan Baoshan found his body trembling. Standing outside the fence, he withdrew from any intention of going in and turned back. An inexpressible feeling crawled upon his heart. He was afraid to be seen. This must be the "party"? He thought. He had known that the Lis were leading a good life, but he was overwhelmed with the scene in front of his eyes. That child wanted to drink a bottle of water which cost 26 yuan! He couldn't help but think of the money in his pocket — that 58 yuan — which his father urged him to return. 58 yuan, in this yard, was only equivalent to two bottles of water. How will Li Yuze or his son look at me, the son of their old neighbor, who makes a special trip and pays a special visit to them just for the purpose of clearing a debt of 58 yuan? Do they still remember that 5 yuan which they lent to their neighbor 53 years ago? Thinking of these, Wan Baoshan suddenly felt frustrated and even turned angry at himself. What am I doing here? I am more than 50 years old. I took such a long trip, made several phone calls, asked about this address, and took some trouble to come here. I come to this luxurious villa just for the purpose of giving its owner a light and wrinkled envelope. It was simply ridiculous!

At the thought of these, he resolved to leave as soon as possible. He turned back and hastened to that hunchback bridge in a brisk pace. After he crossed the bridge, he would not be far from the gate of the manor. But as he was about to go onto the bridge, his legs suddenly failed him — he couldn't move a step! He composed himself and switched the leg, but it didn't work, either. He was shocked and dumbfounded. Am I seized by some supernatural power?[11] He couldn't believe it. After a while, he calmed himself down and slowly turned back — he was trying to walk back to A8. To his surprise, his legs worked! Nonetheless, as he turned again and tried to walk onto the bridge, his legs failed once more.

Wan Baoshan stood there, numb and helpless, like a contemplating philosopher. The sun began to go down in the west and several children were flying kites with upturned faces on the vast meadow extending on both sides of the bridge. Now that he couldn't move a step as if his legs were bewitched, he had to stand there, following those children's eyes and looking up at the sky. There were some "birds" hovering high in the sky: swallows, centipedes, hawks... A black hawk with a red mouth flew the highest, looking down at the ground in a majestic and awe-inspiring manner. An image was suddenly brought alive in Wan Baoshan's mind: On his deathbed, his father spread his arms and looked at him with pleading and forlorn eyes like an old bird in the chilly wind. Looking at the black hawk overhead, Wan Baoshan couldn't help but wonder: Is it my father's soul? Of course, he was not superstitious, but at that moment, his heart was filled with awe and fright. He collected his thoughts, turned around and walked towards the direction of A8. Under the hawk's eyes, his legs moved! There was nothing wrong with his legs! He was sure his legs were well and good.[12]

The hawk flew and circled overhead as if it were urging and escorting him. He looked up at the sky and looked about. The sky was high and the air crisp. There was nobody around. In such a low-density neighborhood one might often found nobody around. Wan Baoshan raised his arm shyly. He was giving his tacit greetings to the hawk above. As he extended his arm bravely, he found something hidden in his body began to crack, melt and gush out. His heart became relaxed and eased a little.[13]

March 19, 2010

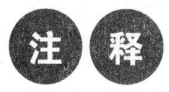 注 释

1. "到底是父亲，一辈子精打细算。" Father never changes! All his life he counts every cent and makes every cent count! count every cent 数钱、数每一分钱，make every cent count 使每一分钱有价值，有意义，make... count 使有价值，有意义。用count every cent and make every cent count来翻译"精打细算"应该是合适的。

2. skin and bone 形容人非常瘦，瘦得皮包骨。表示人瘦的形容词还有slim /

513

slender / willowy / skinny / bony / lean / thin, 可根据语气区别使用。

3. live from hand to mouth 勉强生活，糊口度日。

4. "父亲对自己的不还欠债振振有词，但全家人都明白他更像是强词夺理。" His father spoke in such a plausible and voluble manner, yet the family all knew he was arguing unreasonably to defend himself. plausible (声明、争论等) 似乎是真的、花言巧语的、能说会道的，voluble 喋喋不休的、口若悬河的，argue unreasonably 强词夺理。

5. once in a blue moon 极其罕见的，千载难逢的。

6. put in for 申请。

7. "而到达省会之后，父亲的预谋也没能'得逞'。" Nevertheless, when they arrived at their destination, his father came to know that his elaborate plan would fall flat. "没有得逞" 这里译为 fall flat, 完全失败，没有产生预期的效果。

8. through and through 彻彻底底地。

9. … kept adding highly colored details to it. 不断地添油加醋。

10. "鸟巢" 和 "水立方" 是两个奥运场馆的名字，不能只翻译字面，还应该把其功能说出来，读者才知道这两个馆是干什么的。According to the arrangement, they visited Tian'anmen Square, the National Stadium nicknamed "Bird's Nest" and the National Natatorium nicknamed "Water Cube".

11. "他站在桥下发愣，不相信自己遇见了鬼，不相信这是鬼使神差。"译者在翻译时，把这句处理成了自言自语的问句，这样更能表达人物当时的心情：Am I seized by some supernatural power? He couldn't believe it. "鬼使神差" 译为 seized by some supernatural power。

12. "他确信自己的腿是两条好腿。" He was sure his legs were well and good. well 指健康，good 指正常。

13. "他发现，当他勇敢地把胳膊舒展开来的时候，久已潜藏在身体内的什么东西嘎巴巴地奔涌了出来，他那颗发紧的心也略微感觉到了平安。" As he extended his arm bravely, he found something hidden in his body began to crack, melt and gush out. His heart became relaxed and eased a little. "嘎巴巴地奔涌" 译为 crack, melt and gush out。